# Peace Psychology Book Series

**Series Editor**
Daniel J. Christie

For other titles published in this series, go to
www.springer.com/series/7298

Herbert Blumberg • M. Valerie Kent
A. Paul Hare • Martin F. Davies

# Small Group Research

Implications for Peace Psychology
and Conflict Resolution

 Springer

Herbert Blumberg
Department of Psychology
Goldsmiths College
University of London
New Cross, London
United Kingdom
h.blumberg@gold.ac.uk

A. Paul Hare
Blaustein Institute for Desert Research
Center for Desert Architecture
Ben-Gurion University Negev
Sede Boqer Campus
84990 Sede Boqer
Israel
paulhare@bgumail.bgu.ac.il

M. Valerie Kent
PO Box 16526
Nairobi
Kenya
kent@africaonline.co.ke

Martin F. Davies
Department of Psychology
Goldsmiths College
University of London
New Cross, London
United Kingdom
psa01mfd@gold.ac.uk

ISBN 978-1-4614-0024-0        e-ISBN 978-1-4614-0025-7
DOI 10.1007/978-1-4614-0025-7
Springer New York Dordrecht Heidelberg London

Library of Congress Control Number: 2011933669

Printed on acid-free paper

Springer is part of Springer Science+Business Media (www.springer.com)

*This volume is dedicated to the late A. Paul Hare, an eminent pioneer in small groups research, good-humored activist for conflict resolution and peace, and a mentor, colleague, and friend over a period of decades.*

# Preface

This volume is an independent companion to *Small Group Research: Basic Issues* (Blumberg et al. 2009). Together the two volumes attempt to provide thorough coverage of the small groups literature generally subsequent to our 1994 handbook (see below).

As we said in the introduction to the 2009 volume on basic processes, small group research—studies of friendship, leadership, communication and the like—has grown in its breadth of appeal. Indeed it has come to occupy a substantial place in the literature not only of social psychology and sociology but also of a wide range of other fields and subfields including, among others, international relations, peace studies, business studies, sociology, psychotherapy, social work, and economics.

The number of publications per annum—using consistent search strategies—has also grown apace. For some years we have been engaged in a quest to consolidate and share the gist of the published findings from social psychological and other research concerned with small groups of people. A "small group" is typically one that can engage in "face-to-face social interaction" or its virtual equivalent.

The quest began with Paul Hare's landmark works: a credited collection (Hare et al. 1955, 1965) and a handbook (Hare 1962, 1976).

Our present team went on to publish a new collection (Blumberg et al. 1983), a handbook taking up where the 1976 volume left off (Hare et al. 1994), and a textbook (Hare et al. 1996).

The 1994 handbook—mainly covering work published between 1977 and 1988—cited approximately 5,000 publications–and we knew of several thousand more in the field that we felt were not worth citing for the given purpose. For a subsequent period of rather longer duration (1989 to early 2005), using the same search strategies, we unearthed around 19,000 publications! Much of the increase has been due to growth in academic and other publications generally and (for the present purpose) in peace psychology and some other areas of the behavioral sciences in particular (cf. Blumberg et al. 2006, Chap. 1). Perhaps oddly, even within the psychological literature, there is surprisingly little overlap between peace-psychology research concerned with conflict resolution (primarily but not exclusively in an international context) and—the core of the present volume—small groups research also concerned with applications such as conflict resolution.

As one might imagine, such a large corpus of research, on which the present volume is mainly based, does not lend itself to any one over-arching explanatory paradigm. Nor have we noticed any brand new high-level theories becoming pervasive in the period covered by this volume. What we *have* found, especially, is a very large number of studies that help to contextualize and fill out the range of applicability, and relative applicability, of different perspectives.

The present book is intended to cover several important areas of applied small group research, particularly emphasizing publications from 1988 to 2005—and, selectively, from the "flood" of largely contextualized literature from 2006 to 2009—that are of relevance to peace, conflict resolution, and related areas. This includes six main topics, as delineated in the following chapter summaries.

*Chapter 1, Cooperation, competition and conflict resolution.* This covers small groups research that is distinct from, and (as mooted above) only slightly overlapping with, the material—also on conflict resolution—in our peace psychology volume (Blumberg et al. 2006, Chap. 9 by Hare). A section on core work related to cooperation covers background, contact hypothesis, processes, facilitation and outcomes, and cooperation versus competition. The section on conflict covers key and general concepts, individual background, styles of conflict resolution, experimental variables, communication, special procedures, and guidelines and processes. Resource (collective) dilemmas covers key and general studies, paradigms and theories, individual background (real and perceived), group size, framing of issues, and reward structures. A section on negotiation covers key and general findings, individual differences and perceived power differences, framing and communication, strategies, third-party mediation, and theories, models and suggestions.

*Chapter 2, Bargaining, coalitions, and games: Classified citations.* Categorizes and cites both laboratory and field research. Some prototypical experimental paradigms are as follows: (a) bargaining—laboratory procedures for pairs of participants, emphasizing the distributions of outcomes of a series of offers and counter-offers under a wide variety of circumstances; (b) coalitions—especially the principles whereby parties combine to form winning coalitions and decide on equitable ways of dividing the resultant rewards; and (c) games, especially procedures that elicit cooperation under circumstances (such as that of the Prisoner's Dilemma Game) in which participants acting in concert will achieve a better overall result than if each tried to maximize his or her own immediate rewards.

*Chapter 3, Group dynamics and social cognition.* Covers: Physical setting and background variables; social influence; roles (including leadership); relationships; social interaction including group decision making; intergroup relations; and therapy groups. We have tried, at several junctures, to spell out some of the implications for peace and conflict resolution. (Cognition seems to be under-researched as an explicit perspective in this context, but underpins much existing research and practice related to peace and conflict).

*Chapter 4, The group and the organization.* Covers various aspects of organizations, apart from team performance, which is dealt with in the next chapter. Main topics are: general considerations, networks, groups; theories for small groups and organizations (subsections on functions within functions); typing groups by functional categories; integration and role differentiation; influences between the organization and the small group (goals, norms, and technology); influence of the small group on the organization; self-managing work groups; isolated groups. This chapter—and the next, which deals with teams in organizations—emphasizes the potential applicability to (among others) political organizations and groups of policy-makers, and (for most sections) implications for peacemaking and/or peacebuilding.

*Chapter 5, Team performance.* Following (conceptually) the four Parsonian functions, the first parts of this chapter cover empirical research related to: (a) contextual meaning and the values held by team members; (b) integration and interpersonal matters; (c) goal-attainment—effects, on team performance, of motivation, leadership, and the nature of the task; and (d) research on economic and informational resources. This chapter additionally deals with organizational creativity, learning, team training (including methods of assessment)—all of these topics being relevant to (for example) teams of negotiators, problem-solving groups, and others working together in the service of addressing direct and structural violence.

*Chapter 6, Intergroup relations.* Covers: key and general work; minimal groups; cognitive approaches to the consequences of being in a group, as follows. Ingroup favoritism and bias (includes: Linguistic bias; developmental studies; intergroup differentiation and distinctiveness; optimal distinctiveness theory); social categorization and social identity (includes: individual differences and social identity; social categories, identity and status); multiple category or multiple group membership (includes: perceptions of homogeneity; illusory correlation). Affective consequences: emotion, perceived threat, intergroup anxiety and fear (includes: social category and emotion; threat; intergroup anxiety); behavioral consequences: competition, conflict, aggression; intergroup discontinuity; improving intergroup relations. The contact hypothesis (includes: does contact have generalized consequences? dual identity, overarching categories, reformulated ingroups; contact and attitudes; generating affective ties and the reduction of intergroup anxiety; when does contact work; negative consequences of contact).

*Concluding note.* Group dynamics research and its applicability to conflict resolution represent one of the mainstream content areas of social psychology. (For an alternative comprehensive work on group processes, see J. M. Levine and Hogg 2010; see also Abrams and Hogg 2008.) For those interested explicitly in aspects of peace studies and conflict resolution, however, listings of several hundred core courses are described by Harris and Shuster (2006)—though courses concerned in various other ways with conflict resolution in diverse organizations are even very much more widely prevalent (including, for example, in business administration programs).

Chapters 1 and 2 were written by Blumberg, Chap. 3 by Blumberg and Hare, Chaps. 4 and 5 by Hare, and Chap. 6 by Kent. The chapters can be read independently and can be used as a source for further reading.

# Contents

# Chapter 1
# Cooperation, Competition, and Conflict Resolution

Should we be pleased at the accelerating volume of research related to conflict resolution or awed by the challenge of what remains to be done—or perhaps both?

In the contemporary period, particularly since the 1980s (see Table 1.1), there has been a large amount of excellent research, much of it "bridging" the distinctions between theory and application, and also between lab and field studies. Deutsch et al. (2006) *Handbook of conflict resolution* represents an outstanding example. In addition to new approaches, many of the key perspectives from an earlier period—as compiled by C. G. Smith (1971)—have, by now, been considerably further developed.

The present chapter and the next one continue coverage of topics from two chapters of our previous *Handbook* (Hare et al. 1994, respectively, Chap. 9 on cooperation and conflict resolution and Chap. 10 on mainly laboratory-based research on coalitions, bargaining, and simulation games) that encompassed approximately the fifteen years prior to the end of the Cold War.

Note that research on conflict resolution within Peace Psychology—which has been reviewed by Paul Hare (Blumberg et al. 2006, Chap. 9)—is different from that covered in the present work of small group research, there being surprisingly little overlap.

The sections of the present chapter dwell first on cooperation, then resolution of conflict, resource dilemmas, and finally negotiation. As with other areas of small group research, most of the work is concerned with filling out the contextual dependencies of existing approaches rather than with inventing and applying new paradigms.

If you are wanting a general-purpose checklist to evaluate whether entities are cooperating well—be they countries, power-sharing parties, nongovernmental organizations, or individuals on a peacebuilding team—you might consider looking in turn at harmonious values, interpersonal relations, task accomplishments, and coordination of material and informational resources.

Indeed many of the sections in this chapter are organized according to what we might ironically call a "MIGR" (pronounced "meager"?) progression based on Parsonian functional theory (Hare 1983). The foundation of this progression starts with *Meaning* and basic values, then moves up to *Interpersonal* relations, then *Goal*-orientation and task completion, and finally to economic and informational *Resources*.

H. Blumberg et al., *Small Group Research*, Peace Psychology Book Series,
DOI 10.1007/978-1-4614-0025-7_1, © Springer Science+Business Media, LLC 2012

**Table 1.1** Frequency of "conflict resolution" anywhere in PsycINFO record

| Decade | Number of Records |
| --- | --- |
| 2000s | 3,600 |
| 1990s | 2,860 |
| 1980s | 1,180 |
| 1970s | 420 |
| 1960s and earlier | 200 |

Frequencies are rounded to nearest 20

(We have here reversed an RGIM sequence, partly in order to start with the most "basic" sector. The MIGR sequence represents a descending "cybernetic hierarchy of control," whereby a group's information and resources (R) can be fairly readily updated whereas, at the other extreme, people's values (M) tend to be much more stable.

Previously, resources have been named for *Adaptiveness*, and meaning was designated "*Latent* pattern maintenance," thus providing what had been (and often still is) known as an "AGIL" scheme (Hare 1983), here interchangeable with "RGIM." See also "*Talcott Parsons*" (2010, especially note 167; and see Chap. 4, note 1).

Note that (at the "*I*" and "*R*" levels) interpersonal expectations—on the effects of cooperation or competition, for example—and other cognitive phenomena may moderate a wide variety of findings (Blanck 1993), perhaps particularly including those from studies of collaborative task outcomes. For instance, group members' attributions about outcomes do not necessarily match the actual causes of the outcomes themselves (see also Blumberg et al. 2009, Chap. 2 by Hare). To take an example, when individual feedback to teams performing ambiguous problem-solving tasks indicated (arbitrarily) both (a) the individual's success or failure and (b) the cooperating team's overall success or failure, "successful" individuals did attribute personal responsibility for the group outcome if the team succeeded but not if it failed; "failing" individuals, however, chose an intermediate amount of personal responsibility regardless of the group outcome (Forsyth and Kelley 1994).

For examples of other circumstances in which cognition mediates findings related to group cooperation see Engestroem et al.(1995); Lopez et al. (1997); Makino and Takemura (1993); Meacham and Emont (1989); Singh (1997); Stewart and Moore (1992).

Notwithstanding the overall systematic structure of the topics covered, the arrays of findings presented below do present the reader with something of a serendipiter's journey.

## Cooperation

This section begins by highlighting a number of exciting works—some of them general (and others more applicable to specific contexts), followed by some concerned with background variables. A further subsection, dealing with cooperative processes and the facilitation of cooperative outcomes, is presented according to the aforementioned MIGR progression. (Most of the references for Prisoner's Dilemma and similar Games in Chap. 2 also deal with facilitating cooperation.) The present section on Cooperation concludes with discussions (also following MIGR) of "cooperation versus competition" and of research focusing just on competition.

The mostly positive effects of cooperative settings for task and social aspects of education at all levels have continued to be documented (Hertz-Lazarowitz and Miller 1995). As with the longer-standing jigsaw classroom studies, for instance, over a decade of research (by O'Donnell and Dansereau and others) supports the value of a Scripted Cooperation procedure. In this procedure, dyad members take turns at presenting and critiquing each other's recall of textual information.

Although the jigsaw classroom and scripted cooperation procedures might not be directly applicable in say a peacebuilding context, the *principles* of these approaches and conceptually similar research—such as that dealing with superordinate goals and the contact hypothesis (see Chap. 6)—seem very relevant indeed. Successful progress is especially likely where people or groups can work together on a common goal, on an equal-status basis with the positive approval of authorities, and where each party has something valuable to contribute.

The study of cooperation among adults appears to have matured within various disciplines, but with the task of integrating various approaches still incomplete. In particular, this applies to the merging of social science knowledge (a) with the practicalities of contemporary industrial cooperation—between companies, for example—and (b) with advances in communication technology.

Work summarized by K. G. Smith et al. (1995) emphasizes the importance of interpersonal trust as a foundation for cooperation and coordination. Trust—as well as norms and rules of conduct—ultimately underpins not only the ability of employees from within an institution to work well together both vertically (hierarchically) and horizontally, but also the ability of networks of organizations—through their managers—to work together successfully. Trust is based on psychological factors such as common interests and on structural ones such as proximity over a period of time. No one perspective provides a full understanding of cooperation, but the useful menu includes theories of exchange, attraction, power and conflict, modeling, and social structure.

One is tempted to add "equity" to the prerequisites for cooperative work. This would mirror the "contact hypothesis," whereby prejudice is reduced when people work together face-to-face on an equal-status basis and with the positive sanction of those in authority, and (one might add) with all contributing and all suitably rewarded. However, as documented below, shifts in reward structure do not necessarily change performance.

A discussion of general advances that facilitate cooperation would be incomplete without considering technological progress. The development of electronic Group Decision Support Systems (GDSS) is relevant to cooperative communication, as well as to group problem solving (as discussed in Chap. 8 and also Chap. 7 of Blumberg et al. 2009). Probably the largest well-known example of a cooperatively cumulated database relates to the human genome. Two examples of ongoing issues in smaller contexts have to do with: (a) open systems versus (sometimes helpfully) restrictive ones, such as ordinary e-mail contrasted with a system requiring the sender to include the purpose of a message and, if applicable, to specify the date by which a reply is needed; and (b) balancing the social and task advantages of face-to-face versus teleconferencing contact in (say) deciding between a single- versus multiple-site symposium (Galegher, Kraut, and Egido 1990).

Our previous handbook described Axelrod's (Axelrod 1984) computer tournament, whereby a conditionally benevolent tit-for-tat strategy, in a multiply repeated Prisoner's Dilemma Game (PDG), was especially effective. In a post-Cold-War sequel, Axelrod (1997) models a more complex view of cooperation, whereby "players" may misunderstand one another, may collaborate in building an organization, and may violate agreed norms.

Whether Axelrod's benevolent tit-for-tat strategy can evolve into a stable equilibrium depends on the meaning of "stable equilibrium" and the context of the system, according to Bendor and Swistak (1998). A tit-for-tat strategy may well become a permanent fixture (confirming a "weak" definition of stability) but this need not preclude the simultaneous presence of other strategies (negating a "strong" stability). For instance, in the context of a system where there are no threats to cooperation, conditionally benevolent tit-for-tat and unconditionally benevolent strategies may coexist and moreover be empirically indistinguishable—unless or until some threat does appear (cf. Tudge 2003; see also Sheldon 1999). For a summary of Axelrod's work and subsequent amplifying experiments see Komorita and Parks (1999).

Some contemporary reviews consolidate earlier findings. For example, Deutsch (1989, 1990) summarizes some of the conclusions from his own and colleagues' research. Classic findings from the Kraut-Deutsch "Acme-Bolt Trucking Game" retain contemporary relevance. Two players, "driving" in opposite directions across the same electronic-game field, must agree how to pass through a stretch of single-reversible lane (e.g., by taking turns) or else take a long, expensive detour. Viable solutions are more likely when: participants have a cooperative orientation toward each other, the size of conflict is seen to be small, communication channels are not only open but also facilitated by a neutral third party, "weapons" and threats—such as the possibility of a participant lowering a "gate" across the main road—are unavailable to either party (and, particularly, are not available to *both* parties).

In a two-person point-accumulation laboratory "behavioral strategy" game, a nonpunitive strategy was particularly effective in eliciting cooperation and moreover in realizing high joint outcomes. In conditions of high competitiveness, however, this strategy was particularly effective only when preceded by a "show of strength"(Deutsch 1990). Indeed—as if to echo Sherif's classic findings—even when competitiveness is merely implicit in a paradigm, explicitly joint rewards may be needed to damp down competitive behavior (Blumberg 1997; see also section below on cooperation versus competition).

The (undergraduate) workers in groups may prefer—and expect to be more productive under—equitable distributive reward systems, but (in relevant research) variation in reward systems had no clear consistent effects on actual performance. In particular, in real workplaces, an equal (cooperative egalitarian) distribution of rewards seems at least as effective as a meritocratic one. Indeed economic egalitarianism, as in some forms of worker cooperative, appears to result in *greater* productivity and satisfaction. "If egalitarianism were taken seriously, and the thoughtful effort necessary to establish and maintain such democratic cooperative systems were made, the odds are that we would be more productive and less alienated from ourselves and one another" (Deutsch 1989, p. 152).

The tradition of Deutsch's work on cooperation has been furthered by—among others—(a) Lewicki and Bunker (1995), who link the possible breakdown of cooperation to the stage of trust that has developed (cf. Hwang and Burgers 1997), (b) Vanderslice (1995), who documents organizational threats to cooperative principles (e.g., overconformity and selfish ends) and provides suggestions for improvement, and (c) D. W. Johnson and Johnson (1995), who describe the "potential applications of cooperative learning to educational issues like diversity, globalization, and social and psychological health and development" (Bunker and Rubin 1995, p. 7).

For general paradigms of cooperation and of conflict see Mlicki (1993) and Balawajder (1995). For a sociological theoretical analysis of age as a basis of cooperation and conflict see Henretta (1988). Mechanisms for cultural evolution of cooperation, such as the spread of reciprocity and tribal social "instincts" have been discussed by a variety of researchers (e.g., Bowles and Gintis 2003; Gintis et al. 2003; Hanley et al. 2003; Hammerstein 2003; Mark 2004; Richerson et al. 2003; Eric A. Smith 2003). Henrich and Henrich (2006) discuss mechanisms combining culture and genes.

## *Personal Background*

The effects of group composition, with regard to background variables, are at least partly context-specific. In a computer course, for instance, greater cooperation took place in female-majority and low self-efficacy groups, though males and participants with high self-efficacy or more computer experience offered more task-oriented help (Busch 1996). (Self-efficacy here refers to confidence in one's skills.). Even after cooperative learning, Trinidadian adolescent males continued to base workmate preference on achievement, while females tended to use social class as a basis—though in both cases same race choices decreased (Jules 1991).

Interage cooperation and conflict represent particularly diverse and important phenomena, including biological and role-based age differentiation, and are associated with "the very basic question of how societies are able to reproduce themselves over time" (Henretta 1988, p. 401).

Ability may interact with group composition. Among 6th and 7th graders in cooperative dyads for mathematics mastery, low-ability students had more social interaction and better performance in heterogeneous than in homogeneous groups; for high-ability students, the reverse was true (Hooper and Hannafin 1991).

Among personality variables, (not surprisingly) social value orientation relates to cooperation, with prosocial participants showing high cooperation regardless of others' orientation (Van Lange and Semin-Goossens 1998). Those with individualist or competitive orientation also tended to cooperate with others who were perceived as honest but were inclined to take advantage of those seen as particularly intelligent or as unintelligent.

For other studies linking background and demographic variables with cooperation see Bonaiuto (1997); Grazzani Gavazzi et al. (1996); Mueller (1992); Nowicki et al. (1997); Schmitt (1998).

## Facilitating Cooperation

Brewer's (Brewer 1996; Brewer and Miller 1988) optimal distinctiveness theory posits a basic need for people to assimilate to social ingroups with which they identify, and to differentiate themselves from contrasting outgroups. In a spirit that seems consonant with findings related to the contact hypothesis and the jigsaw classroom (see, e.g., Hare et al. 1996, pp. 149–150), she suggests that one route toward broader cooperation is to encourage differential role assignments (task structures) that "cross-cut" any ingroup/outgroup dichotomy. For example, when respondents' identity to arbitrary designations of "overestimators" or "underestimators" is made salient, there is less outgroup bias in reward allocation when both "overestimators" and "underestimators" are represented within teams that combine requisite skills to solve a problem. Although Brewer is aware that laboratory experiments cannot be automatically extrapolated to political hierarchies, she suggests that conceptualizing different levels of a person's identity as being orthogonal could represent an alternative to the view that multicultural societies must face an uneasy choice between assimilation and separatism.

Some seemingly intractable conflicts, for example, in Northern Ireland and South Africa, arose when societies have been split between the same ingroups and outgroups with respect to a variety of political and social dimensions. With regard to Palestinian and Israeli communities, Kelman (1993) has explored coalitions that cut across conflict lines. (See Bornstein 2003, for conceptually related laboratory research.)

*Meaning (Basic Paradigms)* Analyses by evolutionary biologists indicate that cooperative behavior can be selected-for by evolution only if it aids the solution of specific cognitive problems (Cosmides and Tooby 1992). Such evolution may be effected by selection associated with the needs of small groups living together (Caporael et al. 1989). Using a simulation model, De Vos and Zeggelink (1997) found that a cooperative strategy (of preferring those who have previously helped) is viable in competition with "cheating" strategies if their proportion is not too small (or, in the case of small populations, conditions are relatively harsh).

Cooperation in large groups may depend on the emergence of cooperative social norms—as Stewart (2009) concluded, analyzing historical data from mining camps, where cooperation was needed to secure property rights.

For additional reviews of mechanisms promoting (or diminishing) the evolution of cooperation see Boone (1992); Boyd and Richerson (1992); Reeve (1998);

McElreath et al. (2003); and Troisi (1993). For barriers to intergroup reconciliation and steps to peaceful coexistence see Nadler et al. (2008); and Worchel and Coutant (2008).

For an empirically based theory of cooperative work, applied to computer supported systems see Morley (1994; cf. Finholt and Teasley 1998). For a model relating cooperation to the reduction of intergroup bias see N. Miller and Harrington (1990).

A theory of cooperative behavior can also be based on natural selection (Doebeli et al. 2004; Meyer 1999; Watanabe and Smuts 2004) or on heuristic strategies, and moreover may predict paradoxical findings such as *increased* cooperation with higher payoffs for mutual defection (Buskens and Snijders 1997). Whether natural selection favors cooperation depends on various mechanisms such as kin selection and reciprocity, each of which may function in different ways; cooperation, in turn, is needed for new organization at different levels from the genome to human groupings (Nowak 2006; cf. Nowak and Sigmund 2005).

According to Aktipis (2006) and colleagues, one theme in recent findings is that evolved cooperation, whether derived from human flexibility, cognitive ability or other factors, can be contingent on a party's circumstances.

*Interpersonal Factors* In social dilemmas, cooperation may typically be due to diffusion of internalized individual norms, according to experiments by Kerr and colleagues (e.g., Kerr et al. 1997). Such norms may, in turn, be potentiated by trust among individuals (see above).

Even among six- to seven-year-old children, enhanced cooperation capacity was realized from a program of games designed to encourage mutual acceptance, sharing, and enjoyment (Garaigordobil et al. 1996). Simply engaging in synchronous activities such as singing may strengthen group attachment and yield more cooperation in, for instance, subsequent group economic exercises (Wiltermuth and Heath 2009).

The optimal reward structure for groups may usually depend on the degree of task specialization, and hence of team interdependence, required (Fandt et al. 1993).

As a corollary of Pruitt's goal-expectation hypothesis, cooperation is likely to take place when group members have mutual trust and a common goal entailing cooperation (De Cremer and Stouten 2003). Recategorization may, however, be less likely to take place among low-status groups (Seta et al. 2000).

Various signals and other communicative devices may aid in enhancement and evolution from a cooperative group core (Ahn et al. 2004; Boone and Buck 2003; Cook and Cooper 2003; Taylor and Day 2004). Over time, demographic heterogeneity may have negative and positive effects (Chatman and Flynn 2001).

It has also been suggested that positive intergroup relations can be facilitated by recognizing separate subgroup identities, as well as developing a common group identity (Dovidio, Gaertner, and Esses 2008).

Cooperation (as an independent variable) generally reduces intergroup bias—a very well-established social-psychological finding. A mechanism typically associated with this bias reduction is the reforming of cognitive representations such that a previous outgroup is, for the purpose, merged into the ingroup (Gaertner et al. 1990; see also Chap. 2 for relevant laboratory studies; see also Chap. 6 which, e.g., covers superordinate social identity as a source of developing intergroup cooperation). That is, participants can perceive one main group rather than separate groups. In a de facto extrapolation of this view, Cairns (1982) and others have discussed the potential value of promoting a common "Northern Irish" identity. Common identity plus diversity may, under favorable conditions, promote scientific team creativity (Levine and Moreland 2004).

For additional considerations of interpersonal aspects of cooperative learning see Katovich (1996) and N. Miller and Harrington (1995). For a measure of facilitative group interaction behaviors see Watson and Michaelsen (1988).

*Goal-Directed Factors*  Research in various situations continues to document task and social advantages of shared decision-making (Tjosvold 1988) and other cooperative conditions (Sharan and Shaulov 1990). Reviewing the helpful and unhelpful actions of a group session can aid future achievement (among students at least), especially if the review sessions use a cooperative learning procedure, particularly one that combines student- and teacher-led processing (D. W. Johnson et al. 1990, reporting a study in which high-ability Black students carried out complex problem-solving tasks). For simulation of the sometimes paradoxical relationships among sanctions, cooperation, and defection, see Whitmeyer (2004). Member diversity may facilitate cooperation but—at least in workgroups—this depends on group longevity and the nature of the diversity (King et al. 2009).

As an unfortunate irony, cooperative initiatives among leaders of mutually hostile constituencies may devalue how the leaders are perceived by their own group members (Lundgren 1998; see also Chap. 8 of Blumberg et al. 2009)—an historically familiar problem in many areas including the Middle East and Northern Ireland. Superordinate goals may lead to superordinate identity but should not be confused with each other (Brewer 2000).

For additional considerations as regards goal-directed factors see Cavalier et al. (1995); Curry et al. (1991); Gauthier (1990); Laughlin et al. (1998); Williamson et al. (1992).

*Informational and Other Resources*  For theoretical and practical studies supporting the value and mechanisms of the cooperative integration of information see Chertkoff and Mesch (1997); Finholt and Teasley (1998); Gruber (1990); Halmiova and Potasova (1991); Lakin (1990); John B. Smith (1994); Song et al. (1998). Beyond the small-groups literature see also the *International Journal of Cooperative Information Systems*.

## Cooperation Versus Competition

One might imagine that, if one must compare the two, competition is generally benign and conflict harmful. Tjosvold's (Tjosvold 1998) review makes the reverse case, namely that competition, defined as incompatible goals, may lead to strife, whereas conflict (unconfounded by competition), defined as opposing interests in an interdependent context, may (if faced openly) lead to superior outcomes. To take just one example, he cites a study by Barker et al. (1988), in which managers indicated whom they involved in decision-making and the degree of cooperation in discussing opposing views. Open discussion had a correlation of over 0.6 with effective decision-making. Although more research is needed, Tjosvold (1998) also describes cross-cultural support for the value of cooperative controversy.

Similar premises and conclusions—likewise underpinned by the work of Morton Deutsch and others—emerge from Johnson and Johnson's (D. W. Johnson and Johnson 1989; Roseth et al. 2008) ambitious meta-analysis of research on cooperative, competitive, and individualistic situations. Cooperative interdependence yields not only more achievement and productivity—including high-quality reasoning strategies, new ideas, and superior learning—but also better psychological health, including more liking of self and others. The effects of cooperation (compared with competitive and individualistic situations) on achievement are stronger for studies with greater methodological rigor, but (perhaps fortunately) no statistically significant differences were associated with duration of a study nor type of reward given, nor with ability level, sex, decade of publication, group size, ethnicity, socioeconomic class, age, sample size, setting, nor whether a study was published or unpublished (D. W. Johnson and Johnson 1989, p. 170). Although some individual experiments have shown competition yielding superior results on, for instance, simple activities such as sorting pegs or carrying marbles, the general superiority of cooperation is robust across a wide variety of tasks.

At least in laboratory studies, within-group cooperation may be enhanced by intergroup competition for men but not for women (Van Vugt et al. 2007).

For subsequent publications yielding similar findings see Qin et al. (1995). For additional underlying theories see Bengtsson and Powell (2004) and see also Boone (1992); Edwards (1991); Leik and Meeker (1995); Liebrand et al.(1989). For interpersonal processes see Alper et al. (1998); Bennett (1991); Deberry (1989); Putnam (1997) (covering organizational processes, which are also discussed in Chap. 3). For summary coverage see Van Lange (2000).

Relative advantages (particularly among low-performance individuals) have been found to be contingent on various matters, with for example, cooperative structure being best for extroverted and agreeable members or when accuracy is needed and competitive structures enhance performance speed (Beersma et al. 2003).

For motivation (attitudes toward cooperation) see Brichcin et al. (1994), and for task generalizability (intragroup cooperation facilitating between-group problem-solving) see Keenan and Carnevale (1989) and see also Tauer and Harackiewicz (2004). For other aspects of task and motivation see Griffith and Sell (1988); Hertel and Fiedler (1998); Janssen and Van de Vliert (1996), finding that degree of other-concern (not degree of self-concern) determines cooperativeness; Mitchell and Silver (1990), confirming that individually based goals elicit competition; and

Worchel et al. (1989), finding that cooperation fosters attraction; see also Van Aver-maet et al. (1999).

For discussion of the fairly widespread finding of cooperation being relatively more common than competition within groups than between them see Insko and Wolf (2007). For an insightful overall review of cooperation versus competition see Deutsch (2006).


## Competition

Several studies have focused on the properties of competition itself. Like coopera-tion, competition adaptively causes people to focus on the specific characteristics of the other party (even a fictitious other party!) rather than to rely on stereotyped expectancies (Ruscher and Fiske 1990). Knowing about one's competitors helps one to compete successfully.

As noted above, the value of cooperative interaction is unmistakable. Neverthe-less, for a company or political entity to "be competitive"—in an intergroup mar-ketplace—may be regarded as being a necessity for survival (see also Chap. 3 and K. G. Smith et al. 1992). Indeed, Killman and colleagues have distilled a variety of recommendations for successful competitiveness, focused on internal—within-organization—integration (cooperation) among various elements, including tech-nological and human factors and stakeholders. With regard to being successfully competitive, they conclude, "If one central theme can be said to capture the essence of our model, we would have to choose the theme of teamwork and coordination" (Kilmann et al. 1991, p. 122).

As if to extend this theme, Carnevale and Probst (1997) found, from review-ing several studies, that—ironically—competitive people may, in some contexts, be especially creative and cooperative and therefore effective in circumstances of intergroup conflict.

According to a simulation done by Neal (1997; see also Wellington and Faria 1996), in which groups were made up of members with varying levels of competi-tiveness, it is group cohesiveness—rather than individual competitive disposition—that predicts performance. Decades earlier, of course, Homans (1950) was among the first to consolidate accounts of the importance of cohesiveness and produc-tivity norms. For approaches to understanding the "discontinuity effect" whereby intergroup situations may be more competitive than interindividual ones—includ-ing motivation to work hard (among achievement-oriented people), fear of the out-group, and greed—see Bornstein and Erev (1997); Drigotas et al. (1998); Epstein and Harackiewicz (1992); Schopler and Insko (1992) and, especially, Wildschut et al. (2003). See also Pemberton et al. (1996); Rudisill (1988).

At the interpersonal level, derogation tactics have (perhaps not surprisingly) been attributed to the evolution of intrasexual mate competition (Buss and Dedden 1990). See also Pate et al. (1998).

# Conflict Resolution

Small-group conflict resolution covers a broad array of theoretical and practical topics and spans a variety of levels, from interpersonal to (face-to-face meetings related to) international contexts. For a comprehensive review that is not limited to the current period see Deutsch et al.'s (2006) *Handbook*, already noted above. See also Deutsch's (1994) interim review and Worchel and Simpson's work (1993). For general considerations of reconciliation applicable across levels see Deutsch (2008). For psychological processes such as outgroup bias that need to be addressed in order for postconflict reconciliation to create a lasting peace see Riek et al. (2008). For links between conflict resolution and group processes see Blumberg (2001b).

The present section is concerned with general and theoretical research, followed by background variables, styles of conflict management and resolution, experimental variables, communication procedures, and guidelines. (Also, later in this chapter there is a section concerned with negotiation and mediation, which obviously can be especially relevant to conflict resolution.)

According to Pruitt (1998), essentially these topics might soon be integrated into a unified theory of conflict. In the meantime, his own review organizes the material into four subfields: social dilemmas (covering interdependent outcomes that thus also include Prisoner's Dilemma and social loafing), negotiation, broader conflict (including contention in close relationships and strategic choices), and conflict resolution (including third-party functions and improving intergroup relations). As a common theme running through more than one area, Pruitt (1998, p. 493) notes that cooperation is encouraged by common group membership, attraction, tit-for-tat strategies, and open communication—in other words, by aspects of all four of the "MIGR" sectors described near the outset of the present chapter.

Moreover, according to much research by Deutsch (1994) and his students, the causal linkages tend to be bidirectional. The features that facilitate cooperation are themselves fostered by cooperation. Likewise, competition both follows from and leads to the absence or opposite of those features—that is, may form what Deutsch calls a "malignant social process" that can be reversed but only with difficulty. The "once dominant" dispositional (trait) approach to understanding conflict and other social behavior has been largely supplanted by emphasis on a dynamic interaction of disposition and situation (Deutsch 1994, p. 15)—as if to parallel developments in leadership research discussed in Chap. 6 (written by Kent) of Blumberg et al. (2009) (cf. Rahim 1997). McGrath and colleagues view cooperation and conflict as being connected manifestations of group members coordinating ways of addressing evolved needs (McGrath et al. 1999).

"Conflict settlement" describes a goal intermediate between resolution and management, one in which the parties to a conflict do find an outcome that meets their underlying interests behaviorally even if their attitudes are not shifted (Rubin 1989, 1992). As Rubin notes, it is now more widely accepted that many themes are common across levels (from intrapersonal to international)—the value of third-party mediation, for instance. The research task remains, however, of finding the actual degree of cross-cultural generality of a variety of phenomena such as the need to save face, the importance of prenegotiation and postnegotiation, and the value of different negotiating environments. Rubin gives several helpful suggestions—for instance, the possibility of negotiating from the inside out, (e.g., as in the 1978 Camp David agreements), where a single solution that appears to meet both parties' needs is modified until it is acceptable, rather than the more traditional procedure of bargaining by a series of concessions from parties' initial extreme positions.

For additional analysis of generalizability between interpersonal and international levels of conflict see Rubin and Levinger (1995). In the second edition of a textbook on conflict settlement, Rubin et al. (1994) emphasize that known principles of conflict resolution are still applicable to the post-Cold-War world and, one might add, also to the "post September 11" world.

Worchel and Lundgren (1991) have provided a general easily read review of conflict resolution research, emphasizing aspects that are particularly relevant to community mediation. Pruitt and Olczak (1995) describe a multimodal approach for easing especially severe, unyielding conflicts.

The roots of conflict at any level may of course often relate in part to intergroup prejudice. For many years Dovidio and others have studied latent prejudice, including "aversive racism" (see, e.g., Dovidio and Gaertner 1999). He and colleagues (Dovidio, Maruyama, and Alexander 1998) have highlighted the individual and intergroup factors that shape the nature of perceptions which may foster conflict. They explain that such perceptions lead to how we think, feel, and act toward minority and other groups. And they argue that, despite methodological difficulties, social psychologists should continue to move beyond the laboratory to applied national and international matters.

For a full discussion of some links between prejudice and conflict see Aboud (1992). Other chapters in the same volume cover various developmental aspects of conflict. See also Chap. 6 of the present volume.

## *Paradigms and Topics*

At least a dozen publications, primarily from the 1990s, have described general paradigms, some of them broadly similar to one another, that may be particularly useful for reducing friction in certain contexts or at least for testing hypotheses. As one might by now guess, they are concerned with meaning, interpersonal matters, goal attainment, and resources.

*Basic Meaning* A long-standing conflict may undergo *transformation* when parties improve their relationship by finally reevaluating their defensive postures (Kingsbury 1995). Integrative resolution of strife may be achieved by a series of procedures such as brainstorming for creative solutions and then evaluating and implementing them (Littlefield et al. 1993). In a laboratory study of conflict, pretraining in the desiderata of the conflict resolution model of Wertheim and colleagues (which has some properties in common with Littlefield et al.'s procedures) does facilitate integrative agreements (Feeney and Davidson 1996).

Spears (2008) has discussed the importance of legitimacy in constraining intergroup discrimination though it can also hold back resistance to injustice.

For additional general factorial research on perceived preferences for different modes of conflict resolution see Arnold and Carnevale (1997). For conflict-reducing exercises that can be taught to children see Carlander (1989). For an intriguing formal theory see Levis (1988). For a "graph model" that can provide advice to decision-makers in resolving conflict see Kilgour and Hipel (2005a, b). Aureli and de Waal (2000) discuss, from a variety of perspectives, some evolutionary reasons for natural peacekeeping tendencies (see also Macy 1995).

*Interpersonal Integration* Various aspects of conflict rooted in personal relationships and social interaction have been discussed by a number of authors. Bar-Tal (1990), for example, has discussed the detrimental effects of delegitimization of outgroups.

Dovidio, Saguy, and Shnabel (2009) remind us that conflict is not necessarily negative and opposite to cooperation and that, within a common shared group identity, resolution may depend on a variety of within- and between-group factors. Emphasis on shared interests may help group members to disagree constructively (Chizhik et al. 2009). For large-group systems see Bunker (2006).

For long-term animosities Malloy (2008) suggests that peaceful coexistence may be a more realistic interim goal than resolution.

See also Cahn (1994) for a book on interpersonal conflict; Danielsson and Eveson (1997) for training in social skills and third-party conflict resolution; Hubbard (1997) for a case study of a US-based Jewish-Palestinian discussion group; Kaufmann and Stern (1988) on contract litigation; Schoenbach (1990) for a monograph on the developmental phases of interpersonal conflict and its resolution; and Wallach (2006) for preventing and transforming international and other conflict by using group-relations insights to counter-act irrational processes.

*Goals, Motivation, and Procedures* are implicit in the work of: Ford (1994) on social conflict and bargaining; Coleman (2006b) on power differentials among conflicting parties; Messick et al. (1997), who carried out bargaining experiments demonstrating the difficulty of perceiving others' decision rules; Oots (1990) on bargaining with terrorists as a function of how the terrorist group is organized; and Shnabel and Nadler (2008) on experimentally supported reconciliation based on an "exchange" whereby victims gain power and perpetrators gain an image of morality and social acceptability. Also, as Thompson et al. (2006) have explained, addressable cognitive biases can hamper not only conflicting parties but also negotiators. Even for apparently intractable conflicts, Baron (2008) describes how group and individual processes can be arranged so as to favor a sense of "we-ness" and, in turn, trust and reconciliation.

*Resources* For discussion of the distribution of scarce resources as related to the distribution of information in conflict situations see Levine and Thompson (1996).

For procedures fostering the fair division of resources (e.g., dividing property or settling boundary disputes) see Brams and Taylor (1996).


## Background Variables

In common with much of the other small-groups literature from the 1990s and early 2000s, a large part of the research on conflict resolution has been devoted to "filling out" known paradigms in a broader variety of contexts, including further studying the effects of diverse background variables (see also Chap. 2, by Hare, in Blumberg et al. 2009).

*Sex (and Personality)* When university students described actual interpersonal conflicts and how they coped with them, females were more likely to prefer "indirect" strategies generally whereas males preferred these only when unacquainted with the other party, though other variables such as parties' goals were also relevant (Ohbuchi and Baba 1988). For other broadly parallel studies of effects of parties' sex (and personality/background) see Buunk et al. (1990); Canary et al. (1988); Halpern and Parks (1996); Levy et al. (1997); J. B. Miller (1991); Ohsako and Takahashi (1994); Pilkington et al. (1988). For a study dealing mainly just with personality (conflict mode preference as a function of scales on the Myers-Briggs Type Indicator) see Percival et al. (1992).

*Culture* Well over a dozen studies have looked at the association between culture (and other variables) and styles of conflict resolution, often finding differences, though not always the ones predicted by the researchers. Compared with Anglo-Americans, Taiwan undergraduates ("collectivist culture"), for example, were found not only to be more obliging and avoiding in their conflict styles, as predicted, but also more integrating and compromising (Trubisky et al. 1991). Likewise, compared with their American counterparts, Japanese participants—describing recent interpersonal conflicts—were more likely to render conflicts as covert and to use avoidance and indirect strategies (Ohbuchi and Takahashi 1994).

Of course, individual and subcultural differences within a culture may also affect conflict-resolving strategies. Among engaged Arab-Palestinian men living in Israel, for instance, reasoning was more likely than physical or verbal aggression among those who were not from families that were exposed to violence, those who had egalitarian expectations for marriage, and those classified as androgynous (Haj-Yahia and Edleson 1994). See also Collier (1991) on interaction of sex and culture among Africans, Mexicans, and Anglo-Americans; Duranti (1990) on Samoa; Gabrenya and Hwang (1996) on China; Itoi et al. (1996) on interaction of sex and culture among Japanese and Americans; Kirkbride et al. (1991) on China; Kozan (1990) on Turkey and Jordan.

For other work relating culture to aspects of conflict resolution see Leung and Wu (1990) for an overview. See also Boggs and Chun (1990); Chiu and Kosinski (1994); Faure (1995); Ken-ichi et al. (1997); Kirchmeyer and Cohen (1992); Leung

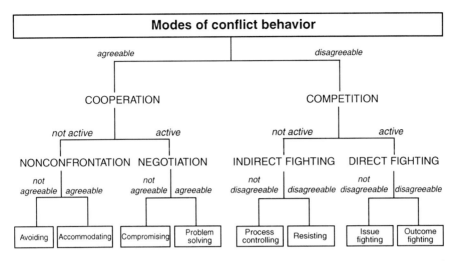

**Fig. 1.1** Refined characterization of modes of conflict behavior in terms of agreeableness and activeness. (Source: E. E. Van de Vliert and M. C. Euwema, Agreeableness and activeness as components of conflict behaviors. *Journal of Personality and Social Psychology*, 1994, 66, 674–687 (Fig. 3, p. 684). © 1994 The American Psychological Association, reprinted with permission)

(1988); Lind et al. (1994); Singelis and Pedersen (1997); Ting-Toomey (1994); Ting-Toomey et al. (1991); Van Oudenhoven et al. (1998); Weisinger and Salipante (1995).

## Styles

Many of the studies cited in the preceding section relate background variables to modes of conflict resolution. Additionally, a substantial literature focuses on the different modes or styles as such. The present discussion starts with a relatively detailed presentation of a scheme that subsumes various others.

The main reported modes can be subsumed under two dimensions, agreeableness and activeness, according to Van de Vliert and Euwema (1994). These are essentially Bales's first two SYMLOG dimensions (Bales and Cohen 1979) and are probably also related, respectively, to agreeableness (and low neuroticism) and extraversion (and openness) from the "Big 5" dimensions (Blumberg 2001a). Van de Vliert and Euwema draw on—and merge—several well-known approaches, both conceptually and also (as an example) in empirical ratings of videotapes of role-plays of two-person conflicts between 82 male Dutch police sergeants, respectively, and a subordinate or superior (actually a professional actor) who had supposedly borrowed a police car for private use. Figure 1.1 shows the proposed merger of several approaches and sources—among them, Bales's interaction process analysis, Osgood's semantic differential, Deutsch's cooperation versus competition, and the five-part taxonomy (avoiding, accommodating, compromising, problem solving, and competing) of Blake and Mouton's conflict grid and subsequently of Kilmann and Thomas's typology, and Horney's moving away/toward/against.

Like Bales before them, Van de Vliert and Euwena conclude not only that the two dimensions that account for the most variance in social interaction are positive-negative and active-passive but also that these are continua and that different situations (in this case, different stages of conflict) have typically different profiles of interaction as rated on these dimensions. No doubt the understanding of conflict could be further enhanced by adding SYMLOG's third dimension, Forward-Backward: rating whether behavior is, or is not, predictable, task-oriented, and serious (conscientious, in "Big 5" terms) rather than emotional. This third dimension could be useful—for example, in understanding particular "terrorist" actions—but would no doubt entail more difficult ratings than the other two dimensions, for such ratings require fuller knowledge of the conflict and the parties, and would also probably be especially dependent on the perspectives of the raters.

The aforementioned scheme does indeed help one to "arrange" and understand the literature on conflict styles. For instance, Fukushima and Ohbuchi (1993) found that strategies (modes) are related to parties' goals—for example, a justice goal goes with a more confrontational (active negative) style than a goal focusing on relations. Roles, too, matter; interpersonal conflicts with a colleague are in many ways similar to those with a social partner but are more likely to show "avoiding" (which is passive and slightly negative) (Pokrajac-Bulian et al. 1996). Profile differences may also apply across "levels," as in the case of participants who felt they would be more likely to use threats (active negative) in intergroup and international disputes but more likely to use promises (active positive) in interpersonal ones (Betz and Fry 1995). In all cases, style may be mediated by attributional processes, as when perceived intentionality in instigating conflict may be associated with anger or violence (active negative) rather than empathy (passive positive) (Betancourt and Blair 1992).

See also Ben-Yoav and Banai (1992); Black (1990); Buzzanell and Burrell (1997); Canary and Spitzberg (1989); Hammock and Richardson (1992); Hammock et al. (1990); Kozan (1990); Leung and Kim (2007); Makino and Takemura (1994); Mapstone (1995); Mills (1997); Ohbuchi and Takahashi (1994); Peirce et al. (1993); Pena and Rodriguez (1996); Richardson et al. (1989); Witte (1989); Witteman (1992).

## *Experimental Variables*

The actual procedures followed in the course of dealing with a conflict may, of course, have profound effects on the outcome. This section (a) begins by describing some general studies (one of them in particular detail) that focus on experimental variables in conflict-resolving procedures and then (b) following the now-familiar "MIGR" progression, in turn notes some studies that emphasize meaning, interpersonal matters, goals, and resources.

In a simulation study concerned with the fictitious "island republic of Cygnus," modeled realistically on the lasting dispute between Greek and Turkish Cypriots, Druckman et al. (1988) compared three prototypical conditions. Participants were students from courses on small-group communication.

In a "values-first" *facilitation* condition of third-party intervention—fashioned loosely after the problem-solving workshops of Burton, Kelman, Doob, and others—participants were said to have taken part in sessions devoted to understanding the relevant culture and values of the conflicting sides and to a shared appreciation of each other's ways of life and respective needs. In an "interests-first" *delinked* condition, based on the separation of (conflicting) values from (more readily compatible differences in specific) interests, parties focused on factual statements and positions on various issues. This was in line with Fisher's now-classic idea of "fractionating conflict," whereby a complicated dispute may be dealt with "one piece at a time," starting with the resolution of smaller issues.

In a third, *embedded* condition, the comparable emphasis was simply on making salient the links between parties' values and positions. Otherwise, the three conditions were strenuously kept comparable with respect to time spent, value complexity, understanding of value content, and other aspects of the situation.

Compared with the embedded condition, the other two procedures were both associated with comparably marked benefits in outcome—for example, more resolutions and a more positive negotiating climate. There were procedural differences between the two effective conditions—for instance, not surprisingly the participants in the values-first facilitation condition (who supposedly had previous experience together in a problem-solving workshop) were more cooperative in discussions at the outset. Although essentially based on roleplaying, Druckman et al.'s method gives a "foothold" for understanding which aspects of complex workshops and issue-based negotiations are responsible for their respective effectiveness. It would be interesting, too, to find out whether (as one suspects) a *dual* focus on facilitation and fractionation could provide even better outcomes or whether the two modes are both productive but essentially incompatible with each other.

In other studies of dispute resolution, various norms (e.g., with regard to communication procedures)—which may cross-cut variables such as value or issue emphasis—have been found to be important. For instance, "voice"—the opportunity to cross-question the accounts given by others (even if the obtained information turns out not to affect the content of an outcome!)—increases the perceived fairness of outcomes (Folger et al. 1996). This seems to be true for both the process stage (when a case is being presented) and the decision stage, and is true for the "voice" not only of disputing parties but also for their representatives, and for the judge or mediator, if any. In the same studies, other closely related aspects of the situation were also important—such as having an appeal mechanism, and a (fair) third-party having control over actual decisions.

For other studies of general procedural parameters see Arnold and Carnevale (1997); Cross and Rosenthal (1999); Fukushima and Ohbuchi (1993); Witteman (1992).

Few studies seem to focus on how experimental procedural aspects of the *"meaning"* of a situation affect conflict. Wilson and Brewer (1993) did find that meaning, in terms of a particular concept—in this case, arguably "deindividuation"—may sometimes help explain the effects of seemingly diverse variables on, for example, the emergence of aggression. Using police patrol-log data from actual confrontations, they found that the degree of violence encountered by the police was associated with—though not, of course, necessarily causally linked to—(greater) number of officers present, number of bystanders, and other aspects of the situation and the degree of anxiety associated with it. Likewise, in a very different context, Singh (1997) found, using a minimal group paradigm, that "harmony" was important. Participants in India divided group rewards in such a way as to "minimize group conflict" in keeping with a goal of fairness and group consonance.

For studies related to *interpersonal* matters see Baron (1988) (the destructive effects of poorly used negative criticism); Farmer and Roth (1998) (on group cohesiveness); Fukushima and Ohbuchi (1996) (the effects, on social goals, of a variety of situational variables); Laursen (1993) (the usually benign impact of conflict on adolescent relationships); and Zumkley and Zumkley-Muenkel (1992) (on mood related to aggressive conflicts and to altruism).

As one might hope, a main concern for studies of experimental procedure is on the impact of how, and how well, people carry out the task of resolving conflict—that is, on *goal-directed* activity, including its interpersonal aspects.

The following finding, for instance, is consistent with the benefits of Druckman's "values first" procedure (based on problem-solving workshops, as described above), but was derived in a wholly different way. In a business setting, dyads formed with high coorientational accuracy—that is, where participants can correctly identify the other party's views and the strategies the other party feels are most likely to yield effective influence—needed to spend less time clarifying their positions, which in turn yielded higher satisfaction with the "conflict process" (Papa and Pood 1988).

For various other studies relevant to goal-directed activity see C. Johnson and Ford (1996) (the impact, on strategy tactics, of dependence and legitimate authority, in role-played conflict); Ohbuchi et al. (1995) (cross-cultural confirmation that collaborative goals yield especially good outcomes); Rouhana and Korper (1996) (how workshop interventions can deal with power asymmetry); and Swingle (1989) (recursive negative effects of experiencing *non*cooperation).

In one of the few studies to focus on *resources* as an experimental variable, social influence was found to be more important than resource scarcity among two-year-olds. Scarcity of resources tended to lead to sharing rather than to increased conflict (Caplan et al. 1991). When duplicate toys were available, many conflicts occurred, although the likelihood of conflict did decrease over time. One could hardly generalize from this study to older ages much less to larger groups, but it does provide support for the view that interpersonal matters "trump" resources; that is, the "MIGR" sequence represents a hierarchy of control (Hare 1983).

## *Communication*

The quality of communication is sufficiently important in resolving conflicts that over a dozen publications in the present period have focused particularly on this special topic, often in the context of interpersonal disputes. For a full review of perspectives on this material (at the interpersonal level)—which is beyond the scope of the present chapter—the reader is referred to Cahn (1990). The first chapter of his collection of recent studies, *Intimates in conflict*, is a review and classification of research including: its dimensions (emotional and critical/rational), levels (essentially what the present chapter has been calling MIGR), and a classification—arguments over particular issues, more encompassing negotiations, unhappy/dissolving relationships. He also looks at the bases of destructive conflict, including: psychological factors such as romantic involvement (which ironically may make bargaining for optimal outcomes *less* likely), relationship dissatisfaction, sex differences in perception and the particular importance of the "health" of the husband's personality; and social factors, such as marital developmental stages, and power and cultural differences.

Perhaps complicating the picture, even similar conflict expressed in different ways may have different optimal ways of being resolved. A taxonomy of interpersonal conflict has been based on informants' guided descriptions of events in their same-sex (nonromantic) or romantic relationships (Baxter et al. 1993). Such instances did not fall on a unidimensional spectrum but included mock (playful) conflicts, repetitive ones, those with third-party involvement, indirect conflict (not expressed verbally), "silent-treatment," episodic, escalatory, one-sided, polite, and tacit. There were broad similarities between friends and romantic partners and between males and females, but there was greater likelihood of indirect and tacit conflicts among friends, especially women.

In a study of the process and outcome of typical disputes between dyads of Chicago high-school students, Stein et al. (1997) devised a method that (fittingly) compromises between the systematic variation of a role-play study and the ecological validity of a real dispute. They measured students' support for each of two dyadic roles in both of two scenarios (delay in returning borrowed money and dropping an old friend when moving to a new school), assigned students (within same-sex and opposite-sex pairs) to the roles of a scenario in accordance with the actual content and strength of their beliefs, and videotaped the resulting negotiations. Judges subsequently and reliably rated and categorized the discourse.

A compromise outcome was especially likely, occurring in 84% of the dyads, when both parties (or at least one) started with high initial knowledge (number of reasons for or against each position). When both parties had low knowledge, outcomes were divided about evenly among compromise, win-loss, and stand-off. Compromise was less likely in male–female dyads than in same-sex ones; win-loss was more likely, with females usually "winning." An experimental intervention of urging compromise had little effect on outcome, though it did increase the level of compromise in mixed-sex dyads.

For other research emphasizing discourse in interpersonal disputes, see Canary and Spitzberg (1990) (attributional biases favoring self); Cloven and Roloff (1991) (value of integrative interaction rather than mulling over disputes); Daly and Wiemann (1994) (relevant system properties of discourse, such as variety, symmetry, and spontaneity); Hama et al. (1988) (motivation and outcome); Sillars and Wilmot (1994) (importance of what are essentially the three SYMLOG dimensions); Sitkin and Bies (1993) (the value of explanations embedded in social accounts); Tutzauer and Roloff (1988) (processes predicting integrative agreements); Vogelzang et al. (1997) (predictive power of words of communality such as "we" versus "you" or "I"). For the analysis of speech acts in higher level (workgroup) conflict see Franz and Jin (1995). For the value of apology in reconciliation see Tavuchis (1991). For general theoretical discussion of the role of communication in conflict see also S. B. Cobb (1991).

For the role of communication more generally in easing—or exacerbating—conflict, see Krauss and Morsella (2006). In order to combat disputants' "common foe" of misunderstanding, they point out the value of reducing noise, taking the other's perspective, trying to understand the other's *intended* meaning, and being an active, questioning listener. To do so may lead to reconciliation and will at least reduce the chances of communication making matters worse. The contact hypothesis (see above) adds additional understanding of when intergroup communication may be especially effective. Olekalns et al. (2008) review communication processes with regard both to the message strategies relevant for conflict management and to goals implicit in negotiation.

Several publications delineate special communication procedures related to the resolution of conflict. Each seems to have its own acronym! Among the matters dealt with are: A multiprocess Affect Infusion Model (AIM) showing, for example, the effect of sadness on conflict-related attributions of self-blame (Forgas 1994); the widespread value of Alternative (nonlitigation) Dispute Resolution (ADR) strategies (Singer 1989); Conflict Elaboration Theory (CET), which de-confounds various social influence phenomena (Perez and Mugny 1996); Consensual Conflict Resolution (CCR) intervention which emphasizes logical discussion, thereby improving solutions (Innami 1994); computerized Decision Support Systems (DSS) or Electronic Meeting Systems (EMS) (Harmon 1998; Sainfort et al. 1990; also, see Chap. 8 of Blumberg et al. (2009), for a detailed discussion of Group Support Systems); and Conflict Management (CM) systems arising from either environmental norms or conscious negotiations (Kuenne 1989).

## Guidelines and Processes

This final section on conflict resolution concerns publications offering practical guidelines and advice about processes. As with several of the previous sections, material is organized according to a "MIGR" progression.

*Meaning* Several approaches deal with conflicts by considering their underlying meaning or significance. According to Kingsbury (1995), many conflicts are rooted in the past and persist only because participants are defensively "locked into" particular values and attitudes. Conflict transformation may follow parties' independent assessment of what would constitute an ideal contemporary relationship. Presumably, problem-solving workshops and fractionation of conflict, discussed above, would be consistent with Kingsbury's views. Indeed his stress on the importance of meeting basic, sometimes primitive needs is aligned with J. Burton's (Burton 1979) approach to problem-solving workshops. For a review of the evolution of problem-solving workshops see Lumsden and Wolfe (1996).

Muldoon (1997), too, emphasizes the importance of "human nature" in the genesis and management of conflict and the need to consider overall context when deciding between, for example, cooperative and adversarial approaches. Ibanez Gracia (1988) stresses, as well, that to understand conflict it is valuable to take a holistic view of social groups as self-organizing systems. Kimmel (2006) and Pedersen (2006) stress the importance of multicultural awareness for both understanding conflict and helping to resolve it.

In a particularly rational approach to the resolution, if not the genesis, of conflict, Sinnott (1993) suggests that "complex thought," covering a broad spectrum of knowledge about a situation, acts symbiotically with conflict so as to promote mature development.

By contrast with the key factors suggested in the preceding paradigms, Stafford and Gibbs (1993) posit that low levels of social control are a primary factor leading to conflict and violence. Although it is an empirical question, one suspects that the relationship is likely to be curvilinear: Some social control is needed for norm-based democratic processing of disputes, but too much social constraint (except when so great as to be totally stifling) would be likely to elicit rebellion.

Rather than positing any particular paradigm as a key to understanding conflict, Bennett et al. (1994) describe the development of INTERACT software, which models interactive decision making and represents a potentially useful tool for concerned parties.

Using a mathematical model rather than a simulation as such, Van Gastel and Paelinck (1992) describe what are effectively parties' utility curves and the nature of "solution spaces." Perhaps conversely, A. Mitchell (2006) suggests a literally philosophical approach for understanding truth and reconciliation.

Finally, for a succinct overview of contributions psychology can make to conflict resolution and peace, see Cairns and Lewis (2003).

*Interpersonal Matters* Already noted, in the section on Cooperation, is the work of Smith et al., on the key importance of trust. An antecedent of trust, as discussed by Tjosvold (1997), is for people (in organizations) to view their goals as positively related; trust, in turn, leads to "constructive controversy" and, with it, creative outcomes (see also Carnevale 2006). Kelman (2008b) posits that mutual acceptance of the other party's identity is a key element in reconciliation and the restoration of trust. See also Janssen et al. (1994); Muluk (2009); Nadler et al. (2008); and Worchel, Coutant-Sassic, and Wong (1993).

In a different chapter of the same book (*Using conflict in organizations*) that includes Tjosvold's paradigm, Baron (1997) offers practical advice for overcoming biased attributions and unwarranted stereotypes.

In everyday contexts such as household divisions of labor, one can specify "collaborative rules" based on people's expectations for working together harmoniously (Goodnow 1996).

Allport's contact hypothesis continues to generate useful research and advice for reducing intergroup conflict (Pettigrew 1998; cf. Corneille 1994). According to this paradigm (see Chap. 6), intergroup prejudice, and hence conflict, can be reduced by sustained task-related social interaction between equal-status members of different groups with the positive support of those in authority. Paradoxically, such contact may be most effective when a person's minority group membership is salient and the person is prototypical of the group (apart from the characteristics being disconfirmed) and hence is less likely to be viewed as an "exception to the rule" (Niens and Cairns 2001). Because people's initial stance may, however, be unaccepting of others whose "outgroup membership" is salient, an optimal sequence for reducing intergroup conflict may be for parties' group identification to be made salient partway through a series of social interactions (Lepore and Brown 2002).

Four ways to reduce intergroup conflict have been described in detail: induce consideration of future consequences, provide independent leadership, foster outgroup empathy, and foster coordination of superordinate goals (Cohen and Insko 2008).

For additional guidelines related to interpersonal matters see Ayoko et al. (2002) (communication management strategies such as checking parties' understanding, as a means of promoting positive aspects of conflict in workgroups); Boardman and Horowitz (1994) (constructive conflict management); Sessa (1996) (training in taking others' perspectives); Shapiro and Liu (2006) (ways of dealing with residual interparty negative emotion); Veenema et al. (1994) (methodological considerations). See also C. T. Miller (1993), who found that higher false consensus bias, whereby people overestimate the popularity of their own viewpoints, is associated with being less likely to favor compromise. Fisher (2006) reviews ways of managing and resolving intergroup conflicts but notes that, happily, most ongoing intergroup relations are cooperative.

*Goal-Directed Activity* Suggestions for "getting on with the task" of resolving conflict are, perhaps not surprisingly, diverse and seem themselves to span a "MIGR" subhierarchy. Providing participants with a broad model or simulation of the "meaning" of the conflict represents one suggestion (Sandole 1989). Galam and Moscovici (1995) reiterate a "theory of power," following from organizational complexity, and associated with conflict and its resolution. Meanwhile, Levine (2009) has been developing and testing a detailed paradigm whereby conflicting parties implement a new mindset for essentially positive collaboration. See Weitzman and Weitzman (2006) for a conceptually similar analysis.

Peterson (1989) reviews "interpersonal" goal conflict and its resolution. According to Kim and Smith (1993), revenge typically escalates conflicts and it is therefore especially important to be vigilant in minimizing others' vengeful behavior—for example, avoid maligning others and apologize for offenses.

"Goal-directed" motivations also merit attention, particularly with regard to adopting stress-reducing strategies, as delineated by Hashimoto (1995). One useful approach to tracking the course of conflict may be to estimate—at different stages of a conflict—the transitional probabilities of going from one state (such as paying attention to own view) to others (such as paying attention to others' views). Nicotera (1994) apparently found that such transitions do not necessarily follow a Markov process. (Any phenomenon—in this case, the phases of an evolving group conflict—following a Markov process requires minimal "historical" knowledge: "If one knows the present state, one does not need to know where one has come from in order to estimate the probabilities of where one will go next.") Instead, for example, at the first stage of a conflict sequence (using undergraduates' written accounts of workplace disputes) participants tended to higher levels of attention to their own views. At the next stage, attention helpfully shifted away from whichever party had just previously been focused on. As yet another set of useful suggestions for actually dealing with (within-group) conflict, Carlander (1989) describes methods that can be taught to children, such as role-playing and discussions that foster cohesiveness.

Retzinger and Scheff (2000) discuss how mediation can address the alienation that may sustain protracted conflicts; and Horton-Deutsch and Horton (2003) suggest that promoting mindfulness may lessen the buildup of intractable conflict. For an analysis and review of intractable conflicts and their possible resolution see Coleman (2006a).

Finally, suggestions regarding informational "resources" (in the form of outcome expectations) within the goal-attainment aspects of conflict resolution are provided by Makoul and Roloff (1998). Based on measures of undergraduates' reasons for withholding complaints, anticipated aggressive responses, anticipated satisfaction, and other variables, they conclude that individuals are most likely to act confrontationally when they are confident of their ability to do so.

*Resources* Positive conflict management is associated with good use of resources (including information). In a particularly apt experimental example: According to Bottger and Yetton (1988), drawing on arguments made by Hall and Watson, "Positive conflict management involves examination of competing knowledge bases, exploration of alternatives, and the willingness of participants to argue for their points of view" (p. 236). In their study, managers and management students, working (mainly) in five-person groups, gave individual opinions about the "moon survival" task and then worked as groups to solve the problem. Both group resources (having a plurality of members with good solutions) and effective conflict management contributed independently to group performance. In particular, when no plurality existed (i.e., limited resources), good performance depended on a good decision scheme (selecting, for each item, the best answer available from members' views), and this in turn depended on positive conflict management. Positive conflict management behaviors (reminiscent of avoiding Groupthink—see Chap. 8 of Blumberg et al. 2009) included: clear logical arguments to support both preferences and decision changes, conflicting parties sharing information that underpins their beliefs, encouraging an expanded range of ideas, suggesting alternatives that might be acceptable to both conflicting parties, and challenging early agreements.

Other advice related to resources in conflict resolution is as follows: If feasible, providing disputants with accurate information about the likely outcome of arbitration increases satisfaction and ratings of fairness (Heuer and Penrod 1994). Indeed, arbitration *prior* to mediation may represent a particularly effective combined strategy (Conlon et al. 2002). To help manage interpersonal conflict, be aware of principles of interpersonal impression formation and their effect on communication in disputes (Spitzberg et al. 1994). Try a computer-aided technique for evaluating and comparing the opinion lists of parties in disagreement (Slater et al. 1989; see also the section on Communication, above). In international conflicts, too, the information implicit in a systems approach may be useful in understanding peacemaking, for example (Kahn and Landau 1988)—this would include awareness of the inertia associated with the status quo (Senese 1997).

## Collective Dilemmas

In collective dilemmas, including those related to scarce resources, a "conflict" can arise not through any "fault" of the participants but because an overall reward structure entraps people into behavior that goes against the common good. After consideration of some relatively general studies, the presentation below turns to theories and paradigms, studies concerned with background variables, some effects of group size and composition, the impact of how a situation is "framed," and properties of the reward structure itself.

In addition to the various studies covered in the present section, references to related work using the PDG and other gaming paradigms are covered in the next chapter. The line between collective dilemmas and Prisoner's Dilemma is, however, a fuzzy one; the typical payoff matrices are broadly similar. In a commons dilemma, as with PDG, everyone is better off if all cooperate (by not overharvesting a resource) than if no one does; but if everyone else cooperates, any given individual will be better off by taking a large harvest. Unlike prototypical PDG, however, resource dilemmas tend to include more than two parties, to be iterative (a given situation is played through several rounds), and to have a resource pool that is updated with each round.

There is also a fairly subtle distinction between some of the work covered in this section—where payoff matrices tend to be explicit and to contrast cooperative and other choices—and those group-decision studies (covered in Chap. 8 of Blumberg et al. 2009) where individuals initially choose among options which the group then discusses and attempts to decide among.

According to Dawes et al. (1990), there are several historical views regarding the origins of cooperation in social dilemmas—a Hobbesian Leviathan state, agreed reciprocal altruism, agreed punishment for defection, and social conscience—but a major factor in a series of their own experiments is simply social identity, for example, with an immediate group. In a typical study of theirs, participants would be given $4 unconditional pay plus a promissory note for $5, which they might lose or keep or double, depending on how many group members "donate" the promissory note to a common pool. Participants are much more likely to contribute resources helpfully to a pool if they are given the opportunity to discuss their situation—thus establishing a social bond—even though formal agreements and side payments are banned from the discussion.

These individual solutions—that is, manipulations aimed at changing the behavior of individual group members—can be particularly easy to implement. They may be subsumed within a decision model, in which participants decide among their options according to their satisfaction with different outcomes and attributions as to how these can be achieved (Samuelson and Messick 1995; see also Kerr and Kaufman-Gilliland 1997).

For discussion of these and other relevant matters see Komorita and Parks (1995); in the course of discussing public goods and resource dilemmas, in the social dilemmas section of their more general review of mixed-motive interaction, they also briefly review organizational dilemmas, whereby workers may form coalitions that reserve a disproportionate share of their organization's resources.

The studies by Dawes and colleagues emphasize one-trial decisions, in order to measure the effects of individuals' social identity even in the absence of motives relevant to an ongoing working relationship with others. By contrast, Suleiman et al. (1996) have studied the effects of sequential actions as such and have found, for example, that if sequence of participation is commonly known, the threat of retaliation may itself induce cooperation. Also, group members may, in effect, take turns over time in making major contributions (Sniezek and May 1990).

Thus all three of Kelman's (Kelman 1961) classic bases of social influence—compliance, identification, and internalization—would seem to be manifest, too, in studies of collective dilemmas.

Reward structures as well as motivational dynamics are featured in real-world examples of social dilemmas, in the concluding chapter of Komorita and Parks's (Komorita and Parks 1994) book on social dilemmas. They cite, for instance, Rutte's account of a Dutch bank where, at the start of each day, work was divided equally among all teams of keypunch operators. After lunch, all remaining work was pooled and again divided equally among teams, with the incentive that everyone could go home when all of the day's work was completed. The unintended result was that people were motivated to work *slowly* in the morning because their unfinished work would be reallocated at lunchtime. The incentive of going home early was rarely achieved and the milieu was unpleasant. In a revised, far more effective scheme, the day's work was still divided equally among teams, but each team could simply go home when it finished. Other cited examples note the importance of salient group identity coupled with monitoring individual behavior (e.g., of energy consumption).

A field study of a social dilemma (1991 water shortage in California) indicated that the presence of a fair procedure (Meaning and Goal-attainment) and identification with the community (Integration) contributed more to conservation than did the severity of the scarcity or favorability of authorities' decisions (Resources) (Tyler and Degoey 1995).

Komorita and Parks stress the need for increased interdisciplinary work and also the importance of reconciling different theoretical approaches—identity theorists, for instance, posit that cooperation is increased with enhanced (common) group identity whereas deindividuation theorists emphasize the value of minimizing (discrepant) group identities. Further theoretical concerns are covered in the next section below.

For a review that emphasizes ways of avoiding the tragedy of the commons see Ostrom et al. (1994). For additional general treatments of these and related matters see Allison and Messick (1990) (establishing that outcomes are multiply determined—for example, best preservation of a common pool when resources are divisible, payoffs are low, and choices can influence others' fate); Erev and Rapoport (1990) (noting the particular importance of knowing about previous *non*cooperative choices); Rutte and Wilke (1992) (applying Pruitt's goal/expectation paradigm, whereby cooperation occurs when parties want to cooperate and expect that others do as well); and Suleiman and Rapoport (1988) (describing a testable model that incorporates uncertainty). See also Messick (1991); Rapoport et al. (1992). For an automated computer system to study commons dilemmas in laboratory and classroom settings see Fusco et al. (1991).

## *Theories and Paradigms*

In their review of theories and strategies for studying social dilemmas Smithson and Foddy (1999) delineate several "core traditions:" social dilemmas as a conflict between motivations for maximization of personal versus collective interests; cooperative evolution from Hobbesian selfish competition; naturally occurring cooperation, such as may arise from social identification (see above); and considerations of rationality and morality. They conclude that there may be multiple mechanisms to ensure human cooperation.

Although the experimental literature on social dilemmas and resource depletion typically focuses on the importance of (human) cooperation, the complex processes of resource allocation also have implications for equity and social inequality. Implications of social dilemma research for social discrimination may well be worth ongoing attention. For instance, Blalock (1991) has provided a tentative paradigm covering a wide range of variables and providing for bidirectional causal paths involving more powerful and weaker actors. As he notes in one example:

> First, there will be a set of competitors for positions, locations in space, school grades, or parental attention and care. Second are those who make allocation decisions that apportion scarce goods or resources among such competitors. The competitors will, in turn, react to these allocation decisions...(p. 4).

Most of the theoretical approaches to social dilemmas are, as one might expect, concerned with resources—Resources being the least stable of the four Parsonian functional areas discussed earlier in this chapter. Cohen-Mansfield (1990) has provided a classification system for group and individual reward systems and a review of relevant literature. Korhonen and Wallenius (1990) demonstrated in a lab experiment that a multicriterion, multiparty resource allocation model may help participant countries of the Council of Mutual Economic Assistance reach consensus on, say, resource allocation for a construction project.

Boone and Macy (2004) emphasize that the reality of environmental and many other contexts may show sufficiently fuzzy uncertainty that parties may not, for some time, know what "game" they are playing much less the distribution of payoffs. Moreover, environmental and other social dilemmas may present themselves in such a way that the perceived interdependent payoff structures are bound in with participants' social identities (Morrison 1999).

Among additional examples of theoretical considerations: Yamagishi and Cook's (Yamagishi and Cook 1993) attempts to bridge social dilemma and social exchange research (putting forward findings on the cooperation advantages of "network-generalized" exchange systems; Bond et al.'s (Bond et al. 1992) application of an expectancy-valence model to differentiate between constructs important for resource allocation and those associated with conflict resolution; Au et al.'s (Au et al. 1998) probabilistic model of criticality (following Rapoport's demonstration that cooperation in contributing to a public good includes a function of whether group members feel that their contributions are critical to the process or outcome); Amnon Rapoport and Suleiman's (1992) equilibrium solutions for resource dilemmas given particular assumptions; Glance and Huberman's (Glance and Huberman 1994) computer simulations of the dynamics of cooperation in structureless and hierarchical (organizational) groups; and experiments by Mulder et al. (2006a, b) demonstrating that, paradoxically, sanctions against noncooperation may sometimes lead to parties perceiving that cooperation is not internally motivated and hence untrustworthy. See also Akimov and Soutchanski's (Akimov and Soutchanski 1994) simulations.

## *Real and Perceived Background Variables*

Typically, studies of collective dilemmas have found no large sex differences— nor groups' sex-composition differences—in cooperation, though women may, on average, be slightly more likely to cooperate and still more likely to report being oriented toward harmonious group relations (Stockard et al. 1988).

Social identification and social values typically have rather substantial effects, as one might expect from the general and theoretical work already mentioned above. Although identification with one's present group can be important, promising to cooperate (unless unanimous) does not in itself seem to predict cooperation in dilemma situations (Dawes et al. 1988). Note that empathy for another group member, whether pre-existing or experimentally induced, may be associated with allocating rewards to particular individuals rather than increasing either one's own payoff or the collective good (Batson et al. 1995). See also Katayama (1995).

To understand cultural differences is especially important in relation to reaching cross-cultural agreements on environmental matters and resource use and may interact with personality and institutional variables (Brett and Kopelman 2004).

The main studied personality construct relevant to cooperation in resource dilemmas seems to be trust in others (possibly similar to (reflected) aggressive mistrust in the General Survey—Kritzer et al. 1974; Blumberg 2001a) and related variables. Trust is mainly relevant when there is concern that cooperation might lead to substantially diminished rewards (Parks and Hulbert 1995). See also De Vries and Wilke (1992); Van Lange and Kuhlman (1990).

Fairness (Wit et al. 1992) and perceived morality of others (Van Lange and Liebrand 1989) both contribute to participants' cooperativeness. (See also Van Dijk and Wilke 1993). Interestingly, if one party is known to have a particularly strong need, then—in cohesive groups—*both* those with high and low needs may make especially small withdrawals from a replenishing resource pool (Sattler 1998, using a survival problem in which supposedly high- or low-thirst participants withdrew water from a simulated community water well and the real rewards were soft drinks!). Cooperativeness may, of course, vary cross-culturally (see, e.g., Parks and Vu 1994). General environmental concern, however, has not been found to be associated with cooperative behavior in a simulated social dilemma even when the simulation concerns a scarce resource (tree harvesting) (Jeffrfey M. Smith and Bell 1992).

A group's supposed past success or failure—against an arbitrary standard with performance held constant—has been found to predict both the cooperativeness of new participants and these participants' perception of their colleagues' cooperativeness and competence (Allison and Kerr 1994).

## Group Size

With larger groups, the efficacy of one's contribution is typically perceived as less than in smaller groups, whether or not the perception is valid (Kerr 1989). One presumes that cooperative choices might accordingly be more likely in smaller groups. In fact group size has typically been studied in conjunction with other variables such as group composition (Chapman 1991) and reward accessibility as a function of size (Rapoport and Bornstein 1989). For instance, Sato (1988) found that the cooperative effect of trust in others occurred only in smaller groups. See also Franzen (1994); Yamagishi (1990, 1992).

## Experimental Procedure: Framing, Communication, and Other Aspects

The specific situation or experimental procedure may of course have a profound effect on behavior in collective dilemmas. This section considers, first, some general studies and then (unsurprisingly!) research that mainly focuses, in turn, on meaning and values, interpersonal matters, goal direction and task completion, and finally resources.

*Framing* One might expect, from prospect theory (discussed in Chap. 8 of Blumberg et al. 2009), that participants in social dilemmas would be especially risk aversive when outcomes are framed in terms of rewards rather than losses. Actual findings seem less orderly, however—perhaps partly because gains or losses can, in principle, occur independently for the pool, the individual, and other participants, and these tend not to be varied parametrically within the same experiment. For instance, participants tended to conform to others' behavior when they could take from a collective pool but to avoid conforming when they could give to such a pool (Fleishman 1988). Likewise, to avoid the destruction of an existing pool, individuals were more willing to contribute than to experience loss, even though the difference was solely in the framing of the situation and not in the amount they thereby got to keep (McDaniel and Sistrunk 1991).

*Communication* Notwithstanding findings reported above as regards the importance of social identity in fostering cooperation, several studies using different methods have found that making identity salient is typically *not* the main effect of communication. Indeed, all of these particular studies have found, in quite different experiments, that a main positive effect of communication was to induce commitments (that are then kept), or to make consensus visible, rather than to foster identity as such (Bouas and Komorita 1996; Kerr and Kaufman-Gilliland 1994; Orbell et al. 1988; see also Bornstein 1992).

*Meaning and Values* In a carefully controlled study in which a variety of qualities were varied experimentally, Chen (1996) evaluated several explanations for cooperation in a public goods problem. (a) *Group identity* (as fostered especially by face-to-face communication or else by pledges that contributed to a group norm, and were measured by a group identity scale) may be a necessary but not sufficient condition for maximizing cooperation. (b) Of particular importance was *criticality*—feeling that one's pledge and contribution will make a difference, measured independently and induced, for instance, by a rule that everyone must contribute an amount equal to the minimum pledge in the group. (c) Also of possible importance in enhancing cooperation is the *minimization of greed and of fear* (of being exploited)—at the pledge stage, the contribution stage, or both.

Criticality may relate to the behavior as well as to the individual. In research that was not itself related to collective dilemmas, Abelson (1995, Chap. 2) describes data that show virtually no difference between 52 self-reported liberal and conservative students as to whether they joined a campus (protest) demonstration. As Abelson noted, the study, however, uses a narrow population, rather small N, and a terse self-report measure on a fairly homogeneous campus. Although attitudes toward campus issues did not distinguish participants from nonparticipants, beliefs in the desirability and efficacy of protest *did*.

Another study, one focused on social traps, demonstrated the importance of self-communication, as it were—that is, contemplating the negative consequences of overharvesting and considering possible alternatives (Neidert and Linder 1990). Some studies (e.g., Bettencourt et al. 1992) demonstrate the importance of aspects of basic values that link with other sectors, such as interpersonal matters (e.g., social orientation of being cooperative versus noncooperative, group identity, instructions that promote interpersonal concern versus task outcome), goal-oriented procedural context (e.g., group behavior at a level of pool under- versus over-use), and resources (reward structure).

Using an interdependence framework for a social dilemma task in a "noisy" environment (that is, one where people occasionally are less cooperative than expected), Klapwijk and Van Lange (2009) found that generosity communicates trust and renders ongoing cooperation more robust.

Evidently, cooperation in social dilemmas follows from a variety of factors spanning the sectors covered in the present review.

*Interpersonal Variables* Simple conformity to others' behavior can be particularly strong, possibly manifest even when it is against participants' own interests (Jeffrey M. Smith and Bell 1994). This is perhaps not surprising, given the general research literature on social conformity. Knowing what others are doing also has some less obvious implications. Although trust (a value) is associated with cooperation, the association depends on interpersonal information—knowing the choices of others and, especially, knowing that they will know one's own choices (Sato 1989). See also Yamagishi (1988).

*Goal Direction (Including Motivation and Rules of Procedure)* Examples of the many procedural variables (some of which have already been mentioned above) that affect individuals' choices favoring pool regeneration are: the self-efficacy of feeling that one's choice might "make a difference" to the group's outcome (Kerr 1992); environmental cues (including random allocation to the role of "guide" rather than "supervisor") making salient a norm such as interpersonal equality of outcome (Samuelson and Allison 1994); punishment for overconsumption (as distinct from punishment for "stealing," which increased mere overconsumption) (Bell et al. 1989). Initial cooperation can be maintained if parties need to maintain their reputations (as in positive feedback on eBay?), if the situation affords opportunities to punish defectors, or simply if people perceive that most other parties are themselves continuing to cooperate (Semmann et al. 2003).

Kugihara (1992) found that fear of an "electric shock" increased traffic jams in a collective escape from a simulated maze. This may seem partly to contradict Mintz's (Mintz 1951) classic finding that reward structure rather than emotional incitement is a primary determinant of cooperation. (Mintz designed a laboratory conceptual rendition of a crowd trying to escape from a confined space, whereby participants needed to remove their cones from a narrow-necked bottle that was slowly filling with water.) Fear of a shock, however, probably *represents* a changed reward structure, unlike the emotional cries that Mintz used.

Relatively subtle differences in procedural rules can influence results—for instance, egalitarianism of contributions and of overall outcomes (Brams and Taylor

1994). See also Tipa and Welsh (2006) regarding real-world resource comanagement by indigenous communities; and Van Avermaet and Van Nieuwkerke (1989) regarding the impact of greed and of fearing others' noncooperation.

*Resources (Including Information)* Merely appealing for cooperation through persuasive messages may be effective in social dilemmas (Rosen and Haaga 1998). Indeed just learning the metaphor of the commons dilemma may be more effective in influencing behavior (littering in a cinema) than a seemingly more informative environmental passage (Mio et al. 1993).

Also, simply varying the sequence in which information is available or the amount of information on which participants need to focus may affect cooperation. Focusing on an entire problem rather than sequentially on its parts, for instance, may encourage cooperation; but if more demanding parts are presented first, then sequential presentation may foster cooperation (Kaufman and Kerr 1993). Perceived complexity of information (being told that previous poor performance was due to task difficulty rather than to personal freedom and overharvesting) may moreover induce structural change (e.g., voting for a group leader) (Samuelson 1991). Having individualized information about each member's contribution may, for example, more effectively induce contributions than having aggregated or no information (Sell and Wilson 1991).

For many findings it may be a moot point whether an effect is due to procedural rules (Goal direction) or participants' knowledge of them (Resources). In any event, knowledge of diminished future resources (high discount rates) may have a chilling effect on cooperation in resource dilemmas (as demonstrated in connection with a need to form whole-group coalitions in order for a group as a whole to reap maximum rewards) (Mannix 1991).

How information is considered may affect outcomes, as when participants "spent" less on security when they had been asked to imagine best-case rather than worst-case scenarios in an international security dilemma (Kramer et al. 1990; indeed, Parks et al. 2003, found similar effects on cooperation to be true more generally in social dilemmas); other factors associated with less expenditure on security were (a) initially high deficits in security and wealth and (b) contributions being framed in terms of economic losses. With computer-mediated communication, cooperation can be established but with more difficulty than in face-to-face situations (Bicchieri and Lev-On 2007).

As discussed briefly above, information provided by the pledges made by other group members—provided that the pledges entail some commitment (Chen and Komorita 1994)—may facilitate cooperation, perhaps by assuaging greed or fear.

Of course perception of others' contributions need not match their actual contributions (unless these too are made known). As an example, players in a social dilemma game may erroneously fail to believe that those others who have high endowments are *more* likely to contribute; contribution likelihood is, moreover, also related to altruism, group size, and criticality (Amnon Rapoport 1988; see also Budescu et al. 1990).

## *Reward Structure*

The reward structure of a social dilemma is crucial both to "entrapment" and cooperative or other solutions, as one will already have inferred from the sections above. A number of studies focus more centrally on the effects of reward arrangements.

Sell and Son (1997) provide a useful comparative review of public goods problems, which usually focus on giving up individual resources (losses), and common pool resource problems, which focus on individual moderation in using a common resource (individual rewards). Their own comparative experiments provide limited support for prospect theory:

> First-time decisions may be especially subject to loss aversion; ... if the setting remains stable, this susceptibility [favoring cooperation in resource dilemmas over public goods situations] remains. If there are setting changes, however, or if group interaction [becomes] involved, other factors ... apparently overwhelm the prospect theory effects, ... [and, instead,] expected utility formulations predict accurately, and cooperation is equivalent for the two kinds of dilemma (p. 134).

As an example, they suggest that initial efforts would be more successfully directed toward *preserving* a rain forest than *creating* a wildlife preserve; moreover, initial success may facilitate further accomplishments.

Simply arranging for costs to be shared can increase the individual probability of volunteering—a finding supported generally in a laboratory study by Weesie and Franzen (1998), though their precise quantitative predictions did not fit the data particularly well.

For other studies dealing with reward structure and closely related variables see, for instance: Aquino et al. (1992) (various effects); Budescu et al. (1992) (multivariate paradigm-based predictions); Hine and Gifford (1996) (certainty about pool size and regeneration rate); Komorita et al. (1993) (unresponsive, unexploitable strategy); Martichuski and Bell (1991) (moral suasion reinforcement for a shared resource rather than for a privatized, divided resource); Weesie (1994) (value of small group size, low costs and high benefits, and certainty about others' preferences). See also Shinotsuka (1989); Van Dijk and Grodzka (1992); White (1994).

## Negotiation

Whatever the nature of a conflict or dilemma, negotiation may well be capable of playing an important part in managing or resolving the situation. Research on psychological aspects of negotiation has been substantial since our earlier *Handbook* (Hare et al. 1994), sufficiently so to warrant this separate section on the topic. Emphasis here is on studies of bargainers, typically "opponent" pairs, primarily—apart from the dedicated subsection, below, on third-party mediation—where there is no mediator (much less a binding arbitrator). The line is blurry between this research and the bargaining literature outlined in the next chapter.

After consideration of some key general works the discussion turns to background variables and perceived differences in power, framing and communication, strategies, third-party mediation, and theoretical paradigms and suggestions. Each of these parts is arranged according to the now-familiar "MIGR" sequence, in some cases preceded by some introductory matters.

## General Considerations

*Meaning* One important conclusion from experimental field research on mediation (Pruitt, Peirce et al. 1993) is that short-term resolution does not predict long-term success. Therefore, mediators might actually do well to focus on parties' development of joint problem-solving skills and a fair hearing rather than on immediate outcomes. As Pruitt et al. explain, this recommendation holds widely, for example, for community mediation and marital therapy, but possibly not universally. In commercial disputes, for instance, contracts may be more significant than the quality of interpersonal relationships.

Somewhat ironically, some non-industrial societies, where routine aggression can threaten social stability, have developed indigenous compulsory mediation systems, which are a source of useful hypotheses for successful mediation in general (Pruitt, Mikolic, Peirce, and Keating 1993). Pruitt et al. cite Merry's list of typical characteristics of such systems: mediation begins at the first sign of conflict, mediators have high status, and community members join in on an imposed solution if need be. They also cite Ury's suggestions that, if there is no other way to avoid aggression, posturing can be substituted for physical struggle (e.g., gangs of boys yelling rather than fighting), the realm of a struggle can be bounded (e.g., workers banning overtime rather than striking fully), and cooling-off periods can be observed, with crisis mediation provided.

Fisher (1994) not only describes, among his case studies, a program of informal workshops for constructively bringing together different parties to conflict but also he places such workshops within the larger context of conflict analysis, confrontation, and resolution.

Much of the contemporary small group research is found outside of core social–psychological contexts, for example in the organizational literature, and this may be especially true of work related to negotiation and conflict resolution. Volumes on research on negotiation in organizations have, for instance, featured sections on the following topics among others: a broader (nonindividual) appreciation of unfair treatment and distrust; environmental disputes; and international conflict in organizational settings (e.g., in-depth consideration of a successful negotiation between General Motors and Toyota and an unsuccessful negotiation between Ford and Toyota) (Lewicki et al. 1997); emotions and attributions; justice in contexts of strong involvement and social identity; and racial and multicultural differences in perspectives on just processes (Bies et al. 1999).

Carnevale (1995) explains the importance of viewing culture as a variable that actually mediates negotiation processes; for instance, acceptable outcomes may be equally likely in cultures (such as, on the whole, the United States) with an individualist orientation as in collectivist ones (Japan and Israel, for instance), but the content of what constitutes an acceptable outcome—and a preferred process for reaching it—may well differ. Some work attempts to integrate negotiation and culture research (Gelfand and Brett 2004). See Tinsley (2004) for a discussion of how culture can inform one's understanding of dispute resolution strategies.

In a meta-analysis of negotiation studies, Druckman (1994) found that compromise was associated with negotiators' orientation, prenegotiation experience, time pressure, and (as one might expect) initial distance between positions. By contrast, the time taken to reach a resolution was best predicted not only by time pressure but also by "size" of issue as well as by prenegotiation experience.

For other general research related to meaning and values see Carnevale (1992); Dbrowski (1990); Dittloff and Harris (1996); Sebenius (1991); Olekalns et al. (1996); and Wall and Blum (1991).

*Interpersonal Context* If negotiation research is to be particularly valuable for understanding real-world situations, it must encompass not only interdependence (including imperfect rationality) but also the context of idiosyncratic interpersonal and intergroup relationships in which the future relationship is as important as the immediate negotiable rewards of an initial encounter (Greenhalgh and Chapman 1995). Relevant variables are amenable to laboratory research, which (for instance) has documented that experimentally induced relationship orientation, as contrasted with an orienting focus on negotiation transactions, may be associated with greater flexibility and, as one might expect, more concern with the importance of the parties' relationship (Greenhalgh and Gilkey 1993).

Pruitt and Carnevale (1993), too, have stressed the existing but relatively "thin" research literature on the social context of negotiation including "social norms, relationships, group processes, mediators, and the broad set of conflict-handling choices within which negotiation is but one" (p. 203).

*Goal Direction and Task Completion* In an apparently meticulous review of research outcomes for two-party explicit bargaining, Thompson (1990b) identifies and covers work in three main approaches. Studies of *individual differences* among bargainers—sex differences, for instance, or scoring high on competitive orientation or on cognitive complexity—typically account for little variance in bargaining outcomes, though future research using contingency paradigms (different optimal individual characteristics in different situations) may possibly prove to be more important.

The second approach covered by Thompson—*Motivation*, as manifest for example in having high experimentally induced aspirations—has a more profound effect. Higher expectations may lead to better individual and possibly joint outcomes (depending on the payoff structure) but the attendant negotiations may be more protracted or indeed can lead to an (unnecessary) impasse. (See also Weingart et al. 1993). Thus the familiar (but not universal) curvilinear relationship between motivation and success may apply, such that when aspirations are especially high or time particularly at a premium, high expectations may yield less payoff overall or per unit of time. The review also highlights possible artifacts in some existing research—to take one example, the possibility that high-joint-aspiration instructions (to find a solution that gives maximum joint profit) may raise the salience of a reward structure being non-zero-sum (a gain by one party is not necessarily at the expense of the other).

Finally among Thompson's perspectives, a more recent *social cognitive* approach has been informative but seems unlikely to provide a thorough account of negotiation outcomes. Research in this tradition has established that heuristic biases in individual decision making (cf. Chap. 8 of Blumberg et al. 2009) may also apply to negotiators, who may—for example—underestimate the commonality of interests between parties. (See also Vorauer and Claude 1998).

Cutting across various approaches, Johnson's (R. A. Johnson 1993) practical text on "negotiation basics" provides information and exercises to aid negotiators in reaching mutually productive outcomes.

*Resources and Information* Also cutting across approaches are (perhaps at root, cognitive) informational problems in reaching agreement. According to Rubin et al.'s (Rubin et al. 1990) analysis, conflicts may arise from: perceived, rather than actual, divergence of interests; informational uncertainty as to others' expectancies; stereotypes about the other side(s) and their negotiators; self-fulfilling preservation of initially incorrect interpersonal expectations.

Some of Rubin et al.'s prescriptive suggestions are as follows: consider inviting a third party; announce and make small positive initiatives (as promulgated in Osgood's "GRIT" method); take advantages of interparty differences (e.g., one party may prefer earlier albeit smaller profits); brainstorm (completely separate from the negotiations); use problem-solving workshops following the format developed by Kelman (2008a) and others (see above). The TRANSCEND approach, developed by Galtung and colleagues (Galtung and Tschudi 2001), also emphasizes cognitive and emotional advantages of creative dialogue in prenegotiation. For other general work emphasizing information see Druckman and Hopmann (1991) and Stein et al. (1996). For key research on negotiation and conflict management particularly in business and management settings, see Bazerman (2005).

## *Background Variables and Perceived Differences*

*Meaning and Basic Values* Negotiation may be more successful and integrative if negotiators are aware of each other's values (e.g., on abortion or the death penalty) that are relevant to a particular negotiation, but it seems best if irrelevant political differences between negotiators are *not* made salient (Keltner and Robinson 1993).

As regards negotiation-specific values: aspiration values generally have a greater effect than minimum goals do on negotiators' demands and on their feelings of success (Thompson 1995a).

Several authors (e.g., Augsburger 1992; Goldman 1994) stress the importance of cultural values on negotiation processes and outcomes. Graham (1993), for example, in examining 17 cultures, concluded that Japanese negotiators had a particular style featuring positive recommendations rather than negative warnings.

Other authors have, for instance, studied the generally modest effects of negotiators' sex (Griffith 1991; Watson 1994; and see various sections above) and of initial trust (Butler 1995).

*Interpersonal Orientations* As one might expect, agreement is facilitated both by liking—which affects one's perception of opponents and their likely actions—and by greater familiarity (which affects perception of the situation) (Druckman and Broome 1991; for a similar finding using a different method see Ross et al. 1997; see also Donohue and Ramesh 1992). Positive mood and high self-esteem affect prenegotiation optimism and postnegotiation evaluations (Kramer, Newton, and Pommerenke 1993).

Simply being an experienced negotiator represents an important interpersonal "background"characteristic—but one that, as several researchers have pointed out, is often missing from laboratory research among naive strangers. Thompson (1990a) found that (experimentally controlled) relevant experience was associated with increased judgmental accuracy, higher aspirations, and greater ability to make interissue tradeoffs ("logrolling skills") and, according to Thompson, to gain more profit.

For some traits, such as risk propensity, successful negotiation seems to depend not on whether the characteristic is low or high but on the degree of interpersonal mismatch (between negotiators) (Ghosh 1993).

*Goal-Attainment* A negotiator's power—for example, availability of alternatives to a negotiated settlement—can be associated with a better self-outcome and, perhaps surprisingly, a better joint outcome as well (Pinkley et al. 1994). In cases of unequal power, higher joint outcome may depend on the weaker party having high aspirations (Mannix and Neale 1993). Of course other variables, such as having a unanimous decision rule rather than a majority one may be relevant (Thompson et al. 1988).

*Resources* Whether one sees a situation as framed from a perspective of losses or gains—the cardinal distinction covered by prospect theory—can affect negotiating, but the effects are complex, dependent, for example, on the other negotiator's frame and on the nature of the issues (Bottom 1998; Olekalns 1997).

In fact we turn now to a more systematic consideration of frame and communication.

## *Framing and Communication*

Common sense suggests that a nonpartisan third party is especially likely to see or frame a conflictual situation in such a way as to appreciate the partisans' common interests as well as their differences. Paradoxically, a partisan who can play the role of a "third party" may, however, have a particularly close vantage point for appreciating the nuances of the situation—hence Hare and Blumberg's (Hare and Blumberg 1979) view that a third-party approach to successful non-violent liberation could include both "partisan" and "nonpartisan" case studies.

Additional conceptual clarity for this paradox has been provided by a series of roleplaying experiments by Thompson (1995b). Overall, partisans are known to be especially unlikely to see genuine common areas of interest—but this effect may be limited to highly involved (actively negotiating) participants. In the roleplaying experiments, partisans who were not highly involved in the proceedings (observers who focused on the values of just one of two participants) made especially accurate judgments about relative interests. Nonpartisans with high involvement (neutral observers who were told that they would later be taking a turn at being actual negotiators) had an intermediate level of accuracy and were more accurate than low-involvement nonpartisans. Interestingly, accountability (being told that they would need to justify their views) damped the accuracy of partisans but augmented it for nonpartisans. Thompson's results, therefore, provide further underpinning for the value of Kelman and others' problem-solving workshops, where partisans (with the support of facilitators) confer informally and away from public glare.

The additional perspectives provided by a highly structured Negotiation Support System may also yield higher and better balanced joint outcomes (Foroughi et al. 1995), though this may be an example of the more general tradeoff whereby better results follow from more time spent exploring a situation's payoff structure. Sufficient time and motivation for systematic exploration should at least yield one of any available Pareto optimal outcomes (where there is no other outcome preferred by both parties—Korhonen et al. 1995).

Simply requiring that a group focus on task or interpersonal matters—rather than there not being any such requirement—may affect outcomes (e.g., how much money is "allocated" to an "AIDS awareness educational program"), possibly in negative ways however (Davis et al. 1998). Indeed, individuals working alone "allocated" even more money than any of the group conditions. Thus, the group decision-making literature (see Chap. 8 of Blumberg et al. 2009) has relevance for understanding the effects of negotiators' frames, with the nature of impact surely being a function of group norms, available information, and other variables.

In another series of roleplaying experiments negotiators who were given a biased proposal (either above or below the middle levels—equivalent to an outcome that an outside mediator would see as unfair) from which to start bargaining also reached biased agreed outcomes, even if they were aware of the initial biases and tried to compensate for them (Korhonen et al. 1995)—a finding broadly consistent with Helson's (Helson 1964) classic adaptation-level paradigm.

For other relatively general work see Turner's (D. B. Turner 1992) work linking communication in negotiation to social interaction between the negotiators and those whom they represent. (See also Putnam and Roloff 1992).

Research on the *meaning* that negotiators assign to situations suggests that one reason that they frequently fail to appreciate their opponents' cognitions, and thereby reach suboptimal outcomes, is that they tend to simplify the situation (Carroll et al. 1988). We are again reminded of the importance and relevance of heuristics, as noted above (under general considerations about negotiation). While acknowledging the importance of emotion (such as resentment and anger) in understanding conflict, Kahneman and Tversky (1995) review the effects of several cognitive biases including optimistic overconfidence in one's ability to predict and control future outcomes, over-weighting of *certain* rather than probable outcomes, and avoidance of outcomes framed as losses rather than gains.

A general understanding of *interpersonal* aspects of frames and communication is probably not yet extant, though one can identify some of the (now familiar) relevant variables. These include: (a) adaptation level—one's opponent becoming *either* more cooperative or more competitive may lead to concessions on both sides (Hilty and Carnevale 1993); (b) a gain or loss frame—findings are complex, but for variable-sum outcomes gain-frame may be especially advantageous when instructions encourage cooperation or one's opponent is loss-framed (Olekalns 1994); (c) the value of impression management (Wall 1991; but see Kumar 1997); (d) the available communications network—for instance, in a three-way conflict, having dyad-only communications may sometimes represent an advantage because a series of two-way trade-offs may lead to a better and more equitable overall solution than more complicated three-way (circular) tradeoffs would (Palmer and Thompson 1995); and (e) facework—for example, in real-life crises, the advantages of negotiators' facilitating others' face-saving as contrasted with crisis perpetrators' typical attempts at own face-saving (Rogan and Hammer 1994).

For a given situation, varying performance *goals* has been found, perhaps not surprisingly, to affect outcomes. Having specific assigned goals, for example, yielded higher performance than self-set "do-your-best" instructions (Northcraft et al. 1994). To paraphrase a more general behavioral principle, negotiators' goals and demands are a joint function of the individual (e.g., strength) and the situation (e.g., whether negative outcomes are possible) (Kuon and Uhlich 1993).

In a seeming reminder of Homans's (Homans 1950) proposition that proximity, liking, and shared work all tend to augment one another (which gave rise to Roger Brown's 1965 analysis of why human interaction does not eventually boil down to something akin to a sugary syrup!), Lawler and Yoon (1993) propose a dynamic potentiating relation among several variables that may affect the process and outcome for a given negotiating situation: equality of power, frequency of communication, positive emotion, and interpersonal cohesiveness. Examples of additional relevant variables are time pressure (Carnevale et al. 1993) and (the advantages of) goal-setting (Fandt et al. 1990) and salience of interparty differences in priorities and perspectives (Kemp and Smith 1994).

The importance of *resources*, including information availability, is implicit in some of the above findings and explicit in other studies. Generating a list of arguments not only in favor of one's own position but also one of potential counterarguments may lead to more flexible offers, especially if there is some delay before negotiators' initial offers are made (Mannix and Innami 1993).

Negotiators' gain- or loss-frames may affect not only their own outcome preferences but also that of mediators—who (in a lab experiment) have proposed better settlements when one, or especially when both, of the negotiators had loss frames (Lim and Carnevale 1995).

The effects of information are not always intuitively obvious. Buyer–seller profit tables in lab studies are often broadly equivalent, but the inherently different frames can yield different results for the two roles. In one study, joint profit (especially for sellers) did indeed increase when buyers and sellers both had complete information (presumably about payoff matrices), but training had a negative effect, with the training of sellers having an especially adverse impact on buyers' expected profits (Gauvin et al. 1990).

For other studies of the effects of what one might call information-based framing see De Dreu et al. (1994); Larrick and Boles (1995); Pinkley (1995); Thompson (1992); Sondak et al. (1995).

## *Strategies*

Pruitt (1991) has provided a superb summary and integrative discussion of negotiation strategies. He notes that negotiators face a choice among three strategies— *contending* by putting one's own case forward (sometimes called competition or distributive bargaining), *problem solving* by working together for a good overall solution with "integrative potential," and *yielding*—plus a fourth "strategy" of inaction or avoidance. After discussing the dynamics of the different strategies, including their simultaneous or sequential use and the strong correlation between the strategies used by different parties to negotiation, he quotes Fisher and Brown's (Fisher and Brown 1988) guidelines for building better working relationships. These span the MIGR domains and include (regardless of what the other party is doing) remaining rational, trying to understand others' positions, communicating before making decisions, being honest and trustworthy, avoiding heavy contentious tactics (in favor of persuasion and being open to persuasion), and being considerate and caring. (Pruitt and Rubin 1999, add a fifth strategy, withdrawing, and discuss how parties' preferences among the strategies are determined.)

Examples of literature fitting within this framework, most of them published subsequently, are as follows. Related to *meaning* and basic concepts: Gillespie and Bazerman's (Gillespie and Bazerman 1997) analysis of integrative solutions where a powerful third-party mediator is essentially an additional negotiator; Callister and Wall's (Callister and Wall 1997) delineation of typically Japanese active but nonassertive techniques such as listening and facilitating communication; Carnevale and Henry's (Carnevale and Henry 1989) empirical validation of the range of mediator strategies; and Kilgour et al.'s (Kilgour et al. 1994) Graph Model for Conflict Resolution (GMCR) software for understanding and supporting negotiation.

*Interpersonal* matters are by definition ubiquitous in negotiation but do not seem to be analyzed primarily on their own within the present literature search. Exceptionally, Ledgerwood et al. (2006) review how persuasion can affect negotiation.

*Goal-attainment* research has covered, for instance: the negative effects of bluffs and threats (Shapiro and Bies 1994); real and perceived coercive power (De Dreu 1995); techniques to facilitate integrative solutions, such as brainstorming, roleplaying, and the separation of objectives and aspirations (Tjosvold and Van de Vliert 1994); and the effects and prevalence of intransigence (Brams and Doherty 1993).

Strategies related to *Resources*, especially information, include: the integrative effects of even one bargaining party providing, or seeking, information (Thompson 1991); the favorable outcomes sometimes achieved by misrepresentation, whether active or by omission (O'Connor and Carnevale 1997); the less flexible bargaining and resultant increase in disagreements by agents with a constituency as compared with principals (Lax and Sebenius 1991); approaches to quantifying concessions (Lootsma et al. 1994); and the prevalence of fixed-sum biases, broadly similar to false consensus (people's overestimation of others' similarity to themselves) (Bottom and Paese 1997). Reviewing information-processing approaches, De Dreu (2005) describes how four major variables may moderate psychological barriers to successful negotiation: power balance, accountability, cooperative motivation, and time pressures.

## Third-Party Mediation

Given the breadth of difficulties that negotiators face, it is hardly surprising that third-party mediators can help in a wide variety of ways. They can reaffirm widespread values such as fairness, facilitate positive interpersonal relations (and help disputants to save face), generally assist in moving a dispute toward resolution, and provide neutral facilities and informal nonthreatening communication channels. Of course one needs to consider the background and experience of the mediators themselves, many of whom use eclectic approaches (Picard 2004).

Esser and Marriott (1995) list several reviews of mediation research prior to the mid-1990s and themselves provide a particularly helpful (generally affirmative) answer to the question of whether laboratory research on mediation is applicable to field situations. They point out that (as one would surmise but might forget, and as has been found to be true in other areas such as psychotherapy research) field research is especially useful in generating hypotheses and lab experiments are typically geared toward their systematic evaluation.

In their summary of findings about mediation tactics, where both field and laboratory research has been carried out, they find generally consistent support for Carnevale's (Carnevale 1986) strategic choice model, which they summarize as follows. Mediators who value the aspirations of the negotiators and perceive common ground between them are especially likely to choose integrative tactics (creatively beneficial to both sides). Those who value aspirations but see little common ground are particularly likely to propose compensation for concessions. Mediators who place little value on disputants' aspirations but do see common ground may simply leave the parties to get on with their own negotiations. Finally, mediators with low value on aspirations who see little common ground may put pressure on bargainers to concede. (For comments on possible refinement of the strategic choice model see Van de Vliert 1992.)

Esser and Marriott also find consistency between a lab study and field studies which have found that as time goes on, in later rounds of negotiation, pressure tactics (e.g., toward lower aspirations) increased.

Similar conclusions about the *effectiveness* of mediation also arise from comparable findings from field and laboratory research (Esser and Marriott 1995). The making of specific settlement proposals increases concession-making, settlements, and quality of settlement. Using an ability to provide rewards (such as economic aid) may also facilitate settlements (but inhibited them in a laboratory study—Idaszak and Carnevale 1989). Among contingent findings: Assertive mediation is more effective in difficult conflicts (here, though, the field results vary in the *direction* of the contingency, which may be curvilinear); paraphrasing (to help communication) is especially effective in difficult situations; and combining issues into package settlements is more effective in low-conflict conditions.

In a survey of 255 professional mediators, Lim and Carnevale (1990) confirmed a contingency view that particular tactics would often be seen as potentially successful in only some disputes.

Mediation research has covered varied arenas such as international disputes and organizational conflicts. The main *dimensions* along which third-party mediation varies, at least in the workplace but reflected generally in some of the results described above, are: degree of involvement and whether the intervention is autocratic or participative (Irving and Meyer 1997). Apparently the solutions to mediated conflicts vary on essentially the same two dimensions as the mediations themselves provided that, for solutions, one (in effect) adds a third—affective-cognitive—dimension (McLaughlin et al. 1991). For a broad review of mediation as a social-psychological process, see Kressel (2006).

An example of the basic *values* inherent in mediation in a particular culture is provided by Wall's (Wall 1990) study of Chinese mediation, based on interviews with five randomly chosen street committees within each of the five mediation sectors of Nanjing. The details are enlightening. Apparently a centuries-old (possibly millennia-old) tradition makes mediation of disputes systematic and ubiquitous in China. The community-agreed mediators, according to Wall's findings, encountered a wide variety of disputes but used a relatively narrow procedural progression that nonetheless drew on a multiplicity of techniques.

Partly in contrast with Western practice, mediators would usually follow this sequence: gather information (whether or not invited to do so); speak to disputants, stressing the good qualities of the other party; ease feelings (e.g., "This is a minor problem," "You are loved by the community"); emphasize socio-emotional persuasion more than conflict content (unless illegal behavior is involved); possibly bring in additional parties; educate or publicly criticize one or both parties; and, when agreement is reached, expect apologies (even very general ones) reciprocated with forgiveness accompanied by tea for all and smiles. As with mediation in the West, cases using more techniques were *more* likely to have successful outcomes.

Intercultural mediation, according to Pedersen (1993, 1994), is most likely to be successful if it emphasizes shared expectations and common ground rather than (possibly culturally defined) "negative" features.

In discussing models of conflict management, Rubin (1994) concludes that both third-party intervention and negotiation can be very helpful; but can also be destructive if misapplied.

For other research that seems particularly relevant to the values related to mediation see Boskey (1994); Conlon et al. (1994); Forlenza (1991); Hale et al. (1991); Keashly et al. (1993); Sheppard et al. (1988); and Witte (1994).

An *interpersonal* laboratory study of third-parties' *role* in disputes found that, compared with "mediators," "intervenors" were more likely to impose solutions, especially when they found disputants to be uncooperative. Moreover, the majority of imposed solutions did not reflect "disputants' underlying interests," especially when the intervenor had "low concern for the disputants' aspirations." The findings were generally consistent with Carnevale's strategic choice model. For other research on mediators' roles see, for example, Bazerman et al. (1992); Burrell et al. (1990); Conlon and Ross (1993).

Mediation may be especially effective toward the *goal* of reducing disputes which otherwise seem particularly intractable. Paradoxically, these may arise when aggrieved disputants extend a conflict into arenas where there is little inherent conflict of interests (McEwen and Milburn 1993), thus in principle giving more room for integrative solutions.

In discussing the process of mediation, Matz (1994) advises mediators to be aware of the dangers of using too much pressure, given that mediation is typically meant to be voluntary and to preserves disputants' autonomy; Matz notes that acceptability (or not) of pressure tactics may depend on very specific "subtleties" in the relationships among the parties. For a further framework related to mediator "mechanisms" see Kaufman and Duncan (1992).

Bridging goal-oriented progress and *resources*, a laboratory study by Harris and Carnevale (1990) found that not only might a third-party offering compensation (positive benefits) be counter-productive—especially if the mediator is seen as having a stake in the result—but also third-party pressure, such as threat of removing benefits, may hasten or improve an outcome.

Resources include, of course, breadth of information and relevant costs. For analysis and advice about mediators' questioning and probing see Burrell (1990). Notwithstanding the Chinese customs described above, in a controlled $2\times2$ (Western) laboratory study, where mediators did or did not use (a) task-oriented techniques (focusing the discussion) and (b) motivation-oriented methods (emphasizing the costs of not reaching agreement), motivation-orientation did not affect outcomes, whereas task-oriented methods were more likely to achieve settlements (albeit compromise ones) (Ross 1990).

For a textbook and theoretical framework covering mediation see Bush and Folger (2005).

## *Additional Theories, Paradigms, and Suggestions*

This chapter concludes with the consideration, in this section on negotiation, of a miscellany of interesting work that does not fit neatly into the preceding discussions.

In her wide-ranging discussion of communication aspects of negotiation, Womack (1990) describes Williams's delineation of characteristics common to effective negotiators. These include (with MIGR aspects added here in parentheses) a command of the relevant facts and laws (R, I), being effective in putting a case (G), and finding it satisfying to use their skills (M, G). Effective negotiators also have self-control and are polite (M, I, G) and, for cooperative negotiation, are sincere and trustworthy (M).

As an example of work emphasizing basic *values* or systems that support negotiation, Brett (1991) advises that high quality group decisions can emerge from conflict provided that suitable training of negotiators takes place, including how to integrate diverse perspectives.

For additional work related to Values (or cutting across several areas) see Bennett and McQuade (1996); Putnam (1994a, b); Roloff and Jordan (1992); Shakun (1995); Thiessen et al. (1998); Tripp and Sondak (1992); Wilkenfeld et al. (1998).

*Interpersonal* matters such as the available communications network can have a marked effect on judgmental accuracy and negotiation outcomes. For example, a clear interpersonal structure of group identity coupled with face-to-face communication may yield better outcomes (Arunachalam and Dilla 1995)—but cf. Sherif's (Sherif 1966) classic work on group conflict and subsequent research on Allport's contact hypothesis (see above) suggesting that these better outcomes might depend on working together with equal status on a common goal with the positive sanction of authorities!

Tracy (1995) puts forward an overall paradigm for negotiation viewed as a decision-making process among living systems engaged in social interaction.

Within the context of social interaction, and like Goffman (1955) before him, Wilson (1992) stresses (and analyzes) the special importance, in negotiation, of saving face. For other studies related to communication and information, see Holmes's (Holmes 1992) work on phases of negotiation and Meerts (1991) on the training of international negotiators.

*Goal-Orientation* Mastenbroek (1991) provides a summary of negotiator training, noting, for example, that experience brings with it increased flexibility. More research about negotiators' agenda-setting is needed, particularly as regards the relative advantages of sequential and simultaneous consideration of different issues, or of some mixture of sequentiality and simultaneity (Balakrishnan et al. 1993); in the meantime, it seems important that this matter at least be considered in the context of any given mediation. For some other aspects of the actual process of negotiation, see Stuhlmacher and Stevenson (1997); Sycara (1990); and Zartman (1991).

With regard to *informational Resources*, Kahneman (1992) provides considerable conceptual clarity by the analysis and description of reference points, anchors, and norms. A fairly detailed consideration seems worthwhile here. (Prospect theory has already been discussed briefly above, but the principles apply not only to conflict resolution in general but also and particularly to negotiations.) A key feature, as manifest in prospect theory, is that people—including disputants—are generally readier to forego rewards than to sustain equivalent losses; the "pain" associated with the loss side of a value-function curve is steeper than the "pleasure" associated with degrees of reward. Thus (leaving aside questions of the proportionality of Just Noticeable Differences), in one of Tversky's examples, if one's current salary is $50,000, the felt difference between new employers' offers of $40,000 and $45,000 is greater than it would be if one's current salary were $35,000.

Negotiations are more likely to fail when negotiators are "risk-prone" (define a situation in terms of losses, such that they are reluctant to abandon the status quo). Findings are borne out in seemingly mundane experiments. Kahneman describes a study by Knetsch, for example: only about 10% of students given equivalent rewards (for completing a questionnaire) of either mugs or chocolate chose to exchange one for the other, despite economic theory predicting that such exchanges should happen about half of the time. The principle of preferring what one already owns does not however apply to commodities that are *meant* to be exchanged—for instance, a seller's stock, a buyer's money, a nation's missiles that are seen as bargaining chips rather than as a genuine source of security.

Kahneman describes his conclusions as being consonant with those arrived at by quite different means in the creative original work of Kurt Lewin: removing stress that holds opponents away from one's own goals is more effective than increasing stress that *pushes* them toward one's goals. "A Lewinian negotiator would ask the following question: what are the main reasons that cause the other side not to do as I wish of their own accord?" (Kahneman 1992, p. 302).

Multiple reference points (in which, e.g., an offer of a $3,000 salary increase is seen as a gain, if compared to present salary, but a loss if compared with an expected rise of $5,000) may, according to Kahneman, fade in and out, like the different realities of an ambiguous figure. The relative "frequencies" with which different reference points are available may determine the central tendency of whether one is, in effect, satisfied or not with (in this example) a particular raise. Negotiators may attempt to emphasize reference points that are favorable to their positions and they may also bring in "anchors," mentioning an extreme but not implausible figure in order to shift expectations as to a fair outcome.

For studies of some other aspects of informational resources—communication and expectations in bargaining—see, for example: Andes (1992); Benbasat et al. (1995); Mannix et al. (1995); Oliver et al. (1994).

Clearly, there should be a general benefit from an increasingly full understanding, and more widespread appreciation, of how negotiators' positions and offers are *perceived*. Guidelines that facilitate tension reduction and integrative solutions are especially to be welcomed.

# Chapter 2
# Bargaining, Coalitions, and Games:
# Classified Citations

Complementing the research on conflict resolution and cooperation—covered in the preceding chapter—is a tradition of studying coalitions, bargaining and "games," especially but not exclusively in the laboratory. Hundreds of studies have modeled a wide variety of "real-world" counterparts. To take just a few examples where understanding can be enhanced by empirically known principles, one notes: the historic 2010 British parliamentary elections showing the pivotal power of the weaker party in a coalition government; process and outcomes of bargaining at every level from inter-personal (indeed, *intra*-personal as well) to international; and a broad variety of inter-party phenomena including, for instance, contrasts between the common good and individual rewards, as mirrored in Prisoner's Dilemma and other "games". Several experimental paradigms have been particularly heavily covered. Three of these are as follows.

In typical *bargaining* procedures, participants may play in pairs consisting of one "buyer" and one "seller." They are assigned "payoff" tables specifying how much each will profit if they can agree (say) to sell a particular quantity of a commodity at a particular "price." They then may take it in turns to make offers which can be accepted or rejected by their co-player. In a variant procedure, they must agree on particular outcomes for each of several "issues."

In many studies of *coalitions*, each participant in a group is assigned a certain amount of "power" or "votes"—and also a level of reward, sometimes manifest as a real payment. Participants typically make offers to join with others provided that they can agree on how their incipient coalition's rewards would be split. If enough participants can agree to join in a coalition or partnership that controls sufficient power or votes, then those players can split the associated rewards.

Finally, various "*gaming*" procedures have been studied, the Prisoner's Dilemma Game (PDG) being perhaps the most famous. Outcomes typically depend on the *joint* choices made by each of a pair of players. Rewards may be arranged in such a way that each player is individually tempted to make one particular choice; if only, however, both could agree to make a different choice, both would be better off. The "sting in the tail" is that if one of the players "defects" to the sub-optimal joint choice, that player receives an especially large reward and the "cooperative" player receives a rather harsh penalty.

H. Blumberg et al., *Small Group Research,* Peace Psychology Book Series,
DOI 10.1007/978-1-4614-0025-7_2, © Springer Science+Business Media, LLC 2012

These paradigms and much of the related classic research have been summarized in a multi-disciplinary variety of publications. See, for example, McClintock (1972, especially the three chapters on coalitions, bargaining, and games) and also Hare et al. (1994, 1996).

At least around 1,000 studies could be delineated and discussed for the present context in the period covered. It would, however, seem to be beyond the interests of most of the readers for this chapter to do so. It is rather useful, however, to have an impression of the scope of the work and, for those having particular interests, the means to retrieve a chosen selection of the studies. Hence the remainder of the present chapter takes the form of a taxonomy and a classified bibliography. We have tried to include a substantial number not only of laboratory studies but also of field applications related to the respective topics. Classified citations follow. The present format is rather compact but one can of course get an idea of the content of each area by consulting the works' titles in the References.

# Bargaining

## *Laboratory and Quasi-Laboratory Studies and Theoretical Papers*

*Reviews and General Studies*  Blumberg (1994); Brams (1990); Chatterjee (1996); Güth and Tietz (1990); Ledyard and Palfrey (1995); Lim and Murnigham (1994); Serrano and Vohra (2002).

*Theoretical Papers and Empirical Tests of Rules of Procedure*  Abdul-Muhmin (2001); Agastya (1996); Babcock and Landeo (2004); Bac and Raff (1996); Baucells and Lippman (2004); Bensaid and Gary-Bobo (1996); Bigoness and DuBose (1992); Blaquière (1994); Blount and Larrick (2000); Bolton and Ockenfels (1998); Bolton and Zwick (1995); Bonacich and Friedkin (1998); Bossert et al. (1996); Boster et al. (1995); Bottom and Paese (1999); Bottom and Studt (1993); Bouckaert (2002); Brams and Kilgour (1996); Brucks and Schurr (1990); Bruttel (2009); Calvó-Armengol (2003); Chang and Liang (1998); Chatterjee and Dutta (1998); Chatterjee and Lee (1998); Church and Zhang (1999); Conley and Wilkie (1996); Dahl and Kienast (1990); Dickinson (2000); Donohue and Roberto (1996); Einy et al. (1999); Esser et al. (1990); Evans (1997); Fershtman (2000); Friedman (1992, 1994); Garratt (1999); Gneezy and Guth (2002); Gneezy et al. (2003); Gomes et al. (1999); Gracia et al. (2000); Güth and Van Damme (1998); Handgraaf et al. (2003); Hoffman et al. (1999); Imai and Salonen (2000); In and Serrano (2004); Inderst (2000); Jones and Jelassi (1990); Kanner (2004); Kibris (2004a, b); Knez and Camerer (1995); Komorita et al. (1989); Kray et al. (2004); Kultti (1999); Kuon and Uhlich (1993); Lahiri (1994); Laskowski and Slonim (1999); Lawler (1992); Lawler and Ford (1993); Lawler et al. (1988); Lax and Sebenius (1991); Lindskold and

Han (1988a); Lopomo (2001); Lu and McAfee (1996); Lusk and Hudson (2004); Mackintosh (1998); Mariotti (1998); Mauleon and Vannetelbosch (2004); McCall (1990); Messick et al. (1997); Meyer (1992); Mo (1994); Moldoveanu and Stevenson (1998); Munier and Zaharia (2002); Myerson (1996); Napel (2003); Nawa et al. (2002); Northcraft, Brodt, and Neale (1995); Ockenfels and Selten (2000); Okada (1996); Oppewal and Tougareva (1992); Paquet et al. (2000); Parco and Rapoport (2004); Pérez-Castrillo and Wettstein (2000); Poulsen (2004); Raith (2000); Ramsay (2004); Rapoport, Weg, and Felsenthal (1990); Rosenmüller (1997); Ross et al. (2002); Schellenberg (1988);Schofield and Parks (2000); Schotter et al. (2000); Schweitzer and DeChurch (2001); Sefton (1992); Shalev (2002); Sloof (2004); Sommers (1993); Sosis et al. (1998); Srivastava (2001); Tauman (2002); Thye (2000); Valenciano and Zarzuelo (1997); Van Cayseele and Furth (1996); Vannetelbosch (1999); Vieth (2003); Weg and Zwick (1999); Weg et al. (1996); Westermark (2003); Yildiz (2003); Zeng (2003); Zwick et al. (1992); Zwick et al. (2000).

*Participants' Characteristics (Gender, Personality, Nationality, and Other Demographic Variables)* Barry and Friedman (1998); Brandstätter and Königstein (2001); Buchan et al. (2004); Calhoun and Smith (1999); Chaudhuri et al. (2003); Costa-Gomes and Zauner (2001); Galinsky et al. (2008); Gunnthorsdottir et al. (2002); Hanany et al. (2007); Katz et al. (2008); Ketelaar and Au (2003); Komorita and Ellis (1988); Maxwell (1992); Murnighan and Saxon (1998); Neu et al. (1988); Nyer and Gopinath (2001); Polzer et al. (1993); Solnick and Schweitzer (1999); Stuhlmacher and Walters (1999); Thompson, Nadler, and Kim (1999).

*Empirical Processes* Abbink et al. (2001); Abbink et al. (2004); Abreu and Sethi (2003); Achterkamp and Akkerman (2003); Allen et al. (1990); Alvarez et al. (2003); Barrett (2004); Battigalli and Siniscalchi (2003); Beisecker et al. (1989); Berninghaus and Güth (2003); Boles et al. (2000); Bolton and Katok (1998); Bolton et al. (2003); Bossert and Peters (2000, 2001); Bottom (1990, 1998); Bottom and Paese (1997); Brams and Doherty (1993); Brunner (1994); Burgos et al. (2002a, b); Busch and Horstmann (1997, 2002); Camerer and Loewenstein (1993); Cardona-Coll (2003); Carpenter (2003b); Chun (2002); Conlon and Ross (1993); Croson et al. (2003); Daniel et al. (1998); Dore (1997); Duane (1991); du Toit (1989); Ellingsen and Robles (2002); Enzle et al. (1992); Esser (1989); Eyuboglu and Buja (1993); Fearon (1994); Fenwick (1997); Ford and Blegen (1992); Frankel (1998); Fukuno and Ohbuchi (1999, 2001, 2003); Fum and Missier (2001); Ghosh (1996); Golann (2004); Hegtvedt and Killian (1999); Hennig-Schmidt et al. (2008); Kambe (1999); Kibris (2002); Kim (2002); Kim and Fragale (2005); Klemisch-Ahlert (1992); Kolb (2004); Kramer et al. (1995); Krämer and Schneider (2003); Kravitz and Gunto (1992); Kritikos and Bolle (2004); Kumar et al. (1995); Large (1999); Lawler (1995); Larrick and Wu (2007); Legut et al. (1995); Lerner (1998); Manzini and Mariotti (2001); Marco Gil (1995); McCabe et al. (1998); McGinn et al. (2003); Miyagawa (2002); Montero (2002); Morgan and Tindale (2002); Morris, Larrick, and Su (1999); Murnighan and Pillutla (1995); Muthoo (1995); Nelson (2002); Ok and Zhou (2000); Olekalns (1991); Ostmann (1992); Ostmann (1996); Paese and Gilin (2000); Pillutla and Murnighan (1995, 2003); Ponsati and Sákovics

(1996); Powell (1996); Ravenscroft et al. (1993); Rojer (1998); Roloff and Jordan (1991); Sebenius (2002); Segendorff (1998); Shapiro (2000); Shell (2001); Son-negård (1996); Sopher (1994); Thompson and DeHarpport (1994); Thompson et al. (2004); Turdaliev (2002); Tutzauer (1990, 1992, 1993); Valley et al. (2002); Van Dijk and Van Knippenberg (1996); Van Dijk et al. (2004); Vanderschraaf and Richards (1997); Viswesvaran and Deshpande (1995); Weg and Smith (1993); Weinberger (2000); Wheeler (2004); Winter (1996); Zott (2002).

*Outcomes* Carpenter (2003a); Chae and Heidhues (2004); Corfman and Lehmann (1993); Dekel and Wolinsky (2003); Handgraaf et al. (2004); Pfingsten and Wagener (2003); Salonen (1998); Tedeschi (1995); Verschuren and Arts (2004); Volij and Winter (2002); Wooders (1998).

## Field Applications

*Cultural and Contextual Effects* Graham et al. (1988); Henrich and Smith (2004); Hill and Gurven (2004); Marlowe (2004); McElreath (2004); Patton (2004); Tinsley (1997); Tracer (2004).

*Formats and Procedural Rules* Blount (1995); Fiske and Tetlock (1997); Graesser (1990); Jap (2003); Keough (1992); Klotz (2004); Kotthoff (1993); López-Paredes et al. (2002); Mandel (2002); Naquin and Paulson (2003); Nygaard and Dahlstrom (2002); Onwujekwe (2004); Scudder (1988); Stroeker and Antonides (1997); Tusing and Dillard (2000); Van Dijk and Van Knippenberg (1998); Walliban (2003).

*Gender and Related Matters* Ishida (2003); Lorber and Bandlamudi (1993); Lundberg and Pollak (2001); Matsumoto (1989); Silvestre (1994); H. W. Smith and Kronauge (1990); Suen et al. (2003); Zick (1992).

*General Considerations and Negotiation* Bazerman et al. (2000). See also Ancona et al. (1991); Banks et al. (2002); Boyle and Lawler (1991); Brodt (1994); Carnevale and Keenan (1992); Connolly et al. (2000); Cutcher-Gershenfeld et al. (2007); DeSimone (2004); Ford (1994); Filzmoser and Vetschera (2008); Forgas (1998); Gullickson (1997); Heifetz and Segev (2004); Johnston and Benton (1988); Komorita and Parks (1995); Lebow (1996); Malhotra and Bazerman (2008); Mintu-Wimsatt and Graham (1998); Morley (2006); Mullen et al. (1991); Pitz (1992); Polzer et al. (1995); Posthuma et al. (2002); Pruitt (1995); Putnam (1993, 1994a, b, 1997); Rapoport (1990); Sebenius (2005); Shell (2006); Stephen and Pham (2008); Van Boven et al. (2003).

*Judicial Contexts* Herzog (2004); McAllister (1990); Pritchard (1990); Beaumont (1995); Becker (1988); Bee and Beronja (1991); Cutcher-Gershenfeld (1994); Devinatz (2004); Elvira and Saporta (2001); Extejt and Russell (1990); Fonstad et al. (2004); Gallagher and Gramm (1997); Gennard (2004); Giacobbe-Miller (1995); Gullickson (1995); Hart (2002); Hebdon and Stern (2003); Hunter and McKersie

(1992); Kelleher (2003); Kelloway (2004); Kelly and Brannick (1990); Kim and Kim (1998); Kramer and Hyclak (2002); Moore and Miljus (1989); Post and Bennett (1994); Putnam et al. (1991); Rose and Danner (1998).

*Miscellaneous* Alvard (2004); Anandalingam (1989); Bose (1996); Cliff and Bruten (1999); Clock of the Long Now (2000); Cohen (1996); Ensminger (2004); Frank (1991); Hagen (2003); Harris and Mowen (2001); Hill (1999); Hull (1999); Kim and Zepeda (2004); Kramer (1995); Lee (2000); Legrenzi et al. (1996); Mulkay et al. (1993); Oots (1990); Rainey (1988); Scudder and Andrews (1995); Snell and Mekies (2001); Woody (1998); Zollman (2008).

*Organizations and Work* Argyres and Liebeskind (1999); Buvik and Reve (2002); Griffin et al. (1995); Hargadon and Sutton (1997); Martinez-Pecino et al. (2008); Marullo and DeLeon (1997); Morley (1992); Oxenbridge and Brown (2002); Shenkar and Yan (2002); Stasavage (2004); Stephenson and Tysoe (1988); Strutton et al. (1993); Sutton and Callahan (1988); Vaccaro and Coward (1993).

*Political Contexts* Blaydes (2004); Cottam (1989); Glad and Rosenberg (1990); Lipschutz (1991, 1993); Maoz and Astorino (1992); Papayoanou (1997); Schelling (2008); Sergeev (1991); A. M. Smith and Stam (2004); Torenvlied and Thomson (2003).

# Coalitions

## *Laboratory and Quasi-Laboratory Studies and Theoretical Papers*

*Reviews and General Studies* Blumberg (1994); Polley (1989); Rapoport (1990); Slikker (2001).

*Theoretical Papers and Empirical Tests of Rules of Procedure* Aknine et al. (2004); Amer et al. (2002); Bloch (1996); Bolton et al. (2003); Boros et al. (1997); Bottom et al. (1996); Boyer (1999); Bruxelles and Kerbrat-Orecchioni (2004); Burani and Zwicker (2003); Chavez and Kimbrough (2004); Esteban and Sákovics (2003); Ferreira (1999); Fukuda and Muto (2004); Gulati and Westphal (1999); Hamiache (1999); Klaus (2001); Komorita et al. (1989); Laruelle and Valenciano (2004); Mannix (1993); Okada (1996); Ray and Vohra (1999); Ray (1996); Schofield and Parks (2000); Sengupta and Sengupta (1996); Eric A. Smith (2003); Sobczak (1988); Van Beest et al. (2004b); Yi (1999).

*Empirical Processes* Beest et al. (2005); Bottom et al. (2000); Carreras (1996); Espinosa and Macho-Stadler (2003); Evans (1996); Fader and Hauser (1988); Gale et al. (2002); Holler and Napel (2004); Komorita and Ellis (1988); Madhavan et al. (2004); Maschler (2004); Nandeibam (2000); Perlinger (2000); Polzer et al. (1998); Simpson and Macy (2001); Van Beest et al. (2004a); Van Beest et al. (2003); Van

Schaik et al. (2004); Vassileva et al. (2002); Vidal (2004); Wagner et al. (2002); Watkins and Rosegrant (1996); Wilke et al. (1996); Yamaguchi (1989, 1991a, b, 1992); Young (1989).

*Stability and Other Outcome Properties* Barberà and Gerber (2003); Belleflamme (2000); Bogomolnaia and Jackson (2002); Cressman et al. (2004); Ho (2002); Milgrom and Roberts (1996); Moldovanu and Winter (1995); Moreno and Wooders (1996); Pápai (2004); Yi (1997).

## *Applications*

*Animal Studies* MacKenzie and Kennedy (1991); Noë (1994); Noë and Sluijter (1995); Öst et al. (2003); Packer et al. (1991); Perrey et al. (2004); Putland (2001); Silk et al. (2004); Vervaecke et al. (2000).

*Community Settings* Armbruster et al. (1999); Berkowitz and Wolff (1996); Boydell and Volpe (2004); Bronheim and Striffler (1999); Conway (2002); Feinberg et al. (2004); Foster-Fishman et al. (2001); Granner and Sharpe (2004); Hays et al. (2000); Keys and Factor (2001); Libby and Austin (2004b); Mansergh et al. (1996); Mayer et al. (1998); McFall et al. (2004); Mitchell et al. (1996); Otis (2004); Sink (1991); Snell-Johns et al. (2003); Wiesenfeld (1997).

*Ethnic Groups* Cosmides et al. (2003); Crowfoot and Chesler (1996); Park (1996); Torres (2002).

*Gender Issues and Similar* Butterwick (2003); Grise-Owens et al. (2004); Lepischak (2004); Martin and Meyerson (1988); Padilla (2004).

*Health and Mental Health* Cramer et al. (2003); Garland et al. (2004); Kegler et al. (1998); Libby and Austin (2002a, 2004); Lindholm et al. (2004); Paine-Andrews et al. (1996); Penner (1995); Philips (2004); Preli and Protinsky (1988); Scavone (1992); Smitson (2001); Visher and Visher (1989); Weiss (1996); Weltz (2003); Zapka et al. (1992).

*Miscellaneous* Benveniste (1989); Coates (1990); Cooren (2001); Dluhy and Kravitz (1990); Dyke (2003); Einspruch and Wunrow (2002); Fanis (2004); Flemons and Tsai (1992); Florin et al. (2000); Galavotti (1989); Grusky et al. (1995); Hagen and Bryant (2003); Huckins (2002); Inniss (1989); Kirsch and Osterling (1995); Kressel (2000); Ma (2001); S. Martinez (1989); Mesquida and Wiener (1996); Mitchell et al. (2004); Mizrahi and Rosenthal (2001); Neighbors and Barta (2004); Nelson (1988); Paul (1996); Pires (1988); Rosen (1996); Shefner (1999); Shipps (2003); Simpson and Cieslik (2002); Stearns and Almeida (2004); Sutherland et al. (1997); Tian (2000); Wolfenstein (1998); Wood and Bohte (2004).

*Organizations* A. T. Cobb (1991); Kenis and Knoke (2002); Mannix and White (1992); Tadepalli (1992).

*Political Groups* Bacharach and Lawler (1988); Bonelli and Simmons (2004a, b); Lai and Reiter (2000); Tedin and Murray (1994); Zurcher and Snow (1990).

# Games

## *Laboratory and Quasi-Laboratory Studies and Theoretical Papers*

*Cooperation* Abbink et al. (2003); Alvard (2004); Bendor et al. (1991); Bilancini and Boncinelli (2009); Boone et al. (2002); R. T. Boone and Macy (1999); Bornstein (2004); Brosig (2002); Cabon-Dhersin and Ramani (2004); Chaudhuri et al. (2002); Cooper et al. (1996); De Dreu et al. (1995); Dinar et al. (1992); Dwyer and Minnegal (1997); Eguíluz et al. (2005); Feeley et al. (1997); Fischer (2009); Fischer and Suleiman (1997); Frank et al. (1993); Friedland (1990); Goren and Bornstein (2000); Güth et al. (1997); Hansen (1990); Hemesath and Pomponio (1998); Huang and Sjöström (2003); Hulbert et al. (2001); Insko et al. (2005); Imhof et al. (2005); Izquierdo and Rafels (2001); Ketelaar and Au (2003); Kiesler et al. (1996); Kim and Webster (2001); Knez and Camerer (2000); Komorita et al. (1991); Lodewijkx (2001); Lopez (1995); Majeski and Fricks (1995); McNamara et al. (2004); Minkler and Miceli (2004); Monterosso et al. (2002); Moreno and Wooders (1998); Mori (1996); Morris et al. (1998); Murnighan (1991); Murnighan and King (1992); Nishizaki et al. (2004); Offerman et al. (2001); Orbell and Dawes (1993); Paese and Stang (1998); Amnon Rapoport and Fuller (1998); Rieskamp and Todd (2006); Scharpf (1990); Schuessler (1989); Signorino (1996); Jeffrey M. Smith and Bell (1992); Srivastava and Lalnunmawii (1989); Stark (2004); Stone et al. (1996); Tsai (1993); Wiseman and Yilankaya (2001); Wu et al. (2009); Zhong et al. (2002).

*Equilibrium* Brandts and MacLeod (1995); Budescu, Rapoport, and Suleiman (1995); Burton and Sefton (2004); Cheng and Zhu (1995); Eichberger and Kelsey (2000); Eliaz (2003); Engl (1995); Groes et al. (1998); Güth (2002); Huettel et al. (2001); Youngse Kim (1996); Maskin and Riley (2003); McKelvey and Palfrey (1995); Ochs (1995); Rapoport, Seale, Erev, and Sundali (1998); Rinott and Scarsini (2000); Sandholm (2003); Schofield and Parks (2000); Shinotsuka and Takamiya (2003); Stanford (1995); Tedeschi (1995); Thoron (2004); Tomala (1999); Van Damme and Hurkens (1996).

*Miscellaneous Games and Constructs—Reviews and General Considerations* Blumberg (1994); Bornstein (2003); Busemeyer and Pleskac (2009); Butler (2007); Charness and Haruvy (2002); Kurzban et al. (2008); Shim (1988); Zwick et al. (2000);

*Miscellaneous Games and Constructs—Background, Demographic Variables, and Rules* Abolafia (1996); Amann and Leininger (1996); Amer et al. (2002); Andreoni and Miller (1995); Attar et al. (2008); Babcock and Landeo (2004); Bacharach and Bernasconi (1997); Badke-Schaub and Strohschneider (1998); Baliga and Evans (2000); Banks et al. (2002); Baye and Hoppe (2003); Bednar and Page (2007); Ben-Ner et al. (2004); Bensaid and Gary-Bobo (1996); Berninghaus et al. (2002); Betz (1995); Bornstein et al. (1994); Bornstein et al. (2004); Bornstein and Rapoport (1988); Bosch-Domènech and Sáez-Martí (2001); Budescu and Rapoport (1994); Budescu et al. (1990); Budescu, Suleiman, and Rapoport (1995); Cabrales et al. (2003); Camerer (2003); Camerer and Loewenstein (1993); Carreras and Freixas (1996); Chakravarty et al. (2000); Colman and Stirk (1998); Curseu and Curseu (2001); Duffy and Feltovich (2002); Fabricatore et al. (2002); Facer et al. (2004); Felsenthal et al. (1998); Gallucci and Perugini (2000); Garratt and Qin (2000); Garson and Stanwyck (1997); Granberg (1999); Granberg and Dorr (1998); Heifetz and Mongin (2001); Henrich et al. (2005); Hine and Gifford (1996); Holler et al. (1992); Holm (2000); Huck et al. (2002); Insko et al. (1988); Israel et al. (1992); Karaul et al. (2000); Kim and Kim (1997); Koller and Milch (2003); Komorita and Carnevale (1992); Kovalenkov and Wooders (2001); Krabbe et al. (1997); Krauss and Wang (2003); Laing and Slotznick (1991); Laskowski and Slonim (1999); Leifer (1988); Lindskold and Han (1988a, b); Lo (1999, 2000); Metha et al. (1994); Michener et al. (1989); D. T. Miller et al. (1998); Morris et al. (2004); Neyman and Okada (2000); Ones and Putterman (2007); Orshan and Zarzuelo (2000); Ostmann (1992); Otten et al. (1995); Pacala et al. (1995); Parks and Vu (1994); Quesada (2002); Rapoport and Au (2001); Reijnierse et al. (1996); Rustichini (1999); Rutledge-Taylor and West (2004); Saijo and Nakamura (1995); Sakurai (1990); Scharlemann et al. (2001); Schellenberg (1990); Schwartz-Shea (2002); Slikker and Van den Nouweland (2001); Stark and Wang (2004); Sterman (1988); Stewart et al. (2003); Stuart (1997); Sugiyama et al. (2004); Suleiman and Budescu (1999); Suleiman and Rapoport (1992); Suleiman et al. (1996); Sundali et al. (1995); Takao and Okura (2001); Tian and Li (1995); Tyson et al. (1988); Van Huyck et al. (1995); Van Schie and Van der Pligt (1995); Weigelt et al. (1989); Werner (1999); West and Lebiere (2001); Whitehead et al. (1996); Wischniewski et al. (2009); Yamagishi and Kiyonari (2000);

*Miscellaneous Games and Constructs—Processes Emerging from Playing* Abele et al. (2004); Anderhub et al. (2004); Anderson (2004); Andreoni et al. (2002); Armantier (2004); Baik et al. (1999); Ben-Porath and Kahneman (2003); Bennett et al. (1994); Betz (1991); Bienenstock and Bonacich (1993); Blume (2003); Bruins et al. (1989); Butler (1992); Camac (1992); Chatterjee et al. (2003); Chen and Plott (1998); Chen et al. (2004); Cheung and Friedman (1997); Cho et al. (2002); Cooper and Stockman (2002); Cotterell et al. (1992); Cressman (1997); Devetag et al. (2000); Devetag and Warglien (2003); Dukerich et al. (1990); Durieu and Solal (2003); Ellingsen and Robles (2002); Enzle et al. (1992); Friedman et al. (2004); Galanos et al. (1993); Gans (1995); Gilboa and Schmeidler (2003); Ginkel and Smith (1999); Gossner and Vieille (2002, 2003); Gray and Stafford (1988); Güth et al. (2003); Güth et al. (1995); Hart and Mas-Colell (2003); Healy and Noussair (2004); Huber (1996); Iizuka et al. (2002); Insko et al. (1993); Israeli (1999); Keren and Wagenaar (1988); Yong-Gwan Kim (1996); Kiyonari et al. (2000); Ladoucer and Dubé (1997); Lambo and Moulen (2002); Langlois and Langlois (1999); Lindskold and Han (1988b); Mannix (1991); Masel (2007); McGinn et al. (2003);

R. I. Miller and Sanchirico (1999); Mookherjee and Sopher (1997); Nelson (2002); Olcina and Peñarrubia (2004); Parks et al. (2002); Rapoport et al. (1993); Rapoport et al. (2002); Roth and Erev (1995); Sandler (1999); Schummer (2000); Sethi and Somanathan (2003); Sheldon (1999); Sobel (2001); Sonnegård (1996); Sonsino and Sirota (2003); Spiegler (2004); Srivastava (2001); Suleiman and Rapoport (1988); Sundali et al. (1995); Taylor and Zwicker (1997); N. E. Turner (1998); Van Assen and Snijders (2004); Watson (1996); Weesie and Franzen (1998); Wilke and Braspenning (1989); Zhang and Norman (1994);

*Miscellaneous Games and Constructs—Outcomes* Boles and Messick (1995); Boros and Gurvich (2000); Dekel and Wolinsky (2003); Fischer, Kubitzki, Guter, and Frey (2007); Funk et al. (2003); Samuelson and Swinkels (2003); Schopler et al. (1991); Willson (2000); Xue (2002).

*Miscellaneous Games and Constructs—Values and Theoretical Perspectives* Asheim (2002); Budescu et al. (1999); Eliaz and Ok (2006); Kremer et al. (1988); Stahl and Wilson (1995); Wayne and Rubinstein (1992).

*Prisoner's Dilemma Game* Antonides (1994); Au and Komorita (2002); Baker and Rachlin (2001, 2002); Batson and Ahmad (2001); Batson and Moran (1999); Bendor et al. (1991); Bolle and Ockenfels (1990); Boone et al. (2002); C. Boone et al. (1999a, b); R. T. Boone and Macy (1999); Brosig (2002); Cooper et al. (1996); Corfman and Lehmann (1994); De Jong et al. (2002); Fader and Hauser (1988); Feeley et al. (1997); Ferguson and Schmitt (1988); Furnham and Quilley (1989); Goren (2001); Goren and Bornstein (1999, 2000); Harris and Madden (2002); Hauk (2003); Hauk and Nagel (2001); Hemesath and Pomponio (1998); Hoffman (1999); Imhof et al. (2005); Insko et al. (1994); Jin et al. (1996); Jones and Zhang (2004); Kassinove et al. (2002); Kay and Ross (2003); Kiesler et al. (1996); Knez and Camerer (2000); Li and Taplin (2002); Liberman et al. (2004); Lopez (1995); McNamara et al. (2004); Messick (2008); Monterosso et al. (2002); Mori (1996); Morris et al. (1995, 1998); Neuberg (1988); Nishizaki et al. (2004); Oda (1997); Anatol, Rapoport (1988); Sheldon et al. (2000); Tomochi (2004); Van Lange, Liebrand, and Kuhlman (1990); Wiseman and Yilankaya (2001); Wolf et al. (2008); Wong and Hong (2005); Yamagishi et al. (2005); Yi and Rachlin (2004).

*Simulation* Affisco and Chanin (1990); Bruschke et al. (1993); Carr and Groves (1998); Chang (2003); Chang et al. (2003); Clark et al. (2003); Diehl (1991); Druckman (1995); Faria and Wellington (2004); Fischer and Suleiman (1997); Frohlich and Oppenheimer (1997); Gaudart (1999); Gosenpud and Miesing (1992); Gosenpud and Washbush (1996); Gotts et al. (2003); Hemmasi and Graf (1992); Hemmasi et al. (1989); Hill and Lance (2002); Hine and Gifford (1997); Hollenbeck et al. (1992); Inglis et al. (2004); Jaffe and Nebenzahl (1990); Johansson and Küller (2002); Joldersma and Geurts (1998); Karasawa (2002a, b); Kashibuchi and Sakamoto (2001); Keeffe et al. (1993); Kirk (2004); Kirts et al. (1991); Kleiman and Kilmer (2009); Klein and Fleck (1990); Koehler (2001); Krackhardt and Stern (1988); Laukka et al. (1995); Li and Baillie (1993); Murnighan (1991); Napier and House (1990); Poplu et al. (2003); Prohaska and Frank (1990); Remus and Edge

(1991); Renaud and Stolovitch (1988); Ross et al. (2001); Rouwette et al. (1998); Schindler (1992); Signorino (1996); Jeffrey M. Smith and Bell (1992); Snow et al. (2002); Stone et al. (1996); Thavikulwat (2004); Trost et al. (1989); Tsai (1993); Tsuchiya and Tsuchiya (2000); Twale (1991); van Eck and Dempsey (2002); Washbush and Gosen (2001); Wellington and Faria (1996); Wheatley et al. (1988); Whiteley and Faria (1989); Williams (1991); Wit and Wilke (1990); Wolfe (1993); Wolfe and Box (1988); Wolfe and Chanin (1993); Wolfe and Roberts (1993).

*Trust* Barr (2004); Berg et al. (1995); Cabon-Dhersin and Ramani (2004); Chaudhuri et al. (2002); Eckel and Wilson (2003); Fang et al. (2002); Gunnthorsdottir et al. (2002); Güth et al. (1997); Insko and Schopler (1998); James (2002); Malhotra (2004); McCabe et al. (1998); McCabe et al. (2003); Mosler (1993); Orbell et al. (1994); Parks, Henager, and Scamahorn (1996); Parks and Hulbert (1995).

*Ultimatum Game* (In the version generally covered by the following references, one player of two suggests a split and the other player may accept or reject it. If accepted, the split is effected; if rejected, neither participant gets anything. Results typically demonstrate that players do not act wholly in self-interest but that an element of fairness is typical. Otherwise second players might logically accept *any* offer in which they get at least something; whereas typically some cultures find many players simply propose 50:50 splits and also find that offers of small amounts get rejected.)

Abbink et al. (2001); Alvard (2004); Bethwaite and Tompkinson (1996); Dickinson (2000); Gneezy et al. (2003); Gurven (2004); Güth et al. (2001); Huck (1999); Humphrey et al. (2004); Larrick and Blount (1997); Munier and Zaharia (2002); Patton (2004); Ruffle (1998); Suleiman (1996); Sum and Gil-White (2004); Tracer (2004); Weg and Smith (1993); Zhong et al. (2002).


## *"Real-World" Applications and Effects*

Alvard and Nolin (2002); Auyeung (2004); Baker et al. (1993); Carment and Rowlands (1998); Chertkoff (1992); Cosgray et al. (1990); Davidson and Newman (1990); Dresner (1989); Edge and Keys (1990); Harrison and Horne (1999); Henrich and Smith (2004); Hornby and Saunders (1989); Keren and Raub (1993); Kolasinski and Gilson (1999); Krebs et al. (2003); Krueger and Acevedo (2008); McCarthy (2002); Moreno and Mayer (2004); Nonami (1996); Pelligra (2007); Sayman et al. (2002); Seo and Nishizaki (1994); Sönmez (1997); Stettler et al. (2004); D. A. Turner (1988); Van Lange et al. (2007); Wit and Wilke (1998).

# Chapter 3
# Group Dynamics and Social Cognition

Social cognition has not really been "missing" from the study of small groups, but the two areas have had largely disparate research literatures until recently. Social identity theory (cf. Deaux 1991) and other cognitive explanations are widely applicable to small-group topics, including setting, personality and background variables, social influence, roles and relationships including leadership, social interaction, group decision-making and cooperation, intergroup relations, and groups in organizational settings. For a wide-range view of the relationship between identity and control in social action, see White (1992).

Cognitive-based explanations partially underpin many—perhaps most—social-psychological findings related to conflict resolution, but relevant cognitive mechanisms are not always made explicit.

A major—and admirable—effort in some recent small groups research has been to attempt some integration with social cognition, a largely separate research area. There is no immediate prospect of "unifying" the two areas. This is partly because these two major areas of social psychology are not, or not yet, themselves unified entities. Deliberate effort has however been applied to understand cognitive aspects of small-groups topics—at the same time rendering "social" cognition more *social* (Ickes and Gonzalez 1996).

One major reason to applaud the simultaneous study of cognition and group effects is simply that they shed light on each other. An important part of the variance in how people interact is, not surprisingly, determined by their perceptions and thoughts. The present chapter includes illustrations of this from virtually every major area of small group research. This chapter is not an occasion for casting disparagement on work that is "purely" cognitive or group-based anymore than the study of biochemistry undermines the value of research based in "undiluted" chemistry or biology, nor does it seem wise just now to present the integration of group dynamics and social cognition from within a single theoretical framework, given that (as demonstrated below) the combinatory work draws productively on a wide variety of paradigms. Finally, cognitive approaches are not here put forward as a way to "rescue" group dynamics. As Steiner (1983) eventually pointed out, and as earlier research handbooks have demonstrated (Hare 1976; Hare et al. 1994), small group research remains alive and well, though its ebb and flow are determined partly by

H. Blumberg et al., *Small Group Research,* Peace Psychology Book Series,
DOI 10.1007/978-1-4614-0025-7_3, © Springer Science+Business Media, LLC 2012

social conditions and their accompanying zeitgeist. Moreland et al. (1994) do document the importance of social cognition—which, according to Mischel (1998), has become virtually synonymous with social psychology—in bolstering interest in group research. Their analysis established this empirically across a sample of articles from specific major journals (including the *Journal of Experimental Social Psychology*) but did not assess the breadth of cognitive influence topically across virtually the entire gamut of group research.

As noted above, cognition was not really "missing" from the study of group dynamics nor of peace psychology—as will become apparent in the present chapter. Indeed the cognition/behavior dichotomy is of course rather artificial (as is the disposition/situation distinction that cross-cuts it). In any case, the weaving of person-perception research into group studies seems beneficial for understanding both areas.

In the early summaries of research on social cognition in small groups, the focus was on the social perception of the self and others (see Hare 1976, pp. 113–130). The topics covered included first impressions, the group basis of perception, perceptual accuracy, perception of friends, self-perception, attribution of causality, changing perception through interaction, perception and adjustment, leader's perception, and from perception to action. Aspects of social cognition related to individual and group decision-making were not included, although mentioned in reviews on decision making, nor was the literature on stereotypes related to minority groups and intergroup relations since the stereotypes were usually based on perception of large categories of persons, not on face-to-face groups. However, the relevance of stereotypes and other aspects of social cognition are now included in this review since perceptions at every system level, from individual, to group, to organization, to society, all play a part in interpersonal behavior.

The "part" also includes, but is not limited to, phenomena that give rise to disputes and the negotiations that can settle them.

Conveniently, many of the main contemporary attempts to integrate group dynamics and social cognition have been brought together in a collection entitled *What's social about social perception* edited by Nye and Brower (1996b). In their introduction to the volume Fiske and Goodwin (1994, 1996) review research and theory on the influence of social factors on perception and list the various topics involving cognition that are relevant, such as accuracy, memory, shared meanings including stereotypes, and the influence of goals and control. In their summary, Nye and Brower (1996a) note the topics that have been covered in the 11 contributions to the volume, including groups as information-processing units, the interchangeability of the self and group, memory systems, focusing attention on the self and other, self-worth, perceptions of leadership, reciprocal perceptions, social construction of identity, ingroups and outgroups, the contact hypothesis, and group development. The strength of the work is its reasonable thoroughness in covering extant research compactly. Ironically, given its breadth, this excellent volume nevertheless does not assess how fully the social-cognition perspective covers the whole range of small-group topics, nor is it organized so as to facilitate this task—which represents an intended goal of this chapter.

Group members' social identities—the social categories, real or symbolic with which they identify—can be especially important in determining their interaction in small groups and they provide a focus for several reviews that essentially deal with cognition and small group behavior (Abrams and Rutland 2008; Abrams et al. 2005; Ellemers Spears, and Doosje 2002; Hogg 2004; Hornsey 2008; J. C. Turner 2000). Like so many constructs that are often conveniently viewed as unidemensional, social identity combines multiple factors, for example importance, commitment, perceived superiority of ingroup, and deference (Roccas et al. 2008; cf. Cameron 2004).

"Triggers" that render a social identity salient may also activate a group "fault-line" with attendant negative outcomes (Chrobot-Mason et al. 2009). By contrast, "social identity complexity"—where members have a variety of different or partly overlapping ingroups—may in general be associated with increased tolerance of outgroups (Roccas and Brewer 2002; see also Crisp and Hewstone 2000b) and less likelihood of polarization and conflict. Where there are multiple group member-ships, participants tend to use heuristics rather than, e.g. algebraic summing to com-bine information (Urada et al. 2007).

Among other topics, social identity in groups has been studied in relation to: mutual influence of the group and the person (Tyler and Smith 1999); group loyalty and related variables such as collective action (Brewer and Silver 2000; Van Vugt and Hart 2004; Zdaniuk and Levine 2001); social power (Tanabe 2001); partisan-ship (Greenwald et al. 2002); and affect (Forgas 2002a, b, c; Thompson and Fine 1999). Ironically, identity with a group may follow from feelings of uncertainty about one's self (Hogg 2007) or from a quest for perceived collective continu-ity (Sani et al. 2008). See also Aron et al. (2004); Barreto and Ellemers (2002b); N. Haslam et al. (2006); Huang (2009); Kashima et al. (2000); Sani and Todman (2002); and Simon et al. (2000).

Social cognition is moreover relevant to linking small group research to other areas of psychology including, e.g. neural bases (Adolphs 2009) and interpersonal problems (Gilovich et al. 1999), comparative (inter-species) research (Emery and Clayton 2009), and to interdisciplinary matters (Hollingshead and Poole 2004; Poole et al. 2004) such as political action (Bliuc et al. 2007; Klandermans and De Weerd 2000).

For publications which review or comment on research on some or all of this chapter's topics, see Brown (1996); Hogg (1996); Howard (1994); Stroebe and Hewstone (1998); Wetherell (1996b). For other "general" work on cognitive aspects of small groups see Abrams (1994); Brewer and Harasty (1996); Gibbons (1990); Hogg and Abrams (1993); Levine et al. (1996); Witte and Davis (1996). For some more specific relevant work that does not seem to fit neatly into any one category, see Biernat and Vescio (1994); Fox and Thornton (1993); Holmes (1997); Latané and Liu (1996); Seidel et al. (1998); Stangor and Duan (1991); Suman (1989); Wilkinson and Kitzinger (1996); Ybema and Buunk (1993).

Research on social identity is relevant to several of the sections of this chapter, as noted below, especially intergroup relations.

Some of the relevant reviews of the literature or collections of articles focus on social perception and do not include topics such as the role of social cognition on decision making, accuracy, or memory. For example, Kunda (1999) in a book entitled *Social cognition: Making sense of people*, organizes the review in three sections:

1. Processes: Concept representation, rules of inference, memory, "hot" [motivated] cognition, and automatic processing.
2. Topics: Group stereotypes, knowledge of other individuals, and knowledge of self.
3. Issues from a cross-cultural perspective.

In texts that cover all of social psychology, such as that by Kassin et al. (2008), we find a chapter on "perceiving persons" that may include a review of research on how "scripts of life" influence perceptions, nonverbal behavior, truth versus deception, attribution theories, information processing in groups, attributions, impression formation, implicit personality theory, the primacy effect, and the self-fulfilling prophecy. Many of these topics have explicit or implicit relevance to social interaction in small groups, intergroup relations, and conflict resolution.

For additional summaries of the literature relating cognition to social behavior see Forgas et al. (2001); Higgins and Sorrentino (1990); Markovsky (1994); Rohrbaugh (1988); Westen (1991).

The findings presented in the present volume and elsewhere are here organized into a progression of small-groups topics. It seems helpful to unfold the topics gradually in an (arguably) intuitively plausible sequence.

One way to assess what has, and has not, been accomplished in building a group/cognition interface is to tour the field of small groups research, with this "interface criterion" in mind. The present "tour" will progress by bringing additional elements "on stage" in approximately the same sequence as that used in the overall organization of this two-volume handbook—Blumberg et al. (2009) and the present volume—and also as used in our previous works (Blumberg 1976; Blumberg et al. 1983; Hare et al. 1994, 1996):[1]

a. The first elements are the pre-existing physical setting and the background and personality variables that people bring with them.
b. Then the effects of others' presence are considered, including the conformity elicited by others' views.
c. Next, with "live" groups now "onstage": The roles and relationships (including leadership roles) among group members.

---

[1] The two books by Hare et al. (1994, 1996) are co-authored but nevertheless have signed chapters. Author's responsibilities were similar, though not identical, in the two volumes. The authorships, on which some of the chapters' introductory analyses in the present volumes are in part based, are as follows (using the 1996 version). Martin Davies: physical setting and background variables (Chaps. 1 and 2), social interaction (Chap. 7), and intergroup relations (Chap. 12). Valerie Kent: social influence (Chaps. 3 and 4) and leadership (Chap. 6). Paul Hare: roles (Chap. 5) and organizational settings (Chap. 11). Herbert Blumberg: group decision making (Chap. 8), and cooperation and bargaining (Chaps. 9 and 10).

d. Ongoing social processes, including the properties of social interaction and also group decision making.
e. Finally, once the live groups have ongoing social interaction, one needs to consider situational (applied) matters, such as conflict resolution generally, and processes in organizations and teams, in intergroup relations, and in therapy groups.

## Physical Setting and Background Variables

The physical situation of a group includes the effects of environment (noise, temperature), material aspects of architecture and room design, and social density and spatial arrangements. The physical environment may facilitate or hinder group processes, and—for the present purpose—it is useful to distinguish between relatively direct effects (as when interpersonal distance makes it hard to hear people seated around a table except for one's neighbors) and more cognitively-mediated ones (as when the ambience of a well-appointed dining room sets the stage for polite conversation). A cognition-based account of these variables would need systematically to explain the extent and mechanisms whereby people's *views* about such dimensions affect the nature and outcome of social interaction. No one, it seems, has yet attempted such a cognitively-oriented account. Some specific findings are relevant, however. For example, group members' needs for regulating the information they receive are associated with the centrality of their seating positions (Koneya 1977; Michelini et al. 1976). Of course one needs a framework to understand these and other effects. An example of such a framework is provided by Mullen and colleagues (Mullen et al. 1996), who have carried out empirical work related to prototypes, discussed below. See also Keyton (1991).

Personal attributes, such as age, sex, personality, and abilities, affect how group members interact with each other. In traditional research on problem-solving groups, for example, males tend to be dominant and task-oriented, and females, friendly and expressive. The specific links (if any) are, however, dependent on context and relate to the functions of particular cognitions and behaviors (LaFrance 2001). For additional research on gender stereotypes and differences in behavior based on gender, see Amancio (1989); Arndt et al. (2002); Bourhis et al. (1992); Breakwell (1990); Carpenter (1994); Cook-Huffman (2000); Fiedler et al. (1993); Grant (1993b); Hunsley et al. (1991); James (1993); Keller and Molix (2008); Kenrick et al. (1994); Nicotera and Rancer (1994); Robinson and Reis (1989); Rudman and Goodwin (2004); and Young (1994).

Many findings are partly cognitive in nature, as when a person's status characteristics help to determine "performance expectation states" in a new group. To take a mundane example, persons who are thought likely to have high task ability are urged to contribute more.

An approach using "prototypes" and "exemplars" cannot "replace" the semi-empirical accounts of the effects, on group processes, of various background dimensions. It does, however, provide a framework for understanding many of these effects.

Relatively large, diverse groups tend to be coded by exemplars; one thinks of the large, "background" group in terms of various individual group members. Proportionately small, salient groups, however, are coded in terms of prototypes (Rosch 1978); one tends to represent such a salient group in terms of a particularly good image of a "typical group member," and one exaggerates the "family resemblance" among members. Although such stereotyping is characteristic of how minorities are viewed, the requisite salience can be achieved for any group simply by verbal instructions to focus on the group rather than on the individual.

Eliot R. Smith and Zarate (1990), in an experimental study with university undergraduates, found that students who learned about group prototypes before encountering individual group members (as might occur through social learning of a stereotype) engaged in more prototype-based processing, relative to students who encountered group members at the outset.

For additional research on prototypes and exemplars, see C. G. Lord et al. (1991); Mullen et al. (1994).

When participants sorted stick figures into groups by sticking them onto a response sheet, an instruction to pay attention to similarities—rather than to each individual figure—yielded fewer and larger categories and also yielded a simpler dimensional structure in the way the figures clustered (Mullen et al. 1996).

For additional research on categories see Gastardo-Conaco (1991); Sedikides and Ostrom (1988).

Various authors also corroborated and extended Hamilton and Gifford's (1976) finding that illusory correlations—erroneous judgments of the relation between two variables—may be involved in the development of stereotypes (cf. Meiser and Hewstone 2006). In the relevant experiments, participants were shown a series of stimulus items that described a member of one of two groups with either a positive or negative trait. More statements described Group A than Group B, and there were more positive than negative statements (for both groups, in the same ratio). When participants are asked which traits are characteristic of which group, they over-estimate the negative characteristics of the minority group. This is because the smaller group is salient, as are the negative traits (which are themselves in a noticeable minority).

In an experiment using more negative traits than positive ones, however, it is the positive traits that become salient, and participants over-estimate the positive characteristics of the minority group. Also, because people are particularly concerned to identify meaningful differences between social categories, traits relevant to evaluative differentiation are especially susceptible to illusory correlation (Haslam, McGarty, and Brown 1996).

For additional research on illusory correlations and stereotypes, see Haslam, McGarty, Oakes, and Turner (1993); McConnell et al. (1994); see also Chap. 6.

Women are still sometimes stereotyped as being unlikely to excel in task skills. One of the ways of surmounting such a barrier is to combine an early demonstration of task skill with a cooperative stance and a style that "attracts others' attention to their high-quality solutions" (Shackelford et al. 1996). For further discussion of stereotyping and ameliorative procedures see below, the section on intergroup relations.

Thus in any given group situation, the personal-background characteristics that are salient (typically, but not necessarily, because they represent minorities) tend to yield impressions of stereotyped, homogeneous groups, and respondents tend to exaggerate the presence of salient traits in these groups. However, when there is more variability in the characteristic that is being judged, a person will be less likely to conclude that the group is homogeneous (see Jetten et al. 1998; Kraus et al. 1993; Lambert 1995, 1998; Linville and Fisher 1993).

Notwithstanding personality variables' known links with attitudes, including cognition and behavior—e.g., between authoritarianism and prejudice—traditional personality variables have not, for the most part, helped to explain cognitive bases of small group processes (Hodson and Sorrentino 2001; Reynolds et al. 2001, 2007). In particular contexts, however, personality variables such as individual or collective self-esteem may be affected by (or may affect) other matters such as group-serving attributional biases or a previously expressed norm of fairness (Ellemers et al. 1999; Hunter et al. 2000; Meeres and Grant 1999; Scheepers et al. 2009; Scholz 2004). If one regards cultural and collective social identities as quasi-personality variables and key determinants of self-concept, then links with small group processes and with properties such as group diversity are of course manifold, as discussed throughout this chapter. For additional examples and analysis see, for example: Abrams and Hogg (2004); Christensen et al. (2004); Haenfler (2004); Mullin and Hogg (1999); Swann et al. (2003, 2004).

Eagly et al. (1994) find serious inadequacies with the rating scale and checklist methods that have generally been used to assess the cognitive and affective bases of attitudes toward social groups. They recommend using open-ended questions that ask participants to write down the beliefs they hold and the affects they experience in relation to the attitude object.

For additional research on stereotypes see Anastasio et al. (1997); Anderson (1990); Biernat and Vescio (1993); Fiske (1993, 2008); Gardner et al. (1995); Mackie, Allison, Worth, and Asuncion (1992); Nakanishi and Kameda (2001); Reicher and Levine (1994); Seta and Seta (1993); Spears, Oakes, Ellemers, and Haslam (1997); Wilder and Shapiro (1991). Stereotyping may interact with other variables such as age, for instance when older adults are more familiar with an outgroup's true characteristics (Chasteen 2005), but such links may often simply go unstudied.

For additional research on cognitive aspects of personality and demographic characteristics of members of small groups see Duckitt (1989); Ellemers et al. (1993); Gaskell and Wright (1997); Goodwin and Soon (1994); Grant (1992); C. T. Miller and Felicio (1990); Sekaquaptewa and Thompson (2002); Uleman et al. (2000); Van Knippenberg and Wilke (1992); Van Twuyver and Van Knippenberg (1998); Wilder (1990); Wilder and Shapiro (1989a); Williams and Sternberg (1988).

## Social Influence

The effects of others' presence represents a small but important part of research on social influence—both generally and with regard to cognitive mediation. The presence of others may facilitate or inhibit behavior depending on, among other things, how it is perceived and the difficulty of the task behavior (Blumberg et al. 2009, Chap. 3 by Kent; Zajonc 1965). The much-studied effect that the size of a group of bystanders has on people helping others, for instance, is a complex interaction of the social-category memberships (including the sex) of the parties concerned (Levine and Crowther 2008). See also Gilbert and Silvera (1996) for a review of "over-helping" and B. N. Smith et al. (2001) on individual differences in social loafing (doing less when one's share of group effort is not evident).

Turning to the wider literature on cognition and social influence, pioneered by Sherif (1936): Respondents' social identities affect when, and to what extent, they will be influenced by communication from others. For example, students were (not surprisingly) more influenced by a speech against drinking and motoring accidents, as causes of brain damage, when the speaker was identified as belonging to a group working toward road safety than one committed to banning the consumption of alcohol (Haslam, McGarty, and Turner 1996). The effect depended, however, on group identity being made salient—that is, participants being asked beforehand whether they agreed with the position of the speaker's group. "Ingroup salience" led, not to mindless processing of the speaker's message, but to *more* careful consideration of the content. Possibly, outgroup salience for a speaker simply causes a message to be seen as "biased" (as in the landmark work of Hovland et al. 1953).

Although a steadfast minority may come to wield positive influence—provided that the minority are consistent and that the majority attribute this consistency to minority group members' confidence in their position (Moscovici 1980)—this influence is likely only if the minority is seen as part of one's ingroup (David and Turner 1996). Self-categorization represents an important determinant of both minority and majority influence (David and Turner 2001a, b). When a group loses its majority status, however, its members may experience decreased identification with the group (Prislin and Christensen 2005). More generally, social identity and self-categorization may be viewed as motivated processes—as part of a strain to reduce subjective uncertainty, for instance—not just as purely cognitive ones (Hogg 2001). For additional research on cognition and the influence of the minority see Clark and Maass (1988); Crano (2001); Kelly (1990b); Moskowitz (1996); Moskowitz and Chaiken (2001); Sanchez-Mazas et al. (1997).

Indeed, it has been argued that principles from stereotyping (associated with group identity, as discussed below) and from social influence can profitably be integrated (Haslam, Oakes et al. 1996). In two experiments, pre-existing stereotypes about Americans and Australians were bolstered when they were endorsed (rather than challenged) by an ingroup or challenged (rather than endorsed) by an outgroup. As Haslam and colleagues have put it, group identity is generally at the "start" of the influence process. This moreover seems true for both normative and informational social influence. Social identity even mediates obedience in studies based on Milgram's paradigm (Collins and Ma 2000; Haslam and Reicher 2006; Reicher and Haslam 2006). A variety of studies confirm the importance of perceived ingroup norms as a source of social influence (Fekadu and Kraft 2002; Kugihara 2001; Mackie and Queller 2000; D. T. Miller and Morrison 2009; Terry and Hogg 2001; Van Knippenberg 2000).

For additional studies linking cognition to social influence see Forgas (2001, 2007); Houser and Ham (2004); Kosmitzki et al. (1994); Lee (2004); D. T. Miller and Prentice (1994); Postmes, Spears, Lee, and Novak (2005); Roussiau and Soubiale (1995); Sassenberg and Postmes (2002); Sinclair et al. (1994); Spears et al. (2001); Weiner (1996); Wilson et al. (1998); Zdaniuk and Levine (1996). Persuasion and social influence are of course important determinants of attitude change; see Wood (2000) for a review of research and see Fleming and Petty (2000) for an integration based on "elaboration likelihood." For a review of social influence including cognitive processes see Forgas and Williams (2001).

In sum, social identity associated with background characteristics and personality is implicated in a wide variety of effects related to interpersonal and intergroup perception. The nature of such perceptions may, in turn, favor—or inhibit—conflict or its resolution or both.

## Roles (Including Leadership)

Roles in general, and leadership roles in particular, are obviously often crucial in determining the course of almost any conflict and of reconciliation. Hence, the importance in this context for having a general understanding of roles and associated cognitive processes.

Roles are defined primarily by the behavioral rights and duties associated with them. This is true of formal roles (such as leader or secretary), informal ones (joker), and transient dramatic roles (protagonist or audience member), as well as those actually defined by characteristic behavior (e.g., nonconformist). The role organization of a group leads to expectations about the potential contributions and status of a group member and such expectations constitute a cognitive component even within the established study of roles.

For related research, see Cast (2003); da Silva and Günther (2000); Hogg (2005a); Hornsey and Jetten (2004); Thoits (2003); Wolfensberger (1995).

Once people are at least acquainted with one another, their knowledge and expectations about each other's roles and skills ("who is good at what") contribute to "transactive" (group) memory systems. This shared knowledge increases productivity. In studies by Moreland, Argote, and Krishnan (1996), radio assembly teams performed better following group rather than individual training. The advantage was not found if the group members merely watched each other in training, without being able to converse, or if the training was limited to "team-building" (experience with a different task), or if participants were assigned to different groups (reshuffled) prior to production testing. In other words, transactive memory systems can be very specific to the particular situation and persons concerned. Park (2008) has shown that even shared cognition about communication rules such as politeness and efficiency impact on satisfaction and productivity.

For additional research on memory and shared knowledge, see Baumeister and Hastings (1997); de la Haye (1990); Hatano and Inagaki (1991).

The study of more formal role differentiation has been concerned especially with leadership roles. In the Lewin et al. (1939) classic laboratory study of leadership styles, democratic leaders were found to elicit better long-term productivity and satisfaction than authoritarian ones. Even prior to that, as well as subsequently, researchers investigated the personality correlates of good leadership (Hare 1976, pp. 278–281) and, more recently, the mediating effects of people's implicit (cognitive) theories of leadership roles. For example, people who identify strongly with a group base leadership perceptions on the group prototypicality of the leader (Fielding and Hogg 1997; Hains et al. 1997; Hogg et al. 1998).

According to Hollander (1958, 1992), leaders who are perceived as conforming and contributing to a group are viewed as being trustworthy and can then "spend" their "idiosyncrasy credits" on being innovative. For an arguably more comprehensive view of leadership attributions, Lord and colleagues (Lord and Maher 1991) find that various information-processing paradigms provide a theoretical and empirical basis for understanding executive leadership; one challenge is to test these views systematically in small-group settings.

A still prominent contemporary approach to the study of leadership, Fiedler's contingency theory, combines cognition and situation. For the Least Preferred Coworker (LPC) scale, respondents are asked to think of the person with whom they have least preferred working and to indicate, for various traits, how positively (high LPC) or negatively (low LPC) they perceive that person. For particularly favorable or unfavorable group situations, leaders with low LPC scores (whom Fiedler assumed task-oriented) have been found to be especially effective. In intermediate situations, high-LPC (social relationship-oriented) leaders are more effective.[2]

People's *perceptions* of a leader's effectiveness may be based, retrospectively, on successful performance outcomes rather than simply on whether a leader matches their prototypical views of a good leader. At least, as Nye and Simonetta's (1996) experiments show, people will make allowances for performance deficits that clearly follow from the situation, such as a leader being obliged to start work with substandard materials. Individual differences are evident and worthy of study, however, as to whether adequate allowances are made, and endure, in complex situations—such as the perceived effects of a large economic stimulus that has helped to prevent financial "meltdown" in a great recession.

---

[2] Recent research, using the System for a Multiple-Level Observation of Groups (SYMLOG) (Bales and Cohen 1979; S. E. Hare and Hare 1996), suggests that Fiedler may have been comparing a social-relationship-oriented leader with one who combines both task and social concerns, since leaders who only emphasize the task—although found in business management teams—are less likely to be found in student populations (Hare et al. 1998).

As the authors mention, outcome is salient in their experimental design. Where it is less salient, leaders are no doubt less judged by results. The point remains, however, that people's judgments play an important part in how a leader is perceived. A person's views about a leader will in turn impact on group productivity and satisfaction—not only directly, but also indirectly through social interaction and the shared views that may emerge. Thus it is often the followers who may determine what constitutes effective leadership (Hogg 2008).

For additional research combining leadership, social identity, and social cognition see Bar-Tal (1998); Choi et al. (2003); De Cremer and Van Vugt (2002); Foddy and Hogg (1999); Garza et al. (1989); Haslam and Platow (2001); Hogg (2005b); Hogg et al. (2006); Hogg and Van Knippenberg (2003); Hogue et al. (2002); Kane et al. (2002); Kohguchi et al. (2002); Meindl (1995); Pavitt et al. (1995); Platow and Van Knippenberg (2001); and Van Vugt and De Cremer (1999).

## Relationships

In contrast to research on roles that is usually focused on formal relations, research on "relationships" is concerned with informal relations, usually between pairs, as persons who are acquainted, friends, or even in love. However, as with roles, persons with informal relationships tend to have expectations for the part played by the other person or persons involved in the relationship. Thus the same types of cognitive judgments that are associated with roles also appear in the analysis of relationships.

As Brewer (2008b) has indicated, most of the literatures on close relationships ("dyadic belonging") and social identity ("collective belonging") are separate despite being potentially mutually applicable, a matter requiring investigation. She cites, however, a variety of empirical studies to support the view that—presumably with regard to the relative importance of various features—the relevant cognitive processes of close-dyadic and group relationships *are* separate or orthogonal rather than being systematically potentiating or compensatory; that is (perhaps depending on what is being measured) the profiles of interaction between groups and between close individuals tend to have a nil or low correlation rather than a positive or negative one.

A utility paradigm of self-disclosure suggests that individuals may, as it were, decide to use disclosure as a means of advancing to their goals for potentially close relationships—and, if so, will monitor their developing relationships and, on the basis of positive and negative perceived utilities, decide about self-disclosure accordingly (Omarzu 2000). Laurenceau et al. (2004) have reviewed more generally how cognitive processes are involved in the advancement of intimate relationships; they, too, emphasize self-disclosure and resultant responsiveness as mechanisms in achieving (sometimes brief) connectedness to others. The attributions of causality made by people seem particularly key to understanding the maintenance and deterioration of close relationships (Karney et al. 2001). Honeycutt and Cantrill (2001) have reviewed typical gender differences in the progression of how developing liaisons are perceived.

International harmony and discord may, in principle, also be subject to mutual monitoring and public self-disclosure, and some supporting evidence derives from the work of Tetlock (1985) and others on integrative complexity; but the investigation of analogous processes largely remains to be done.

For additional work on cognition and close relationships, see Cross and Morris (2003); Fletcher et al. (2000); Fletcher et al. (1999); Foeman and Nance (2002); Gagné and Lydon (2001); Knee et al. (2004); Krahé (2000); Lydon et al. (2008); Medvene et al. (2000); Murray (1999); Noller (2006); Eliot R. Smith et al. (1999).

Obviously, cognitive processes are of importance for human relationships in general; the study of relationships still needs better integration into evolutionary and other paradigms (Reis and Collins 2004).

Interdependence theory may form a basis for understanding the choices that parties may make, based on the rewards and costs to each party that attach not only to each party's actions but also to the joint occurrence of *combinations* of the various parties' choices. The perceived rewards and costs are, however, themselves dependent on the views parties have of one another—i.e., the schemas in their networks of cognitive "structures" (Holmes 2000). It appears that people's social categories and their interpersonal networks are important in identity formation and in their implications for social interaction (Deaux and Martin 2003).

The ability to take on others' perspectives is known to underpin empathic support for others and may help dissolve the perception of outgroups and the adverse orientation towards their members (Ames et al. 2008).

In establishing cultures of peace internationally, social identity and (e.g.) consequent tactfulness and warmth in social interaction seem indeed as important as the literal content of communications (Andersen et al. 2008).

For contemporary research that has been contextualizing the links between cognition and (not necessarily close) relationships see Ely and Roberts (2008); Fitzsimons and Kay (2004); Hahn and Hwang (1999); Hornsey and Jetten (2003); Marrero and Gámez (2004); Metts (2000); J. Miller (2001); Ruscher et al. (2003); Thye et al. (2002); Veríssimo et al. (2003).

For reviews of related research on relationships in general see Aron and Aron (1996); Berscheid (1994); Campbell (1993); Dindia (1997); Fiske and Haslam (1998); Fletcher (1993); Gudykunst and Hammer (1988); Hassebrauck (1995); Hogg and Hains (1996); Hogg, Hardie, and Reynolds (1995); Kelley (1997); Radley (1991); Tesser et al. (1988); Thompson and Holmes (1996); Townsend (1993); Whisman and Allan (1996).

For related work see also Codol et al. (1989); Dudkiewicz (1991); Ellemers and Van Rijswijk (1997); Gao (1996); Hogg and Hardie (1992); Kramer (1996); Kunda and Nisbett (1988); McCullough and Rachal (1998); Moya (1998); Pheterson (1995); Prentice et al. (1994); Steinfeld (1998); Sze (1990); Triandis et al. (1988).

## Social Interaction Including Group Decision Making

Larson and Christensen (1993) note that social cognition occurs in every kind of group problem-solving situation. The cognitive activity involves the acquisition, storage, transmission, manipulation, and use of information for the purpose of creating a group-level intellective product. Such "products" may, for example, relate to harmonious relationships or to dealing with fractious interludes.

Some researchers have paid direct attention to the discourse used by group members in social interaction. Oyserman and Packer (1996), for instance, maintain that social identity and the self are essentially maintained by language, broadly defined. They give examples such as the contrast between what it "means" to be a good student in a blue-collar community in Michigan, or being male or female in inner-city Chicago. As if to support this view experimentally, Steele has found that women and people of color underperform if relevant negative parts of their social identities are made salient (DeAngelis 1996). For instance, black students did worse than whites on a difficult verbal test when told they were taking a test that diagnosed verbal ability. No such differences, due to "stereotype threat," were found when the test was described as a "problem-solving procedure." According to Cadinu et al. (2006), individuals with internal Locus of Control beliefs, although usually performing well, may be particularly susceptible to stereotype threat.

For additional research on social identity see Carbaugh (1996); Dietz-Uhler and Murrell (1998); Lorenzi-Cioldi (1995); Matsui (1990); McKillop et al. (1992); Oyserman and Packer (1996); Smith-Lovin (2003).

The discovery of some previously unknown stigma regarding another person can also change the content of a discussion in a group. Ruscher and Hammer (1994) observed discussion of pairs of university undergraduates to note how a negative revelation of some stigma would disrupt the dyads' shared impressions of the other person. The disrupted dyads now took time to question each other about how the new information would alter their previous impressions. In contrast, when groups discussed controversial topics using an electronic group support system (a form of computer mediated communication), without knowledge of relevant social characteristics of the members, biases of attention and influence were eliminated (Bhappu et al. 1997). Additional evidence for the critical role of social identity in maintaining stereotypes is covered in the section below on intergroup relations. Also below is a discussion of computer-mediated communication.

An interdependence perspective, described above in the context of relationships, also helps one understand the "mutual interconnections" in small-group communication and people's expectations of each other's goals (Holmes 2002) including emotional components (Lawler 2003) and the rewards and costs related to parties' social identities.

In their overview of social identity and communication in small groups, Hogg and Tindale (2005) suggest that identity as manifest in social norms plays a crucial role in many important aspects of social influence, in fact spanning many of the topics covered in this chapter. Indeed the interpretation of many key aspects of identity—age, gender, and authority to name just a few—may typically be established during social interaction (Mokros 2003). This is almost a truism but provides a framework to help, for example, in understanding and analyzing intergroup perceptions and conflicts.

Moreover, identity helps more generally to explain the spread and adoption of ideas and behaviors through communication in a social network, particularly once a "critical mass" for new adoptions is reached (Blume and Durlauf 2006, using economic mathematical models). "Diffusion of innovation" has very broad applicability to phenomena as diverse as the spread of new agricultural techniques and machinery to ideologies leading to inter-group conflict.

Both the origins and amelioration of conflict seem often to be intertwined with communication processes and how they are perceived. Krauss and Morsella (2006) elucidate these links in terms of four paradigms: encoding/decoding (e.g., improve these by reducing "noise"), intentionalist (e.g., conflict may arise because figures of speech such as Khrushchev's "we will bury you" are taken over-literally), perspective taking, and dialogic (value of interactively cooperative communication).

Even familiar communicators may be viewed as having traits that they have merely described as being present in others (Mae et al. 1999). Hence it may, for example, sometimes be important for mediators to emphasize that they do not necessarily share the views and characteristics which they describe.

Singh and Singh (1995) observed four-member group discussions and discovered that participants were more likely to remember accurately statements made by themselves than those made by others. We conclude that for reviews of the literature, do not take our word for it. Take your own word if accurate recall is important for the discussion!

For additional research on social identity and group decisions see M. E. Turner and Pratkanis (1998). For a discussion of the part played by cognitive factors in information processing and interpersonal communication see Wyer and Gruenfeld (1995).

Some of the current approaches to understanding social interaction emphasize nonverbal as well as verbal communication; some are concerned with exchange and equity processes, some with computer-mediated communication, and some with phases of group development. We now turn to these topics, and then conclude this section more generally with material on group decision-making.

*Nonverbal Communication* According to Patterson (1996), theories of nonverbal social interaction (including nonverbal cues linked to verbal communication) invoke both compensation (e.g., turning away if somebody sits too close) and reciprocation (e.g., "turning toward" if a particularly attractive person deliberately sits close). The nonverbal adjustments are mediated by cognitions; expectations are based on labeling, scripts, and attributions about others and about the social interaction.

In his research on nonverbal social interaction, Patterson, to whose work we shall shortly return below, has placed some major social-cognition work into a truly social context. Trope's (Trope and Gaunt 1999) two-stage paradigm of person perception involves (a) an identification process (information is sorted into attribution-relevant categories) followed by (b) a dispositional inference process. Thus, in an experiment where emotion on an actor's face is ambiguously shown: ambiguous calmness (initial perceived category) was seen as less fearful (dispositional) when it was in reaction to a horror film, a Doberman pinscher, or a swarm of bees (Jones 1990). (Thus, presumably you would be seen as especially calm if you display even an ambiguously calm expression if you happen to be viewing a horror film in the company of a dog while being attacked by a swarm of bees!) Similar situational determinants of person perception would be expected to apply to, say, peacekeeping.

Hilton (1995) also records that the social rules governing communication require the listener to go beyond the information given in the message, contrary to the assumption that rational people should operate only on the information explicitly given in judgment tasks. This would seem to support the idea that it is usually better if you "smile when you say that."

Gilbert added a third, fine-tuning stage, to Trope's two stages, which is, however, dependent on adequate time and effort. People may consider context in order to go beyond the dispositional inferences that follow from somebody's explicit verbal content. In one experiment (Gilbert et al. 1992), participants listened to a "dating game" in which male contestants responded in kind to potential female "dates" who espoused either "traditional" or "modern" views about sex roles. Control participants adjusted the face-value disposition (that the male contestants really held traditional or modern views) to take account of the likelihood that the contestants were attempting ingratiation. Experimental participants, who heard an acoustically degraded version of the tape, gleaned as much factual information as the control participants but had to spend so much energy in listening that they failed to fine-tune their attributions and regarded the "traditional" male participants as being genuinely more traditional than the "modern" ones.

Patterson (1996) has demonstrated similar processes when the participants themselves are engaged in social interaction. "Actors" (actually research participants) in a dyad, if asked to make an unfavorable impression, were especially inaccurate in their impressions about the other person and about the other person's impression of themselves. According to Patterson, the lessened accuracy is due to the experimental participants needing to spend energy on the unaccustomed role of giving an unfavorable impression. It does seems possible that the "unfavorable" actors varied in how successfully they put across their intended role and moreover were simply too embarrassed to pay proper attention to the other person's response. (If so, the main point, that perceptual fine-tuning can be impaired by distraction, would still stand.) In theory, the same findings (low accuracy) should apply if the participant's role were varied in other ways—especially high or low dominance or conformity, for example, or mediating in an unfamiliar dispute. It would be enlightening to learn whether less accuracy would indeed be found in such cases. Patterson gives a variety of other excellent suggestions for further research on the "live" study of cognition in social interaction—such as procedures for manipulating and assessing the demands of person perception and of behavior management.

For additional research on perception of nonverbal behavior, see Patterson (1999); Perowne and Mansell (2002); S. W. Smith (1995).

For additional research on attributions, see Darley and Huff (1990); Jones et al. (1989); Thakkar and Kanekar (1989); Wittenbaum and Stasser (1995).

*Distributed Information Systems*  One interesting question about social interaction—especially important within, e.g., conflicting cultures, policy-making groups, and negotiating teams—is whether information "flows evenly" through a social system, and, if not, what are the sources of possible hindrance. Some "filters" seem straightforward, such as interpersonal evaluations being more likely to be discussed reciprocally among friends, and people being more likely to be told the positive things about themselves rather than the negative (Blumberg 1972).

Less obvious is the potentially important information that group members hold but tell to nobody. Transactive memory systems—including the productivity advantages of knowledge about who is good at what—were discussed above, in the section on roles. A perhaps more general picture of groups' "distributed information systems" has been provided by Wittenbaum and Stasser (1996). One of the main findings is that information that is *already* commonly held is the most likely to be shared—indeed shared repeatedly—in the course of discussions. For previously acquainted groups, however, and as a discussion becomes prolonged, individually held information gradually gets put forward—though decisions may still be based on the primacy of early communications emphasizing already-common information.

Exceptionally, although group discussion tends to polarize people's views of another group such as to increase stereotypic appraisal, if counter-stereotypic information is concentrated in just *one* ingroup member, that information is especially likely to be discussed and to influence views of the other group (Brauer et al. 2001). Presumably such counter-stereotypic movement would (in general) facilitate harmony and help to defuse potential conflicts.

Individually held information, which otherwise is less likely to be repeated even if mentioned, is used more in groups with known expert-role assignment. Status (especially leadership) and gender may also affect whether information is used in decision-making. For instance, leaders may be more likely than other members to repeat previously unshared information. If a group is coordinated even tacitly— e.g., if a task is said (by an experimenter) to represent a group decision—members are more likely to recall and draw on others' presumed areas of expertise, thus helping to provide successful coordination for the task.

However, "because the research to date has focused on relatively benign factors ..., we do not know how groups manage information under conditions in which some members can control the need satisfaction of other members, member motives differ from collective goals," or the group is under threat or faces competition (Wittenbaum and Stasser 1996, p. 27). One suspects that these negative factors would undermine the coordination of information. As Zander (1977) has concluded, disparity between individual and group goals has a particularly strong association with low productivity and satisfaction, partly because of poor communication.

For additional research on the relationship between cognitive factors and communication, see De Grada et al. (1999); Leik et al. (1999); Mallubhatla et al. (1991);

McPhee (1995); Pittam (1999); Riva and Galimberti (1998); Seibold et al. (1996); M. E. Turner et al. (1992); Van Ginkel and Van Knippenberg (2009).

For related work, as found in a substantial and diverse literature, see also Andrews (2000); Ball and Giles (1988); Bavelas and Coates (1992); Beck and Orth (1995); Bonito (2002); Burgoon et al. (1996); Cast et al. (1999); Chiu and Khoo (2003); Dietz-Uhler (1999); Douglas (1990); Dugosh et al. (2000); Eliasoph and Lichterman (2003); Georgakopoulou (2002); Hall and Bernieri (2001); Haslam, Jetten, O'Brien, and Jacobs (2004); Houston (1993); Huguet et al. (1998); Hummon (2000); Jones (2001); Kärreman and Alvesson (2001); Kellermann (1995); Lea and Spears (1991); Lesch (1994); Maass et al. (1995); MacGeorge (2001); Mackie, Gastardo-Conaco, and Skelly (1992); Makimura and Yamagishi (2003); Martin and Anderson (1997); Nettle and Dunbar (1997); Nishida (1992); Otten and Mummendey (2002); Parks and Cowlin (1996); Paxton and Moody (2003); Rohde and Stockton (1992); Rouquette (1996); Rubini and Semin (1994); Samter (2002); Samter et al. (1989); Sanders (1991); Santarsiero et al. (1995); Schneider (1994); Schwarz et al. (1991); Sinclair et al. (2005); Strauss (1959, reprinted 1997); Stürmer and Simon (2004); Ting-Toomey (1993); Todorov et al. (2000); Urada and Miller (2000); Vonk (1999); Walther (1997); White and Watkins (2000); Wigboldus et al. (1999); Wiggins (1991); Zucchermaglio et al. (2000).

*Equity* Kimberly (1997) has developed a particularly thorough theoretical integration of group processes covering social norms (such as equality and proportionality in the distribution of rewards) and how these tend to be aligned with the nature of the group (for instance, "primary" egalitarian social groups and "secondary" task ones). One of the main impacts of equity research has to do with people's presumptions (cognitions) that rewards are, or ought to be, equitably distributed.

For additional research on equity, see Hassebrauck (1991); Matsuura (1991); Wagstaff and Perfect (1992).

*Computer-Mediated Communication (CMC)* In a laboratory study comparing conflict in CMC and face-to-face groups (who were given a task to carry out), more conflict about relationships and processes emerged on the first day in the CMC groups, but the differences disappeared by days two and three; task-based conflict was the same from day one (Hobman et al. 2002). It would be worth exploring the generality of such a finding and establishing just which properties of CMC contribute to any such temporary conflict—for instance, restricted communication modalities, enhanced information sharing, or relative anonymity.

Some forms of social action, which may resolve or foment conflict (or both), are clearly rendered more feasible by electronic communication such as internet-based calls to (online or direct) social action (Postmes and Brunsting 2002) or text messaging to mobilize people for collective action (cf. Montiel and Christie 2008).

Using a social identity perspective and text-analyzing software to study email communication among 140 students taking a voluntary ungraded computerized statistics course, Postmes, Spears, and Lea (1999, 2000) established that communication norms emerged from the group's interaction with regard both to the form and content of communications. That is, the norms were socially constructed and locally defined, and conformity to these increased over time. Communication outside the group was moreover governed by different norms. It would be worth exploring further the extent to which these processes differ cross-culturally and between CMC and face-to-face groups—and whether such norms have particular useful (or suboptimal) properties among groups devoted to peace, justice, social action, and conflict resolution.

For additional relevant research on CMC, see Amaral and Monteiro (2002); Bagozziet al. (2007); Baker (2001); Barreto and Ellemers (2002a); Caspi and Blau (2008); Douglas and McGarty (2001); Lee (2006); McKenna and Bargh (2000); Michinov et al. (2004); Postmes, Spears, Sakhel, and De Groot (2001); Riva (2002); Riva and Galimberti (2001); Sassenberg (2002); Sassenberg and Boos (2003); Spears et al. (2002); Taylor and MacDonald (2002); Toranzo et al. (2004); Waskul (2003). The study of CMC, including cognitive and conflict-resolving aspects, is also particularly relevant to organizations and teams (see Chaps. 4 and 5).

*Group Development* The nature of social interaction, and how group members are perceived, may of course vary in the course of a group's development. Worchel (1996, 1998), who summarizes various paradigms for group development, has found that groups progress from formation, through decisions to join, and then into ongoing overlapping cycles. A "cycle" consists of discontent, a precipitating event, group identification, group productivity, individuation, and decay. In Worchel's research—based on field studies of two "rival" universities as well as laboratory experiments—the typical self-perception of being a prototypical group member usually occurs only in early phases of group development. Perception of ingroup homogeneity is found only in middle and later stages, as individuals have or establish their distinctiveness (or simply have more information about the group?). As a group develops, perceived outgroup homogeneity decreases, though the content of outgroup stereotypes tends to remain the same. Over time (e.g., across lab group meetings, though the same could hold true within a single meeting), the familiar preference for cooperation with ingroup and competition with outgroup reverses. Groups tend to be most productive at their mid-life.

Worchel's description is similar to that of Bales and Strodtbeck (1951) on phases in group problem solving. Worchel, along with most other analysts of group development, is describing *process* rather than *content*. In his analysis one does not know the content that the group is being productive about. Thus it would be useful to compare his categories with some form of content analysis—or a more content-oriented classification system such as functional analysis (Hare 1983), which suggests that—both in reality and in members' perceptions—groups will often be concerned successively with their meaning or purpose, the resources needed, roles, task action, and evaluation.

Worchel notes that many studies have used cognition and minimal groups as an endpoint rather than also covering the relevant group dynamics (see below, the discussion of intergroup processes). To complement such experiments, he suggests analyzing videotapes of ongoing laboratory and field groups (even brief ones) to elucidate the "triggers" of group development.

*Group Decision Making* One of the crucial processes involving social interaction is group decision making. In a typical well-established finding, called "choice shift," not only do groups tend to converge on a relatively narrow range of views, but also the focus of that range typically moves to a more extreme response, in the same direction as the group's initial view. Explanations for such shifts have focused on two main processes, both of them partly perceptual: the *informational influence* of *persuasive arguments* and the *normative influence of social comparison*. Both of these processes are inherently cognitive, and have been invoked in a variety of contexts in the present review—particularly with regard to the importance of social identity in determining the nature and extent of influence (see, for instance, the discussion above of Haslam, McGarty, and Turner's work (1996) in the section on social influence). For a discussion of the theory of comparison processes, see Jasso (1993).

How a task is perceived may of course affect the way group members use information presented to them. A study by Wittenbaum, Stasser, and Merry (1996) provides experimental evidence for the tacit coordination of task behavior as a function of the perceived goal of a task and others' expected areas of expertise.

In an effort to simplify the cognitive task of problem identification and problem solving by sets of individuals, the "Nominal Group Technique" was developed, in the 1970s, for sets of individuals whose opinions are combined without having face-to-face meetings (see Chap. 6 for consideration of research by Tajfel and colleagues). In this way, there was the hope of eliminating or minimizing problems such as non-productive digressions or hostile arguments. Fox (1989) describes the method and offers suggestions for its implementation and selective use.

Post-conflict forgiveness and empathy can be positively associated with salience of common ingroup identity and negatively with one-sided ingroup identity, as found by researchers in Chile and Northern Ireland (Noor et al. 2008). Such effects presumably follow at least in part from informal social interaction and decision-making.

Many researchers view social identification as central to group consensus. For reviews, see Curseu (2003) and Kaplan and Wilke (2001). Relevant research covers matters as diverse as the acceptance of political decisions (Leung, Tong, and Lind 2007), the effects of group salience and accountability on expressed attitudes (Joanne R. Smith et al. 2007), and cooperating or not in dealing with (often laboratory-based) social dilemmas (Dawes and Messick 2000, in a special issue on diplomacy and psychology; see also Ando 1999; Bicchieri 2002; De Cremer and Van Dijk 2002; De Cremer et al. 2008; De Cremer and Van Vugt 1999; Jackson 2002a; Eliot R. Smith et al. 2003; Van Vugt and De Cremer 2002).

For cognitive aspects of group decision-making see also Beck and Fisch (2000); Dietz-Uhler (1996); Hodson and Sorrentino (1997); Joanne R. Smith et al. (2007); Testé (2001); M. E. Turner and Pratkanis (1997); Tyler et al. (1996).

The present "tour" of cognitive aspects of basic small group research is now complete with functioning, interacting groups present "on stage." In most areas, "classical" findings involved cognitive processes, and the cognition-behavior links have become increasingly articulated. Several significant applied topics complete the picture: Conflict Resolution (already considered implicitly in the material above as well as in the other sections that follow), Organizations, Intergroup Relations, and Therapy Groups.


## Conflict Resolution

Research about conflict resolution, including some cognitive processes, is covered in Chap. 1. Some publications have, however, been devoted particularly to cognitive aspects of conflict management.

Representative of those focusing on social identity are works by Auerbach (2005); Brewer and Yuki (2007); Tyler and Blader (2001, 2003). Depending on context and values, self-affirmation and heightened salience of an identity can increase tolerance in negotiations (Cohen et al. 2007).

Other works emphasize cognitive aspects of: cooperation and competition (Georgiou et al. 2007), conflict strategy (Sorenson et al. 1999), interdependence and social dilemmas (Chen et al. 2007; Morrison 1999), and negotiation (Barsness and Bhappu 2004; Druckman et al. 2009), including findings that shared identity may arise from a variety of intragroup and intergroup processes and can facilitate multiparty negotiations (Swaab et al. 2008).

See also several of the chapters in Deutsch et al.'s (2006) handbook, which covers many of the foregoing topics as well as, more generally, cognitive subjects such as framing and judgmental biases.


## Organizations

Allard-Poesi (1998) notes that the cognitive approach to the study of organizations assumes the existence of collective representation in organizations. A collective representation is viewed as being related to the socio-cognitive dynamics occurring between group members. Communication and influence processes are critical to the construction of a collective representation.

One fairly well known form of discrimination—with a bearing on how groups function in organizations—is the tendency to attribute the success of own group (or of self) dispositionally to skill, but to attribute success of other group (or other person) externally. Two main varieties of explanation for this bias, according to Forsyth and Kelley (1996), are "hot" motivational theories (such as a self-serving bias) and "cold" cognitive ones. As an example of the latter, people are better at remembering expectation-confirming agencies. In an experiment using six-person configurations (each having two groups of three people each), feedback about individual "performance" (positive, neutral, or negative) was varied independently of the (sub-) group's "success" or "failure" (Forsyth and Kelley 1996). In a set of results mainly supporting a heuristic (cognitive) explanation of bias: (a) "successful" members of "successful" groups claimed more personal responsibility for the outcome (compared with members of "unsuccessful" groups). (b) Equally, they also attributed more responsibility to their group (including the other, less successful members) and (c) all the members of the "unsuccessful" groups typically assigned more responsibility to their two fellow members than to themselves. Women who "failed" had particularly low satisfaction with themselves and their group.

Group processes also apply to larger, more formal entities. The organization is part of the group's "external system," which also includes the society and the environment, thus bringing one full circle to the consideration of background variables. The social-psychological principles that apply to ordinary group processes also apply to behavior in organizations. Most of the effective systems for implementing organizational change still involve face-to-face interaction (or the electronic equivalent) in small groups.

Indeed, while a fairly large proportion of small groups articles in social psychology journals now emphasize intergroup relations and beliefs, intragroup research (on group performance, for instance) has become increasingly well covered in organizational psychology journals (Ferdman 1995; Sanna and Parks 1997).

For organizational settings in particular—which clearly would extend to political and social action contexts—one creative development in the study of social interaction blends case histories with systematic analysis. Donnellon (1996) shows how to prepare a profile derived from a team's history and discourse in order to assess goal attainment and foster improvement. A "cross-functional team" might include, for example, specialists in engineering, manufacturing, quality assurance, and marketing, who voluntarily convene in order to speed the realization of a particularly promising new product. To be successful, such a team might typically and prominently show group identification, interdependence, low social distance, conflict management (constructive confrontation), and effective negotiation. "Identification," to take one example, is manifest in discourse samples where "we" and "our" refer mainly to the team.

One might hope that Donnellon's work could be replicated with larger samples than four companies (including one organization with very successful teams and three with more problematic ones). Truly excellent teams are, however, rather rare so, as regards this particular research, one must for now be satisfied with Donnellon's rich detail and her precise procedures for assessing and improving team quality. Some fragments of situational interactions among factors are already known. For instance, it is only when task interdependence is high that increasing group control over decisions may result in better performance (Liden et al. 1997).

The positive processes and outcomes that Donnellon describes actually increase member satisfaction rather than being at its cost. Although performance goals are not particularly cognitive in nature, team members' *perceptions*—as manifest in Donnellon's discourse analysis—are clearly crucial to the outcomes.

For managing diversity in teams, others make recommendations similar to those of Donnellon. Brewer (1995) suggests emphasizing common team goals and attending carefully to the compositional design of teams. Northcraft, Polzer, Neale, and Kramer (1995) introduce the language of negotiation into the dialogue concerning diversity. Negotiation has also been found to influence leader-member exchange and role differentiation. In an experiment with groups engaged in an organizational problem-solving task, McClane (1991a, b) found that groups whose members experienced higher levels of negotiating latitude tended to have higher overall satisfaction with the leader, the task, and the co-workers.

With regard to diversity in conceptions of a work group's culture, Gruenfeld and Hollingshead (1993) report that, over time, group members become increasingly able or motivated to generate or recognize diversity among their perspectives and to work at incorporating one another's perspectives when constructing shared conceptualizations.

Environmental concerns and globalization provide an opportunity for innovation incorporating a variety of perspectives but individuals' feelings of security and belonging may also be threatened, requiring measures designed to bolster positive outcomes (Van der Zee and Paulus 2008).

For an overview of social cognition in organizations, see Klimoski and Donahue (2001).

For research on work teams, see Hinsz (2004); Lacey and Gruenfeld (1999). See also Dimmock et al. (2005); Driskell et al. (1999, 2000); Rentsch and Woehr (2004); Gundlach et al. (2006); Miles and Kivlighan (2008).

For work on both social identity and team work, see Cicero et al. (2007); Lembke and Wilson (1998).

For additional research on social identity see also Cameira et al. (2002); Dru and Constanza (2003); Elsbach and Bhattacharya (2001); Fielding and Hogg (2000); Platow et al. (2003); Pratkanis and Turner (1999); Postmes and Jetten (2006).

For research with an emphasis on creativity, see Adarves et al. (2006); Bunce and West (1995); Hargadon (1999); Hinkle et al. (1998). See also Bornman and Mynhardt (1991). For other research on cognitive aspects of groups in organizations, see De-Sanctis and Poole (1997); Earley (1997); Harrison and Bazerman (1995); Tyler (1997).

## Intergroup Relations

The analysis of intergroup cooperation, prejudice, and stereotyping has (like research on leadership) embraced both personality and situation. Some of the research on group stereotyping has already been discussed above in the section on personal background variables. Of course stereotyping may also depend on degree of interdependence and other aspects of social relationships (Bogart et al. 1999).

For research that supports the tendency to evaluate aspects of one's own ingroup group more favorably than some outgroup (ingroup bias), see Abelson et al. (1998); Blanz et al. (1995a, b); Crocker and Luhtanen (1990); Islam and Hewstone (1993b); Jetten et al. (1997a, b); Lindeman and Koskela (1994); Long and Manstead (1997); Long et al. (1994); Maass et al. (1996); Marques, Yzerbyt, and Leyens (1988); Marques, Yzerbyt, and Rijsman (1988); Perez and Mugny (1998); Shah et al. (1998); Yoshida and Kubota (1994).

Ingroup bias has also been associated with the tendency to view one's own group as less homogeneous than an outgroup. The tendency to "level" differences within "fields", especially distant ones, and to sharpen differences across fields (a) can be demonstrated literally as a perceptual phenomenon (e.g., by a color gradient across a single visual field which is then divided by a fence-like line into two seemingly homogeneous sub-fields of different hues) and (b) can be argued from an evolutionary perspective in terms of human survival via social groups—cf. maximal distinctiveness theory (Brewer and Roccas 2001; Brown and Zagefka 2005). To extend the analogy a little further: a more distant field (analogous to an outgroup?) may literally be seen as more homogeneous. The grass might literally look greener on the far side of the fence! Indeed, Simon (1992b) notes that both ingroup and outgroup homogeneity effects can occur. He suggests that the perception of relative homogeneity is related to: (a) the minority or majority position of the ingroup, (b) the relevance of the specific attributes or dimensions in question to group members' social identities, and (c) the stereotypes prevailing in society at large. For examples and additional research, see Brewer and Weber (1994); Brown and Smith (1989); Kelly (1988; 1990a, b); Marques et al. (1998); Mullen and Goethals (1990); Sedikides and Ostrom (1993); Simon (1992a; 1993).

For scales developed to measure the extent of ingroup identification and its cognitive and affective components, see Ellemers et al. (1988); Hinkle et al. (1989); Karasawa (1991).

Social perception, at least, is also subject to sometimes marked individual differences. Prejudice is still found to be associated with authoritarianism; that is, clearly some variance is attributable to personality. Indeed, needs for cognitive economy and for self-enhancement are both associated with components of prejudice, namely with social categorization and ingroup favoritism (Stangor and Thompson 2002).

According to the "contact hypothesis" prejudice, regardless of its level in a particular individual or group, can typically be ameliorated by intergroup contact having the following four properties: inter-group social interaction, on an equal-status basis, positively sanctioned by authority, and with a common goal (Allport 1954). Various contemporary analyses of these effects invoke Social Identity Theory— people will change their beliefs and their behavior in the direction of the beliefs and behavior that are seen as prototypical for those social "categories" with which they themselves "identify." For a discussion of "prototypicality" in relation to the analysis of category structure and representation see Oakes et al. (1998).

Spears (2008) has argued that intergroup discrimination and conflict are not an inevitable result of social identity but in effect are ameliorated when a social system is perceived as legitimate. Various communication and other processes facilitate resolution of conflict between different social-identity groups (Stephan 2008a, b). Also, positive intergroup attitudes emerge from fostering appreciation of the value of cultural diversity (Crisp 2008). Moreover—in findings reminiscent of the classical negative correlation between authoritarianism and education level—processes that diminish hostility toward one outgroup tend to be associated with generalized "deprovincialization" and social identity complexity (Brewer 2008a; Pettigrew 1997; see also Brewer 2007a, b).

Prejudice typically stems from ignorance and anxiety, and the four properties of the contact hypothesis work to *de-categorize* group members, shifting respondents' impressions from being based on ingroup/outgroup stereotypes into being more individualized ("exemplar") impressions (Gaertner, Rust, Dovidio, Bachman, and Anastasio 1996). In an earlier laboratory study by Gaertner and colleagues (as described by Gaertner, Rust et al. 1996), the members of paired three-person groups showed less bias in favor of their ingroup if they were induced to conceive of the six persons as individuals or as a six-person group per se rather than as "two subgroups of three persons." Induced perceptions were effected by seating patterns or by inter-team cooperative interaction, both of which were effective. A further study by Gaertner, Rust et al. (1996) extended the findings into a field setting, a multi-cultural secondary school. A "conditions of contact" index, with short sub-scales (derived through factor analysis) was successfully used to predict (a) bias and (b) mediation (of bias) as a function of whether students perceived themselves as members of: one group, equal groups, separate groups, or individuals. The conditions of intergroup contact were found to achieve their favorable effects of de-categorization through various direct and indirect mechanisms.

Findings such as these support the Common Ingroup Identity Model, which proposes that negative intergroup bias—in evaluations, self-disclosure, helping, and other attributes—can be reduced if members conceive of themselves as being in one common group, for at least part of their social identity (Dovidio et al. 1997). For a review, see Gaertner and Dovidio (2005). Dovidio and Gaertner (1996) also discuss practical means for achieving this goal. Likewise, Schmid et al. (2009) have confirmed the association between complex views of social identity and favorable outgroup attitudes in (for instance) Northern Ireland. Effects can be subtle however; comparing a standard to one's self, for instance, tends to increase assimilation or commonness but comparing one's self to a standard may underline the contrast (Mussweiler 2001). For additional research on processes for challenging stereotypes and cultural biases, see Rittner and Nakanishi (1993).

If, however, persons have peripheral membership status in a desirable ingroup, outgroup derogation may be elevated if these persons believe that other ingroup members might learn of their responses (Noel et al. 1995).

When it comes to remembering, people are more likely to remember information related to a stereotype, either pro or con, than unrelated facts (Cano et al. 1991; Fyock and Stangor 1994).

For research on variables related to perceptions of ingroup and outgroup homogeneity, see Bardach and Park (1996); Doosje et al. (1995); Haslam, Oakes, Turner, and McGarty (1995); Haslam, Turner, Oakes, McGarty, and Reynolds (1998); Haslam, Turner, Oakes, Reynolds et al. (1998); Jetten et al. 2004; Kofta (1995); Lorenzi-Cioldi (1993); McGarty et al. (1995); McHoskey and Miller (1994); Ostrom et al. (1993); Park (1990); Reicher and Levine (1994); Simon (1990); Simon and Hamilton (1994); Simon, Micki et al. (1990); Simon and Mummendey (1990); Simon and Pettigrew (1990); Spears, Doosje, and Ellemers (1997); Stroessner and Mackie (1992); Vivian and Berkowitz (1992); Wagner and Ward (1993); Yzerbyt et al. (1998).

For additional research on contact and cooperation, see Brewer (1996); Gaertner et al. (1990, 1994). For research on cognitive aspects of coalitions, bargaining, and games see Bouas and Komorita (1996); Camerer (1988); Coleman (1989); Croson and Marks (1998); Gifford and Hine (1997); Hale et al. (1991); Hardin (1995); Insko et al. (1992); Jin et al. (1996); Kerr (1992); Kiyonari and Yamagishi (1996); Kramer et al. (1993, 1995); Marcus-Newhall et al. (1993); Price (1989); Sidanius (1993); Tetlock (1997); Wetherell (1996a); Wit and Wilke (1992); Yamaguchi (1991a, b). See also Brown et al. (2001); Helbing (1996); Jopling (1993); Karasawa (1995); Mamali (1988); Masulli (1993); O'Connor (1997); Welbourne and Cable (1995). See also Chap. 1, section on facilitating cooperation.

Some meta-analytic integration of the results of research continues to support the phenomenon of ingroup bias (Mullen, Brown, and Smith 1992; see also Platow et al. 1990). High-status groups tend to be more biased, although this effect is moderated by several variables—according to a meta-analysis by Bettencourt et al. (2001). To the extent that such analyses are based on research using the "minimal group paradigm"—where, for example, participants may be assigned to groups according to the color of a paper pinned to their shirt without actual group interaction—some questions have been raised about the value of the findings based on this research design (Rabbie and Schot 1990). Jetten et al. (1996) also comment on the fact that different results can be obtained from observations of minimal groups and natural groups. For additional research using the minimal group paradigm, see Bourhis (1994); Diehl (1989); Finchilescu (1994); Gagnon and Bourhis (1996); Harmon-Jones et al. (1996); Hartstone and Augoustinos (1995); Hong and Harrod (1988); Mlicki (1988); Morales et al. (1998); Platow et al. (1997).

As Brewer (1999) reminds us, ingroup favoritism and prejudice against the outgroup are fairly independent variables, and much outgroup discrimination follows, for instance, from partiality towards own group rather than animosity towards other groups.

How a group's values and issues are perceived by itself and other groups may of course be as important as perception of the group itself. Fiske's Relational Models Theory (Fiske and Haslam 2005) suggests that most inter-party relations are based on one (or at least one at a time) of four norms: free sharing, a pecking order or hierarchy, equity over time, or market pricing. Tetlock and colleagues (Tetlock et al. 2000, 2004) have analyzed proscribed social cognitions—for instance, offering money to shift a "sacred" belief may be counter-productive where tactful mutual compromise might succeed. (For instance, offering Iran a quid-pro-quo for abandoning its nuclear ambitions is, counter-intuitively, seen by knowledgeable participants as being more likely to succeed than offering the quid-pro-quo *plus* a substantial monetary side payment.)

For a variety of other factors affecting the interrelationships among prejudice, cognition, and intergroup processes see Aviram (2009); Bizman and Yinon (2001); Brewer (2001); Crisp and Abrams (2008); Crocker and Garcia (2009); Eidelman and Biernat (2003); Eller and Abrams (2003); Fiske et al. (1999); Gaertner and Insko (2000); Grieve and Hogg (1999); Jonas (2009); Kaiser et al. (2009); Kessler and Mummendey (2008); Mackie and Smith (2002); Nagda and Zúñiga (2003); Petersen and Blank (2003); Reynolds, Turner, and Haslam (2000); Tarrant and North (2004); Vescio et al. (2004).

For additional research and reviews of research on social identity and intergroup relations see an overview by J. C. Turner and Reynolds (2004) and see also Arcuri and Cadinu (1997); Bodenhausen et al. (1998); Branscombe and Ellemers (1998); Branscombe and Wann (1994); Branscombe et al. (1993); Brewer (1993); DeRidder et al. (1992); Brown and Capozza (2006); Doane (1997); Doise (1988); Dovidio, Gaertner, and Validzic (1998); Dovidio, Isen, Guerra, Gaertner, and Rust (1998); Ellemers et al. (1997); Gurin and Markus (1988); Harwood, Terry, and White (1995); Hogg and Abrams (1988); Hogg, Terry, and White (1995); Huddy and Virtanen (1995); Jackson et al. (1996); Kramer and Messick (1998); Lee and Ottati (1995); Mehra et al. (1998); Murrell (1998); Ng (1989); Perdue et al. (1990); Rabbie and Horwitz (1988); Rabbie et al. (1989); Schiffmann and Wicklund (1988); Sidanius et al. (1994); Simon et al. (1995); J. C. Turner and Oakes (1989); Van Knippenberg and Ellemers (1993); Wagner and Zick (1990); Wellen et al. (1998); Worchel, Rothgerber et al. (1998); Yzerbyt et al. (1995); Zani (1992). See also Chap. 6.

It is particularly beyond the scope of the present chapter to review, beyond listing most of them, the post-1999 plethora of publications on the seemingly rather specialized but important matter of relating social identity to intergroup processes and social cognition. For two key reviews see Hogg et al. (2004) and Jussim et al. (2001). The work divides roughly into (a) theoretical, minimal group, and other laboratory studies and (b) applied and field studies—as follows.

Theoretical, minimal group, and other laboratory studies: Aharpour and Brown (2002); Ashmore et al. (2001); Brewer (2009); Brewer and Pierce (2005); Capozza et al. (2000); Costarelli and Callà (2004); Crisp and Beck (2005); De Cremer (2001); Doosje et al. (2002); Eggins et al. (2002); Ellemers et al. (2000); Falomir-Pichastor et al. (2009); Glasford et al. (2009); Gómez et al. (2008); González and Brown (2003); Greenland and Brown (2000); Guimond, Dif, and Aupy (2002); Hecht et al. (2005); Hall and Crisp (2008); Hogg and Mullin (1999); Hogg and Williams (2000); Hornsey and Hogg (2000); Hornsey, Trembath, and Gunthorpe (2004); Hunter et al. (1999); Jackson (2002b); Jackson and Smith (1999); Jetten, Spears et al. (2000); Karasawa (2002a, b); Leach et al. (2008); Lipponen et al. (2003); McKimmie et al. (2003); K. P. Miller et al. (2009); Oishi and Yoshida (2001); Ouwerkerk et al. (2000); Paulsen et al. (2005); Perreault and Bourhis (1999); Reid et al. (2005); Rowley and Moldoveanu (2003); Scheepers (2009); Scheepers, Spears, Doosje, and Manstead (2002; 2003); Michael et al. (2001); Sears et al. (2003); Stellmacher and Petzel (2005); Van Leeuwen et al. (2003); Verkuyten and Hagendoorn (2002); Walker and Smith (2002); Worchel and Coutant (2004); Worchel et al. (2000); Yzerbyt et al. (2003).

Applied and field studies: Bizman and Yinon (2000, 2004); Cairns et al. (2006); Crisp et al. (2001); Drury and Reicher (1999); Gudykunst et al. (1999); Gurin et al. (1999); Hong et al. (2004); Hornsey and Imani (2004); Houston and Andreopoulou (2003); Kuwabara et al. (2007); Lalonde (2002); LaTendresse (2000); Levin and Sidanius (1999); Litvak-Hirsch et al. (2003); Martinot and Audebert (2003); McCoy and Major (2003); Nier et al. (2001); Reicher (2001); Reicher, Cassidy et al. (2006); Schmid et al. (2009); Stott et al. (2001); Tausch, Tam et al. (2007); Tropp and Wright (1999); Verkuyten and Reijerse (2008); Weenig et al. (2004); White (2001); Yuki (2003).

For a review of intergroup relations and cognitive implications such as reducing prejudice and conflict and promoting social solidarity see Dovidio, Gaertner, Esses, and Brewer (2003). See also Hogg and Abrams (2001); Jost (2004); Karakitapoglu and Turk (1999). For relevant aspects of American racial politics, see Sears (2004).

For additional research on other variables, such as self-esteem and intergroup relations, see Crocker et al. (1993); Kirchler et al. (1994); Rabbie and Lodewijkx (1996).

The kind of group being considered may of course have a marked effect on intergroup processes and their perception, as documented in various ways by: Abrams and de Moura (2002); Staub (2001); Kessler and Mummendey (2002); Kumagai and Ohbuchi (2001); Obst, Smith, and Zinkiewicz (2002); Obst, Zinkiewicz, and Smith (2002a, b); Pinter and Greenwald (2004); Sani et al. (2007); Simon and Stürmer (2003); Stott and Drury (2000); Tropp and Brown (2004); Weiloch (2002); Yeung and Stombler (2000).

Many post-1999 studies of cognition and intergroup relations are centrally focused on neither social identity nor prejudice but on a diversity of contextualizing matters. They can be roughly divided into two approximately equal groups: (a) mainly combinations of theoretical and methodological considerations tested in laboratory studies, e.g., work on minimal groups, and (b) mainly applied studies—again as follows.

Theoretical, methodological, laboratory studies: Abrams and Hogg (2001); Albarello and Rubini (2008); Berndsen et al. (1999); Boccato et al. (2003); Boen and Vanbeselaere (2001); Brewer (2000); Cabecinhas (2004); Cadinu and Cerchioni (2001); Cohen (2002); Crisp, Stone, and Hall (2006); Crisp, Walsh, and Hewstone (2006); Cunningham and Platow (2007); Gallois et al. (2005); Gordijn, Yzerbyt, Wigboldus, and Dumont (2006); Hogg and Hains (2001); Hall and Crisp (2005); Harris et al. (2000); Iyer and Leach (2008); Kiyonari (2002); Kwok et al. (2007); Machunsky and Meiser (2009); Mackie et al. (2000); Matheson et al. (2003); McAuliffe et al. (2003); Meiser and Hewstone (2006); Nadler and Halabi (2006); Nagda (2006); Otten (2009); Paladino and Castelli (2008); Pickett et al. (2002); Postmes and Baym (2005); Postmes, Spears, and Lea (2002); Radhakrishnan et al. (2000); Riggio and Riggio (2001); Scheepers, Branscombe, Spears, and Doosje (2002); Scheepers et al. (2006a, b); Schubert and Otten (2002); Stone and Crisp (2007).

Applied studies: Berman and Wittig (2004); Chryssochoou (2000); Corenblum and Stephan (2001); Cunningham (2005); Delmas (2003); Derlega et al. (2002); Dobbs and Crano (2001); Doosje and Branscombe (2003); Dovidio, Gaertner, Niemann, and Snider (2001); Fabick (2002); Halabi and Sonnenschein (2004); Hortaçsu (2000); Hunter (2001); Jetten, Branscombe et al. (2001); Kessler and Mummendey (2001); Lee (2002); Licata and Klein (2002); Liebkind et al. (2006); Liu and Allen (1999); Mullen and Rice (2003); Mummendey et al. (1999); Oetzel and Robbins (2003); Ortiz and Harwood (2007); Pratto et al. (2008); Manfred Schmitt and Maes (2002); Stefan et al. (2003); Struthers et al. (2004); Suleiman (2004); Waldzus et al. (2003); Wenzel et al. (2003); Wolsko et al. (2003); Yzerbyt et al. (2009).

In the flood of research on collective identity, *different* aspects are sometimes treated identically, perhaps out of expedience or insufficient clarity, and conceptually similar matters have on occasion been given different names. A review by Ashmore et al. (2004) goes a long way towards clarifying this situation and moreover to using a sharpened taxonomy to analyze several theoretical approaches to social identity. Among other distinguishable facets of collective identity that they cover are "self-categorization, positive-negative, importance, social embeddedness, behavioral involvement, and content and meaning" (Ashmore et al. 2004, p. 80). See Table 3.1. Among their examples of how the taxonomy can be used to advantage in theoretical paradigms, Ashmore et al. delineate Cross's model in which, for instance, "individual African-Americans must navigate five stages on the path to an integrated sense of racial/cultural self" (p. 106).

**Table 3.1** Elements of collective identity as individual-level constructs

| Element | Definition |
|---|---|
| Self-categorization | Identifying self as a member of, or categorizing self in terms of, a particular social grouping |
| Placing self in social category | Categorizing self in terms of a particular social grouping |
| Goodness of fit/perceived similarity/ Prototypicality | A person's subjective assessment of the degree to which he or she is a prototypical member of the group |
| Perceived certainty of self-identification | The degree of certainty with which a person categorizes self in terms of a particular social grouping |
| Evaluation | The positive or negative attitude that a person has toward the social category in question |
| Private regard | Favorability judgments made by people about their own identities |
| Public regard | Favorability judgments that one perceives others, such as the general public, to hold about one's social category |
| Importance | The degree of importance of a particular group membership to the individual's overall self-concept |
| Explicit importance | The individual's subjective appraisal of the degree to which a collective identity is important to her or his overall sense of self |
| Implicit importance | The placement of a particular group membership in the person's hierarchically organized self-system; the individual is not necessarily consciously aware of the hierarchical position of his or her collective identities |
| Attachment and sense of interdependence | The emotional involvement felt with a group (the degree to which the individual feels at one with the group) |
| Interdependence/mutual fate | Perception of the commonalities in the way group members are treated in society |
| Attachment/affective commitment | A sense of emotional involvement with or affiliative orientation toward the group |
| Interconnection of self and others | The degree to which people merge their sense of self and the group |
| Social embeddedness | The degree to which a particular collective identity is embedded in the person's everyday ongoing social relationships |
| Behavioral involvement | The degree to which the person engages in actions that directly implicate the collective identity category in question |
| Content and meaning | – |
| Self-attributed characteristics | The extent to which traits and dispositions that are associated with a social category are endorsed as self-descriptive by a member of that category |
| Ideology | Beliefs about a group's experience, history, and position in society |
| Narrative | The internally represented story that the person has developed regarding self and the social category in question |
| Collective identity story | The individual's mentally represented narrative of self as a member of a particular social category |
| Group story | The individual's mentally represented narrative of a particular social category of which he or she is a member |

Reprinted with permission from R. D. Ashmore, K. Deaux, and T. McLaughlin-Volpe, An Organizing Framework for Collective Identity: Articulation and Significance of Multidimensionality, *Psychological Bulletin*, 130, 80–114 (Table 1, p. 83). Copyright 2004 by the American Psychological Association.

## Therapy Groups

One question that may apply to groups in general but seems to have arisen particularly in the context of therapy groups is whether the group mainly represents a constructive force or a destructive one. Clearly groups devoted to empowering disadvantaged, oppressed, and war-torn groups have positive goals.

Foulkes (1986) notes that all groups have an *occupation*. In most groups, the occupation takes the form of some sort of decision-making or production. Groups also have a *preoccupation*, a concern for the social-emotional relations of members. For analytic therapy groups, the preoccupation becomes the task, that is to analyze the underlying group dynamics. This involves that analysis of the relatedness of individuals in the group, the location and configuration of any disturbance in relationships, and the nature of communication, both channel and process. The relevance for social perception is that every event in a group is assumed to involve the group as a whole. An event is part of a gestalt, a configuration, of which the event constitutes the figure (foreground) whereas the ground (background) is manifest in the rest of the group. Foulkes describes a *matrix of transpersonal relationships* that is the common shared ground which ultimately determines the meaning and significance of all events upon which all communication, verbal and nonverbal, rests. The events in the group are transpersonal phenomena. They only come into existence through the interaction of two or more people. The individual is a nodal point, an open system. The group acts as a whole through one speaker at a time.

Foulkes saw the group as constructive force while Bion saw it as a destructive one. This issue has been covered particularly thoroughly by Nitsun (1991, 1996), who contrasts the mainly positive forces analyzed by Foulkes with Bion's supposedly negative ones. Perhaps not surprisingly, Nitsun concludes that, particularly in a psychotherapy context, the group can be primarily a positive force but that the group's conductor must be aware of, and deal constructively with, people's (sometimes veridical) *cognitions* of negative forces, which Nitsun calls the anti-group. Nitsun systematically provides a theoretical rationale and a variety of anecdotal examples for such a constructive approach to the real and perceived anti-group. His work provides a useful source of hypotheses for understanding groups in therapeutic and other organizational and general contexts.

M. E. Johnson and Neimeyer (1996) suggest that a social cognitive model is helpful for delineating sources of variance in the interdependent perceptions of members of psychotherapy (as well as other) groups. A's rating of B is a function of A's average emitted ratings, B's average received ratings, a systematic deviation unique to the AB dyad (derived from ratings on at least two occasions), and a constant and error. All of these components are shown to be meaningfully present in one or more contexts from therapy groups.

Since the 1970s much of the small groups research, including that in group therapy and other organizational contexts, has been in (what has been called) an "incrementalist" phase—studying how some major paradigms yield varied outcomes as a function of circumstance (such as setting, personal backgrounds, and role organization). To bring about a renaissance of small groups research, we agree with McGrath (1997) that theory, research, and practice must take seriously the idea that small groups are complex adaptive dynamic systems. Contributing to this goal, it is to be hoped, the recent experimental emphasis on what is still an admittedly patch-work array of cognitive, or at least partly cognitive, explanations may be helping the field to emerge from it's mainly incrementalist period.

# Chapter 4
# The Group and the Organization

## Organizations, Networks, Groups, Teams

The mission and values of an organization are important influences on the social interaction in a small group. Organizations that deliver social services place more emphasis on interpersonal relations while manufacturing organizations are more concerned with the relationships to objects. Cooperation among small group members is more difficult in organizations that value individual performance. The function of the group in relation to the organization determines the appropriate leadership style, degree of role specialization, level of morale, and amount of cohesiveness required for the group task. While the organization affects the small group, the group may also have an influence on the organization. It may set informal norms that reduce organizational output or it may be the key to organizational effectiveness.

Most of the findings on group processes in organizations would apply, directly or potentially, to a broad spectrum of (formal and informal) bodies linked to conflict resolution as well as to peace and also violence. This includes—among many others—political policy-making entities, NGOs, peacekeeping and peacebuilding groups, and direct-action parties. In addition to the findings being helpful in understanding the processes and smooth running of such groups, many of the findings are concerned with learning what might facilitate an egalitarian harmonious ethos in essentially *any* group.

The typical definition of an organization is similar to that proposed by Barnard (1938, p. 73): "The consciously coordinated activities of two or more people." For example, Robey (1986, p. 16), in a textbook on designing organizations, defines an organization as "a system of roles and a stream of activities designed to accomplish shared purposes." A typical definition of a small group is that of Shaw who has written several editions of a popular text on group dynamics. After reviewing some 80 definitions of a group he concluded that a group is: "two or more persons who are interacting with one another in such a manner that each person influences and is influenced by each other person" (Shaw 1976, p. 446). Podolny and Page (1998,

---

This chapter includes material from Chap. 11 on "The Group and the Organization" (Hare et al. 1996) and Chap. 4 on "Groups" (Turniansky and Hare 1998).

H. Blumberg et al., *Small Group Research,* Peace Psychology Book Series,
DOI 10.1007/978-1-4614-0025-7_4, © Springer Science+Business Media, LLC 2012

p. 59) provide a similar definition of a network, although they suggest that a network differs in respect to authority. They define a network as "any collection of actors ($N$ greater than or equal to 2) that pursue repeated, enduring exchange relations with one another and, at the same time, lack a legitimate organizational authority to arbitrate and resolve disputes that may arise during the exchange." However, in a study of five-person exchange networks of university students, Yamagishi et al. (1988) found that the locus of power in their exchange networks was determined by the nature of the network connections (positive, negative, or mixed) and the scarcity of resources, factors that underlie dependency relations.

The main difference between "small" and "large" is of course the number of members. Although organizations are usually composed of a number of small groups, even small groups can have identifiable sub-groups within them. Given the use of electronic media of communication between individuals through phone, fax, and computer, restrictions of spatial arrangements are overcome (McCann and Galbraith 1981, pp 71–72). Communication networks as "information systems" have characteristics similar to those of groups and organizations even though the members do not share the same physical space (Finholt and Sproull 1990). Tichy (1981, p. 237) identified a number of roles in networks including the gatekeeper, liaison, opinion leader, and cosmopolite.

Small networks may be in the form of cliques, cabals, coalitions, or other types. Tichy (1981, p. 228) defines a "clique" as a set of persons who pursue a broad range of purposes over a long period of time, especially to meet expressive and affectional needs. In contrast, he defines a "coalition" as a temporary alliance for limited purposes. In a study of the informal structure in a factory, Burns (1955) contrasted "cliques," which allowed members who were partial failures some protection and chance to withdraw from the institution, with "cabals," which offered the possibility of "illegitimate" control to members who wished to move up in the organization. Homans labels the interaction in informal groups, that is not proscribed by formal work organizational roles, as "elementary social behavior." He observes that "elementary social behavior … is not driven out by institutionalization but survives alongside it, acquiring new reason for existence from it" (Homans 1961, p. 391). In general, people who interact with each other in networks will attach similar meanings to organizational events (Rentsch 1990).

Van Aken et al. (1994) suggest that the formation of networks should not be left to chance. "Affinity groups" can be composed of individuals with similar titles and responsibilities, who meet periodically to share information and address common problems. Their field test of the use of affinity groups in a US government department, a wholesale food distributor, and a university department, indicated that affinity groups can play an instrumental role in an organization's continuous improvement efforts by providing a structured and systematic way of involving white collar and knowledge workers.

Rather than to leave the informal networks to chance formation, it has been proposed that they should be consciously composed by the Chief Executive Office and Senior Executives of a company or other organization. The members of the network would be drawn from across the company's functions, business units, and geography and from different levels in the hierarchy. The networks would function to build trust, encouraging evaluation of business problems from a broad perspective of customers and the company rather than following narrow functional or departmental interests (Charan 1991).

Given the ease with which members of one or several organizations can communicate electronically, in the years beginning with 2000, the same advantages should apply to sets of persons who do not meet face-to-face. However, Kanungo (1998), found that there is a relationship between organizational culture and the use of computer nets. In task-oriented organizations satisfaction with computer-mediated communication and information access was positively related to the degree of use. In contrast, people-oriented organizations displayed a negative relationship between degree of use and satisfaction.

Some definitions of a group, such as that of Shaw, would seem to apply more to informal groups. However, other definitions, such as that of Cartwright and Zander (1968, p. 48) in their classic text on group dynamics, stress the fact that a "full-fledged" group also has a system of interlocking roles and works toward a common goal. Further, although Robey stresses the formal aspects, organizations also have their informal side. Research on organizations tends to focus on the formal side and research on small groups on informal or "elementary" behavior. However, small groups can also be formally organized, especially if they are part of larger formal organizations, and informal networks of individuals can function as organizations.

An additional reason for viewing small groups as small organizations is that much of the research conducted to understand interaction in organizations has actually focused on small groups of persons. Many observers see the small group as a "microcosm" of larger organizations and indeed of whole societies (Slater 1966). Much of the research cited in all major texts on organizations—for example, on authoritarian and democratic group atmospheres (White and Lippitt 1960), on communication networks (Leavitt 1951), and on conformity to norms (Asch 1955)—was all done on small groups.

Among contemporary general works that cover small group research applicable to organizations are those by Borkowski (2005); Brunner et al. (2006) on group relations conferences; Levine and Moreland (2006); Nijstad (2009) on group performance.

Note that research on teams, closely related to viewing small groups as small organizations, represents the subject of the chapter after this one.

# Theories for Small Groups and Organizations

There are no different theories for small groups, usually of less that 30 members, and organizations or for small networks within large networks (Hare 1993). Alvarez and Robin (1992), for example, use functional theory for the analysis of both small groups and organizations.

In terms of functional theory, both fully functioning small groups and large organizations share the following characteristics (Hare 1982 (p. 20), 2003):[1]

1. The members are committed to a set of values that define the overall pattern of
   activity (Meaning, M).
2. The members have accumulated or generated the resources necessary for the task
   at hand (Resources, R).
3. The members have worked out an appropriate form of role differentiation and
   developed a sufficient level of morale for the task (Integration, I).
4. The members have sufficient control, in the form of leadership, to coordinate the
   use of resources by the members playing their roles in the interest of the group's
   (or organization's) values (Goal attainment, G).

## *Functions Within Functions*

It may be sufficient for some levels of analysis to note the success the group or organization has in fulfilling each of the four functions. However, particularly if there
is a failure at any point, it may be desirable to look more closely at the activity in a
functional area, to see just where the problem lies, since to fulfill each function four
sub-functions are necessary which mirror the four main functions.

The easiest example to begin with is in the functional area of producing resources. When a group needs a new piece of equipment, first it is necessary to have
a concept of the type of equipment (Meaning within the Resources area), next tools
that may be required and special materials to make the new product and new skills
by group members (Resources within the Resources area). Next group members'
roles may need to be adjusted to match the production requirements for the new resource (Integration within the Resources area), and finally the new item is produced
(Goal attainment within the Resources area).

Burningham and West (1995, p. 106) provide enough detail of processes within
groups to be able to identify the four sub-functions within the functional areas. They
do not describe the phases within phases in the production of resources, but they do
describe in some detail the phases within phases in the other three functional areas,
except, of course, they do not label them using our terminology. Here we will reproduce their descriptions, leaving aside a word for word translation of their terms, but
providing some summary remarks.

---

[1] Functional theory was developed primarily by Parsons (1961) and was modified by Effrat (1968)
who suggested that the function of "Adaptation," here called "resources," focus on the resources
used by the group in reaching its own Goal attainment, rather than representing the group output to
the larger system, as in Parsons's original formulation. Parsons's label of "Latent pattern maintenance and tension management" for the function of providing the overall meaning of the situation
and the purpose of the group has been shortened to the term "meaning." See also the introduction
to Chap. 1.

*Vision (Meaning)* "Vision is an idea of a valued outcome that represents a higher order goal and motivating force at work." Workgroups with clearly defined objectives are more likely to develop new goal-appropriate methods of working because their efforts have focus and direction. Vision has four parts: clarity (readily understandable), visionary nature (describes a valued outcome that engenders commitment), attainability (practical likelihood of achieving goals), and sharedness (the vision gains acceptance).

*Participatory Safety (Integration)* "Participativeness and safety are characterized as a single psychological construct in which the contingencies are such that involvement in decision making is motivated and reinforced while occurring in an environment that is perceived as interpersonally non-threatening." The more group members participate in decision making through influencing, interacting, and sharing information, the more likely they are to invest in the outcomes of those decisions and to offer new and improved ways of working.

*Task Orientation (Goal-Attainment)* "A shared concern with excellence and quality of task performance in relation to shared vision or outcomes, characterized by evaluations, modifications, control systems, and critical appraisals."

The description of vision includes the sub-functions of meaning (visionary nature), integration (sharedness), and goal-attainment (attainability), but does not refer to the resources necessary to derive the vision. Participative safety focuses on the sub-function of integration, namely participation in decision making. The process is very similar to that of the process of achieving "consensus" as described by Leavitt in 1972 (see Hare 1982, p. 33) and others as an ideal method of making group decisions. The description of task orientation is the only one that alludes to the sub-function of skill of group members in that skills must be present to achieve quality of task performance.

To these three functional areas, Burningham and West (1995, p. 108) added support for innovation, defined as "The expectation, approval, and practical support of attempts to introduce new and improved ways of doing things in the work environment." In their research on groups in an oil company they found that all three aspects of group activity were positively related to group innovativeness.

Although much of the foregoing research and the present account do not refer explicitly to peace nor to international conflict resolution, the same functional concepts are directly applicable to any entity that (for instance) organizes interactive problem-solving sessions.

## Typing Groups by Functional Categories

Using the functional (RGIM) cybernetic hierarchy, it is possible to make some distinctions between the different types of groups (Hare 1992, pp. 19–21). "R" includes resources and equipment. "G" refers to management for specific tasks, by coordinating resources and roles. "I" combines the rules for work with considerations of morale. "M" refers to the overall values and includes creativity that redefines the task and the situation. Crews of boats, planes, or spaceships can be placed at the bottom of the cybernetic hierarchy ("R" level) since their function is bound to a particular type of equipment or technology. Change the technology and you change the nature of the group.

## *Resources (R) Driven Groups*

Crisis organizations (that provide supplies or information) and air crews are examples of resources driven groups, where a large amount of information about the conditions of the plane and the weather must be processed in a short period of time (Foushee 1984). The risk of accidents is increased if pilots need to fly in marginal weather conditions (Bailey et al. 2000).

The roles of the air crew are fixed because of the placement of their seats in the cockpit. For example, in a Boeing 727 the Captain sits in the left seat where he or she tests all emergency warning devices and is the only one who can taxi the aircraft since the nose gear steering wheel is located on the left side of the cockpit. The First Officer, in the right seat, starts the engines and communicates with the tower. The Flight Engineer, in a seat that faces sideways facing a panel that allows one to monitor and control the various sub-systems aboard the aircraft is the only one who can reach the auxiliary power unit (Ginnett 1990, pp. 434–435). For a smaller or larger aircraft the relationship of roles to equipment will be different. To enhance the decision making and communication skills among crew members, resource management training may be used (Nullmeyer and Spiker 2003).

As an example of the dependence of a crew on its technology, Hutchins (1990) describes the navigators on large ships who work with specialized tools. He observes that the tools do not amplify the cognitive abilities of the crew members, but instead transform normally difficult cognitive tasks into easy ones. The nature of the tools affects the division of labor among the crew members and the techniques by which they coordinate their work activities (Seifert and Hutchins 1992). Errors may result from difficulties in verifying automated information, an "automation bias" (Mosier et al. 2001).

Some of the observations made about air crews would also be applicable to any type of group. For example, Hackman (1993), after collecting data from over 300 crews who flew ten different types of aircraft, concluded that an understanding of the behavior and performance of cockpit crews requires careful attention to team-as-a-whole issues, not just the behavior of individual team members. Stout et al. (1994), observing university students in a pilot–copilot flight simulation, reported that team coordination was significantly related to mission performance. Milanovich et al. (1998) reach a similar conclusion in a study of the relations between the captain and the first officer in flight crews. Too often, captains fail to listen and first officers fail to speak. English et al. (2004) report that teams with high team-level conscientiousness perform better.

## *Product (G) Driven Groups*

Moving up, at the "G" level are work teams in business, manufacturing, health, and education. These teams are bound to a product, an object, or the care or education of a person. Change the nature of the product or the service provided and the team must be reorganized. These types of groups are the most frequently studied in the research literature. Although the focus is on the product, in common with groups at other levels of the cybernetic hierarchy, they need to be effective in solving each of the M, I, G, and R functional problems.

The product goal in question might, for instance, be solar-powered water pumps or stand-alone computer workstations to help address poverty-driven structural violence.

Two types of product driven groups that have been treated separately in the literature are "self-managing" groups (that rely on their own leadership resources) and isolated groups (that are often in a confined space in a hostile environment).

*Self-Managing Workgroups* Self-managing groups, often referred as self-directed work teams, have been introduced into the workplace to foster worker empowerment, to reduce levels of management, and to foster cooperation and creativity. For example, in a telecommunications company, self-managing groups, performing customer service, technical support, administrative support, and managerial functions, were more effective than comparable traditionally managed groups that performed the same type of work (Cohen and Ledford 1994).

The aspects of self-management are especially evident when task interdependence is high (Langfred 2000a). During the transition managers need to shift control to the self-directed team members (Douglas and Gardner 2004).

Freedman (1993) suggests that Transactional Analysis can be useful for these groups. This is also true for any other problem solving method that slows down the decision process and helps the problem-solvers to become aware of many factors that are relevant for the decision. For university undergraduates in self-managing workgroups, Druskat and Wolff (1999) found that structured, face-to-face developmental peer appraisal was helpful.

One aspect of self-managing groups involved in manufacturing was a higher quality of exchange relationships between members, compared with more traditional workgroups (Seers et al. 1995). In common with other studies of self-managing groups, these self-managing groups were found to be more cohesive and higher on job satisfaction. Individual and group autonomy may sometimes, however, have a negative effect on cohesiveness (Langfred 2000b). Cohesiveness is also related to employee control over team staffing and perceived fairness (Chansler et al. 2003).

In a study of 60 self-managing teams with 540 employees, Alper et al. (1998) found that teams with highly cooperative goals discussed their opposing views open-mindedly and constructively which in turn developed confidence in team dynamics that contributed to effective team performance. Competitive goals appeared to interfere with constructive controversy, confidence, and effectiveness. See Chap. 1 for some features that foster cooperation.

Based on a clinical model of family development, Neck et al. (1997) suggest that self-managing teams evolve through five phases. The phases, as they develop from a dysfunctional team to a mature and highly effective team, are: chaotic, traditional or dictatorial, imprisoned or "groupthink," ascending or emerging, and team think.

Using the five-factor model of personality for the analysis of the influence of member composition on performance for self-managing teams of university graduate students, Barry and Stewart (1997) report that it is good to have extraverts but not too many. Conscientiousness (of individuals) was unrelated to processes and outcomes at either the individual or group level. According to a study by Mauro et al. (2009), a group composed of a mix of (action-oriented) "locomotors" and (evaluation-oriented) "assessors" optimize the speed of the former and the accuracy of the latter.

In the literature there is a general assertion that self-directed workgroups can "empower" employees and in turn improve quality of performance. Group members do not, however, have to be competent in all aspects of the task since other members can compensate for an individual's areas of deficiency. Members typically feel that their own contribution to the work is more meaningful (Robbins and Fredendall 1995).

Kirkman and Shapiro (1997) caution US organizations that wish to use self-managing work teams in their foreign affiliates since there may be cultural values that interfere with teamwork and especially self-managed teams. Three aspects of cultural values that may inhibit working in teams are the perceived distance between the American values and those of the target culture, an emphasis on individualism rather than collectivism, and the perceived fairness of team-based pay. (For more on the relationship between culture and self-managed work teams see Rafferty and Tapsell 2001.)

Self-managed teams face the same internal functional (M, I, G, R) problems, as Oliver and Roos (2003) report. In responding to the unexpected in a high-velocity environment, teams increased presence, created a context for a shared and emotionally grounded identity (M), and developed a shared set of guiding principles for action, behavior, and decision-making (I). The teams may avoid the "I" problem of dealing with members who engage in "difficult" behaviors (DeLeon 2001). Teams may do well with the "G" function if the leaders design the teams well and engage in hands-on coaching (Wageman 2001). Nevertheless, from their research in two service organizations, Spreitzer, Cohen, and Ledford (1999) report that team leadership was not as importantly related to effectiveness as work design and team characteristics. Participative goal-setting, though, facilitates collective self-actualization and performance (Haslam, Wegge, and Postmes 2009).

Shipper and Manz (1992) suggest an alternative to self-managed groups in which the whole work operation becomes one large empowered group. Everyone is self-managed and can interact directly with everyone else in the system. They describe a company that relies on self-developing groups without managers or bosses. The company has 44 plants and over 5,300 associates. Organizational themes found in the company include a culture and norms supporting employee empowerment and success, a lattice organization structure, no bosses or managers, successful associates working without structure or management, and unstructured research and development for increased creativity and innovation.

If one is concerned about exploitation as a pernicious form of violence, it is helpful to have a variety of such paradigms demonstrating how complex non-hierarchical structures can work well.

*Isolated Groups* Although the team members may be in contact with a distant base they provide an example of teams that need to be self-managed. They not only have to work well together but they have to live together around the clock. Thus issues related to integration (I) find a more dominant place in reports of these team experiences. In addition they usually face the stress of dealing with a hostile environment. They share some of the problems of the Resource driven groups since they are usually dependent on some type of equipment for survival.

Harrison and Connors (1984) describe several types of teams whose mission requires them to operate in "exotic environments," those on space capsules, super tankers, and weather stations. These groups that are isolated from their parent organization are often plagued with interpersonal issues. Santy et al. (1993) mailed crew-debrief questionnaires to US astronauts who flew on space shuttle missions between 1981 and 1990 with one or more crew members from other countries. Nine of the twenty US astronauts responded. They reported 42 incidents of misunderstanding, miscommunication, or interpersonal friction: 9 in the pre-flight period, 26 in-flight, and 7 in the post-flight period. Most of these incidents were rated as having low or medium impact, but five of the in-flight incidents were rated as having high mission impact. The astronauts recommended additions to pre-flight training to prevent multicultural or multinational issues from interfering with mission operations. Similar recommendations would no doubt apply to multi-national peace- and war-related groups.

Kahn and Leon (1994) examined various group climate factors and their relationship to task effectiveness in a team of four female Antarctic expedition members. Daily ratings on mood and behavior indicated that the team functioned well with a highly effective pattern of work and communication. The most commonly reported stressors were interpersonal, especially concerns about the welfare of another team member. Coping with these involved painful problem solving and sharing emotions. The authors concluded that the results confirmed their hypothesis that a female expedition team would be similar to a male or mixed team but with greater sensitivity to emotional concerns.

Leon et al. (1994) kept track of a trek. A 12-person Soviet-American expedition team spent 61 days in a trek by dogsled and cross-country skis from Siberia, across the Bering Strait, to Alaska. Team members kept daily records of the emotional climate and were interviewed at the end of the expedition. Their perception of the fairness of daily task assignments was negatively related to the number of disagreements with other team members. The extent to which one team member helped another was positively associated with assessments of how friendly team members were. Planned stops in villages along the way to promote international harmony enhanced the international objectives but had a negative effect on group cohesiveness.

## Rule (I) Driven Groups

At the "I" level would be (cooperative as well as competitive) sports teams that are rule-driven. They produce nothing. However, the playing field is usually swarming with referees to insure that the game is played within the rules. Change the rules and you have a new game (Kew 1987). Members of sports teams who feel that they have done well playing by the rules in one game and that their whole team has done the same are said to have "collective efficacy." If team members are not clear about their role responsibilities and the behaviors associated with their roles they will lack efficacy (Eys and Carron 2001). If they have won one game they are quite likely to believe they will win the next and to actually perform well (Feltz and Lirgg 1998; Myers, Feltz, and Short 2004; Myers, Payment, and Feltz 2004).

Other studies emphasizing the importance of roles, rules, and social relationships include work by Barr and Saraceno (2009) analyzing the firm as a neural network in a Prisoner's Dilemma type procedure; Casey-Campbell and Marten (2009) reviewing group cohesion; Kolfschoten et al. (2007) on how facilitators can enhance collaboration; Koumakhov (2009) on the importance of shared cognitive/social models of reality; London and Sessa (2007) on development stages for group interaction patterns; Savitsky et al. (2005) on attenuating people's tendency to over-claim the extent of their contribution to a joint task; Xia et al. (2009) on negative social relationships.

## Meaning (M) Driven Groups

At the top of the hierarchy, the "M" level, are scientific research and development teams. They are not bound by existing equipment, product, or rules. Their task is to develop new concepts and to discover new relationships between old or new concepts. Wolpert and Richards (1988, p. 9) writing about "a passion for science" suggest that: "perhaps it is, above all, the thrill of ideas that binds scientists together, it is the passion that drives them and enables them to survive."

When ordinary groups are in a "brainstorming" mode they may have some of the characteristics that are similar to those of the "M" driven groups, although the groups may not contain members who were especially selected for their creative talents. With the introduction of communication between group members via computers, most of the recent research has focused on the number of ideas generated by group members if they are meeting face-to-face, in "nominal" groups where they perform as individuals and someone collects all of their ideas at the end of a session, or in computer mediated groups where each person's ideas can be "posted" on a list without waiting in turn for others to act or respond (cf. Miura 2003). The use of computers or only "nominal" groups cuts out the "production blocking" and "evaluation apprehension" in producing a quantity of ideas as no time is lost taking turns, especially in larger face-to-face groups (Gallupe et al. 1992). Even then, face-to-face groups can do better when assisted by a trained facilitator (Kramer et al. 2001). It also helps if there is no time limit for the task. The members continue as long as they feel they are making progress (Nijstad et al. 1999).

However, research that also considers the "quality" of the ideas reports that nominal brainstorming "groups" can produce ideas that are at least as good as those using electronic brainstorming (Barki and Pinsonneault 2001). People who, however, are shy may not do well in any situation (Bradshaw et al. 1999).

Additional publications relevant to particular Meaning (and values) of a group are by Arrow and Cook (2008); Hornsey et al. (2006); Meyers et al. (2005); Nijstad et al. (2006);Sawyer and DeZutter (2009); Sessa and London (2008); Stapley (2006).

More information concerning factors influencing creativity is provided below in the section on organizational creativity.

## *Integration and Role Differentiation*

In addition to sorting crews and teams by functional specialty (RGIM), they can be classified according to two other criteria, the amount of (a) integration and (b) role differentiation required. Although some merge the two continua (Dyer 1987), they can be kept separate to form at least a two by two table of types of teams that are either high or low on each characteristic. Olmsted made this type of distinction for types of group leadership in his analysis of group activity (Olmsted 1959; see also Olmsted and Hare 1978, p. 14). Sundstrom and Altman (1989, p. 185) have also used this double dichotomy in their typology of work teams.

Sports teams provide the easiest example of this type of classification but entities that, for example, support various forms of non-violent action for social change may also be thus classified. Golf teams are low on both integration and role differentiation. Synchronized swimming teams are high on integration but low on differentiation since all swimmers perform the same activity within a prescribed pattern created by the placement of swimmers. Track teams are low on integration but high on differentiation, with each member of the team performing a different skill at a different time. Football teams (American style) are high on both the need for integration and differentiation. Each type of team requires a different leader style, a different mix of task and social-emotional functions, and thus different solutions to the four functional problems. For some teams the main function of the members is to support the activity of the central person, such as the surgeon in a surgical team or the pilot of an airplane.

## Influences Between the Organization and the Small Group

Most small groups are parts of larger organizations where they must relate to the goals of the organization and to other groups within the organization. Bushe and Johnson (1989) find that organizational variables, the context, account for 41% of the effect on performance, while internal group variables account for 48%. From the organization's point of view, the goals of the organization may come first before being concerned with the relationships between groups (Schein 1988). The organization in turn may be part of some "multi-national" network.

Any action by an individual, a group, or an organization may have an effect on one or more of these system levels. Bales (1999), in his analysis of social interaction systems, pictures these system levels as bubbles within bubbles. The limits of each bubble are represented by a set of dimensions (three for Bales, but there are more, as the research on the "Big 5" indicates). Social interaction, at a moment or over a long period of time, takes place within a set of nested bubbles where individual and group values indicate the direction in which the goal is to be found and the limits of behavior that are appropriate for reaching the goal.

## Goals, Norms, and Technology

The main influence of the organization upon the small group is to set the goal, the mission. Most formal small groups exist in organizations, which become part of the "external system," that includes the society and the environment, setting boundary conditions on the behavior in the small group (Homans 1950, p. 316).

The boundary conditions may influence the ability of a group to make good decisions. Aldag and Fuller (1993) suggest that one of the factors that led to the "groupthink" decisions described by Janis (Janis et al. 1994) was the insulation of the group within the organization. They identify three other classes of antecedents that may be influenced by the organization and can influence decision making:

1. Decision characteristics (importance, time pressure, structure, procedural requirements, task characteristics).
2. Group structure (cohesiveness, leader power, phase of group development).
3. Decision making context (organizational political norms, prior goal-attainment, external threat).

Apparently individual and structural characteristics in a group both predict performance, the former more at early stages and the latter having more effect later on (Lin et al. 2005).

The introduction of advanced manufacturing technology, such as computers, can also affect the work of a small group (Susman 1990; Sussman 1997). With regard to the group task, more skill may be required of members and there may be more task interdependence if two or more workers share the same machine. However, the new technology may make it possible to give the workers timely feedback on their performance and thus reduce costs. With regard to the group dynamics, the introduction of advanced manufacturing technology tends to strengthen group boundaries and make the task more meaningful to the members, especially when the workgroup is able to identify with a completed product. However, time pressure may reduce the time available for solving social-emotional problems related to group performance.

A company may create "cells" (groups of workers) on the shop floor by arranging equipment for some part of the production in close proximity. Members of the same "cell" can then work as a unit to produce their particular part of the manufactured item. Plants with cells are more likely to adopt a "just-in-time" manufacturing philosophy, where items are not stockpiled. Cellular manufacturers place greater responsibility upon shop floor workers. They provide more cross training and job enlargement. They use employee involvement programs as a tool for problem solving and continuous improvement of production processes. There are fewer labor grades, resulting in a flatter hierarchy of labor skills with more workers in the same grade. However, there is greater managerial control over the manufacturing process and the pace of production, with a focus on increasing flexibility and maintaining effective process control (Magjuka and Schmenner 1993).

The "boundary conditions" imposed by the external system may be set in the form of norms governing behavior in roles, or by physical arrangements of the space available for work (Sundstrom and Altman 1989). An example of the latter is given by Homans in his description of the "bank wiring observation room" experiment that was part of the study at the Western Electric Company (Roethlisberger and Dickson 1939). In that experiment, the workers who were placed in the front of the room formed one informal clique and those in the back of the room formed another (Homans 1950, pp. 70–72).

A more recent example is the "open-plan" for offices, an innovation of the 1960s. Internal walls in office building were either removed altogether or replaced with a few partitions. The intention was to facilitate communication, heighten accessibility of fellow workers, and minimize hierarchical barriers. However, the arrangement did not solve workers' attempts to regulate privacy. Workers in open-plan offices complained about the lack of visual and acoustic privacy, compared with workers in conventional walled offices (Sundstrom et al. 1982). Homans notes that informal behavior arising in response to the physical arrangement of the work space or to other aspects of the task may come to be formalized in norms for the group. These norms, in turn, will change more slowly than the behavior of the group members (Homans 1950, p. 412).

Robey (1986, pp. 241–271) describes several types of groups or teams that derive their function from the organizational context: liaison groups, product development teams, matrix groups formed of representatives of different departments, and a "skunk works," a small group of people given freedom to come up with good ideas.

In sum, the organization sets the overall value framework. Group habits are shaped by the organizational context (Gersick and Hackman 1990). Organizational members' performance is controlled through the leaders of small groups (Kerr and Slocum 1981, p. 128). High-performance teams must pay attention to the external factors in the organization, including identifying and establishing relationships with persons who are critical for their performance. In order to be seen as a winning team, team members must let others know that they are winning (Isgar 1993).

## Influence of the Small Group on the Organization

Institutional social change can, but does not always, represent an important facet of addressing difficulties and, more importantly, increasing harmony.

Most of the proposals for bringing about organizational change are implemented by having small numbers of managers or workers in groups learn new ways of decision making (Huse and Cummings 1985) often with computer-supported decision making systems (Poole and DeSanctis 1992). Hackman (1992), while reviewing the literature on group influences on individuals in organizations, notes that although the structure of group norms and the ways that groups enforce adherence to them are important, one should give special attention to the conditions under which influence flows in the opposite direction.

New types of small groups, such as "quality circles" may be introduced as a continuing source of evaluation and new ideas (Buch 1992). When the problem in an organization is diagnosed as a lack of sensitivity to interpersonal relations, managers and workers may be taken through experiences of "sensitivity training" (Van Buskirk and McGrath 1993).

Proposals for change may deal mainly with the cognitive aspects of group performance as in "reconceptualization" (Friedman and Lipshitz 1992) or through attempts to maximize all major functions in a group (Cummings 1981). Unfortunately, in many team-building workshops, tasks that are used to stimulate "creative problem solving" do not permit the solutions at the highest levels of creativity. In addition, "team-building" may be achieved through providing groups with real experiences of changing group methods, rather than by using "workshops" (Hare 1992, pp. 57–61).

Small autonomous groups can be the key to productivity if they are involved in problem solving (Susman 1990). Ancona and Caldwell (1992) report that cross-functional teams can be a blessing or a curse for new product development. The diversity needed for new product design may result in difficulties in communication between team members. However, articles in popular business magazines, such as the *Harvard Business Review*, recommend the formation of teams with a small number of members with complementary skills. These teams can be used for a company's "critical delivery points," where the cost and value of the company's products and services are most directly determined, for example for the management of accounts, customer service, and product design (Katzenbach and Smith 1993). Another name for the type of mixed team that is focused on change is the "task force" (Beer et al. 1990).

The small group sets norms for productivity. Consultants who work with a "human relations" framework try to align the group's norms with those of the organization (Moch and Seashore 1981, p. 218). The early Western Electric studies demonstrated that the norms of the informal small group can either raise productivity, as in the "test room" (Hare 1967) or lower it as in the "bank wiring room" (Roethlisberger and Dickson 1939; cf. Homans 1950, p. 79). Norms can also camouflage the amount of conflict in a group which may be leading to reduced productivity (Sinclair 1992). More recent research confirms the early Western Electric studies; informal networks can cut through formal reporting procedures to "jump start" stalled initiatives and meet extraordinary deadlines. However, they can just as easily sabotage a company's best laid plans by blocking communication and fomenting opposition (Krackhardt and Hanson 1993).

The small group that constitutes the management team in an organization is especially important. Eisenhardt and Schoonhoven (1990) conducted a longitudinal study of factors affecting growth in 98 semiconductor firms in the USA. They found that the firms had greater sales growth when the top management teams were composed of people who had worked together more in the past, when the teams were larger, and when the teams were composed of people with varying amounts of industry experience. In a study of a sample of Fortune 500 companies, the firms most likely to undergo changes in corporate strategy had top management teams with members who were younger, had shorter organization tenure, higher teamwork, higher educational level, higher educational specialization heterogeneity, and higher academic training in the sciences (Wiersema and Bantel 1992).

Another group that is important is the board of directors for a company—or for a formally organized social-action group. If the board is composed of members who are independent and drawn from persons outside the company then the top managers are likely to be rewarded on the basis of objective performance criteria. However, there is a tendency to maximize short run gains, with more diversified products and less emphasis on research and development. If the board of directors is drawn from the inside, the managers will be rewarded by open and subjective appraisal of the quality of the production process (Baysinger and Hoskisson 1989).

Billsberry (1996) observes that there is a downside to the creation of teams in organizations. They say that the chief problem with teams is political, in that almost invariably, their creation undermines some existing distribution of power in a firm.

While it is customary to focus on the commitment of the group members to the values and goals of the whole group, Becker and Billings (1993) note that the focus of commitment is related to such variables as the intent to quit, job satisfaction, prosocial organizational behavior, and certain demographic and contextual variables. Research based on responses of employees suggests four types of commitment: (a) the locally committed, who are attached to their supervisor and work group, (b) the globally committed, who are attached to the top management of the organization, (c) the committed, who are attached to both local and global foci, and (d) the uncommitted, who are attached to neither.

Ancona and Caldwell (1992) report somewhat similar distinctions concerning the level in the organizational hierarchy to which new-product groups in high-technology companies direct their communications. The groups engage in upward communication aimed at molding the views of top management (Meaning), horizontal communication with other groups to coordinate the work and obtain feedback (Integration and Goal-attainment), and horizontal communication outside the organization for a general scanning of the technical and market environment (Resources). The groups develop distinct strategies toward their environment: some specialize in particular external activities, some in multiple external activities, and some remain isolated from the environment.

Before zooming in on the research on team performance (in Chap. 5), we first consider several topics relating to the influence of two system levels at the end of the cybernetic hierarchy of which, at the social system level, organizations, groups, and roles within groups are a part. These systems are environment at the bottom, since it is assumed to have its effect mainly through the biological system, and culture at the top. The influence of two system levels that are lower than that of groups, represented by the personalities and biological nature of the group members, are considered in relation to the integration and resources functions of groups (for further explanation see Hare 1983).

## Environment and Culture

*Environment* Morris, Conrad et al. (1999) take a broad view of health climate. For them, health climate factors included supervisor and coworker support, anti-smoking and pro-exercise attitudes, norms (nutrition, exercise, job tension), employer health orientation, and job flexibility to exercise. They reported differences in perceptions between blue and white collar workers at a manufacturing company where white collar workers reported a more positive perception of health climate, more flexibility to exercise, and a healthier nutrition norm.

Pollack (1998) found that properties of the physical environment and social climate influence group members' feelings of belonging to the group.

For additional research on the influence of environment, see Balser (1997) on the impact of environmental factors on factionalism and schism in social movement organizations.

*Culture* As one aspect of culture, Neal and Biberman (2003) provide an introduction to the special issue of the *Journal of Organizational Change Management* on "The leading edge in research on spirituality and organizations." Suchipriya and Singh (2001), writing from India, note the effect of spiritual tools in attitude building.

Shared "family" values may set off sub-groups within a firm or within a social-action foundation. Haugh and McKee (2003) use the concept of organizational culture and shared values as a means of analyzing the internal operating environment of four smaller firms, each of which has a family dimension to its ownership and management. The shared values of a sense of belonging, honesty, loyalty, trust, and respect were pieced together from multiple data sources during a 12-month ethnographic study of firms in the fish processing industry in Northeast Scotland. These shared values are collectively referred to as embodying a family culture. In the other three firms, the alignment to the values of the family culture served to differentiate between an inner team and peripheral employees. The criteria for membership of the inner team are through alignment to the shared values of the family culture and in this way the inner team in each of the three firms includes family members, some (but not all) supervisory staff, and friends of other members. The contribution of the article is to identify specifically the shared values that underpin the family culture. Further, the research reveals that a universal family culture should not automatically be associated with a family firm, in that it may be a feature of organizational sub-cultures and potentially have relevance to non-family firms.

For more on culture, see Berthon et al. (2001) on managers in cultures focused externally or internally or in organic-process or mechanistic cultures; Blakely et al. (2003) on organizational citizenship behaviors; Giessner and Mummendey (2008) on high-superordinate group salience as facilitating the acceptance of group mergers; J. J. Johnson (2000) on perceptions of supervisory and non-supervisory personnel; J. J. Johnson and McIntye (1998) on job satisfaction; Lok and Crawford (2001) on job satisfaction and commitment; Young and Parker (1999) on collective climate.

*Cross-culture* The importance of facilitative communication in bolstering intercultural harmony in a variety of contexts is widely recognized (Blumberg et al. 2006, especially Chap. 8).

Wang and Chang (1999) investigated the organizational experiences of 30 Chinese corporation immigrants working in American corporations by comparing and contrasting their perceptions of the practice of interpersonal communication in American and Chinese corporations. Workers were divided into two groups; the first group was prompted to hold in mind perceptions about interpersonal communication in American organizations, and the other to hold perceptions about interpersonal communication in Chinese organizations. Three dimensions were found to underlie Chinese perceptions of interpersonal communication in Chinese organizations: Blunt Assertiveness, Smooth Amiability, and Surface Humility. In contrast, those underlying American organizations were: Sophisticated Kindness, Manipulative "Stroking," and Casual Spontaneity. The differences in the dimensions reveal the diverse cognitive frames Chinese professionals use as they attempt to understand communication in American contexts. Issues relating to the adaptation of Chinese working professionals to American culture are also discussed.

Earley (1999) examined the cultural context of power distance in relation to the status characteristics possessed by group members and their influence on group efficacy estimations and performance. Data obtained from 288 senior managers (modal age 30–39 years) from England, France, Thailand, and the USA were used to test the hypothesis that power distance would moderate the influence of member status (gender, education, and age) on collective decisions made by a group. Managers were placed in three-person groups consisting of one person possessing the high status characteristic and two others not having the target trait. Groups performed managerial simulation tasks in which each group read a paragraph describing a fictitious product, chose a medium in which to advertise it, and wrote statements in support of their choice of a medium. Managers also completed questionnaires assessing power distance and other variables followed by collective estimates of group efficacy. Results demonstrate that in high power distance cultures, collective judgments of group capability are more strongly tied to higher rather than to lower status group members' personal judgments. In low power distance cultures, members appear to contribute comparably to collective efficacy judgments.

Aycan et al. (2000) suggest that a Model of Culture Fit explains the way in which socio-cultural environment influences internal work culture and human resource management practices. This model was tested using 1,954 employees from business organizations in ten countries. Participants completed a 57-item questionnaire which measured managerial perceptions of four socio-cultural dimensions, six internal work culture dimensions, and human resource management practices in three areas. Moderated multiple regressions at the individual-level analysis revealed that managers who characterized their socio-cultural environment as fatalistic also assumed that employees, by nature, were not malleable. These managers did not administer job enrichment, empowering supervision, and performance reward contingency. Managers who valued high loyalty assumed that employees should fulfill obligations to one another, and engaged in empowering human resource practices. Managers who perceived paternalism and high power distance in their socio-cultural environment assumed employee reactivity, and furthermore, did not provide job enrichment and empowerment.

Tang et al. (2000) examined the Japanese management philosophy in organizations, and developed a 15-item, four-factor (family orientation and loyalty, open communication, team approach, and manager knowledge) Japanese organizational culture scale. They compared the differences in Japanese organizational culture and other work-related variables between 156 non-unionized employees of one Japanese-owned automobile plant and 144 unionized employees of one US-owned automobile plant in the USA (mean age of overall sample: 40.2 years old). There were no differences in income and education. Employees in the Japanese-owned plant had higher scores for family orientation and loyalty, open communication, team approach, manager knowledge, organizational commitment, organization-based self-esteem, organizational instrumentality, intrinsic satisfaction, and extrinsic satisfaction than those in the US-owned plant. Results are discussed in light of organizational culture and enhancing quality and productivity in the global competitive market.

Cultural values are reflected in a country's laws. Olsen and Kalleberg (2004) examined organizations' use of non-standard work arrangements—fixed-term employees hired directly by the organization, workers from temporary help agencies, and contractors—in the USA and Norway. Their analysis was based on information obtained from surveys of 802 establishments in the USA and 2130 in Norway. They found that Norwegian establishments make greater use of non-standard arrangements than the US establishments; they argue that this is due in part to the greater overall restrictive labor market regulations on hiring and firing regular workers, and greater demand for temporary labor resulting from generous access to leaves of absence in Norway. They also found that certain institutional factors have a similar impact in both countries. First, establishments in the public sector are more likely to use direct-hired temporary workers and less apt to use contractors and temporary help agencies; this pattern is particularly striking in Norway, but is also evident in the USA. Second, highly unionized establishments tend to have the lowest use of non-standard arrangements in both countries.

For more cross-cultural research, see Earley and Mosakowski (2000) on hybrid team culture within trans-national teams.

# Diversity

In the 1990s, a major concern in research on groups was focused on the issue of diversity. The ideology of the USA, where most of the social-psychological research has been performed, no longer assumed that everyone would become very much alike as a result of being dipped, or perhaps thrown, into a "melting pot." It became "politically correct" to recognize differences in background that resulted from gender, race, age, personality, skill, or any other variables that distinguished one group member from another. Since diversity was no longer to be avoided through exclusion of people with certain backgrounds or characteristics, the problem became one of how to make the most of the diversity that was present in the group.

*Diversity and Meaning* To begin, we will find that the meaning of a group activity is affected by the diversity of the characteristics of its members. Also, in contrast to a group composed of members with similar backgrounds, members of diverse groups would seem to expect different behaviors from their group members.

Barak et al. (1998) examined gender and racial/ethnic differences in the diversity perceptions of 2,686 employees of an electronics company located in a multicultural community. Based on social identity and intergroup theories, the authors explored employees' views of the organizational dimension as well as the personal dimension. A factor analysis of the 16-item diversity perceptions scale uncovered four factors along the two hypothesized dimensions: Fairness and Inclusion factors comprising the organizational dimension and Diversity Value and Personal Comfort factors comprising the personal dimension. The analysis revealed that Caucasian men perceived the organization as more fair and inclusive than did Caucasian women or racial/ethnic minority men and women; Caucasian women and racial/ethnic minority men and women saw more value in, and felt more comfortable with, diversity than did Caucasian men.

Competition, as part of the task, may favor homogeneous groups. Pate et al. (1998) conducted an experiment using 500 upper-level undergraduate students enrolled in a principles of management course at a university in the south-western USA. The results of this experiment indicate that the competitive non-diverse groups performed better than did the non-competitive diverse groups in terms of quality of performance. Results also suggest that both the culturally diverse and culturally non-diverse groups outperformed their best individual members' scores when they were matched with competitive situations that enhanced their innate group processing styles. In addition, group performance and synergy were enhanced for nondiverse groups by the competitive situation, but only synergy was promoted within diverse groups by the non-competitive situation. See also Howard and Brakefield (2001) on effects of diversity on performance for groups competing or cooperating.

Timmerman (2000) examined the effects of racial and age diversity on performance in a population of professional sports teams and investigated the moderating effect of team task on team performance. Basketball and baseball were chosen as examples of activities requiring high interdependence and low interdependence respectively. Archival data were gathered from 871 professional basketball teams with 7,944 player-level records and 1,082 professional baseball teams with 20,019 player-level records from 1950–1997. The results revealed that (after controlling for team ability) age diversity and racial diversity were negatively associated with basketball team performance. Diversity on both variables was unrelated to baseball team performance. The results are interpreted in terms of the interaction patterns required in the different sports.

It is best if an organization values common interests rather than individualism (Chatman et al. 1998). When diversity is recognized, however, it could be used in constructing shared conceptions (Gruenfeld and Hollingshead 1993).

For some groups the diversity in the social network may also be important. Reagans and Zuckerman (2001) examined the effects of team diversity on organizational performance. Team leaders and members of 224 corporate research and development teams in 29 industrial corporations completed questionnaires concerning social networks, organizational tenure, and productivity. Additional collected data included productivity measurements. Results show that both network density and heterogeneity influenced team productivity.

Linnehan et al. (2003) report that members of historically excluded racial groups with strong racial identities will be most likely to welcome organizational attempts to become more pluralistic because pluralism means that their valued identities will be respected rather than repressed.

For additional research on diversity, meaning, and identity, see Levine and Kurzban (2006); Paulsen et al. (2005); Van der Zee and Paulus (2008).

*Diversity and Resources* Here we compare information and social diversity. Jehn et al. (1999) explored the influence of three types of workgroup diversity (social category diversity, value diversity, and informational diversity) and two moderators (task type and task interdependence) on workgroup outcomes by using a multi-method field study of 92 employee workgroups in the household goods moving industry. The employees completed surveys that measured diversity, intragroup conflict, task moderator variables, worker morale, and workgroup performance. Their results show that informational diversity positively influenced group performance, mediated by task conflict. Value and social category diversity, task complexity, and task interdependence all moderated this effect. Social category diversity positively influenced group member morale. Value diversity decreased satisfaction, intent to remain, and commitment to the group; relationship conflict mediated the effects of value diversity. The authors discuss the implications of these results for group leaders, managers, and organizations wishing to create and manage a diverse workforce successfully.

Diversity in learning styles, which involve processing information, can help with complex problems. Naumes (1998) conducting research with groups of college students found that the greater number of learning styles present in a group, the better the performance of the group on a complex task requiring interdependence.

Cummings (2004) observes that effective workgroups engage in external knowledge-sharing—the exchange of information, know-how, and feedback with customers, organizational experts, and others outside of the group. This paper argues that the value of external knowledge-sharing increases when workgroups are more structurally diverse. A structurally diverse workgroup is one in which the members, by virtue of their different organizational affiliations, roles, or positions, can expose the group to unique sources of knowledge. It is hypothesized that if members of structurally diverse workgroups engage in external knowledge-sharing, their performance will improve because of this active exchange of knowledge through unique external sources. A field study of 182 workgroups in a Fortune 500 telecommunications firm operationalizes structural diversity as member differences in geographic locations, functional assignments, reporting managers, and business units, as indicated by corporate database records. External knowledge sharing was measured with group member surveys and performance was assessed using senior executive ratings. Ordered logit analyses showed that external knowledge sharing was more strongly associated with performance when workgroups were more structurally diverse.

*Diversity and Integration*  Pelled et al. (1999) present and test an integrative model of the relationships among diversity, conflict, and performance. For their study, 317 members of 45 cross-functional work teams from the electronics divisions of three major corporations completed measures of workgroup diversity, task conflict, emotional conflict, and task routineness. Also, 41 of the team managers completed a group performance measure, and data on group longevity was recorded. Results were analyzed using seemingly unrelated regression and ordinary least squares regression. Findings show that diversity shapes conflict and that conflict, in turn, shapes performance, but these linkages have subtleties. Functional background diversity drives task conflict, but multiple types of diversity drive emotional conflict. Race and tenure diversity are positively associated with emotional conflict, while age diversity is negatively associated with such conflict. Task routineness and group longevity moderates these relationships. Results further show that task conflict has more favorable effects on cognitive task performance than emotional conflict. Overall, these patterns suggest a complex link between workgroup diversity and workgroup functioning.

However, too much diversity in personality types can produce an alien cognitive climate (Kirton and McCarthy 1988). The tensions could reduce work (Brearley 1994) by affecting both task and teamwork motivation (Weaver et al. 1997). An individual might exhibit more anti-social behavior in a diverse group if others appeared to be doing it (Robinson and O'Leary-Kelly 1998).

Thus diversity has its effect on both the roles that individuals will play in a group and on their interpersonal relations. As it affects morale, morale in turn influences the probability of future interaction, the distribution of group rewards, and the extent to which a group is seen as different from other groups (Worchel, Rothgerber et al. 1998).

For additional research on problems related to integration, see Barsade et al. (2000) on the effects of diversity in positive affect among group members; Beersma and De Dreu (2005) on the interaction between task and induced orientation motivation (for a creativity task prosocial groups were better but pro-self groups did better on a planning task); Bunderson and Sutcliffe (2002) on the influence of functional diversity; Jehn et al. (1997) on the effects of diversity on workgroup outcomes (see also Jehn 1997); Eigel and Kuhnert (1996) on work team diversity; Gelfand et al. (2006) on the effects of cultural tightness–looseness; Harrison et al. (1998) on demographic differences and relationship conflict; Mohammed and Angell (2003) on the effect of personality heterogeneity; Mohammed and Angell (2004) on the differential impact of surface-level diversity and deep-level diversity; Sargent and Sue-Chan (2001) on the relation between racio-ethnic diversity and group efficacy. Note that, unsurprisingly, analysis relating to efficacy entails a complex array of factors but that group effectiveness can indeed often be successfully predicted (Gibson and Earley 2007); Zacharias et al. (2008) for a book on modeling group behavior in different cultures.

A variety of approaches have been developed to develop (demographic and job-function) workplace diversity as an asset rather than as a source of conflict and prejudice (Christian et al. 2006; Jehn et al. 2008).

*Diversity and Goal-Attainment* Moreland, Levine, and Wingert (1996) listed the question of "how valuable is diversity" as one of three questions to consider in creating an ideal group. The other two questions were "what is the best group size" and "will any chemistry occur."

After accounting for diversity in race/nationality, gender and age, value diversity predicted greater personal satisfaction, and higher perceived group creativity and effectiveness (Rodriguez 1998). Cady and Valentine (1999) would seem to agree. They used an entropy-based formula to measure team diversity of 50 problem-solving teams. The data were collected in a division of a high-tech, Fortune 500 company. Their results revealed that diversity (race, age, sex, and function) had no impact on quality of innovation, whereas sex and race had a negative and positive impact, respectively, on quantity of innovation.

Usually homogeneity on important variables, culture for example, makes it easier for group members to concentrate on the task. Thomas (1999) reports that culturally homogeneous groups had higher performance than did culturally heterogeneous groups.

Research has reported that groups with diverse member characteristics were more individually-oriented on a first task (Watson, Johnson, Kumar and Critelli 1998), but with task and process feedback caught up with non-diverse groups by the end of a third task. However, in a replication of the experiment (Watson, Johnson, and Merritt 1998) the non-diverse groups were still ahead after the third task.

Some of the dysfunctional consequences of diversity can be reduced by introducing a language of negotiation that makes it possible to conceptualize the fit among the cognitive and physical resources that diverse colleagues bring to a team (Northcraft, Polzer, Neale, and Kramer 1995).

Ancona and Caldwell (1992) were interested in the relationship between diversity and the task activity of groups. They investigated the impact of diversity on communication and group performance in the new-product groups. Both functional and tenure diversity had distinct effects. The greater the functional diversity, the more the group members communicated outside the group's boundaries, and the more external communication, the higher the managerial ratings of innovation. Diversity also affected internal group processes, such as clarifying group goals and setting priorities. In turn, this clarity was associated with high group ratings of overall performance. However, the direct effect of diversity was that it impeded performance. Although it might bring more creativity to problem-solving and product development, it could impede implementation because there was less capability for group work than with homogeneous groups. See Ancona and Caldwell (1998).

Note that, in general, diversity in the sense of having available a variety of perspectives relevant to the task at hand does enhance performance (Page 2007).

For additional research on diversity and goal-attainment see Watson et al. (2002) on learning-team leadership, group process, and team performance.

## *Introducing Diversity*

Naff and Thompson (2000), in a consideration of the impact of teams on the climate for diversity in government, examined the effects of an organizational shift to team-based work structures on diversity-related perceptions of Federal Aviation Administration (FAA) employees. Results were based on responses to surveys of 25,004 FAA employees in the areas of air traffic, research and acquisition, administration, airway facilities, regulation and certification, airports, security, and headquarters. Three measures of diversity climate perceptions were examined: FAA success in elimination of hostile work environment behaviors, success of the model work environment plan, and support for the model work environment principles. Analysis of results, which included controls for minority status, gender, age, supervisory status, agency/job tenure, and work setting, showed a significant overall effect of teamwork and organization on diversity perceptions. The results suggest that involvement in work teams leads to a better diversity climate and greater levels of support for diversity-related initiatives. Teamwork seems to have the strongest relationship with perceived success of the model work environment plan. It is concluded that the positive impact of teamwork is largely centered in changing attitudes rather than behavior. (See also Chaps. 5 and 6).

For additional research on introducing diversity, see Ely (2004) on group diversity, participation in diversity education programs, and performance; Hanover and Cellar (1998) on the effects of a diversity training workshop on self-perceptions of behavior and importance of related management practices.

## Leadership

As the most visible aspect of the goal-attainment function, leadership provides the coordination of the members' roles and group resources in the interest of reaching a group goal that is derived from the overall meaning of the group. The control has more effect if the roles of the members are interdependent (Liden et al. 1997). The amount of coordination required depends upon the nature of the task (Larson and Schaumann 1993). If the "group" is actually a set of specialists, each with an individual task, the leadership is less important. High status individuals as well as formal leaders can be influential—for example, a doctor in a hospital team (Fiorelli 1988). For Intensive Care Units in hospitals the high-performing units were organized with formal hierarchies that combined complementarity with a high degree of centralization (Pettersen 1997).

*Leadership and Meaning* The task can make a difference. Westerberg and Armelius (2000) explored how 245 municipal middle managers perceived their psychosocial and physical work environments, and examined psychosomatic reactions and job satisfaction in departments engaged in different types of activity. They compared male and female managers in these respects. Their results indicated a difference between departments depending on the type of activity. Departments concerned with care and education (i.e., care of the elderly, child care, and schools) showed a tendency to lower values for psychosocial work environment factors and more psychosomatic reactions than the departments geared toward maintenance and production (i.e., street maintenance, power plant, and the recreation office). In the departments concerned with children, female managers were in a majority. In the departments geared toward maintenance and production, male managers predominated. Compared to the men, the women had a higher level of education, lower salaries, more reactions of a psychosomatic nature, lower job satisfaction, and a less satisfying psychosocial work environment.

Hogan (2005), in an article integrating various leadership theories, defines a charismatic leader as one whose power rests upon the devotion to the sanctity, heroism, or exemplary character of an individual person. This style is contrasted with a transformational leader who can bring followers to move beyond their self-interest and commit themselves to a higher moral responsibility. Elsewhere in the literature transformational leadership is often contrasted with transactional leadership, characterized by an everyday "give and take" relationship with followers.

Rai and Sinha (2000) report that superior's transformational leadership style had a significant relationship with commitment. Further, it was found that the facilitating climate enhanced the strength of association of leadership with commitment.

Charismatic leaders may affirm group members' identities. Haslam, Platow, Turner et al. (2001) argue that perceptions of a leader as charismatic are related to the degree to which a leader's behavior serves to affirm and promote an ingroup identity shared with followers. Consistent with this hypothesis, an experimental study ($N = 120$) revealed that independent of organizational performance, a (male) leader was seen as more charismatic in an intergroup context when his previous behavior had been identity-affirming or even-handed rather than identity-negating. Even-handed leaders also tended to be seen as particularly charismatic when they were associated with crisis turnaround, while identity-affirming leaders were protected from negative attributions in the context of crisis decline. These results suggest that social identity and self-categorization processes have a complex role to play in the emergence and perception of charismatic leadership.

For more on charismatic and transformational leaders, see Dvir and Shamir (2003) on follower characteristics and transformational leadership; Jung and Sosik (2002) on transformational leadership and followers' perceptions of empowerment, group cohesiveness, and effectiveness; M. Turner et al. (2002) on managers' moral reasoning and transformational and transactional leadership behaviors. For a comprehensive review of transformational leadership, see Bass and Riggio (2006).

Various aspects of globalization have been cited as positive or negative forces with regard to structural violence and also international peace. Leadership of multinational companies and other organizations may likewise have a variety of effects, and these need to be periodically re-evaluated.

Kets de Vries and Florent-Treacy (2002), based on interviews with over 500 senior executives, explored a number of themes that characterize effective global leaders. They suggest that the ability to be an effective global leader builds on what can be considered to be the traditional competencies of effective leaders. In addition, in studying high-performance organizations, it became clear that the loyalty of the thousands of employees in a global organization could be generated only if the organization's leadership has the capacity to tap into a deep, universal layer of human motivation. Global leaders with this ability understand the existence of employee basic motivational need systems (which include attachment/affiliation and exploration/assertion needs) and work to align the corporate vision, mission, culture, and strategy into these systems. They looked at global leadership's best practices, and specific competencies that relate directly to the role of the global chief executive officer (CEO) and examined how would-be global leaders could best be selected and developed. Those competencies include forging a group identity by speaking to the collective imagination of the workforce and, as already noted, establishing complementarity between the motivational need systems of followers and the demands of the organization.

Indeed a dynamic system often now binds leaders and followers such that "great followers [can] create great leaders" rather than just the other way around (Riggio et al. 2008).

Teams of managers may have problems similar to ordinary teams (see also Chap. 5). For example, team learning may compromise performance for management teams. Bunderson and Sutcliffe (2003) report that although a team learning orientation can encourage adaptive behaviors that lead to improved performance, it is also possible for teams to compromise performance in the near term by overemphasizing learning, particularly when they have been performing well. A test of this proposition in a sample of business unit management teams provides strong support. The results confirm that an appropriate emphasis on learning can have positive consequences for team effectiveness.

For additional research related to leadership and meaning, see Conger et al. (2000) on charismatic leadership and follower effects; Haslam, McGarty et al. (1998) on random selection of leaders; Pillai and Meindl (1998) on charismatic leadership as a function of contextual factors; Van Vianen and Kmieciak (1998) on the relationship between recruiters' perception of the ideal applicant for a managerial position and their perception of organizational climate; Worchel, Jenner, and Hebl (1998) on new leaders who emerge from within or outside the group.

*Leadership and Resources* There are cultural differences in the mix of traits and values that a leader must possess. Den Hartog et al. (1997) provide a comparison between the Netherlands and Poland in managers' perceptions of organizational culture and attributes necessary for leadership effectiveness. In their study, 287 Dutch managers from six organizations and 277 Polish managers from six organizations filled out questionnaires. Results indicate that Polish organizations are seen by their managers as more likely to rely on social norms and procedures to avoid uncertainty, more likely to concentrate power at top management levels, and less likely to encourage future-oriented behaviors, integrate individuals into groups, or encourage organizational members to be fair and kind toward others. Polish managers believe more strongly that autocratic behavior, diplomacy, face saving risk avoidance, administrative skills, isolationism, individualism, and status consciousness are necessary for leadership effectiveness, and less strongly that vision, humane orientation, integrity, and charismatic inspiration are necessary for leadership effectiveness. For similar results, see Maczynski et al. (1997) comparing Polish and Finnish managers and Nasierowski and Mikula (1998) comparing Polish and Canadian managers.

For additional research on leader traits, see Taggar et al. (1999) on leaders who emerged in autonomous work teams.

Although current research has very little to contribute on the subject of member skills or group resources, nevertheless Cannon-Bowers and Salas (1997b) reasonably assert that it is essential to understand the nature of the competencies required to function in a team as a means to define selection criteria, design and conduct training, and to assess team performance in organizations.

Kelly et al. (1990) report that if a group has a task that requires several trials, then any difficulty on the first trial as a result of capacity or capability will be a good predictor of subsequent group performance.

*Leadership and Integration* Leaders, like followers, may need training to learn to play their roles. Jackson et al. (2003) stress the importance of focusing executive development on capability enhancement, to ensure that it is supporting organizational priorities, and on its thorough customization to the corporate context.

For an analysis of command style and team performance in dynamic decision-making tasks, Clancy et al. (2003) note that real-world tasks involving dynamic decision-making are commonly distributed among a number of people, the organizational structure being typically hierarchical in nature. However, the optimal way to divide the responsibility for decision-making among team members is not obvious. They ask, should leaders make all decisions and communicate specific actions for subordinates to carry out? Or should decision-making responsibility be shared, with leaders communicating their intentions to subordinates, who then decide upon appropriate actions and carry these out? This is fundamentally an issue of the relative effectiveness of contrasting command styles. They report a study using teams of three persons—a leader and two subordinates—in a computer-simulated forest firefighting task. The results indicate a marked performance advantage for teams in which the leader is required to command by the communication of intentions rather than by the communication of orders for specific actions. An intention-based command style, which creates a more even distribution of decision-making responsibility across ranks, was found to result in a more equal distribution of the cognitive workload, to take greater advantage of subordinates' local knowledge, and to allow for greater overall team productivity.

Stakeholders can influence management style. Westphal and Khanna (2003) studied the social process by which the corporate elite may have resisted pressure from stakeholders to adopt changes in corporate governance that limit managerial autonomy. They examined (a) how directors who participate in corporate governance changes that reflect greater board control over management may be subjected to a kind of informal social sanctioning, which they refer to as social distancing, on other boards; (b) how the tendency for directors to experience social distancing may be moderated by their status in the corporate elite; and (c) how directors who experience such social control could be deterred from participating subsequently in governance changes that threaten the interests of fellow top managers.

They tested their hypotheses with survey data on processes of social control from a sample of directors and CEOs at Forbes 500 companies and archival data on director participation in four corporate governance changes. Their findings show that (a) directors who participate in governance changes that threaten managerial interests do indeed experience a higher level of social distancing on other boards, particularly when they have low to medium status in the corporate elite, and (b) directors are less likely to participate in such changes if they have recently experienced social distancing (directly or indirectly). They conclude that their theory and empirical tests ultimately address the question of how, or by what social process, boards of directors help maintain the solidarity of the corporate elite and serve the interests of corporate leaders.

For research on leader-member exchange see Cogliser and Schriesheim (2000) and Maslyn and Uhl-Bien (2001).

*Leadership and Goal-Attainment* For an investigation of leader assessment of performance, Short and Palmer (2003) utilized a two-study design to explore performance referents used by CEOs along with characteristics influencing referent orientation (internal versus external). Referent use was identified through content analysis of 119 CEO annual shareholder letters in the restaurant industry. Results suggest that CEOs use a wide variety of primarily internal referents to assess performance. CEOs who integrate external referents into their performance sense-making efforts tend to be from larger and more highly performing organizations. Post hoc analysis revealed that CEOs of larger and younger organizations used a higher percentage of external referents.

Gittell (2001) discusses the effects of span of control on group performance in the flight departure processes of some US airlines. Multi-site surveys, work shadowing, meeting attendance, and work documentation of nine airline departure processes were conducted (span of control refers to the average number of subordinates a supervisor has). Additional collected data included customer complaints, baggage handling, and late arrivals. Results show that small supervisory spans improved performance through positive effects on group processes. Supervisors with smaller spans achieved higher levels of relational coordination among their direct reporters. Findings suggest that supervisors with smaller spans achieve good results through working with and providing intensive coaching and feedback to their direct reporters.

For additional research on leadership and goal-attainment see Durham et al. (1997) on factors influencing team effectiveness; Harms et al. (2007) on effects of personality and motivation; Nye (2002) on attributions of leadership responsibility; Schulz-Hardt and Brodbeck (2008) on a variety of leadership factors that affect performance; Sivasubramaniam et al. (2002) on transformational team leadership behaviors, group potency, and performance.

*Going Back to Meaning for Group Performance* There are several factors that a leader may influence that are related to high performance in groups. For one, rewarding appropriate behavior is important (Chen and Church 1993; C. E. Miller and Komorita 1995; Tindale and Larson 1992). For example, if there are rewards and support for innovation, then innovation will result (Burningham and West 1995). Wageman (1995a, b) investigated the differential effects of task design and reward system on group functioning in a large US corporation where group, individual, and hybrid awards were given to groups of technicians that had group, hybrid, or individual tasks. Groups performed best when their tasks and outcomes were either pure group or pure individual. Hybrid groups performed quite poorly, had low-quality interaction process, and low member satisfaction. See DeMatteo et al. (1998) for an overview of empirical research on team based rewards.

Groups perform better when they have "potency" (Guzzo et al. 1993) or "efficacy" (Durham et al. 1997; Kaplan 1997; Little and Madigan 1997; Silver and Bufanio 1996, 1997); both terms refer to a belief that the group will be effective. Groups with practice at the task do better (Littlepage et al. 1997). This should give them a good reason for feeling efficacious. Even with practice on a task, if a group member quits the group before the second round on the task begins, the departing colleague can arouse a feeling of inequity in the part of those who remain—with a result in a drop in productivity (Sheehan 1993). When it is clear that a team has either won or lost, then team efficacy is affected. For collegiate ice-hockey teams, wins and losses were analyzed across the season (Feltz and Lirgg 1998). Team efficacy increased significantly after a win and decreased significantly after a loss, but player efficacy was not affected.

Groups are less effective if they are victims of "groupthink," when members share an illusion of invulnerability and unanimity and do not fully explore all options before reaching a decision (Peterson et al. 1998; M. E. Turner et al. 1992). However, it is not enough to feel potent or not to feel invulnerable; members of groups must be active in pursuing the group's goal to be effective. As an example, active members of "Quality Circles," groups with an emphasis on the quality of the product, have a lower rate of problem-solving failure and higher net saving for Quality Circles projects than do inactive members (Tang et al. 1993). Van

Aken et al. (1994) recommend a variation of Quality Circles that they call "Affinity Groups." These groups are composed of white collar and knowledge workers with similar titles and responsibilities, who meet periodically to share information and address common problems. Examples from government, private, and educational organizations indicate that the Affinity Groups can play an instrumental role in an organization's continuous improvement efforts by providing a structured and systematic way of involving white collar and knowledge workers.

## Group Support Systems

In the 1990s, there was a sudden interest in resources available to groups in the form of group support systems using computers or telecommunications that made it possible to communicate in different ways for persons sitting in specially equipped rooms, or in different parts of the same organization, or in different geographic locations using "distributed group support systems" (Fellers and Moon 1995). Note that group support systems have already been mentioned as an aspect of integration since part of the effect of introducing group support systems is on the communication network. (See also Blumberg et al., 2009, Chap. 8).

*Group Support Systems and Meaning* To discover which organizations use group support systems, Burris (1998), conducted a review of the literature on computerization of the workplace and found that computerized work organizations typically have fewer hierarchical levels, a bifurcated workforce (that is, divided into two parts), frequently with race and sex segregation, a less formal structure, and diminished use of internal labor markets and reliance instead on external credentialing.

A group task may or may not need special resources. McGrath and colleagues conducted a series of longitudinal studies of groups of university students with a variety of tasks. They compared groups with face-to-face interaction with groups using computer technology (Hollingshead et al. 1993; McGrath 1993; McGrath et al. 1993; McGrath and Berdahl 1998). They reported that group interaction and performance depend upon how well the task and the technology fit each other at a given time and context (McGrath et al. 1993). For idea generating, intellective, and judgment tasks, there were few differences between computer-mediated and face-to-face groups in the quality of the work, but large differences in productivity favoring face-to-face groups (Straus and McGrath 1994).

Technology can be helpful for "virtual" teams, but does not have to be elaborate. Carletta et al. (2000) observed two automotive supply chain teams while they were experimenting with multimedia conferencing in order to determine what support non-collocated teams need and the potential effects of introducing technologies on their group processes. (Collocation entails arranging in proximity those specialists and groups that are likely to need to confer). The observations included meeting recordings and other sources that show the organizational factors affecting teams.

Working in teams requires very close collaboration. Communication technology can help teams if it is used to foster close and relatively informal person-to-person interaction (see also Chap. 6). Organizational constraints on how the technology is introduced favor high-technology, special-purpose installations, but teams can best be supported using relatively modest equipment with desktop access.

As with groups without support systems, time pressure is an aspect of the task (Salanova et al. 2003). Factors that increase motivation are also similar. After conducting an experiment to explore group members' motivation in computer-supported dyads without face-to-face contact, Hertel et al. (2003) report that participants who find that their contribution was valuable increase their motivation in the same way as they would in face-to-face groups. In addition, after conducting a meta-analysis of the literature, Mahmood et al. (2001) report that introducing group support systems faces the same problems as any new technology; if workers think it will be useful then it probably will be. See also Townsend et al. (2001) on desktop video conferencing in virtual workgroups.

*Group Support Systems and Resources* Some of the negative effects of computer support systems may result from information overload. Carey and Kacmar (1997) examined the impact of a group software on task groups of university students. They found that although simple tasks could be accomplished successfully, complex tasks could result in larger error and member dissatisfaction with the medium. When using computers, the participant may have a perception of information overload.

After the introduction of computer support systems for communication in groups, many of the same tasks previously used in group research were analyzed using the new medium. For example, Lam and Schaubroeck (2000) using the hidden profile task, found that as with face-to-face groups it makes a difference if all information is available.

*Group Support Systems and Integration* In a comparison of university student groups using computer support systems where members of some groups were anonymous and others were identified, Jessup et al. (1990) found that group members interacting anonymously using automated decision-support tended to be more critical, more probing, and more likely to generate comments or ideas than when individual contributions were identified. Galegher and Kraut (1990) reached a similar conclusion that computer communication can help reduce barriers to social interaction and can broaden leadership roles. Winquist and Franz (2008), however, describe limitations of the stepladder technique.

If roles are manipulated using the "stepladder" where new members are introduced one at a time, the same effects are reported as with groups without group support systems. Rogelberg et al. (2002) examined whether a structural group intervention, the stepladder technique, can facilitate the task performance of four-person groups ($N = 52$) when using audio-conferencing. Consistent with research conducted on face-to-face groups, the stepladder technique was found to facilitate the decision-making performance of groups interacting via audio-conference.

Although persons communicating by computer have the possibility of not revealing their identities, Postmes and Lea (2000), after a meta-analysis of 12 investigations, found no support for the hypothesis that removing the ability for groups to exert strong social influence on its members improves group decisions. The only reliable effect of anonymity was to lead to more contributions, especially more critical ones.

Lai and Turban (2008) discuss how Web 2.0 and social network developments facilitate communication and otherwise affect group dynamics in organizations.

See also Holsapple and Luo (1999) on the effects of different group-work patterns with group support systems.

*Group Support Systems and Goal-Attainment* Benbasat and Lim (1993), based on a meta-analysis of 31 experimental studies of the effects of using group support systems, concluded that the use of group support systems has positive main effects on decision quality, number of alternatives generated, and equality of participation, but negative main effects in terms of time to reach decision, consensus, and satisfaction.

In support of McGrath's conclusion concerning the importance of the match between the task and the method of communication, Farmer and Hyatt (1994) conducted a study of university students in three types of groups: face-to-face, screen sharing, and audio conferencing. They found that the audio conferencing groups, whose communication channels were poorly matched to task language demands, performed more poorly, made fewer decisions per time period, and used less appropriate strategies than did face-to-face or screen-sharing groups. In contrast, for a brainstorming type task, groups using computer mediation outperformed those using verbal communication because the computer could support a number of communications at the same time, whereas using verbal communication only one idea at a time should be presented (Valacich et al. 1993,).

For most tasks, face-to-face groups seem to do well. Baltes et al. (2002), as a result of a meta-analysis of research comparing decision making in face-to-face versus computer-mediated communication groups, report that computer-mediated communication leads to decreases in group effectiveness, increases in time required to complete tasks, and decreases in member satisfaction compared to face-to-face groups.

Barkhi et al. (1999) would agree. They compared face-to-face and computer mediated communication channels and found that task groups using face-to-face channel outperformed groups using computer-mediated communication.

But there still may be an advantage using special types of computer programs. Jude-York (1998) studied three teams and their uses of technology to enhance team productivity from two large US corporations with global extensions in the computer and telecommunications industries. Innovative socio-technical models were introduced to the teams to improve collaborative work processes and business results. Utilizing the Lotus Notes groupware application Team Room-super, teams made significant improvements in: synergistically building upon each other's work; aligning individual work around business plans; and improving team communication, coordination, and collaboration.

# Summary

The social-psychological theories that apply to behavior in small groups also apply to behavior in organizations (certainly in principle), as well as to small networks and large networks, including those devoted to social action or conflict resolution. This is especially true when the persons in the network are connected through computer-video communication. Both groups and networks may be either formal, having roles designated by their organization, or informal, with roles developed to satisfy the needs of the members in cliques or cabals or to facilitate the achievement of organizational goals.

The main influence of the organization on the small group is to define the mission of the group. The organization is part of the "external system" of the group that includes the society and the environment. In addition to setting the goal for the group, the organization may also have an influence by providing facilities for the task, including the design of the work space and means for electronic communication, or by setting norms for the types of roles that may be played.

In terms of functional theory, some groups are bound more by their equipment, such as air crews, some by the product, such as manufacturing groups, and some by the rules of the game, such as sports teams. Some groups are not bound by any existing equipment, product, or rules but have a task to develop new concepts and discover new relationships, such as scientific research teams. Within each type of group, a further differentiation can be made according to the amount of integration and role differentiation required.

Small groups or informal networks can be the key to increased (or decreased) productivity if they are involved in problem solving or they can develop norms that are counter to those of the organization and decrease productivity. Just as individuals can play different roles in small groups, so small groups can play different roles in organizations. Some of these roles are formal, some informal, and some dramaturgical.

Most of the systems for implementing organizational change involve small groups, for example, by introducing "quality circles" for workers or "team building" for managers.

In the 1990s, a major concern in the USA dealt with the influence of "diversity" in the composition of groups with regard to differences in members' backgrounds in terms of gender, race, age, personality, skills, or other variables. Variance on any of these factors is associated with differences in meaning, resources, integration, and goal-attainment for a group. Members of homogeneous groups may find it easier to get along with each other but diversity in a group may make it easier to solve complex problems.

Leadership is a hardy perennial for research on groups, where a charismatic leader whose power rests upon the devotion to the sanctity, heroism, or exemplary character of an individual person is contrasted with a transformational leader who can bring followers to move beyond their self-interest and commit themselves to a higher moral responsibility. Charismatic leaders may affirm group members' identities while transformational leaders may increase commitment.

In the same period, there was a sudden interest in group support systems that made it possible, using computers or telecommunications, for individuals to make decisions from different geographic locations. Computerized work organizations typically have fewer hierarchical levels, a bifurcated work force, frequently with race and sex segregation, a less formal structure, and diminished use of internal labor markets with reliance instead on external credentialing. The use of group support systems has positive main effects on decision quality, number of ideas generated, and equality of participation, but negative main effects in terms of time to reach a decision, consensus, and satisfaction.

# Chapter 5
# Team Performance

There is a special interest in "teams." However, there is usually no essential difference between the definitions given for groups and teams (see Sundstrom and Altman 1989, p. 176, or Larson and LaFasto 1989, p. 19). All teams are groups, but not all groups are teams. There is an implication that teams have more clearly defined roles, higher morale, and greater productivity (Francis and Young 1979, pp. 6–7; see also Bassin 1988, pp. 65–88; Patten 1988). Shaplin (1964, p. 61) has noted that teams are formally organized and highly structured, for example, a surgical team in a hospital, a football team, or a police antiterrorist team.

Teams often play a crucial role in virtually every aspect of addressing violence and promoting well-being. This chapter, like the previous one, is relevant to peace psychology in at least two ways—(a) applicability of findings to groups working toward peace and conflict resolution, as well as (b) for many of the findings, egalitarian, and conflict-resolving processes in *any* group or organization.

In texts on organizational behavior, one often finds the effective group described as a "team" and instructions given for "team building" (Francis and Young 1979, pp. 6–7; Patten 1988). Some use the term *group* and *team* interchangeably, and in any case, there is mutual relevance between many of the findings in the present chapter and those from other chapters, perhaps especially Chap. 4 on organizations in general. However, Guzzo and Dickson (1996, p. 308), in their review of research on performance and effectiveness of teams in organizations, suggest that teams usually involve more commitment. In everyday and scientific usage, *group* is the most general term. However, group is also used to refer to a set of individuals who have some characteristic in common without actually meeting each other. This is the sense in which the term *nominal group* is used in social psychology. In dictionaries, *team* and *crew* refer to particular types of groups (cf. Simpson and Weiner 1989). The term *team* usually refers to sports groups, and *crew* typically refers to a group of persons managing some form of technology (stage crews and film crews), especially forms of transportation such as boats, aircraft, or spacecraft (Hare 1992, pp. 18–20; 1993, pp. 72–73).

---

This chapter includes material from Chap. 11 on "The Group and the Organization" (Hare et al. 1996) and Chap. 4 on "Groups" (Turniansky and Hare 1998).

H. Blumberg et al., *Small Group Research,* Peace Psychology Book Series,
DOI 10.1007/978-1-4614-0025-7_5, © Springer Science+Business Media, LLC 2012

Many groups have limited role differentiation and their decision-making depends primarily on individual contributions, for example, a jury, a board of trustees, or a personnel evaluation board. If a team does have minimal role differentiation, for example, a wrestling or debating team, the team is likely to be in competition with other teams and to represent some larger organization. The applied literature offers advice for managers on how to make their workgroups into teams (Herrick 1990; Tannenbaum and Yukl 1992; Tindale et al. 1998).

Devine et al. (1999) surveyed 128 US organizations asking about the prevalence, duties, composition, and structure of groups and teams in practice. One sample was randomly selected from the entire population of US organizations; the second sample consisted of organizations known or believed to use teams. Nearly half (48%) of the respondents in the random sample indicated that their organization used some type of team, and ongoing project teams were reported most frequently. Teams were more prevalent in organizations with multiple departments, multiple divisions, higher sales, and more employees. Interpersonal conflict was the best predictor of perceived team effectiveness—having a deleterious effect—but several structural and composition characteristics of the team were related to conflict and/or effectiveness as well. Organizations that reported using teams generally did not support them in terms of team-level performance feedback or compensation practices.

For an integrative review of different frameworks for understanding team behaviors and directions for future research, see Rousseau et al. (2006) and Salas and Wildman (2009).

## Team Performance

In earlier editions of this handbook, the last two chapters served as a summary of the research with reference to performance (Hare 1976, 1994a, b). One chapter compared individuals with groups and a second chapter compared groups of different types. For a summary of research comparing individuals with groups, see the section on "Group Size" in Chap. 5 of Blumberg et al. (2009).

When groups were compared with groups in 1976, the most productive groups were found to be those which could carry out effectively the major steps in the processes of solving task and social–emotional problems. To accomplish this, for a given goal (Meaning, M), the group should have a combination of members' personalities and skills (Resources, R), type of group structure (Integration, I), and experience in the coordination of problem-solving (Goal-attainment, G) that is appropriate for the task. Training or feedback about the performance improved group productivity.

The research during the next period, up to 1994, continued along similar lines. There was now more evidence that high cohesiveness, measured by the members' desire to belong to the group, is associated with high productivity. Although earlier research had indicated that a group size of five persons was optimal for many kinds of discussion tasks, additional research demonstrated that groups would be less efficient if they had either fewer or more members than those actually required for the task. When groups were successful, the success tended to be attributed to the skill and effort of the members. When the group failed, opposing teams or other external features were likely to be blamed for the failure.

These older findings give credence to the perhaps commonsense view that not only must a peacebuilding group, for example, be sufficiently large to accomplish its purpose, but also it may be counterproductive for it to be excessively large.

For the present text, we include here a brief summary of research, using the RGIM perspective, comparing individuals and groups—and groups with groups—with regard to performance. The usual report of research on group productivity includes information about the overall purpose and values of the group (Meaning, M), about the roles and relationships (Integration, I), and about coordination and leadership (Goal-attainment, G), but little about the kinds of equipment that are needed or the skills that the members must have (Resources, R) (cf. Gosenpud 1989; Kline and MacLeod 1997; Weldon and Weingart 1993; and Whitney 1994). Part of the reason is that for laboratory research with university students, no special skills are required and the equipment, if any, is supplied by the experimenter. For applied research with organizations, human relations consultants are not generally called in for technical problems, only for problems of commitment to purpose, morale or role conflict, or difficulties with leadership. However, both task and social–emotional problems are important (Owens et al. 1998). Although it is good for team members to have the necessary technical and team skills, it is even better if they also believe that they do (Mischel and Northcraft 1997).

A comparison of the performance of individuals and groups is provided by Kernan et al. (1994). They were interested in the way that contextual factors, such as task complexity and information, might affect the performance for individuals and groups. Their participants were college students enrolled in management courses who either worked alone or in three-person groups. They performed a simple or complex version of an unfamiliar (to them) truck-routing task. Performance scores were adjusted to prevent incongruent comparison between simple and complex task conditions. Groups were not significantly affected by task complexity or lack of strategy information. Individuals working on complex tasks benefited more from strategy information than did groups.

When individuals and groups were allowed to select their own task goals, both were found to choose goals that required only a modest increase in the performance and were more positive about the situation than if goals had been assigned (Hinsz 1995a; see also Hinsz 1992, 1995b).

Hackman (1992) urges a broad view if one wishes to understand the effects of organizational groups on the beliefs, attitudes, and behaviors of their members. The effects have three different bases: (a) the ambient stimuli that pervade the group setting and impinge on all members of a given group (this set of effects is covered in Chap. 1 by Davies in Blumberg et al. 2009), (b) the discretionary stimuli that members provide to one another selectively, depending on what specific individuals say and do, and (c) the structure of group norms and the ways groups enforce adherence to them. Hackman is interested in the ways that individuals can affect groups as well as the ways that groups can affect individuals. He observes that the factors that differentiate the teams that "go into orbit" and achieve real synergy from those that "crash and burn" have more to do with how the teams are structured and supported than with any inherent virtues or liabilities of teams as performing units (Hackman 1998).

In the next paragraphs, we will look, in turn, at issues related to the four functional problems (RIGM) as they relate to group performance. In the 1950s, life seemed simpler. Thelen (1954) had observed that there were two types of problems in groups, task and social–emotional, at two system levels, the individual and the group. Before the individual can focus on an individual task, the social–emotional conditions for the individual must be satisfactory. After the individuals have solved their own individual task problems, they will have energy to work on the social–emotional problems of the group. Those problems are solved, and energy is available for the group task. The group can be more effective if individual and group goals are combined (Crown and Rosse 1995).

This was before all of the research on friendship and other forms of intimate relationship, especially during the 1990s. Now it is recognized that small groups contain even smaller groups in the form of pairs and other small sets of individuals, usually with informal relationships, but often part of some formal division of labor within the small group.

For a review of theory and research on small group performance and decision-making in the early 2000s, see Kerr and Tindale (2004). For fairly comprehensive reviews of effective teams in organizations and of intervention that can improve the performance, see Kozlowski and Ilgen (2006) and also Marks (2006) and West (2008).

## Task: Meaning (M)

The meaning of group activity may be expressed in terms of a specific task or goal, or in broader terms as a response to a situation or context. The goals are not necessarily the same for all persons in the group (cf. Hinsz 1995c). Some may join because of the high prestige associated with membership, others because their friends have joined, others because they like the particular line of work, and still others because they will acquire information or skills. The reason for joining will influence the style of individual and group activity. For example, if members are all high on the personality dimension of "conscientious" and are very task oriented, then they will develop group norms based on the quality of output rather than quantity (Waung and Brice 1998). Group members are more likely to share a common meaning if they are involved in specific goal setting, especially if progress toward the goal is monitored and rewarded (Widmeyer and Ducharme 1997). The type of goals selected will, in turn, affect the progress toward reaching the goal. If the task is difficult, more effort will result (Whitney 1994). If the task is complex, more time will be spent in planning (Weingart 1992).

A turnover in group membership results in lower performance (Argote et al. 1995). If people drop out, the remaining members are thrown back to "square one" to assess the "meaning of all this" and why someone would not want to remain a member. As new members join, time must be taken from the task until they share the overall meaning of the activity. Even if members never meet face-to-face, a shared goal is important (Weingart and Weldon 1991).

When an individual or a group or an organization becomes aware of the factors that are important in the situation in which it finds itself, it has formed an opinion about "the meaning of all this." The task is to survive in the situation or perhaps creatively change some aspect of the situation. The part of the requirements of the situation that are closest to the individual is the role that the individual should play. The part that is closest to the group is the specific task that must be accomplished and, for the organization, the mission that must be fulfilled.

Choi (2002) notes that with the emergence of new organizational forms such as team-based organizations, external activities have become critical functions for organizational teams.

A meta-analytic review of research on group goals by O'Leary-Kelly et al. (1994) revealed a strong group goal effect on the performance. For interdisciplinary treatment teams in psychiatric hospitals, overall team effectiveness was best predicted by the fulfillment of the task according to prescribed goals (Vinokur-Kaplan 1995). However, for groups where the goals are not prescribed, group members will be more satisfied with the group goal if they have a chance to influence it (Brawley et al. 1993).

At any level (individual, group, or organization), the description of the role, task, or mission will contain a description (explicit or implicit) of the resources that will be needed, the behaviors that will be required, and the level of creativity that will be required to solve the problem. Here, with a focus on the group, we review the research that includes information about meaning and its relationship to aspects of group performance. As noted earlier, for student groups, the task and resources are given by the instructor. Berge (1998) records some of the differences in teamwork between postsecondary classrooms and the workplace.

Meaning and values may, of course, be particularly important for groups devoted to nonviolent conflict resolution or to addressing structural violence.

In this section, we would like to have brought together accounts of research related to meaning in the order in which meaning (including its subphases) would be established for a team. First research on ideas about a possible goal ($M_m$), next developing the resources, in terms of ideas that may be brought together to define the goal in some detail ($M_r$). Next, the parts that individuals or subgroups will play in determining the meaning ($M_i$) which will influence the commitment to the goal. Next, the processes involved, through leadership or other means of decision-making, to bring together the elements of the goal into a unified whole ($M_g$). Then if this process had led to a different conception of the goal of the group than as it was originally conceived, a new definition of the situation (M) might be developed that would govern the activities of the team as it moves through the next phases in group development of securing resources (R), assigning roles (I), and using the resources by persons playing the roles to produce a product (G). However, there is little published data on these phases within phases. We are left with a discussion of overall meaning (M) and, in the sections of this chapter to follow, of the main process phases of Resources, Integration, and Goal-attainment in turn.

For the meaning (M) function, it helps if the team has a goal. Using data from 575 members, leaders, and managers of 145 software development teams, Hoegl and Parboteeah (2003) found that goal setting is directly related to both effectiveness and efficiency.

It is even better to plan to achieve the goal one step at a time (Weldon and Yun 2000). Goals vary. For one group, the goal may be the accuracy in producing reports, for another the task may be simply to sort cards where the "goal" was characterized by the level of difficulty involved (Hinsz and Nickell 2004).

For some group tasks the problem is solved if one group member finds the answer, the "eureka" problems. Brainstorming is an example of a task that does not require participation of everyone. So social loafing may be evident (Hart et al. 2004; see also Chap. 3 by Kent in Blumberg et al. 2009). For other tasks, the kind of equipment (R) and group size (I) make a difference by influencing the work load for individuals and performance (Sebok 2000).

The motivation to achieve a group goal is also influenced by other factors in the situation. For example, intergroup competition may increase the productivity (Mulvey and Ribbens 1999). Or members may have different levels of relationship to other team members, to the team leader, and to an organization of which the team is a part. An individual may value participation at one level but not all levels. Thus, commitment to organization, supervisor, and workgroup may relate differently to intent to quit (Vandenberghe et al. 2004).

As noted earlier, if a simple judgement task does not require any special equipment or individual skills (R), or role differentiation (I), then these aspects of the task may not be included when the task is described. However, the goal-attainment (G) process may be specified where voting may be required and individual opinions combined by majority decision or unanimity. For the record, a majority vote which leaves out extreme positions is found to be more accurate than a requirement of unanimity (Sorkin et al. 1998).

It is better if team members share the process of developing task. Cohen et al. (1999) began with the assumption that "We can't get there unless we know where we are going." They conducted a study of 108 teams from 26 businesses in seven Fortune 500 companies. They found that contextual and process direction-sharing variables positively contribute to teams developing a shared understanding of priorities and work to be done, and also contribute to effectiveness outcomes.

If individual pay is at risk, members are more likely to become involved in goal setting for the group. That is, they have an interest not only in setting a goal but also in the results of achieving it (Guthrieand Hollensbe 2004).

Van Leeuwen and Van Knippenberg (2002) investigated whether the presence of a specific group goal would reduce social matching (i.e., matching one's own performance to the performance expected from others) by serving as an alternative standard. The participants were 53 college students (mean age 20.0 years). As predicted, when there was no specific goal, the participants matched their own performance to the performance expected from other group members. When there was a specific group goal, the women no longer engaged in social matching, although that effect did not emerge among the men. Instead, the women's mean personal performance was close to the performance level representing an equal share of the group goal. Moreover, the participants' perceptions of a fair contribution mediated the performance of the men and the women, both in the presence and the absence of a goal.

In their research, Cunningham and Chelladurai (2004) examined the extent to which (a) the formation of a common in-group identity mitigated the negative effects of functional heterogeneity and (b) group size and relative group performance influenced the formation of a common in-group identity once cross-functional teams are formed. Results of a laboratory experiment with 79 student groups indicate that relative group performance did influence the formation of a common in-group identity and that the in-group identity served to improve affective reactions (i.e., satisfaction and preference to work with the group).

For more research on the relationship between developing a common group identity and group performance, see Witt et al. (1999). For a thorough but somewhat oblique analysis of the main dimensions related to team effectiveness, see LePine et al. (2008).

## Task: Resources (R)

For the function of providing resources for the task, very little research deals with the group decisions about the kinds of resources needed and how to go about making them or finding them. Some attention has been given as to whether individuals who have the necessary skills will be recognized as having them. Bunderson (2003) tested a theory of expertise recognition and utilization in groups that focused on the critical role of members' status cues as indicators of task expertise. The theory draws on status characteristics theory and past research on groups to propose that while attributions of expertise in workgroups will be informed by both specific (i.e., task-relevant) and diffuse (i.e., social category) status cues, the strength of this association will be contingent on the type of cue as well as on characteristics of the group context. So, whereas specific status cues will better predict attributions of expertise in decentralized, longer tenured groups, diffuse status cues will better predict attributions of expertise in centralized, shorter tenured groups. That is, as you get to know others, there is less need to draw on stereotypes as the basis for expectations. Furthermore, attributions of expertise should fully mediate the relationship between members' status cues and intragroup influence. A multilevel test of these hypotheses in a sample of self-managed production teams in a Fortune 100 high-technology firm provided strong support. Group-level analyses confirmed that the alignment of intragroup influence with specific status cues is positively associated with group performance.

Note that expertise at the team level is more complex than at the individual level and—according to analysis by Garrett et al. (2009)—includes six components: subject matter, situational context, interface tool, expert identification, communication, and information flow path.

When experimenters make sure that some group members are "experts," for a group decision, the other members are likely to defer to them (Baumann and Bonner 2004) and give more weight to their opinions (Bonner 2004; Bonner et al. 2002).

Sharing the information between group members can be helpful. However, in an information-rich environment, assigning all information to all members may overload each member's cognitive capabilities (Tindale and Sheffey 2002).

Most of the research related to the resource function records the kinds of skills or types of personalities that will contribute to the group effort. For example, shy people are likely to take only a small part in decision-making (Bradshaw and Stasson 1998). In contrast, group members who are confident of their abilities are more likely to talk (Evered 1998).

If the average of group members' traits that will contribute to teamwork is high, then it is much better. Barrick et al. (1998) examined scores for 652 employees composing 51 work teams. They report that teams that were higher in general mental ability (GMA) and the "Big Five" measures of conscientiousness, agreeableness, extraversion, and emotional stability received higher supervisor ratings for team performance. Positive correlations of team averages on conscientiousness and agreeableness with team performance are also reported by Neuman and Wright (1999) in their research on 79 four-person, human resource work teams. Halfhill et al. (2005), in a field study of intact military teams, also report positive correlations with conscientiousness and agreeableness. Correlations between team performance and means and variances on each of the "Big Five" personality factors are provided by Neuman, Wagner, and Christiansen (1999); for a meta-analysis of such findings see Peeters et al. (2006). According to a different meta-analysis (Bell 2007), personality composition may be more important in field settings, whereas in lab settings the mental ability range and emotional intelligence were the important predictors of performance.

In two studies, Keinan and Koren (2002) allocated 180 students to three-member teams consisting of Type A and Type B personalities in different proportions. Type As are hard workers who are often preoccupied with schedules and the speed of their performance. Type Bs may be more creative, imaginative, and philosophical. The teams performed competitive and noncompetitive tasks. They found that teams consisting primarily of Type A members were more productive than predominantly Type B teams, and that this difference was enhanced when the teams performed competitive tasks. In addition, results show that both Type As and Type Bs were generally more satisfied when teamed up with same-type members.

In addition to personality traits, if special skills are required for a task, such as that of installing and operating communications networks in the US Army Signal Corps, then obviously a high average of team skill predicts high performance (Winkler 1999).

## Task: Integration (I)

Mayer (1998) reports that high-quality decisions are most likely to be made in groups when members participate fully in the process and the group climate is characterized by the presence of respectful behaviors and the absence of negative socio-emotional behaviors. Collective efficacy—or a group's expectation of success—is often an important component of actual performance (Tasa et al. 2007). For high-reflexivity tasks (where teams need to plan and evaluate their performance), high "perceived cooperative outcome interdependence" was associated with increased information sharing and better outcomes (De Dreu 2007).

In research and development groups, as in groups in general, status hierarchies develop which are based, in part, on the external status characteristics of group members (Cohen and Zhou 1991). While most of the external characteristics reflect a group member's past performance, and therefore may be relevant for the group's current activity, gender also has an independent effect on group status, with males being accorded higher status (at the time and places of much of the research).

Status in a group may affect a member's opportunities to have innovative contributions accepted or to learn necessary skills. In a study of a research and development unit in a high-technology manufacturing company, Brooks (1994) identified group learning tasks. She then noted that organizational structures made it difficult for low-power members to carry out the learning tasks. Unequal former power among employees was seen to have a critical influence on the success or failure of learning groups.

One of the features of a group, as a part of the function of Integration, is the communication network. In a new millennium when there is a trend toward "virtual groups" whose members are part of a network and never meet face-to-face, it is reassuring that communication via video was found to be as effective as face-to-face interaction (Olson et al. 1997).

For engineers (aged 26–65) in a US electronics firm, age distributions inside project groups exerted a greater influence than tenure distributions on the frequency of technical communication. The reverse relationship held for technical communication outside the project groups (Zenger and Lawrence 1989). As in ad hoc laboratory groups, both external and internal status characteristics (including gender) affect the ordering of interaction within workgroups (Cohen and Zhou 1991). Usually, low-status members are not listened to (Mallubhatla et al. 1991). For an analysis of the problem of literally being "second string," see Murnighan and Conlon's (Murnighan and Conlon 1991) description of the group dynamic problems of British string quartets. One of the problems they identify is termed the "paradox of the second violinist."

Finer grain distinctions were made concerning the types of communication involved in the roles of team members in new product teams (Ancona and Caldwell 1988). Various sets of activities were identified that group members used to manage their dependence on external groups. Team members carried out scout, ambassador, sentry, and guard activities along with immigrant, captive, and emigrant roles to manage external transactions. High team performance was associated with a fit between the level of boundary activity and the degree of resource dependence.

When there is little role differentiation in a group, members are more likely to engage in "social loafing" and "free riding." Social loafing also occurs if one member has been named the group leader but has no authority (Kerr and Stanfel 1993). The low productivity of the group members is related to low motivation, arising when they perceive no value to contributing, perceive no contingency between their contributions and achieving a desirable outcome, or perceive the costs of contributing to be excessive. (See also Stroebe et al. 1996). Shepperd (1993) suggests three broad categories of solutions: (a) provide incentives for contributing, (b) make contributions indispensable, and (c) decrease the cost of contributing.

For additional research on social loafing, see Hertel et al. (2000) on motivation gains in performance groups; Kerr et al. (2007) on motivational *gains* from stressing social comparisons or the indispensability of an individual's contribution; Miles and Klein (2002) on perception in consequences of free riding; Mulvey and Klein (1998) on the impact of perceived loafing and collective efficacy in group goal processes and group performance; and Sorkin et al. (2001) on signal-detection analysis of group decision-making.

For laboratory studies of team performance and studies of military and industrial teams, we find no reports of groups that need to work out the best set of roles and interpersonal relationships for the task. In common with the functions of meaning and resources, roles and relationships are usually supplied by the experimenter or clearly implied by the task at hand.

Orpen's (Orpen 1997) "stepladder" technique provides examples of an intervention involving roles in group process in order to improve team performance. A core group is formed. Then additional members join one after the other in steps, provided that they have completed the group task individually first, and present their tentative solutions before discussing the task with members of the core group. After completing the problem (the NASA moon landing exercise) individually, 160 management students (mean age 20 years) were randomly assigned to one of 20 four-member groups in either the stepladder condition or the conventional group condition. The stepladder groups produced significantly better decisions than the conventional groups. (See also Rogelberg and O'Connor 1998.) The method is comparable to providing individual training on a task before the new person joins the group.

As another example of the experimenter changing the rules, Penrod and Heuer (1998) conducted two field experiments to examine the consequences of permitting jurors to take notes and direct questions to witnesses during trials. The data for the first experiment were obtained from 29 judges (sitting in 63 trials), 95 lawyers, and 550 jurors—all of whom participated in the same 67 Wisconsin state court trials. Data for the second experiment were obtained from a national sample. The final sample included 75 civil and 85 criminal trials in the courtrooms of 103 different judges from 33 states. Data were supplied by 103 judges, 220 lawyers, and 1,229 jurors. When jurors were told that they could take notes and ask questions they did so. However, with the exception of the finding that juror questions promote juror understanding and alleviate their doubts about the trial evidence, findings reveal relatively little support for the purported advantages of note-taking and questions.

Some research looks for the best combination of group roles for problem-solving groups to see if they already exist in some research teams or if some roles might be added to a team or perhaps used to compose teams with people able to perform these role requirements.

Prichard and Stanton (1999) investigated the potential use of Belbin's Team-Role Theory as a counseling and team development tool for organizations and management consultancies in the UK. Belbin had proposed that the range of useful behaviors that make an effective contribution to team performance is composed of eight clusters (team roles), each of which describes a pattern of behavior characteristic of the way in which one team member interacts with another. These are: plant (innovater), resource investigator, chair, shaper, monitor evaluator, team worker, company worker, and completer–finisher. Prichard and Stanton sought to test Belbin's proposal that teams in which a wide range of team roles are represented perform better than those where there is an imbalance of roles because certain roles are over-represented. The participants in the experiment were aged 23–45 years. The task performance of six teams of four individuals identified as shapers by the Team-Role Self-Perception Inventory (Belbin 2010) was compared with that of six mixed teams of four individuals: one co-ordinator, one plant, one completer finisher, and one team worker. It was found that consistent with Belbin's proposal, the "mixed" teams performed better than teams consisting of shapers alone.

Not everyone agrees. Partington and Harris (1999), also in the UK, noted that accompanying the growing use of teams in the workplace, Belbin's diagnostic instrument for team role self-perception was now widely used for a variety of practical management development purposes, including putting together "balanced" teams. They report that despite the claims of some purists that Belbin's instrument lacks a strong theoretical underpinning, it fills an apparent void in practical team-working literature, even though its applicability is not well understood. They conducted a study using data from 43 teams of MBA students performing a project management simulation exercise and found no significant relationship between team role balance and team performance, although their study did show that the presence or absence of some individual roles can have a positive or negative effect on the performance.

Using another set of types of group roles, S. E. Hare and Hare (2001) used survey data representing varieties of "role repertoires" to simulate small groups and determine an effective five-member composition. For this research, it is assumed that an individual is not limited to playing only one type of role throughout the life of the groups but has a "repertoire" of roles which together cover some part of a three-dimensional social interaction space. Following Bales's SYMLOG paradigm (Bales and Cohen 1979), the three dimensions are active versus passive, friendly versus unfriendly, and conforming versus nonconforming. The data for analysis consisted of survey responses, mostly from members of US organizations that were originally gathered during leadership programs. The Systematic Multiple Level Observation of Groups (SYMLOG) questionnaire is used to inventory "role repertoires," as sets of roles that are multidimensional, dynamic, and sometimes conflicting. The SYMLOG Optimum Profile of behavior for an effective decision-making group served as the criterion of effectiveness that balanced task accomplishment with member satisfaction. The most effective group, with an average profile closest to the SYMLOG norm, had five members playing four primary roles: a social organizer, two democratic task leaders, a team player, and a conservative worker. The simulation illustrates an advantage in the use of "role repertoires" for evaluating group performance and identifying resources, potentials for conflict, and mediation strategies, which might remain hidden if data were used that reported only the primary role for each individual member of a group.

*Emotional Intelligence* As an addition to the measurement of individual task ability that has a long history, tests have now been constructed to measure "emotional intelligence," an aspect of a person's ability to be effective with regard to social–emotional relations with other groups' members. Prati et al. (2003)—in their research on emotional intelligence, leadership effectiveness, and team outcomes—define emotional intelligence as the ability to read and understand others in social contexts, to detect the nuances of emotional reactions, and to utilize such knowledge to influence others through emotional regulation and control.

In common with many psychological tests which used to be only available in the offices of psychologists, the test can be taken using a computer connection to the World Wide Web. The test asks questions in the form of a self-report to determine the extent the respondents can understand emotions shown by others and those exhibited by themselves.

As a sample of research on "emotional intelligence," Offermann et al. (2004) examined the relative contributions of emotional competence (intelligence) and cognitive ability to individual and team performance, team member's attitudes, and leadership perceptions. Focusing on emotional competencies, they predicted that although both cognitive ability and emotional competence would predict performance, cognitive ability would account for more variance on individual tasks, whereas emotional competence would account for more variance in team performance and attitudes. They also predicted that emotional competence would be positively related to team attitudes and both leader emergence and effectiveness. Using a sample of undergraduate business majors who completed tasks alone and as members of teams, their results generally supported the hypotheses.

See also Jordan and Troth (2004) who report that emotional intelligence indicators were positively linked with team performance and were differentially linked to conflict resolution methods and Rapisarda (2002) on emotional competence, group cohesiveness, and high performance.

However, when Feyerherm and Rice (2002) investigated the relationship among a team's emotional intelligence, the team leader's emotional intelligence, and team performance with customer service teams, they found no correlations occurred between members identifying emotions and any performance measure. Team leader emotional intelligence had a neutral to negative relationship with team performance from the team members' perspectives.

*Cohesion* Kozub and McDonnell (2000) examined the relationship between perceived cohesion and collective efficacy in rugby teams. Male athletes ($N = 96$, aged 19–51 years) from seven rugby union clubs completed Widmeyer et al.'s (Widmeyer et al. 1985) Group Environment Questionnaire and a collective efficacy measure designed to assess the athletes' perceptions of their team's functioning in seven performance areas. Multiple regression analyses indicated that the cohesion dimensions accounted for a significant proportion of the variance (32%) in the collective efficacy scores. Inspection of the standardized regression coefficients showed that the task measures of cohesion were stronger predictors of collective efficacy than were the social measures of cohesion. The results were consistent with Spink's (Spink 1990) study of elite volleyball teams and supported the contention of Zaccaro et al. (1995) that properties of the group have great potential to contribute to a team's sense of efficacy.

Here as in other areas, results need to be contextualized. Cohesiveness (interpersonal liking) has larger effect sizes in predicting performance in project teams than in production or service teams, according to a meta-analytic review by Chiocchio and Essiembre (2009). Also, team allegiance may lead to a focus on one's own team's strengths and weaknesses, thus enhancing predictions of success on easy tasks but attenuating predictions of success on difficult ones (Krizan and Windschitl 2007).

*Citizenship* Being a good citizen is one of the general requirements for taking part in group activity. Turnley et al. (2003) examined the relationships between psychological contract fulfillment and three types of employee behavior: in-role performance, organizational citizenship behavior directed at the organization, and organizational citizenship behavior directed at individuals within the organization. Using a sample of 134 supervisor–subordinate dyads, they suggest that the extent of psychological contract-fulfillment is positively related to the performance of all three types of employee behavior. In addition, the results indicate that psychological contract fulfillment is more strongly related to citizenship behavior directed at the organization than to citizenship behavior directed at one's colleagues. Finally, this research investigates if employees' attributions regarding the reasons that psychological contract-breach occurred also impact their work performance. However, the data provide only limited support for the idea that employees are most likely to reduce their work effort when they perceive that the organization has intentionally failed to live up to its commitments.

Dunlop and Lee (2004) investigated the influences of organizational citizenship behavior and workplace deviant behavior (WDB) on business unit performance using data from branches of a fast food organization. Data included measures of WDB and organizational citizenship behavior obtained from staff, ratings of performance provided by supervisors, and objective measures of performance. It was found that WDB was negatively and significantly associated with business unit performance measured both subjectively and objectively. Organizational citizenship behavior, however, failed to contribute to the prediction of business unit performance beyond the level that was achieved by WDB. It appeared, therefore, that the presence of deviant employees among business units impinges upon the performance of the business unit as a whole, whereas organizational citizenship behaviors had comparatively little effect.

Robinson and O'Leary-Kelly (1998) conducted a cross-level field study, involving 187 employees (aged 21–65 years) from 35 groups in 20 organizations, to examine how individuals' antisocial behaviors at work are shaped by the antisocial behavior of their co-workers. They found a positive relationship between the level of antisocial behavior exhibited by an individual and that exhibited by his or her co-workers. They also found that a number of factors moderated this relationship. Finally, they found that dissatisfaction with co-workers was higher when individuals engaged in less antisocial behavior than their co-workers.

For additional research related to citizenship, see Vey and Campbell (2004) on in-role or extra-role organizational citizenship behavior; one asks, which are we measuring?

*Empowerment* Another aspect of integration is whether the individual group members feel "empowered" and able to act on their own or have a say in the way their role should be played. Kirkman and Rosen (2000), on the basis of research with over 100 teams, share insights about the characteristics of empowered teams and what it takes to sustain high team performance. Their findings show that empowered work teams have four characteristics in common: potency, meaningfulness, autonomy, and impact. Four organizational levers of team empowerment are outlined: external leader behavior, production/service responsibilities, the human resource management system, and organizational social structure.

Who can you talk to? Thompson et al. (1998) examined a number of organizational context variables, obtained from three samples in two government agencies. Across samples, a total of 16,460 employees and managers of the Federal Aviation Administration and another federal agency participated. Perceptions of empowerment were then predicted from these context variables. Results show that perception of communication is the strongest predictor of empowerment perceptions across samples and measures. In addition, the size of the communication slope estimate (beta value) did not differ across the samples. The results support the contention that context factors besides teams and restructuring are related to empowerment.

Carless (2004) tested a model in which empowerment was hypothesized to mediate the relationship between psychological climate and job satisfaction. Individual levels of negative affectivity were controlled for. The sample consisted of 174 customer service employees. Support was found for a paradigm in which empowerment mediated the relationship between climate and job satisfaction, the dimensions of meaning and competence were largely responsible for the mediating effects of empowerment.

*Safety* Zohar (2000) presents and tests a group-level model of safety climate to supplement the available organization-level model. Climate perceptions in this case were related to supervisory safety practices rather than to company policies and procedures. The study included 53 workgroups in a single manufacturing company. Climate perceptions significantly predicted microaccident records during the five-month recording period that followed climate measurement, when the effects of group- and individual-level risk factors were controlled. The study establishes an empirical link between safety climate perceptions and objective injury data. (See also Hofmann et al. (2003) on safety climate as an exemplar and leader–member exchange).

For additional research related to integration, see Duffy and Shaw (2000) on envy; Elfenbein and Ambady (2002) on eavesdropping; Emans et al. (2000) on work team's outcome and task interdependence; Losada and Heaphy (2004) on the ratio of positivity to negativity in interaction; Van Dyne and Saavedra (1996) on emotional investment; Sias et al. (2004) on workplace friendship deterioration processes; Totterdell et al. (2004) on organizational networks and employees' effect.

## Task: Goal-Attainment (G)

Having found no examples of research in which group members need to establish the meaning of their activity, nor the resources necessary, nor the roles and relationships that will be optimal, we are not surprised to find a lack of research on which group members are asked to work out a method of decision-making before beginning the task. However, we find one report of groups that did work out new strategies in the face of roadblocks to effectiveness to achieve better performance. Tesluk and Mathieu (1999) investigated how workgroups manage performance barriers in their immediate environment to achieve effectiveness. Relationships were tested using data collected from 473 group members, 88 foremen, and 21 managers pertaining to 88 maintenance and construction road crews in a state department of transportation. Performance constraints were found to have a direct negative relationship with performance. Through problem-management strategies, crews were able to minimize these effects both directly and indirectly by maintaining crew cohesion under more frequent and severe performance problems. In turn, self-management, leadership, and teamwork processes were found to be related to crew use of problem-management actions and strategies.

Research on team performance using laboratory groups of university students generally assumes that the same relationships between (a) group structures and group process variables and (b) group performance that are observed in the laboratory will also be evident in groups functioning in organizations outside the university. Werner and Lester (2001) sought to test this assumption by applying a team effectiveness framework to the performance of student case teams. In their research, they noted whether variables shown to influence work team performance in organizations would affect college student teams working on business case studies. The performance of 107 student case teams from 10 sections of a management class was predicted by using a measure of team structure and four measures of team process. Team process factors were team structure, team spirit, social support, workload sharing, and communication within the group. Team effectiveness was determined by team performance, team satisfaction, and team grade. Results show that satisfaction with the team was significantly and positively related to team structure and three of the process variables. In contrast, although team structure and team spirit were significantly and positively related to grade (on the case project), social support was significantly but negatively related to grade. For another example, see Kline (2001) on predicting team performance by testing a model in a field setting.

Lowrey (2002), drawing on literature from the sociology of work, assumed that subgroups such as design, reporting, and photography have an occupational dimension that does not necessarily serve organizational needs. These subgroups compete for control over work in an environment of normative conflict. This study explores the case of newspaper presentation work, and findings from interviews with 17 visual journalists (newspaper photograph, art, or design directors) reveal several sets of norms at work in decision-making about presentation. Findings also show that visual journalists seek to avoid open conflict with other subgroups, but behind the scenes they attempt to control premises for negotiation. By dodging open conflict, subgroups may be short-circuiting important debates over the way news should be visually framed for audiences.

Okhuysen (2001) presents the evidence for an incremental change process in decision-making groups whereby change unfolds through self-generated interruptions. In the study, 168 students with various levels of group familiarity participated in a problem-solving activity. A formal intervention was allowed to be used in half of the groups. Results found that group members initiate self-interruptions by switching their attention to social concerns (in familiar groups) or to discussion instructions (in groups using formal interventions). During such interruptions, members evaluate activities, propose alternative approaches, and change working strategies. Results suggest that familiarity and formal interventions provide flexible structures that lead to superior performance. A central finding reveals that using a formal intervention in familiar groups hurts performance because pre-established interaction patterns are altered.

Hecht et al. (2002) examined the impact of group potency, group goal commitment, and group ability on group performance. Participants in this study were 143 Officer Cadets, working in 51 groups. Consistent with the hypothesis, group potency contributed to the prediction of group performance over and above group ability. In contrast, group goal commitment did not have a strong relation with group performance. On the basis of these results, it seems that "thinking we can" is an important factor in its own right, regardless of the group's ability.

Tschan (2002) reports that it is better if groups both plan and evaluate their performance (see also Pavitt and Johnson 2001). This is similar to West's recommendations for "reflexivity," although evaluation may be as effective if carried out by individuals as by teams (Gurtner et al. (2007).

De Dreu and Weingart (2003) provide a meta-analysis of research on the associations between relationship conflict, task conflict, team performance, and team member satisfaction. Consistent with past theorizing, results revealed relationship conflict as having strong and negative correlations with both team performance and team member satisfaction. In contrast to what has been suggested in both academic research and introductory textbooks, however, results also revealed task conflict as having strong and negative (instead of the predicted positive) correlations with both team performance and team member satisfaction. A bit of conflict—but only a bit—may be helpful and may account for some positive correlations found in the relevant literature. As predicted, conflict had stronger negative relations with team performance in highly complex (decision-making, project, mixed) than in less complex (production) tasks. Finally, task conflict was less negatively related to team performance when task conflict and relationship conflict were weakly, rather than strongly, correlated (see also Carr et al. 2003).

Guinan et al. (1998) combine a consideration of the effects of resources and goal-attainment. They note that software development projects continue to be over budget and behind schedule, researchers continue to look for ways to improve the likelihood of project success. In this research, the authors juxtapose two different views of what influences software development team performance during the requirements development phase. In an examination of 66 teams from 15 companies, it was found that team skill, managerial involvement, and little variance in team experience enable more effective team processes than do software development tools and methods. Furthermore, development teams exhibit both positive and negative boundary-spanning behaviors. Team members promote and champion their projects to the outside environment, which is considered valuable by project stakeholders. They also, however, guard themselves from their environments; keeping important information a secret from stakeholders negatively predicts performance.

For additional related research, see Allen et al. (2003) on the effects of task and reward interdependence; Bonito (2004) on similarity of notions of an idealized group member; Carmel and Sawyer (1998) on differences in team structure and relationships to users and customers of their products; Chang and Bordia (2001) on group cohesion and group performance; Choi and Kim (1999) on "groupthink"as an example of ineffective problem-solving; Cummings and Cross (2003) on cross-cultural social network research; Drach-Zahavy (2004) on balancing job enrichment practices and the team's need for support; Gibson (2003) on the formation of group efficacy; Harrison et al. (2003) on both continuing and one-shot (single session) teams; Jordan et al. (2002) on group potency, social cohesion, and team member exchange; Kim (2003) on coworker task competence, achievement motivation, and performance; Knoblich and Jordan (2003) on planning for the future; Lam et al. (2004) on effects of group self-esteem; Lee et al. (2002) on group potency as a predictor of performance; LePine (2003) on adaptation of role structure when faced with an unforeseen change; Moon et al. (2004) on adaptation to structural change; Pescosolido (2003) on the beneficial effects of group success; Sosik and Jung (2002) on the effects of culture on group characteristics and performance; Stewart and Barrick (2000) on interdependence and team self-leadership; and Tschan et al. (2000) on different behavior for different tasks.

## *Creativity in Teams*

If the object of team performance (meaning) is not simply to provide an adequate response to the situation or to find an appropriate solution to a problem but to find a solution that is creative at one of Taylor's (Taylor 1959, 1975) levels in terms of skill, combining known elements in new ways, extending theories, or introducing new paradigms, then appropriate solutions to the four functional problems will need to be found. The group members must be motivated to go beyond routine problem-solving, they must have the abilities to do so, the formal and informal roles that make this possible, and a leadership style that brings everything together.

After reviewing theories of creativity, Arbet (1991) concluded that the analysis of levels of creativity is essential, even though a description of levels has been overlooked by most writers on the subject. Generally, when levels of creativity are specified, only two levels are mentioned as related to routine or more unusual tasks. For example, Badke-Schaub and Frankenberger (1998), after an analysis of engineering design processes of teams in industry, divided the processes into (a) phases of routine work and (b) critical situations, where design process takes a new direction.Taylor (1975) identified five levels of creativity with examples of each. As they would appear in art and science, the five levels, ranging from high to low, are as follows:

5 (High)—*New meaning (paradigm)*. A contribution that involves the most abstract ideational principles that underlie a body of knowledge. Examples: Einstein, Freud, and Picasso.
4—*Extension of theory*. Basic principles are understood so that older theories can be extended to cover new areas and modification through alternative approaches is possible. Examples: Jung and Adler elaborate on Freud.
3—*Combinations of known elements*. Ingenuity with material, providing combinations to solve old problems in new ways. Examples: Edison's light and Bell's telephone.
2—*Demonstrating skill*. Contribution or solution that involves skill and a new level of proficiency. Example: Stradivari's violin.
1 (Low)—*Spontaneity*. An action that is different where originality and quality of the product are unimportant. Example: Children's drawings.

For creativity at Level 4, Tyre and von Hippel (1997) suggest moving people around in an organization for a new perspective. They were exploring the nature of adaptations made by engineers in response to user's problems with new technology. They concluded that adaptation was a situated process, in that different organizational settings (a) contain different kinds of clues about the underlying issues, (b) offer different resources for generating and analyzing information, and (c) evoke different assumptions on the part of problem solvers. Hence, their observation that learning how to be creative is often enhanced not just by bringing people together, but by moving them around to confront different sorts of clues, gather different kinds of data, use different kinds of tools, and experience different pressures relevant to a given problem.

Engestroem et al. (1995) offer two other solutions to the problem of enhancing expertise for the solution of problems. Instead of moving people around, they suggest having one individual engaged in multiple ongoing tasks to provide polycontextuality. A second solution is to encourage an individual to cross boundaries, to transport ideas, concepts, and instruments from seemingly unrelated domains to the domain of focal inquiry. Most of the ideas that are new for one group are actually borrowed and adapted from other groups.

For the meaning function, the introduction of "brainstorming" is an example of when the experimenter or group leader defines the task as one calling for new ideas and indicates the way that the brainstorming will be conducted. Dennis et al. (1996)

examined the possibility, for both solitary individuals and interactive groups, that it would make a difference if the major categories of a brainstorming problem were presented simultaneously or sequentially. It did. Participants in the sequential presentation condition generated more ideas than did those in the simultaneous condition in both the individual and the group conditions.

For group resources, Klein and Dologite (2000) report that in some cases, computer support tools can help. Having highly creative members in the group will increase group creativity if creativity-relevant processes within the group are relatively high (Taggar 2001, 2002); thus, team creativity depends at least partly on the average of individual creativity (Pirola-Merlo and Mann 2004).

For the integration function, group members are likely to be more creative if they are in a positive mood (Grawitch et al. 2003a, b); high task and interpersonal cohesiveness are also relevant (Craig and Kelly 1999).

For goal-attainment, innovative projects' success is related to the extent to which there is coordination between resource variables (member contributions and effort) and integration variables (communication, mutual support, and cohesion). For Hoegl and Gemuenden (2001), this set of variables constitutes a measure of "teamwork quality." They report a study in which 575 software development team members (mean age 36.6 years) completed questionnaires and interviews. Their results show that team members' ratings of teamwork quality were significantly associated with team performance as rated by team members, team leaders, and team external managers. However, the magnitude of the relationship between teamwork quality and team performance varied with team members' personal work satisfaction and learning.

Transformational leadership is more likely to bring about the necessary motivation and coordination than transactional leadership for groups of university students doing brainstorming (Jung 2001; see also Chap. 4, section on "Leadership").

## Team Training and Feedback

Group effectiveness is interdependent with organizational context, boundaries, and group development. Sundstrom et al. (1990) list the key factors as: (a) organizational culture, (b) technology and task design, (c) mission clarity, (d) autonomy, (e) rewards, (f) performance feedback, (g) training/consultation, and (h) physical environment. Note that these are the familiar functions with the addition of physical environment. Group boundaries may mediate the impact of organizational context on group development.

The research abstracts that serve as one basis for this review do not provide details of the training programs or feedback methods that are used in organizations to improve the performance of individuals, groups, or the whole organization. Training may be needed at all levels since team members are trying to meet individual, team, and organizational goals. For example, DeShon et al. (2004) report on the effects of training at both the individual and group level.

Usually, the function that is the focus of the training or feedback is given with some indication of its effectiveness. Training is typically given before an individual or group begins a new task or when the task format is about to be changed. Feedback is typically given during the process of work or at the end of some phase of production. Thus, feedback influences the final Meaning phase of individual, group, or organization development when performance is evaluated and new goals and ways of working may be proposed.

Culture can affect the feedback. Morrison et al. (2004) report that research on newcomer feedback-seeking may be based on assumptions that are not universally valid: that newcomers are self-assertive, that they perceive their boss as approachable (low-power distance), and that they need to be proactive to obtain the information that they need (informal, individual socialization process). They conducted surveys with 69 students who had recently begun a full-time MBA program in the USA and 62 students enrolled in a full-time MBA program at the Chinese University of Hong Kong. Individuals from the USA reported more newcomer feedback inquiry than individuals from Hong Kong. This difference was related to cultural differences in self-assertiveness and power distance. These results suggest that some of the implicit assumptions about newcomer feedback-seeking may be less valid outside of the USA. In particular, newcomers within low-individualism and high-power distance societies may be less likely to rely on supervisor-focused feedback inquiry for reducing uncertainty and managing their performance.

For reports on the effects of feedback, see Bailey and Thompson (2000) on the effects of performance feedback on air traffic control team cohesion and coordination; Bradley et al. (2003) who offer a temporal framework for the effects of social–emotional versus task interventions (feedback) on team performance; Marks and Panzer (2004) on the influence of team monitoring which can improve both coordination and the teams' own use of feedback processes; Song et al. (1998) on feedback from external raters that improves cooperation in student lab groups.

Having a chance to practice a task gives group members an opportunity to provide their own feedback. Thus, practice may not make perfect, but it may provide movement in that direction (cf. Hollingshead 1998; Mueller 1997).

*Team Training and Feedback and Meaning* Some research reports training on defining the goal or adapting to a new environment as an aspect of meaning. See Gibson (2001) who, based on a sample of nurses, reports that training for goal setting (M) was best for nurses who were not usually effective since they had not set goals; Sawyer et al. (1999) on training US Air Force personnel to set goals and have priorities, that is, train to overcome typical group productivity problems; Marks et al. (2000) on performance implications of leader briefings and team interaction training for team adaptation to novel environments.

However, the focus of the training is usually either on resources, in terms of individual skills rather than equipment, with which the social–psychological consultant does not deal, roles and interpersonal relationships, or leadership and coordination of the activity. As examples of training for skills, see Brown (2003) on the effect of individual verbal self-guidance training on collective efficacy and team performance; Shebilske et al. (1998) on observation versus hands-on practice of complex skills in dyadic, triadic, and tetradic training teams.

*Team Training and Feedback and Integration* To promote effective groups, May and Schwoerer (1994a) encourage managers to provide for successful job experiences, social modeling, verbal encouragement, and interpreting the stress or anxiety experienced during job performance. They especially emphasize activities in the integrative area by providing groups with training that leads to open communication and relationship building among members, and in the resource/skill areas, by matching the team's complexity and uncertainty with members' skills to reduce the stress experienced by employees. Zander (1994) provides a similar range of advice.

*Team Training and Feedback and Resources* Moreland et al. (1998) advocate developing a transactive memory within workgroups. Their system combines the knowledge possessed by individual group members with a shared awareness of who knows what. When group members need information, but cannot remember it themselves or are uncertain about the accuracy of their memories, they can turn to one another for help. Moreland (1999) notes that for training for transactive memory, it is better if group members are trained together. Moreland and Myaskovsky (2000) record the performance benefits of group training which results in transactive memory rather than improved communication; see also Liang et al. (1995). Anand et al. (1998) suggest that a transactive memory should also be developed at the organizational level.

One way to become aware of who knows what is to actually play each of the group roles in turn. From research on three-person groups of US Navy recruits and trainees performing a simulated radar task, Cannon-Bowers et al. (1998) found that cross-training through positional rotation for highly interdependent tasks was effective in developing interpositional knowledge.

*Team Training and Feedback and Goal-Attainment* Some reports describe training (i.e., the meaning of the activity, M) for both the task (M sub R and M sub G) and relationship (M sub I) functions; for example, Entin and Serfaty (1999) conducted research on training for adaptive team coordination. They hypothesized that highly effective teams adapt to stressful situations by using effective coordination strategies. Such teams draw on shared mental models of the situation and the task environment as well as mutual mental models of interacting team members' tasks and abilities to shift to modes of implicit coordination, and thereby reduce coordination overhead. To test this hypothesis, they developed and implemented a team training procedure designed to train teams to adapt by shifting from explicit to implicit modes of coordination and choosing strategies that are appropriate during periods of high stress and workload conditions. A total of 59 naval officers and 1 civilian participated in the study and were organized into six teams of five individuals each plus controls. Results show that the adaptation-training significantly improved the performance from pre- to post-training and when compared with a control group. Results also show that several underlying team process measures exhibited patterns, indicating that adaptive training improved various team processes, including efficient use of mental models, which, in turn, improved the performance.

As a second example of comprehensive training, Smith-Jentsch et al. (1998) describe Team Dimensional Training (TDT), a strategy for enhancing teams' ability to self-correct, that incorporates developing members' teamwork-related knowledge and skills. Guided team self-correction refers to the use of a facilitator who (a) keeps the team's discussion focused, (b) establishes a positive climate, (c) encourages and reinforces active participation, (d) models effective feedback skills, and (e) coaches team members in stating their feedback in a constructive manner. The model of teamwork on which TDT is based was derived from analyses of performance data from 100 shipboard combat information center teams through the US Navy's Tactical Decision-Making Under Stress research and training program.

In addition, the organizational climate for individual and team training should be supportive. See Lance et al. (2002) who report that for 3,000 US Air Force enlisted men who had been retrained for a different Air Force Specialty, retraining climate was a predictor of retraining success and a moderator of the relationship between cross-job retraining time estimates and time to proficiency in the new job; and see also Facteau et al. (1998) on organizational support for a program of 360-degree feedback from subordinates and peers for supervising managers from a large public utility.

Usually, training and feedback help individuals, teams, and the organization to improve their processes. See Arthur et al. (2003) on effectiveness of training in organizations—a meta-analysis of design and evaluation features; Chowdhury et al. (2002) who report that training business school students in teams can build confidence for later success; Green (2002) who reports that for senior leaders in five large organizations 360-degree feedback resulted in significant, enduring individual, team, and organizational improvements.

However, there are exceptions; for example, Hollingshead (1998) who reports that, for student groups, practice in groups helps the groups but not the individuals; Peterson and Behfar (2003) who report that negative feedback can increase both task (R and G) and relationship (I) conflict.

Group members may provide their own feedback. McFarland and Buehler (1995) report that individuals who perform well within an unsuccessful group have more favorable reactions than equally capable individuals who perform poorly within a successful group. They see this as an instance of the "frog-pond" effect, having to do with whether—as the saying goes—one is a large frog (or fish) in a small pond. They conclude that people focus on their relative standing within their group rather than on their group's overall performance level. They hypothesized that people who value their social groups highly would be more likely to take into account their group's performance level in evaluating themselves. In four studies, the frog-pond effect was strongest among individuals with lower collective self-esteem, an individualistic cultural heritage, or a weaker bond toward a particular social group.

There are more variables to consider. Mesch et al. (1994) are positive about negative feedback. Although groups of university students who received negative feedback were less satisfied, these groups set higher goals, developed more strategies, and performed at higher levels than groups that received positive feedback. Tindale et al. (1991) did not find any effect of positive, negative, or no feedback on group performance. However, individual feedback did make a difference.

"Mentoring" is, in effect, the feedback given over time by the same individual. Mentoring can be used to help individuals and organizations adapt to organizational change (Eby 1997) and can have a positive effect on career optimism (Friedman et al. 1998).

Johnston et al. (1997) provide a set of measures to be used in training for decision-making. Cannon-Bowers and Salas (1997a) review the literature on team performance and training and describe a framework for conceptualizing team performance measures in training. (See also Salas et al. 1997; Stout et al. 1997).

## Stress

Stress for groups at work is a concern since it has negative effects (Driskell et al. 1999; Jex and Thomas 2003).

If group members feel effective, they are less bothered by stress. Jex and Bliese (1999), based on survey data collected from 2,273 US Army soldiers representing 36 companies, found that both self- and collective-efficacy moderated the relationship between stressors and strains. Multilevel random coefficient model results revealed that respondents with strong self-efficacy reacted less negatively in terms of psychological and physical strain to long work hours and work overload than did those reporting low levels of efficacy. In addition, respondents with high levels of self-efficacy responded more positively in terms of job satisfaction to tasks with high significance than did those with low efficacy. The results also revealed that group-level collective efficacy moderated the relationship between work overload and job satisfaction and between task significance and organizational commitment.

Presumably, similar findings would hold for peacekeepers—and would at least represent a working hypothesis for nonmilitary, explicitly nonviolent teams.

Stress also has less effect if group members are high on emotional intelligence (Nikolaou and Tsaousis 2002) or if they have more control over their job (Fernet et al. 2004).

Job insecurity is a form of stress. Sverke et al. (2002) used meta-analytic techniques to estimate how job insecurity relates to its postulated outcomes. Consistent with the conceptual framework, the results indicate that job insecurity has detrimental consequences for employees' job attitudes, organizational attitudes, health, and, to some extent, their behavioral relationship with the organization. The behavioral consequences of insecurity are more detrimental among manual, as compared with nonmanual, workers.

Team culture can also be a variable. Smit and Schabracq (1998) investigated team cultures of middle management teams. Their results show that team cultures have a strong, but "invisible" impact on the performance as well as on health of employees.

Another source of stress can be work/family conflicts. Here, time can be a factor in reducing the stress. Secret and Sprang (2001) utilized the spillover conceptual framework to examine the effects of structural (formal policies) and dynamic (informal supervisory support) aspects of the workplace on the financial stress, time-based problems, and role strain of employed parents. Data were obtained by telephone interview from an availability sample of 374 employed parents in several different workplaces. Logistic regression analyses provided partial support for the hypotheses that each of four groups of different family-friendly policies would affect specific work-family outcomes. One structural component, leave time allowance policy, helped ease the time-based problems of employed parents. The other structural components such as child-care assistance, alternative work arrangements, or stress management programs did not affect the work-family stress variables. Several dynamic components of the work environment, particularly informal supervisory support, were associated with all three measures of work-family stress (see also Behson 2002; Judge and Colquitt 2004).

To provide data for training for stress management, May and Schwoerer (1994b) recommend using a survey of physical symptoms, cumulative trauma disorders (such as the carpel tunnel syndrome), observations, video recordings, and employee interviews about their jobs, tools, and pain experienced at work. As an example of the effects of work stressors, professionals in software development groups were indeed found to be subject to "burnout" under conditions of high stress (Sonnentag et al. 1994). Sokol and Aiello (1993) add that it is helpful to make the intact work unit the target for stress management training.

## Organizational Factors

Recall that with regard to the cybernetic hierarchy, the various system levels are in the order, from the top, cultural (M) system, social system (I) (which includes organization, group, and individual roles), personality system (G), and biological system and environment (R). (With regard to Parsonian functional theory, and its AGIL or MIGR scheme, see also the "Introduction" to Chap. 1 and "Note 1" of Chap. 4.) Although we focus at the organizational level, we will not be surprised if the research also refers to the group and individual level.

*Organization and Motivation (G in the Parsonian Functional Scheme Noted Above)* Gibson and Papa (2000) were interested in the mud, the blood, and the beer (also the name of a rock band) guys as an example of organizational osmosis in blue-collar workgroups. They examined how a common ideological grounding and anticipatory socialization experiences increase identification mechanisms among blue-collar workgroups. A sample consisting of 51 blue-collar employees with 1–33 years of job experience at a major international manufacturing company participated in interviews. Their results show that the workers considered themselves naturally suited to the job, and readily identified one or more parental figures as being responsible for developing their strong work ethic. Almost all had family members working at the plant and had previous knowledge of work there before becoming employed. Hard physical work and demanding work conditions were not only actual conditions at the plant but were perceived to be outward displays of masculinity or machismo. Blue-collar workers reported circumstances that may be termed organizational osmosis, that is, the seemingly effortless adoption of the ideas, values, and culture of an organization on the basis of preexisting socialization experiences. This ideological grounding is influenced by interaction with family, friends, and peers during anticipatory stages. Because these newcomers strongly identify with the values and goals of the organization, they submit to mechanisms of control and discipline in their workgroup.

Members of different departments may have different perceptions of the importance of the organization. Nauta and Sanders (2001) examined (a) differences between departments within organizations with regard to perceptions of their own goals and those of other departments, (b) determinants of these perceived goal differences, and (c) consequences of perceived goal differences in terms of interdepartmental conflict. Interviews were conducted with 41 managers and 85 low-level employees from the manufacturing, planning, and marketing departments of 11 manufacturing plants. Results show that employees in general believed that they pursued goals that were valuable to the organization more strongly than other departments. Manufacturing and marketing employees perceived the largest goal differences with regard to their own department goals. Planning employees perceived the largest goal differences with the manufacturing department with regard to the goals of marketing, and with the marketing department with regard to manufacturing goals. Perceived goal differences were positively related to interdepartmental conflict frequency and seriousness. As regards conflict prevention: among other advantages, this study demonstrates the importance of reducing perceived goal differences, which can be achieved partly by interventions at the organizational level.

In relation to commitment to the organization in contrast to commitment to the unit, Postmes, Tanis, and De Wit (2001) report the results of studies that show that horizontal communications (informal, with proximate colleagues, of socio-emotional content) are less strongly related to levels of commitment at both organizational and unit level, than are vertical communications (strategic information and communication with management). In addition, it was shown that vertical communication from senior management predicts organizational commitment best, whereas commitment with the unit has a higher correlation with vertical communication at that level. Their results are inconsistent with approaches to commitment in organizations and teams that assume commitment stems from interpersonal relations, but more consistent with approaches to organizational commitment based on a social identity approach which tends to focus on social-level antecedents of commitment and identification.

For more research with an organizational emphasis, see Smidts et al. (2001) on employee communication, perceived external prestige, and organizational identification.

*Organization and Resources (R)* The concern about the effective use of human resources by organizations is reflected in special courses and training devoted to "human resource management." Gibb (2001) notes that recent research exploring a range of arguments about trends in human resource management provides contrasting evidence in evaluating the state of human resource management. Methods using either (a) fit with "best practice" or (b) fit with contingencies as ways of evaluating the state of human resource management have been foremost.

Investigating the employees' "point of view" has been proposed as an alternative in some recent studies. The research reported here (Gibb 2001) is based on this alternative method. It describes employees' views of human resource management in their organizations based on a survey of 2,632 employees in 73 companies. The findings show that employees reported areas of strength in human resource management that include training and development, rewards, and levels of personal motivation. Employees also rated the performance of human resource staff highly across a range of services. Notable areas of weakness in human resource management, in employees' estimations, existed in the management of staffing levels, aspects of recruitment and retention, communication, and with levels of morale in the organization as a whole. These findings justify a mixed but overall positive picture of the state of human resource management (Gibb 2001).

*Organization and Integration (I)* One of the aspects of an organization that affects the members' feelings about each other is the extent to which the organizational procedures are ethical (related to *Meaning*) and seen as based on procedural and distributive justice. However, most of the research has been on procedural justice.

One scheme for analyzing justice, especially in organizational settings, uses Greenberg's (Greenberg 1993) four-cell scheme. This includes a distinction between procedural justice (based on whether the means for reaching decisions are fair) and distributive justice (whether the outcome or the resulting distribution of "goods" is equitable). Cross-cutting these two categories is a distinction between justice achieved by structural (formalized) or social means. Procedural justice from structural and social means, respectively, are here called systemic and informational justice. The corresponding terms for distributive justice are configural and interpersonal justice. Social justice is also "interactional" with regard to whether people are treated politely with explanations of procedures and outcomes.

Colquitt et al. (2001) conducted a meta-analytic review of 183 justice studies. The results suggest that although different justice dimensions are moderately to highly related, they contribute incremental explained variance in fairness perceptions. The results also illustrate the overall and unique relationships among distributive, procedural, interpersonal, and informational justice and several major organizational outcomes (e.g., job satisfaction, organizational commitment, evaluation of authority, organizational citizenship behavior, withdrawal, and performance).

Rahim et al. (2000), in a study of 202 currently employed undergraduate students (mean age 22.92 years), examined relationships between employees' perceptions of organizational justice and the styles they use for managing conflict with their supervisors. Regression analysis of questionnaire data indicated that distributive, procedural, and interactional justice were generally positively related to the use of more cooperative conflict management styles (i.e., integrating, obliging, and compromising). Two two-way interaction effects were observed as well, such that higher interactional justice was related to greater use of the integrating style primarily when distributive justice was low and procedural justice was high. Additionally, distributive justice was positively related to use of an avoiding style.

Hauenstein et al. (2001) report that although there are many studies that utilize the constructs of procedural and distributive justice, this research tends to ignore the implications of the bivariate relationship between the two constructs. The stronger the association between the two constructs, the more problematic ignoring this relationship becomes. They conducted a meta-analysis to estimate the relationship between procedural and distributive justice. They also conducted an initial assessment of extent to which the relationship between procedural and distributive justice was context-sensitive. Finally, a series of methodological moderators was evaluated. Their results indicated that the relationship between procedural and distributive justice is strong across all studies. However, this relationship was moderated by research context, and even within research context, there was substantial evidence of variability.

Hendrix et al. (1998) developed and tested a model linking justice perceptions to a series of variables leading to turnover. In their study, 310 full-time employees (aged 18–70 years) completed a justice-perception scale and measures of intrinsic job satisfaction, organizational commitment, attendance motivation, workgroup performance, turnover intentions, and turnover. Positive procedural and distributive justice perceptions were associated with increased intrinsic and extrinsic job satisfaction and organizational commitment. Procedural justice perceptions were positively related to perceptions of workgroup performance. Distributive justice perceptions were negatively related to turnover intentions. Actual turnover was directly influenced by only one factor, turnover intentions, and indirectly by all variables in the model except for workgroup performance perceptions and extrinsic job satisfaction.

Naumann and Bennett (2000) collected data from 220 employees of two banks (mean ages 30 and 32.9 years) who responded to surveys. Workgroup perceptions of cohesion and supervisor visibility in demonstrating procedural justice were associated with the development of procedural justice climate. Procedural justice climate was positively associated with helping behaviors after the effects of individual procedural justice perceptions were controlled for. They conclude that procedural justice climate is an important contextual variable expected to influence work attitudes and behaviors beyond the contributions of individual procedural justice perceptions.

For groups, Naumann and Bennett (2002) examined the effect of procedural justice climate, defined as a distinct group-level cognition about how the workgroup as a whole is treated, on workgroup performance in a sample of 34 workgroups from two organizations. They hypothesized that the relationship between procedural justice climate and performance is indirect, operating through helping behavior. Group-level helping behavior fully mediated the relationship between procedural justice climate and perceived performance. However, the same results were not found when financial performance data were used as a measure of workgroup performance. Implications for the study's findings are discussed. More general questions about the links among team cognition, whether a team "thinks," and deficiencies in complex systems are considered by Cooke et al. (2009).

Adding to this pool of findings for what one might have imagined would be a straightforward relationship: Colquitt et al. (2002) examined antecedents and consequences of procedural justice climate, again defined as a distinct team-level cognition regarding how fairly the team as a whole is treated procedurally, in a sample of manufacturing teams. The purpose was to investigate the relationship between team-level procedural justice and team effectiveness, operationalized in terms of team performance and team absenteeism. A total of 1,747 employees working in 88 teams took part in the study. The results showed that climate level (i.e., the average procedural justice perception within the team) was significantly related to both team performance and team absenteeism. Moreover, the effects of climate level were moderated by climate strength, such that the relationships were more beneficial in stronger climates. In addition, team size and team collectivism were significant antecedents of climate level, and team size and team demographic diversity predicted climate strength.

Colquitt (2004) reported the results of two studies that examined reactions to procedural justice in teams. Both studies predicted that individual members' reactions would be driven not just by their own procedural justice levels but also by the justice experienced by other team members. Study 1 examined intact student teams, whereas Study 2 occurred in a laboratory setting. The results showed that individual members' own justice interacted with others' justice, such that higher levels of role performance occurred when justice was consistent within the team. These effects were strongest in highly interdependent teams and weakest for members who were benevolent with respect to equity sensitivity.

For additional research on justice, see Elovainio (2001) on justice and occupational stress; Forrest (2002) on procedural fairness and conflict; Hegtvedt et al. (2002) on work-family policies; Lamertz (2002) on social relationships of employees with peers and managers and perceptions of organizational justice; Maertz et al. (2004) on procedural justice perceptions and organization attraction; Sinclair (2003) on distributive and procedural justice and team effectiveness; Weaver and Conlon (2003) on organizations that present a facade of choice.

For additional research on ethics, see Cameron et al. (2004) on virtuousness and performance; Treviño et al. (2003) on ethical leadership; Treviño et al. (2001) on ethical climate and ethical culture; and Vitell and Paolillo (2004), on a cross-cultural study.

*Trust* Spreitzer, Noble, Mishra, and Cooke (1999) extend traditional models of group effectiveness by articulating the role that team trust and empowerment play in predicting performance of process improvement work teams. A two-part model is developed—the first part predicting team involvement and the second part predicting team effectiveness. In the first half of the model, it is hypothesized that team trust, empowerment, recognition, and conflict resolution skills enhance levels of team member involvement. In the second half, it is hypothesized that team member involvement, role clarity, and access to information enhance levels of team performance. The model is tested on a sample of 43 process-improvement work teams from a Big Three automotive firm. Multiple referents are used to avoid problems of common method bias. Higher levels of empowerment, trust and conflict resolution (measured together), and recognition are related to team involvement. In turn, greater team involvement along with greater role clarity and access to information are related to higher levels of team performance. Team involvement is found to mediate the relationship between the variables in the first part of the model and team performance.

With a focus on the amount of trust between salespeople and customers, Jap (2001) observed that the use of sales-reps to build trusting relationships and customer satisfaction is a strategic choice in many organizations. Underlying this is an assumption that a trustworthy sales-rep can play a critical role in driving the ultimate success of the firm's strategy to enhance an organizational customer's economic and noneconomic satisfaction. In this research, Jap contends that the customer relationship lifecycle is a critical moderator of the impact of a trustworthy sales-rep on customer satisfaction. Survey results of approximately 1,400 channel customers (e.g., those in mutually dependent organizations) indicate that the consequential value of interpersonal trust in a sales-rep is both time- and context-dependent. The sales-rep plays a minimal role in influencing satisfaction outcomes in the exploration phase of a customer relationship. However, as the relationship progresses through the buildup and mature phases, the interpersonal trust developed with a sales-rep can add tremendous value to a customer's satisfaction with the relationship and the firm's products. When the relationship is in decline, the sales-rep is useful for creating relationship satisfaction, but has an adverse effect on satisfaction with margins (i.e., the parties' evaluation of financial or other return).

Spector and Jones (2004) used survey data from 127 professional-level employees working in eight industries to assess the effects of respondents' trusting stance and (a) the trustee's organization membership (internal or external), (b) the hierarchical relationship (supervisor or peer), and (c) the gender of the trustee, on initial trust level for a new project team member. They found that trusting stance was positively related to initial trust level. They also found an interaction effect between respondent gender and trustee gender on initial trust. Specifically, male initial trust level was higher for a new male team member and lower for a new female team member.

Who trusts? Gilbert and Tang (1998), in an examination of organizational trust antecedents, surveyed 83 managerial employees in a branch of a federal governmental agency located in a large metropolitan city in the southwestern USA. Multiple regression analysis showed that age, marital status, and workgroup cohesion were positively associated with organizational trust. Organizational trust did not differ by either race or gender.

For a comparison of trust and lack of trust, Wells and Kipnis (2001) examined several consequences of trust in terms of influence strategies used and the frequency with which people interact with each other. The study also examined the extent to which the technology of work affects management's dependency on their employees. It was found that distrust of subordinates by 275 managers (mean age 41.5 years) is associated with the use of strong tactics of influence, little dependency on employees, and the use of personal-related characteristics to explain distrust. It was also found that distrust of managers by 267 subordinates (mean age 36.6 years) is associated with the use of strong methods of influence, less interaction, less attempts to influence, and the use of personal-related characteristics to explain lack of trust. These findings have clear implications for understanding the relation among worker trust, dependency, and social influence. The data suggest that both employees and employers could benefit from considering the importance of a trusting relationship in the workplace.

For additional research on trust, see Krosgaard et al. (2002) on employees' trust in managers.

For additional research related to integration, see Duffy and Shaw (2000) on envy; Losada and Heaphy (2004) on the ratio of positivity to negativity in interaction; Sias et al. (2004) on workplace friendship deterioration processes; and Totterdell et al. (2004) on organizational networks and employees' affect.

## Women (Gender)

Some gender differences associated with expectations for behavior and actual behavior between women and men have already been noted in the summaries of research on group and team interaction. However, there is more "political" concern about the extent to which persons of different genders should play different roles than for most of the other variables that affect interaction. So, we also include a separate summary of some of the research on gender at the organizational and group levels—which, of course, relates directly to addressing structural violence.

*Organizational Support* Culture plays a part. Bajdo and Dickson (2001) conducted a cross-cultural examination of the relationship between organizational culture and women's advancement to management in organizations. Data came from the Global Leadership and Organizational Behavior Effectiveness Research Project, a cross-cultural study of societal culture, organizational culture, and leadership. Results of this study indicate that aspects of organizational culture typically associated with women are related to women's progress. In organizations in which organization members reported shared values of high humane orientation and high gender equity, organization members also reported high percentages of women in management relative to other organizations in their society. In addition, organizational leadership cultural practices that emphasized high humane orientation, high gender equity, high-performance orientation, and low-power distance were also related to reports of high percentages of women in management relative to societal norms. Results of regression analysis predicting the percentage of women in management from the dimensions of organizational culture indicated that gender equity practices and values emphasizing humane orientation contributed significantly to the prediction of the percentage of women in management. Organizational cultural practices related to gender equity were found to be the most important predictor of the percentage of women in management.

Law, too, is clearly important. McGauran (2001) reports that in-store equal opportunities policies are effectively neutralized, and furthermore, are neutralized in nationally specific ways which can be related to differences between France and Ireland in the organization of labor market regulation and in women's labor-force participation.

*Women and Meaning* Van Vianen and Fischer (2002) in Study 1 ($N = 327$) investigated gender differences in organizational culture preferences, both in a managerial sample and a sample of nonmanagerial professionals in private sector organizations. It was shown that gender differences only existed in the nonmanagerial groups, with women showing less masculine culture preferences than men did. In Study 2 ($N = 350$), they examined the effects of organizational culture preferences on the ambitions of staff employees and middle-level managers to pursue a career at a top management level in one governmental organization. The results show that organizational culture preferences were predictive for ambition of nonmanagerial employees, but not for that of middle management employees. Overall, women were less ambitious than men, and even ambitious women perceived work–home conflict as an important barrier to career advancement.

For additional related research see Elvira and Cohen (2001) on organizational sex composition labor turnover.

*Women and Resources* Thomas-Hunt and Phillips (2004) examined the effects of member expertise and gender on others' perceptions of expertise, actual—and own perceptions of—influence, and on group performance on a decision-making task. The authors' findings are consistent with social role theory and expectation states theory. Women were *less* influential when they possessed expertise, and having expertise decreased how expert others perceived them to be. Conversely, having expertise was relatively positive for men. These differences were reflected in group performance, as groups with a female expert underperformed groups with a male expert. Thus, contrary to common expectations, possessing expertise did not ameliorate the gender effects often seen in workgroups.

*Women and Integration* Rosen (1998) examined (a) the effects of three types of unwanted sexual experiences in the workplace (gender harassment, unwanted sexual attention, and coercion/imposition) on the psychological well-being of male and female US Army soldiers and (b) the mediating or moderating roles of appraisal of sexual harassment, organizational climate, and the sociodemographic profile of victims. A survey was administered to 1,060 male and 305 female soldiers at three Army posts in the USA. Unwanted sexual experiences were found to be significant predictors of psychological symptoms for male and female soldiers.

Hutson-Comeaux and Kelly (1996) investigated whether interaction style mediates the effect of sex on group task performance, specifically, whether women's more
socio-emotional style facilitated performance on an optimizing task and whether
men's more task-oriented style facilitated performance on a maximizing task. A
total of 400 university women and men worked alone or in same sex triads. Group
interactions were coded according to Bales's (e.g., Bales 1950, 1970). *Interaction
Process Analysis.* Analyses produced the predicted sex-differentiated interaction
styles, such that female groups engaged in more positive socio-emotional behavior
and male groups engaged in more active task behavior. Performance analyses were
also as predicted. Female groups performed significantly better on the optimizing
task, whereas male groups tended to perform better on the maximizing task. However, further analyses revealed that interaction process variables did not appear to
mediate the relationship between sex and task performance.

*Women and Goal-Attainment* What strategies are used by women in high-status
positions? Davies-Netzley (1998) examined women in corporate positions "above
the glass ceiling" and explored their perceptions of corporate mobility and strategies for success in male-dominated elite positions. Through interviews with seven
male (mean age 52 years) and nine female (mean age 50 years) corporate presidents
and chief executive officers in Southern California, it was found that while White
men promote the dominant ideology of individualism and patriarchal gender ideology as explanations of corporate mobility and success, White women emphasize
alternative perspectives by confirming the importance of social networks and peer
similarities for succeeding in elite positions. These women strategically attempt to
increase their cultural capital to negotiate male-dominated networks and maintain
their high-status positions through such measures as obtaining advanced educational degrees or modifying speech and behavior.

For additional research, see Frink et al. (2003) on team performance, cohesion,
leadership, and the gender composition; Talmud and Izraeli (1999) on gender differences in roles as directors.

## Conflicts in Organizations and Groups

DeChurch and Marks (2001) examined the effects of group conflict management
style on group effectiveness. Business school students ($N = 96$; mean age 23.5 years)
participating in a group project completed the Intragroup Conflict Scale (Jehn 1992;
cf. Jehn and Bendersky 2003) concerning task conflict, and the Organizational Conflict Inventory (Rahim 1983) concerning conflict management. Additional collected
data included the course instructor's evaluation of group outcomes. Results show
that the use of agreeable conflict management in response to task conflict was associated with greater group satisfaction. The relationship between task conflict and
group performance was positive when conflict was actively managed, and negative
when it was passively managed. Similarly, task conflict improved group satisfaction

when managed with agreeable behavior, and harmed satisfaction when neutral or disagreeable behaviors were used. They concluded that active conflict management promotes performance and that agreeable conflict management promotes group satisfaction.

Wade-Benzoni (2002) conducted an investigation that includes four studies that examined the allocation of resources across generations in the presence of intergenerational conflict. Participants were 118 MBA graduate students and 89 university administrative staff. Results indicate that the behavior of previous generations influences how a present generation treats future generations (e.g., in the stewardship of future generations' benefits and resources).

Ayoko et al. (2003) present both a qualitative and quantitative examination of workplace conflict, and of the emotional reactions to bullying and counterproductive behaviors. Three studies were undertaken. Data for Study 1 emerged from semistructured interviews conducted with 50 group leaders and members from six workgroups in two large organizations. Interviews were transcribed and analyzed using systematic interpretative techniques. Findings from Study 1 showed that conflict induced a variety of emotional and behavioral responses. Data from Study 2 were collected from 660 employees from seven public sector organizations using a structured open-ended survey. Results from Study 2 revealed that the majority of respondents perceived their managers as bullies. Study 3 surveyed 510 staff in 122 workgroups from five organizations. Regression analysis revealed that differing conflict events were associated with bullying, emotional reactions, and counterproductive behaviors. In particular, prolonged conflict increased incidents of bullying. Higher levels of bullying were predictive of workplace counterproductive behaviors such as purposely wasting company material and supplies, purposely doing one's work incorrectly, and purposely damaging a valuable piece of property belonging to the employer.

Glomb and Liao (2003), in a cross-level study of 149 employees from 25 groups, demonstrate the impact of group social context on individual interpersonal aggression. Their results suggest that both being the target of aggression and the mean level of aggression in a workgroup (absent the target individual) are predictors of employees' reports of engaging in aggression. Effects persisted when individual differences related to aggression, demographics, and situational variables were controlled.

Being unwilling to communicate with other members of an organization is a mild form of aggression. Avtgis (2000) examined the relationship between unwillingness to communicate and quality of organizational relationships of 200 employees of several organizations. Employees completed the Unwillingness to Communicate Scale (Burgoon 1976) and the Organizational Communication Relationships subscale of the International Communication Association Audit (Goldhaber and Rogers 1979). Correlations indicate that people who reported increased communication and high reward in communication also reported greater relational satisfaction and greater perceived organizational influence.

When there is a problem, with whom do individuals seek help? Lee (1997) conducted a laboratory experiment with 64 male and 89 female undergraduates and a field study with 184 physicians and 198 nurses which showed that there was more help seeking between equal status than unequal status individuals. Furthermore, both studies revealed that males sought more help in collective than individualistic organizational norms, though the trend was not apparent for females.

## Time: A Goal-Attainment Variable for Groups and Individuals

What happens over time? Harrison et al. (2002) note that time serves as a medium for collaboration in teams, allowing members to exchange personal and task-related information. They propose that stronger team reward contingencies stimulate collaboration. As time passes, increasing collaboration weakens the effects of surface-level (demographic) diversity on team outcomes but strengthens those of deep-level (psychological) diversity. Also, perceived diversity transmits the impact of actual diversity on team social integration, which, in turn, affects task performance. Results from four waves of data on 144 student project teams support these propositions and the strong relevance of time to research on work team diversity.

Deadlines make a difference. McGrath and colleagues (McGrath 1991; McGrath and Berdahl 1998) have examined the use of time in relation to the task. Groups with deadlines develop at a different pace than those without deadlines. Having a time limit generally results in faster performance but lower creativity (Kelly and Karau 1993).

Waller et al. (2002) tested this assumption that attention to time is a catalyst that motivates groups to pace work under deadline in 38 groups of MBA or master of science students, some working under stable deadlines and others working under changed deadlines. Their results indicate that groups steadily increase the attention to time as deadlines near, rather than sharply increasing such attention at the midpoint, but they engage in task transitions at or near the midpoint of allotted time.

For additional research on time, see Durham et al. (2000) on group goals, time pressure, group efficacy, information-seeking strategy, and performance; Waller et al. (1999) on individuals' time-oriented behavior and group-level polychronic behavior (multitasking).

## Organizational Support for Work

The research reported in this section represents a mix of group and organizational support. Aladwani (2002) collected data from system development project leaders working in 84 US organizations. The findings suggest that higher social integration, and consequently, higher system development project performance is best attained when management provides basic support for the work of the project. The results also reveal that the nature of the relationship between social integration and project performance may be contingent upon some other factors.

As a result of meta-analyses, Svyantek et al. (1999) find that team building impacts positively on workgroup productivity, and Klein et al. (2009) find that it impacts positively on cognitive, affective, and process outcomes as well.

Stinglhamber and Vandenberghe (2003), using a sample of 238 employees, conducted a longitudinal study to examine the linkages between the favorableness of intrinsically and extrinsically satisfying job conditions, perceived organizational support (POS), perceived supervisor support, affective commitment to the organization and supervisor, and turnover. Affective commitment to the supervisor was found to completely mediate the effect of perceived supervisor support on turnover, whereas neither POS nor organizational affective commitment were significantly related to turnover. POS partially mediated the effect of favorable intrinsically satisfying job conditions on organizational affective commitment and fully mediated the effect of extrinsically satisfying job conditions on organizational affective commitment. Finally, perceived supervisor support totally mediated the effect of favorable intrinsically satisfying job conditions on affective commitment to the supervisor.

Lok and Crawford (2004) examined the effects of organizational culture and leadership styles on job satisfaction and organizational commitment in samples of Hong Kong and Australian managers. Statistically significant differences between the two samples were found for measures of innovative and supportive organizational cultures, job satisfaction, and organizational commitment, with the Australian sample having higher mean scores on all these variables. However, differences between the two samples for job satisfaction and commitment were removed after statistically controlling for organizational culture, leadership, and respondents' demographic characteristics. For the combined samples, innovative and supportive cultures, and a consideration leadership style, had positive effects on both job satisfaction and commitment, with the effects of an innovative culture on satisfaction and commitment, and the effect of a consideration leadership style on commitment, being stronger in the Australian sample. Also, an "initiating structure" leadership style had a negative effect on job satisfaction for the combined sample.

Eisenberger et al. (2002), in three studies, investigated the relationships among employees' perception of supervisor support (PSS), POS, and employee turnover. Study 1 found, with 314 employees drawn from a variety of organizations that PSS was positively related to temporal change in POS, suggesting that PSS leads to POS. Study 2 established, with 300 retail sales employees, that the PSS–POS relationship increased with perceived supervisor status in the organization. Study 3 found, with 493 retail sales employees, evidence consistent with the view that POS completely mediated a negative relationship between PSS and employee turnover. These studies suggest that supervisors, to the extent that they are identified with the organization, contribute to POS, and ultimately, to job retention. (See also Acker 2004; and Stinglhamber and Vandenberghe 2004).

Grant-Vallone and Ensher (2001) examined the effect of two types of work and personal life conflict and organizational support on expatriate employees' mental well-being. Workers ($N = 118$; mean age 44 years) at an international agency completed questionnaires concerning general demographic characteristics, conflict between work and personal life, organizational support, depression, and vitality. Results show that work-personal life conflict was related to workers' depression and anxiety. Personal work life conflict was related to health concerns. Organizational support exerted significant main effects on well-being and conflict; however, organizational support did not buffer the effects of conflict on expatriates' well-being. Although organizations are often concerned with personal life interfering with work for expatriates, they should also be concerned with how work is interfering with expatriates' personal lives. Findings suggest that programs addressing both types of conflict are imperative to retaining high-quality employees.

Note that support is just one of several related variables that help address conflict. Among others are availability of problem-solving guidelines, the main motivations and work procedures of all concerned, and of course the emotional, intellectual, and value-oriented "climate" qualities.

Kiewitz et al. (2002) examined the moderating impact of psychological climate on the relationship between perceived organizational politics and both commitment and turnover intent. Data were gathered from 131 restaurant employees (aged 18–51 years) who completed surveys at work. Confirmatory factor analysis revealed that a six-factor conceptualization (supportive management, role clarity, contribution, recognition, self-expression, and challenge) provided the most adequate model representation of the psychological climate construct. Results indicate that politics perceptions interacted with each climate factor (with the exception of challenge) in predicting commitment. Conversely, politics perceptions interacted only with supportive management and self-expression to predict turnover intent.

For more on organizational support, see Hochwarter et al. (2003) on the relationship between politics perceptions and work outcomes; O'Driscoll and Randall (1999) on organizational support and satisfaction and job involvement; Tansky and Cohen (2001) on satisfaction with employee development (self and others) and organizational commitment; and Whitener (2001) on human resource practices, trust-in-management, and organizational commitment.

Bishop et al. (2000) conducted an analysis of data from 380 manufacturing plant employees (average age of 36.9 years) and 9 supervisors. Job performance was related to team commitment; intention to quit was related to organizational commitment; and organizational citizenship behavior was related to both team and organizational commitment. Commitment mediated the relationships between support (including more than organizational support) and the outcome variables.

Parker et al. (2003) report that meta-analytic findings indicate that psychological climate, operationalized as individuals' perceptions of their work environment, does have significant relationships with individuals' work attitudes, motivation, and performance. Structural equation modeling analyses of the meta-analytic correlation matrix indicated that the relationships of psychological climate with employee motivation and performance are fully mediated by employees' work attitudes.

Do socialization tactics provide support? Cable and Parsons (2001) examined how firms' socialization tactics help establish person–organization fit between newcomers and organizations. They used a three-wave longitudinal design that followed 101 individuals (aged 18–44 years) over two years: the authors distributed the first survey before their job search began and the last survey 18 months after their college graduation. Results indicated that newcomers' "subjective fit" perceptions, as well as changes in their values, were associated with two types of socialization tactics: content (i.e., tactics that are sequential and fixed-versus-variable and random) and social aspects (i.e., tactics that emphasize serial and investiture processes rather than disjunctive and divestiture processes). The context dimension of socialization tactics, where socialization is collective and formal (versus individualized and informal), was not related to person–organization fit in this study.

Of course, the effects of "socialization tactics" may vary with context—such as the extent to which roles are clearly defined, the group's ethos (democratic? problem-solving?), and how well the group's ethos matches that of a given individual.

Joshi and Randall (2001) report research results, based on a sample of 151 salespeople, showing that organizational controls affect both the salesperson's task clarity and the salesperson's affective commitment to the organization. Furthermore, results show that task clarity affects the salesperson performance, but it has no effect on customer orientation. Affective commitment, however, has a significant impact on both outcomes.

As a possible example of how context might mediate team support, Byers and Slack (2001) explore the manner in which decisions are made in small leisure businesses and the factors that constrain the decision choices of their owners. The data for the study come from in-depth interviews with 16 small business owners. The results show that these individuals engage primarily in adaptive decision-making. Their decision choices are constrained by factors such as limited time, and the desire to retain control of their business—and they may be unique to the leisure industry, given the fact that in nearly all the cases studied the activity which formed the basis of the business was also the owners' hobby. This latter factor was constraining in that the individuals involved still wished to pursue their hobby while simultaneously operating their business.

## Virtual Teams and Organizations

The research on virtual teams in organizations is similar to the research on group support systems, except that with virtual teams, the only communication between team members is via computer, often without comparison with face-to-face interaction by the same members.

Many NGOs, relief organizations, negotiating bodies, and the like share similar "issues" such as geographically dispersed teams, online donations or sales, and interactive websites. For *any* organizations that work partly online, moreover, there are both unique opportunities and challenges as regards equity and avoiding structural violence.

*Virtual Teams and Organizations and Meaning* The meaning of the work in virtual teams poses problems for the dotcom leader. Brown and Gioia (2002) note that the business model that looks likely to dominate the future in the wake of the convergence between Internet and traditional economies is the "bricks and clicks" organization. The authors conducted an in-depth study of the top executives of a prototypical Fortune 500 company's online division. Researchers tracked and interviewed the president and other top management team (TMT) members over the first 22 months of the launch of the e-business venture. Findings show that two contextual features, the extraordinary speed and the unsettling complexity/ambiguity of the online business environment, profoundly affected not only leadership requirements but also other key managerial processes, including communication, decision-making, and vision. Two substantive themes emerged: (a) coping with organizational identity/image tensions with the offline parent organization and (b) becoming a holographic learning organization. The authors draw upon and extend some of the emerging literature on shared/relational and dispersed leadership to explain how dotcom leaders can adapt to the challenging contextual and substantive features of the e-business environment through the practice of distributive leadership, which can be distinguished from prior related articulations of the concept.

Maznevski and Chudoba (2000) examined technological and group dynamics of global virtual teams and developed a grounded theory of global virtual team processes and performance. Three global virtual teams, which are internationally distributed groups of people with an organizational mandate to make or implement decisions with international components and implications, were observed over a period of 21 months. Global virtual team members completed interviews and questionnaires. Other collected data included observations and company documents. Results show that global virtual teams were assigned tasks that were strategically important and highly complex. The teams rarely met in person, conducting almost all of their interaction and decision-making using communications technology. Effective global virtual team interaction comprises a series of communication incidents, each configured by aspects of the team's structural and process elements. Effective outcomes were associated with a fit among an interaction incident's form, decision process, and complexity. It is concluded that effective global virtual teams sequence these incidents to generate a deep rhythm of regular face-to-face incidents interspersed with less intensive, shorter incidents using various media.

*Virtual Teams and Organizations and Resources* Yoo and Kanawattanachai (2001) examined the developments of transactive memory systems and collective mind and their influence on performance in virtual teams. Building on an emerging body of socio-cognitive literature, it is argued that transactive memory systems and the collective mind are two important variables that explain team performance. This hypothesis was tested with a longitudinal data set collected from 38 virtual teams of graduate management students (mean age 28 years) from six universities in four countries over an eight-week period. Results suggest that the influence of team members' early communication volume on team performance decreases as teams develop transactive memory systems and a collective mind. Results further suggest that the development of a collective mind represents a high-order learning in team settings.

   With regard to the acceptability of groupware—group software—itself, Driskell and Salas (2006) caution that software development must take account of group dynamics including a groups' specific activities.

*Virtual Teams and Organizations and Integration* Aubert and Kelsey (2003) note that trust has been deemed to be critical in ensuring the efficient operation of virtual teams and organizations. Seventy-one business students from two Canadian universities took part in this study. First, the students self-selected their local teammates to form 11 teams. They were subsequently randomly grouped into 11 virtual teams composed of students from both universities. They were asked to conduct a research project and submit a formal report at the end of the semester. Students completed questionnaires at the beginning and the end of the project. This study empirically verifies ability and integrity as being antecedents of trust formation in virtual teams. However, effective team performance was found to be independent of the formation of trust. Further analysis suggests that information symmetry and good communication distinguish high-performance teams from low-performance teams. (See also Chap. 7 of Blumberg et al. 2009).

   Potter and Balthazard (2002) investigated whether or not virtual teams who collaborate via computer-mediated communication also exhibit similar interaction styles, and whether the styles have the same effects on their decision performance and process outcomes as they do with conventional teams. Members of 42 virtual teams ($N = 186$, aged 20–52 years) completed an intellective decision first individually and then collaboratively. Post-task measures captured individual and team performance data as well as process perceptions. An additional post-task tool was able to accurately capture the teams' interaction style. Results show that the interaction styles of virtual teams affect both performance and process outcomes in ways that are directionally consistent with those exhibited by conventional face-to-face teams.

   Gallivan (2001) examined the open-source software movement as an example of a virtual organization and proposes a model that runs contrary to the belief that trust is critical for virtual organizations. Instead, it is argued that various control mechanisms can ensure the effective performance of autonomous agents who participate in virtual organizations. Borrowing from the theory of the McDonaldization of society, the author argues that, given a set of practices to ensure the control, efficiency, predictability, and calculability of processes and outcomes in virtual organizations, effective performance may occur in the absence of trust. A content analysis is employed to examine a set of published case studies of open-source software projects. Results show that, although trust is rarely mentioned, ensuring control is an important criterion for effective performance within open-source software projects. The case studies feature few references to other dimensions of McDonaldization, however, and it is concluded that the open-source software movement relies on many other forms of social control and self-control, which are often unacknowledged in open-source software projects. Through these implicit forms of control, open-source software projects are able to secure the cooperation of the autonomous agents that participate in project teams.

   Montoya-Weiss et al. (2001) examined the effects of temporal coordination on virtual teams supported by an asynchronous communication technology (Lotus

Notes), using a sample of graduate students. Specifically, the authors evaluated the moderating role of a temporal coordination mechanism, process structure, on the relationship between conflict management behavior and virtual team performance. An experiment was conducted with 35 five-person teams in the USA and Japan. Findings show that the way virtual teams manage internal conflict is a crucial factor in their success and that temporal coordination has some significant moderating effects.

Jarvenpaa and Leidner (1998) explore the challenges of creating and maintaining trust in a global virtual team whose members transcend time (!), space, and culture. The challenges are highlighted by integrating recent literature on work teams, computer-mediated communication groups, cross-cultural communication, and interpersonal and organizational trust. To explore these challenges empirically, the authors report on a series of descriptive case studies on global virtual teams whose members were separated by location and culture, were challenged by a common collaborative project, and for whom the only economically and practically viable communication medium was asynchronous and synchronous computer-mediated communication. The results suggest that global virtual teams may experience a form of "swift" trust but such trust appears to be very fragile and temporary.

*Virtual Teams and Organizations and Goal-Attainment* Lee-Kelley (2002) in research on managing the virtual project team noted that shifting work patterns and increasing organizational cooperation have led to electronically integrated "unbounded" organizations and virtual teams. She explored the project manager's leadership style and control in managing changing project boundaries and permeable interfaces. A survey of clinical research projects indicates that project managers are not overly affected by internal market mechanisms or constraints on face-to-face interactions. However, certain project variables such as project objectives, team size, frequency of team changes, and project duration play significant roles in the relationship between the project leader and his/her perception of project difficulties.

Stanton et al. (2003), in a study of virtuality in human supervisory control to assess the effects of psychological and social remoteness, found that in general terms, the results showed that teams working in the same location performed better than teams who were remote from one another.

When information is shared online, teams perform significantly better. Kahai et al. (2004) conducted a laboratory experiment to assess the effects of participative and directive leadership on participation, performance, and satisfaction of 24 undergraduate student workgroups that interacted electronically via a Group Decision Support System to perform a creativity task. Participative and directive leadership were manipulated through confederate leaders who entered scripted comments into the Group Decision Support System. Performance was measured in terms of quality and uniqueness of solutions. Results of partial least-squares analysis indicated that perceptions of both leader participativeness and directiveness were positively related to levels of participation. Participation, in turn, was positively related to performance but negatively related to satisfaction. Problem structure moderated all these relationships except for the relationship between participation and performance (i.e., task makes a difference).

For a review of global virtual team performance, see Zakaria et al. (2008).


## Organizational Creativity

Some studies in this section are of teams that are part of organizations. An important aspect of the relationship between the small group and the organization is the influence that the group has on organizational creativity (Anderson 1992). Whatever the organization can do formally to enhance creativity, the informal group can do or undo, as noted with regard to group norms. The major finding of the Western Electric Studies in the 1930s (Roethlisberger and Dickson 1939) was that informal groups could either encourage or discourage individual productivity. The same is true for creativity. The process begins with the individual's propensity to innovate (Bunce and West 1995).

*Organizational Creativity and Meaning* Although you may not always get what you see, for creativity in organizations, apparently you may get what you reinforce. West (1990) proposed that four psychological constructs (vision, participative safety, climate for excellence, and norms of and support for innovation) can be used to enable prediction of innovation at work. However, two of the concepts, which are group process variables (norms for innovation and participative safety), are more likely to encourage the quantity of attempts to introduce new ideas. Vision and climate for excellence are more product oriented and are more likely to affect the quality of the innovation.

Burningham and West (1995) examined the influence of these four climate factors on rated group innovativeness in a study of 59 members of 13 teams in an oil company. Support for innovation was the most consistent predictor, with negotiated vision and an aim for excellence also serving as predictors.

After reviewing the literature on "organizing for innovation," Dougherty (2006, pp. 430–431) concluded that there were four sets of activities that formed the basis for the development of commercially successful new products by an organization. For each of these activities, she identifies an underlying tension, a problem of normal functioning that disrupts the tension, and particular practices which perpetuate disruption—and at least implicitly, therefore, how such disruptions can be constructively addressed.

1. The innovators must work with potential new customers to identify needs and link these needs with technological possibilities. This activity deals with the "outside versus inside" tension, to keep operations efficient, and avoids an inward emphasis on departmental thought worlds and units and a fixed sense of business.

2. They must organize the flow of work to collaborate across boundaries over problems and solve them within the context of the whole system of attributes that comprise the product. This activity deals with the "new versus old" tension, by managing complexity, and avoids segmentalist thinking and compartmentalization of work, with power based on current work.
3. They must monitor and evaluate their progress. This activity deals with the "determined versus emergent" tension, by controlling multiple activities, and avoids abstracting work into generic standards, with no strategy making.
4. They must develop a sense of commitment which enables participants to take more responsibility without feeling overwhelmed. This activity deals with the "freedom versus responsibility" tension, by accounting for work and results, and avoids the designation of innovation and inclusion as illegitimate.

Evidence that the lack of the various conditions to enhance creativity can lead to "creativity-stifling," is manifest in statements from managers in Nigeria (Mmobuosi 1988).

A higher level of creativity is required for an unusual approach to a problem than for solving a problem in a routine way. The level of creativity required for solution is implicit in the problem. Brophy (1998), after reviewing theories and research concerning creative problem-solving noted that solvable problems vary widely in their complexity, knowledge needs, and the amounts of divergent and convergent thought that are needed. He concluded that the persons, groups, and organizations with different preferences and abilities, knowledge, and work arrangements that best match the character of particular problems will be most creative at the level required.

Coskun et al. (2000) suggest that one technique that may often facilitate group brainstorming is decomposition of the task so that categories of the problem are considered one at a time rather than simultaneously.

Mustonen-Ollila and Lyytinen (2003) identify the factors that affected over 200 information system process innovation adoption decisions in three organizational environments over a period that spanned four decades. The analysis is based on Rogers's (Rogers 1995) theory of Diffusion of Innovations (cf. Katz et al. 1963). The results show that several Diffusion of Innovations factors strongly affect information system process innovation adoption. These include user need recognition, availability of technological infrastructure, past experience, own trials, autonomous work, ease of use, learning by doing, and standards. Yet, a large number of information system process innovation adoptions followed no discernible pattern.

For additional research on organizational innovation see Molleman and Timmerman (2003) on advantages of contingent performance management.

*Organizational Creativity and Resources* For organizational creativity, it helps if the members are diverse in their backgrounds and if they have similar thought patterns.

For related research, see Basadur and Head (2001) on groups with heterogeneous and homogeneous blends of cognitive styles; and Miura and Hida (2004) on creative performance of groups during idea-generation sessions.

*Organizational Creativity and Integration* Interpersonal relations in an organization are important. In Norway, workers from a project-based engineering company were interviewed about aspects of the organization that inhibited or facilitated creativity (Wesenberg 1994). The workers reported little satisfaction of their essential needs through their work. Instead they sought satisfaction through close relationships in their tightly defined and isolated workgroups. Thus, senior managers who advocated a structural orientation toward stimulating creativity were overlooking the potential influence of the informal group. Mueller (1991) agrees as he reports that a "growing body of evidence" indicates that traditional hierarchies are not the most conducive structure for enhancing creativity and innovation at work. Many innovations happen because of the information and support offered by informal channels of communication within an organization. This can be done through "networking" using electronic means of communication. With the advent of the "virtual group" and the "virtual organization," the members of an informal group need no longer be sitting side by side or in the front or back of the room, as they were in the Western Electric study days.

Janssen (2003) notes that although innovative behavior is widely claimed to contribute to long term organizational effectiveness, the price that an individual worker may have to pay for taking an innovative approach has generally not been examined. The hypotheses for a study is that a worker's innovative behavior interacts with his or her job involvement in producing conflict and less satisfactory relations with resisting co-workers who want to prevent innovative change. Moreover, conflict with co-workers is hypothesized to mediate the interactive effect of innovative behavior and job involvement on satisfaction with co-worker relations. These hypotheses were supported in a survey study among 76 secondary school teachers based on supervisor ratings of the teachers' innovative behavior and teachers' self-report data of job involvement, conflict with co-workers, and satisfaction with co-worker relations.

Caldwell and O'Reilly (2003) investigated the role of workgroup norms in promoting innovation in high-technology organizations. Through structured discussions, samples of senior executives identified organizational patterns and norms associated with successful innovation. Based on the results, a survey was developed and administered to a set of managers. Results show four norms associated with increased group innovation: support for risk taking, tolerance of mistakes, teamwork, and speed of action. An instrument to assess these norms is developed.

For additional research on integration, see Grawitch et al. (2003b) on group member mood states and creative performance; Laensisalmi and Kivimäki (1999) on effect of occupational stress; Reid et al. (1999) on collaborative processes in design team meetings; and Troy et al. (2001) on use of market information.

*Organizational Creativity and Goal-Attainment* There should be organizational support for quality and efficiency as well as individual creativity. Miron et al. (2004) examined whether the same personal and contextual characteristics that enhance innovation could also contribute to quality and efficiency. Engineers and technicians ($N = 349$) in 21 units of a large Research and Development company participated in the study. They demonstrated that people have the ability both to be creative and to pay attention to detail, and that an innovative culture does not necessarily compete with a culture of quality and efficiency. Yet, to reach innovative performance creative people need to take the initiative in promoting their ideas, with the possible corresponding price of low performance quality.

Individuals have ideas, but groups carry them out. Axtell et al. (2000) examined the impact of individual perceptions of individual, group, and organizational factors on both elements of innovation. Machine operators ($N = 148$, mean age of 36 years) completed questionnaires. It was found that the suggestion of ideas was more highly related to individual (personal and job) characteristics than the group and organizational characteristics; whereas the implementation of ideas was more strongly predicted by group and organizational characteristics. As expected, interactions were found between the number of suggestions made and group and organizational characteristics, demonstrating how successful implementation of new ideas requires both their formulation in the first place and an appropriately supportive environment.

## Organizational Learning

The same variables that promote organizational creativity also promote organizational learning and good decision-making. The main difference is a matter of focus. In research on creativity, the focus is on the product. In research on learning and decision-making, the focus is on the process. Ideally, organizations not only learn but also use what they learn. Nevis et al. (1997) provide a model of three phases: acquisition, sharing, and utilization. Easterby-Smith (1997) urges a multidisciplinary approach to the subject. For a broad review of organizational learning, see Kozlowski and Bell (2008).

*Organizational Learning and Meaning* For much of the literature, organizational learning is described at two levels: (a) within the system and (b) reviewing the whole system, that is, going back to "M," the meaning of all this. However, an organization is composed of individuals and groups and is part of a society. So, the learning about processes within a system and about the whole system takes place at four levels, for the individual, small group, organization, and society. When organizational culture and group culture are held constant, innovation is related to individual personality. Some studies compare organizations, some groups within organizations, and some individuals within groups. Nordhaug (1994) examined two levels, group and organization with regard to learning through acquisition, exchange, and application of competencies. The group level factors included relationships between colleagues, team-embedded competencies, group norms, groupthink, and the structure and composition of the teams. The organizational level factors consisted of job design, work system, reward system, organizational culture, and organizational design.

We note that the lists of group level variables as well as the organizational level variables include the same items that will be found on any list of factors found to influence any aspect of group or organizational life (cf. J. D. Johnson et al. 1998; West and Wallace 1991). Usually, there are two lists, one for task factors and one for social–emotional factors (Van der Krogt 1998). For learning, the lists include: phases in development (Tompkins 1997); decision rules (Fiol 1994; Laiken 1997); cooperation (Cavalier et al. 1995); basic skills (Carnevale et al. 1990); individual cognitive styles (Tierney 1997); power relationships (Brooks 1997; Carletta et al. 1998; Dovey 1997; Frohman 1997; Swidler and Arditi 1994); and group culture (Levine and Moreland 1991; Tesluk et al. 1997).

Learning depends on feedback after problem-solving (Carley and Harrald 1997). One way of giving individual feedback is to provide a mentor for each protege (Eby 1997). However, if a group or organization is to learn from mistakes, it needs to know a mistake has been made (Edmondson 1996). Not only do some individuals never learn, but apparently some organizations do not learn either. Brunsson (1998) describes "nonlearning organizations" as those that have developed a proficiency for ignoring both problems and solutions to problems. They accomplish this by placing problems and potentially problematic issues with somebody else, to be attended to in future.

In addition to the analysis of learning in face-to-face groups, Araujo (1998) suggests that socio-technical networks be the units of analysis. He advocates a network view of organizations, conceived as a set of interlocking and shifting relations within porous and fluid boundaries.

Note that change, even if handled well, may increase turnover, thus complicating the picture. Baron et al. (2001) examine one mechanism of disruptive effects of change—employee turnover. By analyzing a sample of high-technology start-ups, the authors show that changes in the employment models or blueprints embraced by organizational leaders increase turnover, which, in turn, adversely affects subsequent organizational performance. Turnover associated with organizational change appears to be concentrated among the most senior employees, suggesting "old guard disenchantment" as the primary cause. The results are consistent with the claim of neoinstitutionalist scholars that founders impose cultural blueprints on nascent organizations and with the claim of organizational ecologists that altering such blueprints is disruptive and destabilizing.

Where do most ideas come from, inside or outside the group or organization? Weldon (2000), after conducting case studies of product and process improvements in four workgroups from four different organizations, found that (a) improvements were nearly always a reaction to an immediate problem or a suggestion from someone outside the group; (b) the development and implementation of ideas for change usually took place as group members pursued their normal work activities; and (c) individual ideas for change and individual follow-through were important.

For additional research on organizational learning and meaning, see Bennett et al. (1999) on work climate factors that must support training; Caldwell et al. (2004) on person–environment fit in relation to organizational changes; Castrogiovanni (2002) on change in environment for established manufacturers; Lawrence et al. (2005) on learning and using new technology; Lehman et al. (2002) on functions important for readiness for change; and Schulz (1998) on new rules as a measure of meaning.

*Organizational Learning and Resources* It is best to use high-involvement work practices combined with appropriate human resource practices (Pil and MacDuffie 2000).

*Organizational Learning and Integration* To promote integration organizations should have a collaborative climate (Sveiby and Simons 2002), include customers (Lei and Greer, 2003), and include individuals from outside the organization (Staber 2004).

*Organizational Learning and Goal-attainment* For goal-attainment, it helps to create a collective leadership group in which members play complementary roles (Denis et al. 2001). However, the solving method may need to change first to accommodate change (Tucker et al. 2002).

*Organizational Learning, Final Meaning* Organizations only learn from failure if failures are identified, discussed, and analyzed to see what is wrong. Cannon and Edmondson (2001) examined shared beliefs about failure in organizational workgroups. They argue that the popular ideal of organizational learning from failure is likely to be impeded by powerful psychological and organizational barriers to engaging in behaviors through which this can occur. It is hypothesized that people hold tacit beliefs about appropriate responses to mistakes, problems, and conflict, and that these are shared within and vary between organizational workgroups (H1). These shared beliefs vary in the extent to which they take a learning approach to failure—specifically in the extent to which they endorse identifying, discussing, and analyzing mistakes, problems, and conflicts. It is also hypothesized that effective coaching, clear direction, and a supportive work context influence beliefs related to failure (H2), and that beliefs about failure influence group performance (H3). These hypotheses combine to suggest a theoretical model of antecedents and consequences of shared beliefs about failure in workgroups. The chapter presents empirical evidence from a recent study ($N = 427$ employees) and finds support for Hypotheses 1, 2, and 3. Hypothesis 4—that shared beliefs about failure mediate between the antecedents and the outcome of group performance—was not supported.

## Individual Learning

Should organizational learning be separate from that of group and individual? For some tasks, individuals learning in a group may have more positive effects than learning alone (Lou et al. 2001). It may be even better if there is exposure to both individual and group learning (Brodbeck and Greitemeyer 2000). It helps if the individuals are curious and angry but not anxious (Reio and Callahan 2004). Learning may begin when an individual is faced with a conflict or a crisis (Lehesvirta 2004). New information is more likely to be adopted if it is useful (Sussman and Siegal

2003). This may sound obvious, but it needs to be borne in mind when information is provided! Kleinman et al. (2002), based on research with accounting professionals, argue that the flattening out of traditional hierarchical structures within organizations may be necessary since traditional mentoring and supervisory structures may be inadequate for fostering needed individual learning and personal learning.

## Summary

Functional theory helps one to understand not only organizations in general, including those concerned directly with resolving conflicts, but also teams and their performance. Culture, as a system of shared values, at the top of the cybernetic hierarchy, can play an important part when organizational systems developed in the West are transported to the East. Most of the research on team performance is based on research in the USA where the most productive groups are found to carry out effectively the major steps in solving task and social–emotional problems. For a given goal (Meaning, M), the group should have a combination of members' personalities and skills (Resources, R), type of group structure (Integration, I), and experience in the coordination of problem-solving (Goal-attainment, G) that is appropriate for the task. Training or feedback about performance improves group productivity.

As an aspect of Integration, tests for "emotional intelligence" have now been added to the traditional measures of task ability. Emotional intelligence is part of a person's ability to be effective with regard to social–emotional relations with other group members. Being a good citizen also helps a person play a part in effective group activity.

For creativity in teams, members must be able to go beyond routine problem-solving. "Brainstorming" is one method that can be introduced to influence creativity.

Training and feedback both increase group performance. Training is typically given before a group begins a task or when the task format is about to be changed. Feedback is given during the process of work or at the end of some phase of production. Thus feedback can influence the final Meaning phase of group activity.

Stress can have negative effects that can be offset if group members feel effective, have high emotional intelligence, job security, and few work/family conflicts.

The same four functions that distinguish effective from ineffective groups also apply to organizations. For organizations, one of the aspects that affects the members' feelings about each other is the extent to which the organization's procedures are ethical and seen as based on procedural and distributive justice.

Trust between team members is important as is the trust between salespeople and customers.

There is a greater "political" concern about the extent to which persons of different genders should play different roles than for most other variables that affect social interaction. Organizational cultural practices related to gender equality represent an important predictor of the percentage of women in management. However, women, in particular, are more likely to see the work–home conflict as an important barrier to career advancement.

Time is a goal-attainment variable for groups and individuals. Deadlines make a difference.

The extensive use of computers for organizational decision-making has produced virtual teams and organizations with global virtual teams conducting most of their business using communications technology.

Organizational creativity and learning are similar in that you get what you reinforce. Whatever the organization can do to enhance the creativity, the informal group can either do or undo. Research on organizational creativity focuses on the product. Research on learning and decision-making focuses on the process. The list of group and organizational variables relevant to teams is the same as the list of factors that influence any aspect of organizational life.

# Chapter 6
# Intergroup Relations

The literature on intergroup relations strikingly reflects both continuity and change. Concepts explored in Sherif's three groundbreaking longitudinal summer camp studies have many echoes in current work. Allport's (Allport 1954) reference to the role of contact in the reduction of prejudice, and subsequent theoretical developments, have received considerable attention since our last Handbook (Hare et al. 1994). Pettigrew has produced a steady stream of work related to the field of intergroup relations over more than 50 years and was recently honored in a volume devoted to building on his legacy of improving intergroup relations (Wagner et al. 2008).

Interest in intergroup relations was enlivened in the 1970s by the researches of Tajfel and his colleagues on the minimal group. Whereas Sherif's studies had involved substantial and varied interactions, Tajfel used an arbitrary criterion for group assignment and no face-to-face interaction. This approach took the issues of stereotyping, bias, and discrimination in intergroup relations beyond culture, history, and personality into exploring a common human psychology. Here, the issue that is addressed is how being in, or feeling part of, a group affects relations with members of a different group. People do behave predictably differently toward other groups when they themselves function consciously as part of a group. This applies whether or not they chose to become a member and even if the criteria for membership are trivial and the opportunities for interaction nonexistent.

Accordingly, much of our understanding of intergroup prejudice—a hallmark of structural violence—and of conflict resolution has been buttressed through a variety of cognitive and other paradigms related, among other things, to social identity.

By the late 1980s, the beginning of the period covered by this book, research on intergroup relations was burgeoning, partly because a new generation of researchers was increasingly bringing in ideas more familiar in other areas of psychology. These were far more likely to be about information processing, attributions, heuristics, and biases. In the Sherif studies, social variables were sought to explain intergroup behavior, since random assignment to groups meant that individual differences were excluded from the equation. Recent studies extend and complement the early work and place it in a wider theoretical context. In particular, theories of self-categorization and of social identity have continued to generate considerable

H. Blumberg et al., *Small Group Research,* Peace Psychology Book Series,
DOI 10.1007/978-1-4614-0025-7_6, © Springer Science+Business Media, LLC 2012

research interest. The psychology of intergroup relations represents a very substantial literature devoted to empirical data and, to a much lesser extent, methodology, with complex links with other areas of psychology. Reviews of the growth of the field from its early days to the present can be found in: Randsley de Moura et al. (2008); Nagda et al. (2006); and Hamilton and Hewstone (2007).

Based on the volume and significance of the literature on intergroup relations since the last Handbook (Hare et al. 1994), this chapter will focus on four major themes: the cognitive consequences of perceiving oneself to be a member of a group; the self-group relationship; the emotional consequences of relating to another group; and finally, how intergroup relations may be improved, given the often adverse behavioral consequences of cognitions and feelings in the form of discrimination and conflict. (For cognitive aspects of intergroup relations, see also Chap. 3.)

How groups see and behave toward one another is beset, perhaps even more than other topics in this volume, with problems of defining the term "group." Who are these groups? By what means, for what purpose, are they relating to one another? Although our focus is on small groups, much of the literature includes work in which the term *group* is used much more broadly: defined by gender, race, nation, or language for example. As such, the research may be looking at how these groups see each other, rather than looking at them in interaction in the laboratory or field setting. There is clearly a close connection here with work on prejudice and stereotypes, topics whose history is rooted in the field of individual differences rather than intergroup processes. However, studies which use groups as broad generalizations, which may also present hypothetical situations rather than looking at interaction, are nevertheless often designed to investigate current explanations of well-known intergroup effects. That is particularly the case for cognitive explanations in terms of social identity and self-categorization but also applies to more affective approaches such as those focusing on intergroup anxiety and perceived threat.

## Minimal Groups

Many variables can affect the relations between natural groups, including their history, the wider culture, the attributes upon which membership is based, and the issue of self-selection—any of which may potentially confound research data. Tajfel et al. (1971) used and extended the minimal group paradigm (MGP), involving the establishment of new groups under controlled conditions, making it possible to explore the impact of a range of variables upon behavior. Tajfel initially used supposed preferences for paintings by either Klee or Kandinsky as his rationale to participants for why they were assigned to one group rather than another. The random allocation of participants to groups according to some generally spurious criterion allows study of the consequences of perceiving oneself to be a group member, without all the trappings involved in membership of a natural group. There was no interaction between group members—a truly minimal paradigm. The task for Tajfel's participants was to allocate money either to their own group members or to the other group.

They could not award it to themselves. Given a matrix of choices, participants were more likely to favor their own group; more surprisingly, perhaps, they were more likely to make choices which maximized the difference between the two groups, even if their own group's absolute reward was less than it might be.

Although ingroups are generally found to be favored in minimal group and other intergroup research, this is reflected mainly in the allocation of positive rewards or other positive consequences. Derogation, being actively unfair to outgroups, or delivering noxious stimuli are all less likely than ingroup favoritism—the bias is asymmetrically skewed. Mummendey et al. (1992) compared participants' decisions on the delivery duration of what they believed would be an unpleasant high-pitched tone, and Otten and Moskowitz (2000), looking at affect-based trait inference in minimal groups, also demonstrated ingroup favoritism but not outgroup derogation. See also Halevy et al. (2008).

One explanatory concept for ingroup favoritism is derived from social identity theory (Tajfel and Turner 1986). Many studies have found that increased identity with the group accentuates asymmetry in ingroup–outgroup favoritism and this is addressed more fully later in this chapter. Even in minimal group research this is still a current topic. Hodson et al. (2003) found that greater identification with the group led to discrimination toward the group for positive but not for negative outcomes.

If a person's social identity is partly derived from group affiliations, and given that people prefer a positive to a negative self-concept, social comparison processes will be skewed toward seeing the ingroup favorably relative to others—even in the MGP. Such favorable social comparison can enhance self-esteem and it is assumed higher self-esteem relates to a more positive self-concept.

Hogg and Abrams (1993) suggested that the motive for self-categorizing might be that people seek to reduce subjective uncertainty (see also Hogg and Mullin 1999). In two minimal group studies, Grieve and Hogg (1999) pursued the idea that it is not mere social categorization which leads to discrimination but that a further process of self-categorization must also occur. They manipulated categorization and subjective uncertainty. Finding that intergroup discrimination occurred only in the condition where categorization was accompanied by subjective uncertainty, they concluded that categorization is necessary but not sufficient for discrimination to occur. People reduce uncertainty by self-categorizing, and in these studies discrimination was accompanied by greater identification with the group and by increased self-esteem.

See also Finchilescu (1994) on intergroup attributions in minimal groups.

In two minimal group studies, Jetten, Hogg, and Mullin (2000) tested the related hypothesis that homogeneous groups would be better able to reduce uncertainty than heterogeneous groups. Their findings confirm the role of uncertainty reduction in the motivation of group behavior, which was reflected in the higher level of intergroup differentiation in homogeneous groups in the low certainty condition. In conditions of low certainty, members of homogeneous groups were also most likely to seek feedback from others in the group and were also more likely to change their responses.

For an exploration of the concept of uncertainty reduction and intergroup relations from the perspective of individual differences see Huber and Sorrentino (1996); see also Otten and Bar-Tal (2002) on self-anchoring in relation to need for, and ability to achieve, cognitive structure.

Another possible explanation for favoring the ingroup is derived from equity theory. Here, ingroup-favoring allocations are seen to be based on the sense that they are fair representations of the relative worth of the two groups. In the first of two studies designed to see if equity theory might better explain ingroup-favoring allocations than social identity theory, Platow et al. (1997) directly manipulated relative ingroup and outgroup worth in the MGP. In their second study they assigned participants to conditions according to median splits for *a priori* perceived ingroup worth and for personal self-esteem. Overall, the authors conclude that the evidence supported predictions from social identity theory rather than the relative ingroup worth hypothesis which had been presented by Bruins et al. (1995). See also Falomir-Pichastor et al. (2009); and Hunter et al. (2007).

The direction of causality could go either way—those who have discriminated against the outgroup may consequently have higher self-esteem (see Chin and McClintock 1993). Hunter (2003b), rather than measuring global, trait collective self-esteem in a between-participants experimental design as used in most studies, instead looked at state, category-specific self-esteem in a within-participants design, in which New Zealanders allocated points to anonymous ingroup or anonymous outgroup members (Australians). Those who discriminated against Australians also showed a significant increase in state, category-specific self-esteem. See also Hunter (2003a) on domain-specific self-esteem and ingroup favoritism.

On the other hand, those with higher self-esteem may be more likely to be biased against outgroups.

See also Hogg and Sunderland (1991) on self-esteem and intergroup discrimination; and Petersen and Blank (2003) on bias and state self-esteem.

Hertel et al. (2002) found that people do not just use ingroup norms to judge fairness but, rather, they maintain more general principles of reciprocity or equality by adapting their judgments of fairness according to the behavior they expect from their partner in the interaction.

For other studies of fairness in the MGP, see Amiot and Bourhis (2003); Platow et al. (1990). For majorities–minorities in the MGP, see Yoshida and Kubota (1994). For other studies on the effects of fairness norms, see Jost and Azzi (1996).

At the simplest level, it may be that mere categorization into groups leads to biased judgments and intergroup discrimination and some of the evidence suggests this. Intergroup bias appears to occur automatically, even under minimal group conditions. Ashburn-Nardo et al. (2001) carried out three studies in which they used the Implicit Association Test as a measure of intergroup bias and found that participants more readily associated pleasant words with ingroup names and unpleasant words with outgroup names, however minimal the group and even when perceptions of the outgroup were nonexistent.

Harmon-Jones et al. (1996) found increased intergroup bias in minimal groups in a mortality salience condition (writing essays about death), as did Tam et al. (2007).

See also, Mummendey et al. (2000), on the influence of salience of categorization and valence of evaluation for differentiation in the MGP.

In so far as ingroup favoritism in the minimal group may be a robust phenomenon, it must still be explained. There are, though, some dissenting voices about its robustness: see Rabbie and Schot (1990). Berkowitz (1994) has presented evidence that intergroup bias in the MGP was confounded with participants' expectancies. Gaertner and Insko (2000) were similarly concerned about a possible confound. They looked at whether discrimination which favors the ingroup might in fact be the result of outcome dependence on others. Rather than mere categorization, the effect might be the result of expecting reciprocity from other ingroup members and fearing what the outgroup might do. In two studies where these variables were unconfounded, they found that there were sex differences: Men showed an ingroup reciprocity effect in that they discriminated when they were dependent on ingroup but not on outgroup members. Women, however, favored the ingroup when they were categorized, whatever the dependence structure. The authors suggest there may be biological or environmental constraints which make women more dependent on the ingroup. This somewhat provocative idea will no doubt receive more attention.

For a review of work on minimal groups, including both power and gender in relation to intergroup discrimination see Bourhis (1994). For a citation analysis of Tajfel's work on intergroup relations, see Dumont and Louw (2007).

*Tajfel's Methodology* Bourhis et al. (1997) present a method for scoring allocation strategies measured in the Tajfel matrices, arguing that the matrices are in themselves a subtle measure of intergroup differentiation usable in real and minimal group research.

## Cognitive Approaches to the Consequences of Being in a Group

Ingroups are strongly inclined to favour themselves. They also tend to exaggerate the difference between themselves and the outgroup, to perceive outgroups as more homogeneous than ingroups and to treat deviant ingroup members more harshly than outgroup deviants. They are also more likely to see outgroups in a stereotyped and undifferentiated way, with consequences for their expectations of outgroup behavior and for ingroup members' discriminatory behavior.

### *Ingroup Favoritism and Bias*

Ingroup favoritism would also seem more likely to be manifest when people identify themselves strongly with their ingroup.

Gaertner and Schopler (1998) have questioned the very intergroup nature of what have been seen as intergroup phenomena, including intergroup bias. Revisiting and modifying Campbell's concept of group entitativity in terms of the interconnectedness of the self with others, they found that participants who experienced interaction in groups had a stronger sense of group entitativity (the group as a group) and a stronger sense of the ingroup and outgroup as two separate groups. The effects which they found of these perceptions on intergroup bias give evidence, they argue, for placing the origins of intergroup phenomena in intragroup processes. In a recent study, Newheiser et al. (2009) have presented evidence that while perceived group entitativity predicts intergroup stereotyping and bias, the reverse is also true, that is, prejudice predicts perceived entitativity and mediates the effects of contact and social dominance orientation.

Ingroup favoritism may be reflected in many ways, one of which, according to Betancor et al. (2003) is differentially attributing traits relating to high morality to the ingroup and low morality to the outgroup. Conversely, negative traits which were related to low efficiency were more likely to be ascribed to the ingroup than negative traits related to low morality (the latter being seen as more "diagnostic" or important), whereas those related to low morality were more likely (than low efficiency) to be ascribed to the outgroup.

Other studies on ingroup favoritism and attributional bias: Bettencourt et al. (1997); Moghaddam and Stringer (1988); Ng and Cram (1988); Vrugt and Kraan (1996); Wilberg (1996).

Although it has been argued that ingroup favoritism may reflect interdependence and an expectation of rewards from others in the group, this view does not have a lot of support. A study of reward allocation to ingroups and outgroups in unilateral or multilateral conditions by Tajima (1997) led to the conclusion that ingroup favoritism was the result of psychological group formation not a result of strategic self-interest.

See De Ridder and Tripathi (1992) for several papers on norm violation and intergroup relations; J. C. Martinez (1989) on differential group resources and ingroup bias; and Schruijer and Lemmers (1996) on the effects of norm violation by ingroups and outgroups in the Netherlands.

## Linguistic Bias

The subtlety and pervasiveness of intergroup bias may be reflected in language use. Maass et al. (1989) looked at the linguistic categories that people used to encode and express to others desirable or undesirable behaviors by ingroup or outgroup members. Desirable ingroup behaviors and undesirable outgroup behaviors were coded more abstractly (i.e., more generally), whereas more concrete linguistic categories were used to communicate undesirable ingroup and desirable outgroup behaviors. Thus, they say, stereotypes can be perpetuated in communication.

Even in minimal groups, with no preexisting stereotypes, linguistic bias in favor of the ingroup and with negative descriptions of the outgroup has been shown, increasing with greater group entitativity (Rubini, Moscatelli, and Palmonari 2007).

A study of words used over the past 150 years to refer to immigrant ethnic out-groups in the USA shows what the authors describe as a "sobering picture of the effects of the cognitive representations of immigrants…thinking about ethnic immigrant groups in a simplistic and negative manner" and a corresponding "tendency to exclude" (Mullen 2001, p. 457; cf. Mullen and Rice 2003; Mullen et al. 2007).

For other studies on linguistic bias, see Cole and Leets (1998); Fiedler et al. (1993); Maass et al. (1995); Oehlschlegel and Piontkowski (1997); Schnake and Ruscher (1998); von Hippel et al. (1997).

## Developmental Studies

In the spirit of Sherif's early work, there is a growing number of recent studies on children's perceptions of intergroup relations, although the bulk of the literature has always focused on adult groups. For a review of development processes and intergroup attitudes and a developmental model of subjective group dynamics see Abrams and Rutland (2008).

Many studies focus on intergroup bias and these are mostly structured in terms of social identity or majority/minority status.

A multinational study of 6-year-old children in five culturally diverse countries used measures which unconfounded ingroup favoritism and outgroup derogation. It was very clear that children favored the ingroup. Outgroup derogation was less apparent and more limited, and seemed to reflect the views of the adults of each nation (Bennett et al. 2004).

In a review of the developmental literature on children's intergroup attitudes, Cameron et al. (2001) argue that the consensual view that racial prejudice is expressed in children, even from the age of three years, may well be the result of a research confound between ingroup favoritism and outgroup derogation. Where the two concepts have been distinguished, ingroup bias has been found rather than negativity toward the outgroup. See also Rutland et al. (2007), who have explained children's positive–negative asymmetry in the attribution of traits in terms of normative processes; and Susskind and Hodges (2007) on children's gender-based attributions, distinguishing ingroup favoritism from outgroup derogation.

One way of looking at bias is to measure the response to deviant members of ingroup or outgroup. In a study in which 5–11 year-old children evaluated English and German soccer teams, and also ingroup and outgroup members with normative or nonnormative attitudes toward the teams, all children showed intergroup bias. Favorable evaluations of outgroup deviants and negative evaluations of ingroup deviants increased with age. Only in older children did identification with the ingroup moderate the effects (Abrams, Rutland, and Cameron 2003). Both in that study and in a study of 6–7 and 10–11 year-olds at a summer camp, Abrams, Rutland, Cameron, and Marques (2003) have found age-related differential reaction to ingroup and outgroup deviants, as well as general ingroup bias. They conclude that intergroup and intragroup differentiation occur together, as a way of bolstering ingroup norms, and develop later than simple ingroup bias.

Castelli et al. (2007) studied the importance of intragroup processes in the regulation of intergroup relations among very young children; they found total loyalty to playing with only ingroup children was preferred in preschool and first-grade children but not among 9–11-year olds.

See also Nesdale et al. (2003) on social identity development theory and ethnic ingroup and outgroup attitudes of 9-year-olds in minimal groups; Nesdale et al. (2007; and see Nesdale et al. 2009), again using minimal groups, on children's ratings of ingroup and outgroup similarity and positivity, in relation to self-categorization, intergroup competition, and outgroup ethnicity; Verkuyten (2007) on ingroup favoritism and self-esteem among Dutch and Turkish preadolescents.

Additionally, see Arthur et al. (2008) on developmental intergroup theory and the development of gender stereotyping and prejudice; Banaji et al. (2008) on the early development of intergroup cognition; Bigler and Liben (2006) proposing a developmental intergroup theory to understand the processes by which children learn the targets, stereotypes and prejudices associated with target groups in their culture; Bigler and Liben (2007); Brown and Bigler (2002); Corenblum et al. (1996); Rutland (1999); Verkuyten (2001).

## *Intergroup Differentiation and Distinctiveness*

In addition to ingroup bias and favoritism, there is also a tendency for ingroups to see themselves, "Us," as more different from outgroups, "Them," than is the case in reality. This tendency may operate even at an unconscious level or automatic level. Arguing that automatic behavioral contrast might occur when a social stereotype is activated in circumstances where a comparison between the self and the outgroup stereotype is provoked, Schubert and Häfner (2003) report finding just such an effect, using speed and intellectual performance as behavioral measures of contrast. Furthermore, they report finding in a second study that merely giving subliminal priming of the self while an outgroup stereotype was activated led to automatic behavioral contrast. They consider that social comparison processes may be implicated.

Spears et al. (2004) also report finding automatic behavioral contrast between "Us" and "Them" and again refer to the role of social comparison processes. They found that when neatness was associated with an outgroup rather than with the ingroup, participants colored in pictures more messily. In a second study, those primed with the concept of busy business people reacted more quickly, whereas those primed with their student ingroup identity responded more slowly than controls. Further studies showed that priming us-them comparison reduced the accessibility of words associated with the outgroup stereotype. This was especially the case for more prejudiced participants. Overall, they conclude that when intergroup antagonism is cued or where it is endemic, intergroup differentiation processes operate automatically, based on social comparison and on the role of the self in perception and behavior. See also Gordijn and Stapel (2006).

Ruys et al. (2007) have found unconscious priming to lead to automatic comparison, which affects evaluative responses to information coming from an outgroup; Ledgerwood and Chaiken (2007) found priming affected both automatic assimilation and contrast in relation to group attitudes, dependant on when the group became not merely a context but instead was a comparison point.

See Mummendey and Simon (1989) and Lindeman and Koskela (1994). Both studies include group size and dimension of comparison as variables in intergroup discrimination. See also Degner et al. (2007) as regards priming effects on expression of prejudice and on behavior.

After being categorized into social groups, whether minimal or value-tagged laboratory groups, participants in research by Clement and Krueger (2002) judged other members of their ingroup to be more like themselves than members of the outgroup. Some of the participants were in more than one group and the projection effect was limited to the present ingroup, leading the researchers to conclude that it reflects an anchoring process, limited to the judgment in hand.

See also Holtz (2004); Krueger (1992); Mullen, Dovidio et al. (1992); Reynolds, Turner, and Haslam (2000); Tinoco (1998).

The literature shows a complex relationship between group distinctiveness and the extent to which ingroup members show differentiation on various measures. Jetten et al. (1998) tested their integrative model of social identity and self-categorization theory in a study of ingroup distinctiveness and positive differentiation in both natural and minimal groups. They found, as they had predicted, a curvilinear relationship, with positive differentiation and ingroup bias greatest for intermediate levels of group distinctiveness (manipulated by both intergroup distance and group variability).

Similarly, using both minimal groups and established groups, threats to group distinctiveness and to a member's prototypicality have been found to increase intergroup discrimination and ingroup favoritism (Jetten et al. 1997a). See Jetten et al. (1999) for a review of studies on the effects of group distinctiveness on intergroup behavior and see Spears et al. (2009) on minimal groups.

In circumstances where the ingroup is not very distinctively different from the outgroup, members who strongly identify with the group may be more likely to exhibit positive differentiation or favoritism. Jetten, Spears, and Manstead (2001) found this to be the case whether level of identification was manipulated or merely measured. They argue that group identification is crucial in explaining their results; the emphasis of social identity theory is more explanatory than self-categorization theory. See also Gabarrot et al. (2009) on intergroup similarity and the effect of group norms on discrimination.

In a study of "imposters" (Jetten et al. 2005), the ingroup (vegetarians) and the outgroup (meat-eaters) found an ingroup member eating meat. As expected there was greater derogation of the imposter from ingroup rather than outgroup members. The study was designed to compare social identity theory with the self-categorization hypothesis. Social identity theory would predict that perceptions of low intergroup distinctiveness would lead to greater derogation of the imposter by the ingroup ("reactive distinctiveness"), whereas self-categorization theory would predict greater derogation where there was high intergroup distinctiveness ("reflective distinctiveness"). They found significantly greater derogation in the high intergroup distinctiveness condition.

Jetten et al. (2004) conducted a meta-analysis of the literature on the relationship between distinctiveness and differentiation, looking also at the role of group identification, relevance of the comparison dimension, relevance of the outgroup and the quality of intergroup relations—all predicted by Tajfel and Turner (1979) to play a moderating role in the distinctiveness–differentiation relationship. Overall, there was virtually no effect of distinctiveness on differentiation, but reactive distinctiveness (when "distinctiveness is threatened by a similar outgroup") was found on behavioral measures and reflective distinctiveness (reality-based differentiation) on judgments, with only group identification found to be a moderating variable.

It is clear that self-categorization and social identity theory may both play an explanatory role here. In addition, there may be instrumental reasons, based on their interdependence, for ingroup members to show ingroup bias. Theoretical integration is often suggested in one way or another: Scheepers, Spears, Doosje, and Manstead (2002) point out that their studies show that different conditions lead to intergroup differentiation for differing reasons; they suggest that in seeking to explain intergroup differentiation, social identity approaches should be integrated with interdependence theories. The possible integration of social identity and interdependence approaches to intergroup discrimination in minimal groups is further explored by Stroebe et al. (2007). See also Rubini, Moscatelli, Albarello, and Palmonari (2007) on power, interdependence, and intergroup discrimination in minimal groups.

See also Grant (1993a); Hidaka and Yamaguchi (1997); Jetten et al. (1997b); Mucchi-Faina et al. (2002); Roccas and Schwartz (1993).

## *Optimal Distinctiveness Theory*

Brewer (1991, 1996) has proposed an "optimal distinctiveness" theory, partly as an explanation for the seeming instability of attempts to create merged groups or intergroup cooperation: People simply want to be somewhat different, if perhaps not too much so. It is often found that intergroup discrimination is greater in groups which are numerically in a minority and this was investigated in the context of optimal distinctiveness theory by Leonardelli and Brewer (2001). They found that ingroup identification was necessary for intergroup discrimination. Furthermore, satisfaction with ingroup size and distinctiveness influenced participants' motivations for discriminating against the outgroup.

The concept is considered further in Brewer (2009). See also Vignoles and Moncaster (2007).

# Social Categorization and Social Identity:
# The Self-Group Relationship

Social identity theory predates self-categorization theory but both are still widely in evidence in the literature, with researchers finding support for one or the other or both, or for various integrations thereof. See, for example, Schmitt et al. (2000), who explored an integration of self-evaluation maintenance model of behavior and social identity theory in interpersonal judgments, concluding that the data suggested self-categorization theory could be useful in integrating interpersonal and intergroup perspectives on self-evaluation.

Otten (2009) has argued that social categorization of opponents can affect interpretation, emotional reactions, and consequent behavioral tendencies in conflict situations.

See also Schubert and Otten (2002), who developed graphical scales for the measurement of self-categorization; and Van Bavel and Cunningham (2009) on the overriding of automatic racial and social bias by self-categorization in a novel mixed-race group.

Social identity theory states that identification with the ingroup "category" is a necessary condition for discrimination. The behavioral interaction model, however, rather like realistic conflict theory, regards interdependence and self-interest as fundamental to discrimination.

For a review of the social identity perspective in the study of intergroup relations, see Hogg et al. (2004).

Comparisons between the paradigms tend to favor social identity theory, finding that identification with the group is an important variable in predicting ingroup favoritism, although the relationship with discrimination may be more complex: see Hennessy and West (1999) on small groups in an organizational setting; Perreault and Bourhis (1998) with minimal groups of Canadians/Quebecois allocating money.

In a longitudinal study of the Canadian military, at the beginning and end of a four-year officer training program including Anglophone (majority) and Francophone (minority) recruits, Guimond (2000) found that social identification played a significant role in group socialization, with consequences for the evaluation of outgroups (Francophones, civilians, and immigrants).

For other studies of group identification and ingroup bias, see Doosje and Branscombe (2003); for identification and response to ingroup deviance, see Hutchison and Abrams (2003). See also Kelly (1990a) on minority–majority contexts; Wilder and Shapiro (1991) on outgroup stereotypes; Stott et al. (2001) on hooliganism; and Grant (1993a) on ethnocentrism.

Duckitt and Mphuthing (1998) conclude that there may be two quite different modes of group identification, each having different implications for intergroup behavior. They studied the attitudes of South African Blacks to English Whites, Africaans Whites and Whites in general, before and after the transitional elections in 1994 after the end of apartheid. The researchers used predictions from social identity theory and realistic conflict theory. Both theories predict that group identification will be correlated with negative evaluations of the outgroup when in situations of perceived threat. However, the theories differ in terms of predicted causality. In line with the general prediction, Black identification related only to negative perceptions of Africaans Whites. However, the direction of causality, indicated by longitudinal analysis, showed attitudes influencing identification rather than the reverse, which supports realistic conflict theory rather than social identity theory. Duckitt and Mphuthing thus join others in suggesting that group identification is not a unitary concept.

Among those arguing that social identity may not be a straightforward concept are Jackson and Smith (1999), who have construed it along four different dimensions: perceptions of the intergroup context, ingroup attraction, interdependency beliefs, and depersonalization. In two empirical studies, they identified two types of social identity and these were differentially related to outcome measures, including perceived group homogeneity and evaluations of ingroup and outgroup. More recently Jackson (2002a) has tested a 3D model of group identity in ascribed, achieved, and face-to-face groups, measuring also intergroup bias and perceptions of conflict. The 3D of the model are cognitive, evaluative, and affective ties. The existence of strong affective ties to the group was the best overall predictor of intergroup bias; group identification led to over-positive evaluations of the ingroup. Perceptions of intergroup conflict significantly increased negative evaluations of the outgroup. Jackson (2002c) has also tested the model in terms of the different functions predicted to be served by group identification for majority-group and minority-group members, measuring also perceived intergroup conflict.

From a differing perspective, that of social attraction theories, attraction to the group (that is, depersonalized attraction) was found by Hogg and Hains (1996) to be related to perceptions of prototypicality and of group identification. This depersonalized attraction was an important consequence of self-categorization and was found to be unrelated to interpersonal relations.

Attempting to resolve a sociological approach to identity in which role identities arise from social structure and the psychological perspective of social identity theory, Deaux and Martin (2003) propose, and provide some evidence for, a theoretical model in which level of context is specified. Two levels, social category and interpersonal network, are seen as independent contextual settings.

The problem of relating individual and group identities to intergroup behavior is addressed from another perspective by Worchel et al. (2000). They, like others, feel that inconsistencies in the literature may be resolved if a more complex view of identity is taken. They propose a multidimensional model in which concerns about identity are seen as manifest on four different levels, each with different implications for intergroup behavior, with the salience of each level influenced by a multiplicity of variables. Research suggests that yet more refinements of theory will be necessary.

See also Robins and Foster (1994) on personal versus social identity.

For an overview of social identity theory see Hogg (2006); and for an integration of social identity theory and the theory of planned behavior in a study of decisions about sustainable agriculture, see Fielding et al. (2008).

## Individual Differences, Social Identity, and Self-Esteem

Individual differences influence the relationship between degree of identification and ingroup bias or outgroup discrimination. The most important variable appears to be self-esteem, by definition and empirically. Self-esteem may refer to a trait or to a temporary state and, for either of these, it may be either domain specific or rather more global. Not all studies disambiguate these various possibilities.

See Hunter et al. (1996) for the effects of discrimination on domain-specific self-esteem in adolescents; Meeres and Grant (1999) who tested Hinkle and Brown's 1990 taxonomy of collectivists and individualists; and Verkuyten and Hagendoorn (2002) on favoritism, self-esteem, level of identity, and stimulus valence. See also Branscombe and Wann (1994); James and Greenberg (1989).

Noting the importance placed on the concept of self-esteem by social identity theory, Aharpour and Brown (2002) sought to identify other psychological functions of group identification and also to examine the causal relationships between such functions, degree of identification and intergroup attitudes. For the participants in their study (from different social and national groups) group membership served many functions in addition to self-esteem. Furthermore, ingroup favoritism was apparent only in those groups where identification largely served an interdependence or utilitarian function.

*Individual Differences and Social Identity* Other individual difference variables which have been found significant in relation to the effects of social identity, in at least one study, include allocentrism (Capozza et al. 2000; Carpenter and Radhakrishnan 2002), collectivism (Chen et al. 2002; Verkuyten and Kwa 1996), social dominance orientation (Pratto et al. 2001; Reynolds et al. 2007; Sidanius et al. 1994), need for cognitive economy (Stangor and Thompson 2002), and superiority bias (Hornsey 2003).

A further individual difference has been looked at by Hong et al. (2003), who conducted three studies in Hong Kong at the time of political transition in 1997. They found there were reduced effects of social identification on group orientation in people who viewed human nature as malleable and who saw the dispositions of social groups were seen as changeable. Social identification effects were accentuated in people who saw character and group dispositions as immutable.

*Social Categories, Identity, and Status* The social category in which one finds oneself may be of low status, and hence seemingly not particularly enhancing to self-esteem. Moreover, such categories may be more or less inescapable, whether because of race, for example, or merely because of the manipulations of a laboratory researcher who has just made random assignments to a low-status group with impermeable boundaries and no prospect of changing groups.

For studies on status and the permeability of group boundaries, see Haines and Jost (2000) on the effects of relative powerlessness on stereotyping, affect and memory; and Vanbeselaere et al. (2003) on group permeability and tokenism. See also Boen and Vanbeselaere (2000, 2001, 2002); Jackson et al. (1996); Lalonde and Silverman (1994); Reynolds, Oakes et al. (2000); Rosenthal and Crisp (2006) on reducing stereotypes by blurring intergroup boundaries.

Branscombe et al. (2002) looked at both intergroup status and intragroup evaluation of individual members. In an orthogonal design they measured the effects of these variables on reward allocation and on time given to work on a task meeting either personal needs or group goals. Among other significant differences between conditions, they found that respected members of devalued groups were most likely to withhold rewards from the outgroup and they also donated most time to working to improve the group's image rather than their personal image.

See also Ellemers et al. (2000) on constraints on the expression of intergroup bias, according to relative status and group identification; Noel et al. (1995) on public negativity to outgroups expressed by peripheral ingroup members; Singh et al. (1998) on ingroup bias and fair-mindedness as self-presentation strategies; Van Prooijen and Lam (2007) on the effect of social categorization and intergroup status on the perceived fairness of punishment of ingroup or outgroup members; Wagner and Ward (1993) on outgroup presence and evaluation of the ingroup.

Guimond, Dif, and Aupy (2002) found there to be negative consequences of favorable group outcomes in terms of increased evaluative bias—of high-status group members against the low-status outgroup, and of members of low-status groups in favoring and identifying with the outgroup.

Social comparison theory is important in considering how perceived relative status affects intergroup relations. It has been suggested that one way people can protect their self-esteem is to dismiss comparisons with a higher status outgroup as not relevant. In a study which broadly confirmed their hypothesis that only members of dominant groups suffer from upward comparisons with ingroup members, Martinot et al. (2002) found that members of low-status groups, conversely, did not. In this case, identifying with the ingroup seemed to be a self-protection strategy. The authors suggest that relative group status may affect people's tendency to adopt one self-protection strategy rather than another when faced with upward comparisons.

See also Aberson and Howanski (2002) on the relationship between self-esteem, status, identification, and ingroup bias; Boldry and Kashy (1999) on outgroup favoritism in low-status groups; Ellemers and Van Rijswijk (1997) on status and identity management in minority–majority group relations; Hopkins and Rae (2001); Verkuyten (1997); Zagefka and Brown (2006) on social comparison choices made in several studies with ethnically diverse group members and in a variety of intergroup settings.

People may perceive their higher or lower status as legitimate. If they also believe that individual mobility between groups is possible and endorse such mobility this, according to a status legitimacy hypothesis, will affect the attributions for discrimination made by members of both the higher and the lower status groups. Significant evidence in support of this view is reported by Major et al. (2002) in three studies and with two methodologies. The more that they supported the ideology of individual mobility, the less likely were members of low-status groups to attribute their negative outcomes from high-status groups to discrimination. On the other hand, for members of high-status groups, that ideology of individual mobility was associated with attributions of discrimination about the causes of negative outcomes from low status toward high-status groups.

See also Bettencourt and Bartholow (1998) on the effects of status legitimacy on bias in numerical minorities and majorities; Blanz et al. (1995a) and Otten et al. (2001) on the impact of status differentials and stimulus valence in the allocation of positive and negative outcomes; Eshel (1999) on legitimacy and ingroup bias on planned encounters in Jewish and Arab young people; Grant (1991) on unequal power; Guimond and Dambrum (2002) on relative deprivation and relative gratification; Hornsey et al. (2003) on the effects of differential power and legitimacy on intergroup bias; Jackson (1999) on the effects of status and of group size on intergroup bias and dimensions of identity; Kanning (1999) on status, self-esteem and social conflict; Kirchler et al. (1994) on status differences and adolescent peer groups; Montalban and Gomez (1995); Pettigrew et al. (2008) on prejudice and both group and individual relative deprivation; Platow et al. (1995); Sachdev and Bourhis (1991) on differential power and status in relations between majority and minority groups; Karasawa (2002a, b) on attributions and relative national wealth; Manfred and Maes (2002) on relative deprivation and bias in East and West Germans; Weber et al. (2002) on ingroup prototypicality and the perceived legitimacy of intergroup status differentials.

## *Multiple Category or Multiple Group Membership*

Social identity is not necessarily simple or singular. People belong to many groups, both involuntarily and by choice, which may contribute to part of their identity, as well as influencing whether others see them as "Us" or "Them." While many aspects of intergroup relations are being explained in terms of social identity, there is also a lot of research into the consequences of belonging to more than one social category, identifying with more than one group. As will be seen later, there is also interest in whether intergroup relations can be improved by reconstruing ingroup and outgroups into an overarching common category.

For further consideration of these ideas, see Crisp and Hewstone (2006). See also Crisp (2008); Crisp and Hewstone (2007); Crisp, Walsh, and Hewstone (2006); Roccas and Brewer (2002) on social identity complexity; Verkuyten and Yildiz (2007); and Vescio et al. (1999) on perceiving and responding to multiple categorizable individuals.

Overlapping categories may reduce intergroup differentiation (Vanbeselaere 1996). However, although this was also found to be the case in a later study (Vanbeselaere 2000), it was clear that ingroups were biased against those who were members of a double outgroup.

Roccas (2003) reports three experimental studies in which participants indicated their identification with, and perceived status of, two real or experimental groups of which they were simultaneously members. She found that a group was perceived as having higher status, and this group was identified with more, if the individual was also simultaneously a member of a lower status group. See also Eurich-Fulcer and Schofield (1995).

Merged identities: Van Leeuwen et al. (2003) studied minimal groups, in terms of group bias effects related to the continuation or change of premerger social identity.

*Perceptions of Homogeneity* Ingroup members have widely been found to perceive members of outgroups as more homogeneous than in reality, while perceiving greater variability within their own group. This phenomenon is discussed by Simon (1992a, b). The accuracy of these judgments has been studied by Judd et al. (1991). Outgroup homogeneity effects have also been found in natural and minimal groups by Ostrom and Sedikides (1992). As is generally the case for physical perception, no doubt the phenomenon is partly due to the perspective of greater distance; but the "boundaries" that separate categories must also sharpen the effect.

See also Linville and Fischer (1998) for a consideration of group variability and covariation and their effects on intergroup relations; and Simon (1992a) on intragroup differentiation.

Such differential perceptions of group variability can affect ingroup favoritism, stereotyping and—in a study by Simon, Micki et al. (1990)—also lead to an overestimation of the relative size of the ingroup. Simon and Mummendey (1990) have looked at how relative group size affects ingroup perceptions of a minority outgroup. Simon (1995) has argued that in some studies, such as that by Bartsch and Judd (1993) there has been a confounding of group size, level of abstractedness and frame of reference. The latter study has also been challenged by Haslam and Oakes (1995) in terms of the context-independence of the outgroup homogeneity effect.

The assumption is that ingroups see members of outgroups as all the same because they are defined by their group membership rather than being seen as individuals. However, several factors serve to influence perceptions of ingroup or outgroup variability. These include the extent of members' social identification with the group (Dru and Constanza 2003), and manipulating individuation of ingroup and outgroup members (Vanbeselaere 1988).

See also Helga (2002), who varied the valence of the adjectives presented to participants on which homogeneity judgments were based.

A meta-analytic study of eleven measures of outgroup homogeneity showed that perceived outgroup homogeneity was less strong in minimal than nonminimal groups but that there were systematic discrepancies across the measures used (Boldry et al. 2007).

Guinote et al. (2002) found contrary results for Angolan and Portuguese students living in Portugal. While Portuguese students did show the outgroup homogeneity effect, Angolan students perceived more variability in the outgroup than the ingroup and this finding could not be explained by greater familiarity among ingroup members.

*Illusory Correlation* Illusory correlation refers to the perception that one distinctive stimulus is associated with other stimuli, even though the evidence does not bear out such an association. This seems sometimes to occur because the coincidence of two unusual events yields a phenomenon sufficiently rare as to be memorable and hence more retrievable from memory. The illusory correlation effect has been widely found in people's perceptions of groups and their expectations of the characteristics or behavior of group members.

It is evident from the social cognition literature that negative associations are more difficult to eradicate than positive ones (see Mullen and Johnson 1990, for a review). The combination of a tendency for group members to seek intergroup distinctiveness, to see less variability in outgroups than ingroups and also to recall negative associations, along with the more general illusory correlation effect—all these provide a powerful cognitively biased information-processing underpinning to stereotyping (and see Schaller 1991). Here, stereotyping is seen as a consequence of social cognition processes, enhanced by group processes, rather than rooted in a prejudiced or authoritarian personality.

However, just having the relevant information does not necessarily reduce the illusory correlation effect. Chun and Lee (1999) asked their participants to evaluate two groups based on reading desirable and undesirable behavioral descriptions, varying the difference between the amount of preferential information about the groups. They found that the greater this difference, the greater the illusory correlation effect. Moreover, a second study showed that even when participants were made fully aware of the ratio of desirable to undesirable behaviors, they nonetheless based their evaluations upon the absolute difference in the amount of preferential information, not on the ratios.

The tendency for groups to seek meaningful differences from other groups may also contribute to the illusory correlation effect. A study reported by Berndsen et al. (2001) showed that under conditions of constrained information in which evaluative differences between stimuli were accentuated, illusory correlation effects were related to the participants' evaluative reinterpretations of the stimuli. In a second study, they used the thinking aloud technique to explore the relationship between accentuation and illusory correlation. They conclude that rather than being a simple causal relationship, illusory correlation and the reinterpretation of stimuli were mutually reinforcing, in the process of actively seeking intergroup differences—a conclusion which, they argue, has implications for stereotyping.

It is known that groups tend to seek to differentiate themselves from other groups and that this tendency results in the perception of an illusory correlation between the groups and their behaviors. Berndsen et al. (1999) showed that task instructions can in themselves enhance illusory correlations by generating expectations of group differences. They also were able to show that the illusory correlation effect could be reduced by giving precedence to behaviors rather than to groups. Conversely, the effect was increased where the focus was on groups rather than behaviors.

Berndsen et al. (1998) concluded from their data that the relationship between intragroup similarity and the illusory correlation effect is not simple but curvilinear, a conclusion which could accommodate the contradictory findings of McConnell et al. (1997), where group coherence increased the illusory correlation effect but not if the former were so high that evaluative differentiation between groups became impossible. Thus, intragroup similarity is seen as both a cause and a consequence of differentiation and of the illusory correlation effect.

See also Haslam, McGarty, Oakes, and Turner (1993); C. Johnson and Mullen (1993); Kubota (1997); and see Chap. 3.

## Affective Consequences: Emotion, Perceived Threat, Intergroup Anxiety and Fear

While it is somewhat artificial to separate affect from cognition, such a separation serves to acknowledge the importance of emotion in intergroup relations, relatively neglected in the excitement and interest generated by the perspectives of attribution theory, social identity theory and, more widely, cognitive psychology. The emotional element of intergroup relations, the role of affect in bias and discrimination, did not for a while receive much attention although early theorists and researchers had written of the perceived threat posed by outgroups. Sherif pointed out the place of realistic threat in intergroup relations: in his study, the situation was often win or lose, the boys in one group faced a realistic threat from the other group. The subsequent relative neglect of affective processes has been noted by many, including Greenland and Brown (2000) who, reviewing the evidence, suggested that intergroup anxiety was very closely linked with categorization processes and might well have been an important confounding variable in studies of the effects of intergroup contact. Two studies reported by Hubbert et al. (1999) showed that anxiety and uncertainty in intergroup dyadic encounters decreased in association with perceived increased quality of communication over time. As will be seen in a later section, the consequences of intergroup contact have indeed been found to include the reduction of intergroup anxiety and of perceived threat.

For a consideration of the relationship between affect and prejudice, see Fiske and Ruscher (1993).

Research has shown that, at perhaps the most basic level, certain specific emotional states, induced after the creation of minimal ingroups and outgroups, could automatically give rise to a negative intergroup bias. DeSteno et al. (2004) induced three different states—two negative (anger, sadness) and one neutral. Only participants in the anger condition showed automatic intergroup bias, suggesting that emotional as well as cognitive factors may well be involved.

Maio et al. (2001) have measured physiological arousal experienced by people who are thinking about a group toward which they feel ambivalent and also their information-processing times.

Emotions are often displayed facially and may be differently interpreted by ingroup and outgroup members, an issue explored by Richeson et al. (2007).

Wilder and Simon (1996) reviewed what they termed "the nascent literature that examines the relationship between affect and stereotyping" and how it might apply to intergroup contact. In the same volume, Mackie et al. (1996) consider the many and complex ways in which positive mood may influence intergroup perception and stereotypes, again giving thought to the implications for "pleasant intergroup contact" of the studies they review. In a study of intergroup affect, stereotypes, and behavioral tendencies, Cuddy et al. (2007) found that emotions were better at predicting behavioral tendencies than were stereotypes and also were mediators of links between stereotypes and behavioral tendencies.

It is unlikely that effects of mood or of arousal are simple. This certainly is the conclusion of a review by Bodenhausen et al. (2001): It is not merely a straight-forward equation in which negative emotion is associated with ingroup bias and discrimination, nor that positive affect will somehow make everything all right in intergroup relations. An example of this complexity is found in a study by Dijker et al. (1996), where self-reports of the antecedents of participants' emotional reactions to an ingroup and two different outgroups showed that all provoked different kinds of both positive and negative reactions.

See Haddock et al. (1994) on the moderating role of affect intensity in the relationship between mood and the expression of intergroup attitudes; and see also Arcuri and Cadinu (1997).

The importance of emotions was highlighted in a study by Esses and Dovidio (2002). They presented a video showing discrimination against Blacks or a comparison video, asking their participants, all Whites, to focus either on their emotions or their thoughts whilst watching. Those focusing on their emotions while watching the video that showed discrimination were more willing to have contact with Blacks than were all the other experimental groups, and analysis of the data suggested that this result was mediated by changes in emotions toward Blacks. Other measures, of social policy endorsement toward Blacks and of cognitions about Blacks were not influenced by either focus manipulation. Somewhat similarly, Finlay and Stephan (2000) noted the limited success of information-based programs to influence intergroup relations. They found that Anglo-American participants who read about discrimination against African-Americans but with empathy-inducing instructions showed less ingroup–outgroup bias.

Further evidence of the need for subtlety in understanding the role of emotions in intergroup behavior comes from Mackie et al. (2000) who, in a series of studies, looked at fear, anger, and contempt and the desire to move against or away from the outgroup in a situation where group memberships were made salient and perceived ingroup strength varied. Anger and fear were distinct from each other and anger was more likely when the ingroup was perceived to be strong. Anger against the outgroup mediated the wish to take action against it.

The idea of group-based emotion has gained ground over the past 15 years or so, and it is reviewed by Giner-Sorolla et al. (2007) in their introduction to a special journal issue on the topic. Eliot R. Smith et al. (2007) explore group-based as op-posed to individual emotions and argue, on the basis of their research, that group emotions depend on the person's level of group identification, are shared within the group, and play a part in regulating intergroup and intragroup attitudes and behavior. See also Otten et al. (2009) on motivation and emotion in intergroup relations.

*Social Category and Emotion* Two recent studies of discrimination have used the concepts of Higgins's regulatory focus theory of emotions (Higgins 1997): promotion focus (approaching positive events) and prevention focus (avoiding negative events). Individual self-regulation will incline to one or to the other, but focus can also be either chronic or momentary. Sassenberg, Kessler, and Mummendey (2003) tested the idea that an individual who has self-categorized as a group member will allocate resources in terms of these processes. Participants in their research were asked to allocate positive or negative resources to an ingroup or an outgroup; it was found that promotion focus, both chronic and momentary, was able to explain discrimination in the distribution of resources. Shah et al. (2004) have expressed it as "promoting us or preventing them," and concluded from their studies that there is a relationship between intergroup bias and type of regulatory focus.

Emotional mediation of intergroup responses has also been considered in the context of Smith's social model of emotions (E. R. Smith 1999), in which social categorization is seen to have an impact on emotional reactions and behavior. Yzerbyt et al. (2003) looked at these in people faced with the victims of harmful behavior. The victims were categorized as either members of the same common group as themselves, or as members of an entirely distinct subgroup of the same common group. The extent to which there was identification with the contextually salient subgroup was also measured. Anger and a desire to take offensive action were, as predicted, *higher* when people saw themselves as in the same group as the victims and when they were highly identified with the group.

The same research team looked at reactions in Belgium and the Netherlands one week after the World Trade Center attacks, again with the aim of looking at the possible role of social categorization in emotional and behavioral reactions. If participants' attention was focused on a shared identity with the American victims, more fear, more fear-related behavioral tendencies, and more fear-related behaviors than if the victims were categorized as members of an outgroup (Dumont et al. 2003). See also Gordijn et al. (2001).

Although minimal group studies have, as noted earlier in this chapter, found that people show discrimination more by skewing positive outcomes to favor themselves rather than by allocating negative outcomes to the outgroup, it is inescapably true that some people sometimes behave in terrible ways toward members of outgroups. Research on the authoritarian personality (Adorno et al. 1950) was driven by an attempt to understand prejudice, in the wake of Nazi atrocities. This approach ascribes prejudice to individual differences, which, as Pettigrew (Pettigrew et al. 1958) found in his study of white South Africans, was not an adequate explanation when the sociocultural context supported prejudice—it was "normal." Milgram's studies on factors involved in obedience to authority (see Chap. 4 of Blumberg et al. 2009) looked at factors which might lead people to be prepared to harm others when under orders. That approach does not address how it is that certain people acquire authority in the first place.

Given that discrimination against outgroups, including hostility and violence toward them, can be seen as the wellspring of intergroup research, it is perhaps surprising that an intergroup theory specifically addressing action against the outgroup has only recently been formulated. It is proposed (Leyens et al. 2003) that people ascribe essential human qualities to their ingroup and regard outgroups as less human—a phenomenon called infrahumanization. The process is cognitive and emotional. It is argued that while primary emotions (e.g., fear) are universal, secondary emotions, such as love or resentment are seen to be uniquely human. Although infrahumanization may appear a rather extreme term, it refers to an unconscious process by which people tend to ascribe secondary emotions to their ingroups but not to outgroups. Indeed, they may be reluctant to see outgroups as associated with these emotions at all.

Even without group conflict, high-status and low-status groups displayed infrahumanization. Furthermore, ingroup members behaved less cooperatively toward an outgroup member who expressed secondary emotions. Infrahumanization was reduced by individualizing a member of the outgroup, or by eliciting perspective-taking.

Using a procedure which tested people's conscious memory for associations between ingroup or outgroup with primary or secondary emotions, Gaunt et al. (2002) found that although there were no differences for primary emotions, conscious memory was better for associations between the outgroup and secondary emotions than it was for ingroup-secondary-emotion associations. This finding, they argue, supports the view that people attribute more humanity to ingroups than outgroups.

Further support for the role of infrahumanization processes comes from Vaes et al. (2003), who used "lost email" technique. The email, expressing a secondary, uniquely human emotion, received "nicer" replies if the sender were perceived to be an ingroup rather than an outgroup member. They report further studies, two using a conformity paradigm and also measuring perceived similarity which they proposed to be an underlying mechanism. Their final study showed that, beyond simply depriving outgroup members of positive consequences, ingroup members would take action against the outgroup.

Rodriguez-Bailon and Morales (2003) measured prejudice, perceived humanity, and the perceived values of ingroup and outgroup in a sample of views, held by non-Roma, of both Roma and non-Roma. Those scoring high on prejudice also perceived bigger differences between the values of the two groups and greater differences between ingroup and outgroup humanity.

It seems likely that the concept of infrahumanization and related theory will generate an expanding area of research on intergroup relations.

*Responses to Discrimination* Most of the literature looks at intergroup relations from the point of view of the ingroup. There is, however, some interest in the reaction of victims of discrimination—see Swim and Stangor (1998) for a useful collection of papers addressing the issue of prejudice from the target's perspective. Tropp (2003) has looked at laboratory-generated groups and devalued ethnic groups, finding that exposure to prejudice may lead to negative feelings about contact and cross-group interactions.

See also Boen et al. (2003).

*Threat* Threat may be realistic or perceived. Integrated threat theory incorporates a variety of concepts which have been found to relate threats to intergroup attitudes: realistic threats, symbolic threats, and intergroup anxiety (Stephan and Stephan 2000). In a study of attitudes of Black and White students toward each other's racial group, structural equation modeling of the data revealed the importance of these three threat variables in mediating the effects of negative contact, and ingroup identity, among other variables. This was true more for the negative attitudes of Whites to Blacks than of Blacks to Whites (Stephan et al. 2002). See also Corenblum and Stephan (2001) for work based on integrated threat theory, studying White and First Nation people in Canada. Integrated threat theory was also explored in a study of prejudice among Dutch employees against immigrant workers, showing the mediating role of intergroup anxiety and negative stereotyping (Curseu et al. 2007). See also Tausch et al. (2009) on Hindu–Muslim relations in India; and Tausch, Tam et al. (2007) on the effects of individual-level threat, intergroup anxiety, and group identification on trust and intergroup attitudes in cross-community contact in Northern Ireland.

Discrimination in the face of perceived threat may serve an identity confirmation function or an instrumental function. In a decidedly unusual pair of studies with more than 3,000 participants, Scheepers et al. (2003) first found that self-reports of situations in which participants had discriminated showed that identification with the group predicted both identity confirmation and instrumental functions of discriminatory behavior. The instrumental function arose when the group was perceived to be under threat. In the second study, they asked "die-hard" soccer fans to invent chants in response to one of two situations, either group-reinforcing or group-threatening, and then the functionality of the song was rated. Songs were judged to be more instrumentally functional in the threat situation and more identity confirming in the reinforcing situation although both conditions gave rise (not unexpectedly!) to discriminatory songs.

Similarly, Crisp, Heuston et al. (2007) found that the reaction of soccer fans to their team losing (a social identity threat) would depend on whether they were high or low ingroup identifiers, in terms of emotion and action tendencies. As expected, high identifiers felt angry but not sad, whereas low identifiers felt sad but not angry.

In two other soccer-based studies, which included the concept of threat from a superior team, Leach et al. (2003) examined *schadenfreude* (malicious delight in the misfortunes of another) first of all as manifest in the reactions of one group (Dutch) to their conquest of the German team. *Schadenfreude* was greater for those most interested in soccer, and also where there was a threat of Dutch inferiority, though the second study demonstrated the relevance of salient norms—at least for those less interested in soccer!

Other research on threat and ingroup bias includes the following topics: The effects of threat perceived when members of an outgroup are believed to express a common identity with the ingroup within a superordinate category (Gómez et al. 2008); a socially dominant ingroup (Aebischer and Oberle 2002; Cadinu and Reggiori 2002); the effects of perceived cultural threat or of perceived realistic group conflict on prejudice against Mexican immigrants (Zarate et al. 2004); perceiver threat and discrimination against foreigners in Switzerland (Falomir-Pichastor et al.

2004); realistic threat, symbolic threat, intergroup anxiety, and negative stereotypes as predictors of attitudes to immigrant groups (Stephan et al. 1999); the moderating role of ingroup identification in the effects of realistic and symbolic threats and intergroup anxiety on prejudice (Bizman and Yinon 2001); defensive linguistic consequences of a threat to ethnic identity (Vaes and Wicklund 2002); and stability of status and cardiovascular reactivity in members of minimal groups during intergroup competition and whether seen as threat or challenge (Scheepers 2009).

For a review of intergroup threat theory see Stephan et al. (2009). See also Rudman, Dohn, and Fairchild (2007) on threat and self-esteem compensation; and Tamir and Nadler (2007) on field dependence and intergroup threat.

*Intergroup Anxiety* If people do not have positive past experiences with members of an outgroup then intergroup anxiety may arise. Plant and Devine (2003) proposed that this anxiety would raise hostility toward outgroup members and that interaction with them would be avoided. They confirmed these predictions in two studies of White participants' responses to interacting with Black people—in the second study also finding that people with high anxiety about interacting with a Black person were less likely to return for such an interaction.

The long and troubled history of Black–White relations almost certainly must play a particular part in research findings. Hyers and Swim (1998) focused on this, looking at the immediate effects of such intergroup encounters in terms of intergroup anxiety, affect, cognitions, and behaviors during the encounters. They created groups of various combinations (solo or non-solo status) of African-American (minority group) and European-American (majority group) female students—this variable had very little effect. However, on both cognitive and task-involvement measures, European-Americans were more adversely affected than African-Americans. The authors suggest that the latter have greater intergroup experience and hence were better able to use intergroup coping strategies, in particular mindfulness.

See also Blair et al. (2003) on intergroup anxiety, little intergroup contact and degree of prejudice; Britt et al. (1996) on a person-by-situation approach to intergroup anxiety about interacting with an African-American or a European-American; Stephan and Stephan (1989) on antecedents of intergroup anxiety in Asian-Americans and Hispanic-Americans; and see Abrams et al. (2006) who found that positive intergenerational contact may reduce vulnerability to stereotype threat, reflected in lower group identification, reduced prejudice, and better task performance on the part of the older people in the study.

## Behavioral Consequences: Competition, Conflict, Aggression

*Intergroup Discontinuity* Relations between groups are often more significantly competitive than relations between individuals. This discontinuity between interindividual and intergroup behavior has, over the past 15 years, received considerable attention from Insko and Schopler and their colleagues. In a quantitative review of work in this field, Wildschut et al. (2003) conclude, from looking at 130 comparisons of interindividual and intergroup interactions, that intergroup interactions are on the whole more competitive than the interactions of individuals. They go on to identify four moderating variables, each uniquely associated with the size of the effect, discontinuity being greater when group rather than individual decisions are made, when there is unconstrained communication between participants, when there is severe conflict of interest, and when the opponent's behavior is either unconstrained by the experimenter or else constrained to be cooperative rather than reciprocal. Underpinning these is a theoretical standpoint that the discontinuity effect can be accounted for by the greater greed and fear which arises in the intergroup situation (and see Insko, Schopler et al. 1990; Pemberton et al. 1996).

For another theoretical comparison, this time between Campbell's Realistic Group Conflict Theory and Tajfel and Turner's Social Identity Theory see Insko et al. (1992).

For studies on the effect of intragroup influence on intergroup competition, see Wildschut et al. (2002) and also Van Avermaet et al. (1999); on the role of communication, see Insko et al. (1993); on the effect of a consensus rule, Insko et al. (1988).

The discontinuity effect can be reduced by identifiability (Schopler et al. 1995) and by introducing a concern for longer term outcomes (Insko et al. 1998; Insko et al. 2001). See also Schopler et al. (1994) on the survival of a cooperative tradition in the context of intergroup discontinuity.

For a review of studies on the reduction of the discontinuity effect, see Schopler and Insko (1999). See also Pedersen et al. (2008) on the displacement of triggered aggression on to ingroup or outgroup targets; Stenstrom et al. (2008) on the roles of ingroup identification and outgroup entitativity in vicarious retribution.

For a review on social identity and intergroup conflict, see Jussim et al. (2001). See also Rouhana (1999) on perceptions of national identity by Arab and Jewish high-school students in Israel; and Rudman and Ashmore (2007) on discrimination in relation to predictions from the Implicit Association Test.

Competition may give rise to anxiety: Wilder and Shapiro (1989b) found that competition-induced anxiety played a part in reducing the beneficial impact of an outgroup member's positive behavior. See also Holtz and Miller (2001) on attitude and opinion certainty in intergroup competition.

The basis for conflict (fear versus greed) affected the value of communication between groups in a study of a laboratory model of conflict between teams (Bornstein and Gilula 2003). Communication was of no use in conflicts motivated by greed but was highly effective in fear-based conflicts.

Some research bearing on affect and cognition obviously emphasizes practicalities, as well as the theoretical aspects of intergroup relations. See, for example, Chap. 1 with regard to the work of Cairns and colleagues on Northern Ireland and, complementing the large literature on inter-racial matters, see Casas and Ryan (2010) for relations between the growing Latino population and other Americans.

According to Struch and Schwartz (1989), intergroup aggression is different from ingroup bias and has different predictors. The next section describes some ways in which intergroup relations can be improved.

# The Contact Hypothesis and Improving Intergroup Relations

Sherif showed that contact between groups could, in some circumstances, reduce conflict. Allport (1954) proposed four conditions of contact for optimal consequences of intergroup contact. These were equal status in the situation, common goals, intergroup cooperation, and support from authority. Reducing bias, prejudice and conflict simply through contact is an appealingly simple idea: that increased encounters with the outgroup could reduce prejudice and increase knowledge, seeing "Them" as rather more like "Us," and seeing greater variability among outgroup members. Furthermore, contact may also reduce intergroup anxiety.

Hewstone (2003) concluded that the major mediating variables in predicting the outcome of intergroup contact are:

1. Contact under conditions of equal status (see, e.g., Hubbard 1999).
2. In situations where stereotypes are likely to be disconfirmed. See, for example, Werth and Lord (1992) who found that participants' previous conceptions of typical group member are changed by contact, thus affecting likelihood of generalization.
3. Where there is intergroup cooperation, where participants can get to know each other properly.
4. Where wider social norms support equality.

Pettigrew (1998) in a major review of intergroup contact theory sees these as facilitating rather than necessary conditions for contact to modify intergroup relations. He noted that, despite empirical support for Allport's general idea, there were also problems, including the fact that prejudiced people avoid intergroup contact, thus limiting the nature of research. Perhaps rather more importantly, it does not say what processes are involved, nor how they might generalize. In this substantive review, Pettigrew argues that contact leads to decategorization, salient categorization, and recategorization as a sequential process, with the results shaped by individual differences and societal norms.

For a history and review of the current state of the contact hypothesis, see Dovidio, Gaertner, and Kawakami (2003). For a review of the role of contact in improving intergroup relations, particularly with regard to research on violent conflict, see Tausch et al. (2006). For studies examining the role of wider norms and ideologies in modifying the effects of contact, see Bourhis et al. (2009); Cohen et al. (2006); Jetten et al. (2006); Louis et al. (2007); Vorauer, Gagnon, and Sasaki (2009).

There is more research on the contact hypothesis than on any other aspect of intergroup relations. This in itself suggests that the reality of the research findings is that the idea, while appealing, is certainly not simple. Although contact clearly does reduce intergroup conflict, as shown in the meta-analyses of Pettigrew and Tropp (2006, 2008) there are important moderating variables. Much will depend on what kind of contact, with which members of what kind of group, why, for how long, under what circumstances, whether affective ties are formed, and what negative factors may prevent intergroup contact from diminishing prejudice. Pettigrew and Tropp (2008), above, point out that the three most-studied mediators of contact effects are enhancing knowledge of the outgroup, reducing contact anxiety, and increasing empathy and perspective-taking—and, of these, reducing anxiety and increasing empathy seem to be more effective than increasing knowledge.

However, causality seems not to be unidirectional. Path analysis of data from a longitudinal field survey of ethnic majority and minority groups in Germany, Belgium, and England (Binder et al. 2009) showed lagged contact effects and prejudice effects. Contact reduced prejudice but prejudice, as has been suggested above, was also shown to reduce contact.

See also Brown and Capozza (2006) for a discussion of how motivational, emotional, and cultural influences affect the relationship between contact and both ingroup and outgroup attitudes.

Some research does suggest that simply the extent of opportunity for contacting members of other groups leads to more friendships and personal relations with outgroups—factors which may reduce intergroup hostility (Wagner et al. 2003). Opportunities for contact may increase with the percentage of minority group members, and it is sometimes suggested, especially by politicians, that this increasing ratio would increase ingroup prejudice, as a result of increased perceived threat. Nesdale and Todd (1998) studied intergroup ratios and contact—in university residences with different proportions of Chinese/AngloAustralian students. While they did find some generalized intercultural knowledge and acceptance in relation to intergroup ratios in student halls of residence, they noted that contact was not unqualified in its beneficial effects, particularly for members of the cultural majority. However, Wagner et al. (2006) found, in a study in Germany, that the greater opportunity for contact created by ethnic minorities being a larger percentage of the population in fact reduced prejudice, as contact theory would predict. The moderators of these effects need to be explored and clarified.

*Category-Based Attributions, Stereotypes and Contact* Rothbart (1996), who studied category-based exemplars and stereotype change, says his data are consistent with prototype models of category structure. If contact is with an individual who is too disconfirming of stereotype, then the category is less likely to be activated. With obvious implications although not actually a study of contact, Grier and McGill (2000) looked at "how we explain depends on whom we explain," finding that causal explanations for behavior were influenced by group comparisons and by the extent to which the actor was seen as typical of the group.

Pettigrew's reformulated Group Contact model proposes that the relationship between contact and bias is mediated by changing behavior, ingroup reappraisal, generating affective ties, and learning about the outgroup. Gaertner and Dovidio's Common Ingroup Identity model reflects the three processes which Pettigrew says occur in time sequence, that is, decategorization, salient categorization, and recategorization—and they add a fourth, dual identity (Dovidio, Gaertner, John et al. 2008).

A longitudinal study by Eller and Abrams (2003) offers partial support to both approaches. See also Gaertner and Dovidio (2009); Monteiro et al. (2009); Stone and Crisp (2007); and see Gaertner et al. (2008), who have begun to apply the common ingroup identity model to children as well as adults, which has meant incorporating developmental perspectives into their approach.

## *Dual Identity, Cross-Categorization, Overarching Categories, and Reformulated Ingroups*

The idea that contact might lead to improved intergroup relations by creating a new, more inclusive ingroup (we are all human!) has long had appeal. However, the evidence is not unequivocally supportive. Research on merged groups and on overarching groups often shows that members tend to try to differentiate themselves into subgroups (Hornsey and Hogg 1999) as predicted by Brewer's theory of optimal distinctiveness, discussed earlier in this chapter.

Brewer herself has considered the problem of the instability of superordinate groups and of the frequent failure of cooperative arrangements between ethnic groups to bring about long-term reduction in intergroup prejudice and conflict. In terms of the competing needs for inclusion and for differentiation, essential in her theory, she argues that cross-cutting social roles and identities may be a way in which distinctiveness and cooperation may be maintained in a more stable way.

In this vein Bettencourt and Dorr (1998) found that ingroup favoritism was significantly reduced when they gave research participants cross-cut role assignments in a cooperative setting for members of numerically majority and minority groups. Although category salience and identification were influenced by role assignment, only identification mediated the effect of role assignment on bias. Bettencourt et al. (2007) found that cross-cut role assignments may, in comparison with convergent roles, lead to worsened ingroup attitudes for members of numerical majorities, mediated by ingroup identification, and relative ingroup homogeneity. Klauer et al. (2003) have performed structural analyses on data from their five studies of crossed categorization (by age and gender), stereotyping, and context relevance. They looked at two indices of social categorization—relative subgroup memory and relative dominance or weight of each dimension of categorization. The growth of such research may help to shed light on stereotypes and category activation, and hence their consequences for perception and behavior.

Crisp and Hewstone (2000a) looked at the possible moderating roles of intergroup and affective context on the relationship between crossed-categorization and intergroup bias. They found that, despite different contexts and feedback conditions, the underlying cognitive representations of intergroup structure remained the same. This may pose important questions for those who hope that multiple categorizations may serve to improve intergroup relations.

Crisp et al. (2003) in a computerized minimal group experiment found that priming with an inclusive pronoun ("we") moderated crossed-category evaluations of the composite social group. Urada et al. (2007) used more complex stimuli than those usual in crossed-categorization studies and found that participants seemed to process information arising from multiple group memberships into one of two metacategories, "ingrouplike" and "outgrouplike," depending on the nature of the situation and the task they had to do.

See also Crisp et al. (2002) and Hewstone et al. (1993) on how multiple or crossed categories may improve intergroup relations; and N. Miller et al. (1998) for a theoretical analysis of cross-categorization effects.

In addition, see Amiot et al. (2007) for a longitudinal study on status, equity, and social identification following an intergroup merger; Cunningham (2006) on intergroup bias after recategorization of diverse groups; Dovidio et al. (1997) on recategorization, evaluation, self-disclosure and helping; Greenland and Brown (1999) on categorization, contact and intergroup anxiety; Kessler and Mummendey (2001) on post-recategorization conflict in the common ingroup; Lipponen et al. (2003) on Finnish shipyard workers; and Terry and Callan (1998) on an organizational merger.

An interesting experimental study by Gaertner et al. (2001) showed that when (sixty sets of) two three-person groups were induced to recategorize themselves as either six individuals or as an overarching group of six members, both strategies reduced intergroup bias. These reductions were regarded as being in line with both Brewer's approach to distinctiveness and Turner's self-categorization theory in that different processes were deemed to have been involved. Where participants were led to recategorize themselves into a superordinate group, reduction in bias occurred because the former outgroup members were now seen as more attractive than before. In the condition where each of the six recategorized themselves as separate individuals, intergroup bias decreased because the former ingroup members were seen to be less attractive than they had been before.

González and Brown (2003), pursuing somewhat similar ideas, varied category salience so that participants in a cooperative intergroup task saw themselves as members of a subgroup, a superordinate group, of both the subgroup and superordinate group (a "dual identity" strategy) or fourthly, in a condition where the group was not salient. All conditions of cooperative contact almost eliminated intergroup bias in the immediate situation. Significantly, though, this low level of bias only generalized beyond the immediate situation for those in the "superordinate" or "superordinate and subgroup" categories. See also González and Brown (2006a, b).

For other research on the positive relationship between inductions of dual identity and tolerance, see also Waldzus et al. (2003); Wenzel et al. (2003).

Gaertner et al. (1990) presented findings which they felt showed that the beneficial effects of cooperation in reducing intergroup bias were mediated by changed cognitive representations of the groups. By merging two three-person groups into one, bias was reduced by increasing the perceived attractiveness of members of the former outgroup. Gaertner et al. (1994), using a survey of 1,357 multicultural high-school students, found that reductions in bias were related to stronger common ingroup representations and to a superordinate American identity. Effects of contact were mediated by cognitive representations.

For other studies of common ingroup identity see Gaertner, Rust, Dovidio, Bachman, and Anastasio (1996) on the role of common ingroup identity in the reduction of bias among majority and minority group members; and Hayes et al. (2007) on the effects of integrated religious education in Northern Ireland. See also Gaertner et al. (1990); Gaertner et al. (1994); Nier et al. (2001).

For reviews on common ingroup identity, see Gaertner, Dovidio, and Bachman (1996); and Gaertner, Dovidio, Nier et al. (2000); Gaertner et al. (1999).

## Category Salience

Theories of social identity would also suggest that the blurring or eradication of self-defining group boundaries would threaten the self with negative rather than positive consequences. A further problem may be that by rendering group salience unimportant, or redefining the group, improved relations do not generalize to other groups. What matters, in terms of intergroup relations, is not that group differences should be eradicated but that the differences are firstly made clear (they may be less different than expected), that they are acknowledged in that they remain salient, and that they do not give rise to anxiety or a sense of threat. It has also been suggested that positive intergroup relations can be facilitated by recognizing separate subgroup identities, as well as developing a common group identity (Dovidio, Gaertner, and Esses 2008).

Group salience has been found to be a key moderator of the effects of contact—but how do the effects generalize from the contact individual(s) to the group? It may seem superficially counter-intuitive, but it appears to be important that participants, while engaged in interpersonal contact, maintain their awareness of group membership (Voci and Hewstone 2002; Voci and Hewstone 2003); it may be advantageous if membership salience occurs *part way* through the beneficial contact period.

See Ensari and Miller (2002) on the effects of self-disclosure, typicality, and salience in the reduction of bias in cooperative dyadic intergroup contact. See also Lichtenstein et al. (1997); Brown et al. (1999); Tropp and Bianchi (2007).

## What Does Contact Actually Change: Outgroup Typicality and Perceived Homogeneity

There is evidence that contact can lead to more positive, or at least less negative, social attitudes. It may also make people aware that there is greater variability among members of an outgroup—that is, less homogeneity than they had supposed. Contact can increase outgroup forgiveness and outgroup trust (cf. Hewstone et al. 2005).

Wolsko et al. (2003) found that contact changed perceptions of outgroup variability, but only when the contact was with a person who both disconfirmed the stereotype and, nevertheless, was still seen as typical of the group. Hamburger (1994) discussed the possible effects, on the outgroup stereotype, of contact with an atypical outgroup member. Such effects included a perception of increased outgroup variability.

Wilder (2001) found that the outgroup in his study was most favorably rated when contact (manipulated experimentally) was with a member of the outgroup who was seen to be typical and the interaction was pleasant. However, he further showed that contact was not beneficial if the other were seen as typical but the outgroup stereotype had negative implications for the ingroup. Overall, it appeared that the more typical an outgroup member is seen to be, the greater was the perception of the predictive power of the encounter to other group members.

Desforges et al. (1997) also explored the role of group representativeness in generalization, a component element of the contact hypothesis. They found that generalizing is more likely if a person is seen as representative of the group.

For a dissenting view on the effects of contact see Corneille (1994), who emphasizes ambiguities of the contact hypothesis.

See also Biernat (1990) who assessed people's stereotypes and looked at the role of positive affect in cognitive organization, finding that contact influenced stereotype strength. For a discussion of measurement and conceptual issues relating to stereotypes and contact see Biernat and Crandall (1994). For measurement of contact see McCauley et al. (2001), who have devised an index of intergroup contact and ingroup isolation based upon the proportions of groups in enduring social units.

## Does Contact have Generalized Consequences?

There are different ways in which contact might generalize—from specific members of an outgroup to the wider group as a whole; from the particular outgroup to other outgroups; across situations; across responses (Gaertner and Dovidio 2000; Hewstone 1996). Contact may also provide access to informal social networks (Hewstone 2003). It may also reduce what Schofield and Eurich-Fulcer (2001) see as the "almost automatic fear" experienced by members of a group in response to those of another group.

N. Miller (2002) discussed some of the theoretical issues involved in the generalization of positive intergroup contact, contrasting the approaches of Brewer and Miller (1984) on personalization, Hewstone and Brown's (Hewstone and Brown 1986) social identity theory, and Gaertner and Dovidio's (Gaertner and Dovidio 2000) common ingroup identity model. He concludes that differentiation has cognitive consequences while personalization has significant motivational consequences—both cognitions and motivations being important for generalization.

See Pettigrew (1997) on generalized contact effects of prejudice; see also Pettigrew (1996). Pettigrew introduced the concept of "deprovincialization" to explain a generalized contact effect in which intergroup friendship generalizes to more positive affect toward a far wider range of racial and ethnic outgroups than those with whom people have had direct contact. He explores this further in relation to the idea of social identity complexity—how people think about their ingroups (Pettigrew 2008).

*Contact and Attitudes*  Contact tends to be associated with more positive attitudes toward outgroup members. While the association might imply causality in either direction, statistical path analysis has made clear that, importantly, contact can lead to attitude change. This path seems to be stronger than attitudes leading to behavior—a thorny issue which has beset generations of social psychologists! There is no reason why the causality might not operate in both directions, in a kind of benevolent circularity, as was found by Herek and Capitanio (1996). See also Brown et al. (2001); Hewstone et al. (1994); Liebkind et al. (2000).

In a review, Devine et al. (1996) emphasize the need to consider the motivations and cognitions brought to the encounter by majority and minority group members.

## Generating Affective Ties and the Reduction of Intergroup Anxiety

Affective ties seem clearly to be very important factors in the mediation of the beneficial effects of contact, especially by reducing intergroup anxiety, and by allowing the growth of trust between members of different groups. Islam and Hewstone (1993a) looked at different dimensions of contact—quantitative, qualitative (e.g., equal status, warm), and intergroup (with salience of group membership)—in relation to intergroup anxiety, perceived outgroup variability and intergroup attitudes toward members of majority and minority outgroups in Bangladesh. Quantitative contact significantly influenced perceived outgroup variability, whereas qualitative contact was associated with outgroup attitude. All three forms of contact were associated with reduced intergroup anxiety.

A close friendship with a member of an outgroup may be a predictor of lower intergroup anxiety, though Vonofakou et al. (2007) in three studies of the effects of heterosexuals' friendships with gay men, found that only was the case when the outgroup friend was perceived as highly typical.

The role of intergroup contact in developing trust has been explored by Tropp (2008).

The importance of friendship in intergroup contact has been shown by many researchers. Indeed, Wright et al. (2008) suggest that it would be simpler to describe optimal conditions for successful contact as being those which make friendship more likely, and that the inverse relationship between contact and prejudice is mediated by feelings of friendship.

Contact may occur for many reasons, which include political and structural change or third party intervention. A study of contact initiated by members of an outgroup showed that intergroup anxiety raised ingroup members' perception of threat, anger, and offensive action tendencies (Van Zomeren et al. 2007).

See also Aberson et al. (2004) on relations between whites and African-Americans and between Whites and Latinos; Aboud et al. (2003) on effects on bystanders of intergroup name-calling; Aboud and Sankar (2007) on an intergroup integrated school; Cairns et al. (2006) on ingroup and outgroup affect in the context of religious group membership and intergroup conflict in Northern Ireland; Eller and Abrams (2004) on Anglo-French and Mexican-American relations; Hargie et al. (2002) on contact, trust and friendship between Catholic and Protestant young people in Northern Ireland; Levin et al. (2003), for a longitudinal study of more than two thousand White, Asian, Latino, and African-American college students; Tausch, Hewstone et al. (2007) on cross-community contact in Northern Ireland, social identification, and intergroup anxiety; and Van Laar et al. (2008) on cross-ethnic relationships.

## *Types of Contact*

The research cited above addresses actual contact between members of different groups. In addition, there are now studies of indirect or extended contact, where ingroup members have friends who have contact or friendship with outgroup members, and of imagined contact, where group members are asked to imagine interaction with outgroup members. For a review see R. Turner (2010).

R. Turner, Crisp, and Lambert (2007) found that imagined contact (talking to an outgroup member) led to more positive evaluations, mediated by reduced intergroup anxiety. Stathi and Crisp (2008) concluded from three studies that imagined contacts were most favorable for intergroup relations when the personal self rather than the social self was salient. See also Crisp and Turner (2009) and R. Turner and Crisp (2010).

Crisp and Abrams (2008) present an integrated contact model, examining the processes through which intergroup contact, whether actual or imagined, reduces the impact of stereotypes on behavior via changed perceptions not only of the outgroup but also of the ingroup and the self, which may consequently liberate people from the constraints of negative stereotypes in other domains also.

Pettigrew et al. (2007) found not only that indirect contact (having an ingroup friend who has an outgroup friend) and direct contact are highly intercorrelated but also that indirect and direct contact reduced outgroup prejudice to a comparable degree. They found that they relate to similar personality variables, with authoritarians avoiding contact. The effects of contact are mediated by threat and are negatively related to it. However, for indirect contact it is largely due to perceived collective threat, whereas individual and collective threat are negatively related to direct contact. Pettigrew et al. interpret these findings in the context of group norms. Paolini et al. (2007) also found that direct and indirect friendships reduced outgroup prejudice. For direct contact the effect was larger when the outgroups aroused greater affective rather than cognitive responses; the reverse was true for indirect friendship.

See also Amichai-Hamburger (2008) on innovative intergroup internet-based contact leading to face-to-face contact; Cameron et al. (2006) on different models of extended contact and changing children's attitudes to refugees; and Pettigrew (2009) on secondary, extended effects of contact.

As regards reducing prejudice, see also R. Turner, Hewstone, and Voc (2007) on self-disclosure and intergroup anxiety as mediators of the effect of direct and extended contact.

For studies addressing norms and the link between contact and outgroup discrimination, see Ata et al. (2009) and L. G. E. Smith and Postmes (2009).

## Negative or Ambiguous Consequences of Contact

A body of work suggests that the consequences of contact can be paradoxical, ambiguous, or sometimes negative. Pettigrew himself has suggested that one line of research which needs greater focus is to understand the circumstances in which increased prejudice results from contact, while another is to clarify the moderators and mediating processes behind the effects of contact (Pettigrew 2008).

See also Dovidio, Gaertner, and Saguy (2008) for a review; and see Corneille (1994), who emphasizes the ambiguities of the contact hypothesis.

If the contact situation itself involves negative aspects, such as threat, high anxiety, relative deprivation, or unequal status then the consequences may also be negative. Intergroup contact can lead to false expectations of equality as found by Saguy et al. (2009). Contact may also make minority disadvantage salient, with some negative consequences, as found in a longitudinal study of East and West Germans (Fischer, Maes, and Schmidt 2007).

Vorauer and Sasaki (2009) discuss what they call the ironic effects of empathy in intergroup interaction, having found that empathizing with outgroup members is beneficial only outside, but not within, the context of intergroup interaction. In a similar vein, Vorauer, Martens, and Sasaki (2009) found, from the results of four complex studies of prejudice and intergroup interaction, that cognitive and affective perspective-taking can backfire, with participants low in prejudice behaving toward an outgroup member more negatively than when in other mind-sets. Paradoxically, perspective-taking by high prejudice participants led to somewhat more positive behavior. As with the previously cited study, the beneficial effects of trying to understand were greater outside the interaction situation than within it.

See also Andreychik and Gill (2009) on the diverse consequences for dominant ingroup members of external social explanations for the behavior of low status outgroups; Bilewicz (2007) on historical versus present focus during contact between Polish and Jewish students; Dessel and Rogge (2008) for a review of the empirical literature on intergroup dialogue. Eller et al. (2007) on quality and quantity of contact; Henry and Hardin (2006) on contact, status bias, and prejudice between Whites and Blacks in the USA and between Muslims and Christians in Lebanon; C. S. Johnson et al. (2009) on the content of inter-racial interactions; and Shelton et al. (2009) on the misunderstandings in intergroup contact that can reinforce intergroup prejudice and bias, in this case between Blacks and Whites in the USA.

Behavior may be construed negatively when it comes from an outgroup member, as in Czopp's (Czopp 2008) study of compliments in the form of positive stereotypes.

## Intergroup Conflict and Its Resolution

Intergroup research touches conflicts and stress-points across the world and the breadth of communities studied is itself a sobering reminder of how many groups live uneasily—and worse—with one another. Many of those involved in this area of research to understand are also involved with work on reconciliation and healing, as, for example, Staub on genocide in Rwanda and many other arenas of conflict. See, for example, Staub (2008).

For a review of conflict between individual members of different identity groups and its possible means of resolution, see Stephan (2008a, b). Additional relevant work includes: The role of humiliation in the lack of will to resolve intergroup conflict in Palestinians (Ginges and Atran 2008); a review of the roles of consideration of future consequences, independent leadership, outgroup empathy, and coordination in reducing intergroup conflict (Cohen and Insko 2008); the effect of considering future consequences in an iterated prisoner's dilemma game (Wolf et al. 2009); conflict and cooperation as developmental processes in the life of a group rather than simply positive and negative aspects of group dynamics (Dovidio, Saguy, and Shnabel 2009); the priming of accessible cooperative conflict-schemas (de Zavala et al. 2008); and a review of interventions to enhance intergroup tolerance (Jonas 2009).

See also Fisher (2006) for a general review of intergroup conflict.

For reviews of the social psychology of intergroup reconciliation and the promotion of peace between groups previously in conflict with one another see Hewstone et al. (2008), and Nadler et al. (2008). See also Vollhardt and Bilali (2008) on social psychology's contribution to the study of peace.

See also Subasic and Reynolds (2009) on the policy of "practical reconciliation" between Australian indigenous and nonindigenous people and the failure to address the role of past injustice in current inequality.

Others come to the problems of intergroup relations from wider perspectives in the hope of providing new insights; for example, see Brewer (2007a) on human nature and intergroup relations in which she addresses what she calls the importance of being we; Choi and Bowles (2007) on the coevolution of war and parochial altruism—necessarily jointly evolved, they argue; Mesoudi (2009) on cultural evolutionary theory; Schaller and Neuberg (2008) on evolutionary psychology and understanding stereotypes, prejudice, discrimination, and conflict, with possible implications for their amelioration. See also Amodio (2008) on the social neuroscience of intergroup relations.

## Picture to Be Completed

The picture we have of intergroup relations is very far from complete. We begin to know something of the cognitive and affective factors involved, of their development, and even of biological and evolutionary processes which may be important. Despite the increasingly large and detailed literature on the role of contact in reducing prejudice and hostility toward outgroups, our understanding is still partial, although the identification of mediating variables is leading to many clarifications. Pettigrew (2007) identifies the distinction between primary and secondary emotions made by Leyens and colleagues as a particularly interesting approach for the future. It seems likely that there is much more to learn about the affective processes involved in intergroup relations. The role of affect in cognitive organization is also imperfectly understood, as are the links among affect, cognition, and behavior. The insights of the earliest researchers have proved remarkably enduring but the extent of theoretical development and the body of empirical literature of recent years has given us a much more complex, detailed and layered view. Pettigrew (2006) advocates multilevel approaches to intergroup relations, for enhancing understanding and, at the macrolevel, for developing effective interventions and building on the strengths of intra- and inter-group diversity. The level of conflict in the world continues to provide a tragic setting and an urgent rationale for acquiring greater understanding of outbreaks of murderous hostility between groups and also of their reconciliation. The hope is always that better understanding of intergroup processes at every level will help groups of all kinds and of all sizes to coexist in peace and flourish in diversity.

# References

Abbink, K., Bolton, G. E., Sadrieh, A., & Tang, F.-F. (2001). Adaptive learning versus punishment in ultimatum bargaining. *Games and Economic Behavior, 37*, 1–25.

Abbink, K., Darziv, R., Gilula, Z., Goren, H., Irlenbusch, B., Keren, A., Rockenbach, B., Sadrieh, A., Selten, R., & Zamir, S. (2003). The fisherman's problem: Exploring the tension between cooperative and non-cooperative concepts in a simple game. *Journal of Economic Psychology, 24*, 425–445.

Abbink, K., Sadrieh, A., & Zamir, S. (2004). Fairness, public good, and emotional aspects of punishment behavior. *Theory and Decision, 57*, 25–57.

Abdul-Muhmin, A. (2001). The effect of perceived seller reservation prices on buyers' bargaining behavior in a flexible-price market. *Journal of International Consumer Marketing, 13*(3), 29–45.

Abele, S., Bless, H., & Ehrhart, K.-M. (2004). Social information processing in strategic decision-making: Why timing matters. *Organizational Behavior and Human Decision Processes, 93*, 28–46.

Abelson, R. P. (1995). *Statistics as principled argument.* Hillsdale, NJ, and Hove, UK: Lawrence Erlbaum.

Abelson, R. P., Dasgupta, N., Park, J., & Banaji, M. R. (1998). Perceptions of the collective other. *Personality and Social Psychology Review, 2*, 243–250.

Aberson, C. L., & Howanski, L. M. (2002). Effects of selfesteem, status, and identification on two forms of ingroup bias. *Current Research in Social Psychology, 7*(13), 225–243.

Aberson, C. L., Shoemaker, C., & Tomolillo, C. (2004). Implicit Bias and Contact: The Role of Interethnic Friendships. *Journal of Social Psychology, 144*, 335–348.

Abolafia, M. Y. (1996). Hyperrational gaming. *Journal of Contemporary Ethnography, 25*, 226–250.

Aboud, F. E. (1992). Conflict and group relations. In C. U. Shantz & W. W. Hartup (Eds.), *Conflict in child and adolescent development* (pp. 356–379). New York: Cambridge University Press.

Aboud, F. E., Mendelson, M. J., & Purdy, K. T. (2003). Crossrace peer relations and friendship quality. *International Journal of Behavioral Development, 27*, 165–173.

Aboud, F. E., & Sankar, J. (2007). Friendship and identity in a languageintegrated school. *International Journal of Behavioral Development, 31*, 445–453.

Abrams, D. (1994). Social self-regulation. *Personality and Social Psychology Bulletin, 20*, 473–483.

Abrams, D., & Randsley de Moura, G. (2002). The psychology of collective political protest. In V. C. Ottati, R. S. Tindale, J. Edwards, F. B. Bryant, L. Heath, D. C. O'Connell, Y. Suarez-Balcazar, & E. J. Posavac (Eds.), *The social psychology of politics* (pp. 193–214). New York: Kluwer Academic/Plenum Publishers.

Abrams, D., Eller, A., & Bryant, J. (2006). An age apart: The effects of intergenerational contact and stereotype threat on performance and intergroup bias. *Psychology and Aging, 21*, 691–702.

Abrams, D., & Hogg, M. A. (2001). Comments on the motivational status of self-esteem in social identity and intergroup discrimination. In M. A. Hogg & D. Abrams (Eds.), *Intergroup relations: Essential readings* (pp. 232–244). New York: Psychology Press.

Abrams, D., & Hogg, M. A. (2004). Collective identity: Group membership and self-conception. In M. B. Brewer & M. Hewstone (Eds.), *Self and social identity* (pp. 147–181). Malden: Blackwell Publishing.

Abrams, D., & Hogg, M. A. (2008). Group processes & intergroup relations 10 years on: Development, impact and future directions. *Group Processes and Intergroup Relations, 11*, 419–424.

Abrams, D., Hogg, M. A., Hinkle, S., & Often, S. (2005). The social identity perspective on small groups. In M. S. Poole & A. B. Hollingshead (Eds.), *Theories of small groups: Interdisciplinary perspectives* (pp. 99–137). Thousand Oaks, CA: Sage Publications, Inc.

Abrams, D., & Rutland, A. (2008). The development of subjective group dynamics. In S. R. Levy & M. Killen (Eds.), *Intergroup attitudes and relations in childhood through adulthood* (pp. 47–65). New York: Oxford University Press.

Abrams, D., Rutland, A., & Cameron, L. (2003). The development of subjective group dynamics: Children's judgments of normative and deviant in-group and out-group individuals. *Child Development, 74*, 1–17.

Abrams, D., Rutland, A., Cameron, L., & Marques, J. (2003). The development of subjective group dynamics: When ingroup bias gets specific. *British Journal of Developmental Psychology, 21*, 155–176.

Abreu, D., & Sethi, R. (2003). Evolutionary stability in a reputational model of bargaining. *Games and Economic Behavior, 44*, 195–216.

Achterkamp, M., & Akkerman, A. (2003). Identifying latent conflict in collective bargaining. *Rationality and Society, 15*, 15–43.

Acker, G. (2004). The effect of organizational conditions (role conflict, role ambiguity, opportunities for professional development, and social support) on job satisfaction and intention to leave among social workers in mental health care. *Community Mental Health Journal, 40*, 65–73.

Adarves-Yorno, I., Postmes, T., & Haslam, S. A. (2006). Social identity and the recognition of creativity in groups. *British Journal of Social Psychology, 45*, 479–497.

Adolphs, R. (2009). The social brain: Neural basis of social knowledge. *Annual Review of Psychology, 60*, 693–716.

Adorno, T. W., Frenkel-Brunswik, E., Levinson, D. J., & Sanford, R. N. (1950). *The authoritarian personality*. New York: Harper and Row.

Aebischer, V., & Oberle, D. (2002). Differenciation intergroupes et biais pro-exogroupe chez les membres d'un groupe dominant [Intergroup differentiation and out-group bias in members of a dominant group. *Cahiers Internationaux de Psychologie Sociale*, No. 54, 23–33.

Affisco, J. F., & Chanin, M. N. (1990). An empirical investigation of integrated multicriteria group decision models in a simulation/gaming context. *Simulation and Gaming, 21*, 27–47.

Agastya, M. (1996). Multiplayer bargaining situations: A decision theoretic approach. *Games and Economic Behavior, 12*, 1–20.

Aharpour, S., & Brown, R. (2002). Functions of group identification: An exploratory analysis. *Revue Internationale de Psychologie Sociale, 15*, 157–186.

Ahn, T. K., Janssen, M. A., & Ostrom, E. (2004). Signals, symbols, and human cooperation. In R. W. Sussman & A. R. Chapman (Eds.), *The origins and nature of sociality* (pp. 122–139). Hawthorne, NY: Aldine de Gruyter.

Akimov, V., & Soutchanski, M. (1994). Automata simulation of Nperson social dilemma games. *Journal of Conflict Resolution, 38*, 138–148.

Aknine, S., Pinson, S., & Shakun, M. F. (2004). A multi-agent coalition formation method based on preference models. *Group Decision and Negotiation, 13*, 513–538.

Aktipis, C. A. (2006). Introduction to the special issue on the evolution of cooperation. *Adaptive Behavior, 14*, 191–193.

Aladwani, A. M. (2002). An empirical examination of the role of social integration in system development projects. *Information Systems Journal, 12*, 339–353.

Albarello, F., & Rubini, M. (2008). Relazioni intergruppi e fenomeni di deumanizzazione [Intergroup relations and dehumanisation]. *Psicologia Sociale, 3*, 67–94.

Aldag, R. J., & Fuller, S. R. (1993). Beyond fiasco: A reappraisal of the groupthink phenomenon and a new model of group decision processes. *Psychological Bulletin, 113*, 533–552.

Allard Poesi, F. (1998). Representations and influence processes in groups: Towards a socio-cognitive perspective on cognition in organization. *Scandinavian Journal of Management, 14*, 395–420.

Allen, B. C., Sargent, L. D., & Bradley, L. M. (2003). Differential effects of task and reward interdependence on perceived helping behavior, effort, and group performance. *Small Group Research, 34*, 716–740.

Allen, M., Donohue, W., & Stewart, B. (1990). Comparing hardline and softline bargaining strategies in zero-sum situations using meta-analysis. In M. A. Rahim (Ed.), *Theory and research in conflict management* (pp. 86–103). New York: Praeger Publishers.

Allison, S. T., & Kerr, N. L. (1994). Group correspondence biases and the provision of public goods. *Journal of Personality and Social Psychology, 66*, 688–698.

Allison, S. T., & Messick, D. M. (1990). Social decision heuristics in the use of shared resources. *Journal of Behavioral Decision Making, 3*, 195–204.

Allport, G. W. (1954). *The nature of prejudice*. Reading, MA: Addison-Wesley.

Alper, S., Tjosvold, D., & Law, K. S. (1998). Interdependence and controversy in group decision making: Antecedents to effective self-managing teams. *Organizational Behavior and Human Decision Processes, 74*, 33–52.

Alvard, M. S. (2004). The ultimatum game, fairness, and cooperation among big game hunters. In J. Henrich, R. Boyd, S. Bowles, C. Camerer, E. Fehr, & H. Gintis (Eds.), *Foundations of human sociality* (pp. 413–435). New York: Oxford University Press.

Alvard, M. S., & Nolin, D. A. (2002). Rousseau's whale hunt? Coordination among big-game hunters. *Current Anthropology, 43*, 533–559.

Alvarez, R., & Robin, L. (1992). Organizational structure. In E. F. Borgatta & M. L. Borgatta (Eds.), *Encyclopedia of sociology* (Vol. 3, pp. 1394–1404). New York: Macmillan.

Alvarez, S. A., Barney, J. B., & Bosse, D. A. (2003). Trust and its alternatives. *Human Resource Management, 42*, 393–404.

Amancio, L. (1989). Social differentiation between "dominant" and "dominated" groups: Toward an integration of social stereotypes and social identity. *European Journal of Social Psychology, 19*, 1–10.

Amann, E., & Leininger, W. (1996). Asymmetric all-pay auctions with incomplete information: The two-player case. *Games and Economic Behavior, 14*, 1–18.

Amaral, M. J., & Monteiro, M. B. (2002). To be without being seen: Computer-mediated communication and social identity management. *Small Group Research, 33*, 575–589.

Amer, R., Carreras, F., & Giménez, J. Miguel. (2002). The modified Banzhaf value for games with coalition structure: An axiomatic characterization. *Mathematical Social Sciences, 43*, 45–54.

Ames, D. L., Jenkins, A. C., Banaji, M. R., & Mitchell, J. P. (2008). Taking another person's perspective increases self-referential neural processing. *Psychological Science, 19*, 642–644.

Amichai-Hamburger, Y. (2008). The contact hypothesis reconsidered: Interacting via Internet: Theoretical and practical aspects. In A. Barak (Ed.), *Psychological aspects of cyberspace: Theory, research, applications* (pp. 209–227). New York: Cambridge University Press.

Amiot, C. E., & Bourhis, R. Y. (2003). Discrimination and the positive-negative asymmetry effects: Ideological and normative process. *Personality and Social Psychology Bulletin, 29*, 597–608.

Amiot, C. E., Terry, D. J., & Callan, V. J. (2007). Status, justice, and social identification during an intergroup merger: A longitudinal study. *British Journal of Social Psychology, 46*, 557–577.

Amodio, D. M. (2008). The social neuroscience of intergroup relations. *European Review of Social Psychology, 19*, 1–54.

Anand, V., Manz, C. C., & Glick, W. H. (1998). An organizational memory approach to information management. *Academy of Management Review, 23*, 796–809.

Anandalingam, G. (1989). A multiagent multiattribute approach for conflict resolution in acid rain impact mitigation. *IEEE Transactions on Systems, Man*, and Cybernetics, 19, 1142–1153.

Anastasio, P., Bachman, B., Gaertner, S., & Dovidio, J. (1997). Categorization, recategorization and common ingroup identity. In R. Spears, P. J. Oakes, N. Ellemers, & S. A. Haslam (Eds.),

*The social psychology of stereotyping and group life* (pp. 236–256). Oxford, England: Blackwell Publishers, Inc.

Ancona, D. G., & Caldwell, D. F. (1988). Beyond task and maintenance: Defining external functions in groups. *Group and Organization Studies, 13*, 468–494.

Ancona, D. G., & Caldwell, D. F. (1992). Demography and design: Predictors of new product team performance. *Organization Science, 3*, 321–341.

Ancona, D. G., & Caldwell, D. F. (1998). Rethinking team composition from the outside in. In D. H. Gruenfeld (Ed.), *Composition. Research on managing groups and teams* (Vol. 1, pp. 21–37). Stamford, CT: Jai Press, Inc.

Ancona, D. G., Friedman, R. A., & Kolb, D. M. (1991). The group and what happens on the way to "yes." *Negotiation Journal, 7*, 155–173.

Anderhub, V., Güth, W., & Marchand, N. (2004). Early or late conflict settlement in a variety of games – An experimental study. *Journal of Economic Psychology, 25*, 177–194.

Andersen, S. M., Saribay, A., & Thorpe, J. S. (2008). Simple kindness can go a long way: Relationships, social identity, and engagement. *Social Psychology, 39*, 59–69.

Anderson, C. (2004). Linking micro– to macro-level behavior in the Aggressor-Defender-Stalker Game. *Adaptive Behavior, 12*, 175–185.

Anderson, Neil. (1992). Work group innovation: State-of-theart review. In D. M. Hosking and N. Anderson (Eds.), *Organizational change and innovation: Psychological perspectives and practices in Europe* (pp. 149–160). London: Routledge.

Anderson, Norman H. (1990). Stereotype theory. In N. H. Anderson (Ed.), *Contributions to information integration theory, Vol. 1: Cognition; Vol. 2: Social; Vol. 3: Developmental* (pp. 183–240). Hillsdale, NJ: Lawrence Erlbaum Associates, Inc.

Andes, R. H. (1992). Message dimensions of negotiation. *Negotiation Journal, 8*, 125–130.

Ando, K. (1999). Social identification and a solution to social dilemmas. *Asian Journal of Social Psychology, 2*, 227–235.

Andreoni, J., Brown, P. M., & Vesterlund, L. (2002). What makes an allocation fair? Some experimental evidence. *Games and Economic Behavior, 40*, 1–24.

Andreoni, J., & Miller, J. H. (1995). Auctions with artificial adaptive agents. *Games and Economic Behavior, 10*, 39–64.

Andrews, M. (2000). Forgiveness in Context. *Journal of Moral Education, 29*, 75–86.

Andreychik, M. R., & Gill, M. J. (2009). Ingroup identity moderates the impact of social explanations on intergroup attitudes: External explanations are not inherently prosocial. *Personality and Social Psychology Bulletin, 35*, 1632–1645.

Antonides, G. (1994). Mental accounting in a sequential Prisoner's Dilemma game. *Journal of Economic Psychology, 15*, 351–374.

Aquino, K., Steisel, V., & Kay, A. (1992). The effects of resource distribution, voice, and decision framing on the provision of public goods. *Journal of Conflict Resolution, 36*, 665–687.

Araujo, L. (1998). Knowing and learning as networking. *Management Learning, 29*, 317–336.

Arbet, L. (1991). Reflexions on creativity. *Studia Psychologica, 33*, 175–180.

Arcuri, L., & Cadinu, M. R. (1997). Cognitive and affective factors in the development and maintenance of biased intergroup relations. *Swiss Journal of Psychology Schweizerische Zeitschrift fuer Psychologie Revue Suisse de Psychologie, 56*, 145–155.

Argote, L., Insko, C. A., Yovetich, N., & Romero, A. A. (1995). Group learning curves: The effects of turnover and task complexity on group performance. *Journal of Applied Social Psychology, 25*, 512–529.

Argyres, N. S., & Liebeskind, J. P. (1999). Contractual commitments, bargaining power, and governance inseparability: Incorporating history into transaction cost theory. *Academy of Management Review, 24*, 49–63.

Armantier, O. (2004). Does observation influence learning? *Games and Economic Behavior, 46*, 221–239.

Armbruster, C., Gale, B., Brady, J., & Thompson, N. (1999). Perceived ownership in a community coalition. *Public Health Nursing, 16*, 17–22.

Arndt, J., Greenberg, J., Schimel, J., Pyszczynski, T., & Solomon, S. (2002). To belong or not to belong, that is the question: Terror management and identification with gender and ethnicity. *Journal of Personality and Social Psychology, 83*, 26–43.

Arnold, J. A., & Carnevale, P. J. (1997). Preferences for dispute resolution procedures as a function of intentionality, consequences, expected future interaction, and power. *Journal of Applied Social Psychology, 27*, 371–398.

Aron, A., & Aron, E. N. (1996). Self and self-expansion in relationships. In G. J. O. Fletcher & F. J. Fletcher (Eds.), *Knowledge structures in close relationships: A social psychological approach* (pp. 325–344). Mahwah, NJ: Lawrence Erlbaum Associates, Inc.

Aron, A., McLaughlin-Volpe, T., Mashek, D., Lewandowski, G., Wright, S. C., & Aron, E. N. (2004). Including others in the self. In W. Stroebe & M. Hewstone (Eds.), *European review of social psychology* (Vol. 15, pp. 101–132). Hove, England: Psychology Press/Taylor & Francis (UK), 2004.

Arrow, H., & Cook, J. (2008). Configuring and reconfiguring groups as complex learning systems. In V. I. Sessa & M. London (Eds.), *Work group learning: Understanding, improving and assessing how groups learn in organizations* (pp. 45–72). New York: Taylor & Francis Group/Lawrence Erlbaum Associates.

Arthur, A. E., Bigler, R. S., Liben, L. S., Gelman, S. A., & Ruble, D. N. (2008). Gender stereotyping and prejudice in young children: A developmental intergroup perspective. In S. R. Levy & M. Killen (Eds.), *Intergroup attitudes and relations in childhood through adulthood* (pp. 66–86). New York: Oxford University Press.

Arthur, W., Jr., Bennett, W., Jr., Edens, P. S., & Bell, S. T. (2003). Effectiveness of training in organizations: A meta-analysis of design and evaluation features. *Journal of Applied Psychology, 88*, 234–245.

Arunachalam, V., & Dilla, W. N. (1995). Judgment accuracy and outcomes in negotiation: A causal modeling analysis of decision-aiding effects. *Organizational Behavior and Human Decision Processes, 61*, 289–304.

Asch, S. E. (1955). Opinions and social pressure. *Scientific American, 193*(5), 31–35.

Ashburn-Nardo, L., Voils, C. I., & Monteith, M. J. (2001). Implicit associations as the seeds of intergroup bias: How easily do they take root? *Journal of Personality and Social Psychology, 81*, 789–799.

Asheim, G. B. (2002). On the epistemic foundation for backward induction. *Mathematical Social Sciences, 44*, 121–144.

Ashmore, R. D., Deaux, K., & McLaughlin-Volpe, T. (2004). An organizing framework for collective identity: Articulation and significance of multidimensionality. *Psychological Bulletin, 130*, 80–114.

Ashmore, R. D., Jussim, L., & Wilder, D. (Eds.). (2001). *Social identity, intergroup conflict, and conflict reduction.* New York: Oxford University Press.

Ata, A., Bastian, B., & Lusher, D. (2009). Intergroup contact in context: The mediating role of social norms and group-based perceptions on the contact-prejudice link. *International Journal of Intercultural Relations, 33*, 498–506.

Attar, A., Majumdar, D., Piaser, G., & Porteiro, N. (2008). Common agency games: Indifference and separable preferences. *Mathematical Social Sciences, 56*, 75–95.

Au, W. T., Chen, X. P., & Komorita, S. S. (1998). A probabilistic model of criticality in a sequential public good dilemma. *Organizational Behavior and Human Decision Processes, 75*, 274–293.

Au, W. T., & Komorita, S. S. (2002). Effects of initial choices in the prisoner's dilemma. *Journal of Behavioral Decision Making, 15*, 343–359.

Aubert, B. A., & Kelsey, B. L. (2003). Further understanding of trust and performance in virtual teams. *Small Group Research, 34*, 575–618.

Auerbach, Y. (2005). Conflict resolution, forgiveness and reconciliation in material and identity conflicts. *Humboldt Journal of Social Relations, 29*(2), 41–80.

Augsburger, D. W. (1992). *Conflict mediation across cultures: Pathways and patterns.* Louisville, KY: Westminster/John Knox Press.

Aureli, F., & de Waal, F. B. M. (Eds.). (2000). *Natural conflict resolution.* Berkeley, CA: University of California Press.

Auyeung, L. H. (2004). Building a collaborative online learning community: A case study in Hong Kong. *Journal of Educational Computing Research, 31,* 119–136.

Aviram, R. B. (2009). *The relational origins of prejudice: A convergence of psychoanalytic and social cognitive perspectives.* Lanham, MD: Jason Aronson.

Avtgis, T. A. (2000). Unwillingness to communicate and satisfaction in organizational relationships. *Psychological Reports, 87,* 82–84.

Axelrod, R. M. (1984). *The evolution of cooperation.* New York: Basic Books.

Axelrod, R. M. (1997). *The complexity of cooperation: Agent-based models of competition and collaboration.* Princeton, NJ: Princeton University Press.

Axtell, C. M., Holman, D. J., Unsworth, K. L., Wall, T. D., Waterson, P. E., & Harrington, E. (2000). Shopfloor innovation: Facilitating the suggestion and implementation of ideas. *Journal of Occupational and Organizational Psychology, 73,* 265–285.

Aycan, Z., Kanungo, R. N., Mendonca, M., Yu, K., Deller, J., Stahl, G., & Kurshid, A. (2000). Impact of culture on human resource management practices: A 10–country comparison. *Applied Psychology: An International Review, 49,* 192–221.

Ayoko, O. B., Callan, V. J., & Härtel, C. E. J. (2003). Workplace conflict, bullying and counterproductive behaviors. *International Journal of Organizational Analysis, 11,* 283–301.

Ayoko, O. B., Härtel, C. E. J., & Callan, V. J. (2002). Resolving the puzzle of productive and destructive conflict in culturally heterogeneous workgroups: A communication accommodation theory approach. *International Journal of Conflict Management, 13,* 165–195.

Babcock, L., & Landeo, C. M. (2004). Settlement escrows: An experimental study of a bilateral bargaining game. *Journal of Economic Behavior and Organization, 53,* 401–417.

Bac, M., & Raff, H. (1996). Note: Issuebyissue negotiations: The role of information and time preference. *Games and Economic Behavior, 13,* 125–134.

Bacharach, M., & Bernasconi, M. (1997). The variable frame theory of focal points: An experimental study. *Games and Economic Behavior, 19,* 1–45.

Bacharach, S. B., & Lawler, E. J. (1988). Political alignments in organizations: Contextualization, mobilization, and coordination. In M. A. Neale & R. M. Kramer (Eds.), *Power and influence in organizations* (pp. 67–88). Thousand Oaks, CA: Sage Publications, Inc.

Badke-Schaub, P., & Frankenberger, E. (1998). Approaching the complex network of group design processes in industry: A challenge for research and practice. *International Journal of Cognitive Ergonomics, 2,* 373–381.

Badke-Schaub, P., & Strohschneider, S. (1998). Complex problem solving in the cultural context. *Le Travail Humain: A Bilingual and Multi-Disciplinary Journal in Human Factors, 61,* 1–28.

Bagozzi, R. P., Dholakia, U. M., & Pearo, L. R. K. (2007). Antecedents and consequences of online social interactions. *Media Psychology, 9,* 77–114.

Baik, K. H., Cherry, T. L., Kroll, S., & Shogren, J. F. (1999). Endogenous timing in a gaming tournament. *Theory and Decision, 47,* 1–21.

Bailey, L. L., Peterson, L. M., Williams, K. W., & Thompson, R. C. (2000). Controlled flight into terrain: A study of pilot perspectives in Alaska. *FAA Office of Aviation Medicine Reports,* DOT-FAA-AM–00–28, 1–10, A1–A4, B1–B30.

Bailey, L. L., & Thompson, R. C. (2000). The effects of performance feedback on air traffic control team coordination: A simulation study. *FAA Office of Aviation Medicine Reports,* DOT-FAA-AM–00–25, 1–10.

Bajdo, L. M., & Dickson, M. W. (2001). Perceptions of organizational culture and women's advancement in organizations: A crosscultural examination. *Sex Roles, 45,* 399–414.

Baker, D., Prince, C., Shrestha, L., Oser, R., & Salas, E. (1993). Aviation computer games for crew resource management training. *International Journal of Aviation Psychology, 3,* 143–156.

Baker, F., & Rachlin, H. (2001). Probability of reciprocation in repeated prisoner's dilemma games. *Journal of Behavioral Decision Making, 14,* 51–67.

Baker, F., & Rachlin, H. (2002). Teaching and learning in a probabilistic prisoner's dilemma. *Behavioural Processes, 57,* 211–226.

Baker, P. (2001). Moral panic and alternative identity construction in Usenet. *Journal of Computer-Mediated Communication, 7*(1), [Web-based; unpaginated].

Balakrishnan, P. V., Patton, C., & Lewis, P. A. (1993). Toward a theory of agenda setting in negotiations. *Journal of Consumer Research, 19*, 637–654.

Balawajder, K. (1995). Interpersonal conflict: Internal syndrome. *Polish Psychological Bulletin, 26*, 19–30.

Bales, R. F. (1950). *Interaction process analysis: A method for the study of small groups.* Cambridge, MA: Addison-Wesley Press.

Bales, R. F. (1970). *Personality and interpersonal behavior.* New York: Holt, Rinehart and Winston.

Bales, R. F. (1999). *Social interaction systems: Theory and measurement.* New Brunswick, NJ: Transaction Publishers.

Bales, R. F., & Cohen, S. P. (1979). *SYMLOG: A system for the multiple level observation of groups.* New York: Free Press.

Bales, R. F., & Strodtbeck, F. L. (1951). Phases in group problem-solving. *Journal of Abnormal and Social Psychology, 46*, 485–495.

Baliga, S., & Evans, R. (2000). Renegotiation in repeated games with side-payments. *Games and Economic Behavior, 33*, 159–176.

Ball, P., & Giles, H. (1988). Speech style and employment selection: The Matched Guise Technique. In G. M. Breakwell, H. Foot, & R. Gilmour (Eds.), *Doing social psychology: Laboratory and field exercises* (pp. 121–149). New York: Cambridge University Press.

Balser, D. B. (1997). The impact of environmental factors on factionalism and schism in social movement organizations. *Social Forces, 76*, 199–228.

Baltes, B. B., Dickson, M. W, Sherman, M. P., Bauer, C. C., & LaGanke, J. (2002). Computer-mediated communication and group decision making: A meta-analysis. *Organizational Behavior and Human Decision Processes, 87*, 156–179.

Banaji, M. R., Baron, A. S., Dunham, Y., & Olson, K. (2008). The development of intergroup social cognition: Early emergence, implicit nature, and sensitivity to group status. In S. R. Levy & M. Killen (Eds.), *Intergroup attitudes and relations in childhood through adulthood* (pp. 87–102). New York: Oxford University Press.

Banks, D. T., Hutchinson, J. W., & Meyer, R. J. (2002). Reputation in marketing channels: Repeated-transactions bargaining with two-sided uncertainty. *Marketing Science, 21*, 251–272.

Bar-Tal, D. (1990). Causes and consequences of delegitimization: Models of conflict and ethnocentrism. *Journal of Social Issues, 46*(1), 65–81.

Bar-Tal, D. (1998). Group beliefs as an expression of social identity. In S. Worchel, J. F. Morales, D. Paez, & J.-C. Deschamps (Eds.), *Social identity: International perspectives* (pp. 93–113). London: Sage Publications, Inc.

Barak, M. E. M., Cherin, D. A., & Berkman, S. (1998). Organizational and personal dimensions in diversity climate: Ethnic and gender differences in employee perceptions. *Journal of Applied Behavioral Science, 34*, 82–104.

Barberà, S., & Gerber, A. (2003). On coalition formation: Durable coalition structures. *Mathematical Social Sciences, 45*, 185–203.

Bardach, L., & Park, B. (1996). The effect of ingroup/outgroup status on memory for consistent and inconsistent behavior of an individual. *Personality and Social Psychology Bulletin, 22*, 169–178.

Barker, J., Tjosvold, D., & Andrews, I. R. (1988). Conflict approaches of effective and ineffective managers: A field study in a matrix organization. *Journal of Management Studies, 25*, 167178.

Barkhi, R., Jacob, V. S., & Pirkul, H. (1999). An experimental analysis of face to face versus computer-mediated communication channels. *Group Decision and Negotiation, 8*, 325–347.

Barki, H., & Pinsonneault, A. (2001). Small group brainstorming and idea quality: Is electronic brainstorming the most effective approach? *Small Group Research, 32*, 158–205.

Barnard, C. I. (1938). *The functions of the executive.* Cambridge, MA: Harvard University Press.

Baron, J. N., Hannan, M. T., & Burton, M. D. (2001). Labor pains: Change in organizational models and employee turnover in young, high-tech firms. *American Journal of Sociology, 106*, 960–1012.

Baron, Reuben M. (2008). Reconciliation, trust, and cooperation: Using bottom-up and top-down strategies to achieve peace in the Israeli-Palestinian conflict. In A. Nadler, T. E. Malloy, & J.

D. Fisher (Eds.), *The social psychology of intergroup reconciliation* (pp. 275–298). New York: Oxford University Press.

Baron, Robert A. (1988). Negative effects of destructive criticism: Impact on conflict, self-efficacy, and task performance. *Journal of Applied Psychology, 73,* 199–207.

Baron, Robert A. (1997). Positive effects of conflict: Insights from social cognition. In C. K. W. De Dreu & E. Van de Vliert (Eds.), *Using conflict in organizations* (pp. 177–191). London: Sage Publications, Inc.

Barr, A. (2004). Kinship, familiarity, and trust: An experimental investigation. In J. Henrich, R. Boyd, S. Bowles, C. Camerer, E. Fehr, & H. Gintis (Eds.), *Foundations of human sociality* (pp. 305–334). New York: Oxford University Press.

Barr, J., & Saraceno, F. (2009). Organization, learning and cooperation. *Journal of Economic Behavior and Organization, 70,* 39–53.

Barreto, M., & Ellemers, N. (2002a). The impact of anonymity and group identification on pro-group behavior in computer-mediated groups. *Small Group Research, 33,* 590–610.

Barreto, M., & Ellemers, N. (2002b). The impact of respect versus neglect of self-identities on identification and group loyalty. *Personality and Social Psychology Bulletin, 28,* 629–639.

Barrett, F. J. (2004). Critical moments as "change" in negotiation. *Negotiation Journal, 20,* 213–219.

Barrick, M. R., Stewart, G. L., Neubert, M. J., & Mount, M. K. (1998). Relating member ability and personality to work-team processes and team effectiveness. *Journal of Applied Psychology, 83,* 377–391.

Barry, B., & Friedman, R. A. (1998). Bargainer characteristics in distributive and integrative negotiation. *Journal of Personality and Social Psychology, 74,* 345–359.

Barry, B., & Stewart, G. L. (1997). Composition, process, and performance in self-managed groups: The role of personality. *Journal of Applied Psychology, 82,* 62–78.

Barsade, S. G., Ward, A. J., Turner, J. D. F., & Sonnenfeld, J. A. (2000). To your heart's content: A model of affective diversity in top management teams. *Administrative Science Quarterly, 45,* 802–836.

Barsness, Z. I., & Bhappu, A. D. (2004). At the crossroads of culture and technology: Social influence and information-sharing processes during negotiation. In M. J. Gelfand & J. M. Brett (Eds.), *The handbook of negotiation and culture* (pp. 350–373). Stanford, CA: Stanford University Press.

Bartsch, R. A., & Judd, C. M. (1993). Majority/minority status and perceived ingroup variability revisited. *European Journal of Social Psychology, 23,* 471–483.

Basadur, M., & Head, M. (2001). Team performance and satisfaction: A link to cognitive style within a process framework. *Journal of Creative Behavior, 35,* 227–248.

Bass, B. M., & Riggio, R. E. (2006). *Transformational leadership (2nd ed.).* Mahwah, NJ: Lawrence Erlbaum Associates Publishers.

Bassin, M. (1988). Teamwork at General Foods: New & improved. *Personnel Journal, 67*(5), 62–70.

Batson, C. D., & Ahmad, N. (2001). Empathy-induced altruism in a prisoner's dilemma II: What if the target of empathy has defected? *European Journal of Social Psychology, 31,* 25–36.

Batson, C. D., Batson, J. G., Todd, R. M., Brummett, B. H., Shaw, L. L., & Aldeguer, C. M. R. (1995). Empathy and the collective good: Caring for one of the others in a social dilemma. *Journal of Personality and Social Psychology, 68,* 619–631.

Batson, C. D., & Moran, T. (1999). Empathy-induced altruism in a prisoner's dilemma. *European Journal of Social Psychology, 29,* 909–924.

Battigalli, P., & Siniscalchi, M. (2003). Rationalizable bidding in first-price auctions. *Games and Economic Behavior, 45,* 38–72.

Baucells, M., & Lippman, S. A. (2004). Bargaining with search as an outside option: The impact of the buyer's future availability. *Decision Analysis, 1,* 235–249.

Baumann, M. R., & Bonner, B. L. (2004). The effects of variability and expectations on utilization of member expertise and group performance. *Organizational Behavior and Human Decision Processes, 93,* 89–101.

Baumeister, R. F., & Hastings, S. (1997). Distortions of collective memory: How groups flatter and deceive themselves. In J. W. Pennebaker, D. Paez, & B. Rime (Eds.), *Collective memory of political events: Social psychological perspectives* (pp. 277–293). Mahwah, NJ: Lawrence Erlbaum Associates, Inc.

Bavelas, J. B., & Coates, L. (1992). How do we account for the mindfulness of facetoface dialogue? *Communication Monographs, 59*, 301–305.

Baxter, L. A., Wilmot, W. W., Simmons, C. A., & Swartz, A. (1993). Ways of doing conflict: A folk taxonomy of conflict events in personal relationships. In P. J. Kalbfleisch (Ed.), *Interpersonal communication: Evolving interpersonal relationships* (pp. 89–107). Hillsdale, NJ: Lawrence Erlbaum Associates, Inc.

Baye, M. R., & Hoppe, H. C. (2003). The strategic equivalence of rentseeking, innovation, and patentrace games. *Games and Economic Behavior, 44*, 217–226.

Baysinger, B., & Hoskisson, R. E. (1989). Diversification strategy and R&D intensity in multiproduct firms. *Academy of Management Journal, 32*, 310–332.

Bazerman, M. H. (Ed.). (2005). *Negotiation, decision making and conflict management, Vol 1–3.* Northampton, MA: Edward Elgar Publishing.

Bazerman, M. H., Curhan, J. R., Moore, D. A., & Valley, K. L. (2000). Negotiation. *Annual Review of Psychology, 51*, 279–314.

Bazerman, M. H., Neale, M. A., Valley, K. L., Zajac, E. J., & Kim, Y. M. (1992). The effect of agents and mediators on negotiation outcomes. *Organizational Behavior and Human Decision Processes, Vol 53*, 55–73.

Beaumont, P. B. (1995). *The future of employment relations.* Thousand Oaks, CA: Sage Publications, Inc.

Beck, D., & Fisch, R. (2000). Argumentation and emotional processes in group decision-making: Illustration of a multi-level interaction process analysis approach. *Group Processes and Intergroup Relations, 3*, 183–201.

Beck, D., & Orth, B. (1995). Wer wendet sich an wen?–Muster in der Interaktion kooperierender Kleingruppen [Who is speaking to whom? Channels of communication in intergroup cooperation]. *Zeitschrift fuer Sozialpsychologie, 26*, 92–106.

Becker, B. E. (1988). Concession bargaining: The meaning of union gains. *Academy of Management Journal, 31*, 377–387.

Becker, T. E., & Billings, R. S. (1993). Profiles of commitment: An empirical test. *Journal of Organizational Behavior, 14*, 177–190.

Bednar, J., & Page, S. (2007). Can game(s) theory explain culture? The emergence of cultural behavior within multiple games. *Rationality and Society, 19*, 65–97.

Bee, R. H., & Beronja, T. A. (1991). Attitudinal differences between unionized collegiate professionals. *College Student Journal, 25*, 289–297.

Beer, M., Eisenstat, R., & Spector, B. (1990). *The critical path to corporate renewal.* Boston: Harvard Business School Press.

Beersma, B., & De Dreu, C. K. W. (2005). Conflict's consequences: Effects of social motives on postnegotiation creative and convergent group functioning and performance. *Journal of Personality and Social Psychology, 89*, 358–374.

Beersma, B., Hollenbeck, J. R., Humphrey, S. E., Moon, H., Conlon, D. E., & Ilgen, D. R. (2003). Cooperation, competition, and team performance: Toward a contingency approach. *Academy of Management Journal, 46*, 572–590.

Beest, I. V., Van Dijk, E., De Dreu, C. K. W., & Wilke, H. A. M. (2005). Do-no-harm in coalition formation: Why losses inhibit exclusion and promote fairness cognitions. *Journal of Experimental Social Psychology, 41*, 609–617.

Behson, S. J. (2002). Which dominates? The relative importance of workfamily organizational support and general organizational context on employee outcomes. *Journal of Vocational Behavior, 61*, 53–72.

Beisecker, T., Walker, G., & Bart, J. (1989). Knowledge versus ignorance as bargaining strategies: The impact of knowledge about other's information level. *The Social Science Journal, 26*, 161–172.

Belbin, R. M. (2010). *Management teams : why they succeed or fail* (3rd ed.). Amsterdam: Butterworth-Heinemann, c2010.

Bell, P. A., Petersen, T. R., & Hautaluoma, J. E. (1989). The effect of punishment probability on overconsumption and stealing in a simulated commons. *Journal of Applied Social Psychology, 19*, 1483–1495.

Bell, S. T. (2007). Deep-level composition variables as predictors of team performance: A meta-analysis. *Journal of Applied Psychology, 92*, 595–615

Belleflamme, P. (2000). Stable coalition structures with open membership and asymmetric firms. *Games and Economic Behavior, 30*, 1–21.

Ben-Ner, A., Putterman, L., Kong, F., & Magan, D. (2004). Reciprocity in a two-part dictator game. *Journal of Economic Behavior and Organization, 53*, 333–352.

Ben-Porath, E., & Kahneman, M. (2003). Communication in repeated games with costly monitoring. *Games and Economic Behavior, 44*, 227–250.

Ben-Yoav, O., & Banai, M. (1992). Measuring conflict management styles: A comparison between the MODE and ROC-III instruments using self and peer ratings. *International Journal of Conflict Management, 3*, 237–247.

Benbasat, I., & Lim, L. h. (1993). The effects of group, task, context, and technology variables on the usefulness of group support systems: A meta-analysis of experimental studies. *Small Group Research, 24*, 430–462.

Benbasat, I., Lim, F. J., & Rao, V. S. (1995). A framework for communication support in group work with special reference to negotiation systems. *Group Decision and Negotiation, 4*, 135–158.

Bendor, J., Kramer, R. M., & Stout, S. (1991). When in doubt…: Cooperation in a noisy prisoner's dilemma. *Journal of Conflict Resolution, 35*, 691–719.

Bendor, J., & Swistak, P. (1998). Evolutionary equilibria: Characterization theorems and their implications. *Theory and Decision, 45*, 99–159.

Bengtsson, M., & Powell, W. W. (2004). Introduction: New perspectives on competition and cooperation. *Scandinavian Journal of Management, 20*, 1–8.

Bennett, J. B., Lehman, W. E. K., & Forst, J. K. (1999). Change, transfer climate, and customer orientation: A contextual model and analysis of change-driven training. *Group and Organization Management, 24*, 188–216.

Bennett, M., Barrett, M., Karakozov, R., Kipiani, G., Lyons, E., Pavlenko, V., & Riazanova, T. (2004). Young children's evaluations of the ingroup and of outgroups: A multi-national study. *Social Development, 13*, 124–141.

Bennett, N. (1991). The Emanuel Miller Memorial Lecture 1990: Cooperative learning in classrooms: Processes and outcomes. *Journal of Child Psychology and Psychiatry and Allied Disciplines, 32*, 581–594.

Bennett, P., & McQuade, P. (1996). Experimental dramas: Prototyping a multiuser negotiation simulation. *Group Decision and Negotiation, 5*, 119–136.

Bennett, P., Tait, A., & Macdonagh, K. (1994). INTERACT: Developing software for interactive decisions. *Group Decision and Negotiation, 3*, 351–372.

Bensaid, B., & Gary-Bobo, R. J. (1996). An exact formula for the lion's share: A model of preplay negotiation. *Games and Economic Behavior, 14*, 44–89.

Benveniste, G. (1989). *Mastering the politics of planning: Crafting credible plans and policies that make a difference*. San Francisco: Jossey-Bass.

Berg, J., Dickhaut, J., & McCabe, K. (1995). Trust, reciprocity, and social history. *Games and Economic Behavior, 10*, 122–142.

Berge, Z. L. (1998). Differences in teamwork between post-secondary classrooms and the workplace. *Education and Training, 40*, 194–201.

Berkowitz, B., & Wolff, T. (1996). Rethinking social action and community empowerment: A dialogue. In M. B. Lykes, A. Banuazizi, R. Liem, & M. Morris (Eds.), *Myths about the powerless: Contesting social inequalities* (pp. 296–316). Philadelphia: Temple University Press.

Berkowitz, N. H. (1994). Evidence that subject's expectancies confound intergroup bias in Tajfel's minimal group paradigm. *Personality and Social Psychology Bulletin, 20*, 184–195.

Berman, S. L., & Wittig, M. A. (2004). An Intergroup theories approach to direct political action among African Americans. *Group Processes and Intergroup Relations, 7*, 19–34.

Berndsen, M., McGarty, C., Van Der Pligt, J., & Spears, R. (2001). Meaning-seeking in the illusory correlation paradigm: The active role of participants in the categorization process. *British Journal of Social Psychology, 40*, 209–234.

Berndsen, M., Spears, R., McGarty, C., & Van Der Pligt, J. (1998). Dynamics of differentiation: Similarity as the precursor and product of stereotype formation. *Journal of Personality and Social Psychology, 74*, 1451–1463.

Berndsen, M., Spears, R., Van Der Pligt, J., & McGarty, C. (1999). Determinants of intergroup differentiation in the illusory correlation task. *British Journal of Psychology, 90*, 201–220.

Berninghaus, S. K., Ehrhart, K.-M., & Keser, C. (2002). Conventions and local interaction structures: Experimental evidence. *Games and Economic Behavior, 39*, 177–205.

Berninghaus, S. K., & Güth, W. (2003). Now or later? Endogenous timing of threats. *Theory and Decision, 55*, 235–256.

Berscheid, E. (1994). Interpersonal relationships. *Annual Review of Psychology, 45*, 79–129.

Berthon, P., Pitt, L. F., & Ewing, M. T. (2001). Corollaries of the collective: The influence of organizational culture and memory development on perceived decision-making context. *Journal of the Academy of Marketing Science, 29*, 135–150.

Betancor, V., Leyens, J. -P., Rodriguez, A., & Quiles, M. N. (2003). Atribusion difernetial al endgrupo y al exogrupo de las dimensiones de moralidad y eficacia: Un indicator de favoritismo endogrupal [Differential attributions to the ingroup and outgroup on dimensions of morality and efficiency: An indicator of ingroup favoritism]. *Psicothema, 15*, 407–413.

Betancourt, H., & Blair, I. (1992). A cognition (attribution)emotion model of violence in conflict situations. *Personality and Social Psychology Bulletin, 18*, 343–350.

Bethwaite, J., & Tompkinson, P. (1996). The ultimatum game and nonselfish utility functions. *Journal of Economic Psychology, 17*, 259–271.

Bettencourt, B. A., & Bartholow, B. D. (1998). The importance of status legitimacy for intergroup attitudes among numerical minorities. *Journal of Social Issues, 54*, 759–775.

Bettencourt, B. A., Brewer, M. B., Croak, M. R., & Miller, N. (1992). Cooperation and the reduction of intergroup bias: The role of reward structure and social orientation. *Journal of Experimental Social Psychology, 28*, 301–319.

Bettencourt, B. A., Charlton, K., Dorr, N., & Hume, D. L. (2001). Status differences and in-group bias: A meta-analytic examination of the effects of status stability, status legitimacy, and group permeability. *Psychological Bulletin, 127*, 520–542.

Bettencourt, B. A., Charlton, K., & Kernahan, C. (1997). Numerical representation of groups in cooperative settings: Social orientation effects on ingroup bias. *Journal of Experimental Social Psychology, 33*, 630–659.

Bettencourt, B. A., & Dorr, N. (1998). Cooperative interaction and intergroup bias: Effects of numerical representation and cross-cut role assignment. *Personality and Social Psychology Bulletin, 24*, 1276–1293.

Bettencourt, B. A., Molix, L., Talley, A., & Eubanks, J. P. (2007). Numerical representation and cross-cut role assignments: Majority members' responses under cooperative interaction. *Journal of Experimental Social Psychology, 43*, 553–564.

Betz, B. (1991). Response to strategy and communication in an arms race-disarmament dilemma. *Journal of Conflict Resolution, 35*, 678–690.

Betz, B. (1995). Comparison of GRIT versus GRIT/Tit-For-Tat. *Psychological Reports, 76*, 322.

Betz, B., & Fry, W. R. (1995). The role of group schema in the selection of influence attempts. *Basic and Applied Social Psychology, 16*, 351–365.

Bhappu, A. D., Griffith, T. L., & Northcraft, G. B. (1997). Media effects and communication bias in diverse groups. *Organizational Behavior and Human Decision Processes, 70*, 199–205.

Bicchieri, C. (2002). Covenants without swords: Group identity, norms, and communications in social dilemmas. *Rationality and Society, 14*, 192–228.

Bicchieri, C., & Lev-On, A. (2007). Computer-mediated communication and cooperation in social dilemmas: An experimental analysis. *Politics, Philosophy and Economics, 6*, 139–168.

Bienenstock, E. J., & Bonacich, P. (1993). Game-theory models for exchange networks: Experimental results. *Sociological Perspectives, 36*, 117–135.

Biernat, M. (1990). Stereotypes on campus: How contact and liking influence perceptions of group distinctiveness. *Journal of Applied Social Psychology, 20*, 1485–1513.

Biernat, M., & Crandall, C. S. (1994). Stereotyping and contact with social groups: Measurement and conceptual issues. *European Journal of Social Psychology, 24*, 659–677.

Biernat, M., & Vescio, T. K. (1993). Categorization and stereotyping: Effects of group context on memory and social judgment. *Journal of Experimental Social Psychology, 29*, 166–202.

Biernat, M., & Vescio, T. K. (1994). Still another look at the effects of fit and novelty on the salience of social categories. *Journal of Experimental Social Psychology, 30*, 399–406.

Bies, R. J., Lewicki, R. J., & Sheppard, B. H. (1999). *Research on negotiation in organizations* (Vol. 7). Greenwich, CT: JAI Press.

Bigler, R. S., & Liben, L. S. (2006). A developmental intergroup theory of social stereotypes and prejudice. In R. V. Kail (Ed.), *Advances in child development and behavior* (Vol. 34, pp. 39–89). San Diego, CA: Elsevier Academic Press, 2006.

Bigler, R. S., & Liben, L. S. (2007). Developmental intergroup theory: Explaining and reducing children's social stereotyping and prejudice. *Current Directions in Psychological Science, 16*, 162–166.

Bigoness, W. J., & DuBose, P. B. (1992). Effects of arbitration condition and risk-taking propensity upon bargaining behavior. *International Journal of Conflict Management, 3*, 133–150.

Bilancini, E., & Boncinelli, L. (2009). The co-evolution of cooperation and defection under local interaction and endogenous network formation. *Journal of Economic Behavior and Organization, 70*, 186–195.

Bilewicz, M. (2007). History as an obstacle: Impact of temporal-based social categorizations on Polish-Jewish intergroup contact. *Group Processes and Intergroup Relations, 10*, 551–563.

Billsberry, J. (Ed.). (1996). *The effective manager: Perspectives and illustrations*. Thousand Oaks, CA: Sage.

Binder, J., Zagefka, H., Brown, R., Funke, F., Kessler, T., Mummendey, A., Maquil, A., Demoulin, S., & Leyens, J.-P. (2009). Does contact reduce prejudice or does prejudice reduce contact? A longitudinal test of the contact hypothesis among majority and minority groups in three european countries. *Journal of Personality and Social Psychology, 96*, 843–856.

Bishop, J. W., Scott, K. D., & Burroughs, S. M. (2000). Support, commitment, and employee outcomes in a team environment. *Journal of Management, 26*, 1113–1132.

Bizman, A., & Yinon, Y. (2000). Perceptions of dual identity and separate groups among secular and religious Israeli Jews. *Journal of Social Psychology, 140*, 589–596.

Bizman, A., & Yinon, Y. (2001). Intergroup and interpersonal threats as determinants of prejudice: The moderating role of in-group identification. *Basic and Applied Social Psychology, 23*, 191–196.

Bizman, A., & Yinon, Y. (2004). Intergroup conflict management strategies as related to perceptions of dual identity and separate groups. *Journal of Social Psychology, 144*, 115–126.

Black, D. (1990). The elementary forms of conflict management. In Arizona State U, School of Justice Studies (Ed.), *New directions in the study of justice, law, and social control* (pp. 43–69). New York: Plenum Press.

Blair, Irene V., Park, Bernadette, & Bachelor, Jonathan. (2003). Understanding intergroup anxiety: Are some people more anxious than others? *Group Processes and Intergroup Relations, Vol 6*, 151–169.

Blakely, G. L., Andrews, M. C., & Fuller, J. (2003). Are chameleons good citizens? A longitudinal study of the relationship between self-monitoring and organizational citizenship behavior. *Journal of Business and Psychology, 18*, 131–144.

Blalock, H. M., Jr. (1991). *Understanding social inequality: Modeling allocation processes*. Newbury Park, CA: Sage Publications, Inc.

Blanck, P. D. (Ed.). (1993). *Interpersonal expectations: Theory, research, and applications*. New York: Cambridge University Press.

Blanz, M., Mummendey, A., & Otten, S. (1995a). Perceptions of relative group size and group status: Effects on intergroup discrimination in negative evaluations. *European Journal of Social Psychology, 25*, 231–247.

Blanz, M., Mummendey, A., & Otten, S. (1995b). Positive-negative asymmetry in social discrimination: The impact of stimulus valence and size and status differentials on intergroup evaluations. *British Journal of Social Psychology, 34*, 409–419.

Blaquière, A. (1994). C-optimal threat decision n-tuples in collective bargaining. *Group Decision and Negotiation, 3*, 145–157.

Blaydes, L. (2004). Rewarding impatience: A bargaining and enforcement model of OPEC. *International Organization, 58*, 213–237.

Bliuc, A.-M., McGarty, C., Reynolds, K., & Muntele, D. (2007). Opinion-based group membership as a predictor of commitment to political action. *European Journal of Social Psychology, 37*, 19–32.

Bloch, F. (1996). Sequential formation of coalitions in games with externalities and fixed payoff division. *Games and Economic Behavior, 14*, 90–123.

Blount, S. (1995). When social outcomes aren't fair: The effect of causal attributions on preferences. *Organizational Behavior and Human Decision Processes, 63*, 131–144.

Blount, S., & Larrick, R. P. (2000). Framing the game: Examining frame choice in bargaining. *Organizational Behavior and Human Decision Processes, 81*, 43–71.

Blumberg, H. H. (1972). Communication of interpersonal evaluations. *Journal of Personality and Social Psychology, 23*, 157–162.

Blumberg, H. H. (1976). Group processes. In H. Eysenck and G. Wilson (Eds.), *A textbook of human psychology* (pp. 191–210). Lancaster, England: MTP.

Blumberg, H. H. (1994). Bargaining, coalitions, and games. In A. P. Hare, H. H. Blumberg, M. F. Davies, & M. V. Kent, *Small group research: A handbook* (pp. 237–257). Westport, CT: Ablex Publishing.

Blumberg, H. H. (1997). On taking too much: A point-accumulation procedure for comparing mutual agreement with controlled individual initiatives. *Small Group Research, 28*, 171–193.

Blumberg, H. H. (2001a). The common ground of natural language and social interaction in personality description. *Journal of Research in Personality, 35*, 289–312.

Blumberg, H. H. (2001b, July). The increasing delineation of group process effects related to conflict resolution. Presented at the Seventh International Symposium on the Contributions of Psychology to Peace, under the auspices of the International Union of Psychological Science, [hosted by Ateneo De Manila University], Manila.

Blumberg, H. H., Hare, A. P., & Costin, A. (2006). *Peace Psychology: A comprehensive introduction*. Cambridge, England: Cambridge University Press.

Blumberg, H. H., Hare, A. P., Davies, M. F., & Kent, V. (Eds.). (1983). *Small groups and social interaction* (2 vols.). Chichester, England, and New York: John Wiley & Sons.

Blumberg, H. H., Hare, A. P., Kent, M. V., & Davies, M. F. (2009). *Small group research: Basic issues*. Oxford, England, and New York: Peter Lang.

Blume, L. E. (2003). How noise matters. *Games and Economic Behavior, 44*, 251–271.

Blume, L. E., & Durlauf, S. N. (2006). Identifying social interactions: A review. In J. M. Oakes & J. S. Kaufman (Eds.), *Methods in social epidemiology* (pp. 287–315). San Francisco: Jossey-Bass.

Boardman, S. K., & Horowitz, S. V. (1994). Constructive conflict management and social problems: An introduction. *Journal of Social Issues, 50*(1), 1–12.

Boccato, G., Capozza, D., & Falvo, R. (2003). Bisogno di distintività ed effetto di sovraesclusione dal proprio gruppo [Need for distinctiveness and ingroup overexclusion effect]. *Ricerche di Psicologia, 26*(4), 65–82.

Bodenhausen, G. V., Macrae, C. N., & Garst, J. (1998). Stereotypes in thought and deed: Social-cognitive origins of intergroup discrimination. In C. Sedikides, J. Schopler, & C. A. Insko (Eds.), *Intergroup cognition and intergroup behavior* (pp. 311–335). Mahwah, NJ: Lawrence Erlbaum Associates, Inc., Publishers.

Bodenhausen, G. V., Mussweiler, T., Gabriel, S., & Moreno, K. N. (2001). Affective influences on stereotyping and intergroup relations. In J. P. Forgas (Ed.), *Handbook of affect and social cognition* (pp. 319–343). Mahwah, NJ: Lawrence Erlbaum Associates, Publishers.

Boen, F., & Vanbeselaere, N. (2000). Responding to membership of a low-status group: The effects of stability, permeability and individual ability. *Group Processes and Intergroup Relations, 3*, 41–62.

Boen, F., & Vanbeselaere, N. (2001). Individual versus collective responses to membership in a low-status group: The effects of stability and individual ability. *Journal of Social Psychology, 141*, 765–783.

Boen, F., & Vanbeselaere, N. (2002). The relative impact of socio-structural characteristics on behavioral reactions against membership in a low-status group. *Group Processes and Intergroup Relations, 5*, 299–318.

Boen, F., Vanbeselaere, N., & Snauwaert, B. (2003). How do people classify reactions against different types of discrimination? Two scenario-studies. *Psychologica Belgica, Vol 43*, 215–248.

Bogart, L. M., Ryan, C. S., & Stefanov, M. (1999). Effects of stereotypes and outcome dependency on the processing of information about group members. *Group Processes and Intergroup Relations, 2*, 31–50.

Boggs, S. T., & Chun, M. N. (1990). "Ho'oponopono": A Hawaiian method of solving interpersonal problems. In K. A. Watson-Gegeo, G. M. White, & A. Arno (Eds.), *Disentangling: Conflict discourse in Pacific societies* (pp. 122–160). Stanford, CA: Stanford University Press.

Bogomolnaia, A., & Jackson, M. O. (2002). The stability of hedonic coalition structures. *Games and Economic Behavior, 38*, 201–230.

Boldry, J. G., Gaertner, L., & Quinn, J. (2007). Measuring the measures: A meta-analytic investigation of the measures of outgroup homogeneity. *Group Processes and Intergroup Relations, 10*, 157–178.

Boldry, J. G., & Kashy, D. A. (1999). Intergroup perception in naturally occurring groups of differential status: A social relations perspective. *Journal of Personality and Social Psychology, 77*, 1200–1212.

Boles, T. L., Croson, R. T. A., & Murnighan, J. K. (2000). Deception and retribution in repeated ultimatum bargaining. *Organizational Behavior and Human Decision Processes, 83*, 235–259.

Boles, T. L., & Messick, D. M. (1995). A reverse outcome bias: The influence of multiple reference points on the evaluation of outcomes and decisions. *Organizational Behavior and Human Decision Processes, 61*, 262–275.

Bolle, F., & Ockenfels, P. (1990). Prisoners' Dilemma as a game with incomplete information. *Journal of Economic Psychology, 11*, 69–84.

Bolton, G. E., Chatterjee, K., & McGinn, K. L. (2003). How communication links influence coalition bargaining: A laboratory investigation. *Management Science, 49*, 583–598.

Bolton, G. E., & Katok, E. (1998). Reinterpreting arbitration's narcotic effect: An experimental study of learning in repeated bargaining. *Games and Economic Behavior, 25*, 1–33.

Bolton, G. E., & Ockenfels, A. (1998). Strategy and equity: An ERC-analysis of the Güth—van Damme game. *Journal of Mathematical Psychology, 42*, 215–226.

Bolton, G. E., & Zwick, R. (1995). Anonymity versus punishment in ultimatum bargaining. *Games and Economic Behavior, 10*, 95–121.

Bonacich, P., & Friedkin, N. E. (1998). Unequally valued exchange relations. *Social Psychology Quarterly, 61*, 160–171.

Bonaiuto, M. (1997). Costruzione e validazione di una scala per la misura dell'atteggiamento verso la cooperazione [Construction and validation of a scale for the measurement of attitude toward cooperation]. *Giornale Italiano di Psicologia, 24*, 833–870.

Bond, M. H., Leung, K., & Schwartz, S. (1992). Explaining choices in procedural and distributive justice across cultures. *International Journal of Psychology, 27*, 211–225.

Bonelli, J., & Simmons, L. (2004a). Coalition building and electoral organizing in the passage of anti-discrimination laws: The case of Connecticut. In Y. C. Padilla (Ed.), *Gay and lesbian rights organizing: Community-based strategies* (pp. 35–53). Binghamton, NY: Harrington Park Press/The Haworth Press.

Bonelli, J., & Simmons, L. (2004b). Coalition building and electoral organizing in the passage of anti-discrimination laws: The case of Connecticut. *Journal of Gay and Lesbian Social Services: Issues in Practice, Policy and Research, 16*(3–4), 35–53.

Bonito, J. A. (2002). Methodological and conceptual issues related to interdependence. The analysis of participation in small groups. *Small Group Research, 33*, 412–438.

Bonito, J. A. (2004). Shared cognition and participation in small groups: Similarity of member prototypes. *Communication Research, 31*, 704–730.

Bonner, B. L. (2004). Expertise in group problem solving: Recognition, social combination, and performance. *Group Dynamics: Theory, Research*, and Practice, 8, 277–290.

Bonner, B. L., Baumann, M. R., & Dalal, R. S. (2002). The effects of member expertise on group decision-making and performance. *Organizational Behavior and Human Decision Processes, 88*, 719–736.

Boone, C., De Brabander, B., Carree, M., De Jong, G., Van Olffen, W., & Van Witteloostuijn, A. (2002). Locus of control and learning to cooperate in a prisoner's dilemma game. *Personality and Individual Differences, 32*, 929–946.

Boone, C., De Brabander, B., & Van Witteloostuijn, A. (1999a). The impact of personality on behavior in five Prisoner's Dilemma games. *Journal of Economic Psychology, 20*, 343–377.

Boone, C., De Brabander, B., & Van Witteloostuijn, A. (1999b). Locus of control and strategic behaviour in a prisoner's dilemma game. *Personality and Individual Differences, 27*, 695–706.

Boone, J. L. (1992). Competition, conflict, and the development of social hierarchies. In E. A. Smith & B. Winterhalder (Eds.), *Evolutionary ecology and human behavior* (pp. 301–337). New York: Aldine De Gruyter.

Boone, R. T., & Buck, R. (2003). Emotional expressivity and trustworthiness: the role of nonverbal behavior in the evolution of cooperation. *Journal of Nonverbal Behavior, 27*, 163–182.

Boone, R. T., & Macy, M. W. (1999). Unlocking the doors of the Prisoner's Dilemma: Dependence, selectivity, and cooperation. *Social Psychology Quarterly, 62*, 32–52.

Boone, R. T., & Macy, M. W. (2004). Dependence and cooperation in fuzzy dilemmas: The effects of environmental and endowment uncertainty. In R. Suleiman, D. V. Budescu, I. Fischer, & D. M. Messick (Eds.), *Contemporary psychological research on social dilemmas* (pp. 343–360). New York: Cambridge University Press.

Borkowski, N. (2005). Overview of group dynamics. In N. Borkowski (Ed.), *Organizational behavior in health care* (pp. 311–330). Boston: Jones and Bartlett Publishers.

Bornman, E., & Mynhardt, J. C. (1991). Social identity and intergroup contact in South Africa with specific reference to the work situation. *Genetic, Social*, and General Psychology Monographs, 117, 437–462.

Bornstein, G. (1992). Group decision and individual choice in intergroup competition for public goods. In W. B. G. Liebrand, D. M. Messick, & H. A. M. Wilke (Eds.), *Social dilemmas: Theoretical issues and research findings* (pp. 247–263). Oxford, England: Pergamon Press, Inc.

Bornstein, G. (2003). Intergroup conflict: Individual, group, and collective interests. *Personality and Social Psychology Review, 7*, 129–145.

Bornstein, G. (2004). Cooperation in intergroup social dilemmas. In R. Suleiman, D. V. Budescu, I. Fischer, & D. M. Messick (Eds.), *Contemporary psychological research on social dilemmas* (pp. 227–247). New York: Cambridge University Press.

Bornstein, G., & Erev, I. (1997). The enhancing effect of intergroup competition on group performance. In C. K. W. De Dreu & Van de E. Vliet (Eds.), *Using conflict in organizations* (pp. 116–128). London: Sage Publications, Inc.

Bornstein, G., Erev, I., & Goren, H. (1994). The effect of repeated play in the IPG and IPD team games. *Journal of Conflict Resolution, 38*, 690–707.

Bornstein, G., & Gilula, Z. (2003). Between-group communication and conflict resolution in assurance and chicken games. *Journal of Conflict Resolution, Vol 47*, 326–339.

Bornstein, G., Kugler, T., & Ziegelmeyer, A. (2004). Individual and group decisions in the Centipede game: Are groups more "rational" players? *Journal of Experimental Social Psychology, 40*, 599–605.

Bornstein, G., & Rapoport, A. (1988). Intergroup competition for the provision of step-level public goods: Effects of preplay communication. *European Journal of Social Psychology, 18*, 125–142.

Boros, E., & Gurvich, V. (2000). Stable effectivity functions and perfect graphs. *Mathematical Social Sciences, 39*, 175–194.

Boros, E., Gurvich, V., & Vasin, A. (1997). Stable families of coalitions and normal hypergraphs. *Mathematical Social Sciences, 34*, 107–123.

Bosch-Domènech, A., & Sáez-Martí, M. (2001). Cycles of aggregate behavior in theory and experiment. *Games and Economic Behavior, 36*, 105–137.

Bose, G. (1996). Bargaining economies with patient and impatient agents: Equilibria and intermediation. *Games and Economic Behavior, 14*, 149–172.

Boskey, J. B. (1994). The proper role of the mediator: Rational assessment, not pressure. *Negotiation Journal, 10*, 367–372.

Bossert, W., Nosal, E., & Sadanand, V. (1996). Bargaining under uncertainty and the monotone path solutions. *Games and Economic Behavior, 14*, 173–189.

Bossert, W., & Peters, H. (2000). Multi—attribute decision—making in individual and social choice. *Mathematical Social Sciences, 40*, 327–339.

Bossert, W., & Peters, H. (2001). Minimax regret and efficient bargaining under uncertainty. *Games and Economic Behavior, 34*, 1–10.

Boster, F. J., Kazoleas, D., Levine, T., Rogan, R. G., & Kang, K. H. (1995). The impact of power on communicative persistence, strategic diversity and bargaining outcomes. *Communication Reports, 8*, 136–144.

Bottger, P. C., & Yetton, P. W. (1988). An integration of process and decision scheme explanations of group problem solving performance. *Organizational Behavior and Human Decision Processes, 42*, 234–249.

Bottom, W. P. (1990). Adaptive reference points in integrative bargaining. In K. Borcherding, O. I. Larichev, & D. M. Messick (Eds.), *Contemporary issues in decision making* (pp. 429–447.) Oxford, England: North-Holland.

Bottom, W. P. (1998). Negotiator risk: Sources of uncertainty and the impact of reference points on negotiated agreements. *Organizational Behavior and Human Decision Processes, 76*, 89–112.

Bottom, W. P., Eavey, C. L., & Miller, G. J. (1996). Getting to the core: Coalitional integrity as a constraint on the power of agenda setters. *Journal of Conflict Resolution, 40*, 298–319.

Bottom, W. P., Holloway, J., McClurg, S., & Miller, G. J. (2000). Negotiating a coalition: Risk, quota shaving, and learning to bargain. *Journal of Conflict Resolution, 44*, 147–169.

Bottom, W. P., & Paese, P. W. (1997). False consensus, stereotypic cues, and the perception of integrative potential in negotiation. *Journal of Applied Social Psychology, 27*, 1919–1940.

Bottom, W. P., & Paese, P. W. (1999). Judgment accuracy and the asymmetric cost of errors in distributive bargaining. *Group Decision and Negotiation, 8*, 349–364.

Bottom, W. P., & Studt, A. (1993). Framing effects and the distributive aspect of integrative bargaining. *Organizational Behavior and Human Decision Processes, 56*, 459–474.

Bouas, K. S., & Komorita, S. S. (1996). Group discussion and cooperation in social dilemmas. *Personality and Social Psychology Bulletin, 22*, 1144–1150.

Bouckaert, J. (2002). Bargaining in markets with simultaneous and sequential suppliers. *Journal of Economic Behavior and Organization, 48*, 319–334.

Bourhis, R. Y. (1994). Power, gender, and intergroup discrimination: Some minimal group experiments. In M. P. Zanna & J. M. Olson (Eds.), *The psychology of prejudice: The Ontario symposium, Vol. 7* [Ontario symposium on personality and social psychology, Vol. 7] (pp. 171–208). Hillsdale, NJ: Lawrence Erlbaum Associates, Inc.

Bourhis, R. Y., Cole, R., & Gagnon, A. (1992). Sexe, pouvoir et discrimination: analyse intergroupes des rapports femmes-hommes [Sex, power, and discrimination: Intergroup analysis of rapport between men and women]. *Revue Quebecoise de Psychologie, 13*(1), 103–127.

Bourhis, R. Y., Gagnon, A., & Sachdev, I. (1997). Les matrices de Tajfel: Un guide methodologuque pour la recherche intergroupes [The Tajfel matrices: A methodological approach of intergroup phenomena]. *Cahiers Internationaux de Psychologie Sociale*, No. 34: 11–28.

Bourhis, R. Y., Montreuil, A., Barrette, G., & Montaruli, E. (2009). Acculturation and immigrant-host community relations in multicultural settings. In S. Demoulin, J.-P. Leyens, & J. F. Dovidio (Eds.), *In:Intergroup misunderstandings: Impact of divergent social realities* (pp. 39–61). New York: Psychology Press.

Bowles, S., & Gintis, H. (2003). Origins of human cooperation. In P. Hammerstein (Ed.), *Genetic and cultural evolution of cooperation* (pp. 429–444). Cambridge, MA: MIT Press.

Boyd, R., & Richerson, P. J. (1992). Punishment allows the evolution of cooperation (or anything else) in sizable groups. *Ethology and Sociobiology, 13*, 171–195.

Boydell, K. M., & Volpe, T. (2004). A qualitative examination of the implementation of a community-academic coalition. *Journal of Community Psychology, 32*, 357–374.

Boyer, M. A. (1999). Coalitions, motives, and payoffs: A classroom simulation of mixed-motive negotiations. *Social Science Computer Review, 17*, 305–312.

Boyle, E. H., & Lawler, E. J. (1991). Resolving conflict through explicit bargaining. *Social Forces, 69*, 1183–1204.

Bradley, J., White, B. J., & Mennecke, B. E. (2003). Teams and tasks: A temporal framework for the effects of interpersonal interventions on team performance. *Small Group Research, 34*, 353–387.

Bradshaw, S. D., & Stasson, M. F. (1998). Attributions of shy and not-shy group members for collective group performance. *Small Group Research, 29*, 283–307.

Bradshaw, S. D., Stasson, M. F., & Alexander, D. (1999). Shyness and group brainstorming: Effects on productivity and perceptions of performance. *North American Journal of Psychology, 1*, 267–276.

Brams, S. J. (1990). *Negotiation games: Applying game theory to bargaining and arbitration.* Florence, KY: Taylor & Frances/Routledge.

Brams, S. J., & Doherty, A. E. (1993). Intransigence in negotiations: The dynamics of disagreement. *Journal of Conflict Resolution, 37*, 692–708.

Brams, S. J., & Kilgour, D. M. (1996). Bargaining procedures that induce honesty. *Group Decision and Negotiation, 5*, 239–262.

Brams, S. J., & Taylor, A. D. (1994). Divide the dollar: Three solutions and extensions. *Theory and Decision, 37*, 211–231.

Brams, S. J., & Taylor, A. D. (1996). *Fair division: From cake-cutting to dispute resolution.* Cambridge, England UK: Cambridge University Press.

Brandstätter, H., & Königstein, M. (2001). Personality influences on ultimatum bargaining decisions. *European Journal of Personality, 15*, S53–S70.

Brandts, J., & MacLeod, W. B. (1995). Equilibrium Selection in Experimental Games with Recommended Play. *Games and Economic Behavior, 11*, 36–63.

Branscombe, N. R., & Ellemers, N. (1998). Coping with group-based discrimination: Individualistic versus group-level strategies. In J. K. Swim & C. Stangor (Eds.), *Prejudice: The target's perspective* (pp. 243–266). San Diego, CA: Academic Press, Inc.

Branscombe, N. R., Spears, R., Ellemers, N., & Doosje, B. (2002). Intragroup and intergroup evaluation effects on group behavior. *Personality and Social Psychology Bulletin, 28*, 744–753.

Branscombe, N. R., & Wann, D. L. (1994). Collective self-esteem consequences of outgroup derogation when a valued social identity is on trial. *European Journal of Social Psychology, 24*, 641–657.

Branscombe, N. R., Wann, D. L., Noel, J. G., & Coleman, J. (1993). In-group or out-group extremity: Importance of the threatened social identity. *Personality and Social Psychology Bulletin, 19*, 381–388.

Brauer, M., Judd, C. M., & Jacquelin, V. (2001). The communication of social stereotypes: The effects of group discussion and information distribution on stereotypic appraisals. *Journal of Personality and Social Psychology, 81*, 463–475.

Brawley, L. R., Carron, A. V., & Widmeyer, W. N. (1993). The influence of the group and its cohesiveness on perceptions of group goal-related variables. *Journal of Sport and Exercise Psychology, 15*, 245–260.

Breakwell, G. M. (1990). Social beliefs about gender differences. In C. Fraser & G. Gaskell (Eds.), *The social psychological study of widespread beliefs* (pp. 210–225). New York: Clarendon Press/Oxford University Press.

Brearley, M. (1994). Captains and cricket teams: Therapists and groups. *Group Analysis, 27*, 231–249.

Brett, J. M. (1991). Negotiating group decisions. *Negotiation Journal, 7*, 291–310.

Brett, J., & Kopelman, S. (2004). Cross-cultural perspectives on cooperation in social dilemmas. In Gelfand, J. Michele Brett, M. Jeanne (Eds.), *The handbook of negotiation and culture* (pp. 395–411). Stanford, CA: Stanford University Press.

Brewer, M. B. (1991). The social self: On being the same and different at the same time. *Personality and Social Psychology Bulletin, 17*, 475–482.

Brewer, M. B. (1993). Social identity, distinctiveness, and in-group homogeneity. *Social Cognition, 11*, 150–164.

Brewer, M. B. (1995). Managing diversity: The role of social identities. In S. E. Jackson & M. N. Ruderman (Eds.), *Diversity in work teams: Research paradigms for a changing workplace* (pp. 47–68). Washington, DC: American Psychological Association.

Brewer, M. B. (1996). When contact is not enough: Social identity and intergroup cooperation. *International Journal of Intercultural Relations, 20*, 291–303.

Brewer, M. B. (1999). The psychology of prejudice: Ingroup love or outgroup hate? *Journal of Social Issues, 55*, 429–444.

Brewer, M. B. (2000). Superodinate goals versus superordinate identity as bases of intergroup cooperation. In D. Capozza & R. Brown (Eds.), *Social identity processes: Trends in theory and research* (pp. 117–132). Thousand Oaks, CA: Sage Publications Ltd.

Brewer, M. B. (2001). Ingroup identification and intergroup conflict: When does ingroup love become outgroup hate? In R. D. Ashmore, L. Jussim, & D. Wilder (Eds.), *Social identity, intergroup conflict, and conflict reduction* (pp. 17–41). New York: Oxford University Press.

Brewer, M. B. (2007a). The importance of being we: Human nature and intergroup relations. *American Psychologist, 62*, 728–738.

Brewer, M. B. (2007b). The social psychology of intergroup relations: Social categorization, in-group bias, and outgroup prejudice. In A. W. Kruglanski & E. T. Higgins (Eds.), *Social psychology: Handbook of basic principles* (2nd ed., pp. 695–715). New York: Guilford Press.

Brewer, M. B. (2008a). Deprovincialization: Social identity complexity and outgroup acceptance. In U. Wagner, L. R. Tropp, G. Finchilescu, & C. Tredoux (Eds.), *Improving intergroup relations: Building on the legacy of Thomas F. Pettigrew* (pp. 160–176). Malden: Blackwell Publishing.

Brewer, M. B. (2008b). Social identity and close relationships. In J. P. Forgas & J. Fitness (Eds.), *Social relationships: Cognitive, affective, and motivational processes* (pp. 167–183). New York: Psychology Press.

Brewer, M. B. (2009). Motivations underlying ingroup identification: Optimal distinctiveness and beyond. In S. Otten, K. Sassenberg, & T. Kessler (Eds.), *Intergroup relations: The role of motivation and emotion* (pp. 3–22). New York: Psychology Press.

Brewer, M. B., & Harasty, A. S. (1996). Seeing groups as entities: The role of perceiver motivation. In R. M. Sorrentino & E. T. Higgins (Eds.), *Handbook of motivation and cognition, Vol. 3: The interpersonal context* (pp. 347–370). New York: Guilford Press.

Brewer, M. B., & Miller, N. (1984). Beyond the contact hypothesis: Theoretical perspectives on desegregation. In N. M. Brewer & M. B. Brewer (Eds.), *Groups in contact: The psychology of desegregation* (pp 281–302). Orlando, FL: Academic Press.

Brewer, M. B., & Miller, N. (1988). Contact and cooperation: When do they work? In P. A. Katz & D. A. Taylor (Eds.), *Eliminating racism: Profiles in controversy* (pp. 315–326). New York: Plenum Press.

Brewer, M. B., & Pierce, K. P. (2005). Social identity complexity and outgroup tolerance. *Personality and Social Psychology Bulletin, 31*, 428–437.

Brewer, M. B., & Roccas, S. (2001). Individual values, social identity, and optimal distinctiveness. In C. Sedikides, M. Brewer (Eds.), *Individual Self, Relative Self, Collective Self* (pp. 219–237). Philadelphia: Psychology Press.

Brewer, M. B., & Silver, M. D. (2000). Group distinctiveness, social identification, and collective mobilization. In S. Stryker, T. J. Owens, & R. W. White (Eds.), *Self, identity, and social movements* (pp. 153–171). Minneapolis, MN: University of Minnesota Press.

Brewer, M. B., & Weber, J. G. (1994). Self-evaluation effects of interpersonal versus intergroup social comparison. *Journal of Personality and Social Psychology, 66*, 268–275.

Brewer, M. B., & Yuki, M. (2007). Culture and social identity. In S. Kitayama & D. Cohen (Eds.), *Handbook of cultural psychology* (pp. 307–322). New York: Guilford Press.

Brichcin, W., Janousek, J., Uhlar, P., & Hnilica, K. (1994). Joint problem-solving mediated by a computer network.. *Journal of Russian and East European Psychology, 32*(1), 78–96.

Britt, T. W., Boniecki, K. A., Vescio, T. K., & Biernat, M. (1996). Intergroup anxiety: A person * situation approach. *Personality and Social Psychology Bulletin, 22*, 1177–1188.

Brodbeck, F. C., & Greitemeyer, T. (2000). Effects of individual versus mixed individual and group experience in rule induction on group member learning and group performance. *Journal of Experimental Social Psychology, 36*, 621–648.

Brodt, S. E. (1994). "Inside information" and negotiator decision behavior. *Organizational Behavior and Human Decision Processes, 58*, 172–202.

Bronheim, S. M., & Striffler, N. (1999). A national coalition of communities. In R. N. Roberts & P. R. Magrab (Eds.), *Where children live: Solutions for serving young children and their families* (pp. 73–96). Westport, CT: Ablex Publishing.

Brooks, A. K. (1994). Power and the production of knowledge: Collective team learning in work organizations. *Human Resource Development Quarterly, 5*, 213–235.

Brooks, A. K. (1997). Power and the production of knowledge: Collective team learning in work organizations. In D. F. Russ-Eft, H. S. Preskill, & C. Sleezer (Eds.), *Human resource development review: Research and implications* (pp. 179–205). Thousand Oaks, CA: Sage Publications, Inc.

Brophy, D. R. (1998). Understanding, measuring, and enhancing collective creative problem-solving efforts. *Creativity Research Journal, 11*, 199–229.

Brosig, J. (2002). Identifying cooperative behavior: Some experimental results in a prisoner's dilemma game. *Journal of Economic Behavior and Organization, 47*, 275–290.

Brown, C. S., & Bigler, R. S. (2002). Effects of minority status in the classroom on children's intergroup attitudes. *Journal of Experimental Child Psychology, 83*, 77–110.

Brown, H. (1996). Themes in experimental research on groups from the 1930 s to the 1990s. In M. Wetherell (Ed.), *Identities, groups and social issues* (pp. 9–62). Milton Keynes, England: Open University Press; London: Sage Publications, Inc.

Brown, M. E., & Gioia, D. A. (2002). Making things click: Distributive leadership in an online division of an offline organization. *Leadership Quarterly, 13*, 397–419.

Brown, Roger. (1965). *Social Psychology*. New York: Free Press.

Brown, Rupert, & Capozza, D. (2006a). Motivational, emotional, and cultural influences in social identity processes. In R. Brown & D. Capozza (Eds.), *Social Identities: Motivational, Emotional and Cultural Influences* (pp. 3–29). Hove, England: Psychology Press/Taylor & Francis (UK).

Brown, Rupert, & Capozza, D. (Eds.). (2006b). *Social identities: Motivational, emotional, cultural influences*. Hove, England: Psychology Press.

Brown, Rupert, Maras, P., Masser, B., Vivian, J., & Hewstone, M. (2001). Life on the ocean wave: Testing some intergroup hypotheses in a naturalistic setting. *Group Processes and Intergroup Relations, 4*, 81–97.

Brown, Rupert, & Smith, A. (1989). Perceptions of and by minority groups: The case of women in academia. *European Journal of Social Psychology, 19*, 61–75.

Brown, Rupert, Vivian, J., & Hewstone, M. (1999). Changing attitudes through intergroup contact: The effects of group membership salience. *European Journal of Social Psychology, 29*, 741–764.

Brown, Rupert, & Zagefka, H. (2005). Ingroup affiliations and prejudice. In J. F. Dovidio, P. Glick, & L. A. Rudman (Eds.), *On the nature of prejudice: Fifty years after Allport* (pp. 54–70). Malden: Blackwell Publishing.

Brown, T. C. (2003). The effect of verbal self-guidance training on collective efficacy and team performance. *Personnel Psychology, 56*, 935–964.

Brucks, M., & Schurr, P. H. (1990). The effects of bargainable attributes and attribute range knowledge on consumer choice processes. *Journal of Consumer Research, 16*, 409–419.

Bruins, J. J., Liebrand, W. B., & Wilke, H. A. (1989). About the saliency of fear and greed in social dilemmas. *European Journal of Social Psychology, 19*, 155–161.

Bruins, J., Platow, M. J., & Ng, S. H. (1995). Distributive and procedural justice in interpersonal and intergroup situations: Issues, solutions, and extensions. *Social Justice Research, 8*, 103–121.

Brunner, J. K. (1994). Bargaining with reasonable aspirations. *Theory and Decision, 37*, 311–321.

Brunner, L. D., Nutkevich, A., & Sher, M. (Eds.). (2006). *Group relations conferences: Reviewing and exploring theory, design, roletaking and application.* London: Karnac.

Brunsson, K. (1998). Non-learning organizations. *Scandinavian Journal of Management, 14*, 421–432.

Bruschke, J. C., Gartner, C., & Seiter, J. S. (1993). Student ethnocentrism, dogmatism, and motivation: A study of BAFA BAFA. *Simulation and Gaming, 24*, 9–20.

Bruttel, L. V. (2009). Group dynamics in experimental studies-The Bertrand Paradox revisited. *Journal of Economic Behavior and Organization, 69*, 51–63.

Bruxelles, S., & Kerbrat-Orecchioni, C. (2004). Coalitions in polylogues. *Journal of Pragmatics, 36*, 75–113.

Buch, K. (1992). Quality circles and employee withdrawal behaviors: A cross-organizational study. *Journal of Applied Behavioral Science, 28*, 62–73.

Buchan, N. R., Croson, R. T. A., Johnson, E. J., & Iacobucci, D. (2004). When do fair beliefs influence bargaining behavior? Experimental bargaining in Japan and the United States. *Journal of Consumer Research, 31*, 181–190.

Budescu, D. V., Erev, I., & Zwick, R. (Eds.). (1999). *Games and human behavior: Essays in honor of Amnon Rapoport.* Mahwah, NJ: Lawrence Erlbaum Associates Publishers.

Budescu, D. V., & Rapoport, A. (1994). Subjective randomization in one and two-person games. *Journal of Behavioral Decision Making, 7*, 261–278.

Budescu, D. V., Rapoport, A., & Suleiman, R. (1990). Resource dilemmas with environmental uncertainty and asymmetric players. *European Journal of Social Psychology, 20*, 475–487.

Budescu, D. V., Rapoport, A., & Suleiman, R. (1992). Simultaneous vs. sequential requests in resource dilemmas with incomplete information. *Acta Psychologica, 80*, 297–310.

Budescu, D. V., Rapoport, A., & Suleiman, R. (1995). Common pool resource dilemmas under uncertainty: Qualitative test of equilibrium solutions. *Games and Economic Behavior, 10*, 171–201.

Budescu, D. V., Suleiman, R., & Rapoport, A. (1995). Positional and group size effects in resource dilemmas with uncertain resources. *Organizational Behavior and Human Decision Processes, 61*, 225–238.

Bunce, D., & West, M. A. (1995). Self perceptions and perceptions of group climate as predictors of individual innovation at work. *Applied Psychology: An International Review, 44*, 199–215.

Bunderson, J. S. (2003). Recognizing and Utilizing Expertise in Work Groups: A Status Characteristics Perspective. *Administrative Science Quarterly, 48*, 557–591.

Bunderson, J. S., & Sutcliffe, K. M. (2002). Comparing alternative conceptualizations of functional diversity in management teams: Process and performance effects. *Academy of Management Journal, 45*, 875–893.

Bunderson, J. S., & Sutcliffe, K. M. (2003). Management team learning orientation and business unit performance. *Journal of Applied Psychology, 88*, 552–560.

Bunker, B. B. (2006). Managing conflict through large-group methods. In M. Deutsch, P. T. Coleman, & E. C. Marcus (Eds.), *The handbook of conflict resolution: Theory and practice* (2nd ed., pp. 757–780). Hoboken, NJ: Wiley Publishing.

Bunker, B. B., & Rubin, J. Z. (1995). Introduction: Conflict, cooperation, and justice. In B. B. Bunker & J. Z. Rubin (Eds.), *Conflict, cooperation, and justice: Essays inspired by the work of Morton Deutsch* (pp. 1–9), San Francisco: Jossey-Bass.

Burani, N., & Zwicker, W. S. (2003). Coalition formation games with separable preferences. *Mathematical Social Sciences, 45*, 27–52.

Burgoon, J. K. (1976). The Unwillingness-to-Communicate Scale: Development and validation. *Speech Monographs, 43*(1), 60–69.

Burgoon, J. K., Buller, D. B., Floyd, K., & Grandpre, J. (1996). Deceptive realities. Sender, receiver, and observer perspectives in deceptive conversations. *Communication Research, 23*, 724–748.

Burgos, A., Grant, S., & Kajii, A. (2002a). Bargaining and boldness. *Games and Economic Behavior, 38*, 28–51.

Burgos, A., Grant, S., & Kajii, A. (2002b). Corrigendum to 'Bargaining and boldness' [*Games and Economic Behavior, 38* (2002) 2851], *Games and Economic Behavior, 41*, 165–168.

Burningham, C., & West, M. A. (1995). Individual, climate, and group interaction processes as predictors of work team innovation. *Small Group Research, 26*, 106–117.

Burns, T. (1955). The reference of conduct in small groups: cliques and cabals in occupational milieux. *Human Relations, 8*, 467–486.

Burrell, N. A. (1990). To probe or not to probe: Evaluating mediators' question-asking behaviors. In M. A. Rahim (Ed.), *Theory and research in conflict management* (pp. 54–72). New York: Praeger Publishers.

Burrell, N. A., Donohue, W. A., & Allen, M. (1990). The impact of disputants' expectations on mediation: Testing an interventionist model. *Human Communication Research, 17*, 104–139.

Burris, B. H. (1998). Computerization of the workplace. *Annual Review of Sociology, 24*, 141–157.

Burton, A., & Sefton, M. (2004). Risk, pre-play communication and equilibrium. *Games and Economic Behavior, 46*, 23–40.

Burton, J. (1979). *Deviance, terrorism and war: The process of solving unsolved social and political problems*. Oxford: Robertson.

Busch, L.-A., & Horstmann, I. (1997). A comment on issue-by-issue negotiations. *Games and Economic Behavior, 19*, 144–148.

Busch, L.-A., & Horstmann, I. J. (2002). The game of negotiations: Ordering issues and implementing agreements. *Games and Economic Behavior, 41*, 169–191.

Busch, T. (1996). Gender, group composition, cooperation, and self-efficacy in computer studies. *Journal of Educational Computing Research, 15*, 125–135.

Busemeyer, J. R., & Pleskac, T. J. (2009). Theoretical tools for understanding and aiding dynamic decision making. *Journal of Mathematical Psychology, 53*, 126–138.

Bush, R. A. B., & Folger, J. P. (2005). *The promise of mediation: The transformative approach to conflict* (rev. ed.). San Francisco: Jossey-Bass.

Bushe, G. R., & Johnson, A. L. (1989). Contextual and internal variables affecting task group outcomes in organizations. *Group and Organization Studies, 14*, 462–482.

Buskens, V., & Snijders, C. (1997). "Individual heuristics and the dynamics of cooperation in large groups": Additional results using analytical methods. *Psychological Review, 104*, 792–800.

Buss, D. M., & Dedden, L. A. (1990). Derogation of competitors. *Journal of Social and Personal Relationships. 1990 Aug; Vol 7*, 395–422.

Butler, C. K. (2007). Prospect theory and coercive bargaining. *Journal of Conflict Resolution, 51*, 227–250.

Butler, D. J. (1992). An experimental investigation into the effects of uncertainty on rational behaviour in two-person symmetric games. *Journal of Behavioral Decision Making, 5*, 283–301.

Butler, J. K. (1995). Behaviors, trust, and goal achievement in a win-win negotiating role play. *Group and Organization Management, 20*, 486–501.

Butterwick, S. (2003). Re/searching speaking and listening across difference: Exploring feminist coalition politics through participatory theatre. *International Journal of Qualitative Studies in Education, 16*, 449–465.

Buunk, B. P., Schaap, C., & Prevoo, N. (1990). Conflict resolution styles attributed to self and partner in premarital relationships. *Journal of Social Psychology, 130*, 821–823.

Buvik, A., & Reve, T. (2002). Inter-firm governance and structural power in industrial relationships: The moderating effect of bargaining power on the contractual safeguarding of specific assets. *Scandinavian Journal of Management, 18*, 261–284.

Buzzanell, P. M., & Burrell, N. A. (1997). Family and workplace conflict: Examining metaphorical conflict schemas and expressions across context and sex. *Human Communication Research, 24*, 109–146.

Byers, T., & Slack, T. (2001). Strategic decision-making in small businesses within the leisure industry. *Journal of Leisure Research, 33*, 121–136.

Cabecinhas, R. (2004). Representaçoes sociais, relaçoes intergrupais e cogniçao social [Social representations, intergroup relationships and social cognition]. *Cadernos de Psicologia e Educaçao Paideia, 14*(28), 125–137.

Cable, D. M., & Parsons, C. K. (2001). Socialization tactics and person-organization fit. *Personnel Psychology, 54*, 1–23.

Cabon-Dhersin, M.-L., & Ramani, S. V. (2004). Does trust matter for R&D cooperation? A game theoretic examination. *Theory and Decision, 57*, 143–180.

Cabrales, A., Charness, G., & Corchón, L. C. (2003). An experiment on Nash implementation. *Journal of Economic Behavior and Organization, 51*, 161–193.

Cadinu, M., Maass, A., Lombardo, M., & Frigerio, S. (2006). Stereotype threat: The moderating role of locus of control beliefs. *European Journal of Social Psychology, 36*, 183–197.

Cadinu, M., & Reggiori, C. (2002). Discrimination of a low-status outgroup: The role of ingroup threat. *European Journal of Social Psychology, 32*, 501–515.

Cadinu, M. R., & Cerchioni, M. (2001). Compensatory biases after ingroup threat: "Yeah, but we have a good personality." *European Journal of Social Psychology, 31*, 353–367.

Cady, S. H., & Valentine, J. (1999). Team innovation and perceptions of consideration: What difference does diversity make? *Small Group Research, 30*, 730–750.

Cahn, D. D. (Ed.). (1990). *Intimates in conflict: A communication perspective*. Hillsdale, NJ: Lawrence Erlbaum Associates, Inc.

Cahn, D. D. (Ed.). (1994). *Conflict in personal relationships*. Hillsdale, NJ: Lawrence Erlbaum Associates, Inc.

Cairns, E. (1982). Intergroup conflict in Northern Ireland. In H. Tajfel (Ed.), *Social identity and intergroup relations* (pp. 277–297). Cambridge, England: Cambridge University Press.

Cairns, E., Kenworthy, J., Campbell, A., & Hewstone, M. (2006). The role of in-group identification, religious group membership and inter-group conflict in moderating in-group and outgroup affect. *British Journal of Social Psychology, 45*, 701–716.

Cairns, E., & Lewis, C. A. (2003). Empowering peace. *The Psychologist, 16*(3), 142–143.

Caldwell, D. F., & O'Reilly, C. A., .III (2003). The determinants of team-based innovation in organizations. The role of social influence. *Small Group Research, 34*, 497–517.

Caldwell, S. D., Herold, D. M., & Fedor, D. B. (2004). Toward an understanding of the relationships among organizational change, individual differences, and changes in person-environment fit: A cross-level study. *Journal of Applied Psychology, 89*, 868–882.

Calhoun, P. S., & Smith, W. P. (1999). Integrative bargaining: Does gender make a difference? *International Journal of Conflict Management, 10*, 203–224.

Callister, R. R., & Wall, J. A. Jr. (1997). Japanese community and organizational mediation. *Journal of Conflict Resolution, 41*, 311–328.

Calvó-Armengol, A. (2003). A decentralized market with trading links. *Mathematical Social Sciences, 45*, 83–103.

Camac, C. (1992). Information preferences in a two-person social dilemma. In W. B. G. Liebrand, D. M. Messick, & Wilke, A. M. Hen (Eds.), *Social dilemmas: Theoretical issues and research findings* (pp. 147–161). Elmsford, NY: Pergamon Press.

Cameira, M., Serôdio, R. G., Pinto, I. R., & Marques, J. M. (2002). Efeitos implícitos da pertença e identificaçao grupais na discriminaçao social [Implied effects of group membership and identification on social discrimination]. *Análise Psicológica, 20*, 603–610.

Camerer, C. (1988). Gifts as economic signals and social symbols. *American Journal of Sociology, 94*, 180–214.

Camerer, C. F. (2003). *Behavioral game theory: Experiments in strategic interaction.* New York: Russell Sage Foundation.

Camerer, C. F., & Loewenstein, G. (1993). Information, fairness, and efficiency in bargaining. In B. A. Mellers & J. Baron (Eds.), *Psychological perspectives on justice: Theory and applications* (pp. 155–179). New York: Cambridge University Press.

Cameron, James E. (2004). A three-factor model of social identity. *Self and Identity, 3,* 239–262.

Cameron, Jessica A., Alvarez, J. M., Ruble, D. N., & Fuligni, A. J. (2001). Children's lay theories about ingroups and outgroups: Reconceptualizing research on prejudice. *Personality and Social Psychology Review, 5,* 118–128.

Cameron, K. S., Bright, D., & Caza, A. (2004). Exploring the relationships between organizational virtuousness and performance. *American Behavioral Scientist, 47,* 766–790.

Cameron, L., Rutland, A., Brown, R., & Douch, R. (2006). Changing children's intergroup attitudes toward refugees: Testing different models of extended contact. *Child Development, Vol 77,* 1208–1219.

Campbell, D. T. (1993). Systematic errors to be expected of the social scientist on the basis of a general psychology of cognitive bias. In P. D. Blanck (Ed.), *Interpersonal expectations: Theory, research, and applications* (pp. 25–41). New York: Cambridge University Press.

Canary, D. J., Cunningham, E. M., & Cody, M. J. (1988). Goal types, gender, and locus of control in managing interpersonal conflict. *Communication Research, 15,* 426–446.

Canary, D. J., & Spitzberg, B. H. (1989). A model of the perceived competence of conflict strategies. *Human Communication Research, 15,* 630–649.

Canary, D. J., & Spitzberg, B. H. (1990). Attribution biases and associations between conflict strategies and competence outcomes. *Communication Monographs, 57,* 139–151.

Cannon, M. D., & Edmondson, A. C. (2001). Confronting failure: Antecedents and consequences of shared beliefs about failure in organizational work groups. *Journal of Organizational Behavior, 22,* 161–177.

Cannon-Bowers, J. A., & Salas, E. (1997a). A framework for developing team performance measures in training. In M. T. Brannick, E. Salas, & C. Prince (Eds.), *Team performance assessment and measurement: Theory, methods, and applications* (pp. 45–62). Mahwah, NJ: Lawrence Erlbaum Associates, Inc., Publishers.

Cannon-Bowers, J. A., & Salas, E. (1997b). Teamwork competencies: The interaction of team member knowledge, skills, and attitudes. In H. F. O'Neil, Jr. (Ed.), *Workforce readiness: Competencies and assessment* (pp. 151–174). Mahwah, NJ: Lawrence Erlbaum Associates, Inc., Publishers.

Cannon-Bowers, J. A., Salas, E., Blickensderfer, E., & Bowers, C. A. (1998). The impact of cross-training and workload on team functioning: A replication and extension of initial findings. *Human Factors, 40,* 92–101.

Cano, I., Hopkins, N., & Islam, M. R. (1991). Memory for stereotype-related material: A replication study with real-life social groups. *European Journal of Social Psychology, 21,* 349–357.

Caplan, M., Vespo, J. E., Pedersen, J., & Hay, D. F. (1991). Conflict and its resolution in small groups of one- and two-year-olds. *Child Development, 62,* 1513–1524.

Caporael, L. R., Dawes, R. M., Orbell, J. M., & van de Kragt, A. J. (1989). Selfishness examined: Cooperation in the absence of egoistic incentives. *Behavioral and Brain Sciences, 12,* 683–739.

Capozza, D., Voci, A., & Licciardello, O. (2000). Individualism, collectivism and social identity theory. In D. Capozza & R. Brown (Eds.), *Social identity processes: Trends in theory and research* (pp. 62–80). Thousand Oaks, CA: Sage Publications Ltd.

Carbaugh, D. A. (1996). *Situating selves: The communication of social identities in American scenes.* Albany, NY: State University of New York Press.

Cardona-Coll, D. (2003). Bargaining and strategic demand commitment. *Theory and Decision, 54,* 357–374.

Carey, J. M., & Kacmar, C. J. (1997). The impact of communication mode and task complexity on small group performance and member satisfaction. *Computers in Human Behavior, 13,* 23–49.

Carlander, M. (1989). Konflikter och konfliktbearbetning: En ideskrift foer hemmet, foerskolan, skolan, fritidshemmet och foereningslivet [Conflicts and conflict resolution: An idea paper for home, preschools, schools, youth centers, and organizations]. *Pedagogiska Hjaelpmedel*, No. 40, 65.

Carless, S. A. (2004). Does psychological empowerment mediate the relationship between psychological climate and job satisfaction? *Journal of Business and Psychology, 18*, 405–425.

Carletta, J., Anderson, A. H., & McEwan, R. (2000). The effects of multimedia communication technology on non-collocated teams: A case study. *Ergonomics, 43*, 1237–1251.

Carletta, J., Garrod, S., & Fraser-Krauss, H. (1998). Placement of authority and communication patterns in workplace groups: The consequences for innovation. *Small Group Research, 29*, 531–559.

Carley, K. M., & Harrald, J. R. (1997). Organizational learning under fire: Theory and practice. *American Behavioral Scientist, 40*, 310–332.

Carmel, E., & Sawyer, S. (1998). Packaged software development teams: What makes them different? *Information Technology and People, 11*, 7–19.

Carment, D., & Rowlands, D. (1998). Three's company: Evaluating third-party intervention in intrastate conflict. *Journal of Conflict Resolution, 42*, 572–599.

Carnevale, A. P., Gainer, L. J., & Meltzer, A. S. (1990). Workplace basics: The essential skills employers want. San Francisco: Jossey-Bass Inc, Publishers.

Carnevale, P. J. D. (1986). Strategic choice in mediation. *Negotiation Journal, 2*, 41–56.

Carnevale, P. J. (1992). The usefulness of mediation theory. *Negotiation Journal, 8*, 387–390.

Carnevale, P. J. (1995). Property, culture, and negotiation. In R. M. Kramer & D. M. Messick (Eds.), *Negotiation as a social process: New trends in theory and research* (pp. 309–323). Thousand Oaks, CA: Sage Publications, Inc.

Carnevale, P. J. (2006). Creativity in the outcomes of conflict. In M. Deutsch, P. T. Coleman, & E. C. Marcus (Eds.), *The handbook of conflict resolution: Theory and practice* (2nd ed., pp. 414–435). Hoboken, NJ: Wiley Publishing.

Carnevale, P. J., & Henry, R. A. (1989). Determinants of mediator behavior: A test of the strategic choice model. *Journal of Applied Social Psychology, 19*, 481–498.

Carnevale, P. J., & Keenan, P. A. (1992). The resolution of conflict: Negotiation and third party intervention. In J. F. Hartley & G. M. Stephenson (Eds.), *Employment relations: The psychology of influence and control at work* (pp. 225–245). Malden: Blackwell Publishing.

Carnevale, P. J., O'Connor, K. M., & McCusker, C. (1993). Time pressure in negotiation and mediation. In O. Svenson & A. J. Maule (Eds.), *Time pressure and stress in human judgment and decision making* (pp. 117–127). New York: Plenum Press.

Carnevale, P. J., & Probst, T. M. (1997). Good news about competitive people. In C. K. W. De Dreu & Van de E. Vliert (Eds.), *Using conflict in organizations* (pp. 129–146). London: Sage Publications, Inc.

Carpenter, J. P. (2003a). Bargaining Outcomes as the Result of Coordinated Expectations: An experimental study of sequential bargaining. *Journal of Conflict Resolution, 47*, 119–139.

Carpenter, J. P. (2003b). Is fairness used instrumentally? Evidence from sequential bargaining. *Journal of Economic Psychology, 24*, 467–489.

Carpenter, S. (1994). Characteristics of gender subtypes: Group and individual differences. *Sex Roles, 31*, 167–184.

Carpenter, S., & Radhakrishnan, P. (2002). The relation between allocentrism and perceptions of ingroups. *Personality and Social Psychology Bulletin, 28*, 1528–1537.

Carr, J. Z., Schmidt, A. M., Ford, J. K., & DeShon, R. P. (2003). Climate perceptions matter: A meta-analytic path analysis relating molar climate, cognitive and affective states, and individual level work outcomes. *Journal of Applied Psychology, 88*, 605–619.

Carr, P. D., & Groves, G. (1998). The Internet-based operations simulation game. In J. A. Chambers (Ed.), *Selected papers from the 9th international conference on college teaching and learning* (pp. 15–23). Jacksonville, FL: Florida Community College at Jacksonville.

Carreras, F. (1996). On the existence and formation of partnerships in a game. *Games and Economic Behavior, 12*, 54–67.

Carreras, F., & Freixas, J. (1996). Complete simple games. *Mathematical Social Sciences, 32*, 139–155.

Carroll, J. S., Bazerman, M. H., & Maury, R. (1988). Negotiator cognitions: A descriptive approach to negotiators' understanding of their opponents. *Organizational Behavior and Human Decision Processes, 41*, 352–370.

Cartwright, D., & Zander, A. F. (1968). *Group dynamics: Research and theory.* New York: Harper & Row.

Casas, J. F., & Ryan, C. S. (2010). How Latinos are transforming the United States: Research, theory, and policy. *Journal of Social Issues, 66*, 1–10.

Casey-Campbell, M., & Martens, M. L. (2009). Sticking it all together: A critical assessment of the group cohesion-performance literature. *International Journal of Management Reviews, 11*, 223–246.

Caspi, A., & Blau, I. (2008). Social presence in online discussion groups: Testing three conceptions and their relations to perceived learning. *Social Psychology of Education, 11*, 323–346.

Cast, A. D. (2003). Identities and behavior. In P. J. Burke, T. J. Owens, R. T. Serpe, & P. A. Thoits (Eds.), *Advances in identity theory and research* (pp. 41–53). New York: Kluwer Academic/ Plenum Publishers.

Cast, A. D., Stets, J. E., & Burke, P. J. (1999). Does the self conform to the views of others? *Social Psychology Quarterly, 62*, 68–82.

Castelli, L., De Amicis, L., & Sherman, S. J. (2007). The loyal member effect: On the preference for ingroup members who engage in exclusive relations with the ingroup. *Developmental Psychology, 43*, 1347–1359.

Castrogiovanni, G. J. (2002). Organization task environments: Have they changed fundamentally over time? Journal of Management, 28, 129–150.

Cavalier, J. C., Klein, J. D., Cavalier, & F. J. (1995). Effects of cooperative learning on performance, attitude, and group behaviors in a technical team environment. *Educational Technology Research and Development, 43*(3): 61–71.

Chae, S., & Heidhues, P. (2004). A group bargaining solution. *Mathematical Social Sciences, 48*, 37–53.

Chakravarty, N., Goel, A. M., & Sastry, T. (2000). Easy weighted majority games. *Mathematical Social Sciences, 40*, 227–235.

Chang, A., & Bordia, P. (2001). A multidimensional approach to the group cohesion- group performance relationship. *Small Group Research, 32*, 379–405.

Chang, C., & Liang, M.-Y. (1998). A characterization of the lexicographic Kalai-Smorodinsky solution for n = 3. *Mathematical Social Sciences, 35*, 307–319.

Chang, J. (2003). Use of business simulation games in Hong Kong. *Simulation and Gaming, 34*, 358–366.

Chang, J., Lee, M., Ng, K.-l., & Moon, K.-L. (2003). Business simulation games: The Hong Kong experience. *Simulation and Gaming, 34*, 367–376.

Chansler, P. A., Swamidass, P. M., & Cammann, C. (2003). Self-managing work teams: An empirical study of group cohesiveness in "natural work groups" at a Harley-Davidson Motor Company plant. *Small Group Research, 34*, 101–120.

Chapman, J. G. (1991). The impact of socially projected group composition on behavior in a commons dilemma: A self-attention perspective. *Current Psychology: Research and Reviews, 10*, 183–198.

Charan, Ra. (1991). How networks reshape organizations-for results. *Harvard Business Review, 69*(5), 104–115.

Charness, G., & Haruvy, E. (2002). Altruism, equity, and reciprocity in a gift-exchange experiment: An encompassing approach. *Games and Economic Behavior, 40*, 203–231.

Chasteen, A. L. (2005). Seeing eye-to-eye: Do intergroup biases operate similarly for younger and older adults? *International Journal of Aging and Human Development, 61*, 123–139.

Chatman, J. A., & Flynn, F. J. (2001). The influence of demographic heterogeneity on the emergence and consequences of cooperative norms in work teams. *Academy of Management Journal, 44*, 956–974.

Chatman, J. A., Polzer, J. T., Barsade, S. G., & Neale, M. A. (1998). Being different yet feeling similar: The influence of demographic composition and organizational culture on work processes and outcomes. *Administrative Science Quarterly, 43*, 749–780.

Chatterjee, K. (1996). Game theory and the practice of bargaining. *Group Decision and Negotiation, 5*, 355–369.

Chatterjee, K., & Dutta, B. (1998). Rubinstein auctions: On competition for bargaining partners. *Games and Economic Behavior, 23*, 119–145.

Chatterjee, K., & Lee, C. C. (1998). Bargaining and search with incomplete information about outside options. *Games and Economic Behavior, 22*, 203–237.

Chatterjee, S., Heath, T. B., & Basuroy, S. (2003). Failing to suspect collusion in price-matching guarantees: Consumer limitations in game-theoretic reasoning. *Journal of Consumer Psychology, 13*, 255–267.

Chaudhuri, A., Khan, S. A., Lakshmiratan, A., Py, A.-L., & Shah, L. (2003). Trust and trustworthiness in a sequential bargaining game. *Journal of Behavioral Decision Making, 16*, 331–340.

Chaudhuri, A., Sopher, B., & Strand, P. (2002). Cooperation in social dilemmas, trust and reciprocity. *Journal of Economic Psychology, 23*, 231–250.

Chavez, A. K., & Kimbrough, S. O. (2004). A model of human behavior in coalition formation games. In M. Lovett, C. Schunn, C. Lebiere, & P. Munro (Eds.), *Proceedings of the Sixth International Conference on Cognitive Modeling: ICCCM 2004: Integrating Models* (pp. 70–75). Mahwah, NJ: Lawrence Erlbaum Associates Publishers.

Chen, K.-Y., Fine, L. R., & Huberman, B. A. (2004). Eliminating public knowledge biases in information-aggregation mechanisms. *Management Science, 50*, 983–994.

Chen, K.-Y., & Plott, C. R. (1998). Nonlinear behavior in sealed bid first price auctions. *Games and Economic Behavior, 25*, 34–78.

Chen, X.P. (1996). The group-based binding pledge as a solution to public goods problems. *Organizational Behavior and Human Decision Processes, 66*, 192–202.

Chen, X.-P., & Komorita, S. S. (1994). The effects of communication and commitment in a public goods social dilemma. *Organizational Behavior and Human Decision Processes, 60*, 367–386.

Chen, X.-P., Wasti, S. A., & Triandis, H. C. (2007). When does group norm or group identity predict cooperation in a public goods dilemma? The moderating effects of idiocentrism and allocentrism. *International Journal of Intercultural Relations, 31*, 259–276.

Chen, Y. R., Brockner, J., & Chen, X. P. (2002). Individual-collective primacy and ingroup favoritism: Enhancement and protection effects. *Journal of Experimental Social Psychology, 38*, 482–491.

Chen, Y. R., & Church, A. H. (1993). Reward allocation preferences in groups and organizations. *International Journal of Conflict Management, 4*, 25–59.

Cheng, L. K., & Zhu, M. (1995). Mixe-dstrategy Nash Equilibrium based upon expected utility and quadratic utility. *Games and Economic Behavior, 9*, 139–150.

Chertkoff, J. M. (1992). Do Psychologists Care Whether People Behave as Game Theory Prescribes? *PsycCRITIQUES, 37*, 1053–1054.

Chertkoff, J. M., & Mesch, D. J. (1997). Performance under different contingent reward systems: A reconceptualization of the cooperative-competitive-individualistic literature. In B. Markovsky, M. J. Lovaglia, & L. Troyer (Eds.), *Advances in group processes* (Vol. 14, pp. 1–27). Greenwich, CT: Jai Press, Inc.

Cheung, Y.-W., & Friedman, D. (1997). Individual learning in normal form games: Some laboratory results. *Games and Economic Behavior, 19*, 46–76.

Chin, M. G., & McClintock, C. G. (1993). The effects of intergroup discrimination and social values on level of self-esteem in the minimal group paradigm. *European Journal of Social Psychology, 23*, 63–75.

Chiocchio, F., & Essiembre, H. (2009). Cohesion and performance: A meta-analytic review of disparities between project teams, production teams, and service teams. *Small Group Research, 40*, 382–420.

Chiu, M. M., & Khoo, L. (2003). Rudeness and status effects during group problem solving: Do they bias evaluations and reduce the likelihood of correct solutions? *Journal of Educational Psychology, 95*, 506–523.

Chiu, R. K., & Kosinski, F. A. (1994). Is Chinese conflict-handling behavior influenced by Chinese values? *Social Behavior and Personality, 22*, 81–90.

Chizhik, A. W., Shelly, R. K., & Troyer, L. (2009). Intragroup conflict and cooperation: An introduction. *Journal of Social Issues, 65*, 251–259.

Cho, Y.-H., Luce, R. D., & Truong, L. (2002). Duplex decomposition and general segregation of lotteries of a gain and a loss: An empirical evaluation. *Organizational Behavior and Human Decision Processes, 89*, 1176–1193.

Choi, J. N. (2002). External activities and team effectiveness: Review and theoretical development. *Small Group Research, 33*, 181–208.

Choi, J. N., & Kim, M. U. (1999). The organizational application of groupthink and its limitations in organizations. *Journal of Applied Psychology, 84*, 297–306.

Choi, Jin N., Price, R. H., & Vinokur, A. D. (2003). Self-efficacy changes in groups: Effects of diversity, leadership, and group climate. *Journal of Organizational Behavior, 24*, 357–372.

Choi, Jung-K., & Bowles, S. (2007). The coevolution of parochial altruism and war. *Science, 318*(5850), 636–640.

Chowdhury, S., Endres, M., & Lanis, T. W. (2002). Preparing students for success in team work environments: The importance of building confidence. *Journal of Managerial Issues, 14*, 346–359.

Christensen, P. N., Boldry, J. G., & Kashy, D. A. (2004). Group-based self-evaluation outside of the laboratory: Effects of global versus contextual status. *Personality and Social Psychology Bulletin, 30*, 985–994.

Christian, J., Porter, L. W., & Moffitt, G. (2006). Workplace diversity and group relations: An overview. *Group Processes and Intergroup Relations, 9*, 459–466.

Chrobot-Mason, D., Ruderman, M. N., Weber, T. J., & Ernst, C. (2009). The challenge of leading on unstable ground: Triggers that activate social identity faultlines. *Human Relations, 62*, 1763–1794.

Chryssochoou, X. (2000). Memberships in superordinate level: Re-thinking European union as a multi-national society. *Journal of Community and Applied Social Psychology, 10*, 403–420.

Chun, W. Y., & Lee, H. K. (1999). Effects of the difference in the amount of group preferential information on illusory correlation. *Personality and Social Psychology Bulletin, 25*, 1463–1475.

Chun, Y. (2002). The converse consistency principle in bargaining. *Games and Economic Behavior, 40*, 25–43.

Church, B. K., & Zhang, P. (1999). Bargaining behavior and payoff uncertainty: Experimental evidence. *Journal of Economic Psychology, 20*, 407–429.

Cicero, L., Pierro, A., & Van Knippenberg, D. (2007). Leader group prototypicality and job satisfaction: The moderating role of job stress and team identification. *Group Dynamics: Theory, Research*, and Practice, 11, 165–175.

Clancy, J. M., Elliott, G. C., Ley, T., Omodei, M. M., Wearing, A. J., McLennan, J., & Thorsteinsson, E. B. (2003). Command style and team performance in dynamic decision-making tasks. In S. L. Schneider & J. Shanteau (Eds.), *Emerging perspectives on judgment and decision research* (pp. 586–619). New York: Cambridge University Press.

Clark, A. R., Gjerde, K. A. P., & Skinner, D. (2003). The effects of interdisciplinary instruction on simulation performance. *Simulation and Gaming, 34*, 150–163.

Clark, R. D., & Maass, A. (1988). The role of social categorization and perceived source credibility in minority influence. *European Journal of Social Psychology, 18*, 381–394.

Clement, R. W, & Krueger, J. (2002). Social categorization moderates social projection. *Journal of Experimental Social Psychology, 38*, 219–231.

Cliff, D., & Bruten, J. (1999). Animat market-trading interactions as collective social adaptive behavior. *Adaptive Behavior, 7*, 384–414.

Clock of the Long Now [No authorship indicated]. (2000). The Clock of the Long Now: Time and Responsibility; Serious Play; The Planetary Bargain: Corporate Social Responsibility Comes of Age; New Rules for the New Economy (10 Ways the Network Economy is Changing Every-thing). *Long Range Planning: International Journal of Strategic Management, 33*, 599–614.

Cloven, D. H., & Roloff, M. E. (1991). Sen-semaking activities and interpersonal conflict: Com-municative cures for the mulling blues. *Western Journal of Speech Communication, 55*, 134–158.

Coates, R. C. (1990). *A street is not a home: Solving America's homeless dilemma.* Amherst, NY: Prometheus Books.

Cobb, A. T. (1991). Toward the study of organizational coalitions: Participant concerns and activi-ties in a simulated organizational setting. *Human Relations, 44*, 1057–1079.

Cobb, S. B. (1991). Resolucion de conflictos: una nueva perspectiva [Conflict resolution: A new perspective]. *Acta Psiquiatrica y Psicologica de America Latina, 37*, 31–36.

Codol, J. P., Jarymowicz, M., Kaminska-Feldman, M., & Szuster-Zbrojewicz, A. (1989). Asym-metry in the estimation of interpersonal distance and identity affirmation. *European Journal of Social Psychology, 19*, 11–22.

Cogliser, C. C., & Schriesheim, C. A. (2000). Exploring work unit context and leader-member exchange: A multi-level perspective. *Journal of Organizational Behavior, 21*, 487–511.

Cohen, B. P., & Zhou, X. (1991). Status processes in enduring work groups. *American Sociologi-cal Review, 56*, 179–188.

Cohen, B. D. (2002). Groups to resolve conflicts between groups: Diplomacy with a therapeutic dimension. *Group, 26*, 189–204.

Cohen, G. L., Sherman, D. K., Bastardi, A., Hsu, L., McGoey, M., & Ross, L. (2007). Bridging the partisan divide: Self-affirmation reduces ideological closed-mindedness and inflexibility in negotiation. *Journal of Personality and Social Psychology, 93*, 415–430.

Cohen, M. S. (1996). Transition: From romantic love to the power struggle. *Journal of Imago Relationship Therapy, 1*(2), 19–33.

Cohen, S. G., & Ledford, Gerald E. (1994). The effectiveness of self-managing teams: A quasi-experiment. *Human Relations, 47*, 13–43.

Cohen, S. G., Mohrman, S. A., & Mohrman, A. M., Jr. (1999). We can't get there unless we know where we are going: Direction setting for knowledge work teams. In R. Wageman (Ed.), *Re-search on managing groups and teams: Groups in context* (Vol. 2, pp. 1–31). San Diego, CA: Elsevier Science/JAI Press, 1999.

Cohen, T. R., & Insko, C. A. (2008). War and peace: Possible approaches to reducing intergroup conflict. *Perspectives on Psychological Science, 3*, 87–93.

Cohen, T. R., Montoya, R. M., & Insko, C. A. (2006). Group Morality and Intergroup Relations: Cross-Cultural and Experimental Evidence. *Personality and Social Psychology Bulletin, 32*, 1559–1572.

Cohen-Mansfield, J. (1990). Group and individual reward structures: A conceptual framework for social, educational, and clinical systems. *Journal of Social Behavior and Personality, 5*, 285–303.

Cole, T., & Leets, L. (1998). Linguistic masking devices and intergroup behavior: Further evidence of an intergroup linguistic bias. *Journal of Language and Social Psychology, 17*, 348–371.

Coleman, J. S. (1989). Simulation games and the development of social theory. *Simulation and Games, 20*, 144–164.

Coleman, P. T. (2006a). Intractable conflict. In M. Deutsch, P. T. Coleman, & E. C. Marcus (Eds.), *The handbook of conflict resolution: Theory and practice* (2nd ed., pp. 533–559). Hoboken, NJ: Wiley Publishing.

Coleman, P. T. (2006b). Power and conflict. In M. Deutsch, P. T. Coleman, & E. C. Marcus (Eds.), *The handbook of conflict resolution: Theory and practice* (2nd ed., pp. 120–143). Hoboken, NJ: Wiley Publishing.

Collier, M. J. (1991). Conflict competence within African, Mexican, and Anglo American friend-ships. In S. Ting-Toomey & F. Korzenny (Eds.), *Cross-cultural interpersonal communication* [International and intercultural communication annual, Vol. 15], pp. 132–154). Newbury Park, CA: Sage Publications, Inc.

Collins, B. E., & Ma, L. (2000). Impression management and identity construction in the Milgram social system. In T. Blass (Ed.), *Obedience to authority: Current perspectives on the Milgram paradigm* (pp. 61–90). Mahwah, NJ: Lawrence Erlbaum Associates Publishers.

Colman, A. M., & Stirk, J. A. (1998). Stackelberg reasoning in mixed-motive games: An experimental investigation. *Journal of Economic Psychology, 19,* 279–293.

Colquitt, J. A. (2004). Does the justice of the one interact with the justice of the many? Reactions to procedural justice in teams. *Journal of Applied Psychology, 89,* 633–646.

Colquitt, J. A., Conlon, D. E., Wesson, M. J., Porter, C. O. L. H., & Ng, K. Y. (2001). Justice at the millenium: A meta-analytic review of 25 years of organizational justice research. *Journal of Applied Psychology, 86,* 425–445.

Colquitt, J. A., Noe, R. A., & Jackson, C. L. (2002). Justice in teams: Antecedents and consequences of procedural justice climate. *Personnel Psychology, 55,* 83–109.

Conger, J. A., Kanungo, R. N., & Menon, S. T. (2000). Charismatic leadership and follower effects. *Journal of Organizational Behavior, 21,* 747–767.

Conley, J. P., & Wilkie, S. (1996). An extension of the Nash bargaining solution to nonconvex problems. *Games and Economic Behavior, 13,* 26–38.

Conlon, D. E., Carnevale, P., & Ross, W. H. (1994). The influence of third party power and suggestions on negotiation: The surface value of a compromise. *Journal of Applied Social Psychology, 24,* 1084–1113.

Conlon, D. E., Moon, H., & Ng, K. Y. (2002). Putting the cart before the horse: The benefits of arbitrating before mediating. *Journal of Applied Psychology, 87,* 978–984.

Conlon, D. E., & Ross, W. H. (1993). The effects of partisan third parties on negotiator behavior and outcome perceptions. *Journal of Applied Psychology, 78,* 280–290.

Connolly, T., Arkes, H. R., & Hammond, K. R. (Eds.). (2000). *Judgment and decision making: An interdisciplinary reader (2nd ed.).* New York: Cambridge University Press.

Conway, K. (2002). Booze and beach bans: Turning the tide through community action in New Zealand. *Health Promotion International, 17,* 171–177.

Cook, K. S., & Cooper, R. M. (2003). Experimental studies of cooperation, trust, and social exchange. In E. Ostrom & J. Walker (Eds.), *Trust and reciprocity: Interdisciplinary lessons from experimental research* (pp. 209–244). New York: Russell Sage Foundation.

Cook-Huffman, C. (2000). Who do they say we are? Framing social identity and gender in church conflict. In P. G. Coy & L. M. Woehrle (Eds.), *Social conflicts and collective identities* (pp. 115–132). Lanham, MD: Rowman & Littlefield.

Cooke, N. J., Gorman, J. C., & Rowe, L. J. (2009). An ecological perspective on team cognition. In E. Salas, G. F. Goodwin, & C. S. Burke (Eds.), *Team effectiveness in complex organizations: Cross-disciplinary perspectives and approaches* (pp. 157–182). New York: Routledge/Taylor & Francis Group.

Cooper, D. J., & Stockman, C. K. (2002). Fairness and learning: An experimental examination. *Games and Economic Behavior, 41,* 26–45.

Cooper, R., DeJong, D. V., Forsythe, R., & Ross, T. W. (1996). Cooperation without reputation: Experimental evidence from Prisoner's Dilemma Games. *Games and Economic Behavior, 12,* 187–218.

Cooren, F. (2001). Translation and articulation in the organization of coalitions: The Great Whale River case. *Communication Theory, 11,* 178–200.

Corenblum, B., Annis, R. C., & Young, S. (1996). Effects of own group success or failure on judgements of task performance by children of different ethnicities. *European Journal of Social Psychology, 26,* 777–798.

Corenblum, B., & Stephan, W. G. (2001). White fears and native apprehensions: An integrated threat theory approach to intergroup attitudes. *Canadian Journal of Behavioural Science/Revue canadienne des sciences du comportement, 33,* 251–268.

Corfman, K. P., & Lehmann, D. R. (1993). The importance of others' welfare in evaluating bargaining outcomes. *Journal of Consumer Research, 20,* 124–137.

Corfman, K. P., & Lehmann, D. R. (1994). The prisoner's dilemma and the role of information in setting advertising budgets. *Journal of Advertising, 23*(2), 35–48.

Corneille, O. (1994). Le contact comme mode de resolution du conflit intergroupe: une hypothese toujours bien vivante [Contact as a strategy for resolving intergroup conflict: A persistent hypothesis]. *Cahiers Internationaux de Psychologie Sociale*, No. 23, 40–60.

Cosgray, R. E., Davidhizar, R. E., Grostefon, J. D., Powell, M., & Wringer, P. H. (1990). A Day in the Life of an Inpatient: An experiential game to promote empathy for individuals in a psychiatric hospital. *Archives of Psychiatric Nursing, 4*, 354–359.

Coskun, H., Paulus, P. B., Brown, V., & Sherwood, J. J. (2000). Cognitive stimulation and problem presentation in idea-generating groups. *Group Dynamics: Theory, Research*, and Practice, 4, 307–329.

Cosmides, L., & Tooby, J. (1992). Cognitive adaptations for social exchange. In J. H. Barkow, L. Cosmides, & J. Tooby (Eds.), *The adapted mind: Evolutionary psychology and the generation of culture* (pp. 163–228). New York: Oxford University Press.

Cosmides, L., Tooby, J., & Kurzban, R. (2003). Perceptions of race. *Trends in Cognitive Sciences, 7*, 173–179.

Costa-Gomes, M., & Zauner, K. G. (2001). Ultimatum bargaining behavior in Israel, Japan, Slovenia, and the United States: A social utility analysis. *Games and Economic Behavior, 34*, 238–269.

Costarelli, S., & Callà, R. M. (2004). Self-directed negative affect: The distinct roles of ingroup identification and outgroup derogation. *Current Research in Social Psychology, 10*(2), 13–27.

Cottam, M. L. (1989). Cognitive psychology and bargaining behavior: Peru versus the MNCs. *Political Psychology, 10*, 445–475.

Cotterell, N., Eisenberger, R., & Speicher, H. (1992). Inhibiting effects of reciprocation wariness on interpersonal relationships. *Journal of Personality and Social Psychology, 62*, 658–668.

Craig, T. Y., & Kelly, J. R. (1999). Group cohesiveness and creative performance. *Group Dynamics: Theory, Research, and Practice, 3*, 243–256.

Cramer, M. E., Mueller, K. J., & Harrop, D. (2003). Evaluation informs coalition programming for environmental tobacco smoke reduction. *Journal of Community Health Nursing, 20*, 245–258.

Crano, W. D. (2001). Social influence, social identity, and ingroup leniency. In C. K. W. De Dreu & N. K. De Vries (Eds.), *Group consensus and minority influence: Implications for innovation* (pp. 122–143). Malden: Blackwell Publishing.

Cressman, R. (1997). Local stability of smooth selection dynamics for normal form games. *Mathematical Social Sciences, 34*, 1–19.

Cressman, R., Garay, J., Scarelli, A., & Varga, Z. (2004). The dynamic stability of coalitionist behaviour for two-strategy bimatrix games. *Theory and Decision, 56*, 141–152.

Crisp, R. J. (2008). Recognising complexity in intergroup relations. *The Psychologist, 21*(3), 4.

Crisp, R. J., & Abrams, D. (2008). Improving intergroup attitudes and reducing stereotype threat: An integrated contact model. *European Review of Social Psychology, 19*, 242–284.

Crisp, R. J., & Beck, S. R. (2005). Reducing intergroup bias: The moderating role of ingroup identification. *Group Processes and Intergroup Relations, 8*, 173–185.

Crisp, R. J., Ensari, N., Hewstone, M., & Miller, N. (2002). A dual-route model of crossed categorisation effects. *European Review of Social Psychology, 13*, 35–73.

Crisp, R. J., Heuston, S., Farr, M. J., & Turner, R. N. (2007). Seeing red or feeling blue: Differentiated intergroup emotions and ingroup identification in soccer fans. *Group Processes and Intergroup Relations, 10*(1), 9–26.

Crisp, R. J, & Hewstone, M. (2000a). Crossed categorization and intergroup bias: The moderating roles of intergroup and affective context. *Journal of Experimental Social Psychology, 36*, 357–383.

Crisp, R. J., & Hewstone, M. (2000b). Multiple categorization and social identity. In D. Capozza & R. Brown (Eds.), *Social identity processes: Trends in theory and research* (pp. 149–166). Thousand Oaks, CA: Sage Publications Ltd.

Crisp, R. J., & Hewstone, M. (Eds.). (2006). *Multiple social categorization: Processes, models and applications*. New York: Psychology Press.

Crisp, R. J., & Hewstone, M. (2007). Multiple social categorization. In M. P. Zanna (Ed.), *Advances in experimental social psychology* (Vol. 39, pp. 163–254). San Diego, CA: Elsevier Academic Press, 2007.

Crisp, R. J., Hewstone, M., & Cairns, E. (2001). Multiple identities in Northern Ireland: Hierarchical ordering in the representation of group membership. *British Journal of Social Psychology, 40*, 501–514.

Crisp, R. J., Hewstone, M., Richards, Z., & Paolini, S. (2003). Inclusiveness and crossed categorization: Effects on co-joined category evaluations of in-group and out-group primes. *British Journal of Social Psychology, 42*, 25–38.

Crisp, R. J., Stone, C. H., & Hall, N. R. (2006). Recategorization and subgroup identification: Predicting and preventing threats from common ingroups. *Personality and Social Psychology Bulletin, 32*, 230–243.

Crisp, R. J., & Turner, R. (2009). Can imagined interactions produce positive perceptions? Reducing prejudice through simulated social contact. *American Psychologist, 64*, 231–240.

Crisp, R. J., Walsh, J., & Hewstone, M. (2006). Crossed Categorization in common ingroup contexts. *Personality and Social Psychology Bulletin, 32*, 1204–1218.

Crocker, J., Blaine, B., & Luhtanen, R. (1993). Prejudice, intergroup behaviour and self-esteem: Enhancement and protection motives. In M. A. Hogg & D. Abrams (Eds.), *Group motivation: Social psychological perspectives* (pp. 52–67). London: Harvester Wheatsheaf.

Crocker, J., & Garcia, J. A. (2009). Downward and upward spirals in intergroup interactions: The role of egosystem and ecosystem goals. In T. D. Nelson (Ed.), *Handbook of prejudice, stereotyping, and discrimination* (pp. 229–245). New York: Psychology Press.

Crocker, J., & Luhtanen, R. (1990). Collective self-esteem and ingroup bias. *Journal of Personality and Social Psychology, 58*, 60–67.

Croson, R., Boles, T., & Murnighan, J. K. (2003). Cheap talk in bargaining experiments: Lying and threats in ultimatum games. *Journal of Economic Behavior and Organization, 51*, 143–159.

Croson, R., & Marks, M. (1998). Identifiability of individual contributions in a threshold public goods experiment. *Journal of Mathematical Psychology, 42*, 167–190.

Cross, S. E., & Morris, M. L. (2003). Getting to know you: The relational self-construal, relational cognition, and well-being. *Personality and Social Psychology Bulletin, 29*, 512–523.

Cross, S., & Rosenthal, R. (1999). Three models of conflict resolution: Effects on intergroup expectancies and attitudes. *Journal of Social Issues, 55*, 561–580.

Crowfoot, J. E., & Chesler, M. A. (1996). White men's roles in multicultural coalitions. In B. P. Bowser & R. G. Hunt (Eds.), *Impacts of racism on White Americans* (2nd ed., pp. 202–229). Thousand Oaks, CA: Sage Publications, Inc, 1996.

Crown, D. F., & Rosse, J. G. (1995). Yours, mine, and ours: Facilitating group productivity through the integration of individual and group goals. *Organizational Behavior and Human Decision Processes, 64*, 138–150.

Cuddy, A. J. C., Fiske, S. T., & Glick, P. (2007). The BIAS map: Behaviors from intergroup affect and stereotypes. *Journal of Personality and Social Psychology, 92*, 631–648.

Cummings, J. N. (2004). Work groups, structural diversity, and knowledge sharing in a global organization. *Management Science, 50*, 352–364.

Cummings, J. N., & Cross, R. (2003). Structural properties of work groups and their consequences for performance. *Social Networks, 25*, 197–210.

Cummings, T. G. (1981). Designing effective work groups. In P. C. Nystrom & W. H. Starbuck (Eds.), *Handbook of organizational design* (Vol. 2, pp. 250–271). New York: Oxford University Press.

Cunningham, E., & Platow, M. J. (2007). On helping lower status out-groups: The nature of the help and the stability of the intergroup status hierarchy. *Asian Journal of Social Psychology, 10*, 258–264.

Cunningham, G. B. (2005). The importance of a common in-group identity in ethnically diverse groups. *Group Dynamics: Theory, Research*, and Practice, 9, 251–260.

Cunningham, G. B. (2006). The influence of group diversity on intergroup bias following recategorization. *Journal of Social Psychology, 146*, 533–547.

Cunningham, G. B., & Chelladurai, P. (2004). Affective reactions to cross-functional teams: The impact of size, relative performance, and common in-group identity. *Group Dynamics: Theory, Research,* and Practice, 8, 83–97.

Curry, D. J., Menasco, M. B., & Van Ark, J. W. (1991). Multiattribute dyadic choice: Models and tests. *Journal of Marketing Research, 28,* 259–267.

Curseu, P. L. (2003). *Formal group decision-making: A social-cognitive approach.* ASCR Press.

Curseu, P., & Curseu, A. (2001). Source credibility in decision-making – A game theory approach. *Cognitie Creier Comportament, 5,* 159–178.

Curseu, P. L., Stoop, R., & Schalk, R. (2007). Prejudice toward immigrant workers among Dutch employees: Integrated threat theory revisited. *European Journal of Social Psychology, 37,* 125–140.

Cutcher-Gershenfeld, J. E. (1994). Bargaining over how to bargain in labor-management negotiations. *Negotiation Journal, 10,* 323–335.

CutcherGershenfeld, J., Kochan, T., Ferguson, J.-P., & Barrett, B. (2007). Collective bargaining in the twenty-first century: A negotiations institution at risk. *Negotiation Journal, 23,* 249–265.

Czopp, A. M. (2008). When is a compliment not a compliment? Evaluating expressions of positive stereotypes. *Journal of Experimental Social Psychology, 44,* 413–420.

da Silva, I. R., & Günther, I. d. A. (2000). Papéis Sociais e Envelhecimento em uma Perspectiva de Curso de Vida [Social roles and aging from a life-span perspective]. *Psicologia: Teoria e Pesquisa, 16,* 31–40.

Dahl, J. G., & Kienast, P. K. (1990). The effect of payoff matrix induced competition on the creation of value in negotiation. In M. A. Rahim (Ed.), *Theory and research in conflict management* (pp. 77–85). New York: Praeger Publishers.

Daly, J. A., & Wiemann, J. M. (Eds.). (1994). *Strategic interpersonal communication.* Hillsdale, NJ: Lawrence Erlbaum Associates.

Daniel, T. E., Seale, D. A., & Rapoport, A. (1998). Strategic play and adaptive learning in the sealed-bid bargaining mechanism. *Journal of Mathematical Psychology, 42,* 133–166.

Danielsson, Clare, & Eveson, Susanna. (1997). The community educator: A call for a new profession. *International Journal of Action Methods, 50*(1), 4–16

Darley, J. M., & Huff, C. W. (1990). Heightened damage assessment as a result of the intentionality of the damage-causing act. *British Journal of Social Psychology, 29,* 181–188.

David, B., & Turner, J. C. (1996). Studies in self-categorization and minority conversion: Is being a member of the out-group an advantage? *British Journal of Social Psychology, 35,* 179–199.

David, B., & Turner, J. C. (2001a). Majority and minority influence: A single process self-categorization analysis. In C. K. W. De Dreu & N. K. De Vries (Eds.), *Group consensus and minority influence: Implications for innovation* (pp. 91–121). Malden: Blackwell Publishing.

David, B., & Turner, J. C. (2001b). Self-categorization principles underlying majority and minority influence. In J. P. Forgas & K. D. Williams (Eds.), *Social influence: Direct and indirect processes* (pp. 293–313). New York: Psychology Press.

Davidson, J. A., & Newman, M. (1990). Australian perceptions of the nuclear arms race: A conflict of interests or a misunderstanding? *Australian Psychologist, 25,* 15–24.

Davies-Netzley, S. A. (1998). Women above the glass ceiling: Perceptions on corporate mobility and strategies for success. *Gender and Society, 12,* 339–355.

Davis, J. H., Zarnoth, P., Hulbert, L., Chen, X.-P., Parks, C., & Nam, K. (1998). "The committee charge, framing interpersonal agreement, and consensus models of group quantitative judgment": Corrigendum. *Organizational Behavior and Human Decision Processes, 73,* 102.

Dawes, R. M., & Messick, D. M. (2000). Social dilemmas. *International Journal of Psychology, 35,* 111–116.

Dawes, R. M., van de Kragt, A. J., & Orbell, J. M. (1988). Not me or thee but we: The importance of group identity in eliciting cooperation in dilemma situations: Experimental manipulations. *Acta Psychologica, 68,* 83–97.

Dawes, R. M., van de Kragt, A. J. C., & Orbell, J. M. (1990). Cooperation for the benefit of us-Not me, or my conscience. In J. J. Mansbridge (Ed.), *Beyond self-interest* (pp. 97110). Chicago: University of Chicago Press.

Dbrowski, P. I. (1990). W poszukiwaniu sprawnego negocjatora [In search of a competent negotiator]. *Przeglad Psychologiczny, 33*, 345–351.

De Cremer, D. (2001). Relations of self-esteem concerns, group identification, and selfstereotyping to in-group favoritism. *Journal of Social Psychology, 141*, 389–400.

De Cremer, D., & Stouten, J. (2003). When do people find cooperation most justified? The effect of trust and self-other merging in social dilemmas. *Social Justice Research, 16*, 41–52.

De Cremer, D., & Van Dijk, E. (2002). Reactions to group success and failure as a function of identification level: A test of the goal-transformation hypothesis in social dilemmas. *Journal of Experimental Social Psychology, 38*, 435–442.

De Cremer, D., Van Knippenberg, D., Van Dijk, E., & Van Leeuwen, E. (2008). Cooperating if one's goals are collective-based: Social identification effects in social dilemmas as a function of goal transformation. *Journal of Applied Social Psychology, 38*, 1562–1579.

De Cremer, D., & Van Vugt, M. (1999). Social identification effects in social dilemmas: A transformation of motives. *European Journal of Social Psychology, 29*, 871–893.

De Cremer, D., & Van Vugt, M. (2002). Intergroup and intragroup aspects of leadership in social dilemmas: A relational model of cooperation. *Journal of Experimental Social Psychology, 38*, 126–136.

De Dreu, C. K. W. (1995). Coercive power and concession making in bilateral negotiation. *Journal of Conflict Resolution, 39*, 646–670.

De Dreu, C. K. W. (2005). A PACT against conflict escalation in negotiation and dispute resolution. *Current Directions in Psychological Science, 14*, 149–152.

De Dreu, C. K. W. (2007). Cooperative outcome interdependence, task reflexivity, and team effectiveness: A motivated information processing perspective. *Journal of Applied Psychology, 92*, 628–638.

De Dreu, C. K. W., Carnevale, P. J. D., Emans, B. J. M., & Van de Vliert, E. (1994). Effects of gain/loss frames in negotiation: Loss aversion, mismatching, and frame adoption. *Organizational Behavior and Human Decision Processes, 60*, 90–107.

De Dreu, C. K. W.., & Weingart, L. R. (2003). Task versus relationship conflict, team performance, and team member satisfaction: A meta-analysis. *Journal of Applied Psychology, 88*, 741–749.

De Dreu, C. K. W.., Yzerbyt, V. Y., & Leyens, J.-P. (1995). Dilution of stereotype-based cooperation in mixed-motive interdependence. *Journal of Experimental Social Psychology, 31*, 575–593.

De Grada, E., Kruglanski, A. W., Mannetti, L., & Pierro, A. (1999). Motivated cognition and group interaction: Need for closure affects the contents and processes of collective negotiations. *Journal of Experimental Social Psychology, 35*, 346–365.

De Jong, P. J., Peters, M., De Cremer, D., & Vranken, C. (2002). Blushing after a moral transgression in a prisoner's dilemma game: Appeasing or revealing? *European Journal of Social Psychology, 32*, 627–644.

de la Haye, A. M. (1990). La memoire des personnes: II. Construction cognitive des individus et des groupes [Person memory: II. Cognitive construction of individuals and groups]. *Annee Psychologique, 90*, 93–108.

de Moura. See Randsley de Moura.

De Ridder, R., & Tripathi, R. C. (Eds.). (1992). *Norm violation and intergroup relations*. Oxford, England UK: Clarendon Press/Oxford University Press.

De Ridder, R., Schruijer, S. G. L., & Tripathi, R. C. (1992). Norm violation as a precipitating factor of negative intergroup relations. In R. De Ridder & R. C. Tripathi (Eds.), *Norm violation and intergroup relations* (pp. 3–37). Oxford, England: Clarendon Press/Oxford University Press.

De Vos, H., & Zeggelink, E. (1997). Reciprocal altruism in human social evolution: The viability of reciprocal altruism with a preference for "old-hel-pingpartners". *Evolution and Human Behavior, 18*, 261–278.

De Vries, S., & Wilke, H. A. M. (1992). Constrained egoism and resource management under uncertainty. In W. B. G. Liebrand, D. M. Messick, & H. A. M. Wilke (Eds.), *Social dilemmas: Theoretical issues and research findings* (pp. 81–99). Oxford, England: Pergamon Press, Inc.

de Zavala, A., Federico, C. M., Cislak, A., & Sigger, J. (2008). Need for closure and competition in intergroup conflicts: Experimental evidence for the mitigating effect of accessible conflict-schemas. *European Journal of Social Psychology, 38*, 84–105.

DeAngelis, Tori. (1996, October). Minorities' performance is hampered by stereotypes. *[APA] Monitor, 27*(10), 38.

Deaux, K. (1991). Social identities: Thoughts on structure and change. In R. C. Curtis (Ed.), *The relational self: Theoretical convergences in psychoanalysis and social psychology* (pp. 77–93). New York: Guilford Press.

Deaux, K., & Martin, D. (2003). Interpersonal networks and social categories: Specifying levels of context in identity processes. *Social Psychology Quarterly, 66*, 101–117.

Deberry, S. T. (1989). The effect of competitive tasks on liking of self and other. *Social Behavior and Personality, 17*, 67–80.

DeChurch, L. A., & Marks, M. A. (2001). Maximizing the benefits of task conflict: The role of conflict management. *International Journal of Conflict Management, 12*, 4–22.

Degner, J., Wentura, D., Gniewosz, B., & Noack, P. (2007). Hostility-related prejudice against Turks in adolescents: Masked affective priming allows for a differentiation of automatic prejudice. *Basic and Applied Social Psychology, 29*, 245–256.

Dekel, E., & Wolinsky, A. (2003). Rationalizable outcomes of large private-value– firstprice discrete auctions. *Games and Economic Behavior, 43*, 175–188.

DeLeon, L. (2001). Accountability for individuating behaviors in self-managing teams. *Organization Development Journal, 19*(4), 7–19.

Delmas, F. (2003). Le biais pro endogroupe dans le paradigme des groupes minimaux: L'hypothèse soumission/élaboration [Intergroup bias in minimal group paradigm: The submission/elaboration hypothesis]. *Revue Internationale de Psychologie Sociale, 16*, 73–98.

DeMatteo, J. S., Eby, L. T., & Sundstrom, E. (1998). Team-based rewards: Current empirical evidence and directions for future research. In B. M. Staw & L. L. Cummings (Eds.), *Research in organizational behavior, Vol. 20: An annual series of analytical essays and critical reviews* (pp. 141–183). Greenwich, CT: Jai Press, Inc.

Den Hartog, D. N., Maczynski, J., Motowidlo, S. J., Jarmuz, S., Koopman, P., Thierry, H., & Wilderom, C. P. M. (1997). Cross-cultural perceptions of leadership: A comparison of leadership and societal and organizational culture in the Netherlands and Poland. *Polish Psychological Bulletin, 28*, 255–267.

Denis, J.-L., Lamothe, L., & Langley, A. (2001). The dynamics of collective leadership and strategic change in pluralistic organizations. *Academy of Management Journal, 44*, 809–837.

Dennis, A. R., Valacich, J. S., Connolly, T., & Wynne, B. E. (1996). Process structuring in electronic brainstorming. *Information Systems Research, 7*, 268–277.

Derlega, V. J., Cukur, C. S., Kuang, J. C., & Forsyth, D. R. (2002). Interdependent construal of self and the endorsement of conflict resolution strategies in interpersonal, intergroup and international disputes. *Journal of Cross-Cultural Psychology, 33*, 610–625.

DeSanctis, G., & Poole, M. S. (1997). Transitions in teamwork in new organizational forms. In B. Markovsky, M. J. Lovaglia, & L. Troyer (Eds.), *Advances in group processes* (Vol. 14, pp. 157–176). Greenwich, CT: Jai Press, Inc.

Desforges, D. M., Lord, C. G., Pugh, M. A., Sia, T. L., Scarberry, N. C., & Ratcliff, C. D. (1997). Role of group representativeness in the generalization part of the contact hypothesis. *Basic and Applied Social Psychology, 19*, 183–204.

DeShon, R. P., Kozlowski, S. W. J., Schmidt, A. M., Milner, K. R., & Wiechmann, D. (2004). A multiple-goal, multilevel model of feedback effects on the regulation of individual and team performance. *Journal of Applied Psychology, 89*, 1035–1056.

DeSimone, B. A. (2004). Making the deal: A guide to successful negotiation. *Optometry: Journal of the American Optometric Association, 75*, 55–59.

Dessel, A., & Rogge, M. E. (2008). Evaluation of intergroup dialogue: A review of the empirical literature. *Conflict Resolution Quarterly, 26*, 199–238.

DeSteno, D., Dasgupta, N., Bartlett, M., & Cajdric, A. (2004). Prejudice from Thin Air: The effect of emotion on automatic intergroup attitudes. *Psychological Science, 15*, 319–324.

Deutsch, M. (1989). Equality and economic efficiency: Is there a trade-off? In N. Eisenberg, J. Reykowski, & E. Staub (Eds.), *Social and moral values: Individual and societal perspectives* (pp. 139–153). Hillsdale, NJ: Lawrence Erlbaum Associates, Inc.

Deutsch, M. (1990). Cooperation, conflict, and justice. In Wheelan, & A. Susan Pepitone, A. A. V. Emm (Eds.), *Advances in field theory* (pp. 149–164). Newbury Park, CA: Sage Publications, Inc.

Deutsch, M. (1994). Constructive conflict resolution: Principles, training, and research. *Journal of Social Issues, 50*(1), 13–32.

Deutsch, M. (2006). Cooperation and competition. In M. Deutsch, P. T. Coleman, & E. C. Marcus (Eds.), *The handbook of conflict resolution: Theory and practice* (2nd ed., pp. 23–42). Hoboken, NJ: Wiley Publishing.

Deutsch, Morton. (2008). Reconciliation after destructive intergroup conflict. In A. Nadler, T. E. Malloy, & J. D. Fisher (Eds.), *The social psychology of intergroup reconciliation* (pp. 471–485). New York: Oxford University Press.

Deutsch, M., Coleman, P. T., & Marcus, E. C. (Eds.). (2006). *The handbook of conflict resolution: Theory and practice* (2nd ed.). Hoboken, NJ: Wiley.

Devetag, G., & Warglien, M. (2003). Games and phone numbers: Do short term memory bounds affect strategic behavior? *Journal of Economic Psychology, 24*, 189–202.

Devetag, M. G., Legrenzi, P., & Warglien, M. (2000). Focusing strategies in reasoning about games. In W. Schaeken, De G. Vooght, A. Vandierendonck, & G. d'Ydewalle (Eds.), *Deductive reasoning and strategies* (pp. 287–299). Mahwah, NJ: Lawrence Erlbaum Associates Publishers.

Devinatz, V. G. (2004). A response to the British Journal of Industrial Relations Symposium on the Human Rights Watch Report: A Minimum Program for Promoting Collective Bargaining Rights as a Human Right. *Employee Responsibilities and Rights Journal, 16*, 13–23.

Devine, D. J., Clayton, L. D., Philips, J. L., Dunford, B. B., & Melner, S. B. (1999). Teams in organizations: Prevalence, characteristics, and effectiveness. *Small Group Research, 30*, 678–711.

Devine, P. G., Evett, S. R., & Vasquez-Suson, K. A. (1996). Exploring the interpersonal dynamics of intergroup contact. In R. M. Sorrentino & E. T. Higgins (Eds.), *Handbook of motivation and cognition, Vol. 3: The interpersonal context* (pp. 423–464). New York: Guilford Press.

Dickinson, D. L. (2000). Ultimatum decision-making: A test of reciprocal kindness. *Theory and Decision, 48*, 151–177.

Diehl, B. J. (1991). CRISIS: A process evaluation. *Simulation and Gaming, 22*, 293–307.

Diehl, M. (1989). Dichotomie und Diskriminierung: Die Auswirkungen von Kreuzkategorisierungen auf die Diskriminierung im Paradigma der minimalen Gruppen [Dichotomy and discrimination: The effects of cross-categorizations on discrimination in a minimal-group paradigm]. *Zeitschrift fuer Sozialpsychologie, 20*, 92–102.

Dietz-Uhler, B. (1996). The escalation of commitment in political decision-making groups: A social identity approach. *European Journal of Social Psychology, 26*, 611–629.

Dietz-Uhler, B. (1999). Defensive reactions to group-relevant information. *Group Processes and Intergroup Relations, 2*, 17–29.

Dietz-Uhler, B., & Murrell, A. (1998). Effects of social identity and threat on selfe-steem and group attributions. *Group Dynamics, 2*, 24–35.

Dijker, A. J., Koomen, W., Van Den Heuvel, H., & Frijda, N. H. (1996). Perceived antecedents of emotional reactions in inter-ethnic relations. *British Journal of Social Psychology, 35*, 313–329.

Dimmock, J. A., Grove, J. R., & Eklund, R. C. (2005). Reconceptualizing team identification: New dimensions and their relationship to intergroup bias. *Group Dynamics: Theory, Research*, and Practice, 9, 75–86.

Dinar, A., Ratner, A., & Yaron, D. (1992). Evaluating cooperative game theory in water resources. *Theory and Decision, 32*, 1–20.

Dindia, K. (1997). Self-disclosure, self-identity, and relationship development: A transactional/dialectical perspective. In S. Duck (Ed.), *Handbook of personal relationships: Theory, research and interventions* (2nd ed., pp. 411–426). Chichester, England: John Wiley & Sons, Inc.

Dittloff, S. A., & Harris, K. L. (1996). A contingency approach to understanding negotiator behavior as a function of worldmindedness and expected future interaction. *Journal of Psychology, 130*, 59–70.

Dluhy, M. J., & Kravitz, S. L. (1990). *Building coalitions in the human services*. Thousand Oaks, CA: Sage Publications, Inc.

Doane, A. W., Jr. (1997). Dominant group ethnic identity in the United States: The role of "hidden" ethnicity in intergroup relations. *Sociological Quarterly, 38*, 375–397.

Dobbs, M., & Crano, W. D. (2001). Outgroup accountability in the minimal group paradigm: Implications for aversive discrimination and social identity theory. *Personality and Social Psychology Bulletin, 27*, 355–364.

Doebeli, M., Hauert, C., & Killingback, T. (2004). The evolutionary origin of cooperators and defectors. *Science, 306*(5697), 859–862.

Doise, W. (1988). Individual and social identities in intergroup relations. *European Journal of Social Psychology, 18*, 99–111.

Donnellon, A. (1996). *Team talk: The power of language in team dynamics*. Boston, MA: Harvard University Business School Press.

Donohue, W. A., & Ramesh, C. N. (1992). Negotiator-opponent relationships. In L. L. Putnam & M. E. Roloff (Eds.), *Communication and negotiation* (pp. 209–232). Newbury Park, CA: Sage Publications.

Donohue, W. A., & Roberto, A. J. (1996). An empirical examination of three models of integrative and distributive bargaining. *International Journal of Conflict Management, 7*, 209–229.

Doosje, B., & Branscombe, N. R. (2003). Attributions for the negative historical actions of a group. *European Journal of Social Psychology, 33*, 235–248.

Doosje, B., Ellemers, N., & Spears, R. (1995). Perceived intragroup variability as a function of group status and identification. *Journal of Experimental Social Psychology, 31*, 410–436.

Doosje, B., Spears, R., & Ellemers, N. (2002). Social identity as both cause and effect: The development of group identification in response to anticipated and actual changes in the intergroup status hierarchy. *British Journal of Social Psychology, 41*, 57–76.

Dore, M. (1997). On playing fair: Professor Binmore on game theory and the social contract. *Theory and Decision, 43*, 219–239.

Dougherty, D. (2006). Organizing for innovation in the 21st century. In S. Clegg, C. Hardy, & W. Nord (Eds.), *Handbook of organization studies* (2nd ed., pp. 598–617). London: Sage.

Douglas, C., & Gardner, W. L. (2004). Transition to self-directed work teams: Implications of transition time and self-monitoring for managers' use of influence tactics. *Journal of Organizational Behavior, 25*, 47–65.

Douglas, K. M., & McGarty, C. (2001). Identifiability and self-presentation: Computer-mediated communication and intergroup interaction. *British Journal of Social Psychology, 40*, 399–416.

Douglas, W. (1990). Uncertainty, information-seeking, and liking during initial interaction. *Western Journal of Speech Communication, 54*, 66–81.

Dovey, K. (1997). The learning organization and the organization of learning: Power, transformation and the search for form in learning organizations. *Management Learning, 28*, 331–349.

Dovidio, J. F., & Gaertner, S. L. (1996). Affirmative action, unintentional racial biases, and intergroup relations. *Journal of Social Issues, 52*(4), 51–75.

Dovidio, J. F., & Gaertner, S. L. (1999). Reducing prejudice: Combating intergroup biases. *Current Directions in Psychological Science, 8*, 101–105.

Dovidio, J. F., Gaertner, S. L., & Esses, V. M. (2008). Cooperation, common identity, and intergroup contact. In B. A. Sullivan, M. Snyder, & J. L. Sullivan (Eds.), *Cooperation: The political psychology of effective human interaction* (pp. 143–159). Malden: Blackwell Publishing.

Dovidio, J. F., Gaertner, S. L., Esses, V. M., & Brewer, M. B. (2003). Social conflict, harmony, and integration. In T. Millon & M. J. Lerner (Eds.), *Handbook of psychology: Personality and social psychology* (Vol. 5, pp. 485–506). Hoboken, NJ: John Wiley & Sons Inc, 2003.

Dovidio, J. F., Gaertner, S. L., John, M.-S., Halabi, S., Saguy, T., Pearson, A. R., & Riek, B. M. (2008). Majority and minority perspectives in intergroup relations: The role of contact, group representations, threat, and trust in intergroup conflict and reconciliation. In A. Nadler,

T. E. Malloy, & J. D. Fisher (Eds.), *The social psychology of intergroup reconciliation* (pp. 227–253). New York: Oxford University Press.

Dovidio, J. F., Gaertner, S. L., & Kawakami, K. (2003). Intergroup contact: The past, present, and the future. *Group Processes and Intergroup Relations, 6*, 5–20.

Dovidio, J. F., Gaertner, S. L., Niemann, Y. F., & Snider, K. (2001). Racial, ethnic, and cultural differences in responding to distinctiveness and discrimination on campus: Stigma and common group identity. *Journal of Social Issues, 57*, 167–188.

Dovidio, J. F., Gaertner, S. L., Saguy, T., & Halabi, S. (2008). From when to why: Understanding how contact reduces bias. In U. Wagner, L. R. Tropp, G. Finchilescu, & C. Tredoux (Eds.), *Improving intergroup relations: Building on the legacy of Thomas F. Pettigrew* (pp. 75–90). Malden: Blackwell Publishing.

Dovidio, J. F., Gaertner, S. L., & Validzic, A. (1998). Intergroup bias: Status, differentiation, and a common in-group identity. *Journal of Personality and Social Psychology, 75*, 109–120.

Dovidio, J. F., Gaertner, S. L., Validzic, A., Matoka, K., Johnson, B., & Frazier, S. (1997). Extending the benefits of recategorization: Evaluations, self-disclosure, and helping. *Journal of Experimental Social Psychology, 33*, 401–420.

Dovidio, J. F., Isen, A. M., Guerra, P., Gaertner, S. L., & Rust, M. (1998). Positive affect, cognition, and the reduction of intergroup bias. In C. Sedikides, J. Schopler, & C. A. Insko (Eds.), *Intergroup cognition and intergroup behavior* (pp. 337–366). Mahwah, NJ: Lawrence Erlbaum Associates, Inc., Publishers.

Dovidio, J. F., Maruyama, G., & Alexander, M. G. (1998). A social psychology of national and international group relations. *Journal of Social Issues, 54*, 831–846.

Dovidio, J. F., Saguy, T., & Shnabel, N. (2009). Cooperation and conflict within groups: Bridging intragroup and intergroup processes. *Journal of Social Issues, 65*, 429–449.

Drach-Zahavy, A. (2004). The proficiency trap: How to balance enriched job designs and the team's need for support. *Journal of Organizational Behavior, 25*, 979–996.

Dresner, M. (1989). Changing energy end-use patterns as a means of reducing global-warming trends. *Journal of Environmental Education, 21*(2), 41–46.

Drigotas, S. M., Insko, C., & Schopler, J. (1998). Mere categorization and competition: A closer look at social identity theory and the discontinuity effect. In S. Worchel, J. F. Morales, D. Paez, & J.-C. Deschamps (Eds.), *Social identity: International perspectives* (pp. 180–198). London: Sage Publications, Inc.

Driskell, J. E., & Salas, E. (2006). Groupware, group dynamics, and team performance. In C. Bowers, E. Salas, & F. Jentsch (Eds.), *Creating high-tech teams: Practical guidance on work performance and technology* (pp. 11–34). Washington, DC: American Psychological Association.

Driskell, J. E., Salas, E., & Johnston, J. (1999). Does stress lead to a loss of team perspective? *Group Dynamics: Theory, Research*, and Practice, 3, 291–302.

Driskell, J. E., Salas, E., & Johnston, J. (2000). Does stress lead to a loss of team perspective? *Human Performance in Extreme Environments, 5*(1), 69–76.

Dru, V., & Constanza, C. (2003). Effet de l'identification sociale et du résultat d'une compétition collective sur les jugements d'homogénéité [Effects of social identification and collective competition on homegeneity judgments]. *Cahiers Internationaux de Psychologie Sociale*, No. 57, 102–108.

Druckman, D. (1994). Determinants of compromising behavior in negotiation: A meta-analysis. *Journal of Conflict Resolution, 38*, 507–556.

Druckman, D. (1995). The educational effectiveness of interactive games. In D. Crookall & K. Arai (Eds.), *Simulation and gaming across disciplines and cultures: ISAGA at a watershed* (pp. 178–187). Thousand Oaks, CA: Sage Publications, Inc.

Druckman, D., & Broome, B. J. (1991). Value differences and conflict resolution: Familiarity or liking? *Journal of Conflict Resolution, 35*, 571–593.

Druckman, D., Broome, B. J., & Korper, S. H. (1988). Value differences and conflict resolution: Facilitation or delinking? *Journal of Conflict Resolution, 32*, 489–510.

Druckman, D., & Hopmann, P. T. (1991). Content analysis. In V. A. Kremenyuk (Ed.), *International negotiation: Analysis, approaches, issues* (pp. 244–263). San Francisco: Jossey-Bass Inc, Publishers.

Druckman, D., Olekalns, M., & Smith, P. L. (2009). Interpretive filters: Social cognition and the impact of turning points in negotiation. *Negotiation Journal, 25*, 13–40.

Drury, J., & Reicher, S. (1999). The intergroup dynamics of collective empowerment: Substantiating the social identity model of crowd behavior. *Group Processes and Intergroup Relations, 2*, 381–402.

Druskat, V. U., & Wolff, S. B. (1999). Effects and timing of developmental peer appraisals in self-managing work groups. *Journal of Applied Psychology, 84*, 58–74.

du Toit, P. (1989). Bargaining about bargaining: Inducing the self-negating prediction in deeply divided societies: The case of South Africa. *Journal of Conflict Resolution, 33*, 210–230.

Duane, M. J. (1991). To grieve or not to grieve: Why "reduce it to writing?" *Public Personnel Management, 20*, 83–90.

Duckitt, J. (1989). Authoritarianism and group identification: A new view of an old construct. *Political Psychology, 10*, 63–84.

Duckitt, John, & Mphuthing, Thobi. (1998). Group identification and intergroup attitudes: A longitudinal analysis in South Africa. *Journal of Personality and Social Psychology, 74*, 80–85.

Dudkiewicz, M. (1991). Identyfikacja z grupa a wrogosc i przyjacielskosc. Podejscie do analizy zwawiska w sietle koncepcji J. C. Turnera i J. Rabbiego [Group identification, hostility, and friendship: The Turner and Rabbie approaches]. *Przeglad Psychologiczny, 34*, 455–466.

Duffy, J., & Feltovich, N. (2002). Do actions speak louder than words? An experimental comparison of observation and cheap talk. *Games and Economic Behavior, 39*, 1–27.

Duffy, M. K., & Shaw, J. D. (2000). The Salieri Syndrome: Consequences of envy in groups. *Small Group Research, 31*, 3–23.

Dugosh, K. L., Paulus, P. B., Roland, E. J., & Yang, H.-C. (2000). Cognitive stimulation in brainstorming. *Journal of Personality and Social Psychology, 79*, 722–735.

Dukerich, J., Weigelt, K., & Schotter, A. (1990). A game theory analysis of dual discrimination. *Organizational Behavior and Human Decision Processes, 47*, 21–41.

Dumont, K., & Louw, J. (2007). A citation analysis of Henri Tajfel's work on intergroup relations. *International Journal of Psychology, 44*, 46–59.

Dumont, M., Yzerbyt, V., Wigboldus, D., & Gordijn, E. H. (2003). Social categorization and fear reactions to the September 11th terrorist attacks. *Personality and Social Psychology Bulletin, 29*, 1509–1520.

Dunlop, P. D., & Lee, K. (2004). Workplace deviance, organizational citizenship behavior, and business unit performance: the bad apples do spoil the whole barrel. *Journal of Organizational Behavior, 25*, 67–80.

Duranti, Alessandro. (1990). Doing things with words: Conflict, understanding, and change in a Samoan fono. In K. A. Watson-Gegeo & G. M. White (Eds.), *Disentangling: Conflict discourse in Pacific societies* (pp. 459–489). Stanford, CA: Stanford University Press.

Durham, C. C., Knight, D., & Locke, E. A. (1997). Effects of leader role, team-set goal difficulty, efficacy, and tactics on team effectiveness. *Organizational Behavior and Human Decision Processes, 72*, 203–231.

Durham, C. C., Locke, E. A., Poon, J. M. L., & McLeod, P. L. (2000). Effects of group goals and time pressure on group efficacy, information-seeking strategy, and performance. *Human Performance, 13*, 115–138.

Durieu, J., & Solal, P. (2003). Adaptive play with spatial sampling. *Games and Economic Behavior, 43*, 189–195.

Dvir, T., & Shamir, B. (2003). Follower developmental characteristics as predicting transformational leadership: A longitudinal field study. *Leadership Quarterly, 14*, 327–344.

Dwyer, P. D., & Minnegal, M. (1997). Sago games: Cooperation and change among Sago producers of Papua New Guinea. *Evolution and Human Behavior, 18*, 89–108.

Dyer, W. G. (1987). *Teambuilding* (2nd ed.). Reading, MA: Addison-Wesley.

Dyke, N. V. (2003). Crossing movement boundaries: Factors that facilitate coalition protest by American college students, 1930–1990. *Social Problems, 50*, 226–250.

Eagly, A. H., Mladinic, A., & Otto, S. (1994). Cognitive and affective bases of attitudes toward social groups and social policies. *Journal of Experimental Social Psychology, 30*, 113–137.

Earley, P. C. (1997). *Face, harmony, and social structure: An analysis of organizational behavior across cultures*. New York: Oxford University Press.

Earley, P. C. (1999). Playing follow the leader: Status-determining traits in relation to collective efficacy across cultures. *Organizational Behavior and Human Decision Processes, 80*, 192–212.

Earley, P. C., & Mosakowski, E. (2000). Creating hybrid team cultures: An empirical test of transnational team functioning. *Academy of Management Journal, 43*, 26–49.

Easterby-Smith, M. (1997). Disciplines of organizational learning: Contributions and critiques. *Human Relations, 50*, 1085–1113.

Eby, L. T. (1997). Alternative forms of mentoring in changing organizational environments: A conceptual extension of the mentoring literature. *Journal of Vocational Behavior, 51*, 125–144.

Eckel, C. C., & Wilson, R. K. (2003). The human face of game theory: Trust and reciprocity in sequential games. In E. Ostrom & J. Walker (Eds.), *Trust and reciprocity: Interdisciplinary lessons from experimental research* (pp. 245–274). New York: Russell Sage Foundation.

Edge, A., & Keys, B. (1990). Cross-cultural learning in a multinational business environment. *Journal of Management Development, 9*, 43–49.

Edmondson, A. C. (1996). Learning from mistakes is easier said than done: Group and organizational influences on the detection and correction of human error. *Journal of Applied Behavioral Science, 32*, 5–28.

Edwards, J. (1991). Co-operation and competition: Two sides of the same coin? *Irish Journal of Psychology, 12*, 76–82.

Effrat, A. (1968). Editor's introduction. [Applications of Parsonian theory]. *Sociological Inquiry, 38*, 97–103.

Eggins, R. A., Haslam, S. A., & Reynolds, K. J. (2002). Social identity and negotiation: Subgroup representation and superordinate consensus. *Personality and Social Psychology Bulletin, 28*, 887–899.

Eguíluz, V. M., Zimmermann, M. G., Cela-Conde, C. J., & San Miguel, M. (2005). Cooperation and the emergence of role differentiation in the dynamics of social networks. *American Journal of Sociology, 110*, 977–1008.

Eichberger, J., & Kelsey, D. (2000). Non-additive beliefs and strategic equilibria. *Games and Economic Behavior, 30*, 183–215.

Eidelman, S., & Biernat, M. (2003). Derogating black sheep: Individual or group protection? *Journal of Experimental Social Psychology, 39*, 602–609.

Eigel, K. M., & Kuhnert, K. W. (1996). Personality diversity and its relationship to managerial team productivity. In M. N. Ruderman, M. W. Hughes-James, & S. E. Jackson (Eds.), *Selected research on work team diversity* (pp. 75–98). Washington, DC: American Psychological Association.

Einspruch, E. L., & Wunrow, J. J. (2002). Assessing youth/adult partnership: The Seven Circles (AK) experience. *Journal of Drug Education, 32*, 1–12.

Einy, E., Holzman, R., & Monderer, D. (1999). On the least core and the Mas-Colell bargaining set. *Games and Economic Behavior, 28*, 181–188.

Eisenberger, R., Stinglhamber, F., Vandenberghe, C., Sucharski, I. L., & Rhoades, L. (2002). Perceived supervisor support: Contributions to perceived organizational support and employee retention. *Journal of Applied Psychology, 87*, 565–573.

Eisenhardt, K. M., & Schoonhoven, C.-B. (1990). Organizational growth: linking founding team, strategy, environment, and growth among U.S. semiconductor ventures, 1978–1988. *Administrative Science Quarterly, 35*, 504–529.

Elfenbein, H. A., & Ambady, N. (2002). Predicting workplace outcomes from the ability to eavesdrop on feelings. *Journal of Applied Psychology, 87*, 963–971.

Eliasoph, N., & Lichterman, P. (2003). Culture in Interaction. *American Journal of Sociology, 108*, 735–794.

Eliaz, K. (2003). Nash equilibrium when players account for the complexity of their forecasts. *Games and Economic Behavior, 44*, 286–310.

Eliaz, K., & Ok, E. A. (2006). Indifference or indecisiveness? Choice-theoretic foundations of incomplete preferences. *Games and Economic Behavior, 56*, 61–86.

Ellemers, N., Kortekaas, P., & Ouwerkerk, J. W. (1999). Self-categorisation, commitment to the group and group self-esteem as related but distinct aspects of social identity. *European Journal of Social Psychology, 29*, 371–389.

Ellemers, N., Spears, R., & Doosje, B. (1997). Sticking together of falling apart: In-group identification as a psychological determinant of group commitment versus individual mobility. *Journal of Personality and Social Psychology, 72*, 617–626.

Ellemers, N., Spears, R., & Doosje, B. (2002). Self and social identity. *Annual Review of Psychology, 53*, 161–186.

Ellemers, N., Van Dyck, C., Hinkle, S., & Jacobs, A. (2000). Intergroup differentiation in social context: Identity needs versus audience constraints. *Social Psychology Quarterly, 63*, 60–74.

Ellemers, N., Van Knippenberg, A., De Vries, N., & Wilke, H. (1988). Social identification and permeability of group boundaries. *European Journal of Social Psychology, 18*, 497–513.

Ellemers, N., & Van Rijswijk, W. (1997). Identity needs versus social opportunities: The use of group-level and individual-level identity management strategies. *Social Psychology Quarterly, 60*, 52–65.

Ellemers, N., Wilke, H., & Van Knippenberg, A. (1993). Effects of the legitimacy of low group or individual status on individual and collective status-enhancement strategies. *Journal of Personality and Social Psychology, 64*, 766–778.

Eller, A., & Abrams, D. (2003). "Gringos" in Mexico: Cross-sectional and longitudinal effects of language school-promoted contact on intergroup bias. *Group Processes and Intergroup Relations, 6*, 55–75.

Eller, A., & Abrams, D. (2004). Come together: Longitudinal comparisons of Pettigrew's reformulated intergroup contact model and the Common Ingroup Identity Model in Anglo-French and Mexican-American contexts. *European Journal of Social Psychology, 34*, 229–256.

Eller, A., Abrams, D., Viki, G. T., Imara, D. A., & Peerbux, S. (2007). Stay cool, hang loose, admit nothing: Race, intergroup contact, and public-police relations. *Basic and Applied Social Psychology, 29*, 213–224.

Ellingsen, T., & Robles, J. (2002). Does evolution solve the hold-up problem? *Games and Economic Behavior, 39*, 28–53.

Elovainio, M., Kivimäki, M., & Helkama, K. (2001). Organizational justice evaluations, job control, and occupational strain. *Journal of Applied Psychology, 86*, 418–424.

Elsbach, K. D., & Bhattacharya, C. B. (2001). Defining who you are by what you're not: Organizational disidentification and the National Rifle Association. *Organization Science, 12*, 393–413.

Elvira, M. M., & Cohen, L. E. (2001). Location matters: A cross-level analysis of the effects of organizational sex composition on turnover. *Academy of Management Journal, 44*, 591–605.

Elvira, M. M., & Saporta, I. (2001). How does collective bargaining affect the gender pay gap? *Work and Occupations, 28*, 469–490.

Ely, R. J. (2004). A field study of group diversity, participation in diversity education programs, and performance. *Journal of Organizational Behavior, 25*, 755–780.

Ely, R. J., & Roberts, L. M. (2008). Shifting frames in team-diversity research: From difference to relationships. In A. P. Brief (Ed.), *Diversity at work* (pp. 175–201). New York: Cambridge University Press.

Emans, B., Van Der Vegt, G., & Van de Vliert, E. (2000). Interplay of task and outcome interdependence in generating work team members' affective responses-some new findings. In M. Vartiainen, F. Avallone, & N. Anderson (Eds.), *Innovative theories, tools, and practices in work and organizational psychology* (pp. 111–124). Ashland, OH: Hogrefe & Huber Publishers.

Emery, N. J., & Clayton, N. S. (2009). Comparative social cognition. *Annual Review of Psychology, 60*, 87–113.

Engestroem, Y., Engestroem, R., & Kaerkkaeinen, M. (1995). Polycontextuality and boundary crossing in expert cognition: Learning and problem solving in complex work activities. *Learning and Instruction, 5*, 319–336.

Engl, G. (1995). Lower hemicontinuity of the Nash Equilibrium correspondence. *Games and Economic Behavior, 9*, 151–160.

English, A., Griffith, R. L., & Steelman, L. A. (2004). Team performance: The effect of team conscientiousness and task type. *Small Group Research, 35*, 643–665.

Ensari, N., & Miller, N. (2002). The out-group must not be so bad after all: The effects of disclosure, typicality, and salience on intergroup bias. *Journal of Personality and Social Psychology, 83*, 313–329.

Ensminger, J. (2004). Market integration and fairness: Evidence from Ultimatum, dictator, and public goods experiments in East Africa. In J. Henrich, R. Boyd, S. Bowles, C. Camerer, E. Fehr, & H. Gintis (Eds.), *Foundations of human sociality* (pp. 356–381). New York: Oxford University Press.

Entin, E. E., & Serfaty, D. (1999). Adaptive team coordination. *Human Factors, 41*, 312–325.

Enzle, M. E., Harvey, M. D., & Wright, E. F. (1992). Implicit role obligations versus social responsibility in constituency representation. *Journal of Personality and Social Psychology, 62*, 238–245.

Epstein, J. A., & Harackiewicz, J. M. (1992). Winning is not enough: The effects of competition and achievement orientation on intrinsic interest. *Personality and Social Psychology Bulletin, 18*, 128–138.

Erev, I., & Rapoport, A. (1990). Provision of step-level public goods: The sequential contribution mechanism. *Journal of Conflict Resolution, 34*, 401–425.

Eshel, Y. (1999). Effects of in-group bias on planned encounters of Jewish and Arab youths. *Journal of Social Psychology, 139*, 768–783.

Espinosa, M. P., & Macho-Stadler, I. (2003). Endogenous formation of competing partnerships with moral hazard. *Games and Economic Behavior, 44*, 172–183.

Esser, J. K. (1989). Agreement pressure and opponent strategies in oligopoly bargaining. *Personality and Social Psychology Bulletin, 15*, 596–603.

Esser, J. K., Calvillo, M. J., Scheel, M. R., & Walker, J. L. (1990). Oligopoly bargaining: Effects of agreement pressure and opponent strategies. *Journal of Applied Social Psychology, 20*, 1256–1271.

Esser, J. K., & Marriott, R. G. (1995). Mediation tactics: A comparison of field and laboratory research. *Journal of Applied Social Psychology, 25*, 1530–1546.

Esses, V. M., & Dovidio, J. F. (2002). The role of emotions in determining willingness to engage in intergroup contact. *Personality and Social Psychology Bulletin, 28*, 1202–1214.

Esteban, J., & Sákovics, J. (2008). Theory of agreements in the shadow of conflict: The genesis of bargaining power. *Theory and Decision, 65*, 227–252.

Eurich-Fulcer, R., & Schofield, J. W. (1995). Correlated versus uncorrelated social categorizations: The effect on intergroup bias. *Personality and Social Psychology Bulletin, 21*, 149–159.

Evans, R. A. (1996). Value, consistency, and random coalition formation. *Games and Economic Behavior, 12*, 68–80.

Evans, R. (1997). Coalitional bargaining with competition to make offers. *Games and Economic Behavior, 19*, 211–220.

Evered, L. J. (1998). Participant confidence-competence and performance in variable collaborative groups. *Journal of Research and Development in Education, 31*, 63–68.

Extejt, M. M., & Russell, C. J. (1990). The role of individual bargaining behavior in the pay setting process: A pilot study. *Journal of Business and Psychology, 5*, 113–126.

Eys, M. A., & Carron, A. V. (2001). Role ambiguity, task cohesion, and task self-efficacy. *Small Group Research, 32*, 356–373.

Eyuboglu, N., & Buja, A. (1993). Dynamics of channel negotiations: Contention and reciprocity. *Psychology and Marketing, 10*, 47–65.

Fabick, S. D. (2002). Us & them: Reducing the risk of terrorism. In C. E. Stout (Ed.), *The psychology of terrorism: Clinical aspects and responses* (Vol. II, pp. 226–241). Westport, CT: Praeger Publishers/Greenwood Publishing Group, 2002.

Fabricatore, C., Nussbaum, M., & Rosas, R. (2002). Playability in action videogames: A qualitative design model. *Human-Computer Interaction, 17*, 311–368.

Facer, K., Joiner, R., Stanton, D., Reid, J., Hull, R., & Kirk, D. (2004). Savannah: Mobile gaming and learning? *Journal of Computer Assisted Learning, 20*, 399–409.

Facteau, C. L., Facteau, J. D., Schoel, L. C., Russell, J. E. A., & Poteet, M. L. (1998). Reactions of leaders to 360–degree feedback from subordinates and peers. *Leadership Quarterly, 9*, 427–448.

Fader, P. S., & Hauser, J. R. (1988). Implicit coalitions in a generalized Prisoner's Dilemma. *Journal of Conflict Resolution, 32*, 553–582.

Falomir-Pichastor, J. M., Gabarrot, F., & Mugny, G. (2009). Conformity and identity threat: The role of ingroup identification. *Swiss Journal of Psychology/Schweizerische Zeitschrift für Psychologie/Revue Suisse de Psychologie, 68*, 79–87.

Falomir-Pichastor, J. M., Muñoz-Rojas, D., Invernizzi, F., & Mugny, G. (2004). Perceived ingroup threat as a factor moderating the influence of ingroup norms on discrimination against foreigners. *European Journal of Social Psychology, 34*, 135–153.

Fandt, P. M., Cady, S. H., & Sparks, M. R. (1993). The impact of reward interdependency on the synergogy model of cooperative performance: Designing an effective team environment. *Small Group Research, 24*, 101–115.

Fandt, P. M., Richardson, W. D., & Conner, H. M. (1990). The impact of goal setting on team simulation experience. *Simulation and Gaming, 21*, 411–422.

Fang, C., Kimbrough, S. O., Valluri, A., Zheng, Z., & Pace, S. (2002). On adaptive emergence of trust behavior in the game of stag hunt. *Group Decision and Negotiation, 11*, 449–467.

Fanis, M. (2004). Collective action meets prospect theory: An application to coalition building in Chile, 197–375. *Political Psychology, 25*, 363–388.

Faria, A. J., & Wellington, W. J. (2004). A survey of simulation game users, former-users, and never-users. *Simulation and Gaming, 35*, 178–207.

Farmer, S. M., & Hyatt, C. W. (1994). Effects of task language demands and task complexity on computer-mediated work groups. *Small Group Research, 25*, 331–366.

Farmer, S. M., & Roth, J. (1998). Conflict-handling behavior in work groups: Effects of group structure, decision processes, and time. *Small Group Research, 29*, 669–713.

Faure, G. O. (1995). Conflict formulation: Going beyond culture-bound views of conflict. In B. B. Bunker & J. Z. Rubin (Eds.), *Conflict, cooperation, and justice: Essays inspired by the work of Morton Deutsch* (pp. 39–57). San Francisco: Jossey-Bass Inc, Publishers.

Fearon, J. D. (1994). Signaling versus the balance of power and interests: An empirical test of a crisis bargaining model. *Journal of Conflict Resolution, 38*, 236–269.

Feeley, T. H., Tutzauer, F., Rosenfeld, H. L., & Young, M. J. (1997). Cooperation in an infinite-choice continuous-time prisoner's dilemma. *Simulation and Gaming, 28*, 442–459.

Feeney, M. C., & Davidson, J. A. (1996). Bridging the gap between the practical and the theoretical: An evaluation of a conflict resolution model. *Peace and Conflict: Journal of Peace Psychology, 2*, 255–269.

Feinberg, M. E., Greenberg, M. T., & Osgood, D. W. (2004). Readiness, functioning, and perceived effectiveness in community prevention coalitions: A study of communities that care. *American Journal of Community Psychology, 33*, 163–176.

Fekadu, Z., & Kraft, P. (2002). Expanding the theory of planned behaviour: The role of social norms and group identification. *Journal of Health Psychology, 7*, 33–43.

Fellers, J. W., & Moon, D. K. (1995). Distance education in the future: Exploring the application of distributed group support systems. *Group Decision and Negotiation, 4*, 273–286

Felsenthal, D. S., Machover, M., & Zwicker, W. (1998). The bicameral postulates and indices of a priori voting power. *Theory and Decision, 44*, 83–116.

Feltz, D. L., & Lirgg, C. D. (1998). Perceived team and player efficacy in hockey. *Journal of Applied Psychology, 83*, 557–564.

Fenwick, H. (1997). Charge bargaining and sentence discount: The victim's perspective. *International Review of Victimology, 5*, 23–36.

Ferdman, B. M. (1995). Cultural identity and diversity in organizations: Bridging the gap between group differences and individual uniqueness. In M. M. Chemers, S. Oskamp, & M. Costanzo (Eds.), *Diversity in organizations: New perspectives for a changing workplace* [Claremont symposium on applied social psychology, Vol. 8], pp. 37–61). Thousand Oaks, CA: Sage Publications, Inc.

Ferguson, E. D., & Schmitt, S. (1988). Gender-linked stereotypes and motivation affect performance in the Prisoner's Dilemma Game. *Perceptual and Motor Skills, 66,* 703–714.

Fernet, C., Guay, F., & Senécal, C. (2004). Adjusting to job demands: The role of work self-determination and job control in predicting burnout. *Journal of Vocational Behavior, 65,* 39–56.

Ferreira, J. L. (1999). Endogenous formation of coalitions in noncooperative games. *Games and Economic Behavior, 26,* 40–58.

Fershtman, C. (2000). A note on multi-issue two-sided bargaining: Bilateral procedures. *Games and Economic Behavior, 30,* 216–227.

Feyerherm, A. E., & Rice, C. L. (2002). Emotional intelligence and team performance: The good, the bad and the ugly. *International Journal of Organizational Analysis, 10,* 343–362.

Fiedler, K., Semin, G. R., & Finkenauer, C. (1993). The battle of words between gender groups: A language-based approach to intergroup processes. *Human Communication Research, 19,* 409–441.

Fielding, K. S., & Hogg, M. A. (1997). Social identity, self-categorization, and leadership: A field study of small interactive groups. *Group Dynamics, 1,* 39–51.

Fielding, K. S., & Hogg, M. A. (2000). Working hard to achieve self-defining group goals: A social identity analysis. *Zeitschrift für Sozialpsychologie, 31,* 191–203.

Fielding, K. S., Terry, D. J., Masser, B. M., & Hogg, M. A. (2008). Integrating social identity theory and the theory of planned behaviour to explain decisions to engage in sustainable agricultural practices. *British Journal of Social Psychology, 47,* 23–48.

Filzmoser, M., & Vetschera, R. (2008). A classification of bargaining steps and their impact on negotiation outcomes. *Group Decision and Negotiation, 17,* 421–443.

Finchilescu, G. (1994). Intergroup attributions in minimal groups. *Journal of Social Psychology, 134,* 111–118.

Finholt, T., & Sproull, L. S. (1990). Electronic groups at work. *Organization Science, 1,* 41–64

Finholt, T. A., & Teasley, S. D. (1998). The need for psychology in research on computer-supported cooperative work. *Social Science Computer Review, 16,* 40–52.

Finlay, K. A., & Stephan, W. G. (2000). Improving intergroup relations: The effects of empathy on racial attitudes. *Journal of Applied Social Psychology, 30,* 1720–1737.

Fiol, C. M. (1994). Consensus, diversity, and learning in organizations. *Organization Science, 5,* 403–420.

Fiorelli, J. S. (1988). Power in work groups: Team member's perspectives. *Human Relations, 41,* 1–12.

Fischer, I. (2009). Friend or foe: Subjective expected relative similarity as a determinant of cooperation. *Journal of Experimental Psychology: General, 138,* 341–350.

Fischer, I., & Suleiman, R. (1997). Election frequency and the emergence of cooperation in a simulated intergroup conflict. *Journal of Conflict Resolution, 41,* 483–508.

Fischer, P., Kubitzki, J., Guter, S., & Frey, D. (2007). Virtual driving and risk taking: Do racing games increase risk-taking cognitions, affect, and behaviors? *Journal of Experimental Psychology: Applied, 13,* 22–31.

Fischer, R., Maes, J., & Schmitt, M. (2007). Tearing down the 'Wall in the head'? Culture contact between Germans. *International Journal of Intercultural Relations, 31,* 163–179.

Fisher, R., & Brown, S. (1988). *Getting together: Building a relationship that gets to yes.* Boston: Houghton Mifflin.

Fisher, R. J. (1994). Generic principles for resolving intergroup conflict. *Journal of Social Issues, 50*(1), 47–66.

Fisher, R. J. (2006). Intergroup conflict. In M. Deutsch, P. T. Coleman, & E. C. Marcus (Eds.), *The handbook of conflict resolution: Theory and practice* (2nd ed., pp. 176–196). Hoboken, NJ: Wiley Publishing.

Fiske, A. P., & Haslam, N. (1998). Prerequisites for satisfactory relationships. In L. H. Meyer, H.-S. Park, M. Grenot-Scheyer, I. Schwartz, & B. Harry (Eds.), *Making friends: The influences of culture and development* [Children, youth & change: Sociocultural perspectives, Vol. 3] (pp. 385–392). Baltimore: Paul H. Brookes Publishing Co.

Fiske, A. P., & Haslam, N. (2005). The four basic social bonds: Structures for coordinating interaction. In M. W. Baldwin (Ed.), *Interpersonal cognition* (pp. 267–298). New York: Guilford Press.

Fiske, A. P., & Tetlock, P. E. (1997). Taboo trade-offs: Reactions to transactions that transgress the spheres of justice. *Political Psychology, 18*, 255–297.

Fiske, S. T. (1993). Controlling other people: The impact of power on stereotyping. *American Psychologist, 48*, 621–628.

Fiske, S. T. (2008). From Lewin and Allport to Pettigrew: Modern practical theories. In U. Wagner, L. R. Tropp, G. Finchilescu, & C. Tredoux (Eds.), *Improving intergroup relations: Building on the legacy of Thomas F. Pettigrew* (pp. 27–41). Malden: Blackwell Publishing.

Fiske, S. T., & Goodwin, S. A. (1994). Social cognition research and small group research, a West Side Story or...? *Small Group Research, 25*, 147–171.

Fiske, S. T., & Goodwin, S. A. (1996). Introduction: *Social cognition research and small group research, a* West Side Story *or ...?* In J. L. Nye & A. M. Brower (Eds.), *What's social about social cognition? Research on socially shared cognition in small groups* (pp. xiii-xxxiii). Thousand Oaks, CA: Sage.

Fiske, S. T., & Ruscher, J. B. (1993). Negative interdependence and prejudice: Whence the affect? In D. M. Mackie & D. L. Hamilton (Eds.), *Affect, cognition, and stereotyping: Interactive processes in group perception* (pp. 239–268). San Diego, CA: Academic Press, Inc.

Fiske, S. T., Xu, J., Cuddy, A. C., & Glick, P. (1999). (Dis)respecting versus (dis)liking: Status and interdependence predict ambivalent stereotypes of competence and warmth. *Journal of Social Issues, 55*, 473–489.

Fitzsimons, G. M., & Kay, A. C. (2004). Language and interpersonal cognition: Causal effects of variations in pronoun usage on perceptions of closeness. *Personality and Social Psychology Bulletin, 30*, 547–557.

Fleishman, J. A. (1988). The effects of decision framing and others' behavior on cooperation in a social dilemma. *Journal of Conflict Resolution, 32*, 162–180.

Fleming, M. A., & Petty, R. E. (2000). Identity and persuasion: An elaboration likelihood approach. In D. J. Terry & M. A. Hogg (Eds.), *Attitudes, behavior, and social context: The role of norms and group membership* (pp. 171–199). Mahwah, NJ: Lawrence Erlbaum Associates Publishers.

Flemons, D. G., & Tsai, Y.-m. (1992). Cross-generational coalitions and well-being: A multivariate analysis of social network data. *Journal of Family Psychology, 6*, 195–198.

Fletcher, G. J. O. (1993). Cognition in close relationships. *New Zealand Journal of Psychology, 22*(2), 69–81.

Fletcher, G. J. O., Simpson, J. A., & Thomas, G. (2000). Ideals, perceptions, and evaluations in early relationship development. *Journal of Personality and Social Psychology, 79*, 933–940.

Fletcher, G. J. O., Simpson, J. A., Thomas, G., & Giles, L. (1999). Ideals in intimate relationships. *Journal of Personality and Social Psychology, 76*, 72–89.

Florin, P., Mitchell, R., Stevenson, J., & Klein, I. (2000). Predicting intermediate outcomes for prevention coalitions: A developmental perspective. *Evaluation and Program Planning, 23*, 341–346.

Foddy, M., & Hogg, M. A. (1999). Impact of leaders on resource consumption in social dilemmas: The intergroup context. In M. Foddy, M. Smithson, S. Schneider, & M. Hogg (Eds.), *Resolving social dilemmas: Dynamic, structural, and intergroup aspects* (pp. 309–330). New York: Psychology Press.

Foeman, A., & Nance, T. (2002). Building new cultures, reframing old images: Success strategies of interracial couples. *Howard Journal of Communications, 13*, 237–249.

Folger, R., Cropanzano, R., Timmerman, T. A., Howes, J. C., & Mitchell, D. (1996). Elaborating procedural fairness: Justice becomes both simpler and more complex. *Personality and Social Psychology Bulletin, 22*, 435–441.

Fonstad, N. O., McKersie, R. B., & Eaton, S. C. (2004). Interest-based negotiations in a transformed labor-management setting. *Negotiation Journal, 20*, 5–11.

Ford, R. (1994). Conflict and bargaining. In M. Foschi & E. J. Lawler (Eds.), *Group processes: Sociological analyses* (pp. 231–256). Chicago, IL: Nelson-Hall Publishers.

Ford, R., & Blegen, M. A. (1992). Offensive and defensive use of punitive tactics in explicit bargaining. *Social Psychology Quarterly, 55*, 351–362.

Forgas, J. P. (1994). Sad and guilty? Affective influences on the explanation of conflict in close relationships. *Journal of Personality and Social Psychology, 66*, 56–68.

Forgas, J. P. (1998). On feeling good and getting your way: Mood effects on negotiator cognition and bargaining strategies. *Journal of Personality and Social Psychology, 74*, 565–577.

Forgas, J. P. (2001). On being moody but influential: The role of affect in social influence strategies. In J. P. Forgas & K. D. Williams (Eds.), *Social influence: Direct and indirect processes* (pp. 147–166). New York: Psychology Press.

Forgas, J. P. (2002a). Feeling and doing: Affective influences on interpersonal behavior. *Psychological Inquiry, 13*, 1–28.

Forgas, J. P. (2002b). Feeling and thinking: The influence of affect on social cognition and behavior. In L. Bäckman & C. von Hofsten (Eds.), *Psychology at the turn of the millennium, Vol. 1: Cognitive, biological, and health perspectives* (pp. 455–480). Hove, England: Psychology Press/Taylor & Francis (UK), 2002.

Forgas, J. P. (2002c). Toward understanding the role of affect in social thinking and behavior. *Psychological Inquiry, 13*, 90–102.

Forgas, J. P. (2007). When sad is better than happy: Negative affect can improve the quality and effectiveness of persuasive messages and social influence strategies. *Journal of Experimental Social Psychology, 43*, 513–528.

Forgas, J. P., & Williams, K. D. (Eds.). (2001). *Social influence: Direct and indirect processes*. New York: Psychology Press.

Forgas, J. P., Williams, K. D., & Wheeler, L. (Eds.). (2001). *The social mind: Cognitive and motivational aspects of interpersonal behavior*. New York: Cambridge University Press.

Forlenza, S. G. (1991). Mediation and psychotherapy: Parallel processes. In K. G. Duffy, J. W. Grosch, & P. V. Olczak (Eds.), *Community mediation: A handbook for practitioners and researchers* (pp. 227–239). New York: Guilford Press.

Foroughi, A., Perkins, W. C., & Jelassi, M. T. (1995). An empirical study of an interactive, session-oriented computerized negotiation support system (NSS). *Group Decision and Negotiation, 4*, 485–512.

Forrest, K. D. (2002). Voiceless, The effects of unfair procedures on recipients and observers in small groups. *Current Research in Social Psychology, 8*(5), 62–84.

Forsyth, D. R., & Kelley, K. N. (1994). Attribution in groups: Estimations of personal contributions to collective endeavors. *Small Group Research, 25*, 367–383.

Forsyth, D. R., & Kelley, K. N. (1996). Heuristic-based biases in estimations of personal contributions to collective endeavors. In J. L. Nye & A. M. Brower (Eds.), *What's social about social cognition? Research on socially shared cognition in small groups* (pp. 106–123). Thousand Oaks, CA: Sage.

Foster-Fishman, P. G., Berkowitz, S. L., Lounsbury, D. W., Jacobson, S., & Allen, N. A. (2001). Building collaborative capacity in community coalitions: A review and integrative framework. *American Journal of Community Psychology, 29*, 241–261.

Foulkes, S. H. (1986, first published 1975). *Group Analytic Psychotherapy: Method and Principles*. London: Maresfield Library.

Foushee, H. C. (1984). Dyads and triads at 35,000 feet: Factors affecting group process and aircrew performance. *American Psychologist, 39*, 885–893.

Fox, S., & Thornton, G. C. (1993). Implicit Distribution Theory: The influence of cognitive representation of differentiation on actual ratings. *Perceptual and Motor Skills, 76*, 259–276.

Fox, W. M. (1989). The improved Nominal Group Technique (NGT). *Journal of Management Development, 8*, 20–27.

Francis, D., & Young, D. (1979). *Improving Work Groups*. San Diego, CA: University Associates.

Frank, R. H. (1991). Economics. In M. Maxwell (Ed.), *The sociobiological imagination* (pp. 91–110). Albany, NY: State University of New York Press.

Frank, R. H., Gilovich, T., & Regan, D. T. (1993). The evolution of one-shot cooperation: An experiment. *Ethology and Sociobiology, 14*, 247–256.

Frankel, D. M. (1998). Creative bargaining. *Games and Economic Behavior, 23*, 43–53.

Franz, C. R., & Jin, K. G. (1995). The structure of group conflict in a collaborative work group during information systems development. *Journal of Applied Communication Research, 23*, 108–127.

Franzen, A. (1994). Gruppengroe-Se und die Stabilitaet der Kooperation im Commons Dilemma [Group size and the stability of cooperation in a commons dilemma]. *Zeitschrift fuer Sozialpsychologie, 25*, 307–314.

Freedman, L. D. (1993). TA tools for self-managing work teams. *Transactional Analysis Journal, 23*, 104–109.

Friedland, N. (1990). Attribution of control as a determinant of cooperation in exchange interactions. *Journal of Applied Social Psychology, 20*, 303–320.

Friedman, E., Shor, M., Shenker, S., & Sopher, B. (2004). An experiment on learning with limited information: nonconvergence, experimentation cascades, and the advantage of being slow. *Games and Economic Behavior, 47*, 325–352.

Friedman, R., Kane, M., & Cornfield, D. B. (1998). Social support and career optimism: Examining the effectiveness of network groups among Black managers. *Human Relations, 51*, 1155–1177.

Friedman, R. A. (1992). From theory to practice: Critical choices for "mutual gains" training. *Negotiation Journal, 8*, 91–98.

Friedman, R. A. (1994). Missing ingredients in mutual gains bargaining theory. *Negotiation Journal, 10*, 265–280.

Friedman, V. J., & Lipshitz, R. (1992). Teaching people to shift cognitive gears: Overcoming resistance on the road to Model II. *Journal of Applied Behavioral Science, 28*, 118–136.

Frink, D. D., Robinson, R. K., Reithel, G., Arthur, M. M., Ammeter, A. P., Ferris, G. R., Kaplan, D. M., & Morrisette, H. S. (2003). Gender demography and organizational performance. *Group and Organization Management, 28*, 127–147.

Frohlich, N., & Oppenheimer, J. A. (1997). Tests of leadership solutions to collective action problems. *Simulation and Gaming, 28*, 181–197.

Frohman, A. L. (1997). Igniting organizational change from below: The power of personal initiative. *Organizational Dynamics, 25*(3), 39–53.

Fukuda, E., & Muto, S. (2004). Dynamic coalition formation in the Apex Game. *Theory and Decision, 56*, 153–163.

Fukuno, M., & Ohbuchi, K.. (1999). Procedural and distributive fairness in rejection of unequal offers. *Tohoku Psychologica Folia, 58*, 11–18.

Fukuno, M., & Ohbuchi, K.-I. (2001). Respondent's rejection of unequal offer as protecting one's identity in ultimatum bargaining. *Japanese Journal of Social Psychology, 16*, 184–192.

Fukuno, M., & Ohbuchi, K.-I. (2003). Procedural fairness in ultimatum bargaining: Effects of interactional fairness and formal procedure on respondents' reactions to unequal offers. *Japanese Psychological Research, 45*, 152–161.

Fukushima, O., & Ohbuchi, K. I. (1993). Multiple goals and resolution strategies in interpersonal conflicts. *Tohoku Psychologica Folia, 52*, 20–27.

Fukushima, O., & Ohbuchi, K. i. (1996). Antecedents and effects of multiple goals in conflict resolution. *International Journal of Conflict Management, 7*, 191–208.

Fum, D., & Missier, F. D. (2001). Modeling counteroffer behavior in dyadic distributive negotiation. In E. M. Altmann, A. Cleeremans, C. D. Schunn, & W. D. Gray (Eds.), *Proceedings of the 2001 Fourth International Conference on Cognitive Modeling* (pp. 85–90). Mahwah, NJ: Lawrence Erlbaum Associates Publishers.

Funk, J. B., Buchman, D. D., Jenks, J., & Bechtoldt, H. (2003). Playing violent video games, desensitization, and moral evaluation in children. *Journal of Applied Developmental Psychology, 24*, 413–436.

Furnham, A., & Quilley, R. (1989). The Protestant work ethic and the Prisoner's Dilemma Game. *British Journal of Social Psychology, 28*, 79–87.

Fusco, M. E., Bell, P. A., Jorgensen, M. D., & Smith, J. M. (1991). Using a computer to study the commons dilemma. *Simulation and Gaming, 22*, 67–74.

Fyock, J., & Stangor, C. (1994). The role of memory biases in stereotype maintenance. *British Journal of Social Psychology, 33*, 331–343.

Gabarrot, F., Falomir-Pichastor, J. M., & Mugny, G. (2009). Being similar versus being equal: Intergroup similarity moderates the influence of in-group norms on discrimination and prejudice. *British Journal of Social Psychology, 48*, 253–273.

Gabrenya, W. K., Jr., & Hwang, K. K. (1996). Chinese social interaction: Harmony and hierarchy on the good earth. In M. H. Bond (Ed.), *The handbook of Chinese psychology* (pp. 309–321). Hong Kong, Hong Kong: Oxford University Press.

Gaertner, L., & Insko, C. A. (2000). Intergroup discrimination in the minimal group paradigm: Categorization, reciprocation, or fear? *Journal of Personality and Social Psychology, 79*, 77–94.

Gaertner, L., & Schopler, J. (1998). Perceived ingroup entitativity and intergroup bias: An interconnection of self and others. *European Journal of Social Psychology, 28*, 963–980.

Gaertner, S. L., & Dovidio, J. F. (2000). The aversive form of racism. In C. Stangor (Ed.), *Stereotypes and prejudice: Essential readings* (289–304). New York: Psychology Press.

Gaertner, S. L., & Dovidio, J. F. (2005). Understanding and Addressing Contemporary Racism: From Aversive Racism to the Common In-group Identity Model. *Journal of Social Issues, 61*, 615–639.

Gaertner, S. L., & Dovidio, J. F. (2009). A common ingroup identity: A categorization-based approach for reducing intergroup bias. In T. D. Nelson (Ed.), *Handbook of prejudice, stereotyping, and discrimination* (pp. 489–505). New York: Psychology Press.

Gaertner, S. L., Dovidio, J. F., & Bachman, B. A. (1996). Revisiting the contact hypothesis: The induction of a common ingroup identity. *International Journal of Intercultural Relations, 20*, 271–290.

Gaertner, S. L., Dovidio, J. F., Guerra, R., Rebelo, M., Monteiro, M. B., Riek, B. M., & Houlette, M. A. (2008). The common in-group identity model: Applications to children and adults. In S. R. Levy & M. Killen (Eds.), *Intergroup attitudes and relations in childhood through adulthood* (pp. 204–219). New York: Oxford University Press.

Gaertner, S. L., Dovidio, J. F., Nier, J. A., Banker, B. S., Ward, C. M., Houlette, M., & Loux, S. (2000). The Common Ingroup Identity Model for reducing intergroup bias: Progress and challenges. In R. Brown & D. Capozza (Eds.), *Social identity processes: Trends in theory and research* (pp. 133–148). London: Sage Publications Ltd.

Gaertner, S. L., Dovidio, J. F., Rust, M. C., Nier, J. A., Banker, B. S., Ward, C. M., Mottola, G. R., & Houlette, M. (1999). Reducing intergroup bias: Elements of intergroup cooperation. *Journal of Personality and Social Psychology, 76*, 388–402.

Gaertner, S. L., Mann, J. A., Dovidio, J. F., Murrell, A. J., & Pomare, M. (1990). How does cooperation reduce intergroup bias? *Journal of Personality and Social Psychology, 59*, 692–704.

Gaertner, S. L., Mann, J. A., Dovidio, J. F., Murrell, A. J., & Pomare, M. (2000). How does cooperation reduce intergroup bias? In C. Stangor (Ed.), *Stereotypes and prejudice: Essential readings* (pp. 435–450). New York: Psychology Press. [Reprinted from *JPSP*, 1990].

Gaertner, S. L., Mann, J., Murrell, A., & Dovidio, J. F. (2001). Reducing intergroup bias: The benefits of recategorization. In M. A. Hogg & D. Abrams (Eds.), *Intergroup relations: Essential readings* (pp. 356–369). Philadelphia: Psychology Press.

Gaertner, S. L., Rust, M. C., Dovidio, J. F., Bachman, B. A., & Anastasio, P. A. (1994). The contact hypothesis: The role of a common ingroup identity on reducing intergroup bias. *Small Group Research, 25*, 224–249.

Gaertner, S. L., Rust, M. C., Dovidio, J. F., Bachman, B. A., & Anastasio, P. A. (1996). The contact hypothesis: The role of a common ingroup identity on reducing intergroup bias among majority and minority group members. In J. L. Nye & A. M. Brower (Eds.), *What's social about social cognition? Research on socially shared cognition in small groups* (pp. 230–260). Thousand Oaks, CA: Sage Publications, Inc.

Gagné, F. M., & Lydon, J. E. (2001). Mind-set and close relationships: When bias leads to (in)accurate predictions. *Journal of Personality and Social Psychology, 81*, 85–96.

Gagnon, A., & Bourhis, R. Y. (1996). Discrimination in the minimal group paradigm: Social identity or self-interest? *Personality and Social Psychology Bulletin, 22*, 1289–1301.

Galam, S., & Moscovici, S. (1995). Towards a theory of collective phenomena: III. Conflicts and forms of power. *European Journal of Social Psychology, 25*, 217–229.

Galanos, A. N., Cohen, H. J., & Jackson, T. W. (1993). Medical education in geriatrics: The lasting impact of the aging game. *Educational Gerontology, 19*, 675–682.

Galavotti, C. (1989). Implementation. In C. M. Bonjean, M. T. Coleman, & I. Iscoe (Eds.), *Community care of the chronically mentally ill: Proceedings of the sixth Robert Lee Sutherland Seminar in Mental Health* (pp. 91–95). Austin, TX: Hogg Foundation for Mental Health.

Gale, K., Martin, K., & McQueen, G. (2002). Triadic assessment. *Assessment and Evaluation in Higher Education, 27*, 557–567.

Galegher, J., & Kraut, R. E. (1990). Technology for intellectual teamwork: Perspectives on research and design. In J. Galegher, R. E. Kraut, & C. Egido (Eds.), *Intellectual teamwork: Social and technological foundations of cooperative work* (pp. 1–20). Hillsdale, NJ: Lawrence Erlbaum Associates, Inc.

Galegher, J., Kraut, R. E., & Egido, C. (Eds.). (1990). *Intellectual teamwork: Social and technological foundations of cooperative work*. Hillsdale, NJ: Lawrence Erlbaum Associates, Inc.

Galinsky, A. D., Maddux, W. W., Gilin, D., & White, J. B. (2008). Why it pays to get inside the head of your opponent: The differential effects of perspective taking and empathy in negotiations. *Psychological Science, 19*, 378–384.

Gallagher, D. G., & Gramm, C. L. (1997). Collective bargaining and strike activity. In D. Lewin, Mitchell, & J. B. Daniel Zaidi, A. Mahmoo (Eds.), *The human resource management handbook, Parts 1–3* (pp. 65–93). San Diego, CA: Elsevier Science/JAI Press.

Gallivan, M. J. (2001). Striking a balance between trust and control in a virtual organization: A content analysis of open source software case studies. *Information Systems Journal, 11*, 277–304.

Gallois, C., McKay, S., & Pittam, J. (2005). Intergroup communication and identity: Intercultural, organizational, and health communication. In K. L. Fitch & R. E. Sanders (Eds.), *Handbook of language and social interaction* (pp. 231–250). Mahwah, NJ: Lawrence Erlbaum Associates Publishers.

Gallucci, M., & Perugini, M. (2000). An experimental test of a game-theoretical model of reciprocity. *Journal of Behavioral Decision Making, 13*, 367–389.

Gallupe, R. B., Dennis, A. R., Cooper, W. H., Valacich, J. S., Bastianutti, L. M., & Nunamaker, J. (1992). Electronic brainstorming and group size. *Academy of Management Journal, 35*, 350–369.

Galtung, J., & Tschudi, F. (2001). Crafting peace: On the psychology of the TRANSCEND approach. In D. J. Christie, R. V. Wagner, & D. D. Winter (Eds.), *Peace, conflict, and violence: Peace psychology for the 21st century* (pp. 210–222). Upper Saddle River, NJ: Prentice Hall/Pearson Education.

Gans, J. S. (1995). Best replies and adaptive learning. *Mathematical Social Sciences, 30*, 221–234.

Gao, G. (1996). Self and OTHER: A Chinese perspective on interpersonal relationships. In W. B. Gudykunst, S. Ting-Toomey, & T. Nishida (Eds.), *Communication in personal relationships across cultures* (pp. 81–101). Thousand Oaks, CA: Sage Publications, Inc.

Garaigordobil, M., Maganto, C., & Etxeberria, J. (1996). Effects of a cooperative game program on socio-affective relations and group cooperation capacity. *European Journal of Psychological Assessment, 12*, 141–152.

Gardner, R. C., MacIntyre, P. D., & Lalonde, R. N. (1995). The effects of multiple social categories on stereotyping. *Canadian Journal of Behavioural Science, 27*, 466–483.

Garland, B., Crane, M., Marino, C., Stone-Wiggins, B., Ward, A., & Friedell, G. (2004). Effect of community coalition structure and preparation on the subsequent implementation of cancer control activities. *American Journal of Health Promotion, 18*, 424–434.

Garratt, R. (1999). On Bargaining for an indivisible good. *Games and Economic Behavior, 26*, 186–192.

Garratt, R., & Qin, C.-Z. (2000). On market games when agents cannot be in two places at once. *Games and Economic Behavior, 31*, 165–173.

Garrett, S. K., Caldwell, B. S., Harris, E. C., & Gonzalez, M. C. (2009). Six dimensions of expertise: A more comprehensive definition of cognitive expertise for team coordination. *Theoretical Issues in Ergonomics Science, 10*, 93–105.

Garson, B. E., & Stanwyck, D. J. (1997). Locus of control and incentive in self-managing teams. *Human Resource Development Quarterly, 8*, 247–258.

Garza, R. T., Lipton, J. P., & Isonio, S. A. (1989). Group ethnic composition, leader ethnicity, and task performance: An application of social identity theory. *Genetic, Social*, and General Psychology Monographs, 115, 295–314.

Gaskell, G. D., & Wright, D. B. (1997). Group differences in memory for a political event. In J. W. Pennebaker, D. Paez, & B. Rime (Eds.), *Collective memory of political events: Social psychological perspectives* (pp. 175–189). Mahwah, NJ: Lawrence Erlbaum Associates, Inc.

Gastardo-Conaco, M. C. (1991). Complex social categories. *Philippine Journal of Psychology, 24*(1), 1–11.

Gaudart, H. (1999). Games as teaching tools for teaching English to speakers of other languages. *Simulation and Gaming, 30*, 283–291.

Gaunt, R., Leyens, J. P., & Demoulin, S. (2002). Intergroup relations and the attribution of emotions: Control over memory for secondary emotions associated with the ingroup and outgroup. *Journal of Experimental Social Psychology, 38*, 508–514.

Gauthier, D. (1990). Maximization constrained: The rationality of cooperation. In P. K. Moser (Ed.), *Rationality in action: Contemporary approaches* (pp. 315–334). New York: Cambridge University Press.

Gauvin, S., Lilien, G. L., & Chatterjee, K. (1990). The impact of information and computer based training on negotiators' performance. *Theory and Decision, 28*, 331–354.

Gelfand, M. J., & Brett, J. M. (2004). Integrating negotiation and culture research. In M. J. Gelfand & J. M. Brett (Eds.), *The handbook of negotiation and culture* (pp. 415–428). Stanford, CA: Stanford University Press.

Gelfand, M. J., Nishii, L. H., & Raver, J. L. (2006). On the nature and importance of cultural tightness-looseness. *Journal of Applied Psychology, 91*, 1225–1244.

Gennard, J. (2004). UNI Europa Graphical's approach to the co-ordination of national level collective bargaining within a European context. *Employee Relations, 26*, 531–549.

Georgakopoulou, A. (2002). Narrative and identity management: Discourse and social identities in a tale of tomorrow. *Research on Language and Social Interaction, 35*, 427–451.

Georgiou, I., Becchio, C., Glover, S., & Castiello, U. (2007). Different action patterns for cooperative and competitive behaviour. *Cognition, 102*, 415–433.

Gersick, C. J., & Hackman, J. R. (1990). Habitual routines in task-performing groups. *Organizational Behavior and Human Decision Processes, 47*, 65–97.

Ghosh, D. (1993). Risk propensity and conflict behavior in dyadic negotiation: Some evidence from the laboratory. *International Journal of Conflict Management, 4*, 223–247.

Ghosh, D. (1996). Nonstrategic delay in bargaining: An experimental investigation. *Organizational Behavior and Human Decision Processes, 67*, 312–325.

Giacobbe-Miller, J. K. (1995). A test of the group values and control models of procedural justice from the competing perspectives of labor and management. *Personnel Psychology, 48*, 115–142.

Gibb, S. (2001). The state of human resource management: Evidence from employees' views of HRM systems and staff. *Employee Relations, 23*, 318–336.

Gibbons, F. X. (1990). The impact of focus of attention and affect on social behaviour. In C. W. Ra (Ed.)y *Shyness and embarrassment: Perspectives from social psychology* (pp. 119–143). New York: Cambridge University Press.

Gibson, C. B. (2001). Me and us: Differential relationships among goal-setting training, efficacy and effectiveness at the individual and team level. *Journal of Organizational Behavior, 22*, 789–808.

Gibson, C. B. (2003). The efficacy advantage: Factors related to the formation of group efficacy. *Journal of Applied Social Psychology, 33,* 2153–2186.

Gibson, C. B., & Earley, P. C. (2007). Collective cognition in action: Accumulation interaction, examination, and accommodation in the development and operation of group efficacy beliefs in the workplace. *Academy of Management Review, 32,* 438–458.

Gibson, M. K., & Papa, M. J. (2000). The mud, the blood, and the beer guys: Organizational osmosis in blue-collar work groups. *Journal of Applied Communication Research, 28,* 68–88.

Giessner, S. R., & Mummendey, A. (2008). United we win, divided we fail? Effects of cognitive merger representations and performance feedback on merging groups. *European Journal of Social Psychology, 38,* 412–435.

Gifford, R., & Hine, D. W. (1997). "I'm cooperative, but you're greedy": Some cognitive tendencies in a commons dilemma. *Canadian Journal of Behavioural Science, 29,* 257–265.

Gilbert, D. T., McNulty, S. E., Giuliano, T. A., & Benson, J. E. (1992). Blurry words and fuzzy deeds: The attribution of obscure behavior. *Journal of Personality and Social Psychology, 62,* 18–25.

Gilbert, D. T., & Silvera, D. H. (1996). Overhelping. *Journal of Personality and Social Psychology, 70,* 678–690.

Gilbert, J. A., & Tang, T. L. P. (1998). An examination of organizational trust antecedents. *Public Personnel Management, 27,* 321–338.

Gilboa, I., & Schmeidler, D. (2003). A derivation of expected utility maximization in the context of a game. *Games and Economic Behavior, 44,* 184–194.

Gillespie, J. J., & Bazerman, M. H. (1997). Parasitic integration: Win-win agreements containing losers. *Negotiation Journal, 13,* 271–282.

Gilovich, T., Kruger, J., & Savitsky, K. (1999). Everyday egocentrism and everyday interpersonal problems. In R. M. Kowalski & M. R. Leary (Eds.), *The social psychology of emotional and behavioral problems: Interfaces of social and clinical psychology* (pp. 69–95). Washington, DC: American Psychological Association.

Giner-Sorolla, R., Mackie, D. M., & Smith, E. R. (2007). Special issue on intergroup emotions: Introduction. *Group Processes and Intergroup Relations, 10,* 5–8.

Ginges, J., & Atran, S. (2008). Humiliation and the inertia effect: Implications for understanding violence and compromise in intractable intergroup conflicts. *Journal of Cognition and Culture, 8,* 281–294.

Ginkel, J., & Smith, A. (1999). So you say you want a revolution: A game theoretic explanation of revolution in repressive regimes. *Journal of Conflict Resolution, 43,* 291–316.

Ginnett, R. C. (1990). Airline Cockpit Crew. In J. R. Hackman (Ed.), *Groups That Work (and Those That Don't): Creating conditions for effective teamwork* (pp. 427–448). San Francisco: Jossey-Bass.

Gintis, H., Bowles, S., Boyd, R., & Fehr, E. (2003). Explaining altruistic behavior in humans. *Evolution and Human Behavior, 24,* 153–172.

Gittell, J. H. (2001). Supervisory span, relational coordination, and flight departure performance: A reassessment of postbureaucracy theory. *Organization Science, 12,* 468–483.

Glad, B., & Rosenberg, J. P. (1990). Bargaining under fire: Limit setting and maintenance during the Korean War. In G. Bett (Ed.)y *Psychological dimensions of war* (pp. 181–200). Thousand Oaks, CA: Sage Publications, Inc.

Glance, N. S., & Huberman, B. A. (1994). Social dilemmas and fluid organizations. In K. M. Carley & M. J. Prietula (Eds.), *Computational organization theory* (pp. 217–239). Hillsdale, NJ: Lawrence Erlbaum Associates, Inc.

Glasford, D. E., Dovidio, J. F., & Pratto, F. (2009). I continue to feel so good about us: In-group identification and the use of social identity-enhancing strategies to reduce intragroup dissonance. *Personality and Social Psychology Bulletin, 35,* 415–427.

Glomb, T. M., & Liao, H. (2003). Interpersonal aggression in work groups: Social influence, reciprocal, and individual effects. *Academy of Management Journal, 46,* 486–496.

Gneezy, U., & Guth, W. (2002). On competing rewards standards-An experimental study of ultimatum bargaining. *Journal of Socio-Economics, 31,* 599–607.

Gneezy, U., Haruvy, E., & Roth, A. E. (2003). Bargaining under a deadline: Evidence from the reverse ultimatum game. *Games and Economic Behavior, 45*, 347–368.

Goffman, E. (1955). On face-work: An analysis of ritual elements in social interaction. *Psychiatry: Journal for the Study of Interpersonal Processes, 18*, 213–231.

Golann, D. (2004). Death of a Claim: The Impact of Loss Reactions on Bargaining. *Negotiation Journal, 20*, 539–553.

Goldhaber, G. M., & Rogers, D. P. (1979). *Auditing organizational communication systems: The ICA commmunication audit.* Dubuque, IA: Kendall/Hunt Pub. Co.

Goldman, A. (1994). The centrality of "ningensei" to Japanese negotiating and interpersonal relationships: Implications for U.S.-Japanese communication. *International Journal of Intercultural Relations, 18*, 29–54.

Gomes, A., Hart, S., & Mas-Colell, A. (1999). Finite horizon bargaining and the consistent field. *Games and Economic Behavior, 27*, 204–228.

Gómez, A., Dovidio, J. F., Huici, C., Cuadrado, I., & Gaertner, S. L. (2008). The other side of we: When outgroup members express common identity. *Personality and Social Psychology Bulletin, 34*, 1613–1626.

González, R., & Brown, R. (2003). Generalization of positive attitude as a function of subgroup and superordinate group identifications in intergroup contact. *European Journal of Social Psychology, 33*, 195–214.

González, R., & Brown, R. (2006a). Dual identities in intergroup contact: Group status and size moderate the generalization of positive attitude change. *Journal of Experimental Social Psychology, Vol 42*, 753–767.

González, R., & Brown, R. (2006b). Intergroup contact and levels of categorization: Effects on intergroup emotions. In R. Brown & D. Capozza (Eds.), *Social Identities: Motivational, Emotional and Cultural Influences* (pp. 259–277). Hove, England: Psychology Press/Taylor & Francis.

Goodnow, J. J. (1996). Collaborative rules: How are people supposed to work with one another? In P. B. Baltes & U. M. Staudinger (Eds.), *Interactive minds: Life-span perspectives on the social foundation of cognition* (pp. 163–197). New York: Cambridge University Press.

Goodwin, R., & Soon, A. P. Y. (1994). Self-monitoring and relationship adjustment: A cross-cultural analysis. *Journal of Social Psychology, 134*, 35–39.

Gordijn, E. H., & Stapel, D. A. (2006). Behavioural effects of automatic interpersonal versus intergroup social comparison. *British Journal of Social Psychology, 45*, 717–729.

Gordijn, E. H., Wigboldus, D., & Yzerbyt, V. (2001). Emotional consequences of categorizing victims of negative outgroup behavior as ingroup or outgroup. *Group Processes and Intergroup Relations, 4*, 317–326.

Gordijn, E. H., Yzerbyt, V., Wigboldus, D., & Dumont, M. (2006). Emotional reactions to harmful intergroup behavior. *European Journal of Social Psychology, 36*, 15–30.

Goren, H. (2001). The effect of out-group competition on individual behavior and out-group perception in the Intergroup Prisoner's Dilemma (IPD) game. *Group Processes and Intergroup Relations, 4*, 160–182.

Goren, H., & Bornstein, G. (1999). Reciprocation and learning in the Intergroup Prisoner's Dilemma Game. In D. V. Budescu, I. Erev, & R. Zwick (Eds.), *Games and human behavior: Essays in honor of Amnon Rapoport* (pp. 299–314). Mahwah, NJ: Lawrence Erlbaum Associates Publishers.

Goren, H., & Bornstein, G. (2000). The effects of intragroup communication on intergroup cooperation in the repeated Intergroup Prisoner's Dilemma (IPD) game. *Journal of Conflict Resolution, 44*, 700–719.

Gosenpud, J. (1989). The prediction of simulation performance as it is affected by time. *Simulation and Games, 20*, 319–350.

Gosenpud, J. J., & Miesing, P. (1992). The relative influence of several factors on simulation performance. *Simulation and Gaming, 23*, 311–325.

Gosenpud, J., & Washbush, J. (1996). Total enterprise simulation performance as a function of Myers-Briggs personality type. *Simulation and Gaming, 27*, 184–205.

Gossner, O., & Vieille, N. (2002). How to play with a biased coin? *Games and Economic Behavior,* *41,* 206–226.

Gossner, O., & Vieille, N. (2003). Strategic learning in games with symmetric information. *Games and Economic Behavior, 42,* 25–47.

Gotts, N. M., Polhill, J. G., & Law, A. N. R. (2003). Agent-based simulation in the study of social dilemmas. *Artificial Intelligence Review, 19,* 3–92.

Gracia, F. J., Arcos, J. L., & Caballer, A. (2000). Influencia de la presión temporal en el trabajo en grupo en función del tipo de tarea y del canal de comunicación [Time pressure influence on group work by task type and communication channel]. *Psicothema, 12,* 241–246.

Graesser, C. C. (1990). A social averaging theorem for group decision making. In N. H. Anderson (Ed.), *Contributions to information integration theory, Vol. 1: Cognition; Vol. 2: Social; Vol. 3: Developmental. (pp* 1–40). Hillsdale, NJ, England: Lawrence Erlbaum Associates, Inc, 1990.

Graham, J. L. (1993). The Japanese negotiation style: Characteristics of a distinct approach. *Negotiation Journal, 9,* 123–140.

Graham, J. L., Kim, D. K., Lin, C.-y., & Robinson, M. (1988). Buyer-seller negotiations around the Pacific rim: Differences in fundamental exchange processes. *Journal of Consumer Research, 15,* 48–54.

Granberg, D. (1999). A new version of the Monty Hall Dilemma with unequal probabilities. *Behavioural Processes, 48,* 25–34.

Granberg, D., & Dorr, N. (1998). Further exploration of two-stage decision making in the Monty Hall dilemma. *American Journal of Psychology, 111,* 561–579.

Granner, M. L., & Sharpe, P. A. (2004). Evaluating community coalition characteristics and functioning: A summary of measurement tools. *Health Education Research, 19,* 514–532.

Grant, P. R. (1991). Ethnocentrism between groups of unequal power under threat in intergroup competition. *Journal of Social Psychology, 131,* 21–28.

Grant, P. R. (1992). Ethnocentrism between groups of unequal power in response to perceived threat to social identity and valued resources. *Canadian Journal of Behavioural Science, 24,* 348–370.

Grant, P. R. (1993a). Ethnocentrism in response to a threat to social identity. *Journal of Social Behavior and Personality, 8,* 143–154.

Grant, P. R. (1993b). Reactions to intergroup similarity: Examination of the similarity/differentiation and the similarity/attraction hypotheses. *Canadian Journal of Behavioural Science, 25,* 28–44.

Grant-Vallone, E. J., & Ensher, E. A. (2001). An examination of work and personal life conflict, organizational support and employee health among international expatriates. *International Journal of Intercultural Relations, 25,* 261–278.

Grawitch, M. J., Munz, D. C., Elliott, E. K., & Mathis, A. (2003). Promoting creativity in temporary problem-solving groups: The effects of positive mood and autonomy in problem definition on idea-generating performance. *Group Dynamics: Theory, Research,* and Practice, 7, 200–213.

Grawitch, M. J, Munz, D. C., & Kramer, T. J. (2003). Effects of member mood states on creative performance in temporary workgroups. *Group Dynamics, 7,* 41–54.

Gray, L. N., & Stafford, M. C. (1988). On choice behavior in individual and social situations. *Social Psychology Quarterly, 51,* 58–65.

Grazzani Gavazzi, I., Groppo, M., Confalonieri, E., & Calvino, E. (1996). Piani condivisi non riusciti ed emozioni: una prospettiva cross-culturale [Thwarted shared plans and emotions: A cross-cultural perspective]. *Ricerche di Psicologia, 20*(3), 133–160.

Green, B. (2002). Listening to leaders: Feedback on 360–degree feedback one year later. *Organization Development Journal, 20*(1), 8–16.

Greenberg, J. (1993). The social side of fairness: Interpersonal and informational classes of organizational justice. In R. Cropanzano (Ed.), *Justice in the work place: Approaching fairness in human resource management* (pp. 79–103). Hillsdale, NJ: Erlbaum.

Greenhalgh, L., & Chapman, D. I. (1995). Joint decision making: The inseparability of relationships and negotiation. In R. M. Kramer & D. M. Messick (Eds.), *Negotiation as a social pro-*

*cess: New trends in theory and research* (pp. 166–185). Thousand Oaks, CA: Sage Publications, Inc.

Greenhalgh, L., & Gilkey, R. W. (1993). The effect of relationship orientation on negotiators' cognitions and tactics. *Group Decision and Negotiation, 2*, 167–183.

Greenland, K., & Brown, R. (1999). Categorization and intergroup anxiety in contact between British and Japanese nationals. *European Journal of Social Psychology, 29*, 503–521.

Greenland, K., & Brown, R. (2000). Categorization and intergroup anxiety in intergroup contact. In D. Capozza & R. Brown (Eds.), *Social identity processes: Trends in theory and research* (pp. 167–183). Thousand Oaks, CA: Sage Publications Ltd.

Greenwald, A. G., Pickrell, J. E., & Farnham, S. D. (2002). Implicit partisanship: Taking sides for no reason. *Journal of Personality and Social Psychology, 83*, 367–379.

Grier, S. A., & McGill, A. L. (2000). How we explain depends on whom we explain: The impact of social category on the selection of causal comparisons and causal explanations. *Journal of Experimental Social Psychology, 36*, 545–566.

Grieve, P. G., & Hogg, M. A. (1999). Subjective uncertainty and intergroup discrimination in the minimal group situation. *Personality and Social Psychology Bulletin, 25*, 926–940.

Griffin, M. A., Tesluk, P. E., & Jacobs, R. R. (1995). Bargaining cycles and work-related attitudes: Evidence for threat-rigidity effects. *Academy of Management Journal, 38*, 1709–1725.

Griffith, C. E. (1991). Personality and gender as factors in interpersonal negotiation. *Journal of Social Behavior and Personality, 6*, 915–928.

Griffith, W. I., & Sell, J. (1988). The effects of competition on allocators' preferences for contributive and retributive justice rules. *European Journal of Social Psychology, 18*, 443–455.

Grise-Owens, E., Vessels, J., & Owens, L. W. (2004). Organizing for change: One city's journey toward justice. In Y. C. Padilla (Ed.), *Gay and lesbian rights organizing: Community-based strategies* (pp. 1–15). Binghamton, NY: Harrington Park Press/The Haworth Press.

Groes, E., Jacobsen, H. J., Sloth, B., & Tranæs, T. (1998). Nash equilibrium with lower probabilities. *Theory and Decision, 44*, 37–66.

Gruber, H. E. (1990). The cooperative synthesis of disparate points of view. In I. Rock (Ed.), *The legacy of Solomon Asch: Essays in cognition and social psychology* (pp. 143–158). Hillsdale, NJ: Lawrence Erlbaum Associates, Inc.

Gruenfeld, D. H., & Hollingshead, A. B. (1993). Sociocognition in work groups: The evolution of group integrative complexity and its relation to task performance. *Small Group Research, 24*, 383–405.

Grusky, O., Bonacich, P., & Webster, C. (1995). The coalition structure of the four-person family. *Current Research in Social Psychology, 1*(3), 16–29.

Gudykunst, W. B., & Hammer, M. R. (1988). The influence of social identity and intimacy of interethnic relationships on uncertainty reduction processes. *Human Communication Research, 14*, 569–601.

Gudykunst, W. B., Nishida, T., Morisaki, S., & Ogawa, N. (1999). The influence of students' personal and social identities on their perceptions of interpersonal and intergroup encounters in Japan and the United States. *Japanese Journal of Social Psychology, 15*, 47–58.

Guimond, S. (2000). Group socialization and prejudice: The social transmission of intergroup attitudes and beliefs. *European Journal of Social Psychology, 30*, 335–354.

Guimond, S., & Dambrum, M. (2002). When prosperity breeds intergroup hostility: The effects of relative deprivation and relative gratification on prejudice. *Personality and Social Psychology Bulletin, 28*, 900–912.

Guimond, S., Dif, S., & Aupy, A. (2002). Social identity, relative group status and intergroup attitudes: When favorable outcomes change intergroup relations... for the worse. *European Journal of Social Psychology, 32*, 739–760.

Guinan, P. J., Cooprider, J. G., & Faraj, S. (1998). Enabling software development team performance during requirements definition: A behavioral versus technical approach. *Information Systems Research, 9*, 101–125.

Guinote, A., Aveiro, Mafalda S. S., & da Mata, S. C. (2002). Stereotypes and perception of group variability: The case of Angolans in Portugal [Esterotipos e percepcao de variabilidade de grupo: O caso dos angolanos residentes em Portugal]. *Psicologia: Revista da Associacao Portuguesa Psicologia, 16*(1), 199–208.

Gulati, R., & Westphal, J. D. (1999). Cooperative or controlling? The effects of CEO-board relations and the content of interlocks on the formation of joint ventures. *Administrative Science Quarterly, 44*, 473–506.

Gullickson, T. (1995). Review of *Psychology applied to work: An introduction to industrial and organizational psychology. PsycCRITIQUES, 40*, 177.

Gullickson, T. (1997). Review of *The art of bargaining. PsycCRITIQUES, 42*, 758.

Gundlach, M., Zivnuska, S., & Stoner, J. (2006). Understanding the relationship between individualism-collectivism and team performance through an integration of social identity theory and the social relations model. *Human Relations, 59*, 1603–1632.

Gunnthorsdottir, A., McCabe, K., & Smith, V. (2002). Using the Machiavellianism instrument to predict trustworthiness in a bargaining game. *Journal of Economic Psychology, 23*, 49–66.

Gurin, P., & Markus, H. (1988). Group identity: The psychological mechanisms of durable salience. *Revue Internationale de Psychologie Sociale, 1*, 257–274.

Gurin, P., Peng, T., Lopez, G., & Nagda, B. A. (1999). Context, identity, and intergroup relations. In D. A. Prentice & D. T. Miller (Eds.), *Cultural divides: Understanding and overcoming group conflict* (pp. 133–170). New York: Russell Sage Foundation.

Gurtner, A., Tschan, F., Semmer, N. K., & Nägele, C. (2007). Getting groups to develop good strategies: Effects of reflexivity interventions on team process, team performance, and shared mental models. *Organizational Behavior and Human Decision Processes, 102*, 127–142.

Gurven, M. (2004). Does market exposure affect economic game behavior? The Ultimatum game and the public goods game among the Tsimane' of Bolivia. In J. Henrich, R. Boyd, S. Bowles, C. Camerer, E. Fehr, & H. Gintis (Eds.), *Foundations of human sociality* (pp. 194–231). New York: Oxford University Press.

Güth, W. (2002). On the inconsistency of equilibrium refinement. *Theory and Decision, 53*, 371–392.

Güth, W., Huck, S., & Müller, W. (2001). The relevance of equal splits in Ultimatum Games. *Games and Economic Behavior, 37*, 161–169.

Güth, W., Kliemt, H., & Ockenfels, A. (2003). Fairness versus efficiency: An experimental study of (mutual) gift giving. *Journal of Economic Behavior and Organization, 50*, 465–475.

Güth, W., Ockenfels, P., & Ritzberger, K. (1995). On durable goods monoplies: An experimental study of intrapersonal price competition and price discrimination over time. *Journal of Economic Psychology, 16*, 247–274.

Güth, W., Ockenfels, P., & Wendel, M. (1997). Cooperation based on trust. An experimental investigation. *Journal of Economic Psychology, 18*, 15–43.

Güth, W., & Tietz, R. (1990). Ultimatum bargaining behavior: A survey and comparison of experimental results. *Journal of Economic Psychology, 11*, 417–449.

Güth, W., & Van Damme, E. (1998). Information, strategic behavior, and fairness in ultimatum bargaining: An experimental study. *Journal of Mathematical Psychology, 42*, 227–247.

Guthrie, J. P., & Hollensbe, E. C. (2004). Group Incentives and Performance: A Study of Spontaneous Goal Setting, Goal Choice and Commitment. *Journal of Management, 30*, 263–284.

Guzzo, R. A., & Dickson, M. W. (1996). Teams in organizations: Recent research on performance and effectiveness. *Annual Review of Psychology, 47*, 307–338.

Guzzo, R. A., Yost, P. R., Campbell, R. J., & Shea, G. P. (1993). Potency in groups: Articulating a construct. *British Journal of Social Psychology, 32*, 87–106.

Hackman, J. R. (1992). Group influences on individuals in organizations. In M. D. Dunnette & L. M. Hough (Eds.), *Handbook of industrial and organizational psychology* (2nd ed., Vol. 3, pp. 199–267). Palo Alto, CA: Consulting Psychologists Press, Inc.

Hackman, J. R. (1993). Teams, leaders, and organizations: New directions for crew-oriented flight training. In E. L. Wiener, B. G. Kanki, & R. L. Helmreich (Eds.), *Cockpit resource management* (pp. 47–69). San Diego, CA: Academic Press, Inc.

Hackman, J. R. (1998). Why teams don't work. In R. S. Tindale, L. Heath, J. Edwards, E. J. Posavac, F. B. Bryant, Y. Suarez-Balcazar, E. Henderson-King, & J. Myers (Eds.), *Theory and research on small groups* [Social psychological applications to social issues, Vol. 4] (pp. 245–267). New York: Plenum Press.

Haddock, G., Zanna, M. P., & Esses, V. M. (1994). Mood and the expression of intergroup attitudes: The moderating role of affect intensity. *European Journal of Social Psychology, 24,* 189–205.

Haenfler, R. (2004). Collective identity in the Straight Edge Movement: How diffuse movements foster commitment, encourage individualized participation, and promote cultural change. *Sociological Quarterly, 45,* 785–805.

Hagen, E. H. (2003). The bargaining model of depression. In P. Hammerstein (Ed.), *Genetic and cultural evolution of cooperation* (pp. 95–123). Cambridge, MA: MIT Press.

Hagen, E. H., & Bryant, G. A. (2003). Music and dance as a coalition signaling system. Human Nature, 14, 21–51.

Hahn, D.-W., & Hwang, S.-J. (1999). Test of similarity-attraction hypothesis in group performance situation. *Korean Journal of Social and Personality Psychology, 13*(1), 255–275.

Haines, E. L., & Jost, J. T. (2000). Placating the powerless: Effects of legitimate and illegitimate explanation on affect, memory, and stereotyping. *Social Justice Research, 13,* 219–236.

Hains, S. C., Hogg, M. A., & Duck, J. M. (1997). Self-categorization and leadership: Effects of group prototypicality and leader stereotypicality. *Personality and Social Psychology Bulletin, 23,* 1087–1099.

Haj-Yahia, M. M., & Edleson, J. L. (1994). Predicting the use of conflict resolution tactics among engaged Arab-Palestinian men in Israel. *Journal of Family Violence, 9,* 47–62.

Halabi, R., & Sonnenschein, N. (2004). The Jewish-Palestinian encounter in a time of crisis. *Journal of Social Issues, 60,* 373–387.

Hale, C. L., Bast, C., & Gordon, B. (1991). Communication within a dispute mediation: Interactants' perceptions of the process. *International Journal of Conflict Management, 2,* 139–158.

Halevy, N., Bornstein, G., & Sagiv, L. (2008). "In-group love" and "out-group hate" as motives for individual participation in intergroup conflict: A new game paradigm. *Psychological Science, 19,* 405–411.

Halfhill, T., Nielsen, T. M., Sundstrom, E., & Weilbaechear, A. (2005). Group personality composition and performance in military service teams. *Military Psychology, 17,* 41–54.

Hall, J. A., & Bernieri, F. J. (Eds.). (2001). *Interpersonal sensitivity: Theory and measurement.* Mahwah, NJ: Lawrence Erlbaum Associates Publishers.

Hall, N. R., & Crisp, R. J. (2005). Considering multiple criteria for social categorization can reduce intergroup bias. *Personality and Social Psychology Bulletin, 31,* 1435–1444.

Hall, N. R., & Crisp, R. J. (2008). Assimilation and contrast to group primes: The moderating role of ingroup identification. *Journal of Experimental Social Psychology, 44,* 344–353.

Halmiova, O., & Potasova, A. (1991). The effect of social communication and subjective measures of certainty-uncertainty.. *Studia Psychologica, 33,* 159–163.

Halpern, J. J., & Parks, J. M. (1996). Vive La Difference: Differences between males and females in process and outcomes in a low-conflict negotiation. *International Journal of Conflict Management, 7,* 45–70.

Hama, Y., Sinotsuka, H., & Toda, M. (1988). A study of utterances to opposing opinions: A preliminary investigation. *Japanese Journal of Experimental Social Psychology, 28,* 55–64.

Hamburger, Y. (1994). The contact hypothesis reconsidered: Effects of the atypical outgroup member on the outgroup stereotype. *Basic and Applied Social Psychology, 15,* 339–358.

Hamiache, G. (1999). A new axiomatization of the Owen value for games with coalition structures. *Mathematical Social Sciences, 37,* 281–305.

Hamilton, D. L., & Gifford, R. K. (1976). Illusory correlation in interpersonal perception: A cognitive basis of stereotypic judgments. *Journal of Experimental Social Psychology, 12,* 392–407.

Hamilton, D. L., & Hewstone, M. (2007). Conceptualising group perception: A 35–year evolution. In M. Hewstone, H. A. W. Schut, J. B. F. De Wit, K. Van Den Bos, & M. S. Stroebe (Eds.), *The scope of social psychology: Theory and applications* (pp. 87–106). New York: Psychology Press.

Hammerstein, P. (2003). Understanding cooperation: An interdisciplinary challenge. In P. Hammerstein (Ed.), *Genetic and cultural evolution of cooperation* (pp. 1–6). Cambridge, MA: MIT Press.

Hammock, G. S., & Richardson, D. R. (1992). Aggression as one response to conflict. *Journal of Applied Social Psychology, 22*, 298–311.

Hammock, Georgina S., Richardson, Deborah R., Pilkington, Constance J., & Utley, Mary. (1990). Measurement of conflict in social relationships. *Personality and Individual Differences, 11*, 577–583.

Hanany, E., Kilgour, D. M., & Gerchak, Y. (2007). Final-offer arbitration and risk aversion in bargaining. *Management Science, 53*, 1785–1792.

Handgraaf, M. J. J., Van Dijk, E., & De Cremer, D. (2003). Social Utility in Ultimatum Bargaining. *Social Justice Research, 16*, 263–283.

Handgraaf, M. J. J., Van Dijk, E., Wilke, H. A. M., & Vermunt, R. C. (2004). Evaluability of outcomes in ultimatum bargaining. *Organizational Behavior and Human Decision Processes, 95*, 97–106.

Hanley, J., Orbell, J., & Morikawa, T. (2003). Conflict, interpersonal assessment, and the evolution of cooperation: Simulation results. In E. Ostrom & J. Walker (Eds.), *Trust and reciprocity: Interdisciplinary lessons from experimental research* (pp. 170–206). New York: Russell Sage Foundation.

Hanover, J. M. B., & Cellar, D. F. (1998). Environmental factors and the effectiveness of workforce diversity training. *Human Resource Development Quarterly, 9*, 105–124.

Hansen, G. P. (1990). A cooperation-competition PK experiment with computerized horse races. *Journal of Parapsychology, 54*, 21–33.

Hardin, R. (1995). *One for all: The logic of group conflict.* Princeton, NJ: Princeton University Press.

Hare, A. P. (1962). *Handbook of small group research.* New York: Free Press of Glencoe.

Hare, A. P. (1967). Small group development in the relay assembly testroom. *Sociological Inquiry, 37*, 169–182.

Hare, A. P. (1976). *Handbook of small group research* (2nd ed.). New York: Free Press.

Hare, A. P. (1982). *Creativity in small groups.* Beverly Hills, CA: Sage.

Hare, A. P. (1983). A functional interpretation of interaction. In H. H. Blumberg, A. P. Hare, V. Kent, & M. F. Davies (Eds.), *Small groups and social interaction* (Vol. 2, pp. 429–447). Chichester and New York: John Wiley & Sons.

Hare, A. P. (1992). Moreno's sociometric study at the Hudson School for Girls. *Journal of Group Psychotherapy, Psychodrama and Sociometry, 45*(1), 24–39.

Hare, A. P. (1993). Small groups in organizations. In R. T. Golembiewski (Ed.), *Handbook of Organizational Behavior* (pp. 61–89). New York: Marcel Dekker.

Hare, A. P. (1994a). Group versus group. In: A. P. Hare, H. H. Blumberg, M. F. Davies, & M. V. Kent, *Small group research: A handbook* (pp. 271–281). Norwood, NJ: Ablex Publishing Corp.

Hare, A. P. (1994b). Individual versus group. In: A. P. Hare, H. H. Blumberg, M. F. Davies, & M. V. Kent, *Small group research: A handbook* (pp. 261–270). Norwood, NJ: Ablex Publishing Corp.

Hare, A. P. (2003). Roles, relationships, and groups in organizations: Some conclusions and recommendations. *Small Group Research, 34*, 123–154.

Hare, A. P., & Blumberg, H. H. (Eds.). (1979). *Liberation without violence: A third party approach.* London: Rex Collings.

Hare, A. P., Blumberg, H. H., Davies, M. F., & Kent, M. V. (1994). *Small group research: A handbook.* Norwood, NJ: Ablex.

Hare, A. P., Blumberg, H. H., Davies, M. F., & Kent, M. V. (1996). *Small groups: An introduction.* Westport, CT: Praeger/Greenwood Press.

Hare, A. P., Borgatta, E. F., & Bales, R. F. (Eds.). (1955). *Small groups: Studies in social interaction.* New York: Knopf.

Hare, A. P., Borgatta, E. F., & Bales, R. F. (Eds.). (1965). *Small groups: Studies in social interaction* (rev. ed.). New York: Knopf.

Hare, A. P., Hare, S. E., & Blumberg, H. H. (1998). Wishful thinking: Who has the least preferred co-worker? *Small Group Research, 29*, 419–435.

Hare, S. E., & Hare, A. P. (Eds.). (1996). *SYMLOG field theory: Organizational consultation, value differences, personality and social perception.* Westport, CT: Praeger.

Hare, S. E., & Hare, A. P. (2001). Role repertoires of members in an effective small group: A simulation. *International Journal of Action Methods, 54*, 91–115.

Hargadon, A. B. (1999). Group cognition and creativity in organizations. In R. Wageman (Ed.), *Research on managing groups and teams: Groups in context* (Vol. 2, pp. 137–155). San Diego, CA: Elsevier Science/JAI Press, 1999.

Hargadon, A., & Sutton, R. I. (1997). Technology brokering and innovation in a product development firm. *Administrative Science Quarterly, 42*, 716–749.

Hargie, O. D. W., Dickson, D. A., & Rainey, S. (2002). Religious difference, inter-group trust, attraction, and disclosure amongst young people in Northern Ireland. *International Journal of Adolescence and Youth, 10*, 213–235.

Harmon, J. (1998). Electronic meetings and intense group conflict: Effects of a policy-modeling performance support system and an audio communication support system on satisfaction and agreement. *Group Decision and Negotiation, 7*, 131–155.

Harmon-Jones, E., Greenberg, J., Solomon, S., & Simon, L. (1996). The effects of mortality salience on intergroup bias between minimal groups. *European Journal of Social Psychology, 26*, 677–681.

Harms, P. D., Roberts, B. W., & Wood, D. (2007). Who shall lead? An integrative personality approach to the study of the antecedents of status in informal social organizations. *Journal of Research in Personality, 41*, 689–699.

Harris, A. C., & Madden, G. J. (2002). Delay discounting and performance on the prisoner's dilemma game. *Psychological Record, 52*, 429–440.

Harris, E. G., & Mowen, J. C. (2001). The influence of cardinal-, central-, and surface-level personality traits on consumers' bargaining and complaint intentions. *Psychology and Marketing, 18*, 1155–1185.

Harris, I. M., & Shuster, A. L. (2006). *Global directory of peace studies and conflict resolution programs* (7th ed.). San Francisco, CA: Peace and Justice Studies Association (PJSA) and International Peace Research Association Foundation (IPRAF).

Harris, K. L., & Carnevale, P. J. (1990). Chilling and hastening: The influence of third-party power and interests on negotiation. *Organizational Behavior and Human Decision Processes, 47*, 138–160.

Harris, P., Middleton, W., & Joiner, R. (2000). The typical student as an in-group member: Eliminating optimistic bias by reducing social distance. *European Journal of Social Psychology, 30*, 235–253.

Harrison, A. A., & Connors, M. M. (1984). Groups in exotic environments. *Advances in Experimental Social Psychology, 18*, 49–87.

Harrison, D. A., Mohammed, S., McGrath, J. E., Florey, A. T., & Vanderstoep, S. W. (2003). Time matters in team performance: Effects of member familiarity, entrainment and task discontinuity on speed and quality. *Personnel Psychology, 56*, 633–669.

Harrison, D. A., Price, K. H., & Bell, M. P. (1998). Beyond relational demography: Time and the effects of surface- and deep-level diversity on work group cohesion. *Academy of Management Journal, 41*, 96–107.

Harrison, D. A., Price, K. H., Gavin, J. H., & Florey, A. T. (2002). Time, teams, and task performance: Changing effects of diversity on group functioning. *Academy of Management Journal, 45*, 1029–1045.

Harrison, J. R., & Bazerman, M. H. (1995). Regression to the mean, expectation inflation, and the winner's curse in organizational contexts. In R. M. Kramer & D. M. Messick (Eds.), *Negotiation as a social process: New trends in theory and research* (pp. 69–94). Thousand Oaks, CA: Sage Publications, Inc.

Harrison, Y., & Horne, J. A. (1999). One night of sleep loss impairs innovative thinking and flexible decision making. *Organizational Behavior and Human Decision Processes, 78*, 128–145.

Hart, J. W., Karau, S. J., Stasson, M. F., & Kerr, N. A. (2004). Achievement motivation, expected coworker performance, and collective task motivation: Working hard or hardly working? *Journal of Applied Social Psychology, 34*, 984–1000.

Hart, S., & Mas-Colell, A. (2003). Regret-based continuous-time dynamics. *Games and Economic Behavior, 45*, 375–394.

Hart, S. M. (2002). The pay equity bargaining process in Newfoundland: Understanding cooperation and conflict by incorporating gender and class. *Gender, Work and Organization, 9*, 355–371.

Hartstone, M., & Augoustinos, M. (1995). The minimal group paradigm: Categorization into two versus three groups. *European Journal of Social Psychology, 25*, 179–193.

Harwood, J., Giles, H., & Ryan, E. B. (1995). Aging, communication, and intergroup theory: Social identity and intergenerational communication. In J. F. Nussbaum & J. Coupland (Eds.), *Handbook of communication and aging research* (pp. 133–159). Mahwah, NJ: Lawrence Erlbaum Associates, Inc.

Hashimoto, T. (1995). Interpersonal conflicts as stressors: A perspective for stress reduction strategies. *Japanese Journal of Experimental Social Psychology, 35*, 185–193.

Haslam, N., Bastian, B., Bain, P., & Kashima, Y. (2006). Psychological essentialism, Implicit theories, and intergroup relations. *Group Processes and Intergroup Relations, 9*, 63–76.

Haslam, S. A., Jetten, J., O'Brien, A., & Jacobs, E. (2004). Social identity, social influence and reactions to potentially stressful tasks: Support for the self-categorization model of stress. *Stress and Health: Journal of the International Society for the Investigation of Stress, 20*, 3–9.

Haslam, S. A., McGarty, C., & Brown, P. M. (1996). The search for differentiated meaning is a precursor to illusory correlation. *Personality and Social Psychology Bulletin, 22*, 611–619.

Haslam, S. A., McGarty, C., Brown, P. M., Eggins, R. A., Morrison, B. E., & Reynolds, K. J. (1998). Inspecting the emperor's clothes: Evidence that random selection of leaders can enhance group performance. *Group Dynamics, 2*, 168–184.

Haslam, S. A., McGarty, C., Oakes, P. J., & Turner, J. C. (1993). Social comparative context and illusory correlation: Testing between ingroup bias and social identity models of stereotype formation. *Australian Journal of Psychology, 45*, 97–101.

Haslam, S. A., McGarty, C., & Turner, J. C. (1996). Salient group memberships and persuasion: The role of social identity in the validation of beliefs. In J. L. Nye & A. M. Brower (Eds.), *What's social about social cognition? Research on socially shared cognition in small groups* (pp. 29–57). Thousand Oaks, CA: Sage.

Haslam, S. A., & Oakes, P. J. (1995). How context-independent is the outgroup homogeneity effect? A response to Bartsch and Judd. *European Journal of Social Psychology, 12*, 469–475.

Haslam, S. A., Oakes, P. J., McGarty, C., Turner, J. C., Reynolds, K. J., & Eggins, R. A. (1996). Stereotyping and social-influence: The mediation of stereotype applicability and sharedness by the views of in-group and out-group members. *British Journal of Social Psychology, 35*, 369–397.

Haslam, S. A., Oakes, P. J., Turner, J. C., & McGarty, C. (1995). Social categorization and group homogeneity: Changes in the perceived applicability of stereotype content as a function of comparative context and trait favourableness. *British Journal of Social Psychology, 34*, 139–160.

Haslam, S. A., & Platow, M. J. (2001). The link between leadership and followership: How affirming social identity translates vision into action. *Personality and Social Psychology Bulletin, 27*, 1469–1479.

Haslam, S. A., Platow, M. J., Turner, J. C., Reynolds, K. J., McGarty, C., Oakes, P. J., Johnson, S., Ryan, M. K., & Veenstra, K. (2001). Social identity and the romance of leadership: The importance of being seen to be "doing it for us." *Group Processes and Intergroup Relations, 4*, 191–205.

Haslam, S. A., & Reicher, S. (2006). Stressing the group: Social identity and the unfolding dynamics of responses to stress. *Journal of Applied Psychology, 91*, 1037–1052.

Haslam, S. A., Turner, J. C., Oakes, P. J., McGarty, C., & Reynolds, K. J. (1998). The group as a basis for emergent stereotype consensus. In W. Stroebe & M. Hewstone (Eds.), *European Review of Social Psychology* (Vol. 8, pp. 203–239). Chichester, England: John Wiley & Sons, Inc.

Haslam, S. A., Turner, J. C., Oaks, P. J., Reynolds, K. J., Eggins, R. A., Nolan, M., & Tweedie, J. (1998). When do stereotypes become really consensual? Investigating the group-based dynamics of the concensualization process. *European Journal of Social Psychology, 28*, 755–776.

Haslam, S. A., Wegge, J., & Postmes, T. (2009). Are we on a learning curve or a treadmill? The benefits of participative group goal setting become apparent as tasks become increasingly challenging over time. *European Journal of Social Psychology, 39*, 430–446.

Hassebrauck, M. (1991). Emotionale Konsequenzen dyadischer Unausgewogenheit: Eine experimentelle Untersuchung zum Einflu[s von Fehlattributionen [Emotional consequences of dyadic inequity: An experiment testing the influence of misattributions]. *Zeitschrift fuer Sozialpsychologie, 22*, 181–192.

Hassebrauck, M. (1995). Kognitionen von Beziehungsqualitaet: Eine Prototypenanalyse [Cognitions of relationship quality: A prototype analysis]. *Zeitschrift fuer Sozialpsychologie, 26*, 160–172.

Hatano, G., & Inagaki, K. (1991). Sharing cognition through collective comprehension activity. In L. B. Resnick, J. M. Levine, & S. D. Teasley (Eds.), *Perspectives on socially shared cognition* (pp. 331–348). Washington, DC: American Psychological Association.

Hauenstein, N. M. A., McGonigle, T., & Flinder, S. W. (2001). A meta-analysis of the relationship between procedural justice and distributive justice: Implications for justice research. *Employee Responsibilities and Rights Journal, 13*, 39–56.

Haugh, H. M., & McKee, L. (2003). "It's just like a family"–shared values in the family firm. *Community, Work and Family, 6*, 141–158.

Hauk, E. (2003). Multiple Prisoner's Dilemmma games with(out) an outside option: An experimental study. *Theory and Decision, 54*, 207–229.

Hauk, E., & Nagel, R. (2001). Choice of partners in multiple two-person prisoner's dilemma games: An experimental study. *Journal of Conflict Resolution, 45*, 770–793.

Hayes, B. C., McAllister, I., & Dowds, L. (2007). Integrated education, intergroup relations, and political identities in Northern Ireland. *Social Problems, 54*, 454–482.

Hays, C. E., Hays, S. P., DeVille, J. O., & Mulhall, P. F. (2000). Capacity for effectiveness: The relationship between coalition structure and community impact. *Evaluation and Program Planning, 23*, 373–379.

Healy, P., & Noussair, C. (2004). Bidding behavior in the price is right game: An experimental study. *Journal of Economic Behavior and Organization, 54*, 231–247.

Hebdon, R., & Stern, R. (2003). Do public-sector strike bans really prevent conflict? *Industrial Relations: A Journal of Economy and Society, 42*, 493–512.

Hecht, M. L., Jackson, R. L., II, & Pitts, M. J. (2005). Culture: Intersections of intergroup and identity theories. In J. Harwood & H. Giles (Eds.), *Intergroup communication: Multiple perspectives* (pp. 21–42). New York: Peter Lang Publishing.

Hecht, T. D., Allen, N. J., Klammer, J. D., & Kelly, E. C. (2002). Group beliefs, ability, and performance: The potency of group potency. *Group Dynamics: Theory, Research, and Practice, 6*, 143–152.

Hegtvedt, K. A., Clay-Warner, J., & Ferrigno, E. D. (2002). Reactions to injustice: Factors affecting workers' resentment toward family-friendly policies. *Social Psychology Quarterly, 65*, 386–400.

Hegtvedt, K. A., & Killian, C. (1999). Fairness and emotions: Reactions to the process and outcomes of negotiations. *Social Forces, 78*, 269–303.

Heifetz, A., & Mongin, P. (2001). Probability logic for Type Spaces. *Games and Economic Behavior, 35*, 31–53.

Heifetz, A., & Segev, E. (2004). The evolutionary role of toughness in bargaining. *Games and Economic Behavior, 49*, 117–134.

Helbing, D. (1996). A stochastic behavioral model and a "microscopic" foundation of evolutionary game theory. *Theory and Decision, 40*, 149–179.

Helga, T. (2002). Motivációs tényezok hatása a sztereotip tulajdonságok odaítélésére [Motivational factors in stereotype-attribution process]. *Erdélyi Pszichológiai Szemle, 3*, 425–454.

Helson, H. (1964). *Adaptation level theory: An experimental and systematic approach to behavior.* New York: Harper.

Hemesath, M., & Pomponio, X. (1998). Cooperation and culture: Students from China and the United States in a prisoner's dilemma. *Cross-Cultural Research: The Journal of Comparative Social Science, 32*, 171–184.

Hemmasi, M., & Graf, L. A. (1992). Managerial skills acquisition: A case for using business policy simulations. *Simulation and Gaming, 23*, 298–310.

Hemmasi, M., Graf, L. A., & Kellogg, C. E. (1989). A comparison of the performance, behaviors, and analysis strategies of MBA versus BBA students in a simulation environment. *Simulation and Games, 20*, 15–30.

Hendrix, W. H., Robbins, T., Miller, J., & Summers, T. P. (1998). Effects of procedural and distributive justice on factors predictive of turnover. *Journal of Social Behavior and Personality, 13*, 611–632.

Hennessy, J., & West, M. A. (1999). Intergroup behavior in organizations: A field test of social identity theory. *Small Group Research, 30*, 361–382.

Hennig-Schmidt, H., Li, Z.-Y., & Yang, C. (2008). Why people reject advantageous offers-Non-monotonic strategies in ultimatum bargaining Evaluating a video experiment run in PR China. *Journal of Economic Behavior and Organization, 65*, 373–384.

Henretta, J. C. (1988). Conflict and cooperation among age strata. In J. E. Birren, V. L. Bengtson, & D. E. Deutschman (Eds.), *Emergent theories of aging* (pp. 385–404). New York: Springer Publishing Co.

Henrich, J., Boyd, R., Bowles, S., Camerer, C., Fehr, E., Gintis, H., McElreath, R., Alvard, M., Barr, A., Ensminger, J., Henrich, N. S., Hill, K., Gil-White, F., Gurven, M., Marlowe, F. W., Patton, J. Q., & Tracer, D. (2005). "Economic man" in cross-cultural perspective: Behavioral experiments in 15 small-scale societies. *Behavioral and Brain Sciences, 28*, 795–855.

Henrich, J., & Henrich, N. (2006). Culture, evolution and the puzzle of human cooperation. *Cognitive Systems Research, 7*, 220–245.

Henrich, J., & Smith, N. (2004). Comparative experimental evidence from Machiguenga, Mapuche, Huinca, and American populations. In J. Henrich, R. Boyd, S. Bowles, C. Camerer, E. Fehr, & H. Gintis (Eds.), *Foundations of human sociality* (pp. 126–167). New York: Oxford University Press.

Henry, P. J., & Hardin, C. D. (2006). The contact hypothesis revisited: Status bias in the reduction of implicit prejudice in the United States and Lebanon. *Psychological Science, 17*, 862–868.

Herek, Gregory M., & Capitanio, John P. (1996). "Some of my best friends": Intergroup contact, concealable stigma, and heterosexuals' attitudes toward gay men and lesbians. *Personality and Social Psychology Bulletin, 22*, 412–424.

Herrick, N. (1990). *Joint management and employee participation: Labor and management at the crossroads.* San Francisco, CA: Jossey-Bass.

Hertel, G., Aarts, H., & Zeelenberg, M. (2002). What do you think is "fair"?: Effects of ingroup norms and outcome control on fairness judgments. *European Journal of Social Psychology, 32*, 327–341.

Hertel, G., Deter, C., & Konradt, U. (2003). Motivation gains in computer-supported groups. *Journal of Applied Social Psychology, 33*, 2080–2105.

Hertel, G., & Fiedler, K. (1998). Fair and dependent versus egoistic and free: Effects of semantic and evaluative priming on the "Ring Measure of Social Values". *European Journal of Social Psychology, 28*, 49–70.

Hertel, G., Kerr, N. L., & Messé, L. A. (2000). Motivation gains in performance groups: Paradigmatic and theoretical developments on the Köhler effect. *Journal of Personality and Social Psychology, 79*, 580–601.

Hertz-Lazarowitz, R., & Miller, N. (Eds.). (1995). *Interaction in cooperative groups: The theoretical anatomy of group learning.* New York: Cambridge University Press.

Herzog, S. (2004). Plea bargaining practices: Less covert, more public support? *Crime and Delinquency, 50*, 590–614.

Heuer, L., & Penrod, S. (1994). Predicting the outcomes of disputes: Consequences for disputant reactions to procedures and outcomes. *Journal of Applied Social Psychology, 24*, 260–283.

Hewstone, M. (1996). Contact and categorization: Social psychological interventions to change intergroup relations. In C. N. Macrae, C. Stangor, & M. Hewstone (Eds.), *Stereotypes and stereotyping* (pp. 323–368). New York: Guilford Press.

Hewstone, M. (2003). Intergroup contact: Panacea for prejudice? *The Psychologist, 16*, 352–355.

Hewstone, M., & Brown, R. (Eds.). (1986). *Contact and conflict in intergroup encounters.* Cambridge, MA: Basil Blackwell.

Hewstone, M. Cairns, E., Voci, A., Paolini, S., McLernon, F., Crisp, R. J., Niens, U., & Craig, J. (2005). Intergroup contact in a divided society: Challenging segregation in Northern Ireland. In D. Abrams, M. A. Hogg, & J. M. Marques (Eds.), *The social psychology of inclusion and exclusion* (pp. 265–292). New York: Psychology Press.

Hewstone, M., Carpenter, J., Franklyn-Stokes, A., & Routh, D. (1994). Intergroup contact between professional groups: Two evaluation studies. *Journal of Community and Applied Social Psychology, 4*, 347–363.

Hewstone, M., Islam, M. R., & Judd, C. M. (1993). Models of crossed categorization and intergroup relations. *Journal of Personality and Social Psychology, 64*, 779–793.

Hewstone, M., Kenworthy, J. B., Cairns, E., Tausch, N., Hughes, J., Tam, T., Voci, A., von Hecker, U., & Pinder, C. (2008). Stepping stones to reconciliation in Northern Ireland: Intergroup contact, forgiveness, and trust. In A. Nadler, T. E. Malloy, & J. D. Fisher (Eds.), *The social psychology of intergroup reconciliation* (pp. 199–226). New York: Oxford University Press.

Hidaka, Y., & Yamaguchi, S. (1997). Effects of the perception of intergroup difference between ingroup and outgroup upon ingroup consensus estimation. *Japanese Journal of Experimental Social Psychology, 37*, 165–176.

Higgins, E. T. (1997). Beyond pleasure and pain. *American Psychologist, 52*, 1280–1300.

Higgins, E. T., & Sorrentino, R. M. (1990). *Handbook of motivation and cognition. Vol. 2: Foundations of social behavior.* New York: Guilford Press.

Hill, J. L., & Lance, C. G. (2002). Debriefing stress. *Simulation and Gaming, 33*, 490–503.

Hill, K., & Gurven, M. (2004). Economic experiments to examine fairness and cooperation among the Ache Indians of Paraguay. In J. Henrich, R. Boyd, S. Bowles, C. Camerer, E. Fehr, & H. Gintis (Eds.), *Foundations of human sociality* (pp. 382–412). New York: Oxford University Press.

Hill, M. (1999). Barter: Ethical considerations in psychotherapy. *Women and Therapy, 22*, 81–91.

Hilton, D. J. (1995). The social context of reasoning: Conversational inference and rational judgment. *Psychological Bulletin, 118*, 248–271.

Hilty, J. A., & Carnevale, P. J. (1993). Black-hat/white-hat strategy in bilateral negotiation. *Organizational Behavior and Human Decision Processes, 55*, 444–469.

Hine, D. W., & Gifford, R. (1996). Individual restraint and group efficiency in commons dilemmas: The effects of two types of environmental uncertainty. *Journal of Applied Social Psychology, 26*, 993–1009.

Hine, D. W., & Gifford, R. (1997). What harvesters really think about in commons dilemma simulations: A grounded theory analysis. *Canadian Journal of Behavioural Science/Revue canadienne des sciences du comportement, 29*, 180–194.

Hinkle, S., Taylor, L. A., Fox-Cardamone, D. L., & Crook, K. F. (1989). Intragroup identification and intergroup differentiation: A multicomponent approach. *British Journal of Social Psychology, 28*, 305–317.

Hinkle, S., Taylor, L. A., Fox-Cardamone, L., & Ely, P. G. (1998). Social identity and aspects of social creativity: Shifting to new dimensions of intergroup comparison. In S. Worchel, J. F. Morales, D. Paez, & J.-C. Deschamps (Eds.), *Social identity: International perspectives* (pp. 166–179). London: Sage Publications, Inc.

Hinsz, V. B. (1992). Social influences on the goal choices of group members. *Journal of Applied Social Psychology, 22*, 1297–1317.

Hinsz, V. B. (1995a). Goal-setting by groups performing an additive task: A comparison with individual goal-setting. *Journal of Applied Social Psychology, 25*, 965–990.

Hinsz, V. B. (1995b). Group and individual decision-making for task-performance goals-processes in the establishment of goals in groups. *Journal of Applied Social Psychology, 25*, 353–370.

Hinsz, V. B. (1995c). Mental models of groups as social system: Considerations of specification and assessment. *Small Group Research, 26*, 200–233.

Hinsz, V. B. (2004). Metacognition and mental models in groups: An illustration with metamemory of group recognition memory. In E. Salas & S. M. Fiore (Eds.), *Team cognition: Understanding the factors that drive process and performance* (pp. 33–58). Washington, DC: American Psychological Association.

Hinsz, V. B., & Nickell, G. S. (2004). Positive reactions to working in groups in a study of group and individual goal decision making. *Group Dynamics: Theory, Research,* and Practice, *8*, 253–264.

Ho, S. (2002). Evolutionary stable coalition structure. *Nonlinear Dynamics, Psychology,* and Life Sciences, *6*, 159–172.

Hobman, E. V., Bordia, P., Irmer, B., & Chang, A. (2002). The expression of conflict in computer-mediated and face-to-face groups. *Small Group Research, 33*, 439–465.

Hochwarter, W. A., Kacmar, C., Perrewé, P. L., & Johnson, D. (2003). Perceived organizational support as a mediator of the relationship between politics perceptions and work outcomes. *Journal of Vocational Behavior, 63*, 438–456.

Hodson, G., Dovidio, J. F., & Esses, V. M. (2003). Ingroup identification as a moderator of positive-negative asymmetry in social discrimination. *European Journal of Social Psychology, 33*, 215–233.

Hodson, G., & Sorrentino, R. M. (1997). Groupthink and uncertainty orientation: Personality differences in reactivity to the group situation. *Group Dynamics, 1*, 144–155.

Hodson, G., & Sorrentino, R. M. (2001). Just who favors in in-group? Personality differences in reactions to uncertainty in the minimal group paradigm. *Group Dynamics: Theory, Research,* and Practice, 5, 92–101.

Hoegl, M., & Gemuenden, H. G. (2001). Teamwork quality and the success of innovative projects: A theoretical concept and empirical evidence. *Organization Science, 12*, 435–449.

Hoegl, M., & Parboteeah, K. P. (2003). Goal setting and team performance in innovative projects: On the moderating role of teamwork quality. *Small Group Research, 34*, 3–19.

Hoffman, A. J., Gillespie, J. J., Moore, D. A., Wade-Benzoni, K. A., Thompson, L. L., & Bazerman, M. H. (1999). A mixed-motive perspective on the economics versus environmental debate. *American Behavioral Scientist, 42*, 1254–1276.

Hoffman, R. (1999). The independent localisations of interaction and learning in the repeated prisoner's dilemma. *Theory and Decision, 47*, 57–72.

Hofmann, D. A., Morgeson, F. P., & Gerras, S. J. (2003). Climate as a moderator of the relationship between leader-member exchange and content specific citizenship: Safety climate as an exemplar. *Journal of Applied Psychology, 88*, 170–178.

Hogan, D. B. (2005). Leadership: Toward and integration of classical and current theories. In A. P. Hare, E. Sjovold, H. G. Baker, and J. Powers (Eds.), *Analysis of social interaction systems: SYMLOG research and applications* (pp. 68–131). Lanham, MD: University Press of America.

Hogg, M. A. (1996). Social identity, self-categorization, and the small group. In E. H. Witte & J. H. Davis (Eds.), *Understanding group behavior, Vol. 2: Small group processes and interpersonal relations. Understanding group behavior* (pp. 227–253). Mahwah, NJ: Lawrence Erlbaum Associates, Inc.

Hogg, M. A. (2001). Self-categorization and subjective uncertainty resolution: Cognitive and motivational facets of social identity and group membership. In J. P. Forgas, K. D. Williams, & L. Wheeler (Eds.), *The social mind: Cognitive and motivational aspects of interpersonal behavior* (pp. 323–349). New York: Cambridge University Press.

Hogg, M. A. (2004). Social categorization, depersonalization, and group behavior. In M. B. Brewer & M. Hewstone (Eds.), *Self and social identity* (pp. 203–231). Malden: Blackwell Publishing.

Hogg, M. A. (2005a). All animals are equal but some animals are more equal than others: Social identity and marginal membership. In K. D. Williams, J. P. Forgas, & W. von Hippel (Eds.),

*The social outcast: Ostracism, social exclusion, rejection, and bullying* (pp. 243–261). New York: Psychology Press.

Hogg, M. A. (2005b). Social identity and leadership. In D. M. Messick & R. M. Kramer (Eds.), *The psychology of leadership: New perspectives and research* (pp. 53–80). Mahwah, NJ: Lawrence Erlbaum Associates Publishers.

Hogg, M. A. (2006). Social Identity Theory. In P. J. Burke (Ed.), *Contemporary social psychological theories* (pp. 111–136). Stanford, CA; Stanford University Press.

Hogg, M. A. (2007). Uncertainty-identity theory. In M. P. Zanna (Ed.), *Advances in experimental social psychology* (Vol. 39, pp. 69–126). San Diego, CA: Elsevier Academic Press, 2007.

Hogg, M. A. (2008). Social identity processes and the empowerment of followers. In R. E. Riggio, I. Chaleff, & J. Lipman-Blumen (Eds.), *The art of followership: How great followers create great leaders and organizations* (pp. 267–276). San Francisco: Jossey-Bass.

Hogg, M. A., & Abrams, D. (1988). *Social identifications: A social psychology of intergroup relations and group processes*. London: Routledge.

Hogg, M. A., & Abrams, D. (1993). Towards a single-process uncertainty-reduction model of social motivation in groups. In M. A. Hogg & D. Abrams (Eds.), *Group motivation: Social psychological perspectives* (pp. 173–190). London: Harvester Wheatsheaf.

Hogg, M. A., & Abrams, D. (Eds.). (2001). *Intergroup relations: Essential readings*. New York: Psychology Press.

Hogg, M. A., Abrams, D., Otten, S., & Hinkle, S. (2004). The social identity perspective: Intergroup relations, self-conception, and small groups. *Small Group Research, 35*, 246–276.

Hogg, M. A., Fielding, K. S., Johnson, D., Masser, B., Russell, E., & Svensson, A. (2006). Demographic category membership and leadership in small groups: A social identity analysis. *Leadership Quarterly, 17*, 335–350.

Hogg, M. A., & Hains, S. C. (1996). Intergroup relations and group solidarity: Effects of group identification and social beliefs on depersonalized attraction. *Journal of Personality and Social Psychology, 70*, 295–309.

Hogg, M. A., & Hains, S. C. (2001). Intergroup relations and group solidarity: Effects of group identification and social beliefs on depersonalized attraction. In M. A. Hogg & D. Abrams (Eds.), *Intergroup relations: Essential readings* (pp. 110–128). New York: Psychology Press.

Hogg, M. A., Hains, S. C., & Mason, I. (1998). Identification and leadership in small groups: Salience, frame of reference, and leader stereotypicality effects on leader evaluations. *Journal of Personality and Social Psychology, 75*, 1248–1263.

Hogg, M. A., & Hardie, E. A. (1992). Prototypicality, conformity and depersonalized attraction: A self-categorization analysis of group cohesiveness. *British Journal of Social Psychology, 31*, 41–56.

Hogg, M. A., Hardie, E. A., & Reynolds, K. J. (1995). Prototypical similarity, self-categorization, and depersonalized attraction: A perspective on group cohesiveness. *European Journal of Social Psychology, 25*, 159–177.

Hogg, M. A., & Mullin, B. A. (1999). Joining groups to reduce uncertainty: Subjective uncertainty reduction and group identification. In D. Abrams & M. A. Hogg (Eds.), *Social identity and social cognition* (pp. 249–279). Malden: Blackwell Publishing.

Hogg, M. A., & Sunderland, J. (1991). Self-esteem and intergroup discrimination in the minimal group paradigm. *British Journal of Social Psychology, 30*, 51–62.

Hogg, M. A., Terry, D. J., & White, K. M. (1995). A tale of two theories: A critical comparison of identity theory with social identity theory. *Social Psychology Quarterly, 58*, 255–269.

Hogg, M. A., & Tindale, R. S. (2005). Social identity, influence, and communication in small groups. In J. Harwood & H. Giles (Eds.), *Intergroup communication: Multiple perspectives* (pp. 141–164). New York: Peter Lang Publishing.

Hogg, M. A., & Van Knippenberg, D. (2003). Social Identity and Leadership Processes in Groups. In M. P. Zanna (Ed.), *Advances in experimental social psychology* (Vol. 35, pp. 1–52). San Diego, CA: Elsevier Academic Press, 2003.

Hogg, M. A., & Williams, K. D. (2000). From I to we: Social identity and the collective self. *Group Dynamics: Theory, Research*, and Practice, *4*, 81–97.

Hogue, M. B., Yoder, J. D., & Ludwig, J. (2002). Increasing initial leadership effectiveness: Assisting both women and men. *Sex Roles, 46,* 377–384.

Hollander, E. P. (1958). Conformity, status, and idiosyncrasy credit. *Psychological Review, 65,* 117–127.

Hollander, E. P. (1992). The essential interdependence of leadership and followership. *Current Directions in Psychological Science, 1,* 71–75.

Hollenbeck, J. R., Ilgen, D. R., Phillips, J. M., & Hedlund, J. (1994). Decision risk in dynamic two-stage contexts: Beyond the status quo. *Journal of Applied Psychology, 79,* 592–598.

Holler, M. J., Host, V., & Kristensen, K. (1992). Decisions on strategic markets: An experimental study. *Scandinavian Journal of Management, 8,* 133–146.

Holler, M. J., & Napel, S. (2004). Monotonicity of power and power measures. *Theory and Decision, 56,* 93–111.

Hollingshead, A. B. (1998). Group and individual training: The impact of practice on performance. *Small Group Research, 29,* 254–280.

Hollingshead, A. B., McGrath, J. E., & O'Connor, K. M. (1993). Group task-performance and communication technology: A longitudinal study of computer-mediated versus face-to-face work groups. *Small Group Research, 24,* 307–333.

Hollingshead, A. B., & Poole, M. S. (2004). Interdisciplinary theoretical perspectives of small groups part II. *Small Group Research, 35,* 243–245.

Holm, H. J. (2000). Gender-based focal points. *Games and Economic Behavior, 32,* 292–314.

Holmes, D. (Ed.). (1997). *Virtual politics: Identity and community in cyberspace.* London: Sage Publications, Inc.

Holmes, J. G. (2000). Social relationships: The nature and function of relational schemas. *European Journal of Social Psychology, 30,* 447–495.

Holmes, J. G. (2002). Interpersonal expectations as the building blocks of social cognition: An interdependence theory perspective. *Personal Relationships, 9,* 1–26.

Holmes, M. E. (1992). Phase structures in negotiation. In L. L. Putnam & M. E. Roloff (Eds.), *Communication and negotiation* (pp. 83–105). Newbury Park, CA: Sage Publications, Inc.

Holsapple, C. E, & Luo, W. H. (1999). Effects of experience-based work patterns in a GSS environment. *Group Decision and Negotiation, 8,* 305–324.

Holtz, R. (2004). Group Cohesion, Attitude Projection, and Opinion Certainty: Beyond Interaction. *Group Dynamics: Theory, Research, and Practice, 8,* 112–125.

Holtz, R., & Miller, N. (2001). Intergroup competition, attitudinal projection, and opinion certainty: Capitalizing on conflict. *Group Processes and Intergroup Relations, 4,* 61–73.

Homans, G. C. (1950). *The human group.* Harcourt, Brace/Random House.

Homans, G. C. (1961). *Social behavior: Its elementary forms.* New York : Harcourt, Brace and World.

Honeycutt, J. M., & Cantrill, J. G. (2001). *Cognition, communication, and romantic relationships.* Mahwah, NJ: Lawrence Erlbaum Associates Publishers.

Hong, O. P., & Harrod, W. J. (1988). The role of reasons in the ingroup bias phenomenon. *European Journal of Social Psychology, 18,* 537–545.

Hong, Y.-y., Chan, G., Chiu, C.-y., Wong, R. Y. M., Hansen, I. G., Lee, S.-l., Tong, Y.-y., & Fu, H.-y. (2003). How are social identities linked to self-conception and intergroup orientation? The moderating effect of implicit theories. *Journal of Personality and Social Psychology, 85,* 1147–1160.

Hong, Y.-y., Coleman, J., Chan, G., Wong, R. Y. M., Chiu, C.-y., Hansen, I. G., Lee, S.-l., Tong, Y.-y., & Fu, H.-y. (2004). Predicting intergroup bias: The interactive effects of implicit theory and social identity. *Personality and Social Psychology Bulletin, 30,* 1035–1047.

Hooper, Simon, & Hannafin, Michael J. (1991). The effects of group composition on achievement, interaction, and learning efficiency during computer-based cooperative instruction. *Educational Technology Research and Development. 39*(3), 27–40.

Hopkins, N., & Rae, C. (2001). Intergroup differentiation: Stereotyping as a function of status hierarchy. *Journal of Social Psychology, 141,* 323–333.

Hornby, T.-A., & Saunders, D. (1989). Using the SIMPLEX game format to examine current issues in the life of applied psychologists. *Educational and Child Psychology, 6*(3, Pt 1), 75–94.

Hornsey, M. J. (2003). Linking Superiority Bias in the Interpersonal and Intergroup Domains. *Journal of Social Psychology, 143*, 479–491.

Hornsey, M. J. (2008). Social identity theory and self-categorization theory: A historical review. *Social and Personality Psychology Compass, 2*, 204–222.

Hornsey, M. J., Blackwood, L., Louis, W., Fielding, K., Mavor, K., Morton, T., O'Brien, A., Paasonen, K.-E., Smith, J., & White, K. M. (2006). Why do people engage in collective action? Revisiting the role of perceived effectiveness. *Journal of Applied Social Psychology, 36*, 1701–1722.

Hornsey, M. J., & Hogg, M. A. (1999). Subgroup differentiation as a response to an overly-inclusive group: A test of optimal distinctiveness theory. *European Journal of Social Psychology, 29*, 543–550.

Hornsey, M. J., & Hogg, M. A. (2000). Subgroup relations: A comparison of mutual intergroup differentiation and common ingroup identity models of prejudice reduction. *Personality and Social Psychology Bulletin, 26*, 242–256.

Hornsey, M. J., & Imani, A. (2004). Criticizing groups from the inside and the outside: An identity perspective on the intergroup sensitivity effect. *Personality and Social Psychology Bulletin, 30*, 365–383.

Hornsey, M. J., & Jetten, J. (2003). Not being what you claim to be: Impostors as sources of group threat. *European Journal of Social Psychology, 33*, 639–657.

Hornsey, M. J., & Jetten, J. (2004). The individual within the group: Balancing the need to belong with the need to be different. *Personality and Social Psychology Review, 8*, 248–264.

Hornsey, M. J, Spears, R., Cremers, I., & Hogg, M. A. (2003). Relations between high and low power groups: The importance of legitimacy. *Personality and Social Psychology Bulletin, 29*, 216–227.

Hornsey, M. J., Trembath, M., & Gunthorpe, S. (2004). "You can criticize because you care": Identity attachment, constructiveness, and the intergroup sensitivity effect. *European Journal of Social Psychology, 34*, 499–518.

Hortaçsu, N. (2000). Intergroup relations in a changing political context: The case of veiled and unveiled university students in Turkey. *European Journal of Social Psychology, 30*, 733–744.

Horton-Deutsch, S. L., & Horton, J. M. (2003). Mindfulness: Overcoming intractable conflict. *Archives of Psychiatric Nursing, 17*, 186–193.

Houser, R. A., & Domokos-Cheng Ham, M. A. (2004). *Gaining power and control through diversity and group affiliation.* Westport, CT: Praeger Publishers/Greenwood Publishing Group.

Houston, D. M., & Andreopoulou, A. (2003). Tests of both corollaries of social identity theory's self-esteem hypothesis in real group settings. *British Journal of Social Psychology, 42*, 357–370.

Houston, G. (1993). *Being and belonging: Group, intergroup and gestalt.* Chichester, England UK: John Wiley and Sons.

Hovland, C. I., Janis, I. L., & Kelley, H. H. (1953). *Communication and persuasion: Psychological studies of opinion change.* New Haven, CT: Yale University Press.

Howard, Jack L., & Brakefield, J. T. (2001). Effects of diversity on performance: The effects of task type. *Employee Responsibilities and Rights Journal, 13*, 147–154.

Howard, Judith A. (1994). A social cognitive conception of social structure. *Social Psychology Quarterly, 57*, 210–227.

Huang, C.-Y., & Sjöström, T. (2003). Consistent solutions for cooperative games with externalities. *Games and Economic Behavior, 43*, 196–213.

Huang, M. (2009). A conceptual framework of the effects of positive affect and affective relationships on group knowledge networks. *Small Group Research, 40*, 323–346.

Hubbard, A. S. (1997). Face-to-face at arm's length: Conflict norms and extra-group relations in grassroots dialogue groups. *Human Organization, 56*, 265–274.

Hubbard, A. S. (1999). Cultural and status differences in intergroup conflict resolution: A longitudinal study of a Middle East dialogue group in the United States. *Human Relations, 52*, 303–325.

Hubbert, K. N., Gudykunst, W. B., & Guerrero, S. L. (1999). Intergroup communication over time. *International Journal of Intercultural Relations, 23*, 13–46.

Huber, G. L., & Sorrentino, R. M. (1996). Uncertainty in interpersonal and intergroup relations: An individual-differences perspective. In R. M. Sorrentino & E. T. Higgins (Eds.), *Handbook of motivation and cognition, Vol. 3: The interpersonal context* (pp. 591–619). New York: Guilford Press.

Huber, O. (1996). Buying protection in a multistage investment task. *Acta Psychologica, 92*, 153–167.

Huck, S. (1999). Responder behavior in ultimatum offer games with incomplete information. *Journal of Economic Psychology, 20*, 183–206.

Huck, S., Müller, W., & Normann, H.-T. (2002). To Commit or not to commit: Endogenous timing in experimental duopoly markets. *Games and Economic Behavior, 38*, 240–264.

Huckins, K. D. (2002). Communication in religious lobbying: Making meaning, creating power. *Journal of Media and Religion, 1*, 121–134.

Huddy, L., & Virtanen, S. (1995). Subgroup differentiation and subgroup bias among Latinos as a function of familiarity and positive distinctiveness. *Journal of Personality and Social Psychology, 68*, 97–108.

Huettel, S. A., Lockhead, G., & Glensberg, A. (2001). Psychologically rational choice: Selection between alternatives in a multiple-equilibrium game. *Cognitive Systems Research, 1*, 143–160.

Huguet, P., Latané, B., & Bourgeois, M. (1998). The emergence of a social representation of human rights via interpersonal communication: Empirical evidence for the convergence of two theories. *European Journal of Social Psychology, 28*, 831–846.

Hulbert, L. G., Corrêa da Silva, M. L., & Adegboyega, G. (2001). Cooperation in social dilemmas and allocentrism: A social values approach. *European Journal of Social Psychology, 31*, 641–657.

Hull, J. M. (1999). Bargaining with God: Religious development and economic socialization. *Journal of Psychology and Theology, 27*, 241–249.

Hummon, N. P. (2000). Utility and dynamic social networks. *Social Networks, 22*, 221–249.

Humphrey, S. E., Ellis, A. P. J., Conlon, D. E., & Tinsley, C. H. (2004). Understanding customer reactions to brokered ultimatums: Applying negotiation and justice theory. *Journal of Applied Psychology, 89*, 466–482.

Hunsley, J., Silver, R. C., & Lee, C. M. (1991). Anticipating meeting a peer: Cognitive processes in distressed and nondistressed women. *Canadian Journal of Behavioural Science, 23*, 411–422.

Hunter, J. A. (2001). Self-esteem and in-group bias among members of a religious social category. *Journal of Social Psychology, 141*, 401–411.

Hunter, J. A. (2003a). Ingroup favoring allocations and domain specific self esteem in the minimal group setting. *Current Research in Social Psychology*, Vol 8(13), 176–186.

Hunter, J. A. (2003b). State, category specific collective self esteem and intergroup discrimination. *Current Research in Social Psychology, 8*(10), 139–148.

Hunter, J. A., O'Brien, K. S., & Grocott, A. C. (1999). Social identity, domain specific self-esteem and intergroup evaluation. *Current Research in Social Psychology, 4*(6), 160–177.

Hunter, J. A., O'Brien, K., & Stringer, M. (2007). Threats to identity, self-esteem and intergroup discrimination. *Social Behavior and Personality, 35*, 937–942.

Hunter, J. A., Platow, M. J., Howard, M. L., & Stringer, M. (1996). Social identity and intergroup evaluative bias: Realistic categories and domain specific self-esteem in a conflict setting. *European Journal of Social Psychology, 26*, 631–647.

Hunter, J. A., Reid, J. M., Stokell, N. M., & Platow, M. J. (2000). Social attribution, self-esteem, and social identity. *Current Research in Social Psychology, 5*(7), 97–125.

Hunter, L. W., & McKersie, R. B. (1992). Can "mutual gains" training change labor-management relationships? *Negotiation Journal, 8*, 319–330.

Huse, E. F., & Cummings, T. G. (1985). *Organization development and change* (3rd ed.). St. Paul, MN: West Pub. Co.

Hutchins, E. (1990). The technology of team navigation. In J. Galegher, R. E. Kraut, & C. Egido (Eds.), *Intellectual teamwork: Social and technological foundations of cooperative work* (191–220). Hillsdale, NJ: Lawrence Erlbaum Associates.

Hutchison, P., & Abrams, D. (2003). Ingroup identification moderates stereotype change in reaction to ingroup deviance. *European Journal of Social Psychology, 33,* 497–506.

Hutson-Comeaux, S. L., & Kelly, J. R. (1996). Sex differences in interaction style and group task performance: The process-performance relationship. *Journal of Social Behavior & Personality, 11,* 255–275.

Hwang, P., & Burgers, W. P. (1997). Properties of trust: An analytical view. *Organizational Behavior and Human Decision Processes, 69,* 67–73.

Hyers, L. L., & Swim, J. K. (1998). A comparison of the experiences of dominant and minority group members during an intergroup encounter. *Group Processes and Intergroup Relations, 1,* 143–163.

Ibanez Gracia, T. (1988). El conflicto social: Perspectivas clasicas y enfoque renovador [Social conflict: Classical views and a modern approach]. *Boletin de Psicologia Spain,* No. *18,* 7–21.

Ickes, W., & Gonzalez, R. (1996). "Social" cognition and *social* cognition: From the subjective to the intersubjective. In J. L. Nye & A. M. Brower (Eds.), *What's social about social cognition? Research on socially shared cognition in small groups* (pp. 285–308). Thousand Oaks, CA: Sage.

Idaszak, J. R., & Carnevale, P. J. (1989). Third party power: Some negative effects of positive incentives. *Journal of Applied Social Psychology, 19,* 499–516.

Iizuka, H., Yamamoto, M., Suzuki, K., & Ohuchi, A. (2002). Bottom-up consensus formation in voting games. *Nonlinear Dynamics, Psychology,* and Life Sciences, *6,* 185–195.

Imai, H., & Salonen, H. (2000). The representative Nash solution for two-sided bargaining problems. *Mathematical Social Sciences, 39,* 349–365.

In, Y., & Serrano, R. (2004). Agenda restrictions in multi-issue bargaining. *Journal of Economic Behavior and Organization, 53,* 385–399.

Inderst, R. (2000). Multi-issue bargaining with endogenous agenda. *Games and Economic Behavior, 30,* 64–82.

Inglis, S., Sammon, S., Justice, C., Cuneo, C., Miller, S., Rice, J., Roy, D., & Warry, W. (2004). Cross-cultural simulation to advance student inquiry. *Simulation and Gaming, 35,* 476–487.

Innami, I. (1994). The quality of group decisions, group verbal behavior, and intervention. *Organizational Behavior and Human Decision Processes, 60,* 409–430.

Inniss, L. B. (1989). Collaboration. In C. M. Bonjean, M. T. Coleman, & I. Iscoe (Eds.), *Community care of the chronically mentally ill: Proceedings of the sixth Robert Lee Sutherland Seminar in Mental Health* (pp. 97–101). Austin, TX: Hogg Foundation for Mental Health.

Insko, C. A., Hoyle, R. H., Pinkley, R. L., Hong, G., Slim, R. M., Dalton, B., Lin, Y.-H. W., Ruffin, P. P., Dardis, G. J., Bernthal, P. R., & Schopler, J. (1988). Individual-group discontinuity: The role of a consensus rule. *Journal of Experimental Social Psychology, 24,* 505–519.

Insko, C. A., Kirchner, J. L., Pinter, B., Efaw, J., & Wildschut, T. (2005). Interindividual-intergroup discontinuity as a function of trust and categorization: The paradox of expected cooperation. *Journal of Personality and Social Psychology, 88,* 365–385.

Insko, C. A., & Schopler, J. (1998). Differential distrust of groups and individuals. In C. Sedikides, J. Schopler, & C. A. Insko (Eds.), *Intergroup cognition and intergroup behavior* (pp. 75–107). Mahwah, NJ: Lawrence Erlbaum Associates Publishers.

Insko, C. A., Schopler, J., Drigotas, S. M., Graetz, K. A., Kennedy, J., Cox, C., & Bornstein, G. (1993). The role of communication in interindividual-intergroup discontinuity. *Journal of Conflict Resolution, 37,* 108–138.

Insko, C. A., Schopler, J., Gaertner, L., Wildschut, T., Kozar, R., Pinter, B., Finkel, E. J., Brazil, D. M., Cecil, C. L., & Montoya, M. R. (2001). Interindividual-intergroup discontinuity reduction through the anticipation of future interaction. *Journal of Personality and Social Psychology, 80,* 95–111.

Insko, C. A., Schopler, J., Graetz, K. A., Drigotas, S. M., Currey, D. P., Smith, S. L., Brazil, D., & Bornstein, G. (1994). Interindividual-intergroup discontinuity in the prisoner's dilemma game. Insko, *Journal of Conflict Resolution, 38,* 87–116.

Insko, C. A., Schopler, J., Hoyle, R. H., Dardis, G. J., & Graetz, K. A. (1990). Individual/group discontinuity as a function of fear and greed. *Journal of Personality and Social Psychology, 58*, 68–79.

Insko, C. A., Schopler, J., Kennedy, J. F., Dahl, K. R., Graetz, K. A., & Drigotas, S. M. (1992). Individual-group discontinuity from the differing perspectives of Campbell's Realistic Group Conflict Theory and Tajfel and Turner's Social Identity Theory. *Social Psychology Quarterly, 55*, 272–291.

Insko, C. A., Schopler, J., Pemberton, M. B., Wieselquist, J., McIlraith, S. A., Currey, D. P., & Gaertner, L. (1998). Long-term outcome maximization and the reduction of interindividual-intergroup discontinuity. *Journal of Personality and Social Psychology, 75*, 695–711.

Insko, C. A., & Wolf, S. T. (2007). Situational variance in intergroup conflict: Matrix correlations, matrix interactions, and social support. In M. Hewstone, Schut, A. W. Henk, J. B. F. De Wit, K. Van Den Bos, & M. S. Stroebe (Eds.), *The scope of social psychology: Theory and applications* (pp. 139–158). New York: Psychology Press.

Irving, P. G., & Meyer, J. P. (1997). A multidimensional scaling analysis of managerial third-party conflict intervention strategies. *Canadian Journal of Behavioural Science, 29*, 7–18.

Isgar, T. (1993). *The ten minute team: 10 steps to building high performing teams* (2nd ed.). Boulder, CO: Seluera Press.

Ishida, J. (2003). The role of intrahousehold bargaining in gender discrimination. *Rationality and Society, 15*, 361–380.

Islam, M. R., & Hewstone, M. (1993a). Dimensions of contact as predictors of intergroup anxiety, perceived out-group variability, and out-group attitude: An integrative model. *Personality and Social Psychology Bulletin, 19*, 700–710.

Islam, M. R., & Hewstone, M. (1993b). Intergroup attributions and affective consequences in majority and minority groups. *Journal of Personality and Social Psychology, 64*, 936–950.

Israel, R. D., Dolan, T. A., & Caranasos, G. J. (1992). Gerontopoly: Development and testing of a new game in geriatric education. *Gerontology and Geriatrics Education, 12*(4), 17–30.

Israeli, E. (1999). Sowing doubt optimally in two-person repeated games. *Games and Economic Behavior, 28*, 203–216.

Itoi, R., Ohbuchi, Ken I., & Fukuno, M. (1996). A cross-cultural study of preference of accounts: Relationship closeness, harm severity, and motives of account making. *Journal of Applied Social Psychology, 26*, 913–934.

Iyer, A., & Leach, C. W. (2008). Emotion in inter-group relations. *European Review of Social Psychology, 19*, 86–124.

Izquierdo, J. M., & Rafels, C. (2001). Average Monotonic Cooperative Games. *Games and Economic Behavior, 36*, 174–192.

Jackson, J. W. (1999). How variations in social structure affect different types of intergroup bias and different dimensions of social identity in a multi-intergroup setting. *Group Processes and Intergroup Relations, 2*, 145–173.

Jackson, J. W. (2002a). Intergroup Attitudes as a Function of Different Dimensions of Group Identification and Perceived Intergroup Conflict. *Self and Identity, 1*, 11–33.

Jackson, J. W. (2002b). Reactions to social dilemmas are influenced by group identification motives. In S. P. Shohov (Ed.), *Advances in psychology research* (Vol. 16, pp. 167–183). Hauppauge, NY: Nova Science Publishers, 2002.

Jackson, J. W. (2002c). The relationship between group identity and intergroup prejudice is moderated by sociostructural variation. *Journal of Applied Social Psychology, 32*, 908–933.

Jackson, J. W., & Smith, E. R. (1999). Conceptualizing social identity: A new framework and evidence for the impact of different dimensions. *Personality and Social Psychology Bulletin, 25*, 120–135.

Jackson, L. A., Sullivan, L. A., Harnish, R., & Hodge, C. N. (1996). Achieving positive social identity: Social mobility, social creativity, and permeability of group boundaries. *Journal of Personality and Social Psychology, 70*, 241–254.

Jackson, S., Farndale, E., & Kakabadse, A. (2003). Executive development: Meeting the needs of top teams and boards. *Journal of Management Development, 22*, 185–265.

Jaffe, E. D., & Nebenzahl, I. D. (1990). Group interaction and business game performance. *Simulation and Gaming, 21,* 133–146.

James, H. S., Jr. (2002). The trust paradox: A survey of economic inquiries into the nature of trust and trustworthiness. *Journal of Economic Behavior and Organization, 47,* 291–307.

James, K. (1993). Conceptualizing self with in-group stereotypes: Context and esteem precursors. *Personality and Social Psychology Bulletin, 19,* 117–121.

James, K., & Greenberg, J. (1989). In-group salience, intergroup comparison, and individual performance and self-esteem. *Personality and Social Psychology Bulletin, 15,* 604–616.

Janis, I. L., Deutsch, M., Krauss, R. M., Moorhead, G., Ference, R., & Neck, C. P. (1994). Groups and individual behavior. In W. A. Lesko (Ed.), *Readings in social psychology: General, classic, and contemporary selections* (2nd ed., pp. 328–354). Needham Heights, MA: Allyn & Bacon, 1994.

Janssen, O. (2003). Innovative behaviour and job involvement at the price of conflict and less satisfactory relations with co-workers. *Journal of Occupational and Organizational Psychology, 76,* 347–364.

Janssen, O., & Van de Vliert, E. (1996). Concern for the other's goals: Key to (de)-escalation of conflict. *International Journal of Conflict Management, 7,* 99–120.

Janssen, O., Van de Vliert, E., & Euwema, M. (1994). Interdependentie, zelf-ander-motivatie en conflictgedrag in organisaties [Interdependence, self/other motivation, and conflict behavior in organizations]. *Nederlands Tijdschrift voor de Psychologie en haar Grensgebieden, 49,* 15–26.

Jap, S. D. (2001). The strategic role of the salesforce in developing customer satisfaction across the relationship lifecycle. *Journal of Personal Selling and Sales Management, 21*(2), 95–108.

Jap, S. D. (2003). An exploratory study of the introduction of online reverse auctions. *Journal of Marketing, 67*(3), 96–107.

Jarvenpaa, S. L., & Leidner, D. E. (1998). Communication and trust in global virtual teams. *Journal of Computer-Mediated Communication, 3*(4), [Web-based; unpaginated].

Jasso, G. (1993). Building the theory of comparison processes: Construction of postulates and derivation of predictions. In J. Berger & M. Zelditch, Jr. (Eds.), *Theoretical research programs: Studies in the growth of theory* (pp. 213–264). Stanford, CA: Stanford University Press.

Jehn, K. A. (1992). The impact of intragroup conflict on effectiveness: A multimethod examination of the benefits and detriments of conflict. Unpublished doctoral dissertation, Northwestern University.

Jehn, K. A. (1997). Affective and cognitive conflict in work groups: Increasing performance through value-based intragroup conflict. In C. K. W. De Dreu & E. Van de Vliert (Eds.), *Using conflict in organizations* (pp. 87–100). London: Sage Publications, Inc.

Jehn, K. A., & Bendersky, C. (2003). Intragroup conflict in organizations: A contingency perspective on the conflict-outcome relationship. In R. M. Kramer & B. M. Staw (Eds.), *Research in organizational behavior: An annual series of analytical essays and critical reviews* (Vol 25, pp. 187–242). Oxford, England: Elsevier Science.

Jehn, K. A., Chadwick, C., & Thatcher, S. M. B. (1997). To agree or not to agree: The effects of value congruence, individual demographic dissimilarity, and conflict on workgroup outcomes. *International Journal of Conflict Management, 8,* 287–305.

Jehn, K. A., Greer, L. L., & Rupert, J. (2008). Diversity, conflict, and their consequences. In A. P. Brief (Ed.), *Diversity at work* (pp. 127–174). New York: Cambridge University Press.

Jehn, K. A., Northcraft, G. B., & Neale, M. A. (1999). Why differences make a difference: A field study of diversity, conflict, and performance in workgroups. *Administrative Science Quarterly, 44,* 741–763.

Jessup, L. M., Connolly, T., & Tansik, D. A. (1990). Toward a theory of automated group work: The deindividuating effects of anonymity. *Small Group Research, 21,* 333–348.

Jetten, J., Branscombe, N. R., Schmitt, M. T., & Spears, R. (2001). Rebels with a cause: Group identification as a response to perceived discrimination from the mainstream. *Personality and Social Psychology Bulletin, 27,* 1204–1213.

Jetten, J., Hogg, M. A., & Mullin, B. A. (2000). In-group variability and motivation to reduce subjective uncertainty. *Group Dynamics, 4,* 184–198.

Jetten, J., McAuliffe, B. J., Hornsey, M. J., & Hogg, M. A. (2006). Differentiation between and within groups: The influence of individualist and collectivist group norms. *European Journal of Social Psychology, Vol 36*, 825–843.

Jetten, J., Spears, R., Hogg, M. A., & Manstead, A. S. R. (2000). Discrimination constrained and justified: Variable effects of group variability and in-group identification. *Journal of Experimental Social Psychology, 36*, 329–356.

Jetten, J., Spears, R., & Manstead, A. S. R. (1996). Intergroup norms and intergroup discrimination: Distinctive self-categorization and social identity effects. *Journal of Personality and Social Psychology, 71*, 1222–1233.

Jetten, J., Spears, R., & Manstead, A. S. R. (1997a). Distinctiveness threat and prototypicality: Combined effects on intergroup discrimination and collective self-esteem. *European Journal of Social Psychology, 27*, 635–657.

Jetten, J., Spears, R., & Manstead, A. S. R. (1997b). Strength of identification and intergroup differentiation: The influence of group norms. *European Journal of Social Psychology, 27*, 603–609.

Jetten, J., Spears, R., & Manstead, A. S. R. (1998). Defining dimensions of distinctiveness: Group variability makes a difference to differentiation. *Journal of Personality and Social Psychology, 74*, 1481–1492.

Jetten, J., Spears, R., & Manstead, A. S. R. (1999). Group distinctiveness and intergroup discrimination. In N. Ellemers, R. Spears, & B. Doosje (Eds.), *Social identity: Context, commitment, content* (pp. 107–126). Oxford, England: Blackwell Science Ltd.

Jetten, J., Spears, R., & Manstead, A. S. R. (2001). Similarity as a source of differentiation: The role of group identification. *European Journal of Social Psychology, 31*, 621–640.

Jetten, J., Spears, R., & Postmes, T. (2004). Intergroup distinctiveness and differentiation: A meta-analytic integration. *Journal of Personality and Social Psychology, 86*, 862–879.

Jetten, J., Summerville, N., Hornsey, M. J., & Mewse, A. J. (2005). When differences matter: intergroup distinctiveness and the evaluation of impostors. *European Journal of Social Psychology, 35*, 609–620.

Jex, S. M., & Bliese, P. D. (1999). Efficacy beliefs as a moderator of the impact of workre-lated stressors: A multilevel study. *Journal of Applied Psychology, 84*, 349–361.

Jex, S. M., & Thomas, J. L. (2003). Relations between stressors and group perceptions: Main and mediating effects. *Work and Stress, 17*, 158–169.

Jin, N., Hayashi, N., & Shinotsuka, H. (1996). An experimental study of prisoner's dilemma network: Formation of committed relations among PD partners. *Japanese Journal of Experimental Social Psychology, 35*, 292–303.

Johansson, M., & Küller, R. (2002). TRAFFIC JAM: Psychological assessment of a gaming simulation. *Simulation and Gaming, 33*, 67–88.

Johnson, C. S., Olson, M. A., & Fazio, R. H. (2009). Getting acquainted in interracial interactions: Avoiding intimacy but approaching race. *Personality and Social Psychology Bulletin, 35*, 557–571.

Johnson, C., & Ford, R. (1996). Dependence power, legitimacy, and tactical choice. *Social Psychology Quarterly, 59*, 126–139.

Johnson, C., & Mullen, B. (1993). The determinants of differential group evaluations in distinctiveness-based illusory correlations in stereotyping. *British Journal of Social Psychology, 32*, 253–263.

Johnson, D. W., & Johnson, R. T. (1989). *Cooperation and competition: Theory and research.* Edina, MN: Interaction Book Company.

Johnson, D. W., & Johnson, R. T. (1995). Social interdependence: Cooperative learning in education. In B. B. Bunker & J. Z. Rubin (Eds.), *Conflict, cooperation, and justice: Essays inspired by the work of Morton Deutsch* (pp. 205–251), San Francisco: Jossey-Bass.

Johnson, D. W., Johnson, R. T., Stanne, M. B., & Garibaldi, A. (1990). Impact of group processing on achievement in cooperative groups. *Journal of Social Psychology, 130*, 507–516.

Johnson, J. D., La France, B. H., Meyer, M., Speyer, J. B., & Cox, D. (1998). The impact of formalization, role conflict, role ambiguity, and communication quality on perceived organizational innovativeness in the Cancer Information Service. *Evaluation and the Health Professions, 21,* 27–51.

Johnson, J. J. (2000). Differences in supervisor and non-supervisor perceptions of quality culture and organizational climate. *Public Personnel Management, 29,* 119–128.

Johnson, J. J., & McIntye, C. L. (1998). Organizational culture and climate correlates of job satisfaction. *Psychological Reports, 82,* 843–850.

Johnson, M. E., & Neimeyer, R. A. (1996). Perceptual sets and stimulus values: The social relations model in group psychotherapy. In J. L. Nye & A. M. Brower (Eds.), *What's social about social cognition? Research on socially shared cognition in small groups* (pp. 154–174). Thousand Oaks, CA: Sage.

Johnson, R. A. (1993). *Negotiation basics: Concepts, skills, and exercises.* Newbury Park, CA: Sage Publications, Inc.

Johnston, J. H., Smith-Jentsch, K. A., & Cannon Bowers, J. A. (1997). Performance measurement tools for enhancing team decision-making training. In M. T. Brannick, E. Salas, & C. Prince (Eds.), *Team performance assessment and measurement: Theory, methods, and applications* (pp. 311–327). Mahwah, NJ: Lawrence Erlbaum Associates, Inc., Publishers.

Johnston, W. J., & Benton, W. C. (1988). Bargaining, negotiations, and personal selling. In W. F. Van Raaij, G. M. Van Veldhoven, & K.-E. Wärneryd (Eds.), *Handbook of economic psychology* (pp. 448–471). New York: Kluwer Academic/Plenum Publishers.

Joldersma, C., & Geurts, J. L. A. (1998). Simulation/gaming for policy development and organizational change. *Simulation and Gaming, 29,* 391–399.

Jonas, K. J. (2009). Interventions enhancing intergroup tolerance. In S. Otten, K. Sassenberg, & T. Kessler (Eds.), *Intergroup relations: The role of motivation and emotion* (pp. 284–303). New York: Psychology Press.

Jones, B. H., & Jelassi, M. T. (1990). The effect of computer intervention and task structure on bargaining outcome. *Theory and Decision, 28,* 355–377.

Jones, E. E. (1990). *Interpersonal perception.* New York: Freeman.

Jones, E. E., Flammer, A., Grob, A., Luethi, R., Augoustinos, M., Swap, W. C., Ossoff, E. P., Rubin, J. Z., & Fletcher, G. J. O. (1989). Attribution theory. In J. P. Forgas & J. M. Innes (Eds.), *Recent advances in social psychology: An international perspective* (pp. 63–125). Amsterdam: North-Holland.

Jones, K. W. (2001). "I've called 'em tom-ah-toes all my life and I'm not going to change!": Maintaining linguistic control over English identity in the U.S. *Social Forces, 79,* 1061–1094.

Jones, M., & Zhang, J. (2004). Rationality and bounded information in repeated games, with application to the iterated Prisoner's Dilemma. *Journal of Mathematical Psychology, 48,* 334–354.

Jopling, D. (1993). Cognitive science, other minds, and the philosophy of dialogue. In U. Neisser (Ed.), *The perceived self: Ecological and interpersonal sources of self-knowledge* (pp. 290–309). New York: Cambridge University Press.

Jordan, M. H., Feild, H. S., & Armenakis, A. A. (2002). The relationship of group process variables and team performance: A team-level analysis in a field setting. *Small Group Research, 33,* 121–150.

Jordan, P. J., & Troth, A. C. (2004). Managing emotions during team problem solving: Emotional intelligence and conflict resolution. *Human Performance, 17,* 195–218.

Joshi, A. W., & Randall, S. (2001). The indirect effects of organizational controls on salesperson performance and customer orientation. *Journal of Business Research, 54,* 1–9.

Jost, J. T. (2004). A perspectivist looks at the past, present, and (perhaps) the future of intergroup relations: A quixotic defense of system justification theory. In J. T. Jost, M. R. Banaji, & D. A. Prentice (Eds.), *Perspectivism in social psychology: The yin and yang of scientific progress* (pp. 215–230). Washington, DC: American Psychological Association.

Jost, J. T., & Azzi, A. E. (1996). Microjustice and macrojustice in the allocation of resources between experimental groups. *Journal of Social Psychology, 136,* 349–365.

Judd, C. M., Ryan, C. S., & Park, B. (1991). Accuracy in the judgment of in-group and out-group variability. *Journal of Personality and Social Psychology, 61,* 366–379.

Jude-York, D. (1998). Technology enhanced teamwork: Aligning individual contributions for superior team performance. *Organization Development Journal, 16*(3), 73–82.

Judge, T. A., & Colquitt, J. A. (2004). Organizational justice and stress: The mediating role of work-family conflict. *Journal of Applied Psychology, 89*, 395–404.

Jules, Vena. (1991). Interaction dynamics of cooperative learning groups in Trinidad's secondary schools. *Adolescence. 26*, 931–949.

Jung, D. I. (2001). Transformational and transactional leadership and their effects on creativity in groups. *Creativity Research Journal, 13*, 185–195.

Jung, D. I., & Sosik, J. J. (2002). Transformational leadership in work groups: The role of empowerment, cohesiveness, and collective-Efficacy on perceived group performance. *Small Group Research, 33*, 313–336.

Jussim, L., Ashmore, R. D., & Wilder, D. (2001). Introduction: Social identity and intergroup conflict. In R. D. Ashmore, L. Jussim, & D. Wilder (Eds.), *Social identity, intergroup conflict, and conflict reduction* (pp. 3–14). New York: Oxford University Press.

Kahai, S. S., Sosik, J. J., & Avolio, B. J. (2004). Effects of participative and directive leadership in electronic groups. *Group and Organization Management, 29*, 67–105.

Kahn, L. S., & Landau, J. H. (1988). *Peacemaking: A systems approach to conflict management.* Lanham, MD: University Press of America.

Kahn, P. M., & Leon, G. R. (1994). Group climate and individual functioning in an all-women Antarctic expedition team. *Environment and Behavior, 26*, 669–697.

Kahneman, D. (1992). Reference points, anchors, norms, and mixed feelings. *Organizational Behavior and Human Decision Processes, 51*, 296–312.

Kahneman, D., & Tversky, A. (1995). Conflict resolution: A cognitive perspective. In K. J. Arrow (Ed.), *Barriers to conflict resolution* (pp. 45–60). [New York]: W. W. Norton. [Rprinted in M. H. Bazerman (Ed.), *Negotiation, decision making and conflict management* (Vol. 1–3, pp. 116–134). Northampton, MA: Edward Elgar Publishing, 2005].

Kaiser, C. R., Hagiwara, N., Malahy, L. W., & Wilkins, C. L. (2009). Group identification moderates attitudes toward ingroup members who confront discrimination. *Journal of Experimental Social Psychology, 45*, 770–777.

Kambe, S. (1999). Bargaining with imperfect commitment. *Games and Economic Behavior, 28*, 217–237.

Kane, T. D., Zaccaro, S. J., Tremble, T., Jr., & Masuda, A. D. (2002). An examination of the leaders' regulation of groups. *Small Group Research, 33*, 65–120.

Kanner, M. D. (2004). Framing and the role of the second actor: An application of prospect theory to bargaining. *Political Psychology, 25*, 213–239.

Kanning, U. P. (1999). Self-esteem related behavior and social conflicts in hospitals [Selbstwertdienliches verhalten und soziale konflikte im krankenhaus]. *Gruppendynamik, 30*, 207–229.

Kanungo, S. (1998). An empirical study of organizational culture and network-based computer use. *Computers in Human Behavior, 14*, 79–91.

Kaplan, I. T. (1997). Relationships between group efficacy, goals, and performance: A comment on Silver and Bufanio (SGR, 1996). *Small Group Research, 28*, 556–558.

Kaplan, M. F., & Wilke, H. (2001). Cognitive and social motivation in group decision making. In J. P. Forgas, K. D. Williams, & L. Wheeler (Eds.), *The social mind: Cognitive and motivational aspects of interpersonal behavior* (pp. 406–428). New York: Cambridge University Press.

Karakitapoglu, Z. (1999). Gruplar Arasi Iliskiler: Sosyal Psikolojik Yaklasimlara Toplu Bir Bakis [Intergroup Relations: A review of Social Psychological Approaches]. *Türk Psikoloji Yazilari, 1*(3), 51–78.

Karasawa, K. (2002a). Identification with an ingroup and a super-ordinate group and support provision toward outgroups: An examination in a simulated society game. *Japanese Journal of Psychology, 73*, 18–25.

Karasawa, K. (2002b). Responsibility attribution and support provision in an intergroup context: An examination in a simulated society game. *Japanese Psychological Research, 44*, 196–208.

Karasawa, M. (1991). Toward an assessment of social identity: The structure of group identification and its effects on in-group evaluations. *British Journal of Social Psychology, 30*, 293–307.

Karasawa, M. (1995). Group distinctiveness and social identity of a low-status group. *Journal of Social Psychology, 135*, 329–338.

Karaul, M., Korilis, Y. A., & Orda, A. (2000). A market-based architecture for management of geographically dispersed, replicated Web servers. *Decision Support Systems, 28*, 191–204.

Karney, B. R., McNulty, J. K., & Frye, N. E. (2001). A social-cognitive perspective on the maintenance and deterioration of relationship satisfaction. In J. Harvey & A. Wenzel (Eds.), *Close romantic relationships: Maintenance and enhancement* (pp. 195–214). Mahwah, NJ: Lawrence Erlbaum Associates Publishers.

Kärreman, D., & Alvesson, M. (2001). Making newsmakers: Conversational identity at work. *Organization Studies, 22*, 59–89.

Kashibuchi, M., & Sakamoto, A. (2001). The educational effectiveness of a simulation/game in sex education. *Simulation and Gaming, 32*, 331–343.

Kashima, E. S., Kashima, Y., & Hardie, E. A. (2000). Self-typicality and group identification: Evidence for their separateness. *Group Processes and Intergroup Relations, 3*, 97–110.

Kassin, S. M., Fein, S., Markus, H., & Brehm, S. S. (2008). *Social psychology* (7th ed.). Boston: Houghton Mifflin.

Kassinove, H., Roth, D., Owens, S. G., & Fuller, J. R. (2002). Effects of trait anger and anger expression style on competitive attack responses in a wartime prisoner's dilemma game. *Aggressive Behavior, 28*, 117–125.

Katayama, M. (1995). The differences between individualists and cooperators: Interpersonal cognition of resource allocation. *Japanese Journal of Psychology, 66*, 83–90.

Katovich, M. A. (1996). Cooperative bases of control: Toward an interactionist conceptualization. *Social Science Journal, 33*, 257–271.

Katz, E., Levin, M. L., & Hamilton, H. (1963). Traditions of research on the diffusion of innovation. *American Sociological Review, 28*, 237–252.

Katz, R., Amichai-Hamburger, Y., Manisterski, E., & Kraus, S. (2008). Different orientations of males and females in computer-mediated negotiations. *Computers in Human Behavior, 24*, 516–534.

Katzenbach, J. R., & Smith, D. K. (1993). *The wisdom of teams: Creating the high-performance organization*. Boston: Harvard Business School.

Kaufman, C. M., & Kerr, N. L. (1993). Small wins: Perceptual focus, efficacy, and cooperation in a stage-conjunctive social dilemma. *Journal of Applied Social Psychology, 23*, 3–20.

Kaufman, S., & Duncan, G. T. (1992). A formal framework for mediator mechanisms and motivations. *Journal of Conflict Resolution, 36*, 688–708.

Kaufmann, P. J., & Stern, L. W. (1988). Relational exchange norms, perceptions of unfairness, and retained hostility in commercial litigation. *Journal of Conflict Resolution, 32*, 534–552.

Kay, A. C., & Ross, L. (2003). The perceptual push: The interplay of implicit cues and explicit situational construals on behavioral intentions in the Prisoner's Dilemma. *Journal of Experimental Social Psychology, 39*, 634–643.

Keashly, L., Fisher, R. J., & Grant, P. R. (1993). The comparative utility of third party consultation and mediation within a complex simulation of intergroup conflict. *Human Relations, 46*, 371–393.

Keeffe, M. J., Dyson, D. A., & Edwards, R. R. (1993). Strategic management simulations: A current assessment. *Simulation and Gaming, 24*, 363–368.

Keenan, P. A., & Carnevale, P. J. (1989). Positive effects of within-group cooperation on between-group negotiation. *Journal of Applied Social Psychology, 19*, 977–992.

Kegler, M. C., Steckler, A., Malek, S. H., & McLeroy, K. (1998). A multiple case study of implementation in 10 local Project ASSIST coalitions in North Carolina. *Health Education Research, 13*, 225–238.

Keinan, G., & Koren, M. (2002). Teaming up Type As and Bs: The effects of group composition on performance and satisfaction. *Applied Psychology: An International Review, 51*, 425–445.

Kelleher, T. (2001). PR and conflict: A theoretical review and case study of the 2001 University of Hawaii faculty strike. *Journal of Communication Management, 8*, 184–196.

Keller, J., & Molix, L. (2008). When women can't do math: The interplay of self-construal, group identification, and stereotypic performance standards. *Journal of Experimental Social Psychology, 44*, 437–444.

Kellermann, K. (1995). The conversation MOP: A model of patterned and pliable behavior. In D. E. Hewes (Ed.), *The cognitive bases of interpersonal communication* (pp. 181–221). Hillsdale, NJ: Lawrence Erlbaum Associates, Inc.

Kelley, H. H. (1997). Expanding the analysis of social orientations by reference to the sequential-temporal structure of situations. *European Journal of Social Psychology, 27*, 373–404.

Kelloway, E. K. (2004). Labor unions and occupational safety: Conflict and cooperation. In J. Barling, Frone, Michael R.;(Eds.), *The psychology of workplace safety* (pp. 249–264). Washington, DC: American Psychological Association.

Kelly, A., & Brannick, T. (1990). The impact of state pay policy and collective bargaining structure on the character of industrial conflict. *International Journal of Conflict Management, 1*, 175–190.

Kelly, C. (1988). Intergroup differentiation in a political context. *British Journal of Social Psychology, 27*, 319–332.

Kelly, C. (1990a). Social identity and intergroup perceptions in minority/majority contexts. *Human Relations, 43*, 583–599.

Kelly, C. (1990b). Social identity and levels of influence: When a political minority fails. *British Journal of Social Psychology, 29*, 289–301.

Kelly, J. R., & Karau, S. J. (1993). Entrainment of creativity in small groups. *Small Group Research, 24*, 179–198.

Kelly, J. R., Futoran, G. C., & McGrath, J. E. (1990). Capacity and capability: Seven studies of entrainment of task performance rates. *Small Group Research, 21*, 283–314.

Kelman, H. C. (1961). Processes of opinion change. *Public Opinion Quarterly. 25*, 57–78.

Kelman, H. C. (1993). Coalitions across conflict lines: The interplay of conflicts within and between the Israeli and Palestinian communities. In S. Worchel and J. Simpson (Eds.), *Conflict between people and groups* (pp. 236–258). Chicago: Nelson-Hall.

Kelman, H. C. (2008a). Evaluating the contributions of interactive problem solving to the resolution of ethnonational conflicts. *Peace and Conflict: Journal of Peace Psychology, 14*, 29–60. [Checked against Kelman's article in peace psychology newsletter, 18(2) 2009 PP newsletter]

Kelman, H. C. (2008b). Reconciliation from a social-psychological perspective. In A. Nadler, T. E. Malloy, & J. D. Fisher (Eds.), *The social psychology of intergroup reconciliation* (pp. 15–32). New York: Oxford University Press.

Keltner, D., & Robinson, R. J. (1993). Imagined ideological differences in conflict escalation and resolution. *International Journal of Conflict Management, 4*, 249–262.

Kemp, K. E., & Smith, W. P. (1994). Information exchange, toughness, and integrative bargaining: The roles of explicit cues and perspective-taking. *International Journal of Conflict Management, 5*, 5–21.

Ken-ichi, O., Kei-Ichiro, I., Ikuo, S., Tyler, T. R., & Lind, E. A. (1997). Goals and tactics in within- and between-culture conflicts. *Tohoku Psychologica Folia, 56*, 1–13.

Kenis, P., & Knoke, D. (2002). How organizational field networks shape interorganizational tie-formation rates. *Academy of Management Review, 27*, 275–293.

Kenrick, D. T., Neuberg, S. L., Zierk, K. L., & Krones, J. M. (1994). Evolution and social cognition: Contrast effects as a function of sex, dominance, and physical attractiveness. *Personality and Social Psychology Bulletin, 20*, 210–217.

Keough, C. M. (1992). Bargaining arguments and argumentative bargainers. In L. L. Putnam & M. E. Roloff (Eds.), *Communication and negotiation* (pp. 109–127). Thousand Oaks, CA: Sage Publications, Inc.

Keren, G., & Raub, W. (1993). Resolving social conflicts through hostage posting: Theoretical and empirical considerations. *Journal of Experimental Psychology: General, 122*, 429–448.

Keren, G., & Wagenaar, W. A. (1988). Chance and skill in gambling: A search for distinctive features. *Social Behaviour, 3*, 199–217.

Kernan, M. C., Bruning, N. S., & Miller-Guhde, L. (1994). Individual and group performance: Effects of task complexity and information. *Human Performance, 7*, 273–289.

Kerr, N. L. (1989). Illusions of efficacy: The effects of group size on perceived efficacy in social dilemmas. *Journal of Experimental Social Psychology, 25*, 287–313.

Kerr, N. L. (1992). Efficacy as a causal and moderating variable in social dilemmas. In W. B. G. Liebrand, D. M. Messick, & H. A. M. Wilke (Eds.), *Social dilemmas: Theoretical issues and research findings* (pp. 59–80). Oxford, England: Pergamon Press, Inc.

Kerr, N. L., Garst, J., Lewandowski, D. A., & Harris, S. E. (1997). That still, small voice: Commitment to cooperate as an internalized versus a social norm. *Personality and Social Psychology Bulletin, 23*, 1300–1311.

Kerr, N. L., & Kaufman-Gilliland, C. M. (1994). Communication, commitment, and cooperation in social dilemma. *Journal of Personality and Social Psychology, 66*, 513–529.

Kerr, N. L., & Kaufman-Gilliland, C. M. (1997). "…and besides, I probably couldn't have made a difference anyway": Justification of social dilemma defection via perceived self-inefficacy. *Journal of Experimental Social Psychology, 33*, 211–230.

Kerr, N. L., Messé, L. A., Seok, D.-H., Sambolec, E. J., Lount, R. B., Jr., & Park, E. S. (2007). Psychological mechanisms underlying the Köhler motivation gain. *Personality and Social Psychology Bulletin, 33*, 828–841.

Kerr, N. L., & Stanfel, J. A. (1993). Role schemata and member motivation in task groups. *Personality and Social Psychology Bulletin, 19*, 432–442.

Kerr, N. L., & Tindale, R. S. (2004). Group performance and decision making. *Annual Review of Psychology, 55*, 623–655.

Kerr, S., & Slocum, J. J. W. (1981). Controlling the performances of people in organizations. In P. C. Nystrom & W. H. Starbuck (Eds.), *Handbook of organizational design: Volume 2. Remodeling organizations and their environments* (pp. 116–134). Oxford University Press.

Kessler, T., & Mummendey, A. (2001). Is there any scapegoat around? Determinants of intergroup conflicts at different categorization levels. *Journal of Personality and Social Psychology, 81*, 1090–1102.

Kessler, T., & Mummendey, A. (2002). Sequential or parallel processes? A longitudinal field study concerning determinants of identity-management strategies. *Journal of Personality and Social Psychology, 82*, 75–88.

Kessler, T., & Mummendey, A. (2008). Prejudice and intergroup relations. In M. Hewstone, W. Stroebe, & K. Jonas (Eds.), *Introduction to social psychology* (4th ed., pp. 290–314). Malden: Blackwell Publishing, 2008.

Ketelaar, T., & Au, W. T. (2003). The effects of feelings of guilt on the behaviour of uncooperative individuals in repeated social bargaining games: An affect-as-information interpretation of the role of emotion in social interaction. *Cognition and Emotion, 17*, 429–453.

Kets de Vries, M. F. R., & Florent-Treacy, E. (2002). Global leadership from A to Z: Creating high commitment organizations. *Organizational Dynamics, 30*, 295–309.

Kew, F. (1987). Contested rules: An explanation of how games change. *International Review for the Sociology of Sport, 22*, 125–135.

Keys, C. B., & Factor, A. R. (2001). Building community coalitions with people with disabilities and their families: An empowerment approach. *Journal of Prevention and Intervention in the Community, 21*(2), 91–112.

Keyton, J. (1991). Evaluating individual group member satisfaction as a situational variable. *Small Group Research, 22*, 200–219.

Kibris, Ö. (2002). Misrepresentation of utilities in bargaining: Pure exchange and public good economies. *Games and Economic Behavior, 39*, 91–110.

Kibris, Ö. (2004a). Egalitarianism in ordinal bargaining: The Shapley-Shubik rule. *Games and Economic Behavior, 49*, 157–170.

Kibris, Ö. (2004b). Ordinal invariance in multicoalitional bargaining. *Games and Economic Behavior, 46*, 76–87.

Kiesler, S., Sproull, L., & Waters, K. (1996). A prisoner's dilemma experiment on cooperation with people and human-like computers. *Journal of Personality and Social Psychology, 70*, 47–65.

Kiewitz, C., Hochwarter, W. A., Ferris, G. R., & Castro, S. L. (2002). The role of psychological climate in neutralizing the effects of organizational politics on work outcomes. *Journal of Applied Social Psychology, 32*, 1189–1207.

Kilgour, D. M., & Hipel, K. W. (2005a). The Graph model for conflict resolution: Past, present, and future. *Group Decision and Negotiation, 14*, 441–460.

Kilgour, D. M., & Hipel, K. W. (2005b). Introduction to the special issue on the graph model for conflict resolution. *Group Decision and Negotiation, 14*, 439–440.

Kilgour, D. M., Hipel, K. W., & Fang, L. (1994). Negotiation support using the graph model for conflict resolution. *Group Decision and Negotiation, 3*, 29–46.

Kilmann, R. H., Shelleman, J., & Uzzi, B. (1991). Integrating different approaches for achieving competitiveness. In R. H. Kilmann & I. Kilmann (Eds.), *Making organizations competitive: Enhancing networks and relationships across traditional boundaries* (pp. 108–126). San Francisco: Jossey-Bass Inc, Publishers.

Kim, D.-H., & Kim, D. H. (1997). A system dynamics model for a mixed-strategy game between police and driver. *System Dynamics Review, 13*, 33–52.

Kim, J., & Zepeda, L. (2004). Factors affecting children's participation and amount of labor on family farms. *Journal of Safety Research, 35*, 391–401.

Kim, M. U., & Kim, H. S. (1998). Union commitment and company commitment: Their relationship and antecedents. *Korean Journal of Industrial and Organizational Psychology, 11*(1), 113–135.

Kim, P. H. (2003). When Private Beliefs Shape Collective Reality: The Effects of Beliefs About Coworkers on Group Discussion and Performance. *Management Science, 49*, 801–815.

Kim, P. H., & Fragale, A. R. (2005). Choosing the Path to bargaining power: An empirical comparison of BATNAs and contributions in negotiation. *Journal of Applied Psychology, 90*, 373–381.

Kim, S. H., & Smith, R. H. (1993). Revenge and conflict escalation. *Negotiation Journal, 9*, 37–43.

Kim, S. H., & Webster, J. M. (2001). Getting competitors to cooperate: A comparison of three reciprocal strategies. *Representative Research in Social Psychology, 25*, 9–19.

Kim, Yong-Gwan. (1996). Evolutionary analyses of tacit communication in Van Huyck, Battalio, and Beil's Game experiments. *Games and Economic Behavior, 16*, 218–237.

Kim, Youngse. (1996). Equilibrium selection in n-person coordination games. *Games and Economic Behavior, 15*, 203–227.

Kim, Youngse. (2002). Satisficing and fairness in ultimatum bargaining game experiments. *Risk, Decision and Policy, 7*, 235–247.

Kimberly, J. C. (1997). *Group processes and structures: A theoretical integration.* Lanham, MD: University Press of America.

Kimmel, P. R. (2006). Culture and conflict. In M. Deutsch, P. T. Coleman, & E. C. Marcus (Eds.), *The handbook of conflict resolution: Theory and practice* (2nd ed., pp. 625–648). Hoboken, NJ: Wiley Publishing.

King, E. B., Hebl, M. R., & Beal, D. J. (2009). Conflict and cooperation in diverse workgroups. *Journal of Social Issues, 65*, 261–285.

Kingsbury, S. (1995). Incremental change and transformation in persons and systems. In F. Massarik (Ed.), *Advances in organization development* (Vol. 3, pp. 119–126). Norwood, NJ: Ablex Publishing Corp.

Kirchler, E., Palmonari, A., & Pombeni, M. L. (1994). Social categorization processes as dependent on status differences between groups: A step into adolscents' peer-groups. *European Journal of Social Psychology, 24*, 541–563.

Kirchmeyer, C., & Cohen, A. (1992). Multicultural groups: Their performance and reactions with constructive conflict. *Group and Organization Management, 17*, 153–170.

Kirk, J. J. (2004). The making of a gaming-simulation course: A personal tale. *Simulation and Gaming, 35*, 85–93.

Kirkbride, P. S., Tang, S. F., & Westwood, R. I. (1991). Chinese conflict preferences and negotiating behaviour: Cultural and psychological influences. *Organization Studies, 12*, 365–386.

Kirkman, B. L., & Rosen, B. (2000). Powering up teams. *Organizational Dynamics, 28*(3), 48–66.

Kirkman, B. L., & Shapiro, D. L. (1997). The impact of cultural values on employee resistance to teams: Toward a model of globalized self-managing work team effectiveness. *Academy of Management Review, 22*, 730–757.

Kirsch, H. W., & Osterling, J. (1995). Coalition building in an emerging democracy: The development of a national drug-abuse prevention plan in Paraguay. In H. W. Kirsch (Ed.), *Drug lessons & education programs in developing countries* (pp. 297–309). New Brunswick, NJ: Transaction Publishers.

Kirton, M. J., & McCarthy, R. M. (1988). Cognitive climate and organizations. *Journal of Occupational Psychology, 61*, 175–184.

Kirts, C. A., Tumeo, M. A., & Sinz, J. M. (1991). The COMMONS GAME: Its instructional value when used in a natural resources management context. *Simulation and Gaming, 22*, 5–18.

Kiyonari, T. (2002). Expectations of a generalized exchange system and ingroup favoritism: An experimental study of bounded reciprocity. *Japanese Journal of Psychology, 73*, 1–9.

Kiyonari, T., Tanida, S., & Yamagishi, T. (2000). Social exchange and reciprocity: Confusion or a heuristic? *Evolution and Human Behavior, 21*, 411–427.

Kiyonari, T., & Yamagishi, T. (1996). Distrusting outsiders as a consequence of commitment formation. *Japanese Journal of Experimental Social Psychology, 36*, 56–67.

Klandermans, B., & De Weerd, M. (2000). Group identification and political protest. In S. Stryker, T. J. Owens, & R. W. White (Eds.), *Self, identity, and social movements* (pp. 68–90). Minneapolis, MN: University of Minnesota Press.

Klapwijk, A., & Van Lange, P. A. M. (2009). Promoting cooperation and trust in "noisy" situations: The power of generosity. *Journal of Personality and Social Psychology, 96*, 83–103.

Klauer, K. C., Ehrenberg, K., & Wegener, I. (2003). Crossed categorization and stereotyping: Structural analyses, effects patterns, and dissociative effects of context relevance. *Journal of Experimental Social Psychology, 39*, 332–354.

Klaus, B. (2001). Coalitional strategy-proofness in economies with single-dipped preferences and the assignment of an indivisible object. *Games and Economic Behavior, 34*, 64–82.

Kleiman, M., & Kilmer, B. (2009). The dynamics of deterrence. *PNAS Proceedings of the National Academy of Sciences of the United States of America, 106*, 14230–14235.

Klein, C., DiazGranados, D., Salas, E., Le, H., Burke, C. S., Lyons, R., & Goodwin, G. F. (2009). Does team building work? *Small Group Research, 40*, 181–222.

Klein, E. E., & Dologite, D. G. (2000). The role of computer support tools and gender composition in innovative information system idea generation by small groups. *Computers in Human Behavior, 16*, 111–139.

Klein, R. D., & Fleck, R. A. (1990). International business simulation/gaming: An assessment and review. *Simulation and Gaming, 21*, 147–165.

Kleinman, G., Siegel, P., & Eckstein, C. (2002). Teams as a learning forum for accounting professionals. *Journal of Management Development, 21*, 427–460.

Klemisch-Ahlert, M. (1992). Distributive justice of bargaining and risk sensitivity. *Theory and Decision, 32*, 303–318.

Klimoski, R. J., & Donahue, L. M. (2001). Person perception in organizations: An overview of the field. In M. London (Ed.), *How people evaluate others in organizations* (pp. 5–43). Mahwah, NJ: Lawrence Erlbaum Associates Publishers.

Kline, T. J. B. (2001). Predicting team performance: Testing a model in a field setting. *Journal for Specialists in Group Work, 26*, 185–197.

Kline, T. J. B., & MacLeod, M. (1997). Predicting organizational team performance. *Organization Development Journal, 15*(4), 77–84.

Klotz, A. (2004). Review of *The Power of Legitimacy: Assessing the Role of Norms in Crisis Bargaining*. *Political Psychology, 25*, 142–145.

Knee, C. R., Patrick, H., Vietor, N. A., & Neighbors, C. (2004). Implicit theories of relationships: Moderators of the link between conflict and commitment. *Personality and Social Psychology Bulletin, 30*, 617–628.

Knez, M. J., & Camerer, C. F. (1995). Outside options and social comparison in Three-Player Ultimatum Game experiments. *Games and Economic Behavior, 10*, 65–94.

Knez, M., & Camerer, C. (2000). Increasing cooperation in prisoner's dilemmas by establishing a precedent of efficiency in coordination games. *Organizational Behavior and Human Decision Processes, 82*, 194–216.

Knoblich, G., & Jordan, J. S. (2003). Action coordination in groups and individuals: Learning anticipatory control. *Journal of Experimental Psychology: Learning, Memory, and Cognition, 29*, 1006–1016.

Koehler, D. H. (2001). Instability and convergence under simple-majority rule: Results from simulation of committee choice in two-dimensional space. *Theory and Decision, 50*, 305–332.

Kofta, M. (1995). Stereotype of a group as-a–whole: The role of diabolic causation schema. *Polish Psychological Bulletin, 26*, 83–96.

Kohguchi, H., Sakata, K., & Kurokawa, M. (2002). An Examination of the Effectiveness of Multiple Leaders in the Intergroup Context. *Japanese Journal of Experimental Social Psychology, 42*, 40–54.

Kolasinski, E. M., & Gilson, R. D. (1999). Ataxia following exposure to a virtual environment. *Aviation, Space, and Environmental Medicine, 70*, 264–269.

Kolb, D. M. (2004). Staying in the Game or Changing It: An Analysis of Moves and Turns in Negotiation. *Negotiation Journal, 20*, 253–268.

Kolfschoten, G. L., Hengst-Bruggeling, M. D., & De Vreede, G.-J. (2007). Issues in the design of facilitated collaboration processes. *Group Decision and Negotiation, 16*, 347–361.

Koller, D., & Milch, B. (2003). Multi-agent influence diagrams for representing and solving games. *Games and Economic Behavior, 45*, 181–221.

Komorita, S. S., Aquino, K. F., & Ellis, A. L. (1989). Coalition bargaining: A comparison of theories based on allocation norms and theories based on bargaining strength. *Social Psychology Quarterly, 52*, 183–196.

Komorita, S. S., & Carnevale, P. (1992). Motivational arousal vs. decision framing in social dilemmas. In W. B. G. Liebrand, D. M. Messick, & H. A. M. Wilke (Eds.), *Social dilemmas: Theoretical issues and research findings* (pp. 209–223). Elmsford, NY: Pergamon Press.

Komorita, S. S., Chan, D. K., & Parks, C. (1993). The effects of reward structure and reciprocity in social dilemmas. *Journal of Experimental Social Psychology, 29*, 252–267.

Komorita, S. S., & Ellis, A. L. (1988). Level of aspiration in coalition bargaining. *Journal of Personality and Social Psychology, 54*, 421–431.

Komorita, S. S., Hilty, J. A., & Parks, C. D. (1991). Reciprocity and cooperation in social dilemmas. *Journal of Conflict Resolution, 35*, 494–518.

Komorita, S. S., & Parks, C. D. (1994). *Social dilemmas*. Dubuque, IA: Brown and Benchmark.

Komorita, S. S., & Parks, C. D. (1995). Interpersonal relations: Mixed-motive interaction. *Annual Review of Psychology, 46*, 183–207.

Komorita, S. S., & Parks, C. D. (1999). Reciprocity and cooperation in social dilemmas: Review and future directions. In D. V. Budescu, I. Erev, & R. Zwick (Eds.), *Games and human behavior: Essays in honor of Amnon Rapoport* (pp. 315–330). Mahwah, NJ: Lawrence Erlbaum Associates Publishers.

Koneya, M. (1977). Privacy regulation in small and large groups. *Group and Organization Studies, 2*, 324–335.

Korhonen, P., Oretskin, N., Teich, J., & Wallenius, J. (1995). The impact of a biased starting position in a single negotiation text type mediation. *Group Decision and Negotiation, 4*, 357–374.

Korhonen, P., & Wallenius, J. (1990). Supporting individuals in group decision-making. *Theory and Decision, 28*, 313–329.

Kosmitzki, C., Cheng, J. Y., & Chik, S. W. K. (1994). Do national stereotypes apply equally to individual members of social minority and majority groups? *Journal of Social Psychology, 134*, 395–397.

Kotthoff, H. (1993). Disagreement and concession in disputes: On the context sensitivity of preference structures. *Language in Society, 22*, 193–216.

Koumakhov, R. (2009). Conventions in Herbert Simon's theory of bounded rationality. *Journal of Economic Psychology, 30*, 293–306.

Kovalenkov, A., & Wooders, M. H. (2001). Epsilon cores of games with limited side payments nonemptiness and equal treatment. *Games and Economic Behavior, 36,* 193–218.

Kozan, M. K. (1990). Relationships of hierarchy and topics to conflict management styles: A comparative study. In M. A. Rahim (Ed.), *Theory and research in conflict management* (pp. 174–187). New York: Praeger Publishers.

Kozlowski, S. W. J., & Bell, B. S. (2008). Team learning, development, and adaptation. In V. I. Sessa & M. London (Eds.), *Work group learning: Understanding, improving and assessing how groups learn in organizations* (pp. 15–44). New York: Taylor & Francis Group/Lawrence Erlbaum Associates.

Kozlowski, S. W. J., & Ilgen, D. R. (2006). Enhancing the effectiveness of work groups and teams. *Psychological Science in the Public Interest, 7,* 77–124.

Kozub, S. A., & McDonnell, J. F. (2000). Exploring the relationship between cohesion and collective efficacy in rugby teams. *Journal of Sport Behavior, 23,* 120–129.

Krabbe, P. F. M., Essink-Bot, M.-L., & Bonsel, G. J. (1997). The comparability and reliability of five health-state valuation methods. *Social Science and Medicine, 45,* 1641–1652.

Krackhardt, D., & Hanson, J. (1993) Informal Networks: The Company Behind the Chart. *Harvard Business Review, 71*(4)), 104–111.

Krackhardt, D., & Stern, R. N. (1988). Informal networks and organizational crises: An experimental simulation. *Social Psychology Quarterly, 51,* 123–140.

Krahé, B. (2000). Sexual scripts and heterosexual aggression. In T. Eckes & H. M. Trautner (Eds.), *The developmental social psychology of gender* (pp. 273–292). Mahwah, NJ: Lawrence Erlbaum Associates Publishers.

Kramer, J. K., & Hyclak, T. (2002). Why strikes occur: Evidence from the capital markets. *Industrial Relations: A Journal of Economy and Society, 41,* 80–93.

Kramer, R. M. (1995). In dubious battle: Heightened accountability, dysphoric cognition, and self-defeating bargaining behavior. In R. M. Kramer & D. M. Messick (Eds.), *Negotiation as a social process: New trends in theory and research* (pp. 95–120). Thousand Oaks, CA: Sage Publications, Inc.

Kramer, R. M. (1996). Divergent realities and convergent disappointments in the hierarchic relation: Trust and the intuitive auditor at work. In R. M. Kramer & T. R. Tyler (Eds.), *Trust in organizations: Frontiers of theory and research* (pp. 216–245). Thousand Oaks, CA: Sage Publications, Inc.

Kramer, R. M., & Messick, D. M. (1998). Getting by with a little help from our enemies: Collective paranoia and its role in intergroup relations. In C. Sedikides, J. Schopler, & C. A. Insko (Eds.), *Intergroup cognition and intergroup behavior* (pp. 233–255). Mahwah, NJ: Lawrence Erlbaum Associates, Inc., Publishers.

Kramer, R. M., Meyerson, D., & Davis, G. (1990). How much is enough? Psychological components of 'guns versus butter' decisions in a security dilemma. *Journal of Personality and Social Psychology, 58,* 984–993.

Kramer, R. M., Newton, E., & Pommerenke, P. L. (1993). Self-enhancement biases and negotiator judgment: Effects of self-esteem and mood. *Organizational Behavior and Human Decision Processes, 56,* 110–133.

Kramer, R. M., Pommerenke, P., & Newton, E. (1993). The social context of negotiation: Effects of social identity and interpersonal accountability on negotiator decision making. *Journal of Conflict Resolution, 37,* 633–654.

Kramer, R. M., Shah, P. P., & Woerner, S. L. (1995). Why ultimatums fail: Social identity and moralistic aggression in coercive bargaining. In R. M. Kramer & D. M. Messick (Eds.), *Negotiation as a social process: New trends in theory and research* (pp. 285–308). Thousand Oaks, CA: Sage Publications, Inc.

Kramer, T. J., Fleming, G. P., & Mannis, S. M. (2001). Improving face-to-face brainstorming through modeling and facilitation. *Small Group Research, 32,* 533–557.

Krämer, U. S., & Schneider, G. (2003). Faire Formeln: Psychologische und prozedurale Einflussfaktoren auf die Lösung von distributiven Konflikten [Fair Formulas: Psychological and

Procedural Determinants in the Resolution of Redistributive Conflicts]. *Kölner Zeitschrift für Soziologie und Sozialpsychologie, 55*(1), 55–78.

Kraus, S., Ryan, C. S., Judd, C. M., Hastie, R., & Park, B. (1993). Use of mental frequency distributions to represent variability among members of social categories. *Social Cognition, 11*, 22–43.

Krauss, R. M., & Morsella, E. (2006). Communication and conflict. In M. Deutsch, P. T. Coleman, & E. C. Marcus (Eds.), *The handbook of conflict resolution: Theory and practice* (2nd ed., pp. 144–157). Hoboken, NJ: Wiley. [Also in 1st ed., Deutsch & Coleman (Eds.), 2000, pp. 131–143.]

Krauss, S., & Wang, X. T. (2003). The psychology of the Monty Hall problem: Discovering psychological mechanisms for solving a tenacious brain teaser. *Journal of Experimental Psychology: General, 132*, 3–22.

Kravitz, D. A., & Gunto, S. (1992). Decisions and perceptions of recipients in ultimatum bargaining games. *Journal of Socio-Economics, 21*, 65–84.

Kray, L. J., Reb, J., Galinsky, A. D., & Thompson, L. (2004). Stereotype reactance at the bargaining table: The effect of stereotype activation and power on claiming and creating value. *Personality and Social Psychology Bulletin, 30*, 399–411.

Krebs, C. P., Costelloe, M., & Jenks, D. (2003). Drug control policy and smuggling innovation: A game-theoretic analysis. *Journal of Drug Issues, 33*, 133–160.

Kremer, J., Gallagher, A., Somerville, P., & Traylen, G. (1988). Social categorization and behaviour in mixed-motive games: A Northern Ireland study. *Social Behaviour, 3*, 229–236.

Kressel, G. M. (2000). The students' strike and Simmel's model of triadic relationships. *Megamot, 40*, 316–322.

Kressel, K. (2006). Mediation revisited. In M. Deutsch, P. T. Coleman, & E. C. Marcus (Eds.), *The handbook of conflict resolution: Theory and practice* (2nd ed., pp. 726–756). Hoboken, NJ: Wiley Publishing.

Kritikos, A., & Bolle, F. (2004). Punishment as a public good. When should monopolists care about a consumer boycott? *Journal of Economic Psychology, 25*, 355–372.

Kritzer, H. M., Hare, A. P., & Blumberg, H. H. (1974). The General Survey: A short measure of five personality dimensions. *Journal of Psychology, 86*, 165–172.

Krizan, Z., & Windschitl, P. D. (2007). Team allegiance can lead to both optimistic and pessimistic predictions. *Journal of Experimental Social Psychology, 43*, 327–333.

Krosgaard, M. A., Brodt, S. E., & Whitener, E. M. (2002). Trust in the face of conflict: The role of managerial trustworthy behavior and organizational context. *Journal of Applied Psychology, 87*, 312–319.

Krueger, J. (1992). On the overestimation of between-group differences. In W. Stroebe & M. Hewstone (Eds.), *European review of social psychology* (Vol. 3, pp. 31–56). Chichester, England: John Wiley & Sons.

Krueger, J. I., & Acevedo, M. (2008). A game-theoretic view of voting. *Journal of Social Issues, 64*, 467–485.

Kubota, K. (1997). Intergroup discrimination and illusory correlation induced by social category: Minority, majority, and outsider. *Japanese Journal of Psychology, 68*, 120–128.

Kuenne, R. E. (1989). Conflict management in mature rivalry. *Journal of Conflict Resolution, 33*, 554–566.

Kugihara, N. (1992). Collective behavior in an emergency: Escaping from a human maze. *Japanese Journal of Experimental Social Psychology, 31*, 246–255.

Kugihara, N. (2001). Effects of aggressive behaviour and group size on collective escape in an emergency: A test between a social identity model and deindividuation theory. *British Journal of Social Psychology, 40*, 575–598.

Kultti, K. (1999). Equivalence of Auctions and Posted Prices. *Games and Economic Behavior, 27*, 106–113.

Kumagai, T., & Ohbuchi, K.-I. (2001). The effect of collective self-esteem and group membership on aggression of 'third-party victims.' *Tohoku Psychologica Folia, 60*, 35–44.

Kumar, N., Scheer, L. K., & Steenkamp, J.-B. E. M. (1995). The effects of supplier fairness on vulnerable resellers. *Journal of Marketing Research, 32*, 54–65.

Kumar, R. (1997). The role of affect in negotiations: An integrative overview. *Journal of Applied Behavioral Science, 33*, 84–100.

Kunda, Z. (1999). *Social cognition: Making sense of people.* Cambridge, MA: MIT Press.

Kunda, Z., & Nisbett, R. E. (1988). Predicting individual evaluations from group evaluations and vice versa: Different patterns for self and other? *Personality and Social Psychology Bulletin, 14*, 326–334.

Kuon, B., & Uhlich, G. R. (1993). The negotiation agreement area: An experimental analysis of two-person characteristic function games. *Group Decision and Negotiation, 2*, 323–345.

Kurzban, R., Rigdon, M. L., & Wilson, B. J. (2008). Incremental approaches to establishing trust. *Experimental Economics, 11*, 370–389.

Kuwabara, K., Willer, R., Macy, M. W., Mashima, R., Terai, S., & Yamagishi, T. (2007). Culture, identity, and structure in social exchange: A web-based trust experiment in the United States and Japan. *Social Psychology Quarterly, 70*, 461–479.

Kwok, W. W., Wright, B., & Kashima, Y. (2007). Constructing intergroup relationships in social communication. *Japanese Psychological Research, 49*, 121–135.

Lacey, R., & Gruenfeld, D. (1999). Unwrapping the work group: How extra-organizational context affects group behavior. In R. Wageman (Ed.), *Research on managing groups and teams: Groups in context* (Vol. 2, pp. 157–177). San Diego, CA: Elsevier Science/JAI Press, 1999.

Ladoucer, R., & Dubé, D. (1997). Erroneous perceptions in generating random sequences: Identification and strength of a basic misconception in gambling behavior. *Swiss Journal of Psychology/Schweizerische Zeitschrift für Psychologie/Revue Suisse de Psychologie, 56*, 256–259.

Laensisalmi, H., & Kivimäki, M. (1999). Factors associated with innovative climate: What is the role of stress? *Stress Medicine, 15*, 203–213.

LaFrance, M. (2001). Gender and social interaction. In R. K. Unger (Ed.), *Handbook of the psychology of women and gender* (pp. 245–255). Hoboken, NJ: John Wiley & Sons Inc.

Lahiri, S. (1994). Some concepts of distributive justice in bargaining problems. *Group Decision and Negotiation, 3*, 133–143.

Lai, B., & Reiter, D. (2000). Democracy, political similarity and international alliances, 1816–1992. *Journal of Conflict Resolution, 44*, 203–227.

Lai, L. S. L., & Turban, E. (2008). Groups formation and operations in the Web 2.0 environment and social networks. *Group Decision and Negotiation, 17*, 387–402.

Laiken, M. E. (1997). Collaborative processes for collaborative organizational design: The role of reflection, dialogue and polarity management in creating an environment for organizational learning. *Organization Development Journal, 15*(4), 35–42.

Laing, J. D., & Slotznick, B. (1991). When anyone can veto: A laboratory study of committees governed by unanimous rule. *Behavioral Science, 36*, 179–195.

Lakin, F. (1990). Visual languages for cooperation: A performing medium approach to systems for cooperative work. In J. Galegher, R. E. Kraut, & C. Egido (Eds.), *Intellectual teamwork: Social and technological foundations of cooperative work* (pp. 453–488). Hillsdale, NJ: Lawrence Erlbaum Associates, Inc.

Lalonde, R. N. (2002). Testing the social identity-intergroup differentiation hypothesis: "We're not American eh"! *British Journal of Social Psychology, 41*, 611–630.

Lalonde, R. N., & Silverman, R. A. (1994). Behavioral preferences in response to social injustice: The effects of group permeability and social identity salience. *Journal of Personality and Social Psychology, 66*, 78–85.

Lam, S. S. K., & Schaubroeck, J. (2000). Improving group decisions by better pooling information: A comparative advantage of group decision support systems. *Journal of Applied Psychology, 85*, 565–573.

Lam, S. S. K., Schaubroeck, J., & Brown, A. D. (2004). Esteem maintenance among groups: Laboratory and field studies of group performance cognitions. *Organizational Behavior and Human Decision Processes, 94*, 86–101.

Lambert, A. J. (1995). Stereotypes and social judgment: The consequences of group variability. *Journal of Personality and Social Psychology, 68*, 388–403.

Lambert, A. J., Barton, L., Lickel, B. A., & Wells, J. (1998). The influence of group variability and processing goals on the ease of making decisions about social categories. *Personality and Social Psychology Bulletin, 24*, 807–820.

Lambo, L. D., & Moulen, J. (2002). Ordinal equivalence of power notions in voting games. *Theory and Decision, 53*, 313–325.

Lamertz, K. (2002). The social construction of fairness: Social influence and sense making in organizations. *Journal of Organizational Behavior, 23*, 19–37.

Lance, C. E., Kavanagh, M. J., & Brink, K. E. (2002). Retraining climate as a predictor of retraining success and as a moderator of the relationhip between cross-job retraining time estimates and time to proficiency in the new job. *Group and Organization Management, 27*, 294–317.

Langfred, C. W. (2000a). The paradox of self-management: Individual and group autonomy in work groups. *Journal of Organizational Behavior, 21*, 563–585.

Langfred, C. W. (2000b). Work-group design and autonomy: A field study of the interaction between task interdependence and group autonomy. *Small Group Research, 31*, 54–70.

Langlois, C., & Langlois, J.-P. P. (1999). Behavioral issues of rationality in international interaction: An empirical appraisal. *Journal of Conflict Resolution, 43*, 818–839.

Large, M. D. (1999). The effectiveness of gifts as unilateral initiatives in bargaining. *Sociological Perspectives, 42*, 525–542.

Larrick, R. P., & Blount, S. (1997). The claiming effect: Why players are more generous in social dilemmas than in ultimatum games. *Journal of Personality and Social Psychology, 72*, 810–825.

Larrick, R. P., & Boles, T. L. (1995). Avoiding regret in decisions with feedback: A negotiation example. *Organizational Behavior and Human Decision Processes, 63*, 87–97.

Larrick, R. P., & Wu, G. (2007). Claiming a large slice of a small pie: Asymmetric disconfirmation in negotiation. *Journal of Personality and Social Psychology, 93*, 212–233.

Larson, C. E., & LaFasto, F. M. J. (1989). *Teamwork: What must go right/what can go wrong.* Thousand Oaks, CA: Sage Publications, Inc.

Larson, J. R., & Christensen, C. (1993). Groups as problem-solving units: Toward a new meaning of social cognition. *British Journal of Social Psychology. 32*, 5–30.

Larson, J. R., & Schaumann, L. J. (1993). Group goals, group coordination, and group member motivation. *Human Performance. 6*, 49–69.

Laruelle, A., & Valenciano, F. (2004). On The meaning of Owen-Banzhaf coalitional value in voting situations. *Theory and Decision, 56*, 113–123.

Laskowski, M. C., & Slonim, R. L. (1999). An asymptotic solution for sealed bid common-value auctions with bidders having asymmetric information. *Games and Economic Behavior, 28*, 238–255.

Latané, B., & Liu, J. H. (1996). The intersubjective geometry of social space. *Journal of Communication, 46*(4), 26–34.

LaTendresse, D. (2000). Social identity and intergroup relations within the hospital. *Journal of Social Distress and the Homeless, 9*, 51–69.

Laughlin, P. R., Shupe, E. I., & Magley, V. J. (1998). Effectiveness of positive hypothesis testing for cooperative groups. *Organizational Behavior and Human Decision Processes, 73*, 27–38.

Laukka, S. J., Järvilehto, T., Alexandrov, Y. I., & Lindqvist, J. (1995). Frontal midline theta related to learning in a simulated driving task. *Biological Psychology, 40*, 313–320.

Laurenceau, J.-P., Rivera, L. M., Schaffer, A. R., & Pietromonaco, P. R. (2004). Intimacy as an Interpersonal Process: Current Status and Future Directions. In D. J. Mashek & A. P. Aron (Eds.), *Handbook of closeness and intimacy* (pp. 61–78). Mahwah, NJ: Lawrence Erlbaum Associates Publishers.

Laursen, B. (1993). The perceived impact of conflict on adolescent relationships. *Merrill Palmer Quarterly, 39*, 535–550.

Lawler, E. J. (1992). Power processes in bargaining. *Sociological Quarterly, 33*, 17–34.

Lawler, E. J. (1995). "Power processes in bargaining": Erratum. *Sociological Quarterly, 36*, [218].

Lawler, E. J. (2003). Interaction, emotion, and collective identities. In P. J. Burke, T. J. Owens, R. T. Serpe, & P. A. Thoits (Eds.), *Advances in identity theory and research* (pp. 135–149). New York: Kluwer Academic/Plenum Publishers.

Lawler, E. J., & Ford, R. (1993). Metatheory and friendly competition in theory growth: The case of power processes in bargaining. In J. Berger & M. Zelditch, Jr (Eds.), *Theoretical research programs: Studies in the growth of theory* (pp. 172–210). Stanford, CA: Stanford University Press.

Lawler, E. J., Ford, R. S., & Blegen, M. A. (1988). Coercive capability in conflict: A test of bilateral deterrence versus conflict spiral theory. *Social Psychology Quarterly, 51*, 93–107.

Lawler, Edward J, & Yoon, Jeongkoo. (1993). Power and the emergence of commitment behavior in negotiated exchange. *American Sociological Review, 58*, 465–481.

Lawrence, T. B., Mauws, M. K., Dyck, B., & Kleysen, R. F. (2005). The politics of organizational learning: Integrating power into the 4I framework. *Academy of Management Review, 30*, 180–191.

Lax, D. A., & Sebenius, J. K. (1991). Negotiating through an agent. *Journal of Conflict Resolution, 35*, 474–493.

Lea, M., & Spears, R. (1991). Computer-mediated communication, de-individuation and group decision-making. *International Journal of Man-Machine Studies, 34*, 283–301.

Leach, C. W., Spears, R., Branscombe, N. R., & Doosje, B. (2003). Malicious pleasure: Schadenfreude at the suffering of another group. *Journal of Personality and Social Psychology, 84*, 932–943.

Leach, C. W., Van Zomeren, M., Zebel, S., Vliek, M. L. W., Pennekamp, S. F., Doosje, B., Ouwerkerk, J. W., & Spears, R. (2008). Group-level self-definition and self-investment: A hierarchical (multicomponent) model of in-group identification. *Journal of Personality and Social Psychology, 95*, 144–165.

Leavitt, H. J. (1951). Some effects of certain communication patterns on group performance. *Journal of Abnormal and Social Psychology, 46*, 38–50.

Lebow, R. N. (1996). *The art of bargaining*. Baltimore, MD: Johns Hopkins University Press.

Ledgerwood, A., & Chaiken, S. (2007). Priming us and them: Automatic assimilation and contrast in group attitudes. *Journal of Personality and Social Psychology, 93*, 940–956.

Ledgerwood, A., Chaiken, S., Gruenfeld, D. H., & Judd, C. M. (2006). Changing minds: Persuasion in negotiation and conflict resolution. In M. Deutsch, P. T. Coleman, & E. C. Marcus (Eds.), *The handbook of conflict resolution: Theory and practice* (2nd ed., pp. 455–485). Hoboken, NJ: Wiley Publishing.

Ledyard, J. O., & Palfrey, T. R. (1995). Introduction. *Games and Economic Behavior, 10*, 1–5.

Lee, C., Tinsley, C. H., & Bobko, P. (2002). An investigation of the antecedents and consequences of group-level confidence. *Journal of Applied Social Psychology, 32*, 1628–1652.

Lee, D. Y. (2000). Retail bargaining behaviour of American and Chinese customers. *European Journal of Marketing, 34*, 190–206.

Lee, E.-J. (2004). Effects of visual representation on social influence in computer-mediated communication: Experimental tests of the social identity model of deindividuation effects. *Human Communication Research, 30*, 234–259.

Lee, E.-J. (2006). When and how does depersonalization increase conformity to group norms in computer-mediated communication? *Communication Research, 33*, 423–447.

Lee, F. (1997). When the going gets tough, do the tough ask for help? Help seeking and power motivation in organizations. *Organizational Behavior and Human Decision Processes, 72*, 336–363.

Lee, K. S. (2002). Building intergroup relations after September 11. *Analyses of Social Issues and Public Policy, 2*(1), 131–141.

Lee, Y. T., & Ottati, V. (1995). Perceived in-group homogeneity as a function of group membership salience and stereotype threat. *Personality and Social Psychology Bulletin, 21*, 610–619.

Lee-Kelley, L. (2002). Situational leadership: Managing the virtual project team. *Journal of Management Development, 21*, 461–476.

Legrenzi, P., Politzer, G., & Girotto, V. (1996). Contract proposals: A sketch of a grammar. *Theory and Psychology, 6*, 247–265.

Legut, J., Potters,. A. M., & Tijs, S. H. (1995). A transfer property of equilibrium payoffs in economies with land. *Games and Economic Behavior, 10*, 355–367.

Lehesvirta, T. (2004). Learning processes in a work organization: From individual to collective and/or vice versa? *Journal of Workplace Learning, 16*, 92–100.

Lehman, W. E. K., Greener, J. M., & Simpson, D. D. (2002). Assessing organizational readiness for change. *Journal of Substance Abuse Treatment, 22*, 197–209.

Lei, D., & Greer, C. R. (2003). The empathetic organization. *Organizational Dynamics, 32*(2), 142–164.

Leifer, E. M. (1988). Trails of involvement: Evidence for local games. *Sociological Forum, 3*, 499–524.

Leik, R. K., & Meeker, B. F. (1995). Computer simulation for exploring theories: Models of interpersonal cooperation and competition. *Sociological Perspectives, 38*, 463–482.

Leik, R. K., Owens, T. J., & Tallman, I. (1999). Interpersonal commitments: The interplay of social networks and individual identities. In J. M. Adams & W. H. Jones (Eds.), *Handbook of interpersonal commitment and relationship stability* (pp. 239–256). Dordrecht, Netherlands: Kluwer Academic Publishers.

Lembke, S., & Wilson, M. G. (1998). Putting the "Team" into teamwork: Alternative theoretical contributions for contemporary management practice. *Human Relations, 51*, 927–944.

Leon, G. R., Kafner, R., Hoffman, R. G., & Dupre, L. (1994). Group processes and task effectiveness in a Soviet-American expedition team. *Environment and Behavior, 26*, 149–165.

Leonardelli, G. J., & Brewer, M. B. (2001). Minority and majority discrimination: When and why. *Journal of Experimental Social Psychology, 37*, 468–485.

LePine, J. A. (2003). Team adaptation and postchange performance: Effects of team composition in terms of members' cognitive ability and personality. *Journal of Applied Psychology, 88*, 27–39.

LePine, J. A., Piccolo, R. F., Jackson, C. L., Mathieu, J. E., & Saul, J. R. (2008). A meta-analysis of teamwork processes: Tests of a multidimensional model and relationships with team effectiveness criteria. *Personnel Psychology, 61*, 273–307.

Lepischak, B. (2004). Building community for Toronto's lesbian, gay, bisexual, transsexual and transgender youth. In Y. C. Padilla (Ed.), *Gay and lesbian rights organizing: Community-based strategies* (pp. 81–98). Binghamton, NY: Harrington Park Press/The Haworth Press.

Lepore, L., & Brown, R. (2002). The role of awareness: Divergent automatic stereotype activation and implicit judgment correction. *Social Cognition, 20*, 321–351.

Lerner, A. (1998). A pie allocation among sharing groups. *Games and Economic Behavior, 22*, 316–330.

Lesch, C. L. (1994). Observing theory in practice: Sustaining consciousness in a coven. In L. R. Frey (Ed.), *Group communication in context: Studies of natural groups* (pp. 57–82). Hillsdale, NJ: Lawrence Erlbaum Associates, Inc.

Leung, K. (1988). Some determinants of conflict avoidance. *Journal of Cross-Cultural Psychology, 19*, 125–136.

Leung, K., & Wu, P. G. (1990). Dispute processing: A cross-cultural analysis. In R. W. Brislin (Ed.), *Applied cross-cultural psychology* [Cross-cultural research and methodology series, Vol. 14], pp. 209–231). Newbury Park, CA: Sage Publications, Inc.

Leung, K., Tong, K.-K., & Lind, E. A. (2007). Realpolitik versus fair process: Moderating effects of group identification on acceptance of political decisions. *Journal of Personality and Social Psychology, 92*, 476–489.

Leung, T., & Kim, M.-S. (2007). Eight conflict handling styles: Validation of model and instrument. *Journal of Asian Pacific Communication, 17*, 173–198.

Levin, S., & Sidanius, J. (1999). Social dominance and social identity in the United States and Israel: Ingroup favoritism or outgroup derogation? *Political Psychology, 20*, 99–126.

Levin, S., Van Laar, C., & Sidanius, J. (2003). The effects of ingroup and outgroup friendship on ethnic attitudes in college: A longitudinal study. *Group Processes and Intergroup Relations, Vol 6*, 76–92.

Levine, J. M., Bogart, L. M., & Zdaniuk, B. (1996). Impact of anticipated group membership on cognition. In R. M. Sorrentino & E. T. Higgins (Eds.), *Handbook of motivation and cognition, Vol. 3: The interpersonal context* (pp. 531–569). New York: Guilford Press.

Levine, J. M., & Hogg, M. A. (Eds.). (2010). *Encyclopedia of group processes & intergroup relations*. Thousand Oaks, CA: Sage.

Levine, J. M., & Moreland, R. L. (1991). Culture and socialization in work groups. In L. B. Resnick, J. M. Levine, & S. D. Teasley (Eds.), *Perspectives on socially shared cognition* (pp. 257–279). Washington, DC: American Psychological Association.

Levine, J. M., & Moreland, R. L. (2004). Collaboration: The social context of theory development. *Personality and Social Psychology Review, 8*, 164–172.

Levine, J. M., & Moreland, R. L. (Eds.). (2006). *Small groups*. New York: Psychology Press.

Levine, J. M., & Thompson, L. (1996). Conflict in groups. In E. T. Higgins & A. W. Kruglanski (Eds.), *Social psychology: Handbook of basic principles* (pp. 745–776). New York: Guilford Press.

Levine, M., & Crowther, S. (2008). The responsive bystander: How social group membership and group size can encourage as well as inhibit bystander intervention. *Journal of Personality and Social Psychology, 95*, 1429–1439.

Levine, S. S., & Kurzban, R. (2006). Explaining clustering in social networks: Towards an evolutionary theory of cascading benefits. *Managerial and Decision Economics, 27*, 173–187.

Levine, S. (2009). *Getting to resolution: Turning conflict into collaboration (2nd ed.)*. San Francisco: Berrett-Koehler Publishers.

Levis, A. J. (1988). *Conflict analysis: The formal theory of behavior: A theory and its experimental validation*. Manchester Village, VT: Normative Publications.

Levy, S. Y., Wambolt, F. S., & Fiese, B. H. (1997). Family-of-origin experiences and conflict resolution behaviors of young adult dating couples. *Family Process, 36*, 297–310.

Lewicki, R. J., Bies, R. J., & Sheppard, B. H. (Eds.). (1997). *Research on negotiation in organizations, Vol. 6*. Greenwich, CT: Jai Press, Inc.

Lewicki, R. J., & Bunker, B. B. (1995). Trust in relationships: A model of development and decline. In B. B. Bunker & J. Z. Rubin (Eds.), *Conflict, cooperation, and justice: Essays inspired by the work of Morton Deutsch* (pp. 133–173). San Francisco: Jossey-Bass Inc, Publishers.

Lewin, K., Lippitt, R., & White, R. K. (1939). Patterns of aggressive behavior in experimentally created social climates. *Journal of Social Psychology, 10*, 271–299.

Leyens, J. Ph., Cortes, B. P., Demoulin, S., Dovidio, J., Fiske, S. T., Gaunt, R., Paladino, M. P., Rodriguez-Torres, R. T., & Vaes, V. (2003). Emotional prejudice, essentialism, and nationalism. *European Journal of Social Psychology, 33*, 709–717.

Li, E. Y., & Baillie, A. S. (1993). Mixing case method with business games: Student evaluations. *Simulation and Gaming, 24*, 336–355.

Li, S., & Taplin, J. E. (2002). Examining whether there is a disjunction effect in Prisoner's Dilemma games. *Chinese Journal of Psychology, 44*, 25–46.

Liang, D. W., Moreland, R., & Argote, L. (1995). Group versus individual training and group performance: The mediating factor of transactive memory. *Personality and Social Psychology Bulletin, 21*, 384–393.

Libby, M. K., & Austin, M. J. (2002). Building a coalition of non-profit agencies to collaborate with a county health and human services agency: The Napa county behavioral health committee of the Napa coalition of non-profits. *Administration in Social Work, 26*(4), 81–99.

Libby, M. K., & Austin, M. J. (2004a). Building a coalition of nonprofit agencies to collaborate with a county health and human services agency. In M. J. Austin (Ed.), *Changing welfare services: Case studies of local welfare reform programs* (pp. 267–283). Binghamton, NY: Haworth Social Work Practice Press.

Libby, M. K., & Austin, M. J. (2004b). A community partnership approach to serving the homeless. In M. J. Austin (Ed.), *Changing welfare services: Case studies of local welfare reform programs* (pp. 231–250). Binghamton, NY: Haworth Social Work Practice Press.

Liberman, V., Samuels, S. M., & Ross, L. (2004). The name of the game: Predictive power of reputations versus situational labels in determining Prisoner's Dilemma Game moves. *Personality and Social Psychology Bulletin, 30*, 1175–1185.

Licata, L., & Klein, O. (2002). Does European citizenship breed xenophobia?: European identification as a predictor of intolerance towards immigrants. *Journal of Community and Applied
Social Psychology, 12*, 323–337.

Lichtenstein, R., Alexander, J. A., Jinnett, K., & Ullman, E. (1997). Embedded intergroup relations
in interdisciplinary teams: Effects on perceptions of level of team integration. *Journal of Applied Behavioral Science, 33*, 413–434.

Liden, R. C., Wayne, S. J., & Bradway, L. K. (1997). Task interdependence as a moderator of the
relation between group control and performance. *Human Relations, 50*, 169–181.

Liebkind, K., Haaramo, J., & Jasinskaja-Lahti, I. (2000). Effects of contact and personality on
intergroup attitudes of different professionals. *Journal of Community and Applied Social Psychology, 10*, 171–181.

Liebkind, K., Henning-Lindblom, A., & Solheim, E. (2006). Ingroup favouritism and outgroup
derogation among Swedish-speaking Finns. *Nordic Psychology, 58*, 262–278 [also cited as
pp. 57–73].

Liebrand, Wim B., Poppe, Matthijs, & Wilke, Henk A. (1989). Cooeperatie en competitie: Een
inleiding [Cooperation and competition: An introduction]. *Nederlands Tijdschrift voor de Psychologie en haar Grensgebieden, 44*, 195–200.

Lim, R. G., & Carnevale, P. J. (1990). Contingencies in the mediation of disputes. *Journal of Personality and Social Psychology, Vol 58*, 259–272.

Lim, R. G., & Carnevale, P. J. (1995). Influencing mediator behavior through bargainer framing.
*International Journal of Conflict Management, 6*, 349–368.

Lim, S. G.-S., & Murnigham, J. K. (1994). Phases, deadlines, and the bargaining process. *Organizational Behavior and Human Decision Processes, 58*, 153–171.

Lin, Z., Yang, H., Arya, B., Huang, Z., & Li, D. (2005). Structural versus individual perspectives
on the dynamics of group performance: Theoretical exploration and empirical investigation.
*Journal of Management, 31*, 354–380.

Lind, E. A., Huo, Y. J., & Tyler, T. R. (1994) .... And justice for all: Ethnicity, gender, and preferences for dispute resolution procedures. *Law and Human Behavior, 18*, 269–290.

Lindeman, M., & Koskela, P. (1994). Group size, controllability of group membership, and comparative dimension as determinants of intergroup discrimination. *European Journal of Social
Psychology, 24*, 267–278.

Lindholm, M., Ryan, D., Kadushin, C., Saxe, L., & Brodsky, A. (2004). "Fighting back" against
substance abuse: The structure and function of community coalitions. *Human Organization,
63*, 265–276.

Lindskold, S., & Han, G. (1988a). GRIT as a foundation for intergrative bargaining. *Personality
and Social Psychology Bulletin, 14*, 335–345.

Lindskold, S., & Han, G. (1988b). Group resistance to influence by a conciliatory member. *Small
Group Behavior, 19*, 19–34.

Linnehan, F., Konrad, A. M., Reitman, F., Greenhalgh, A., & London, M. (2003). Behavioral goals
for a diverse organization: The effects of attitudes, social norms, and racial identity for Asian
Americans and Whites. *Journal of Applied Social Psychology, 33*, 1331–1359.

Linville, P. W., & Fischer, G. W. (1993). Exemplar and abstraction models of perceived group variability and stereotypicality. *Social Cognition, 11*, 92–125.

Linville, P. W., & Fischer, G. W. (1998). Group variability and covariation: Effects on intergroup
judgment and behavior. In C. Sedikides, J. Schopler, & C. A. Insko (Eds.), *Intergroup cognition and intergroup behavior* (pp. 123–150). Mahwah, NJ: Lawrence Erlbaum Associates, Inc.,
Publishers.

Lipponen, J., Helkama, K., & Juslin, M. (2003). Subgroup identification, superordinate identification and intergroup bias between the subgroups. *Group Processes and Intergroup Relations,
6*, 239–250.

Lipschutz, R. D. (1991). Bargaining among nations: Culture, history, and perceptions in regime
formation. *Evaluation Review, 15*, 46–74.

Lipschutz, R. D. (1993). "Bargaining among nations: Culture, history, and perceptions in regime
formation": Erratum. *Evaluation Review, 17*, 663.

Little, B. L., & Madigan, R. M. (1997). The relationship between collective efficacy and performance in manufacturing work teams. *Small Group Research, 28*, 517–534.

Littlefield, L., Love, A., Peck, C., & Wertheim, E. H. (1993). A model for resolving conflict: Some theoretical, empirical and practical implications. *Australian Psychologist, 28*, 80–85.

Littlepage, G., Robison, W., & Reddington, K. (1997). Effects of task experience and group experience on group performance, member ability, and recognition of expertise. *Organizational Behavior and Human Decision Processes, 69*, 133–147.

Litvak-Hirsch, T., Bar-On, D., & Chaitin, J. (2003). Whose House is This? Dilemmas of Identity Construction in the Israeli-Palestinian Context. *Peace and Conflict: Journal of Peace Psychology, 9*, 127–148.

Liu, J. H., & Allen, M. W. (1999). Evolution of political complexity in Maori Hawke's Bay: Archaeological history and its challenge to intergroup theory in psychology. *Group Dynamics: Theory, Research, and Practice, 3*, 64–80.

Imhof, L. A., Fudenberg, D., & Nowak, M. A. (2005). Evolutionary cycles of cooperation and defection. *PNAS Proceedings of the National Academy of Sciences of the United States of America, 102*, 10797–10800.

Lo, K. C. (1999). Extensive form games with uncertainty averse players. *Games and Economic Behavior, 28*, 256–270.

Lo, K. C. (2000). Epistemic conditions for agreement and stochastic independence of epsilon-contaminated beliefs. *Mathematical Social Sciences, 39*, 207–234.

Lodewijkx, H. F. M. (2001). Individual-group continuity in cooperation and competition under varying communication conditions. *Current Research in Social Psychology, 6*(12), 166–182.

Lok, P., & Crawford, J. (2001). Antecedents of organizational commitment and the mediating role of job satisfaction. *Journal of Managerial Psychology, 16*, 594–613.

Lok, P., & Crawford, J. (2004). The effect of organisational culture and leadership style on job satisfaction and organisational commitment: A cross-national comparison. *Journal of Management Development, 23*, 321–338.

London, M., & Sessa, V. I. (2007). The development of group interaction patterns: How groups become adaptive, generative, and transformative learners. *Human Resource Development Review, 6*, 353–376.

Long, K. M., & Manstead, A. S. R. (1997). Group immersion and intergroup differentiation: Contextual shifts in categorization. *British Journal of Social Psychology, 36*, 291–303.

Long, K. M., Spears, R., & Manstead, A. S. R. (1994). The influence of personal and collective self-esteem on strategies of social differentiation. *British Journal of Social Psychology, 33*, 313–329.

Lootsma, F. A., Sluijs, J. M., & Wang, S. Y. (1994). Pairwise comparison of concessions in negotiation processes. *Group Decision and Negotiation, 3*, 121–131.

Lopez, F. G., Gover, M. R., Leskela, J., Sauer, E. M., Schirmer, L., & Wyssmann, J. (1997). Attachment styles, shame, guilt, and collaborative problem-solving orientations. *Personal Relationships, 4*, 187–199.

Lopez, L. C. (1995). Correlations of selected cognitive styles with cooperation in a prisoner's dilemma game. *Psychological Reports, 77*, 242.

López-Paredes, A., Hernández-Iglesias, C., & Gutiérrez, J. P. (2002). Towards a new experimental socio-economics: Complex behaviour in bargaining. *Journal of Socio-Economics, 31*, 423–429.

Lopomo, G. (2001). Optimality and robustness of the English Auction. *Games and Economic Behavior, 36*, 219–240.

Lorber, J., & Bandlamudi, L. (1993). The dynamics of marital bargaining in male infertility. *Gender and Society, 7*, 32–49.

Lord, C. G., Desforges, D. M., Ramsey, S. L., Trezza, G. R., & Lepper, M. R. (1991). Typicality effects in attitude)ehavior consistency: Effects of category discrimination and category knowledge. *Journal of Experimental Social Psychology, 27*, 550–575.

Lord, R. G., & Maher, K. G. (1991). *Leadership and information processing: Linking perception and performance*. London: Unwin Hyman.

Lorenzi-Cioldi, F. (1993). They all look alike, but so do we...sometimes: Perceptions of in-group and out-group homogeneity as a function of sex and context. *British Journal of Social Psychology, 32,* 111–124.

Lorenzi-Cioldi, F. (1995). The self in collection and aggregate groups. In I. Lubek, R. Van Hezewijk, G. Pheterson, & C. W. Tolman (Eds.), *Trends and issues in theoretical psychology* (pp. 46–52). New York: Springer Publishing Co, Inc.

Losada, M., & Heaphy, E. (2004). The role of positivity and connectivity in the performance of business teams: A nonlinear dynamics model. *American Behavioral Scientist, 47,* 740–765.

Lou, Y., Abrami, P. C., & d'Apollonia, S. (2001). Small group and individual learning with technology: A meta-analysis. *Review of Educational Research, 71,* 449–521.

Louis, W. R., Duck, J. M., Terry, D. J., Schuller, R. A., & Lalonde, R. N. (2007). Why Do Citizens Want to Keep Refugees Out? Threats, Fairness and Hostile Norms in the Treatment of Asylum Seekers. *European Journal of Social Psychology, 37,* 53–73.

Lowrey, W. (2002). Word people vs. picture people: Normative differences and strategies for control over work among newsroom subgroups. *Mass Communication and Society, 5,* 411–432.

Lu, X., & McAfee, R. P. (1996). The evolutionary stability of auctions over bargaining. *Games and Economic Behavior, 15,* 228–254.

Lumsden, M., & Wolfe, R. (1996). Evolution of the problem-solving workshop: An introduction to social-psychological approaches to conflict resolution. *Peace and Conflict: Journal of Peace Psychology, 2,* 37–67.

Lundberg, S., & Pollak, R. A. (2001). Bargaining and distribution in families. In Thornton, A (Ed.). *The well-being of children and families: Research and data needs* (pp. 314–338). Ann Arbor, MI: The University of Michigan Press.

Lundgren, D. C. (1998). Members' changes in attitude toward cooperative and antagonistic leaders in a competitive intergroup situation. *Psychological Reports, 82,* 254.

Lusk, J. L., & Hudson, D. (2004). Effect of monitor-subject cheap talk on ultimatum game offers. *Journal of Economic Behavior and Organization, 54,* 439–443.

Lydon, J. E., Menzies-Toman, D., Burton, K., & Bell, C. (2008). If-then contingencies and the differential effects of the availability of an attractive alternative on relationship maintenance for men and women. *Journal of Personality and Social Psychology, 95,* 50–65.

Ma, J. (2001). Job Matching and coalition formation with utility or disutility of co-workers. *Games and Economic Behavior, 34,* 83–103.

Maass, A., Ceccarelli, R., & Rudin, S. (1996). Linguistic intergroup bias: Evidence for in-group-protective motivation. *Journal of Personality and Social Psychology, 71,* 512–526.

Maass, A., Milesi, A., Zabbini, S., & Stahlberg, D. (1995). Linguistic intergroup bias: Differential expectancies or in-group protection? *Journal of Personality and Social Psychology, 68,* 116–126.

Maass, A., Salvi, D., Arcuri, L., & Semin, G. R. (1989). Language use in intergroup contexts: The linguistic intergroup bias. *Journal of Personality and Social Psychology, 57,* 981–993.

MacGeorge, E. L. (2001). Support providers' interaction goals: The influence of attributions and emotions. *Communication Monographs, 68,* 72–97.

Machunsky, M., & Meiser, T. (2009). Mood and cognition in intergroup judgment. In S. Otten, K. Sassenberg, & T. Kessler (Eds.), *Intergroup relations: The role of motivation and emotion* (pp. 83–100). New York: Psychology Press.

MacKenzie, K. R., & Kennedy, J. L. (1991). Primate ethology and group dynamics. In S. Tuttman (Ed.), *Psychoanalytic group theory and therapy: Essays in honor of Saul Scheidlinger* (pp. 357–377). Madison, CT: International Universities Press, Inc.

Mackie, D. M., Allison, S. T., Worth, L. T., & Asuncion, A. G. (1992). The impact of outcome biases on counterstereotypic inferences about groups. *Personality and Social Psychology Bulletin, 18,* 44–51.

Mackie, D. M., Devos, T., & Smith, E. R. (2000). Intergroup emotions: Explaining offensive action tendencies in an intergroup context. *Journal of Personality and Social Psychology, 79,* 602–616.

Mackie, D. M., Gastardo-Conaco, M., & Skelly, J. J. (1992). Knowledge of the advocated position and the processing of in-group and out-group persuasive messages. *Personality and Social Psychology Bulletin, 18,* 145–151.

Mackie, D. M., & Queller, S. (2000). The impact of group membership on persuasion: Revisiting "Who says what to whom with what effect?" In D. J. Terry & M. A. Hogg (Eds.), *Attitudes, behavior, and social context: The role of norms and group membership* (pp. 135–155). Mahwah, NJ: Lawrence Erlbaum Associates Publishers.

Mackie, D. M., Queller, S., Stroessner, S. J., & Hamilton, D. L. (1996). Making stereotypes better or worse: Multiple roles for positive affect in group impressions. In R. M. Sorrentino & E. T. Higgins (Eds.), *Handbook of motivation and cognition, Vol. 3: The interpersonal context* (pp. 371–396). New York: Guilford Press.

Mackie, D. M., & Smith, E. R. (Eds.). (2002). *From prejudice to intergroup emotions: Differentiated reactions to social groups.* New York: Psychology Press.

Mackintosh, K. H. (1998). Bargaining policies and social exchange: Review of a neglected concept. *Journal of Socio-Economics, 27,* 565–585.

Macy, M. W. (1995). PAVLOV and the evolution of cooperation: An experimental test. *Social Psychology Quarterly, 58,* 74–87.

Maczynski, J., Lindell, M., Motowidlo, S. J., Sigfrids, C., & Jarmuz, S. (1997). A comparison of organizational and societal culture in Finland and Poland. *Polish Psychological Bulletin, 28,* 269–278.

Madhavan, R., Gnyawali, D. R., & He, J. (2004). Two's company, three's a crowd? Triads in cooperative-competitive networks. *Academy of Management Journal, 47,* 918–927.

Mae, L., Carlston, D. E., & Skowronski, J. J. (1999). Spontaneous trait transference to familiar communications: Is a little knowledge a dangerous thing? *Journal of Personality and Social Psychology, 77,* 233–246.

Maertz, C. P., Jr., Bauer, T. N., Mosley, D. C., Jr., Posthuma, R. A., & Campion, M. A. (2004). Do procedural justice perceptions in a selection testing context predict applicant attraction and intention toward the organization? *Journal of Applied Social Psychology, 34,* 125–145.

Magjuka, R. J., & Schmenner, R. W. (1993). Cellular manufacturing, group technology, and human resource management: An international study. *International Journal of Management, 10,* 405–412.

Mahmood, M. A., Hall, L., & Swanberg, D. L. (2001). Factors affecting information technology usage: A meta-analysis of the empirical literature. *Journal of Organizational Computing and Electronic Commerce, 11,* 107–130.

Maio, G. R., Greenland, K., Bernard, M., & Esses, V. M. (2001). Effects of intergroup ambivalence on information processing: The role of physiological arousal. *Group Processes and Intergroup Relations, 4,* 355–372.

Majeski, S. J., & Fricks, S. (1995). Conflict and cooperation in international relations. *Journal of Conflict Resolution, 39,* 622–645.

Major, B., Gramzow, R. H., McCoy, S. K., Levin, S., Schmader, T., & Sidanius, J. (2002). Perceiving personal discrimination: The role of group status and legitimizing ideology. *Journal of Personality and Social Psychology, 82,* 269–282.

Makimura, Y., & Yamagishi, T. (2003). Ongoing group interaction, ingroup favoritism, and reward allocation. *Japanese Journal of Psychology, 73,* 488–493.

Makino, K., & Takemura, K. (1993). Japanese concessional behaviors as interpersonal interaction. *Psychological Reports. Feb; Vol 72,* 103–109.

Makino, K., & Takemura, K. (1994). Cognitive structure of Japanese concessional behaviors. *Psychological Reports, 74,* 771–778.

Makoul, G., & Roloff, M. E. (1998). The role of efficacy and outcome expectations in the decision to withhold relational complaints. *Communication Research, 25,* 5–29.

Malhotra, D. (2004). Trust and reciprocity decisions: The differing perspectives of trustors and trusted parties. *Organizational Behavior and Human Decision Processes, 94,* 61–73.

Malhotra, D., & Bazerman, M. H. (2008). Psychological influence in negotiation: An introduction long overdue. *Journal of Management, 34,* 509–531.

Malloy, T. E. (2008). Intergroup relations and reconciliation: Theoretical analysis and method-ological implications. In A. Nadler, T. E. Malloy, & J. D. Fisher (Eds.), *The social psychology of intergroup reconciliation* (pp. 345–365). New York: Oxford University Press.

Mallubhatla, R., Pattipati, K. R., Kleinman, D. L., & Tang, Z. B. (1991). A model of distributed team information processing under ambiguity. *IEEE Transactions on Systems, Man, and Cybernetics, 21*, 713–725.

Mamali, Catalin. (1988). Tipuri de intercunoastere si comportament cognitiv interpersonal [Types of interknowledge and the cognitive interpersonal behavior]. *Revista de Psihologie, 34*, 229–244.

Mandel, D. R. (2002). Beyond mere ownership: Transaction demand as a moderator of the endowment effect. *Organizational Behavior and Human Decision Processes, 88*, 737–747.

Mannix, E. A. (1991). Resource dilemmas and discount rates in decision making groups. *Journal of Experimental Social Psychology, 27*, 379–391.

Mannix, E. A. (1993). Organizations as resource dilemmas: The effects of power balance on coalition formation in small groups. *Organizational Behavior and Human Decision Processes, 55*, 1–22.

Mannix, E. A., & Innami, I. (1993). The effects of argument preparation and timing of first offer on negotiators' cognitions and performance. *Group Decision and Negotiation, 2*, 347–362.

Mannix, E. A., & Neale, M. A. (1993). Power imbalance and the pattern of exchange in dyadic negotiation. *Group Decision and Negotiation, 2*, 119–133.

Mannix, E. A., Tinsley, C. H., & Bazerman, M. (1995). Negotiating over time: Impediments to integrative solutions. *Organizational Behavior and Human Decision Processes, 62*, 241–251.

Mannix, E. A., & White, S. B. (1992). The impact of distributive uncertainty on coalition formation in organizations. *Organizational Behavior and Human Decision Processes, 51*, 198–219.

Mansergh, G., Rohrbach, L. A., Montgomery, S. B., Pentz, M. A., & Johnson, C. A. (1996). Process evaluation of community coalitions for alcohol and other drug abuse prevention: A case study comparison of researcher- and community-initiated models. *Journal of Community Psychology, 24*, 118–135.

Manzini, P., & Mariotti, M. (2001). Perfect equilibria in a model of bargaining with arbitration. *Games and Economic Behavior, 37*, 170–195.

Maoz, Z., & Astorino, A. (1992). The cognitive structure of peacemaking: Egypt and Israel, 1970–1978. *Political Psychology, 13*, 647–662.

Mapstone, E. (1995). Rational men and conciliatory women: Graduate psychologists construct accounts of argument. *Feminism and Psychology, 5*, 61–83.

Marco Gil, M. d. C. (1995). Efficient solutions for bargaining problems with claims. *Mathematical Social Sciences, 30*, 57–69.

Marcus-Newhall, A., Miller, N., Holtz, R., & Brewer, M. B. (1993). Cross-cutting category membership with role assignment: A means of reducing intergroup bias. *British Journal of Social Psychology, 32*, 125–146.

Mariotti, M. (1998). Extending Nash's axioms to nonconvex problems. *Games and Economic Behavior, 22*, 377–383.

Mark, N. (2004). Cultural transmission, disproportionate prior exposure, and the evolution of cooperation. *American Sociological Review, 69*, 144–149.

Markovsky, B. (1994). Social perception. In M. Foschi & E. J. Lawler (Eds.), *Group processes: Sociological analyses* (pp. 73–94). Chicago, IL: Nelson-Hall Publishers.

Marks, M. (2006). Editorial: The science of team effectiveness. *Psychological Science in the Public Interest, 7*(3), i.

Marks, M. A., & Panzer, F. J. (2004). The Influence of Team Monitoring on Team Processes and Performance. *Human Performance, Vol 17*, 25–41.

Marks, M. A., Zaccaro, S. J., & Mathieu, J. E. (2000). Performance implications of leader briefings and team-interaction training for team adaptation to novel environments. *Journal of Applied Psychology, 85*, 971–986.

Marlowe, F. (2004). Dictators and Ultimatums in an egalitarian society of Hunter-Gatherers: The Hadza of Tanzania. In J. Henrich, R. Boyd, S. Bowles, C. Camerer, E. Fehr, & H. Gintis (Eds.), *Foundations of human sociality* (pp. 168–193). New York: Oxford University Press.

Marques, J. M., Paez, D., & Abrams, D. (1998). Social identity and intragroup differentiation as subjective social control. In S. Worchel, J. F. Morales, D. Paez, & J.-C. Deschamps (Eds.), *Social identity: International perspectives* (pp. 124–141). London: Sage Publications, Inc.

Marques, J. M., Yzerbyt, V. Y., & Leyens, J. P. (1988). The "Black Sheep Effect": Extremity of judgments towards ingroup members as a function of group identification. *European Journal of Social Psychology, 18*, 1–16.

Marques, J. M., Yzerbyt, V. Y., & Rijsman, J. B. (1988). Context effects on intergroup discrimination: In-group bias as a function of experimenter's provenance. *British Journal of Social Psychology, 27*, 301–318.

Marrero, H., & Gámez, E. (2004). Comprensión de las relaciones interpersonales en el contexto de narraciones de episodios de interacción [Comprehending relationship in the context of narratives about interpersonal interactions]. *Estudios de Psicología, 25*, 45–56.

Martichuski, D. K., & Bell, P. A. (1991). Reward, punishment, privatization, and moral suasion in a commons dilemma. *Journal of Applied Social Psychology, 21*, 1356–1369.

Martin, J., & Meyerson, D. (1988). Women and power: Conformity, resistance, and disorganized coaction. In M. A. Neale & R. M. Kramer (Eds.), *Power and influence in organizations* (pp. 311–348). Thousand Oaks, CA: Sage Publications, Inc.

Martin, M. M., & Anderson, C. M. (1997). Aggressive communication traits: How similar are young adults and their parents in argumentativeness, assertiveness, and verbal aggressiveness. *Western Journal of Communication, 61*, 299–314.

Martinez, J. C. (1989). The ingroup bias as a function of differences in resources within groups. *European Journal of Social Psychology, 19*, 251–254.

Martinez, S. (1989). Child care and federal policy. In J. S. Lande, S. W. Scarr, & N. Gunzenhauser (Eds.), *Caring for children: Challenge to America* (pp. 111–124). Hillsdale, NJ, England: Lawrence Erlbaum Associates, Inc.

Martinez-Pecino, R., Munduate, L., Medina, F. J., & Euwema, M. C. (2008). Effectiveness of mediation strategies in collective bargaining. *Industrial Relations: A Journal of Economy and Society, 47*, 480–495.

Martinot, D., & Audebert, O. (2003). Relation entre estime de soi et identification ethnique dans des contextes scolaires menaçants pour l'identité ethnique des élèves [Relationship between self-esteem and ethnic identification in an intergroup comparison context threatening the ethnic identity]. *Cahiers Internationaux de Psychologie Sociale*, No. 58, 28–38.

Martinot, D., Redersdorff, S., Guimond, S., & Dif, S. (2002). Ingroup versus outgroup comparisons and self-esteem: The role of group status and ingroup identification. *Personality and Social Psychology Bulletin, 28*, 1586–1600.

Marullo, G., & DeLeon, P. H. (1997). Professional involvement in the employment process. *Professional Psychology: Research and Practice, 28*, 411–412.

Maschler, M. (2004). Encouraging a coalition formation. *Theory and Decision, 56*, 25–34.

Masel, J. (2007). A Bayesian model of quasi-magical thinking can explain observed cooperation in the public good game. *Journal of Economic Behavior and Organization, 64*, 216–231.

Maskin, E., & Riley, J. (2003). Uniqueness of equilibrium in sealed high-bid auctions. *Games and Economic Behavior, 45*, 395–409.

Maslyn, J. M., & Uhl-Bien, M. (2001). Leader-member exchange and its dimensions: Effects of self-effort and other's effort on relationship quality. *Journal of Applied Psychology, 86*, 697–708.

Mastenbroek, W. F. G. (1991). Development of negotiating skills. In V. A. Kremenyuk (Ed.), *International negotiation: Analysis, approaches, issues* (pp. 379–399). San Francisco: Jossey-Bass Inc, Publishers.

Masulli, I. (1993). Cognitive maps and social change. In E. Laszlo & I. Masulli (Eds.), *The evolution of cognitive maps: New paradigms for the twenty-first century* [World futures general evolution studies, Vol. 5], pp. 169–180). Langhorne, PA: Gordon and Breach Science Publishers.

Matheson, K., Cole, B., & Majka, K. (2003). Dissidence from within: Examining the effects of intergroup context on group members' reactions to attitudinal opposition. *Journal of Experimental Social Psychology, 39*, 161–169.

Matsui, M. (1990). Interpersonal anxiety and the self-others cognitive system: A study of the self-identity system. *Japanese Journal of Psychology, 61*, 94–102.

Matsumoto, Y. (1989). Effects of issue-prominence upon interpersonal conflict. *Japanese Journal of Experimental Social Psychology, 29*, 1–11.

Matsuura, H. (1991). An examination in mutual comparison of perception of equity in intimate pairs. *Japanese Journal of Experimental Social Psychology, 31*, 155–166.

Matz, D. E. (1994). Mediator pressure and party autonomy: Are they consistent with each other? *Negotiation Journal, 10*, 359–365.

Mauleon, A., & Vannetelbosch, V. (2004). Bargaining with endogenous deadlines. *Journal of Economic Behavior and Organization, 54*, 321–335.

Mauro, R., Pierro, A., Mannetti, L., Higgins, E. T., & Kruglanski, A. W. (2009). The perfect mix: Regulatory complementarity and the speed-accuracy balance in group performance. *Psychological Science, 20*, 681–685.

Maxwell, D. (1992). Gender differences in mediation style and their impact on mediator effectiveness. *Mediation Quarterly, 9*, 353–364.

May, D. R., & Schwoerer, C. E. (1994a). Developing effective work teams: Guidelines for fostering work team efficacy. *Organization Development Journal, 12*(3), 29–39.

May, D. R., & Schwoerer, C. E. (1994b). Employee health by design: Using employee involvement teams in ergonomic job redesign. *Personnel Psychology, 47*, 861–876.

Mayer, J. P., Soweid, R., Dabney, S., Brownson, C., Goodman, R. M., & Brownson, R. C. (1998). Practices of successful community coalitions: A multiple case study. *American Journal of Health Behavior, 22*, 368–369.

Mayer, M. E. (1998). Behaviors leading to more effective decisions in small groups embedded in organizations. *Communication Reports, 11*, 123–132.

Maznevski, M. L., & Chudoba, K. M. (2000). Bridging space over time: Global virtual team dynamics and effectiveness. *Organization Science, 11*, 473–492.

McAllister, H. A. (1990). Effects of eyewitness evidence on plea-bargain decisions by prosecutors and defense attorneys. *Journal of Applied Social Psychology, 20*, 1461–1473.

McAuliffe, B. J., Jetten, J., Hornsey, M. J., & Hogg, M. A. (2003). Individualist and collectivist norms: When it's ok to go your own way. *European Journal of Social Psychology, 33*, 57–70.

McCabe, K. A., Rassenti, S. J., & Smith, V. L. (1998). Reciprocity, trust, and payoff privacy in extensive form bargaining. *Games and Economic Behavior, 24*, 10–24.

McCabe, K. A., Rigdon, M. L., & Smith, V. L. (2003). Positive reciprocity and intentions in trust games. *Journal of Economic Behavior and Organization, 52*, 267–275.

McCall, B. P. (1990). Interest arbitration and the incentive to bargain: A principal-agent approach. *Journal of Conflict Resolution, 34*, 151–167.

McCann, J., & Galbraith, J. R. (1981). Interdepartmental Relations. In P. C. Nystrom & W. H. Starbuck (Eds.), *Handbook of Organizational Design, Volume 2: Remodelling Organizations* (pp. 60–84), New York: Oxford University Press.

McCarthy, B. (2002). New economics of sociological criminology. *Annual Review of Sociology, 28*, 417–442.

McCauley, C., Plummer, M., Moskalenko, S., & Mordkoff, J. T. (2001). The exposure index: A measure of intergroup contact. *Peace and Conflict: Journal of Peace Psychology, 7*, 321–336.

McClane, W. E. (1991a). Implications of member role differentiation: Analysis of a key concept in the LMX model of leadership. *Group and Organization Studies, 16*, 102–113.

McClane, W. E. (1991b). The interaction of leader and member characteristics in the leader-member exchange (LMX) model of leadership. *Small Group Research, 22*, 283–300.

McClintock, C. G. (Ed.). (1972). Experimental social psychology. New York: Holt, Rinehart and Winston.

McConnell, A. R., Sherman, S. J., & Hamilton, D. L. (1994). Illusory correlation in the perception of groups: An extension of the distinctiveness-based account. *Journal of Personality and Social Psychology, 67*, 414–429.

McConnell, A. R., Sherman, S. J., & Hamilton, D. L. (1997). Target entitativity: Implications for information processing about individual and group targets. *Journal of Personality and Social Psychology, 72*, 750–762.

McCoy, S. K., & Major, B. (2003). Group identification moderates emotional responses to perceived prejudice. *Personality and Social Psychology Bulletin, 29*, 1005–1017.

McCullough, M. E., Rachal, K. C., Sandage, S. J., Worthington, E. L., Jr., Brown, S. W., & Hight, T. L. (1998). Interpersonal forgiving in close relationships: II. Theoretical elaboration and measurement. *Journal of Personality and Social Psychology, 75*, 1586–1603.

McDaniel, W. C., & Sistrunk, F. (1991). Management dilemmas and decisions: Impact of framing and anticipated responses. *Journal of Conflict Resolution, 35*, 21–42.

McElreath, R. (2004). Community structure, mobility, and the strength of norms in an African society: the Sangu of Tanzania. In J. Henrich, R. Boyd, S. Bowles, C. Camerer, E. Fehr, & H. Gintis (Eds.), *Foundations of human sociality* (pp. 335–355). New York: Oxford University Press.

McElreath, R., Clutton-Brock, T. H., Fehr, E., Fessler, D. M. T., Hagen, E. H., Hammerstein, P., Kosfeld, M., Milinski, M., Silk, J. B., Tooby, J., & Wilson, M. I. (2003). Group Report: The role of cognition and emotion in cooperation. In P. Hammerstein (Ed.), *Genetic and cultural evolution of cooperation* (pp. 125–152). Cambridge, MA: MIT Press.

McEwen, C. A., & Milburn, T. W. (1993). Explaining a paradox of mediation. *Negotiation Journal, 9*, 23–36.

McFall, S., Norton, B. L., & McLeroy, K. R. (2004). A qualitative evaluation of rural community coalitions. *International Quarterly of Community Health Education, 23*, 311–326.

McFarland, C., & Buehler, R. (1995). Collective self-esteem as a moderator of the frog-pond effect in reactions to performance feedback. *Journal of Personality and Social Psychology, 68*, 1055–1070.

McGarty, C., Haslam, S. A., Hutchinson, K. J., & Grace, D. M. (1995). Determinants of perceived consistency: The relationship between group entitativity and the meaningfulness of categories. *British Journal of Social Psychology, 34*, 237–256.

McGauran, A.-M. (2001). Masculine, feminine or neutral? In-company equal opportunities policies in Irish and French MNC retailing. *International Journal of Human Resource Management, 12*, 754–771.

McGinn, K. L., Thompson, L., & Bazerman, M. H. (2003). Dyadic processes of disclosure and reciprocity in bargaining with communication. *Journal of Behavioral Decision Making, 16*, 17–34.

McGrath, J. E. (1991). Time, interaction, and performance (TIP): A theory of groups. *Small Group Research, 22*, 147–174.

McGrath, J. E. (1993). The JEMCO workshop: Description of a longitudinal study. *Small Group Research, 24*, 285–306.

McGrath, J. E. (1997). Small group research, that once and future field: An interpretation of the past with an eye to the future. *Group Dynamics: Theory, Research, and Practice, 1*, 7–27.

McGrath, J. E., Arrow, H., & Berdahl, J. L. (1999). Cooperation and conflict as manifestations of coordination in small groups. *Polish Psychological Bulletin, 30*, 1–14.

McGrath, J. E., Arrow, H., Gruenfeld, D. H., Hollingshead, A. B., & O'Connor, K. M. (1993). Groups, tasks, and technology: The effects of experience and change. *Small Group Research, 24*, 406–420.

McGrath, Joseph E., & Berdahl, Jennifer L. (1998). Groups, technology, and time: Use of computers for collaborative work. In R. S. Tindale, L. Heath, J. Edwards, E. J. Posavac, F. B. Bryant, Y. Suarez-Balcazar, E. Henderson-King, & J. Myers (Eds.), *Theory and research on small groups* [Social psychological applications to social issues, Vol. 4] (pp. 205–228). New York: Plenum Press.

McHoskey, J. W., & Miller, A. G. (1994). Effects of constraint identification, processing mode, expectancies, and intragroup variability on attributions toward group members. *Personality and Social Psychology Bulletin, 20*, 266–276.

McKelvey, R. D., & Palfrey, T. R. (1995). Quantal response equilibria for normal form games. *Games and Economic Behavior, 10*, 6–38.

McKenna, Katelyn Y. A., & Bargh, John A. (2000). Plan 9 from cyberspace: The implications of the Internet for personality and social psychology. *Personality and Social Psychology Review, 4*, 57–75.

McKillop, K. J., Berzonsky, M. D., & Schlenker, B. R. (1992). The impact of self-presentations on self-beliefs: Effects of social identity and self-presentational context. *Journal of Personality, 60*, 789–808.

McKimmie, B. M., Terry, D. J., Hogg, M. A., Manstead, A. S. R., Spears, R., & Doosje, B. (2003). I'm a hypocrite, but so is everyone else: Group support and the reduction of cognitive dissonance. *Group Dynamics: Theory, Research*, and Practice, *7*, 214–224.

McLaughlin, M. E., Carnevale, P., & Lim, R. G. (1991). Professional mediators' judgments of mediation tactics: Multidimensional scaling and cluster analyses. *Journal of Applied Psychology, 76*, 465–472.

McNamara, J. M., Barta, Z., & Houston, A. I. (2004). Variation in behaviour promotes cooperation in the Prisoner's Dilemma game. *Nature, 428*, 745–748.

McPhee, R. D. (1995). Cognitive perspectives on communication: Interpretive and critical responses. In D. E. Hewes (Ed.), *The cognitive bases of interpersonal communication* (pp. 225–246). Hillsdale, NJ: Lawrence Erlbaum Associates, Inc.

Meacham, J. A., & Emont, N. C. (1989). The interpersonal basis of everyday problem solving. In J. D. Sinnott (Ed.), *Everyday problem solving: Theory and applications* (pp. 7–23). New York: Praeger Publishers.

Medvene, L. J., Teal, C. R., & Slavich, S. (2000). Including the other in self: Implications for judgments of equity and satisfaction in close relationships. *Journal of Social and Clinical Psychology, 19*, 396–419.

Meeres, S. L., & Grant, P. R. (1999). Enhancing collective and personal self-esteem through differentiation: Further exploration of Hinkle & Brown's taxonomy. *British Journal of Social Psychology, 38*, 21–34.

Meerts, P. (1991). Training of negotiators. In V. A. Kremenyuk (Ed.), *International negotiation: Analysis, approaches, issues* (pp. 400–408). San Francisco: Jossey-Bass Inc, Publishers.

Mehra, A., Kilduff, M., & Brass, D. J. (1998). At the margins: A distinctiveness approach to the social identity and social networks of underrepresented groups. *Academy of Management Journal, 41*, 441–452.

Meindl, J. R. (1995). The romance of leadership as a follower-centric theory: A social constructionist approach. *Leadership Quarterly, 6*, 329–341.

Meiser, T., & Hewstone, M. (2006). Illusory and spurious correlations: Distinct phenomena or joint outcomes of exemplar-based category learning? *European Journal of Social Psychology, 36*, 315–336.

Mesch, D. J., Farh, J. L., & Podsakoff, P. M. (1994). Effects of feedback sign on group goal setting, strategies, and performance. *Group and Organization Management, 19*, 309–333.

Mesoudi, A. (2009). How cultural evolutionary theory can inform social psychology and vice versa. *Psychological Review, 116*, 929–952.

Mesquida, C. G., & Wiener, N. I. (1996). Human collective aggression: A behavioral ecology perspective. *Ethology and Sociobiology, 17*, 247–262.

Messick, D. M. (1991). Social dilemmas, shared resources, and social justice. In H. Steensma & R. Vermunt, *Social justice in human relations, Volume 2: Societal and psychological consequences of justice and injustice* (pp. 49–69). New York: Plenum Press.

Messick, D. (2008). Must good guys finish last? In J. I. Krueger (Ed.), *Rationality and social responsibility: Essays in honor of Robyn Mason Dawes* (pp. 233–244). New York: Psychology Press.

Messick, D. M., Moore, D. A., & Bazerman, M. H. (1997). Ultimatum bargaining with a group: Underestimating the importance of the decision rule. *Organizational Behavior and Human Decision Processes, 69*, 87–101.

Metha, J., Starmer, C., & Sugden, R. (1994). Focal points in pure coordination games: An experimental investigation. *Theory and Decision, 36*, 163–185.

Metts, S. (2000). Face and facework: Implications for the study of personal relationships. In K. Dindia & S. Duck (Eds.), *Communication and personal relationships* (pp. 77–93). New York: John Wiley & Sons Ltd.

Meyer, H.-D. (1992). Norms and self-interest in ultimatum bargaining: The prince's prudence. *Journal of Economic Psychology, 13*, 215–232.

Meyer, P. (1999). The sociobiology of human cooperation: The interplay of ulitmate and proximate causes. In J. M. G. Van der Dennen, D. Smillie, & D. R. Wilson (Eds.), *The Darwinian heritage and sociobiology* (pp. 49–65). Westport, CT: Praeger Publishers/Greenwood Publishing Group.

Meyers, R. A., Berdahl, J. L., Brashers, D., Considine, J. R., Kelly, J. R., Moore, C., Peterson, J. L., & Spoor, J. R. (2005). Understanding groups from a feminist perspective. In M. S. Poole & A. B. Hollingshead (Eds.), *Theories of small groups: Interdisciplinary perspectives* (pp. 241–276). Thousand Oaks, CA: Sage Publications, Inc.

Michelini, R. L., Passalacqua, R., Cusimano, J. (1976). Effects of Seating Arrangement on Group Participation. *Journal of Social Psychology, 99*, 179–186.

Michener, H. A., Salzer, M. S., & Richardson, G. D. (1989). Extensions of value solutions in constant-sum non-sidepayment games. *Journal of Conflict Resolution, 33*, 530–553.

Michinov, N., Michinov, E., & Toczek-Capelle, M.-C. (2004). Social identity, group processes, and performance in synchronous computer-mediated communication. *Group Dynamics: Theory, Research, and Practice, 8*, 27–39.

Milanovich, D. M., Driskell, J. E., Stout, R. J., & Salas, E. (1998). Status and cockpit dynamics: A review and empirical study. *Group Dynamics, 2*, 155–167.

Miles, J. A., & Klein, H. J. (2002). Perception in consequences of free riding. *Psychological Reports, 90*, 215–225.

Miles, J. R., & Kivlighan, D. M., Jr. (2008). Team cognition in group interventions: The relation between coleaders' shared mental models and group climate. *Group Dynamics: Theory, Research, and Practice, 12*, 191–209.

Milgram, S. (1963). Behavioral study of obedience. *Journal of Abnormal and Social Psychology, 67*, 371–378.

Milgrom, P., & Roberts, J. (1996). Coalition-proofness and correlation with arbitrary communication possibilities. *Games and Economic Behavior, 17*, 113–128.

Miller, Carol T. (1993). Majority and minority perceptions of consensus and recommendations for resolving conflicts about land use regulation. *Personality and Social Psychology Bulletin, 19*, 389–398.

Miller, Carol T., & Felicio, D. M. (1990). Person-positivity bias: Are individuals liked better than groups? *Journal of Experimental Social Psychology, 26*, 408–420.

Miller, Charles E., & Komorita, S. S. (1995). Reward allocation in task-performing groups. *Journal of Personality and Social Psychology, 69*, 80–90.

Miller, D. T., & Morrison, K. R. (2009). Expressing deviant opinions: Believing you are in the majority helps. *Journal of Experimental Social Psychology, 45*, 740–747.

Miller, D. T., & Prentice, D. A. (1994). Collective errors and errors about the collective. *Personality and Social Psychology Bulletin, 20*, 541–550.

Miller, D. T., Downs, J. S., & Prentice, D. A. (1998). Minimal conditions for the creation of a unit relationship: The social bond between birthdaymates. *European Journal of Social Psychology, 28*, 475–481.

Miller, J. (2001). Family and community integrity. *Journal of Sociology and Social Welfare, 28*(4), 23–44.

Miller, J. B. (1991). Women's and men's scripts for interpersonal conflict. *Psychology of Women Quarterly, 15*, 15–29.

Miller, K. P., Brewer, M. B., & Arbuckle, N. L. (2009). Social identity complexity: Its correlates and antecedents. *Group Processes and Intergroup Relations, 12*, 79–94.

Miller, N. (2002). Personalization and the promise of contact theory. *Journal of Social Issues, 58*, 387–410.

Miller, N., & Harrington, H. J. (1990). A model of social category salience for intergroup relations: Empirical tests of relevant variables. In P. J. D. Drenth, J. A. Sergeant, & R. J. Takens (Eds.), *European perspectives in psychology, Vol. 3: Work and organizational, social and economic, cross-cultural* (pp. 205–220). Chichester, England: John Wiley & Sons.

Miller, N., & Harrington, H. J. (1995). Social categorization and intergroup acceptance: Principles for the design and development of cooperative learning teams. In R. Hertz-Lazarowitz & N. Miller (Eds.), *Interaction in cooperative groups: The theoretical anatomy of group learning* (pp. 203–227). New York: Cambridge University Press.

Miller, N., Gross, S., & Holtz, R. (1991). Social projection and attitudinal certainty. In J. Suls & T. A. Wills (Eds.), *Social comparison: Contemporary theory and research* (pp. 177–209). Hillsdale, NJ: Lawrence Erlbaum Associates, Inc.

Miller, N., Urban, L. M., & Vanman, E. J. (1998). A theoretical analysis of crossed social categorization effects. In C. Sedikides, J. Schopler, & C. A. Insko (Eds.), *Intergroup cognition and intergroup behavior* (pp. 393–420). Mahwah, NJ: Lawrence Erlbaum Associates, Inc., Publishers.

Miller, R. I., & Sanchirico, C. W. (1999). The role of absolute continuity in "merging of opinions" and "rational learning." *Games and Economic Behavior, 29*, 170–190.

Mills, B. (1997). An exploratory examination of relationships between contact boundary styles and conflict resolution styles. *Organization Development Journal, 15*(4), 17–25.

Minkler, L. P., & Miceli, T. J. (2004). Lying, integrity, and cooperation. *Review of Social Economy, 62*, 27–50.

Mintu-Wimsatt, A., & Graham, J. L. (1998). Antecedents and outcomes of problem-solving: A look at Canadian negotiators. In T. A. Scandura & M. G. Serapio (Eds.), *Research in international business and international relations: Leadership and innovation in emerging markets* (Vol. 7, pp. 117–137). San Diego, CA: Elsevier Science/JAI Press, 1998.

Mintz, A. (1951). Non-adaptive group behavior. *Journal of Abnormal and Social Psychology, 46*, 150–159. PA 54:2982.

Mio, J. S., Thompson, S. C., & Givens, G. H. (1993). The commons dilemma as metaphor: Memory, influence, and implications for environmental conservation. *Metaphor and Symbolic Activity, 8*, 23–42.

Miron, E., Erez, M., & Naveh, E. (2004). Do personal characteristics and cultural values that promote innovation, quality, and efficiency compete or complement each other? *Journal of Organizational Behavior, 25*, 175–199.

Mischel, L. J., & Northcraft, G. B. (1997). "I think we can, I think we can...": The role of efficacy beliefs in group and team effectiveness. In B. Markovsky, M. J. Lovaglia, & L. Troyer (Eds.), *Advances in group processes* (Vol. 14, pp. 177–197). Greenwich, CT: Jai Press, Inc.

Mischel, W. (1998). Metacognition at the hyphen of social-cognitive psychology. *Personality and Social Psychology Review, 2*, 84–86.

Mitchell, A. (2006). When philosophical assumptions matter. In N. N. Potter (Ed.), *Trauma, truth and reconciliation: Healing damaged relationships* (pp. 111–126). New York: Oxford University Press.

Mitchell, R. E., Stevenson, J. F., & Florin, P. (1996). A typology of prevention activities: Applications to community coalitions. *Journal of Primary Prevention, 16*, 413–436.

Mitchell, R. E., Stone-Wiggins, B., Stevenson, J. F., & Florin, P. (2004). Cultivating capacity: Outcomes of a statewide support system for prevention coalitions. *Journal of Prevention and Intervention in the Community, 27*(2), 67–87.

Mitchell, T. R., & Silver, W. S. (1990). Individual and group goals when workers are interdependent: Effects on task strategies and performance. *Journal of Applied Psychology, 75*, 185–193.

Miura, A. (2003). Effects of communication medium and goal setting of group brainstorming. In K.-S. Yang, K.-K. Hwang, P. B. Pedersen, & I. Daibo (Eds.), *Progress in Asian social psychology: Conceptual and empirical contributions* (pp. 199–215). Westport, CT: Praeger Publishers/ Greenwood Publishing Group.

Miura, A., & Hida, M. (2004). Synergy between diversity and similarity in group-idea generation. *Small Group Research, 35*, 540–564.

Miyagawa, E. (2002). Subgame-perfect implementation of bargaining solutions. *Games and Economic Behavior, 41,* 292–308.

Mizrahi, T., & Rosenthal, B. B. (2001). Complexities of coalition building: Leaders' successes, strategies, struggles and solutions. *Social Work, 46,* 63–78.

Mlicki, M. K. (1993). Collective action: A tentative model. In T. Airaksinen & W. W. Gasparski (Eds.), *Practical philosophy and action theory* [Praxiology: The international annual of practical philosophy and methodology, Vol. 2] (pp. 103–118). New Brunswick, NJ: Transaction Publishers.

Mlicki, P. P. (1988). Warunki budowania tozsamosci spolecznej a dyskryminacyjne zachowania miedzygrupowe w paradygmacie minimalnej grupy [Conditions of social identity construction and inter-group discriminative behavior in the minimal group paradigm]. *Studia Psychologiczne, 26*(1–2), 103–133.

Mmobuosi, I. B. (1988). Problems of creativity and organisational change: The experiences of some chief executives. *Leadership and Organization Development Journal, 9,* 23–31.

Mo, J. (1994). The logic of two-level games with endogenous domestic coalitions. *Journal of Conflict Resolution, 38,* 402–422.

Moch, M., & Seashore, S. E. (1981). How norms affect behaviors in and of corporations. In P. C. Nystrom and W. H. Starbuck (Eds.), *Handbook of organizational design.* Oxford, England: Oxford University Press.

Moghaddam, F. M., & Stringer, P. (1988). Out-group similarity and intergroup bias. *Journal of Social Psychology, 128,* 105–115.

Mohammed, S., & Angell, L. C. (2003). Personality heterogeneity in teams: Which differences make a difference for team performance? *Small Group Research, 34,* 651–677.

Mohammed, S., & Angell, L. C. (2004). Surface– and deep-level diversity in workgroups: Examining the moderating effects of team orientation and team process on relationship conflict. *Journal of Organizational Behavior, 25,* 1015–1039.

Mokros, H. B. (2003). *Identity matters: Communication based explorations and explanations.* Cresskill, NJ: Hampton Press.

Moldovanu, B., & Winter, E. (1995). Order independent equilibria. *Games and Economic Behavior, 9,* 21–34.

Moldoveanu, M. C., & Stevenson, H. H. (1998). Ethical universals in practice: An analysis of five principles. *Journal of Socio-Economics, 27,* 721–752.

Molleman, E., & Timmerman, H. (2003). Performance management when innovation and learning become critical performance indicators. *Personnel Review, 32,* 93–113.

Montalban, F. M., & Gomez, L. (1995). Efectos de la discrepancia de estatus sobre el comportamiento intergrupal [Effects of status discrepancy on intergroup behaviour]. *Revista de Psicologia Social, 10,* 219–233.

Monteiro, M. B., Guerra, R., & Rebelo, M. (2009). Reducing prejudice: Common ingroup and dual identity in unequal status intergroup encounters. In S. Demoulin, J.-P. Leyens, & J. F. Dovidio (Eds.), *Intergroup misunderstandings: Impact of divergent social realities* (pp. 273–290). New York: Psychology Press.

Montero, M. (2002). Non-cooperative bargaining in apex games and the kernel. *Games and Economic Behavior, 41,* 309–321.

Monterosso, J., Ainslie, G., Mullen, P. A.-C. P. T., & Gault, B. (2002). The fragility of cooperation: A false feedback study of a sequential iterated prisoner's dilemma. *Journal of Economic Psychology, 23,* 437–448.

Montiel, C. J., & Christie, D. J. (2008). Conceptual Frame for a Psychology of Nonviolent Democratic Transitions: Positioning Across Analytical Layers. In F. M. Moghaddam, R. Harre & N. Lee (Eds.), *Global Conflict Resolution Through Positioning Analysis* (pp. 261–280). New York: Springer.

Montoya Weiss, M. M., Massey, A. P., & Song, M. (2001). Getting it together: Temporal coordination and conflict management in global virtual teams. *Academy of Management Journal, 44,* 1251–1262.

Mookherjee, D., & Sopher, B. (1997). Learning and decision costs in experimental constant sum games. *Games and Economic Behavior, 19,* 97–132.

Moon, H., Hollenbeck, J. R., Humphrey, S. E., Ilgen, D. R., West, B., Ellis, A. P. J., & Porter, C. O. L. H. (2004). Asymmetric adaptability: Dynamic team structures as one-way streets. *Academy of Management Journal, 47*, 681–695.

Moore, W., & Miljus, R. C. (1989). Integration of collective bargaining and formal worker participation processes: Boon or barrier to worker rights? *Employee Responsibilities and Rights Journal, 2*, 217–231.

Morales, J. F., Lopez-Saez, M., & Vega, L. (1998). Discrimination and beliefs on discrimination in individualists and collectivists. In S. Worchel, J. F. Morales, D. Paez, & J.-C. Deschamps (Eds.), *Social identity: International perspectives* (pp. 199–210). London: Sage Publications.

Moreland, R. L. (1999). Transactive memory: Learning who knows what in work groups and organizations. In L. L. Thompson, J. M. Levine, & D. M. Messick (Eds.), *Shared cognition in organizations: The management of knowledge* (pp. 3–31). Mahwah, NJ: Lawrence Erlbaum Associates Publishers.

Moreland, R. L., Argote, L., & Krishnan, R. (1996). Socially shared cognition at work: Transactive memory and group performance. In J. L. Nye & A. M. Brower (Eds.), *What's social about social cognition? Research on socially shared cognition in small groups* (pp. 57–84). Thousand Oaks, CA: Sage.

Moreland, R. L., Argote, L., & Krishnan, R. (1998). Training people to work in groups. In R. S. Tindale, L. Heath, J. Edwards, E. J. Posavac, F. B. Bryant, Y. Suarez-Balcazar, E. Henderson-King, & J. Myers (Eds.), *Theory and research on small groups* [Social psychological applications to social issues, Vol. 4] (pp. 37–60). New York: Plenum Press.

Moreland, R. L., Hogg, M. A., & Hains, S. C. (1994). Back to the future: Social psychological research on groups. *Journal of Experimental Social Psychology, 30*, 527–555.

Moreland, R. L., Levine, J. M., & Wingert, M. L. (1996). Creating the ideal group: Composition effects at work. In E. H. Witte & J. H. Davis (Eds.), *Understanding group behavior, Vol. 2: Small group processes and interpersonal relations. Understanding group behavior* (pp. 11–35). Mahwah, NJ: Lawrence Erlbaum Associates, Inc.

Moreland, R. L., & Myaskovsky, L. (2000). Exploring the performance benefits of group training: Transactive memory or improved communication? *Organizational Behavior and Human Decision Processes, 82*, 117–133.

Moreno, D., & Wooders, J. (1996). Coalition-proof equilibrium. *Games and Economic Behavior, 17*, 80–112.

Moreno, D., & Wooders, J. (1998). An experimental study of communication and coordination in noncooperative games. *Games and Economic Behavior, 24*, 47–76.

Moreno, R., & Mayer, R. E. (2004). Personalized messages that promote science learning in virtual environments. *Journal of Educational Psychology, 96*, 165–173.

Morgan, P. M., & Tindale, R. S. (2002). Group vs individual performance in mixed-motive situations: Exploring an inconsistency. *Organizational Behavior and Human Decision Processes, 87*, 44–65.

Mori, K. (1996). Effects of trust and communication on cooperative choice in a two-person prisoner's dilemma game. *Japanese Journal of Experimental Social Psychology, 35*, 324–336.

Morley, I. E. (1992). Intra-organizational bargaining. In J. F. Hartley & G. M. Stephenson (Eds.), *Employment relations: The psychology of influence and control at work* (pp. 203–224). Malden: Blackwell Publishing.

Morley, I. E. (1994). Computer Supported Cooperative Work and engineering product design. In J. H. E. Andriessen & R. A. Roe (Eds.), *Telematics and work* (pp. 231–260). Hove, England: Lawrence Erlbaum Associates, Inc.

Morley, I. E. (2006). Negotiation and bargaining. In O. Hargie (Ed.), *The handbook of communication skills* (3rd ed., pp. 403–425). New York: Routledge, 2006.

Morris, C. S., Hancock, P. A., & Shirkey, E. C. (2004). Motivational effects of adding context relevant stress in PC-based game training. *Military Psychology, 16*, 135–147.

Morris, M. W., Larrick, R. P., & Su, S. K. (1999). Misperceiving negotiation counterparts: When situationally determined bargaining behaviors are attributed to personality traits. *Journal of Personality and Social Psychology, 77*, 52–67.

Morris, M. W., Sim, D. L. H., & Girotto, V. (1995). Time of decision, ethical obligation, and causal illusion: Temporal cues and social heuristics in the prisoner's dilemma. In R. M. Kramer & D. M. Messick (Eds.), *Negotiation as a social process: New trends in theory and research* (pp. 209–239). Thousand Oaks, CA: Sage Publications, Inc.

Morris, M. W., Sim, D. L. H., & Girotto, V. (1998). Distinguishing sources of cooperation in the one-round prisoner's dilemma: Evidence for cooperative decisions based on the illusion of control. *Journal of Experimental Social Psychology, 34*, 494–512.

Morris, W. R., Conrad, K. M., Marcantonio, R. J., Marks, B. A., & Ribisl, K. M. (1999). Do blue-collar workers perceive the worksite health climate differently than white-collar workers? *American Journal of Health Promotion, 13*, 319–324.

Morrison, B. (1999). Interdependence, the group, and social cooperation: A new look at an old problem. In M. Foddy, M. Smithson, S. Schneider, & M. Hogg (Eds.), *Resolving social dilemmas: Dynamic, structural, and intergroup aspects* (pp. 295–308). New York: Psychology Press.

Morrison, E. W., Chen, Y.-R., & Salgado, S. R. (2004). Cultural differences in newcomer feedback seeking: A comparison of the United States and Hong Kong. *Applied Psychology: An International Review, 53*, 1–22.

Moscovici, S. (1980). Towards a theory of conversion behavior. *Advances in Experimental Social Psychology, 13*, 209–239.

Mosier, K. L., Skitka, L. J., Dunbar, M., & McDonnell, L. (2001). Aircrews and automation bias: The advantages of teamwork? *International Journal of Aviation Psychology, 11*, 1–14.

Moskowitz, G. B. (1996). The mediational effects of attributions and information processing in minority social influence. *British Journal of Social Psychology, 35*, 47–66.

Moskowitz, G. B., & Chaiken, S. (2001). Mediators of minority social influence: Cognitive processing mechanisms revealed through a persuasion paradigm. In C. K. W. De Dreu & N. K. De Vries (Eds.), *Group consensus and minority influence: Implications for innovation* (pp. 60–90). Malden: Blackwell Publishing.

Mosler, H.-J. (1993). Self-dissemination of environmentally-responsible behavior: The influence of trust in a commons dilemma game. *Journal of Environmental Psychology, 13*, 111–123.

Moya, M. (1998). Social identity and interpersonal relationships. In S. Worchel, J. F. Morales, D. Paez, & J.-C. Deschamps (Eds.), *Social identity: International perspectives* (pp. 154–165). London: Sage Publications, Inc.

Mucchi-Faina, A., Costarelli, S., & Romoli, C. (2002). The effects of intergroup context of evaluation on ambivalence toward the ingroup and the outgroup. *European Journal of Social Psychology, 32*, 247–259.

Mueller, R. K. (1991). Corporate networking: How to tap unconventional wisdom. In J. Henry (Ed.), *Creative management* (pp. 153–162). Thousand Oaks, CA: Sage Publications.

Mueller, G. F. (1992). Psychological and communicational influences on coordination effectiveness. *Basic and Applied Social Psychology, 13*, 337–350.

Mueller, G. F. (1997). Impact of verbal expressions on coordination. *Swiss Journal of Psychology Schweizerische Zeitschrift fuer Psychologie Revue Suisse de Psychologie, 56*, 175–181.

Mulden, B. (1997). *The heart of conflict.* New York: Berkley.

Mulder, L. B., Van Dijk, E., De Cremer, D., & Wilke, H. A. M. (2006a). Undermining trust and cooperation: The paradox of sanctioning systems in social dilemmas. *Journal of Experimental Social Psychology, 42*, 147–162.

Mulder, L. B., Van Dijk, E., De Cremer, D., & Wilke, H. A. M. (2006b). When sanctions fail to increase cooperation in social dilemmas: Considering the presence of an alternative option to defect. *Personality and Social Psychology Bulletin, 32*, 1312–1324.

Mulkay, M., Clark, C., & Pinch, T. (1993). Laughter and the profit motive: The use of humor in a photographic shop. *Humor: International Journal of Humor Research, 6*, 163–193.

Mullen, B. (2001). Ethnophaulisms for ethnic immigrant groups. *Journal of Social Issues, 57*, 457–475.

Mullen, B., Brown, R., & Smith, C. (1992). Ingroup bias as a function of salience, relevance, and status: An integration. *European Journal of Social Psychology, 22*, 103–122.

Mullen, B., Calogero, R. M., & Leader, T. I. (2007). A social psychological study of ethnonyms: Cognitive representation of the in-group and intergroup hostility. *Journal of Personality and Social Psychology, 92,* 612–630.

Mullen, B., Dovidio, J. F., Johnson, C., & Copper, C. (1992). In-group/out-group differences in social projection. *Journal of Experimental Social Psychology, 28,* 422–440.

Mullen, B., & Goethals, G. R. (1990). Social projection, actual consensus and valence. *British Journal of Social Psychology, 29,* 279–282.

Mullen, B., & Johnson, C. (1990). Distinctiveness-based illusory correlations and stereotyping: A meta-analytic integration. *British Journal of Social Psychology, 29,* 11–27.

Mullen, B., Johnson, C., & Anthony, T. (1994). Relative group size and cognitive representations of ingroup and outgroup: The phenomenology of being in a group. *Small Group Research, 25,* 250–266.

Mullen, B., & Rice, D. R. (2003). Ethnophaulisms and exclusions: The behavioral consequences of cognitive representation of ethnic immigrant groups. *Personality and Social Psychology Bulletin, 29,* 1056–1067.

Mullen, B., Rozell, D., & Johnson, C. (1996). The phenomenology of being in a group: Complexity approaches to operationalizing cognitive representation. In J. L. Nye & A. M. Brower (Eds.), *What's social about social cognition? Research on socially shared cognition in small groups* (pp. 205–229). Thousand Oaks, CA: Sage.

Mullen, J. D., & Roth, B. M. (1991). *Decision-making: Its logic and practice.* Savage, MD: Rowman & Littlefield/Rowman and All.

Mullin, B.-A., & Hogg, M. A. (1999). Motivations for group membership: The role of subjective importance and uncertainty reduction. *Basic and Applied Social Psychology, 21,* 91–102.

Muluk, H. (2009). Memory for sale: How groups "distort" their collective memory for reconciliation purposes and building peace. In C. J. Montiel & N. M. Noor (Eds.), *Peace psychology in Asia* (pp. 105–122). New York: Springer Science + Business Media.

Mulvey, P. W., & Klein, H. J. (1998). The impact of perceived loafing and collective efficacy in group goal processes and group performance. *Organizational Behavior and Human Decision Processes, 74,* 62–87.

Mulvey, P. W., & Ribbens, B. A. (1999). The effects of intergroup competition and assigned group goals on group efficacy and group effectiveness. *Small Group Research, 30,* 651–677.

Mummendey, A., Klink, A., Mielke, R., Wenzel, M., & Blanz, M. (1999). Socio-structural characteristics of intergroup relations and identity management strategies: Results from a field study in East Germany. *European Journal of Social Psychology, 29,* 259–285.

Mummendey, A., Otten, S., Berger, U., & Kessler, T. (2000). Positive-negative asymmetry in social discrimination: Valence of evaluation and salience of categorization. *Personality and Social Psychology Bulletin, 26,* 1258–1270.

Mummendey, A., & Simon, B. (1989). Better or different? III. The impact of importance of comparison dimension and relative in-group size upon intergroup discrimination. *British Journal of Social Psychology, 28,* 1–16.

Mummendey, A., Simon, B., Dietze, C., Grünert, M., Haeger, G., Kessler, S., Lettgen, S., & Schäferhoff, S. (1992). Categorization is not enough: Intergroup discrimination in negative outcome allocation. *Journal of Experimental Social Psychology, 28,* 125–144.

Munier, B., & Zaharia, C. (2002). High stakes and acceptance behavior in ultimatum bargaining: A contribution from an international experiment. *Theory and Decision, 53,* 187–207.

Murnighan, J. K. (1991). Cooperating when you know your outcomes will differ. *Simulation and Gaming, 22,* 463–475.

Murnighan, J. K., & Conlon, D. E. (1991). The dynamics of intense work groups: A study of British string quartets. *Administrative Science Quarterly, 36,* 165–186.

Murnighan, J. K., & King, T. R. (1992). The effects of leverage and payoffs on cooperative behavior in asymmetric dilemmas. In W. B. G. Liebrand, D. M. Messick, & H. A. M. Wilke (Eds.), *Social dilemmas: Theoretical issues and research findings* (pp. 163–182). Elmsford, NY: Pergamon Press.

Murnighan, J. K., & Pillutla, M. M. (1995). Fairness versus self-interest: Asymmetric moral imperatives in ultimatum bargaining. In R. M. Kramer & D. M. Messick (Eds.), *Negotiation as a social process: New trends in theory and research* (pp. 240–267). Thousand Oaks, CA: Sage Publications, Inc.

Murnighan, J. K., & Saxon, M. S. (1998). Ultimatum bargaining by children and adults. *Journal of Economic Psychology, 19*, 415–445.

Murray, S. L. (1999). The quest for conviction: Motivated cognition in romantic relationships. *Psychological Inquiry, 10*, 23–34.

Murrell, A. J. (1998). To identify or not to identity: Preserving, ignoring, and sometimes destroying racial (social) identity. In J. L. Eberhardt & S. T. Fiske (Eds.), *Confronting racism: The problem and the response* (pp. 188–201). Thousand Oaks, CA: Sage Publications, Inc.

Mussweiler, T. (2001). Focus of comparison as a determinant of assimilation versus contrast in social comparison. *Personality and Social Psychology Bulletin, 27*, 38–47.

Mustonen-Ollila, E., & Lyytinen, K. (2003). Why organizations adopt information system process innovations: A longitudinal study using Diffusion of Innovation theory. *Information Systems Journal, 13*, 275–297.

Muthoo, A. (1995). A bargaining model with players' perceptions on the retractability of offers. *Theory and Decision, 38*, 85–98.

Myers, N. D., Feltz, D. L., & Short, S. E. (2004). Collective efficacy and team performance: A longitudinal study of collegiate football teams. *Group Dynamics: Theory, Research, and Practice, 8*, 126–138.

Myers, N. D., Payment, C. A., & Feltz, D. L. (2004). Reciprocal relationships between collective efficacy and team performance in women's ice hockey. *Group Dynamics: Theory, Research, and Practice, 8*, 182–195.

Myerson, R. B. (1996). John Nash's contribution to economics. *Games and Economic Behavior, 14*, 287–295.

Nadler, A., & Halabi, S. (2006). Intergroup helping as status relations: Effects of status stability, identification, and type of help on receptivity to high-status group's help. *Journal of Personality and Social Psychology, 91*, 97–110.

Nadler, A., Malloy, T. E., & Fisher, J. D. (Eds.). (2008). *The social psychology of intergroup reconciliation*. New York: Oxford University Press.

Naff, K. C., & Thompson, R. C. (2000). The impact of teams on the climate for diversity in government: The FAA experience. *FAA Office of Aviation Medicine Reports*, DOT-FAA-AM–00–27, 1–15, A1.

Nagda, B. A. (2006). Breaking barriers, crossing borders, building bridges: Communication processes in intergroup dialogues. *Journal of Social Issues, 62*, 553–576.

Nagda, B. A., Tropp, L. R., & Paluck, E. L. (2006). Looking back as we look ahead: Integrating research, theory, and practice on intergroup relations. *Journal of Social Issues, 62*, 439–451.

Nagda, B. (R.) A., & Zúñiga, X. (2003). Fostering meaningful racial engagement through intergroup dialogues. *Group Processes and Intergroup Relations, 6*, 111–128.

Nakanishi, D., & Kameda, T. (2001). Emergent influence of stereotypic beliefs in group problem-solving. *Japanese Journal of Psychology, 71*, 469–476.

Nandeibam, S. (2000). Distribution of coalitional power under probabilistic voting procedures. *Mathematical Social Sciences, 40*, 63–84.

Napel, S. (2003). Aspiration adaptation in the ultimatum minigame. *Games and Economic Behavior, 43*, 86–106.

Napier, H. S., & House, W. C. (1990). Simulated versus actual firms: A ratio interaction matrix comparison. *Simulation and Gaming, 21*, 166–180.

Naquin, C. E., & Paulson, G. D. (2003). Online bargaining and interpersonal trust. *Journal of Applied Psychology, 88*, 113–120.

Nasierowski, W., & Mikula, B. (1998). Culture dimensions of Polish managers: Hofstede's indices. *Organization Studies, 19*, 495–509.

Naumann, S. E., & Bennett, N. (2000). A case for procedural justice climate: Development and test of a multilevel model. *Academy of Management Journal, 43*, 881–889.

Naumann, S. E., & Bennett, N. (2002). The effects of procedural justice climate on work group performance. *Small Group Research, 33*, 361–377.

Naumes, M. J. (1998). Individual differences in learning style and group performance. In R. R. Hoffman, M. F. Sherrick, & J. S. Warm (Eds.), *Viewing psychology as a whole: The integrative science of William N Dember.* (pp. 541–558). Washington, DC: American Psychological Association.

Nauta, A., & Sanders, K. (2001). Causes and consequences of perceived goal differences between departments within manufacturing organizations. *Journal of Occupational and Organizational Psychology, 74,* 321–342.

Nawa, N. E., Shimohara, K., Katai, O., & Sun, R. (2002). On fairness and learning agents in a bargaining model with uncertainty. *Cognitive Systems Research, 3,* 555–578.

Neal, D. J. (1997). Group competitiveness and cohesion in a business simulation. *Simulation and Gaming, 28,* 460–476.

Neal, J., & Biberman, J. (2003). Introduction: The leading edge in research on spirituality and organizations. *Journal of Organizational Change Management, 16,* 363–366.

Neck, C. P., Connerley, M. L., & Manz, C. C. (1997). Toward a continuum of self-managing team development. In M. M. Beyerlein, D. A. Johnson, & S. T. Beyerlein (Eds.), *Advances in interdisciplinary studies of work teams* (Vol. 4, pp. 193–216). Greenwich, CT: Jai Press, Inc.

Neidert, Gregory P., & Linder, Darwyn E. (1990). Avoiding social traps: Some conditions that maintain adherence to restricted consumption. *Social Behaviour, 5,* 261–284.

Neighbors, M., & Barta, K. (2004). School Nurse Summer Institute: A Model for Professional Development. *Journal of School Nursing, 20,* 134–138.

Nelson, R. E. (1988). Social network analysis as intervention tool: Examples from the field. *Group and Organization Studies, 13,* 39–58.

Nelson, W. R., Jr. (2002). Equity or intention: It is the thought that counts. *Journal of Economic Behavior and Organization, 48,* 423–430.

Nesdale, D., Griffiths, J. A., Durkin, K., & Maass, A. (2007). Effects of group membership, intergroup competition and out-group ethnicity on children's ratings of in-group and out-group similarity and positivity. *British Journal of Developmental Psychology, 25,* 359–373.

Nesdale, D., Maass, A., Kiesner, J., Durkin, K., Griffiths, J., & James, B. (2009). Effects of peer group rejection and a new group's norms on children's intergroup attitudes. *British Journal of Developmental Psychology, 27,* 799–814.

Nesdale, D., & Todd, P. (1998). Intergroup ratio and the contact hypothesis. *Journal of Applied Social Psychology, 28,* 1196–1217.

Nettle, D., & Dunbar, R. I. M. (1997). Social markers and the evolution of reciprocal exchange. *Current Anthropology, 38,* 93–99.

Neu, J., Graham, J. L., & Gilly, M. C. (1988). The influence of gender on behaviors and outcomes in a retail buyer-seller negotiation simulation. *Journal of Retailing, 64,* 427–451.

Neuberg, S. L. (1988). Behavioral implications of information presented outside of conscious awareness: The effect of subliminal presentation of trait information on behavior in the Prisoner's Dilemma Game. *Social Cognition, 6,* 207–230.

Neuman, G. A., & Wright, J. (1999). Team effectiveness: Beyond skills and cognitive ability. *Journal of Applied Psychology, 84,* 376–389.

Neuman, G. A., Wagner, S. H., & Christiansen, N. D. (1999). The relationship between work-team personality composition and the job performance of teams. *Group and Organization Management, 24,* 28–45.

Nevis, E. C., DiBella, A. J., & Gould, J. M. (1997). Understanding organizations as learning systems. In D. F. Russ-Eft, H. S. Preskill, & C. Sleezer (Eds.), *Human resource development review: Research and implications* (pp. 274–298). Thousand Oaks, CA: Sage Publications, Inc.

Newheiser, A.-K., Tausch, N., Dovidio, J. F., & Hewstone, M. (2009). Entitativity and prejudice: Examining their relationship and the moderating effect of attitude certainty. *Journal of Experimental Social Psychology, 45,* 920–926.

Neyman, A., & Okada, D. (2000). Repeated games with bounded entropy. *Games and Economic Behavior, 30,* 228–247.

Ng, S. H. (1989). Intergroup behaviour and the self. *New Zealand Journal of Psychology, 18*(1), 1–12.

Ng, S. H., & Cram, F. (1988). Intergroup bias by defensive and offensive groups in majority and minority conditions. *Journal of Personality and Social Psychology, 55*, 749–757.

Nicotera, A. M. (1994). The use of multiple approaches to conflict: A study of sequences. *Human Communication Research, 20*, 592–621.

Nicotera, A. M., & Rancer, A. S. (1994). The influence of sex on self-perceptions and social stereotyping of aggressive communication predispositions. *Western Journal of Communication, 58*, 283–307.

Niens, U., & Cairns, E. (2001). Intrastate violence. In D. J. Christie, R. V. Wagner, & D. D. Winter (Eds.), (2001), *Peace, conflict, and violence: Peace psychology for the 21st Century* (pp. 39–48). Upper Saddle River, NJ: Prentice Hall.

Nier, J. A., Gaertner, S. L., Dovidio, J. F., Banker, B. S., Ward, C. M., & Rust, M. C. (2001). Changing interracial evaluations and behavior: The effects of a common group identity. *Group Processes and Intergroup Relations, 4*, 299–316.

Nijstad, B. A. (2009). *Group performance*. New York: Psychology Press.

Nijstad, B. A., Stroebe, W., & Lodewijkx, H. F. M. (1999). Persistence of brainstorming groups: How do people know when to stop? *Journal of Experimental Social Psychology, 35*, 165–185.

Nijstad, B. A., Stroebe, W., & Lodewijkx, H. F. M. (2006). The illusion of group productivity: A reduction of failures explanation. *European Journal of Social Psychology, 36*, 31–48.

Nikolaou, I., & Tsaousis, I. (2002). Emotional intelligence in the workplace: Exploring its effects on occupational stress and organizational commitment. *International Journal of Organizational Analysis, 10*, 327–342.

Nishida, K. (1992). Effects of conversation act on conversation strategy and interpersonal cognition. *Japanese Journal of Psychology, 63*, 319–325.

Nishizaki, I., Sakawa, M., & Katagiri, H. (2004). Influence of environmental changes on cooperative behavior in the Prisoner's Dilemma game on an artificial social model. *Applied Artificial Intelligence, 18*, 651–671.

Nitsun, M. (1991). The anti-group: Destructive forces in the group and their therapeutic potential. *Group Analysis, 24*, 7–20.

Nitsun, M. (1996). *The anti-group: Destructive forces in the group and their creative potential.* London: Routledge.

Nitsun, M. (1991). The anti-group: Destructive forces in the group and their therapeutic potential. *Group Analysis, 24*, 7–20.

Noë, R. (1994). A model of coalition formation among male baboons with fighting ability as the crucial parameter. *Animal Behaviour, 47*, 211–213.

Noë, R., & Sluijter, A. A. (1995). Which adult male savanna baboons form coalitions? *International Journal of Primatology, 16*, 77–105.

Noel, J. G., Wann, D. L., & Branscombe, N. R. (1995). Peripheral ingroup membership status and public negativity toward outgroups. *Journal of Personality and Social Psychology, 68*, 127–137.

Noller, P. (2006). Nonverbal communication in close relationships. In V. Manusov & M. L. Patterson (Eds.), *The Sage handbook of nonverbal communication* (pp. 403–420). Thousand Oaks, CA: Sage Publications, Inc.

Nonami, H. (1996). The self-sacrificing minority and saving victims of environmental problems as a social conflict situation. *Psychologia: An International Journal of Psychology in the Orient, 39*, 33–41.

Noor, M., Brown, R., Gonzalez, R., Manzi, J., & Lewis, C. A. (2008). On positive psychological outcomes: What helps groups with a history of conflict to forgive and reconcile with each other? *Personality and Social Psychology Bulletin, 34*, 819–832.

Nordhaug, O. (1994). Structural learning barriers in organizations. *Scandinavian Journal of Educational Research, 38*, 299–313.

Northcraft, G. B., Brodt, S. E., & Neale, M. A. (1995). Negotiating with nonlinear subjective utilities: Why some concessions are more equal than others. *Organizational Behavior and Human Decision Processes, 63*, 298–310.

Northcraft, G. B., Neale, M. A., & Earley, P. C. (1994). Joint effects of assigned goals and training on negotiator performance. *Human Performance, 7*, 257–272.

Northcraft, G. B., Polzer, J., Neale, M. A., & Kramer, R. M. (1995). Diversity, social identity, and performance: Emergent social dynamics in cross-functional teams. In S. E. Jackson & M. N. Ruderman (Eds.), *Diversity in work teams: Research paradigms for a changing workplace* (pp. 69–96). Washington, DC: American Psychological Association.

Nowak, M. A. (2006). Five rules for the evolution of cooperation. *Science, 314*(5805), 1560–1563.

Nowak, M. A., & Sigmund, K. (2005). Evolution of indirect reciprocity. *Nature, 437*, 1291–1298.

Nowicki, S., Jr., Fost, L., & Naik, M. (1997). The impact of cooperative and competitive instructions on the performance of friendly and hostile complementary mixed-sex dyads. *Journal of Research in Personality, 31*, 512–522.

Nullmeyer, R. T., & Spiker, V. A. (2003). The importance of crew resource management behaviors in mission performance: Implications for training evaluation. *Military Psychology, 15*, 77–96.

Nye, J. L. (2002). The eye of the follower: Information processing effects on attributions regarding leaders of small groups. *Small Group Research, 33*, 337–360.

Nye, J. L. & Brower, A. M. (1996a). What *is* social about social cognition research? In J. Nye & A. M. Brower (Eds.), *What's social about social cognition: Social cognition in small groups* (pp. 311–323). Newbury Park, CA: Sage Publications.

Nye, J. L., & Brower, A. M. (Eds.). (1996b). *What's social about social cognition? Research on socially shared cognition in small groups.* Thousand Oaks, CA: Sage Publications, Inc.

Nye, J. L., & Simonetta, L. G. (1996). Followers' perceptions of group leaders: The impact of recognition-based and inference-based processes. In J. L. Nye & A. M. Brower (Eds.), *What's social about social cognition? Research on socially shared cognition in small groups* (pp. 124–153). Thousand Oaks, CA: Sage.

Nyer, P. U., & Gopinath, M. (2001). Bargaining behavior and acculturation: A cross-cultural investigation. *Journal of International Consumer Marketing, 14*(23), 101–122.

Nygaard, A., & Dahlstrom, R. (2002). Role stress and effectiveness in horizontal alliances. *Journal of Marketing, 66*(2), 61–82.

Oakes, P., Haslam, S. A., & Turner, J. C. (1998). The role of prototypicality in group influence and cohesion: Contextual variation in the graded structure of social categories. In S. Worchel, J. F. Morales, D. Paez–, & J.-C. Deschamps (Eds.), *Social identity: International perspectives* (pp. 75–92). London: Sage Publications, Inc.

Obst, P., Smith, S. G., & Zinkiewicz, L. (2002). An exploration of sense of community, Part 3: Dimensions and predictors of psychological sense of community in geographical communities. *Journal of Community Psychology, 30*, 119–133.

Obst, P., Zinkiewicz, L., & Smith, S. G. (2002a). Sense of community in science fiction fandom, Part 1: Understanding sense of community in an international community of interest. *Journal of Community Psychology, 30*, 87–103.

Obst, P., Zinkiewicz, L., & Smith, S. G. (2002b). Sense of community in science fiction fandom, Part 2: Comparing neighborhood and interest group sense of community. *Journal of Community Psychology, 30*, 105–117.

Ochs, J. (1995). Games with unique, mixed strategy equilibria: An experimental study. *Games and Economic Behavior, 10*, 202–217.

Ockenfels, A., & Selten, R. (2000). An experiment on the hypothesis of involuntary truth-signalling in bargaining. *Games and Economic Behavior, 33*, 90–116.

O'Connor, K. M. (1997). Groups and solos in context: The effects of accountability on team negotiation. *Organizational Behavior and Human Decision Processes, 72*, 384–407.

O'Connor, Kathleen M., & Carnevale, Peter J. (1997). A nasty but effective negotiation strategy: Misrepresentation of a common-value issue. *Personality and Social Psychology Bulletin. 23*, 504–515.

Oda, R. (1997). Biased face recognition in the prisoner's dilemma game. *Evolution and Human Behavior, 18*, 309–315.

O'Driscoll, M. P., & Randall, D. M. (1999). Perceived organisational support, satisfaction with rewards, and employee job involvement and organisational commitment. *Applied Psychology: An International Review, 48*, 197–209.

Oehlschlegel, S., & Piontkowski, U. (1997). Topic progression and social categorization. *Journal of Language and Social Psychology, 16*, 444–455.

Oetzel, J. G., & Robbins, J. (2003). Multiple identities in teams in a cooperative supermarket. In L. R. Frey (Ed.), *Group communication in context: Studies of bona fide groups* (2nd ed., pp. 183–206). Mahwah, NJ: Lawrence Erlbaum Associates Publishers.

Offerman, T., Potters, J., & Verbon, H. A. A. (2001). Cooperation in an overlapping generations experiment. *Games and Economic Behavior, 36*, 264–275.

Offermann, L. R., Bailey, J. R., Vasilopoulos, N. L., Seal, C., & Sass, M. (2004). The relative contribution of emotional competence and cognitive ability to individual and team performance. *Human Performance, 17*, 219–243.

Ohbuchi, K. i., & Baba, R. (1988). Selection of influence strategies in interpersonal conflicts: Effects of sex, interpersonal relations, and goals. *Tohoku Psychologica Folia, 47*, 63–73.

Ohbuchi, K. i., Fukushima, O., & Fukuno, M. (1995). Reciprocity and cognitive bias reactions to interpersonal conflicts. *Tohoku Psychologica Folia, 54*, 53–60.

Ohbuchi, K. I., & Takahashi, Y. (1994). Cultural styles of conflict management in Japanese and Americans: Passivity, covertness, and effectiveness of strategies. *Journal of Applied Social Psychology, 24*, 1345–1366.

Ohsako, H., & Takahashi, S. (1994). Effects of "Amae" on interpersonal emotions and conflict-solution strategies in interpersonal conflict situations. *Japanese Journal of Experimental Social Psychology, 34*, 44–57.

Oishi, C., & Yoshida, F. (2001). The effect of in-group-outgroup comparison context on black sheep effect: An analysis from a social identity perspective. *Japanese Journal of Psychology, 71*, 445–453.

Ok, E. A., & Zhou, L. (2000). The Choquet bargaining solutions. *Games and Economic Behavior, 33*, 249–264.

Okada, A. (1996). A noncooperative coalitional bargaining game with random proposers. *Games and Economic Behavior, 16*, 97–108.

Okhuysen, G. A. (2001). Structuring change: Familiarity and formal interventions in problem-solving groups. *Academy of Management Journal, 44*, 794–808.

Olcina, G., & Peñarrubia, C. (2004). Hold up and intergenerational transmission of preferences. *Journal of Economic Behavior and Organization, 54*, 111–132.

O'Leary-Kelly, A. M., Martocchio, J. J., & Frink, D. D. (1994). A review of the influence of group goals on group performance. *Academy of Management Journal, 37*, 1285–1301.

Olekalns, M. (1991). The balance of power: Effects of role and market forces on negotiated outcomes. *Journal of Applied Social Psychology, 21*, 1012–1033.

Olekalns, M. (1994). Context, issues and frame as determinants of negotiated outcomes. *British Journal of Social Psychology, 33*, 197–210.

Olekalns, M. (1997). Situational cues as moderators of the frame-outcome relationship. *British Journal of Social Psychology, 36*, 191–209.

Olekalns, M., Putnam, L. L., Weingart, L. R., & Metcalf, L. (2008). Communication processes and conflict management. In C. K. W. De Dreu & M. J. Gelfand (Eds.), *The psychology of conflict and conflict management in organizations* (pp. 81–114). New York: Taylor & Francis Group/ Lawrence Erlbaum Associates.

Olekalns, M., Smith, P. L., & Kibby, R. (1996). Social value orientations and negotiator outcomes. *European Journal of Social Psychology, 26*, 299–313.

Oliver, D., & Roos, j. (2003). Dealing with the unexpected: Critical incidents in the LEGO Mindstorms team. *Human Relations, 56*, 1057–1082.

Oliver, R. L., Balakrishnan, P. V., & Barry, B. (1994). Outcome satisfaction in negotiation: A test of expectancy disconfirmation. *Organizational Behavior and Human Decision Processes, 60*, 252–275.

Olmsted, M. S. (1959). *The small group*. New York: Random House.

Olmsted, M. S., & Hare, A. P. (1978). *The small group* (2nd ed.). New York: Random House.

Olsen, K. M., & Kalleberg, A. L. (2004). Non-standard work in two different employment regimes: Norway and the United States. *Work, Employment and Society, 18*, 321–348.

Olson, J. S., Olson, G. M., & Meader, D. (1997). Face-to-face group work compared to remote group work with and without video. In K. E. Finn, A. J. Sellen, & S. Wilbur (Eds.), *Video-mediated communication: Computers, cognition, and work* (pp. 157–172). Mahwah, NJ: Lawrence Erlbaum Associates, Inc., Publishers.

Omarzu, J. (2000). A disclosure decision model: Determining how and when individuals will self-disclose. *Personality and Social Psychology Review, 4*, 174–185.

Ones, U., & Putterman, L. (2007). The ecology of collective action: A public goods and sanctions experiment with controlled group formation. *Journal of Economic Behavior and Organization, 62*, 495–521.

Onwujekwe, O. (2004). Criterion and content validity of a novel structured haggling contingent valuation question format versus the bidding game and binary with follow-up format. *Social Science and Medicine, 58*, 525–537.

Oots, K. L. (1990). Bargaining with terrorists: Organizational considerations. *Terrorism, 13*, 145–158.

Oppewal, H., & Tougareva, E. (1992). A three-person ultimatum game to investigate effects of differences in need, sharing rules and observability on bargaining behaviour. *Journal of Economic Psychology, 13*, 203–213.

Orbell, J. M., & Dawes, R. M. (1993). Social welfare, cooperators' advantage, and the option of not playing the game. *American Sociological Review, 58*, 787–800.

Orbell, J. M., van de Kragt, A. J., & Dawes, R. M. (1988). Explaining discussion-induced cooperation. *Journal of Personality and Social Psychology, 54*, 811–819.

Orbell, J., Dawes, R., & Schwartz-Shea, P. (1994). Trust, social categories, and individuals: The case of gender. *Motivation and Emotion, 18*, 109–128.

Orpen, C. (1997). Using the stepladder technique to improve team performance. *Psychological Studies, 42*, 24–28.

Orshan, G., & Zarzuelo, J. M. (2000). The bilateral consistent prekernel for NTU games. *Games and Economic Behavior, 32*, 67–84.

Ortiz, M., & Harwood, J. (2007). A social cognitive theory approach to the effects of mediated intergroup contact on intergroup attitudes. *Journal of Broadcasting and Electronic Media, 51*, 615–631.

Öst, M., Ydenberg, R., Kilpi, M., & Lindström, K. (2003). Condition and coalition formation by brood-rearing common eider females. *Behavioral Ecology, 14*, 311–317.

Ostmann, A. (1992). The interaction of aspiration levels and the social field in experimental bargaining. *Journal of Economic Psychology, 13*, 233–261.

Ostmann, A. (1996). Representing interactional judgments in multilateral bargaining symlog scores, orlik clusters, and behavioral variation. *Small Group Research, 27*, 450–470.

Ostrom, E., Gardner, R., & Walker, J. (1994). *Rules, Games, and Common-Pool Resources*. Ann Arbor, MI: University of Michigan Press.

Ostrom, T. M., Carpenter, S. L., Sedikides, C., & Li, F. (1993). Differential processing of in-group and out-group information. *Journal of Personality and Social Psychology, 64*, 21–34.

Ostrom, T. M., & Sedikides, C. (1992). Out-group homogeneity effects in natural and minimal groups. *Psychological Bulletin, 112*, 536–552.

Otis, M. D. (2004). One community's path to greater social justice: Building on earlier successes. In Y. C. Padilla (Ed.), *Gay and lesbian rights organizing: Community-based strategies* (pp. 17–33). Binghamton, NY: Harrington Park Press/The Haworth Press.

Otten, G.-J., Borm, P., Storcken, T., & Tijs, S. (1995). Effectivity functions and associated claim game correspondences. *Games and Economic Behavior, 9*, 172–190.

Otten, S. (2009). Social categorization, intergroup emotions, and aggressive interactions. In S. Otten, K. Sassenberg, & T. Kessler (Eds.), *Intergroup relations: The role of motivation and emotion* (pp. 162–181). New York: Psychology Press.

Otten, S., & Bar-Tal, Y. (2002). Self-anchoring in the minimal group paradigm: The impact of need and ability to achieve cognitive structure. *Group Processes and Intergroup Relations, 5*, 267–284.

Otten, S., & Moskowitz, G. B. (2000). Evidence for implicit evaluative in-group bias: Affect-biased spontaneous trait inference in a minimal group paradigm. *Journal of Experimental Social Psychology, 36*, 77–89.

Otten, S., & Mummendey, A. (2002). Social discrimination and aggression: A matter of perspective-specific divergence? In C. F. Graumann & W. Kallmeyer (Eds.), *Perspective and perspectivation in discourse* (pp. 233–250). Amsterdam: John Benjamins Publishing Company.

Otten, S., Mummendey, A., & Blanz, M. (2001). Intergroup discrimination in positive and negative outcome allocations: Impact of stimulus valence, relative group status, and relative group size. In M. A. Hogg & D. Abrams (Eds.), *Intergroup relations: Essential readings* (pp. 188–204). Philadelphia: Psychology Press.

Otten, S., Sassenberg, K., & Kessler, T. (Eds.). (2009). *Intergroup relations: The role of motivation and emotion.* New York: Psychology Press.

Ouwerkerk, J. W., De Gilder, D., & De Vries, N. K. (2000). When the going gets tough, the tough get going: Social identification and individual effort in intergroup competition. *Personality and Social Psychology Bulletin, 26*, 1550–1559.

Owens, D. A., Mannix, E. A., & Neale, M. A. (1998). Strategic formation of groups: Issues in task performance and team member selection. In D. H. Gruenfeld (Ed.), *Composition. Research on managing groups and teams* (Vol. 1, pp. 149–165). Stamford, CT: Jai Press, Inc.

Oxenbridge, S., & Brown, W. (2002). The two faces of partnership? An assessment of partnership and co-operative employer/trade union relationships. *Employee Relations, 24*, 262–276.

Oyserman, D., & Packer, M. J. (1996). Social cognition and self-concept: A socially contextualized model of identity. In J. L. Nye & A. M. Brower (Eds.), *What's social about social cognition? Research on socially shared cognition in small groups* (pp. 175–201). Thousand Oaks, CA: Sage Publications, Inc.

Pacala, J. T., Boult, C., Bland, C., & O'Brien, J. (1995). Aging game improves medical students' attitudes toward caring for elders. *Gerontology and Geriatrics Education, 15*(4), 45–57.

Packer, C., Gilbert, D. A., Pusey, A. E., & O'Brien, S. J. (1991). A molecular genetic analysis of kinship and cooperation in African lions. *Nature, 351*, 562–565.

Padilla, Y. C. (Ed.). (2004). *Gay and lesbian rights organizing: Community-based strategies.* Binghamton, NY: Harrington Park Press/The Haworth Press.

Paese, P. W., & Gilin, D. A. (2000). When an adversary is caught telling the truth: Reciprocal cooperation versus self-interest in distributive bargaining. *Personality and Social Psychology Bulletin, 26*, 79–90.

Paese, P. W., & Stang, S. J. (1998). Adaptation-level phenomena and the prevalence of cooperation. *Social Psychology Quarterly, 61*, 172–183.

Page, S. E. (2007). *The difference: How the power of diversity creates better groups, firms, schools, and societies.* Princeton, NJ: Princeton University Press.

Paine-Andrews, A., Fawcett, S. B., Richter, K. P., Berkley, J. Y., Williams, E. L., & Lopez, C. M. (1996). Community coalitions to prevent adolescent substance abuse: The case of the "Project Freedom" Replication Initiative. *Journal of Prevention and Intervention in the Community, 14*(1–2), 81–99.

Paladino, M.-P., & Castelli, L. (2008). On the immediate consequences of intergroup categorization: Activation of approach and avoidance motor behavior toward ingroup and outgroup members. *Personality and Social Psychology Bulletin, 34*, 755–768.

Palmer, L. G., & Thompson, L. (1995). Negotiation in triads: Communication constraints and tradeoff structure. *Journal of Experimental Psychology: Applied, 1*, 83–94.

Paolini, S., Hewstone, M., & Cairns, E. (2007). Direct and indirect intergroup friendship effects: Testing the moderating role of the affective-cognitive bases of prejudice. *Personality and Social Psychology Bulletin, 33*, 1406–1420.

Papa, M. J., & Pood, E. A. (1988). Coorientational accuracy and differentiation in the management of conflict. *Communication Research, 15*, 400–425.

Pápai, S. (2004). Unique stability in simple coalition formation games. *Games and Economic Behavior, 48*, 337–354.

Papayoanou, P. A. (1997). Intra-alliance bargaining and U.S. Bosnia policy. *Journal of Conflict Resolution, 41*, 91–116.

Paquet, R., Gaétan, I., & Bergeron, J.-G. (2000). Does interest-based bargaining (IBB) really make a difference in collective bargaining outcomes? *Negotiation Journal, 16*, 281–296.

Parco, J. E., & Rapoport, A. (2004). Enhancing honesty in bargaining under incomplete information: An experimental study of the bonus procedure. *Group Decision and Negotiation, 13*, 539–562.

Park, E. J. W. (1996). Our L. A.? Korean Americans in Los Angeles after the civil unrest. In M. J. Dear, H. E. Schockman, & G. Hise (Eds.), *Rethinking Los Angeles* (pp. 153–169). Thousand Oaks, CA: Sage Publications, Inc.

Park, H. S. (2008). The effects of shared cognition on group satisfaction and performance: Politeness and efficiency in group interaction. *Communication Research, 35*, 88–108.

Parker, C. P., Baltes, B. B., Young, S. A., Huff, J. W., Altmann, R. A., Lacost, H. A., & Roberts, J. E. (2003). Relationships between psychological climate perceptions and work outcomes: A meta-analytic review. *Journal of Organizational Behavior, 24*, 389–416.

Parks, C. D., & Cowlin, R. A. (1996). Acceptance of uncommon information into group discussion when that information is or is not demonstable. *Organizational Behavior and Human Decision Processes, 66*, 307–315.

Parks, C. D., Henager, R. F., & Scamahorn, S. D. (1996). Trust and reactions to messages of intent in social dilemmas. *Journal of Conflict Resolution, 40*, 134–151.

Parks, C. D., & Hulbert, L. G. (1995). High and low trusters' responses to fear in a payoff matrix. *Journal of Conflict Resolution, 39*, 718–730.

Parks, C. D., Rumble, A. C., & Posey, D. C. (2002). The effects of envy on reciprocation in a social dilemma. *Personality and Social Psychology Bulletin, 28*, 509–520.

Parks, C. D., Sanna, L. J., & Posey, D. C. (2003). Retrospection in social dilemmas: How thinking about the past affects future cooperation. *Journal of Personality and Social Psychology, 84*, 988–996.

Parks, C. D., & Vu, A. D. (1994). Social dilemma behavior of individuals from highly individualist and collectivist cultures. *Journal of Conflict Resolution, 38*, 708–718.

Parsons, T. (1961). *Theories of society: Foundations of modern sociological theory*. New York: Free Press.

Partington, D., & Harris, H. (1999). Team role balance and team performance: An empirical study. *Journal of Management Development, 18*, 694–705.

Pate, S., Watson, W. E., & Johnson, L. (1998). The effects of competition on the decision quality of diverse and nondiverse groups. *Journal of Applied Social Psychology, 28*, 912–923.

Patten, T. H., Jr. (1988). *Fair pay: The managerial challenge of comparable job worth and job evaluation*. San Francisco, CA: Jossey-Bass.

Patterson, M. L. (1996). Social behavior and social cognition: A parallel process approach. In J. L. Nye & A. M. Brower (Eds.), *What's social about social cognition? Research on socially shared cognition in small groups* (pp. 87–105). Thousand Oaks, CA: Sage.

Patterson, M. L. (1999). The evolution of a parallel process model of nonverbal communication. In P. Philippot, R. S. Feldman, & E. J. Coats (Eds.), *The social context of nonverbal behavior* (pp. 317–347). New York: Cambridge University Press.

Patton, J. Q. (2004). Coalitional effects on reciprocal fairness in the ultimatum game: A case from the Ecuadorian Amazon. In J. Henrich, R. Boyd, S. Bowles, C. Camerer, E. Fehr, & H. Gintis (Eds.), *Foundations of human sociality* (pp. 96–124). New York: Oxford University Press.

Paul, L. C. (1996). Impact of nutrition-related coalitions on welfare reform and food security in a rural state. *Journal of Nutrition Education, 28*, 119–122.

Paulsen, N., Graham, P., Jones, E., Callan, V. J., & Gallois, C. (2005). Organizations as intergroup contexts: Communication, discourse, and identification. In J. Harwood & H. Giles (Eds.), *Intergroup communication: Multiple perspectives* (pp. 165–188). New York: Peter Lang Publishing.

Pavitt, C., & Johnson, K. K. (2001). The association between group procedural MOPs and group discussion procedure. *Small Group Research, 32*, 595–624.

Pavitt, C., Whitchurch, G. G., McClurg, H., & Petersen, N. (1995). Melding the objective and subjective sides of leadership: Communication and social judgments in decision making groups. *Communication Monographs, 62*, 243–264.

Paxton, P., & Moody, J. (2003). Structure and sentiment: Explaining emotional attachment to group. *Social Psychology Quarterly, 66*, 34–47.

Pedersen, P. (1993). Mediating multicultural conflict by separating behaviors from expectations in a cultural grid. *International Journal of Intercultural Relations, 17*, 343–353.

Pedersen, P. (1994). "Mediating multicultural conflict by separating behaviors from expectations in a cultural grid": *Erratum. International Journal of Intercultural Relations, 18*, 157–158.

Pedersen, P. (2006). Multicultural conflict resolution. In M. Deutsch, P. T. Coleman, & E. C. Marcus (Eds.), *The handbook of conflict resolution: Theory and practice* (2nd ed., pp. 649–670). Hoboken, NJ: Wiley Publishing.

Pedersen, W. C., Bushman, B. J., Vasquez, E. A., & Miller, N. (2008). Kicking the (barking) dog effect: The moderating role of target attributes on triggered displaced aggression. *Personality and Social Psychology Bulletin, 34*, 1382–1395.

Peeters, M. A. G., Van Tuijl, H. F. J. M., Rutte, C. G., & Reymen, I. M. M. J. (2006). Personality and team performance: A meta-analysis. *European Journal of Personality, 20*, 377–396.

Peirce, R. S., Pruitt, D. G., & Czaja, S. J. (1993). Complainant-respondent differences in procedural choice. *International Journal of Conflict Management, 4*, 199–222.

Pelled, L. H., Eisenhardt, K. M., & Xin, K. R. (1999). Exploring the black box: An analysis of work group diversity, conflict, and performance. *Administrative Science Quarterly, 44*, 1–28.

Pelligra, V. (2007). The not-so-fragile fragility of goodness: The responsive quality of fiduciary relationships. In L. Bruni & P. L. Porta (Eds.), *Handbook on the economics of happiness* (pp. 290–317). Northampton, MA: Edward Elgar Publishing.

Pemberton, M. B., Insko, C. A., & Schopler, J. (1996). Memory for and experience of differential competitive behavior of individuals and groups. *Journal of Personality and Social Psychology, 71*, 953–966.

Pena, F., & Rodriguez, D. (1996). Caracteristicas individuales y estilos de gestion del conflicto [Individual characteristics and conflict resolution style]. *Boletin de Psicologia Spain, 52*, 47–70.

Penner, S. (1995). A study of coalitions among HIV/AIDS service organizations. *Sociological Perspectives, 38*, 217–239.

Penrod, S., & Heuer, L. (1998). Improving group performance: The case of the jury. In R. S. Tindale, L. Heath, J. Edwards, E. J. Posavac, F. B. Bryant, Y. Suarez-Balcazar, E. Henderson-King, & J. Myers (Eds.), *Theory and research on small groups* [Social psychological applications to social issues, Vol. 4] (pp. 127–152). New York: Plenum Press.

Percival, T. Q., Smitheram, V., & Kelly, M. (1992). Myers-Briggs Type Indicator and conflicthandling intention: An interactive approach. *Journal of Psychological Type, 23*, 10–16.

Perdue, C. W., Dovidio, J. F., Gurtman, M. B., & Tyler, R. B. (1990). Us and them: Social categorization and the process of intergroup bias. *Journal of Personality and Social Psychology, 59*, 475–486.

Perez, J. A., & Mugny, G. (1996). The conflict elaboration theory of social influence. In E. H. Witte & J. H. Davis (Eds.), *Understanding group behavior, Vol. 2: Small group processes and interpersonal relations. Understanding group behavior* (pp. 191–210). Mahwah, NJ: Lawrence Erlbaum Associates, Inc.

Perez, J. A., & Mugny, G. (1998). Categorization and social influence. In S. Worchel, J. F. Morales, D. Paez, & J.-C. Deschamps (Eds.), *Social identity: International perspectives* (pp. 142–153). London: Sage Publications, Inc.

Pérez-Castrillo, D., & Wettstein, D. (2000). Implementation of bargaining sets via simple mechanisms. *Games and Economic Behavior, 31*, 106–120.

Perlinger, T. (2000). Voting power in an ideological spectrum: The Markov-Pólya index. *Mathematical Social Sciences, 40*, 215–226.

Perowne, S., & Mansell, W. (2002). Social anxiety, self-focused attention, and the discrimination of negative, neutral and positive audience members by their non-verbal behaviours. *Behavioural and Cognitive Psychotherapy, 30*, 11–23.

Perreault, S., & Bourhis, R. Y. (1998). Social identification, interdependence and discrimination. *Group Processes and Intergroup Relations, 1*, 49–66.

Perreault, S., & Bourhis, R. Y. (1999). Ethnocentrism, social identification, and discrimination. *Personality and Social Psychology Bulletin, 25*, 92–103.

Perrey, S., Barrett, H. C., & Manson, J. H. (2004). White-faced capuchin monkeys show triadic awareness in their choice of allies. *Animal Behaviour, 67*, 165–170.

Pescosolido, A. T. (2003). Group efficacy and group effectiveness: The effects of group efficacy over time on group performance and development. *Small Group Research, 34*, 20–42.

Petersen, L.-E., & Blank, H. (2003). Ingroup bias in the minimal group paradigm shown by three-person groups with high or low state self-esteem. *European Journal of Social Psychology, 33*, 149–162.

Peterson, D. R. (1989). Interpersonal goal conflict. In L. A. Pervin (Ed.), *Goal concepts in personality and social psychology* (pp. 327–361). Hillsdale, NJ: Lawrence Erlbaum Associates, Inc.

Peterson, R. S., & Behfar, K. J. (2003). The dynamic relationship between performance feedback, trust, and conflict in groups: A longitudinal study. *Organizational Behavior and Human Decision Processes, 92*, 102–112.

Peterson, R. S., Owens, P. D., Tetlock, P. E., Fan, E. T., & Martorana, P. (1998). Group dynamics in top management teams: Groupthink, vigilance, and alternative models of organizational failure and success. *Organizational Behavior and Human Decision Processes, 73*, 272–305.

Pettersen, I. J. (1997). Hierarchy and complementarity-joint predictors of group effectiveness? *Scandinavian Journal of Management, 13*, 77–93.

Pettigrew, T. (1996). *How to think like a social scientist*. New York: HarperCollins.

Pettigrew, T. F. (1997). Generalized intergroup contact effects on prejudice. *Personality and Social Psychology Bulletin, 23*, 173–185.

Pettigrew, T. F. (1998). Intergroup contact theory. *Annual Review of Psychology, 49*, 65–85.

Pettigrew, T. F. (2006). The advantages of multilevel approaches. *Journal of Social Issues, 62*, 615–620.

Pettigrew, T. F. (2007). Probing the complexity of intergroup prejudice. *International Journal of Psychology, 44*, 40–42.

Pettigrew, T. F. (2008). Future directions for intergroup contact theory and research. *International Journal of Intercultural Relations, 32*, 187–199.

Pettigrew, T. F. (2008). Reflections on core themes in intergroup research. In U. Wagner, L. R. Tropp, G. Finchilescu, & C. Tredoux (Eds.), *Improving intergroup relations: Building on the legacy of Thomas F. Pettigrew* (pp. 283–303). Malden: Blackwell Publishing.

Pettigrew, T. F. (2009). Secondary transfer effect of contact: Do intergroup contact effects spread to noncontacted outgroups? *Social Psychology, 40*, 55–65.

Pettigrew, T. F., Allport, G. W., & Barnett, E. O. (1958). Binocular resolution and perception of race in South Africa. *British Journal of Psychology, 49*, 265–278.

Pettigrew, T. F., Christ, O., Wagner, U., Meertens, R. W., van Dick, R., & Zick, A. (2008). Relative deprivation and intergroup prejudice. *Journal of Social Issues, 64*, 385–401.

Pettigrew, T. F., Christ, O., Wagner, U., & Stellmacher, J. (2007). Direct and indirect intergroup contact effects on prejudice: A normative interpretation. *International Journal of Intercultural Relations, 31*, 411–425.

Pettigrew, T. F., & Tropp, L. R. (2000). Does intergroup contact reduce prejudice: Recent meta-analytic findings. In S. Oskamp (Ed.), *Reducing prejudice and discrimination* (pp. 93–114). Mahwah, NJ: Lawrence Erlbaum Associates, Publishers.

Pettigrew, T. F., & Tropp, L. R. (2006). A meta-analytic test of intergroup contact theory. *Journal of Personality and Social Psychology, 90*, 751–783.

Pettigrew, T. F., & Tropp, L. R. (2008). How does intergroup contact reduce prejudice? Meta-analytic tests of three mediators. *European Journal of Social Psychology, 38*, 922–934.

Pfingsten, A., & Wagener, A. (2003). Bargaining solutions as social compromises. *Theory and Decision, 55*, 359–389.

Pheterson, G. (1995). Group identity and social relations: Divergent theoretical conceptions in the United States, the Netherlands, and France. In I. Lubek, R. Van Hezewijk, G. Pheterson, & C. W. Tolman (Eds.), *Trends and issues in theoretical psychology* (pp. 66–72). New York: Springer Publishing Co, Inc.

Philips, M. E. (2004). Action research and development coalitions in health care. *Action Research, 2*, 349–370.

Picard, C. A. (2004). Exploring an integrative framework for understanding mediation. *Conflict Resolution Quarterly, 21*, 295–311.

Pickett, C. L., Silver, M. D., & Brewer, M. B. (2002). The impact of assimilation and differentiation needs on perceived group importance and judgments of ingroup size. *Personality and Social Psychology Bulletin, 28*, 546–558.

Pil, F. K., & MacDuffie, J. P. (2000). The adoption of high-involvement work practices. In C. Ichniowski, D. I. Levine, C. Olson, & G. Strauss (Eds.), *The American workplace: Skills, compensation, and employee involvement* (pp. 137–171). New York: Cambridge University Press.

Pilkington, C. J., Richardson, D. R., & Utley, M. E. (1988). Is conflict stimulating? Sensation seekers' responses to interpersonal conflict. *Personality and Social Psychology Bulletin, 14*, 596–603.

Pillai, R., & Meindl, J. R. (1998). Context and charisma: A "meso" level examination of the relationship of organic structure, collectivism, and crisis to charismatic leadership. *Journal of Management, 24*, 643–671.

Pillutla, M. M., & Murnighan, J. K. (1995). Being fair or appearing fair: Strategic behavior in ultimatum bargaining. *Academy of Management Journal, 38*, 1408–1426.

Pillutla, M. M., & Murnighan, J. K. (2003). Fairness in bargaining. *Social Justice Research, 16*, 241–262.

Pinkley, R. L. (1995). Impact of knowledge regarding alternatives to settlement in dyadic negotiations: Whose knowledge counts? *Journal of Applied Psychology, 80*, 403–417.

Pinkley, R. L., Neale, M. A., & Bennett, R. J. (1994). The impact of alternatives to settlement in dyadic negotiation. *Organizational Behavior and Human Decision Processes, 57*, 97–116.

Pinter, B., & Greenwald, A. G. (2004). Exploring implicit partisanship: Enigmatic (but genuine) group identification and attraction. *Group Processes and Intergroup Relations, 7*, 283–296.

Pires, M. A. (1988). Building coalitions with external constituencies. In R. L. Heath (Ed.), *Strategic issues management: How organizations influence and respond to public interests and policies* (pp. 185–198). San Francisco: Jossey-Bass.

Pirola-Merlo, A., & Mann, L. (2004). The relationship between individual creativity and team creativity: Aggregating across people and time. *Journal of Organizational Behavior, 25*, 235–257.

Pittam, J. (1999). The historical and emergent enactment of identity in language. *Research on Language and Social Interaction, 32*, 111–117.

Pitz, G. F. (1992). From Bible to Baseball: Principles of Rational Negotiation. *PsycCRITIQUES, 37*, 240–241.

Plant, E. A., & Devine, P. G. (2003). The antecedents and implications of interracial anxiety. *Personality and Social Psychology Bulletin*, Vol *29*, 790–801.

Platow, M. J., Harley, K., Hunter, J. A., Hanning, P., Shave, R., & O'Connell, A. (1997). Interpreting in-group-favouring allocations in the minimal group paradigm. *British Journal of Social Psychology, 36*, 107–117.

Platow, M. J., McClintock, C. G., & Liebrand, W. B. (1990). Predicting intergroup fairness and ingroup bias in the minimal group paradigm. *European Journal of Social Psychology, 20*, 221–239.

Platow, M. J., O'Connell, A., Shave, R., & Hanning, P. (1995). Social evaluations of fair and unfair allocators in interpersonal and intergroup situations. *British Journal of Social Psychology, 34*, 363–381.

Platow, M. J., & Van Knippenberg, D. (2001). A social identity analysis of leadership endorsement: The effects of leader ingroup prototypicality and distributive intergroup fairness. *Personality and Social Psychology Bulletin, 27*, 1508–1519.

Platow, M. J., Wenzel, M., & Nolan, M. (2003). The importance of social identity and self-categorization processes for creating and responding to fairness. In S. A. Haslam, D. Van Knippenberg, M. J. Platow, & N. Ellemers (Eds.), *Social identity at work: Developing theory for organizational practice* (pp. 261–276). New York: Psychology Press.

Podolny, J. M., & Page, K. L. (1998). Network forms of organization. *Annual Review of Sociology, 24*, 57–76.

Pokrajac-Bulian, A., Kardum, I., & Susanj, Z. (1996). Styles of handling interpersonal conflict in various social interactions. *Studia Psychologica, 38*, 163–176.

Pollack, B. N. (1998). The impact of the sociophysical environment on interpersonal communication and feelings of belonging in work groups. In J. Sanford & B. R. Connell (Eds.), *People, places and public policy* (pp. 71–78). Edmond, OK: Environmental Design Research Association.

Polley, R. B. (1989). Coalition, mediation, and scapegoating: General principles and cultural variation. *International Journal of Intercultural Relations, 13*, 165–181.

Polzer, J. T., Mannix, E. A., & Neale, M. A. (1995). Multiparty negotiation in its social context. In R. M. Kramer & D. M. Messick (Eds.), *Negotiation as a social process: New trends in theory and research* (pp. 123–142). Thousand Oaks, CA: Sage Publications, Inc.

Polzer, J. T., Mannix, E. A., & Neale, M. A. (1998). Interest alignment and coalitions in multiparty negotiation. *Academy of Management Journal, 41*, 42–54.

Polzer, J. T., Neale, M. A., & Glenn, P. O. (1993). The effects of relationships and justification in an interdependent allocation task. *Group Decision and Negotiation, 2*, 135–148.

Ponsati, C., & Sákovics, J. (1996). Multiperson Bargaining over Two Alternatives. *Games and Economic Behavior*, Vol *12*, 226–244.

Poole, M. S., & DeSanctis, G. (1992). Microlevel structuration in computer-supported group decision making. *Human Communication Research. 19*, 5–49.

Poole, M. S., Hollingshead, A. B., McGrath, J. E., Moreland, R. L., & Rohrbaugh, J. (2004). Interdisciplinary perspectives on small groups. *Small Group Research, 35*, 3–16.

Poplu, G., Baratgin, J., Mavromatis, S., & Ripoll, H. (2003). What Kind of Process Underlie Decision Making in Soccer Simulation? An Implicit-Memory Investigation. *International Journal of Sport and Exercise Psychology, 1*, 390–405.

Post, F. R., & Bennett, R. J. (1994). Use of the collaborative collective bargaining process in labor negotiations. *International Journal of Conflict Management, 5*, 34–61.

Posthuma, R. A., Dworkin, J. B., & Swift, M. S. (2002). Mediator tactics and sources of conflict: Facilitating and inhibiting effects. *Industrial Relations: A Journal of Economy and Society, 41*, 94–109.

Postmes, T., & Baym, N. (2005). Intergroup dimensions of the internet. In J. Harwood & H. Giles (Eds.), *Intergroup communication: Multiple perspectives* (pp. 213–238). New York: Peter Lang Publishing.

Postmes, T., & Brunsting, S. (2002). Collective action in the age of the Internet: Mass communication and online mobilization. *Social Science Computer Review, 20*, 290–301.

Postmes, T., & Jetten, J. (2006). *Individuality and the group: Advances in social identity.* London: Sage.

Postmes, T., & Lea, M. (2000). Social processes and group decision making: Anonymity in group decision support systems. *Ergonomics, 43*, 1252–1274.

Postmes, T., Spears, R., & Lea, M. (1999). Social identity, normative content, and "deindividuation" in computer-mediated groups. In N. Ellemers, R. Spears, & B. Doosje (Eds.), *Social identity: Context, commitment, content* (pp. 164–183). Oxford, England: Blackwell Science.

Postmes, T., Spears, R., & Lea, M. (2000). The formation of group norms in computer-mediated communication. *Human Communication Research, 26*, 341–371.

Postmes, T., Spears, R., & Lea, M. (2002). Intergroup differentiation in computer-mediated communication: Effects of depersonalization. *Group Dynamics: Theory, Research, and Practice, 6*, 3–16.

Postmes, T., Spears, R., Lee, A. T., & Novak, R. J. (2005). Individuality and social influence in groups: Inductive and deductive routes to group identity. *Journal of Personality and Social Psychology, 89*, 747–763.

Postmes, T., Spears, R., Sakhel, K., & De Groot, D. (2001). Social influence in computer-mediated communication: The effects of anonymity on group behavior. *Personality and Social Psychology Bulletin, 27*, 1243–1254.

Postmes, T., Tanis, M., & De Wit, B. (2001). Communication and commitment in organizations: A social identity approach. *Group Processes and Intergroup Relations, 4*, 227–246.

Potter, R. E., & Balthazard, P. A. (2002). Virtual team interaction styles: Assessment and effects. *International Journal of Human-Computer Studies, 56*, 423–443.

Poulsen, A. U. (2004). On efficiency, tie-breaking rules and role assignment procedures in evolutionary bargaining. *Mathematical Social Sciences, 47*, 233–243.

Powell, R. (1996). Bargaining in the shadow of power. *Games and Economic Behavior, 15*, 255–
289.

Prati, L. M., Douglas, C., Ferris, G. R., Ammeter, A. P., & Buckley, M. R. (2003). Emotional intelligence, leadership effectiveness, and team outcomes. *International Journal of Organizational
Analysis, 11*, 21–40.

Pratkanis, A. R., & Turner, M. E. (1999). Groupthink and preparedness for the Loma Prieta earth-
quake: A social identity maintenance analysis of causes and preventions. In R. Wageman (Ed.),
*Research on managing groups and teams: Groups in context* (Vol. 2, pp. 115–136). San Diego,
CA: Elsevier Science/JAI Press, 1999.

Pratto, F., Hegarty, P. J., & Korchmaros, J. D. (2008). How communication practices and category norms lead people to stereotype particular people and groups. In Y. Kashima, K. Fiedler,
& P. Freytag (Eds.), *Stereotype dynamics: Language-based approaches to the formation, maintenance, and transformation of stereotypes* (pp. 293–313). Mahwah, NJ: Lawrence Erlbaum
Associates Publishers.

Pratto, F., Sidanius, J., Stallworth, L. M., & Malle, B. F. (2001). Social dominance orientation:
A personality variable predicting social and political attitudes. In M. A. Hogg & D. Abrams
(Eds.), *Intergroup relations: Essential readings* (pp. 30–59). Philadelphia: Psychology Press.

Preli, R., & Protinsky, H. (1988). Aspects of family structures in alcoholic, recovered, and nonal-
coholic families. *Journal of Marital and Family Therapy, 14*, 311–314.

Prentice, D. A., Miller, D. T., & Lightdale, J. R. (1994). Asymmetries in attachments to groups
and to their members: Distinguishing between common-identity and common-bond groups.
*Personality and Social Psychology Bulletin, 20*, 484–493.

Price, V. (1989). Social identification and public opinion: Effects of communicating group conflict. *Public Opinion Quarterly, 53*, 197–224.

Prichard, J. S., & Stanton, N. A. (1999). Testing Belbin's team role theory of effective groups.
*Journal of Management Development, 18*, 652–665.

Prislin, R., & Christensen, P. N. (2005). Social change in the aftermath of successful minority
influence. *European Review of Social Psychology, 16*, 43–73.

Pritchard, D. (1990). Homicide and bargained justice. In R. Surette (Ed.), *The media and criminal justice policy: Recent research and social effects* (pp. 143–152). Springfield, IL, England:
Charles C Thomas, Publisher.

Prohaska, C. R., & Frank, E. J. (1990). Using simulations to investigate management decision
making. *Simulation and Gaming, 21*, 48–58.

Pruitt, D. G. (1991). Strategy in negotiation. In V. A. Kremenyuk (Ed.), *International negotiation:
Analysis, approaches, issues* (pp. 78–89). San Francisco: Jossey-Bass Inc, Publishers.

Pruitt, D. G. (1995). Networks and collective scripts: Paying attention to structure in bargaining
theory. In R. M. Kramer & D. M. Messick (Eds.), *Negotiation as a social process: New trends
in theory and research* (pp. 37–47). Thousand Oaks, CA: Sage Publications, Inc.

Pruitt, D. G. (1998). Social conflict. In D. T. Gilbert, S. T. Fiske, & G. Lindzey (Eds.), *The handbook of social psychology* (4th ed., Vol. 2, pp. 470–503). Boston: Mcgraw-Hill.

Pruitt, D. G., & Carnevale, P. J. (1993). *Negotiation in social conflict*. Pacific Grove, CA: Brooks/
Cole Publishing Co.

Pruitt, D. G., & Olczak, P. V. (1995). Beyond hope: Approaches to resolving seemingly intractable
conflict. In B. B. Bunker & J. Z. Rubin (Eds.), *Conflict, cooperation, and justice: Essays inspired by the work of Morton Deutsch* (pp. 59–92). San Francisco: Jossey-Bass Inc, Publishers.

Pruitt, D. G., Mikolic, J. M., Peirce, R. S., & Keating, M. (1993). Aggression as a struggle tactic
in social conflict. In R. B. Felson & J. T. Tedeschi (Eds.), *Aggression and violence: Social interactionist perspectives* (pp. 99–118). Washington, DC: American Psychological Association.

Pruitt, D. G., Peirce, R. S., Zubek, J. M., McGillicuddy, N. B., & Welton, G. L. (1993). In S.
Worchel & J. A. Simpson, *Conflict between people and groups: Causes, processes and resolutions* (pp. 60–75). Chicago: Nelson-Hall.

Pruitt, D., & Rubin, J. Z. (1999). Strategic choice. In R. J. Lewicki, D. M. Saunders, & J. W. Minton (Eds.), *Negotiation: Readings, exercises, and cases* (3rd ed., pp. 14–31). Boston: Irwin/The McGraw-Hill Companies.

Putland, D. (2001). Has sexual selection been overlooked in the study of avian helping behavior? *Animal Behaviour, 62*, 811–814.

Putnam, L. L. (1993). Spanning the interdisciplinary boundary in conflict research. *PsycCRITIQUES, 38*, 57–58.

Putnam, L. L. (1994a). Challenging the assumptions of traditional approaches to negotiation. *Negotiation Journal, 10*, 337–346.

Putnam, L. L. (1994b). Productive conflict: Negotiation as implicit coordination. *International Journal of Conflict Management, 5*, 284–298.

Putnam, L. L. (1997). Productive conflict: Negotiation as implicit coordination. In C. K. W. De Dreu & E. Van de Vliert (Eds.), *Using conflict in organizations* (pp. 147–160). Thousand Oaks, CA: Sage Publications, Inc.

Putnam, L. L., & Roloff, M. E. (Eds.). (1992). *Communication and negotiation.* Newbury Park, CA: Sage Publications, Inc.

Putnam, L. L., Van Hoeven, S. A., & Bullis, C. A. (1991). The role of rituals and fantasy themes in teachers' bargaining. *Western Journal of Speech Communication, 55*, 85–103.

Qin, Z., Johnson, D. W., & Johnson, R. T. (1995). Cooperative versus competitive efforts and problem solving. *Review of Educational Research, 65*, 129–143.

Quesada, A. (2002). Belief system foundations of backward induction. *Theory and Decision, 53*, 393–403.

Rabbie, J. M., & Horwitz, M. (1988). Categories versus groups as explanatory concepts in intergroup relations. *European Journal of Social Psychology, 18*, 117–123.

Rabbie, J. M., & Lodewijkx, H. F. M. (1996). A behavioral interaction model: Toward an integrative theoretical framework for studying intra– and intergroup dynamics. In E. H. Witte & J. H. Davis (Eds.), *Understanding group behavior, Vol. 2: Small group processes and interpersonal relations. Understanding group behavior* (pp. 255–294). Mahwah, NJ: Lawrence Erlbaum Associates, Inc.

Rabbie, J. M., & Schot, J. C. (1990). Group behavior in the minimal group paradigm: Fact or fiction? In P. J. D. Drenth, J. A. Sergeant, & R. J. Takens (Eds.), *European perspectives in psychology, Vol. 3: Work and organizational, social and economic, cross-cultural* (pp. 251–263). Chichester, England: John Wiley & Sons.

Rabbie, J. M., Schot, J. C., & Visser, L. (1989). Social identity theory: A conceptual and empirical critique from the perspective of a behavioural interaction model. *European Journal of Social Psychology, 19*, 171–202.

Radhakrishnan, P., Kuhn, K. M., & Gelfand, M. J. (2000). The role of allocentrism on perceptions and reactions to congruity. *International Journal of Intercultural Relations, 24*, 725–740.

Radley, A. (1991). Solving a problem together: A study of thinking in small groups. *Journal of Phenomenological Psychology, 22*, 39–59.

Rafferty, J., & Tapsell, J. (2001). Self-managed work teams and manufacturing strategies: Cultural influences in the search for team effectiveness and competitive advantage. *Human Factors and Ergonomics in Manufacturing, 11*, 19–34.

Rahim, M.. (1983). Measurement of organizational conflict. *Journal of General Psychology, Vol 109*, 189–199.

Rahim, M. A. (1997). Styles of managing organizational conflict: A critical review and synthesis of theory and research. In M. A. Rahim, R. T. Golembiewski, & L. E. Pate (Eds.), *Current topics in management* (Vol. 2, pp. 61–77). Greenwich, CT: Jai Press, Inc.

Rahim, M. A., Magner, N. R., & Shapiro, D. L. (2000). Do justice perceptions influence styles of handling conflict with supervisor?: What justice perceptions, precisely? *International Journal of Conflict Management, 11*, 9–31.

Rai, S., & Sinha, A. K. (2000). Transformational leadership, organizational commitment, and facilitating climate. *Psychological Studies, 45*, 33–42.

Rainey, L. C. (1988). The experience of dying. In H. Wass, F. M. Berardo, & R. A. Neimeyer (Eds.), *Dying: Facing the facts* (2nd ed., pp. 137–157). New York: Hemisphere Publishing Corp/Harper & Row Publishers, 1988.

Raith, M. G. (2000). Fair-negotiation procedures. *Mathematical Social Sciences, 39*, 303–322.

Ramsay, K. W. (2004). Politics at the water's edge: Crisis bargaining and electoral competition. *Journal of Conflict Resolution, 48*, 459–486.

Randsley de Moura, G., Leader, T., Pelletier, J., & Abrams, D. (2008). Prospects for group processes and intergroup relations research: A review of 70 years' progress. *Group Processes and Intergroup Relations, 11*, 575–596.

Rapisarda, B. A. (2002). The impact of emotional intelligence on work team cohesiveness and performance. *International Journal of Organizational Analysis, 10*, 363–379.

Rapoport, Amnon. (1988). Provision of step-level public goods: Effects of inequality in resources. *Journal of Personality and Social Psychology, 54*, 432–440.

Rapoport, Amnon. (1990). *Experimental studies of interactive decisions.* New York: Kluwer Academic/Plenum Publishers.

Rapoport, Amnon, & Au, W. T. (2001). Bonus and penalty in common pool resource dilemmas under uncertainty. *Organizational Behavior and Human Decision Processes, 85*, 135–165.

Rapoport, Amnon, & Bornstein, G. (1989). Solving public good problems in competition between equal and unequal size groups. *Journal of Conflict Resolution, 33*, 460–479.

Rapoport, Amnon, Budescu, D. V., & Suleiman, R. (1993). Sequential requests from randomly distributed shared resources. *Journal of Mathematical Psychology, 37*, 241–265.

Rapoport, Amnon, Budescu, D. V., Suleiman, R., & Weg, E. (1992). Social dilemmas with uniformly distributed resources. In W. B. G. Liebrand, D. M. Messick, & H. A. M. Wilke (Eds.), *Social dilemmas: Theoretical issues and research findings* (pp. 43–57). Elmsford, NY: Pergamon Press.

Rapoport, Amnon, & Fuller, M. A. (1998). Coordination in noncooperative three-person games under different information structures. *Group Decision and Negotiation, 7*, 363–382.

Rapoport, Amnon, Seale, D. A., & Winter, E. (2002). Coordination and learning behavior in large groups with asymmetric players. *Games and Economic Behavior, 39*, 111–136.

Rapoport, Amnon, Seale, D. A., Erev, I., & Sundali, J. A. (1998). Equilibrium play in large group market entry games. *Management Science, 44*, 119–141.

Rapoport, Amnon, & Suleiman, R. (1992). Equilibrium solutions for resource dilemmas. *Group Decision and Negotiation, 1*, 269–294.

Rapoport, Amnon, Weg, E., & Felsenthal, D. S. (1990). Effects of fixed costs in two-person sequential bargaining. *Theory and Decision, 28*, 47–71.

Rapoport, Anatol. (1988). Experiments with n-person social traps: I. Prisoner's Dilemma, Weak Prisoner's Dilemma, Volunteer's Dilemma, and Largest Number. *Journal of Conflict Resolution, 32*, 457–472.

Ravenscroft, S. P., Haka, S. F., & Chalos, P. (1993). Bargaining behavior in a transfer pricing experiment. *Organizational Behavior and Human Decision Processes, 55*, 414–443.

Ray, D., & Vohra, R. (1999). A theory of endogenous coalition structures. *Games and Economic Behavior, 26*, 286–336.

Ray, I. (1996). Coalition-proof correlated equilibrium: A definition. *Games and Economic Behavior, 17*, 56–79.

Reagans, R., & Zuckerman, E. W. (2001). Networks, diversity, and productivity: The social capital of corporate R&D teams. *Organization Science, 12*, 502–517.

Reeve, H. Kern. (1998). Acting for the good of others: Kinship and reciprocity with some new twists. In C. B. Crawford, D. L. Krebs, & C. A. Insko (Eds.), *Handbook of evolutionary psychology: Ideas, issues, and applications* (pp. 43–85). Mahwah, NJ: Lawrence Erlbaum Associates, Inc., Publishers.

Reicher, S. D. (2001). The St. Pauls' riot: An explanation of the limits of crowd action in terms of a social identity model. In M. A. Hogg & D. Abrams (Eds.), *Intergroup relations: Essential readings* (pp. 302–315). New York: Psychology Press.

Reicher, S., Cassidy, C., Wolpert, I., Hopkins, N., & Levine, M. (2006). Saving Bulgaria's Jews: An analysis of social identity and the mobilisation of social solidarity. *European Journal of Social Psychology, 36*, 49–72.

Reicher, S., & Haslam, S. A. (2006). On the agency of individuals and groups: Lessons from the BBC Prison Study. In T. Postmes & J. Jetten (Eds.), *Individuality and the group: Advances in social identity* (pp. 237–257). Thousand Oaks, CA: Sage Publications, Inc.

Reicher, S., & Levine, M. (1994). Deindividuation, power relations between groups and the expression of social identity: The effects of visibility to the out-group. *British Journal of Social Psychology, 33*, 145–163.

Reid, F. J. M., Reed, S., & Edworthy, J. (1999). Design visualization and collaborative interaction in undergraduate engineering teams. *International Journal of Cognitive Ergonomics, 3*, 235–259.

Reid, S. A., Giles, H., & Harwood, J. (2005). A self-categorization perspective on communication and intergroup relations. In J. Harwood & H. Giles (Eds.), *Intergroup communication: Multiple perspectives* (pp. 241–263). New York: Peter Lang Publishing.

Reijnierse, H., Maschler, M., Potters, J., & Tijs, S. (1996). Simple Flow Games. *Games and Economic Behavior, 16*, 238–260.

Reio, T. G., Jr., & Callahan, J. L. (2004). Affect, curiosity, and socialization-related learning: A path analysis of antecedents to job performance. *Journal of Business and Psychology, 19*, 3–22.

Reis, H. T., & Collins, W. A. (2004). Relationships, human behavior, and psychological science. *Current Directions in Psychological Science, 13*, 233–237.

Remus, W., & Edge, A. G. (1991). Does adding a formal leader improve the performance of a team in a business simulation? *Simulation and Gaming, 22*, 498–501.

Renaud, L., & Stolovitch, H. (1988). Simulation gaming: An effective strategy for creating appropriate traffic safety behaviors in five-year-old children. *Simulation and Games, 19*, 328–345.

Rentsch, J. R. (1990). Climate and culture: Interaction and qualitative differences in organizational meanings. *Journal of Applied Psychology, 75*, 668–681.

Rentsch, J. R., & Woehr, D. J. (2004). Quantifying congruence in cognition: Social relations modeling and team member schema similarity. In E. Salas & S. M. Fiore (Eds.), *Team cognition: Understanding the factors that drive process and performance* (pp. 11–31). Washington, DC: American Psychological Association.

Retzinger, S., & Scheff, T. (2000). Emotion, alienation and narratives: Resolving intractable conflict. *Mediation Quarterly, 18*, 71–85.

Reynolds, K. J., Oakes, P. J., Haslam, S. A., Nolan, M. A., & Dolnik, L. (2000). Responses to powerlessness: Stereotyping as an instrument of social conflict. *Group Dynamics, 4*, 275–290.

Reynolds, K. J., Turner, J. C., & Haslam, S. A. (2000). When are we better than them and they worse than us? A closer look at social discrimination in positive and negative domains. *Journal of Personality and Social Psychology, 78*, 64–80.

Reynolds, K. J., Turner, J. C., Haslam, S. A., & Ryan, M. K. (2001). The role of personality and group factors in explaining prejudice. *Journal of Experimental Social Psychology, 37*, 427–434.

Reynolds, K. J., Turner, J. C., Haslam, S. A., Ryan, M. K., Bizumic, B., & Subasic, E. (2007). Does personality explain in-group identification and discrimination? Evidence from the minimal group paradigm. *British Journal of Social Psychology, 46*, 517–539.

Richardson, D. R., Hammock, G. S., Lubben, T., & Mickler, S. (1989). The relationship between love attitudes and conflict responses. *Journal of Social and Clinical Psychology, 8*, 430–441.

Richerson, P. J., Boyd, R. T., & Henrich, J. (2003). Cultural evolution of human cooperation. In P. Hammerstein (Ed.), *Genetic and cultural evolution of cooperation* (pp. 357–388). Cambridge, MA: MIT Press.

Richeson, J., Dovidio, J. F., Shelton, J. N., & Hebl, M. (2007). Implications of ingroup—outgroup membership for interpersonal perceptions: Faces and emotion. In U. Hess & P. Philippot (Eds.), *Group dynamics and emotional expression* (pp. 7–32). New York: Cambridge University Press.

Riek, B. M., Gaertner, S. L., Dovidio, J. F., Brewer, M. B., Mania, E. W., & Lamoreaux, M. J. (2008). A social-psychological approach to postconflict reconciliation. In A. Nadler, T. E. Malloy, & J. D. Fisher (Eds.), *The social psychology of intergroup reconciliation* (pp. 255–273). New York: Oxford University Press.

Rieskamp, J., & Todd, P. M. (2006). The evolution of cooperative strategies for asymmetric social interactions. *Theory and Decision, 60,* 69–111.

Riggio, R. E., Chaleff, I., & Lipman-Blumen, J. (Eds.). (2008). *The art of followership: How great followers create great leaders and organizations.* San Francisco: Jossey-Bass.

Riggio, R. E., & Riggio, H. R. (2001). Self-report measurement of interpersonal sensitivity. In J. A. Hall & F. J. Bernieri (Eds.), *Interpersonal sensitivity: Theory and measurement* (pp. 127–142). Mahwah, NJ: Lawrence Erlbaum Associates Publishers.

Rinott, Y., & Scarsini, M. (2000). On the number of pure strategy Nash equilibria in random games. *Games and Economic Behavior, 33,* 274–293.

Rittner, B., & Nakanishi, M. (1993). Challenging stereotypes and cultural biases through small group process. *Social Work with Groups, 16*(4), 5–23.

Riva, G. (2002). Communicating in CMC: Making order out of miscommunication. In L. Anolli, R. Ciceri, & G. Riva (Eds.), *Say not to say: New perspectives on miscommunication* (pp. 197–227). Amsterdam: IOS Press.

Riva, G., & Galimberti, C. (1998). Computer-mediated communication: Identity and social interaction in an electronic environment. *Genetic, Social,* and General Psychology Monographs, 124, 434–464.

Riva, G., & Galimberti, C. (2001). Virtual communication: Social interaction and identity in an electronic environment. In G. Riva & F. Davide (Eds.), *Communications through virtual technologies: Identity, community and technology in the communication age* [Reprint] (pp. 23–46). Amsterdam: IOS Press.

Robbins, T. L., & Fredendall, L. D. (1995). The empowering role of self-directed work teams in the quality focused organization. *Organization Development Journal, Vol 13*(1), 33–42.

Robey, D. (1986). *Designing organizations: A macro perspective.* Homewood, IL: Irwin.

Robins, E. M., & Foster, D. (1994). Social identity versus personal identity: An investigation into the interaction of group and personal status with collective self-esteem on ingroup favouritism. *South African Journal of Psychology, 24,* 115–121.

Robinson, L. F., & Reis, H. T. (1989). The effects of interruption, gender, and status on interpersonal perceptions. *Journal of Nonverbal Behavior, 13,* 141–153.

Robinson, S. L., & O'Leary-Kelly, A. M. (1998). Monkey see, monkey do: The influence of work groups on the antisocial behavior of employees. *Academy of Management Journal, 41,* 658–672.

Roccas, S. (2003). Identification and status revisited: The moderating role of self-enhancement and self—transcendence values. *Personality and Social Psychology Bulletin, 29,* 726–736.

Roccas, S., & Brewer, M. (2002). Social identity complexity. *Personality and Social Psychology Review, 6,* 88–106.

Roccas, S., Sagiv, L., Schwartz, S., Halevy, N., & Eidelson, R. (2008). Toward a unifying model of identification with groups: Integrating theoretical perspectives. *Personality and Social Psychology Review, 12,* 280–306.

Roccas, S., & Schwartz, S. H. (1993). Effects of intergroup similarity on intergroup relations. *European Journal of Social Psychology, 23,* 581–595.

Rodriguez, R. A. (1998). Challenging demographic reductionism: A pilot study investigating diversity in group composition. *Small Group Research, 29,* 744–759.

Rodriguez-Bailon, R., & Morales, M. M. (2003). Perceived values—differences as a process involved in the intergroup relationship between gypsies and non—gypsies [La diferencia percibida en valores como proceso vinculado a las relaciones intergrupales de payos y gitanos]. *Psicothema, 15,* 176–182.

Roethlisberger, F. J., & Dickson, W. J. (1939). *Management and the worker.* Cambridge, MA: Harvard University Press.

Rogan, R. G., & Hammer, M. R. (1994). Crisis negotiations: A preliminary investigation of face-work in naturalistic conflict discourse. *Journal of Applied Communication Research, 22,* 216–231.

Rogelberg, S. G., & O'Connor, M. S. (1998). Extending the stepladder technique: An examination of self-paced stepladder groups. *Group Dynamics, 2*, 82–91.

Rogelberg, S. G., O'Connor, M. S., & Sederburg, M. (2002). Using the stepladder technique to facilitate the performance of audioconferencing. *Journal of Applied Psychology, 87*, 994–1000.

Rogers, E. M. (1995). *Diffusion of innovations* (4th ed.). New York: Free Press.

Rohde, R. I., & Stockton, R. (1992). The effect of structured feedback on goal attainment, attraction to the group, and satisfaction with the group in small group counseling. *Journal of Group Psychotherapy, Psychodrama and Sociometry, 44*, 172–180.

Rohrbaugh, J. (1988). Cognitive conflict tasks and small group processes. In B. Brehmer & C. R. B. Joyce (Eds.), *Human judgment: The SJT view* [Advances in psychology, 54] (pp. 199–226). Amsterdam: North-Holland.

Rojer, M. (1998). Rechtvaardigheid van het proces en de uitkomsten van cao-onderhandelingen [Procedural and distributional justice of collective bargaining]. *Gedrag en Organisatie, 11*, 401–412.

Roloff, M. E., & Jordan, J. M. (1991). The influence of effort, experience, and persistence on the elements of bargaining plans. *Communication Research, 18*, 306–332.

Roloff, M. L., & Jordan, J. M. (1992). Achieving negotiation goals: The "fruits and foibles" of planning ahead. In L. L. Putnam & M. E. Roloff (Eds.), *Communication and negotiation* (pp. 21–45). Newbury Park, CA: Sage Publications, Inc.

Rosch, E. (1978). Principles of categorization. In E. Rosch & B. B. Lloyd (Eds.), *Cognition and categorization* (pp. 27–48). Hillsdale, NJ: Lawrence Erlbaum.

Rose, S., & Danner, M. J. E. (1998). Money matters: The art of negotiation for women faculty. In L. H. Collins, J. C. Chrisler, & K. Quina (Eds.), *Career strategies for women in academe: Arming Athena* (pp. 157–186). Thousand Oaks, CA: Sage Publications, Inc.

Rosen, J., & Haaga, D. A. F. (1998). Facilitating cooperation in a social dilemma: A persuasion approach. *Journal of Psychology, 132*, 143–153.

Rosen, L. N. (1998). Psychological effects of sexual harassment, appraisal of harassment, and organizational climate among U.S. Army soldiers. *Military Medicine, 163*, 63–67.

Rosen, S. M. (1996). Dismantling the postwar social contract. In M. B. Lykes, A. Banuazizi, R. Liem, & M. Morris (Eds.), *Myths about the powerless: Contesting social inequalities* (pp. 337–347). Philadelphia: Temple University Press.

Rosenmüller, J. (1997). Bargaining with incomplete information: An axiomatic approach. *Theory and Decision, 42*, 105–146.

Rosenthal, H. E. S., & Crisp, R. J. (2006). Reducing stereotype threat by blurring intergroup boundaries. *Personality and Social Psychology Bulletin, 32*, 501–511.

Roseth, C. J., Johnson, D. W., & Johnson, R. T. (2008). Promoting early adolescents' achievement and peer relationships: The effects of cooperative, competitive, and individualistic goal structures. *Psychological Bulletin, 134*, 223–246.

Ross, W. H. (1990). An experimental test of motivational and content control on dispute mediation. *Journal of Applied Behavioral Science, 26*, 111–118.

Ross, W. H., Brantmeier, C., & Ciriacks, T. (2002). The impact of hybrid dispute-resolution procedures on constituent fairness judgments. *Journal of Applied Social Psychology, 32*, 1151–1188.

Ross, W. H., Jr., Fischer, D., Baker, C., & Buchholz, K. (1997). University residence hall assistants as mediators: An investigation of the effects of disputant and mediatory relationship on intervention preferences. *Journal of Applied Social Psychology. 27*, 664–707.

Ross, W. H., Jr., Pollman, W., Perry, D., Welty, J., & Jones, K. (2001). Interactive video negotiator training: A preliminary evaluation of the McGill Negotiation Simulator. *Simulation and Gaming, 32*, 451–468.

Roth, A. E., & Erev, I. (1995). Learning in extensive-form games: Experimental data and simple dynamic models in the intermediate term. *Games and Economic Behavior, 8*, 164–212.

Rothbart, M. (1996). Category-exemplar dynamics and stereotype change. *International Journal of Intercultural Relations, 20*, 305–321.

Rouhana, N. N. (1999). Differentiation in understanding one's own and the adversary's identity in protracted intergroup conflict: Zionism and Palestinianism. *Journal of Applied Social Psychology, 29,* 1999–2023.

Rouhana, N. N., & Korper, S. H. (1996). Dealing with the dilemmas posed by power asymmetry in intergroup conflict. *Negotiation Journal, 12,* 353–366.

Rouquette, M. L. (1996). Social representations and mass communication research. *Journal for the Theory of Social Behaviour, 26,* 221–231.

Rousseau, V., Aubé, C., & Savoie, A. (2006). Teamwork behaviors: A review and an integration of frameworks. *Small Group Research, 37,* 540–570.

Roussiau, Nicolas, & Soubiale, Nadege. (1995). Approche experimentale de la modification d'une representation sociale sous l'effet de la communication d'un message [Modification of a social representation in response to communication of a message: An experimental approach]. *Bulletin de Psychologie, 49*(422), 88–99.

Rouwette, E. A. J. A., Fokkema, E., Van Kuppevelt, H. J. J., & Peters, V. A. M. (1998). Measuring MARCO POLIS management game's influence on market orientations. *Simulation and Gaming, 29,* 420–431.

Rowley, T. J., & Moldoveanu, M. (2003). When will stakeholder groups act? An interest and–identity-based model of stakeholder group mobilization. *Academy of Management Review, 28,* 204–219.

Rubin, J. Z. (1989). Some wise and mistaken assumptions about conflict and negotiation. *Journal of Social Issues, 45*(2), 195–209.

Rubin, J. Z. (1992). Conflict, negotiation, and peace: Psychological perspectives and roles. In S. Staub & P. Green (Eds.), *Psychology and social responsibility: Facing global challenges* (pp. 121–144). New York: New York University Press.

Rubin, J. Z. (1994). Models of conflict management. *Journal of Social Issues, 50*(1), 33–45.

Rubin, J. Z., Kim, S. H., & Peretz, N. M. (1990). Expectancy effects and negotiation. *Journal of Social Issues, 46*(2), 125–139.

Rubin, J. Z., & Levinger, G. (1995). Levels of analysis: In search of generalizable knowledge. In B. B. Bunker & J. Z. Rubin (Eds.), *Conflict, cooperation, and justice: Essays inspired by the work of Morton Deutsch* (pp. 13–38). San Francisco: Jossey-Bass Inc, Publishers.

Rubin, J. Z., Pruitt, D. G., & Kim, S. H. (1994). *Social conflict: Escalation, stalemate, and settlement (2nd ed.).* New York: Mcgraw-Hill Book Company.

Rubini, M., Moscatelli, S., Albarello, F., & Palmonari, A. (2007). Group power as a determinant of interdependence and intergroup discrimination. *European Journal of Social Psychology, 37,* 1203–1221.

Rubini, M., Moscatelli, S., & Palmonari, A. (2007). Increasing group entitativity: Linguistic intergroup discrimination in the minimal group paradigm. *Group Processes and Intergroup Relations, 10,* 280–296.

Rubini, M., & Semin, G. R. (1994). Language use in the context of congruent and incongruent ingroup behaviours. *British Journal of Social Psychology, 33,* 355–362.

Rudisill, M. E. (1988). Sex differences in various cognitive and behavioral parameters in a competitive situation. *International Journal of Sport Psychology, 19,* 296–310.

Rudman, L. A., & Ashmore, R. D. (2007). Discrimination and the Implicit Association Test. *Group Processes and Intergroup Relations, 10,* 359–372.

Rudman, L. A., Dohn, M. C., & Fairchild, K. (2007). Implicit self-esteem compensation: Automatic threat defense. *Journal of Personality and Social Psychology, 93,* 798–813.

Rudman, L. A., & Goodwin, S. A. (2004). Gender differences in automatic in-group bias: Why do women like women more than men like men? *Journal of Personality and Social Psychology, 87,* 494–509.

Ruffle, B. J. (1998). More Is better, but fair is fair: Tipping in Dictator and Ultimatum Games. *Games and Economic Behavior, 23,* 247–265.

Ruscher, J. B., & Fiske, S. T. (1990). Interpersonal competition can cause individuating processes. *Journal of Personality and Social Psychology, 58,* 832–843.

Ruscher, J. B., & Hammer, E. D. (1994). Revising disrupted impressions through conversation. *Journal of Personality and Social Psychology, 66,* 530–541.

Ruscher, J. B., Santuzzi, A. M., & Hammer, E. Y. (2003). Shared impression formation in the cognitively interdependent dyad. *British Journal of Social Psychology, 42,* 411–425.

Rustichini, A. (1999). Minimizing regret: The general case. *Games and Economic Behavior, 29,* 224–243.

Rutland, A. (1999). The development of national prejudice, in-group favouritism and self-stereotypes in British children. *British Journal of Social Psychology, 38,* 55–70.

Rutland, A., Brown, R. J., Cameron, L., Ahmavaara, A., Arnold, K., & Samson, J. (2007). Development of the positive-negative asymmetry effect: Ingroup exclusion norm as a mediator of children's evaluations on negative attributes. *European Journal of Social Psychology, 37,* 171–190.

Rutledge-Taylor, M. F., & West, R. L. (2004). Cognitive modeling versus game theory: Why cognition matters. In M. Lovett, C. Schunn, C. Lebiere, & P. Munro (Eds.), *Proceedings of the Sixth International Conference on Cognitive Modeling: ICCCM 2004: Integrating Models* (pp. 255–260). Mahwah, NJ: Lawrence Erlbaum Associates Publishers.

Rutte, C. G., & Wilke, H. A. M. (1992). Goals, expectations and behavior in a social dilemma situation. In W. B. G. Liebrand, D. M. Messick, & H. A. M. Wilke (Eds.), *Social dilemmas: Theoretical issues and research findings* (pp. 289–305). Oxford, England: Pergamon Press, Inc.

Ruys, K. I., Spears, R., Gordijn, E. H., & De Vries, N. K. (2007). Automatic contrast: Evidence that automatic comparison with the social self affects evaluative responses. *British Journal of Psychology, 98,* 361–374.

Sachdev, I., & Bourhis, R. Y. (1991). Power and status differentials in minority and majority group relations. *European Journal of Social Psychology, 21,* 1–24.

Saguy, T., Tausch, N., Dovidio, J. F., & Pratto, F. (2009). The irony of harmony: Intergroup contact can produce false expectations for equality. *Psychological Science, 20,* 114–121.

Saijo, T., & Nakamura, H. (1995). The "spite" dilemma in voluntary contribution mechanism experiments. *Journal of Conflict Resolution, 39,* 535–560.

Sainfort, F. C., Gustafson, D. H., Bosworth, K., & Hawkins, R. P. (1990). Decision support systems effectiveness: Conceptual framework and empirical evaluation. *Organizational Behavior and Human Decision Processes, 45,* 232–252.

Sakurai, M. M. (1990). Modeling strategic threats: A competitive test of the Harsanyi function H(S) and characteristic function v(S). *Journal of Conflict Resolution, 34,* 74–91.

Salanova, M., Llorens, S., Cifre, E., Martínez, I. M., & Schaufeli, W. B. (2003). Perceived collective efficacy, subjective well-being, and task performance among electronic work groups: An experimental study. *Small Group Research, 34,* 43–73.

Salas, E., Cannon-Bowers, J. A., & Johnston, J. H. (1997). How can you turn a team of experts into an expert team?: Emerging training strategies. In C. E. Zsambok & G. Klein (Eds.), *Naturalistic decision making* Expertise: Research and applications. (pp. 359–370). Mahwah, NJ: Lawrence Erlbaum Associates, Inc.

Salas, E., & Wildman, J. L. (2009). Ten critical research questions: The need for new and deeper explorations. In E. Salas, G. F. Goodwin, & C. S. Burke (Eds.), *Team effectiveness in complexorganizations: Cross-disciplinary perspectives and approaches* (pp. 525–546). New York: Routledge/Taylor & Francis Group.

Salonen, H. (1998). Egalitarian solutions for n-person bargaining games. *Mathematical Social Sciences, 35,* 291–306.

Samter, W. (2002). How gender and cognitive complexity influence the provision of emotional support: A study of indirect effects. *Communication Reports, 15,* 5–16.

Samter, W., Burleson, B. R., & Baden-Murphy, L. (1989). Behavioral complexity is in the eye of the beholder: Effects of cognitive complexity and message complexity on impressions of the source of comforting messages. *Human Communication Research, 15,* 612–629.

Samuelson, C. D. (1991). Perceived task difficulty, causal attributions, and preferences for structural change in resource dilemmas. *Personality and Social Psychology Bulletin, 17,* 181–187.

Samuelson, C. D., & Allison, S. T. (1994). Cognitive factors affecting the use of social decision heuristics in resource-sharing tasks. *Organizational Behavior and Human Decision Processes, 58,* 1–27.

Samuelson, C. D., & Messick, D. M. (1995). Let's make some new rules: Social factors that make freedom unattractive. In R. M. Kramer & D. M. Messick (Eds.), *Negotiation as a social process: New trends in theory and research* (pp. 48–68). Thousand Oaks, CA: Sage Publications.

Samuelson, L., & Swinkels, J. M. (2003). Evolutionary stability and lexicographic preferences. *Games and Economic Behavior, 44*, 332–342.

Sanchez-Mazas, M., Mugny, G., & Falomir, J. M. (1997). Minority influence and intergroup relations: Social comparison and validation processes in the context of xenophobia in Switzerland. *Swiss Journal of Psychology Schweizerische Zeitschrift fuer Psychologie Revue Suisse de Psychologie, 56*, 182–192.

Sanders, R. E. (1991). The two-way relationship between talk in social interactions and actors' goals and plans. In K. Tracy (Ed.), *Understanding face-to-face interaction: Issues linking goals and discourse* (pp. 167–188). Hillsdale, NJ: Lawrence Erlbaum Associates, Inc.

Sandholm, W. H. (2003). Evolution and equilibrium under inexact information. *Games and Economic Behavior, 44*, 343–378.

Sandler, T. (1999). Alliance formation, alliance expansion, and the core. *Journal of Conflict Resolution, 43*, 727–747.

Sandole, D. J. D. (1989). Simulation as a basis for consciousness raising: Some encouraging signs for conflict resolution. In D. Crookall & D. Saunders (Eds.), *Communication and simulation: From two fields to one theme* (pp. 127–140). Clevedon, England: Multilingual Matters.

Sani, F., Bowe, M., & Herrera, M. (2008). Perceived collective continuity: Seeing groups as temporally enduring entities. In F. Sani (Ed.), *Self continuity: Individual and collective perspectives* (pp. 159–172). New York: Psychology Press.

Sani, F., Bowe, M., Herrera, M., Manna, C., Cossa, T., Miao, X., & Zhou, Y. (2007). Perceived collective continuity: Seeing groups as entities that move through time. *European Journal of Social Psychology, 37*, 1118–1134.

Sani, F., & Todman, J. (2002). Should we stay or should we go? A social psychological model of schisms in groups. *Personality and Social Psychology Bulletin, 28*, 1647–1655.

Sanna, L. J., & Parks, C. D. (1997). Group research trends in social and organizational psychology: Whatever happened to intragroup research? *Psychological Science, 8*, 261–267.

Santarsiero, L. J., Baker, R. C., & McGee, T. F. (1995). The effects of cognitive pretraining on cohesion and self-disclosure in small groups: An analog study. *Journal of Clinical Psychology, 51*, 403–409.

Santy, P. A., Holland, A. W., Looper, L., & Marcondes-North, R. (1993). Multicultural factors in the space environment: Results of an international shuttle crew debrief. *Aviation, Space, and Environmental Medicine, 64*, 196–200.

Sargent, L. D., & Sue-Chan, C. (2001). Does diversity affect group efficacy? The intervening role of cohesion and task interdependence. *Small Group Research, 32*, 426–450.

Sassenberg, K. (2002). Common bond and common identity groups on the Internet: Attachment and normative behavior in on-topic and off-topic chats. *Group Dynamics: Theory, Research, and Practice, 6*, 27–37.

Sassenberg, K., & Boos, M. (2003). Attitude change in computer-mediated communication: Effects of anonymity and category norms. *Group Processes and Intergroup Relations, 6*, 405–422.

Sassenberg, K., Kessler, T., & Mummendey, A.,. (2003). Less negative = more positive? Social discrimination as avoidance or approach. *Journal of Experimental Social Psychology, 39*, 48–58.

Sassenberg, K., & Postmes, T. (2002). Cognitive and strategic processes in small groups: Effects of anonymity of the self and anonymity of the group on social influence. *British Journal of Social Psychology, 41*, 463–480.

Sato, K. (1988). Trust and group size in a social dilemma. *Japanese Psychological Research, 30*, 88–93.

Sato, K. (1989). Trust and feedback in a social dilemma. *Japanese Journal of Experimental Social Psychology, 29*, 123–128.

Sattler, D. N. (1998). The need principle in social dilemmas. *Journal of Social Behavior and Personality, 13*, 667–678.

Savitsky, K., Van Boven, L., Epley, N., & Wight, W. M. (2005). The unpacking effect in allocations of responsibility for group tasks. *Journal of Experimental Social Psychology, 41*, 447–457.

Sawyer, J. E., Latham, W. R., Pritchard, R. D., & Bennett, W. R., Jr. (1999). Analysis of work group productivity in an applied setting: Application of a time series panel design. *Personnel Psychology, 52*, 927–967.

Sawyer, R. K., & DeZutter, S. (2009). Distributed creativity: How collective creations emerge from collaboration. *Psychology of Aesthetics, Creativity*, and the Arts, 3, 81–92.

Sayman, S., Hoch, S. J., & Raju, J. S. (2002). Positioning of store brands. *Marketing Science, 21*, 378–397.

Scavone, K. A. (1992). State creative arts therapies coalitions: Models and challenges. *The Arts in Psychotherapy, 19*, 57–60.

Schaller, M. (1991). Social categorization and the formation of group stereotypes: Further evidence for biased information processing in the perception of group-behavior correlations. *European Journal of Social Psychology, 21*, 25–35.

Schaller, M., & Neuberg, S. L. (2008). Intergroup prejudices and intergroup conflicts. In C. Crawford & D. Krebs (Eds.), *Foundations of evolutionary psychology* (pp. 401–414). New York: Taylor & Francis Group/Lawrence Erlbaum Associates.

Scharlemann, J. P. W., Eckel, C. C., Kacelnik, A., & Wilson, R. K. (2001). The value of a smile: Game theory with a human face. *Journal of Economic Psychology, 22*, 617–640.

Scharpf, F. W. (1990). Decision rules, decision styles, and policy choices. In R. L. Kahn & M. N. Zald (Eds.), *Organizations and nation-states: New perspectives on conflict and cooperation* (pp. 309–354). San Francisco: Jossey-Bass.

Scheepers, D. (2009). Turning social identity threat into challenge: Status stability and cardiovascular reactivity during inter-group competition. *Journal of Experimental Social Psychology, 45*, 228–233.

Scheepers, D., Branscombe, N. R., Spears, R., & Doosje, B. (2002). The emergence and effects of deviants in low and high status groups. *Journal of Experimental Social Psychology, 38*, 611–617.

Scheepers, D., Spears, R., Doosje, B., & Manstead, A. S. R. (2002). Integrating identity and instrumental approaches to intergroup differentiation: Different contexts, different motives. *Personality and Social Psychology Bulletin, 28*, 1455–1467.

Scheepers, D., Spears, R., Doosje, B., & Manstead, A. S. R. (2003). Two functions of verbal intergroup discrimination: Identity and instrumental motives as a result of group identification and threat. *Personality and Social Psychology Bulletin, 29*, 568–577.

Scheepers, D., Spears, R., Doosje, B., & Manstead, A. S. R. (2006a). Diversity in in-group bias: Structural factors, situational features, and social functions. *Journal of Personality and Social Psychology, 90*, 944–960.

Scheepers, D., Spears, R., Doosje, B., & Manstead, A. S. R. (2006b). The social functions of ingroup bias: Creating, confirming, or changing social reality. *European Review of Social Psychology, 17*, 359–396.

Scheepers, D., Spears, R., Manstead, A. S. R., & Doosje, B. (2009). The influence of discrimination and fairness on collective self-esteem. *Personality and Social Psychology Bulletin, 35*, 506–515.

Schein, E. H. (1988). Intergroup problems in organizations. In R. Katz (Ed.), *Managing professionals in innovative organizations: A collection of readings* (pp. 325–331). Cambridge, MA: Ballinger Publishing Co/Harper & Row Publishers, Inc.

Schellenberg, J. A. (1988). A comparative test of three models for solving "the bargaining problem." *Behavioral Science, 33*, 81–96.

Schellenberg, J. A. (1990). *Primitive games*. Boulder, CO: Westview Press.

Schelling, T. C. (2008). Bargaining, communication, and limited war. *Negotiation and Conflict Management Research, 1*, 198–217.

Schiffmann, R., & Wicklund, R. A. (1992). The minimal group paradigm and its minimal psychology: On equating social identity with arbitrary group membership. *Theory and Psychology, 2*, 29–50.

Schindler, R. M. (1992). A coupon is more than a low price: Evidence from a shopping-simulation study. *Psychology and Marketing, 9*, 431–451.

Schmid, K., Hewstone, M., Tausch, N., Cairns, E., & Hughes, J. (2009). Antecedents and consequences of social identity complexity: Intergroup contact, distinctiveness threat, and outgroup attitudes. *Personality and Social Psychology Bulletin, 35*, 1085–1098.

Schmitt, D. R. (1998). Social behavior. In K. A. Lattal & M. Perone (Eds.), *Handbook of research methods in human operant behavior* (pp. 471–505). New York: Plenum Press.

Schmitt, Manfred, & Maes, J. (2002). Stereotypic ingroup bias as self-defense against relative deprivation: Evidence from a longitudinal study of the German unification process. *European Journal of Social Psychology, 32*, 309–326.

Schmitt, Michael T., & Branscombe, N. R. (2001). The good, the bad, and the manly: Threats to one's prototypicality and evaluations of fellow in-group members. *Journal of Experimental Social Psychology, 37*, 510–517.

Schmitt, Michael T., Silvia, P. J, & Branscombe, N. R. (2000). The intersection of self-evaluation maintenance and social identity theories: Intragroup judgment in interpersonal and intergroup contexts. *Personality and Social Psychology Bulletin, 26*, 1598–1606.

Schnake, S. B., & Ruscher, J. B. (1998). Modern racism as a predictor of the linguistic intergroup bias. *Journal of Language and Social Psychology, 17*, 484–491.

Schneider, A. K. (1994). Effective responses to offensive comments. *Negotiation Journal, 10*, 107–115.

Schoenbach, P. (1990). *Account episodes: The management or escalation of conflict.* Cambridge, England: Cambridge University Press.

Schofield, J. W., & Eurich-Fulcer, R. (2001). When and how school desegregation improves intergroup relations. In R. Brown & S. L. Gaertner (Eds.), *Blackwell handbook of social psychology: Intergroup processes* (pp.475–494). Oxford: Blackwell.

Schofield, N., & Parks, R. (2000). Nash equilibrium in a spatial model of coalition bargaining. *Mathematical Social Sciences, 39*, 133–174.

Scholz, R. (2004). Self-esteem and the Process of its Reassessment in Multicultural Groups: Renegotiating the Symbolic Social Order. *Group Analysis, 37*, 525–535.

Schopler, J., & Insko, C. A. (1992). The discontinuity effect in interpersonal and intergroup relations: Generality and mediation. *European Review of Social Psychology, 3*, 121–151.

Schopler, J., & Insko, C. A. (1999). The reduction of the interindividual-intergroup discontinuity effect: The role of future consequences. In M. Foddy, M. Smithson, S. Schneider, & M. Hogg (Eds.), *Resolving social dilemmas: Dynamic, structural, and intergroup aspects* (pp. 281–293). Philadelphia: Psychology Press.

Schopler, J., Insko, C. A., Currey, D., Smith, S., Brazil, D., Riggins, T., Gaertner, L., & Peterson, S. (1994). The survival of a cooperative tradition in the intergroup discontinuity context. *Motivation and Emotion, 18*, 301–315.

Schopler, J., Insko, C. A., Drigotas, S. M., Wieselquist, J., Pemberton, M. B., & Cox, C. (1995). The role of identifiability in the reduction of interindividual-intergroup discontinuity. *Journal of Experimental Social Psychology, 31*, 553–574.

Schopler, J., Insko, C. A., Graetz, K. A., Drigotas, S. M., & Smith, V. A. (1991). The generality of the individual-group discontinuity effect: Variations in positivity-negativity of outcomes, players' relative power, and magnitude of outcomes. *Personality and Social Psychology Bulletin, 17*, 612–624.

Schotter, A., Zheng, W., & Snyder, B. (2000). Bargaining through agents: An experimental study of delegation and commitment. *Games and Economic Behavior, 30*, 248–292.

Schruijer, S. G. L., & Lemmers, L. (1996). Explanations and evaluations by Turks and Dutchmen of norm violating ingroup and outgroup behaviour. *Journal of Community and Applied Social Psychology, 6*, 101–107.

Schubert, T. W., & Häfner, M. (2003). Contrast from social stereotypes in automatic behavior. *Journal of Experimental Social Psychology, 39*, 577–584.

Schubert, T. W, & Otten, S. (2002). Overlap of self, ingroup, and outgroup: Pictorial measures of self-categorization. *Self and Identity, 1*, 353–376.

Schuessler, R. (1989). Exit threats and cooperation under anonymity. *Journal of Conflict Resolution, 33*, 728–749.

Schulz, M. (1998). Limits to bureaucratic growth: The density dependence of organizational rule births. *Administrative Science Quarterly, 43*, 845–876.

Schulz-Hardt, S., & Brodbeck, F. C. (2008). Group performance and leadership. In M. Hewstone, W. Stroebe, & K. Jonas (Eds.), *Introduction to social psychology (4th ed.)* (pp. 264–289). Malden: Blackwell Publishing.

Schummer, J. (2000). Eliciting preferences to assign positions and compensation. *Games and Economic Behavior, 30*, 293–318.

Schwarz, N., Strack, F., Hilton, D. J., & Naderer, G. (1991). Base rates, representativeness, and the logic of conversation: The contextual relevance of "irrelevant" information. *Social Cognition, 9*, 67–84.

Schwartz-Shea, P. (2002). Theorizing gender for experimental game theory: Experiments with "sex status" and "merit status" in an asymmetric game. *Sex Roles, 47*, 301–319.

Schweitzer, M. E., & DeChurch, L. A. (2001). Linking frames in negotiations: Gains, losses and conflict frame adoption. *International Journal of Conflict Management, 12*, 100–113.

Scudder, J. N. (1988). The influence of power upon powerful speech: A social-exchange perspective. *Communication Research Reports, 5*, 140–145.

Scudder, J. N., & Andrews, P. H. (1995). A comparison of two alternative models of powerful speech: The impact of power and gender upon the use of threats. *Communication Research Reports, 12*, 25–33.

Sears, D. O. (2004). Continuities and contrasts in American racial politics. In J. T. Jost, M. R. Banaji, & D. A. Prentice (Eds.), *Perspectivism in social psychology: The yin and yang of scientific progress* (pp. 233–245). Washington, DC: American Psychological Association.

Sears, D. O., Huddy, L., & Jervis, R. (Eds.). (2003). *Oxford handbook of political psychology*. New York: Oxford University Press.

Sebenius, J. K. (1991). Negotiation analysis. In V. A. Kremenyuk (Ed.), *International negotiation: Analysis, approaches, issues* (pp. 203–215). San Francisco: Jossey-Bass Inc, Publishers.

Sebenius, J. K. (2002). Caveats for cross-border negotiators. *Negotiation Journal, 18*, 121–133.

Sebenius, J. K. (2005). Negotiation analysis: A characterization and review. In M. H. Bazerman (Ed.), *Negotiation, decision making and conflict management* (Vol. 1–3, pp. 18–41). Northampton, MA: Edward Elgar Publishing, 2005.

Sebok, A. (2000). Team performance in process control: Influences of interface design and staffing levels. *Ergonomics, 43*, 1210–1236.

Secret, M., & Sprang, G. (2001). The effects of family-friendly workplace environments on work-family stress of employed parents. *Journal of Social Service Research, 28*, 21–45.

Sedikides, C., & Ostrom, T. M. (1988). Are person categories used when organizing information about unfamiliar sets of persons? *Social Cognition, 6*, 252–267.

Sedikides, C., & Ostrom, T. M. (1993). Perceptions of group variability: Moving from an uncertain crawl to a purposeful stride. *Social Cognition, 11*, 165–174.

Seers, A., Petty, M. M., & Cashman, J. F. (1995). Team-member exchange under team and traditional management: A naturally occurring quasi-experiment. *Group and Organization Management, 20*, 18–38.

Sefton, M. (1992). Incentives in simple bargaining games. *Journal of Economic Psychology, 13*, 263–276.

Segendorff, B. (1998). Delegation and threat in bargaining. *Games and Economic Behavior, 23*, 266–283.

Seibold, D. R., Meyers, R. A., & Sunwolf (1996). Communication and influence in group decision making. In R. Y. Hirokawa & M. S. Poole (Eds.), *Communication and group decision making* (2nd ed., pp. 242–268). Thousand Oaks, CA: Sage Publications, Inc.

Seidel, S. D., Stasser, G. L., & Collier, S. A. (1998). Action identification theory as an explanation of social performance. *Group Dynamics, 2*, 147–154.

Seifert, C. M., & Hutchins, E. L. (1992). Error as opportunity: Learning in a cooperative task. *Human-Computer Interaction, 7*, 409–435.

Sekaquaptewa, D., & Thompson, M. (2002). The differential effects of solo status on members of high– and low-status groups. *Personality and Social Psychology Bulletin, 28*, 694–707.

Sell, J., & Son, Y. (1997). Comparing public goods with common pool resources: Three experiments. *Social Psychology Quarterly, 60,* 118–137.

Sell, J., & Wilson, R. K. (1991). Levels of information and contributions to public goods. *Social Forces, 70,* 107–124.

Semmann, D., Krambeck, H.-J., & Milinski, M. (2003). Volunteering leads to rock-paper-scissors dynamics in a public goods game. *Nature, 425,* 390–393.

Senese, P. D. (1997). Costs and demands: International sources of dispute challenges and reciprocation. *Journal of Conflict Resolution, 41,* 407–427.

Sengupta, A., & Sengupta, K. (1996). A property of the core. *Games and Economic Behavior, 12,* 266–273.

Seo, F., & Nishizaki, I. (1994). Conflict resolution with robustness in international negotiations: A game theoretic approach. *Group Decision and Negotiation, 3,* 47–68.

Sergeev, V. M. (1991). Metaphors for understanding international negotiation. In V. A. Kremenyuk (Ed.), *International negotiation: Analysis, approaches, issues* (pp. 58–64). San Francisco: Jossey-Bass.

Serrano, R., & Vohra, R. (2002). Bargaining and bargaining sets. *Games and Economic Behavior, 39,* 292–308.

Sessa, V. I. (1996). Using perspective taking to manage conflict and affect in teams. *Journal of Applied Behavioral Science, 32,* 101–115.

Sessa, V. I., & London, M. (2008). Group learning: An introduction. In V. I. Sessa & M. London (Eds.), *Work group learning: Understanding, improving and assessing how groups learn in organizations* (pp. 3–13). New York: Taylor & Francis Group/Lawrence Erlbaum Associates.

Seta, C. E., Seta, J. J., & Culver, J. (2000). Recategorization as a method for promoting intergroup cooperation: Group status matters. *Social Cognition, 18,* 354–376.

Seta, J. J., & Seta, C. E. (1993). Stereotypes and the generation of compensatory and noncompensatory expectancies of group members. *Personality and Social Psychology Bulletin, 19,* 722–731.

Sethi, R., & Somanathan, E. (2003). Understanding reciprocity. *Journal of Economic Behavior and Organization, 50,* 1–27.

Shackelford, S., Wood, W., & Worchel, S. (1996). Behavioral styles and the influence of women in mixed-sex groups. *Social Psychology Quarterly, 59,* 284–293.

Shah, J. Y., Brazy, P. C., & Higgins, E. T. (2004). Promoting us or preventing them: Regulatory focus and manifestations of intergroup bias. *Personality and Social Psychology Bulletin, 30,* 433–446.

Shah, J. Y., Kruglanski, A. W., & Thompson, E. P. (1998). Membership has its (epistemic) rewards: Need for closure effects on in-group bias. *Journal of Personality and Social Psychology, 75,* 383–393.

Shakun, M. F. (1995). Restructuring a negotiation with evolutionary systems design. *Negotiation Journal, 11,* 145–150.

Shalev, J. (2002). Loss aversion and bargaining. *Theory and Decision, 52,* 201–232.

Shapiro, Daniel L. (2000). Supplemental joint brainstorming: Navigating past the perils of traditional bargaining. *Negotiation Journal, 16,* 409–419.

Shapiro, Daniel, & Liu, V. (2006). Psychology of a stable peace. In M. Fitzduff & C. Stout (Eds.), *The psychology of resolving global conflicts: From war to peace (Vol. 1): Nature vs. nurture* (pp. 307–329). Westport, CT: Praeger Security International, 2006.

Shapiro, Debra L., & Bies, R. J. (1994). Threats, bluffs, and disclaimers in negotiations. *Organizational Behavior and Human Decision Processes, 60,* 14–35.

Shaplin, J. T. (1964). Toward a Theoretical Rationale for Team Teaching. In J. T. Shaplin & H. F. Olds, Jr., *Team teaching* (pp. 57–98). New York: Harper & Row.

Sharan, S., & Shaulov, A. (1990). Cooperative learning, motivation, and academic achievement. In S. Sharan (Ed.), *Cooperative learning: Theory and research* (pp. 173–202). New York: Praeger Publishers.

Shaw, M. E. (1976). *Group dynamics: The psychology of small group behavior.* New York: McGraw-Hill.

Shebilske, W. L., Jordon, J. A., Goettl, B. P., & Paulus, L. E. (1998). Observation versus hands-on practice of complex skills in dyadic, triadic, and tetradic training-teams. *Human Factors, 40*, 525–540.

Sheehan, E. P. (1993). The effects of turnover on the productivity of those who stay. *Journal of Social Psychology. 133*, 699–706.

Shefner, J. (1999). Sponsors and the urban poor: Resources or restrictions? *Social Problems, 46*, 376–397.

Sheldon, K. M. (1999). Learning the lessons of tit-for-tat: Even competitors can get the message. *Journal of Personality and Social Psychology, 77*, 1245–1253.

Sheldon, K. M., Sheldon, M. S., & Osbaldiston, R. (2000). Prosocial values and group assortation within an N-person Prisoner's Dilemma Game. *Human Nature, 11*, 387–404.

Shell, G. R. (2001). Bargaining styles and negotiation: The Thomas-Kilmann Conflict Mode Instrument in negotiation training. *Negotiation Journal, 17*, 155–174.

Shell, G. R. (2006). *Bargaining for advantage: Negotiation strategies for reasonable people (2nd ed.).* New York: Penguin Books/Penguin Group (USA).

Shelton, J. N., Dovidio, J. F., Hebl, M., & Richeson, J. A. (2009). Prejudice and intergroup interaction. In S. Demoulin, J.-P. Leyens, & J. F. Dovidio (Eds.), *In:Intergroup misunderstandings: Impact of divergent social realities* (pp. 21–38). New York: Psychology Press.

Shenkar, O., & Yan, A. (2002). Failure as a consequence of partner politics: Learning from the life and death of an international cooperative venture. *Human Relations, 55*, 565–601.

Sheppard, B. H., Saunders, D. M., & Minton, J. W. (1988). Procedural justice from the third-party perspective. *Journal of Personality and Social Psychology, 54*, 629–637.

Shepperd, J. A. (1993). Productivity loss in performance groups: A motivation analysis. *Psychological Bulletin, 113*, 67–81.

Sherif, M. (1936). *The psychology of social norms.* New York, NY: Harper.

Sherif, M. (1966). *In common predicament: Social psychology of intergroup conflict and cooperation.* Boston: Houghton Mifflin.

Shim, J. P. (1988). The visual interactive computer-aided approach to teaching zero-sum/non-zero-sum games. *Social Science Computer Review, 6*, 392–397.

Shinotsuka, H. (1989). Resource size, group size, cost and other's strategy in a social dilemma game. *Japanese Journal of Experimental Social Psychology, 29*, 107–121.

Shinotsuka, T., & Takamiya, K. (2003). The weak core of simple games with ordinal preferences: Implementation in Nash equilibrium. *Games and Economic Behavior, 44*, 379–389.

Shipper, F., & Manz, C. C. (1992). Employee self-management without formally designated teams: An alternative road to empowerment. *Organizational Dynamics, 20*(3), 48–61.

Shipps, D. (2003). Pulling together: Civic capacity and urban school reform. *American Educational Research Journal, 40*, 841–878.

Shnabel, N., & Nadler, A. (2008). A needs-based model of reconciliation: Satisfying the differential emotional needs of victim and perpetrator as a key to promoting reconciliation. *Journal of Personality and Social Psychology, 94*, 116–132.

Short, J. C., & Palmer, T. B. (2003). Organizational performance referents: An empirical examination of their content and influences. *Organizational Behavior and Human Decision Processes, 90*, 209–224.

Sias, P. M., Heath, R. G., Perry, T., Silva, D., & Fix, B. (2004). Narratives of workplace friendship deterioration. *Journal of Social and Personal Relationships, 21*, 321–340.

Sidanius, J. (1993). The psychology of group conflict and the dynamics of oppression: A social dominance perspective. In S. Iyengar & W. J. McGuire (Eds.), *Explorations in political psychology* (pp. 183–219). Durham, NC: Duke University Press.

Sidanius, J., Pratto, F., & Mitchell, M. (1994). In-group identification, social dominance orientation, and differential intergroup social allocation. *Journal of Social Psychology, 134*, 151–167.

Signorino, C. S. (1996). Simulating international cooperation under uncertainty: The effects of symmetric and asymmetric noise. *Journal of Conflict Resolution, 40*, 152–205.

Silk, J. B., Alberts, S. C., & Altmann, J. (2004). Patterns of coalition formation by adult female baboons in Amboseli, Kenya. *Animal Behaviour, 67*, 573–582.

Sillars, A. L., & Wilmot, W. W. (1994). Communication strategies in conflict and mediation. In J. A. Daly & J. M. Wiemann (Eds.), *Strategic interpersonal communication* (pp. 163–190). Hillsdale, NJ: Lawrence Erlbaum Associates, Inc.

Silver, W. S., & Bufanio, K. M. (1996). The impact of group efficacy and group goals on group task performance. *Small Group Research, 27*, 347–359.

Silver, W. S., & Bufanio, K. M. (1997). Reciprocal relationships, causal influences, and group efficacy: A reply to Kaplan. *Small Group Research, 28*, 559–562.

Silvestre, A. J. (1994). Brokering: A process for establishing long-term and stable links with gay male communities for research and public health education. *AIDS Education and Prevention, 6*, 65–73.

Simon, B. (1990). Soziale Kategorisierung und differentielle Wahrnehmung von Ingroup und Outgroup-Homogenitaet [Social categorization and differential perception of ingroup and- outgroup homogeneity]. *Zeitschrift fuer Sozialpsychologie, 21*, 298–313.

Simon, B. (1992a). Intragroup differentiation in terms of ingroup and outgroup attributes. *European Journal of Social Psychology, 22*, 407–413.

Simon, B. (1992b). The perception of ingroup and outgroup homogeneity: Reintroducing the intergroup context. In W. Stroebe & M. Hewstone (Eds.), *European review of social psychology* (Vol. 3, pp. 1–30). Chichester, England: John Wiley & Sons.

Simon, B. (1993). On the asymmetry in the cognitive construal of ingroup and outgroup: A model of egocentric social categorization. *European Journal of Social Psychology, 23*, 131–147.

Simon, B. (1995). The perception of ingroup and outgroup homogeneity: On the confounding of group size, level of abstractness and frame of reference: A reply to Bartsch and Judd. *European Journal of Social Psychology, 12*, 463–468.

Simon, B., & Hamilton, D. L. (1994). Self-stereotyping and social context: The effects of relative in-group size and in-group status. *Journal of Personality and Social Psychology, 66*, 699–711.

Simon, B., Mlicki, P., Johnston, L., Caetano, A., Warawicki, M., Van Knippenberg, A., & De Ridder, R. (1990). The effects of ingroup and outgroup homogeneity on ingroup favouritism, stereotyping and overestimation of relative ingroup size. *European Journal of Social Psychology, 20*, 519–523.

Simon, B., & Mummendey, A. (1990). Perceptions of relative group size and group homogeneity: We are the majority and they are all the same. *European Journal of Social Psychology, 20*, 351–356.

Simon, B., Pantaleo, G., & Mummendey, A. (1995). Unique individual or interchangeable group member? The accentuation of intragroup differences versus similarities as an indicator of the individual self versus the collective self. *Journal of Personality and Social Psychology, 69*, 106–119.

Simon, B., & Pettigrew, T. F. (1990). Social identity and perceived group homogeneity: Evidence for the ingroup homogeneity effect. *European Journal of Social Psychology, 20*, 269–286.

Simon, B., & Stürmer, S. (2003). Respect for group members: Intragroup determinants of collective identification and group-serving behavior. *Personality and Social Psychology Bulletin, 29*, 183–193.

Simon, B., Stürmer, S., & Steffens, K. (2000). Helping individuals or group members? The role of individual and collective identification in AIDS volunteerism. *Personality and Social Psychology Bulletin, 26*, 497–506.

Simpson, B., & Macy, M. W. (2001). Collective action and power inequality: Coalitions in exchange networks. *Social Psychology Quarterly, 64*, 88–100.

Simpson, D., & Cieslik, M. (2002). Education Action Zones, empowerment and parents. *Educational Research, 44*, 119–128.

Simpson, J. A., & Weiner, E. S. C. (Eds.). (1989). *Oxford English Dictionary*. Oxford: Clarendon Press.

Sinclair, Amanda. (1992). The tyranny of a team ideology. *Organization Studies. 13*, 611–626.

Sinclair, Andrea L. (2003). The effects of justice and cooperation on team effectiveness. *Small Group Research, 34*, 74–100.

Sinclair, R. C., Mark, M. M., & Clore, G. L. (1994). Mood-related persuasion depends on (mis) attributions. *Social Cognition, 12,* 309–326.

Sinclair, S., Huntsinger, J., Skorinko, J., & Hardin, C. D. (2005). Social tuning of the self: Consequences for the self-evaluations of stereotype targets. *Journal of Personality and Social Psychology, 89,* 160–175.

Singelis, T. M., & Pedersen, P. (1997). Conflict and mediation across cultures. In K. Cushner & R. W. Brislin (Eds.), *Improving intercultural interactions: Modules for cross-cultural training programs, Vol. 2. Multicultural aspects of counseling series, No. 8* (pp. 184–204). Thousand Oaks, CA: Sage Publications, Inc.

Singer, L. R. (1989). The quiet revolution in dispute settlement. *Mediation Quarterly, 7,* 105–113.

Singh, B., & Singh, T. (1995). Remembering self– and other-initiated ideas in group discussion. *Psychological Studies, 40,* 36–38.

Singh, R. (1997). Group harmony and interpersonal fairness in reward allocation: On the loci of the moderation effect. *Organizational Behavior and Human Decision Processes, 72,* 158–183.

Singh, R., Choo, W. M., & Poh, L. L. (1998). In-group bias and fair-mindedness as strategies of self-presentation in intergroup perception. *Personality and Social Psychology Bulletin, 24,* 147–162.

Sink, D. W. (1991). Transorganizational development in urban policy coalitions. *Human Relations, 44,* 1179–1195.

Sinnott, J. D. (1993). Use of complex thought and resolving intragroup conflicts: A means to conscious adult development in the workplace. In J. Demick, P. M. Miller, & P. M. Miller (Eds.), *Development in the workplace* (pp. 155–175). Hillsdale, NJ: Lawrence Erlbaum Associates, Inc.

Sitkin, S. B., & Bies, R. J. (1993). Social accounts in conflict situations: Using explanations to manage conflict. *Human Relations, 46,* 349–370.

Sivasubramaniam, N., Murry, W. D., Avolio, B. J., & Jung, D. I. (2002). A longitudinal model of the effects of team leadership and group potency on group performance. *Group and Organization Management, 27,* 66–96.

Slater, Patrick, Chetwynd, J., & Farnsworth, J. (1989). Analyzing disagreement with logical equivalence matrixes. *International Journal of Personal Construct Psychology, 2,* 443–457.

Slater, Philip E. (1966). *Microcosm: Structural, psychological, and religious evaluation in groups.* New York: J. Wiley.

Slikker, M. (2001). Coalition formation and potential games. *Games and Economic Behavior, 37,* 436–448.

Slikker, M., & Van Den Nouweland, A. (2001). A one-stage model of link formation and payoff division. *Games and Economic Behavior, 34,* 153–175.

Sloof, R. (2004). Finite horizon bargaining with outside options and threat points. *Theory and Decision, 57,* 109–142.

Smidts, A., Pruyn, A. Th. H., & Van Riel, C. B. M. (2001). The impact of employee communication and perceived external prestige on organizational identification. *Academy of Management Journal, 44,* 1051–1062.

Smit, I., & Schabracq, M. (1998). Team cultures, stress and health. *Stress Medicine, 14,* 13–19.

Smith, A., & Stam, A. C. (2004). Bargaining and the nature of war. *Journal of Conflict Resolution, 48,* 783–813.

Smith, B. N., Kerr, N. A., Markus, M. J., & Stasson, M. F. (2001). Individual differences in social loafing: Need for cognition as a motivator in collective performance. *Group Dynamics: Theory, Research, and Practice, 5,* 150–158.

Smith, C. G. (Ed.). (1971). *Conflict resolution: [Contributions of the behavioral sciences].* `Notre Dame, IN: University of Notre Dame Press.

Smith, Eliot R. (1999). Affective and cognitive implications of a group becoming part of the self: New models of prejudice and of the self-concept. In D. Abrams & M. A. Hogg (Eds.), *Social identity and social cognition* (pp. 183–196). Wiley-Blackwell (1999).

Smith, Eliot R., & Zarate, M. A. (1990). Exemplar and prototype use in social categorization. *Social Cognition, 8,* 243–262.

Smith, Eliot R., Jackson, J. W., & Sparks, C. W. (2003). Effects of inequality and reasons for inequality on group identification and cooperation in social dilemmas. *Group Processes and Intergroup Relations, 6*, 201–220.

Smith, Eliot R., Murphy, J., & Coats, S. (1999). Attachment to groups: Theory and management. *Journal of Personality and Social Psychology, 77*, 94–110.

Smith, Eliot R., Seger, C. R., & Mackie, D. M. (2007). Can emotions be truly group level? Evidence regarding four conceptual criteria. *Journal of Personality and Social Psychology, 93*, 431–446.

Smith, Eric A. (2003). Human cooperation: Perspectives from behavioral ecology. In P. Hammerstein (Ed.), *Genetic and cultural evolution of cooperation* (pp. 401–427.)y Cambridge, MA: MIT Press.

Smith, H. W., & Kronauge, C. (1990). The politics of abortion: Husband notification legislation, self-disclosure, and marital bargaining. *Sociological Quarterly, 31*, 585–598.

Smith, Jeffrey M., & Bell, P. A. (1992). Environmental concern and cooperative/competitive behavior in a simulated commons dilemma. *Journal of Social Psychology, 132*, 461–468.

Smith, Jeffrey M., & Bell, P. A. (1994). Conformity as a determinant of behavior in a resource dilemma. *Journal of Social Psychology, 134*, 191–200.

Smith, Joanne R., Terry, D. J., & Hogg, M. A. (2007). Social identity and the attitude-behaviour relationship: Effects of anonymity and accountability. *European Journal of Social Psychology, 37*, 239–257.

Smith, John B. (1994). *Collective intelligence in computer-based collaboration*. Hillsdale, NJ: Lawrence Erlbaum Associates, Inc.

Smith, K. G., Carroll, S. J., & Ashford, S. J. (1995). Intra– and interorganizational cooperation: Toward a research agenda. *Academy of Management Journal, 38*, 7–23.

Smith, K. G., Grimm, C. M., & Gannon, M. J. (1992). *Dynamics of competitive strategy*. Newbury Park, CA: Sage Publications, Inc.

Smith, L. G. E., & Postmes, T. (2009). Intra-group interaction and the development of norms which promote inter-group hostility. *European Journal of Social Psychology, 39*, 130–144.

Smith, S. W. (1995). Perceptual processing of nonverbal-relational messages. In D. E. Hewes (Ed.), *The cognitive bases of interpersonal communication* (pp. 87–112). Hillsdale, NJ: Lawrence Erlbaum Associates, Inc.

Smith-Jentsch, K. A., Zeisig, R. L., Acton, B., & McPherson, J. A. (1998). Team dimensional training: A strategy for guided team self-correction. In J. A. Cannon-Bowers & E. Salas (Eds.), *Making decisions under stress: Implications for individual and team training* (pp. 271–297). Washington, DC: American Psychological Association.

Smith-Lovin, L. (2003). Self, identity, and interaction in an ecology of identities. In P. J. Burke, T. J. Owens, R. T. Serpe, & P. A. Thoits (Eds.), *Advances in identity theory and research* (pp. 167–178). New York: Kluwer Academic/Plenum Publishers.

Smithson, M., & Foddy, M. (1999). Theories and strategies for the study of social dilemmas. In M. Foddy, M. Smithson, S. Schneider, & M. Hogg (Eds.), *Resolving social dilemmas: Dynamic, structural, and intergroup aspects* (pp. 1–14). Philadelphia, PA: Psychology Press (Taylor & Francis).

Smitson, W. S. (2001). Managed mental health care: A home grown product. *Administration and Policy in Mental Health, 28*, 229–234.

Snell, J. C., & Mekies, S. (2001). Replaceable professors: An observation. *Journal of Instructional Psychology, 28*, 111–112.

Snell-Johns, J., Imm, P., Wandersman, A., & Claypoole, J. (2003). Roles assumed by a community coalition when creating environmental and policy-level changes. *Journal of Community Psychology, 31*, 661–670.

Sniezek, J. A., & May, D. R. (1990). Conflict of interests and commitment in groups. *Journal of Applied Social Psychology, 20*, 1150–1165.

Snow, S. C., Gehlen, F. L., & Green, J. C. (2002). Different ways to introduce a business simulation: The effect on student performance. *Simulation and Gaming, 33*, 526–532.

Sobczak, J. (1988). Formowanie koalicji w swietle wybranych koncepcji teoretycznych [Forma-tion of coalition in the light of selected theoretical conceptions]. *Przeglad Psychologiczny, 31*, 947–961.

Sobel, J. (2001). Manipulation of preferences and relative utilitarianism. *Games and Economic Behavior, 37*, 196–215.

Sokol, M. B., & Aiello, J. R. (1993). Implications for team focused stress management training. *Consulting Psychology Journal: Practice and Research, 45*(4), 1–10.

Solnick, S. J., & Schweitzer, M. E. (1999). The influence of physical attractiveness and gender on ultimatum game decisions. *Organizational Behavior and Human Decision Processes, 79*, 199–215.

Sommers, P. M. (1993). The influence of salary arbitration on player performance. *Social Science Quarterly, 74*, 439–443.

Sondak, H., Neale, M. A., & Pinkley, R. (1995). The negotiated allocation of benefits and burdens: The impact of outcome valence, contribution, and relationship. *Organizational Behavior and Human Decision Processes, 64*, 249–260.

Song, C., Sommer, S. M., & Hartman, A. E. (1998). The impact of adding an external rater on interdepartmental cooperative behaviors of workers. *International Journal of Conflict Man-agement, 9*, 117–138.

Sönmez, T. (1997). Games of manipulation in marriage problems. *Games and Economic Behavior, 20*, 169–176.

Sonnegård, J. (1996). Determination of first movers in sequential bargaining games: An experi-mental study. *Journal of Economic Psychology, 17*, 359–386.

Sonnentag, S., Brodbeck, F. C., Heinbokel, T., & Stolte, W. (1994). Stressor-burnout relationship in software development teams. *Journal of Occupational and Organizational Psychology, Vol 67*, 327–341.

Sonsino, D., & Sirota, J. (2003). Strategic pattern recognition-experimental evidence. *Games and Economic Behavior, 44*, 390–411.

Sopher, B. (1994). Concession behavior in a bargaining game: A laboratory test of the risk domi-nance principle. *Journal of Conflict Resolution, 38*, 117–137.

Sorenson, R. L., Morse, E. A., & Savage, G. T. (1999). A test of the motivations underlying choice of conflict strategies in the dual-concern model. *International Journal of Conflict Manage-ment, 10*, 25–44.

Sorkin, R. D., Hays, C. J, & West, R. (2001). Signal-detection analysis of group decision making. *Psychological Review, 108*, 183–203.

Sorkin, R. D., West, R., & Robinson, D. E. (1998). Group performance depends on the majority rule. *Psychological Science, 9*, 456–463.

Sosik, J. J, & Jung, D. I. (2002). Work-group characteristics and performance in collectivistic and individualistic cultures. *Journal of Social Psychology, 142*, 5–23.

Sosis, R., Feldstein, S., & Hill, K. (1998). Bargaining theory and cooperative fishing participation on Ifaluk atoll. *Human Nature, 9*, 163–203.

Spears, R. (2008). Social identity, legitimacy, and intergroup conflict: The rocky road to reconcili-ation. In A. Nadler, T. E. Malloy, & J. D. Fisher (Eds.), *The social psychology of intergroup reconciliation* (pp. 319–344). New York: Oxford University Press.

Spears, R., Doosje, B., & Ellemers, N. (1997). Self-stereotyping in the face of threats to group status and distinctiveness: The role of group identification. *Personality and Social Psychology Bulletin, 23*, 538–553.

Spears, R., Gordijn, E., Dijksterhuis, A., & Stapel, D. A. (2004). Reaction in Action: Intergroup Contrast in Automatic Behavior. *Personality and Social Psychology Bulletin, 30*, 605–616.

Spears, R., Jetten, J., Scheepers, D., & Cihangir, S. (2009). Creative distinctiveness: Explaining in-group bias in minimal groups. In S. Otten, K. Sassenberg, & T. Kessler (Eds.), *Intergroup relations: The role of motivation and emotion* (pp. 23–40). New York: Psychology Press.

Spears, R., Lea, M., Corneliussen, R. A., Postmes, T., & ter Haar, W. (2002). Computer-mediated communication as a channel for social resistance: The strategic side of SIDE. *Small Group Research, 33*, 555–574.

Spears, R., Oakes, P. J., Ellemers, N., & Haslam, S. A. (Eds.). (1997). *The social psychology of stereotyping and group life*. Oxford, England: Blackwell Publishers, Inc.

Spears, R., Postmes, T., Lea, M., & Watt, S. E. (2001). A SIDE view of social influence. In J. P. Forgas & K. D. Williams (Eds.), *Social influence: Direct and indirect processes* (pp. 331–350). New York: Psychology Press.

Spector, M. D., & Jones, G. E. (2004). Trust in the workplace: Factors affecting trust formation between team members. *Journal of Social Psychology, 144*, 311–321.

Spiegler, R. (2004). Simplicity of beliefs and delay tactics in a concession game. *Games and Economic Behavior, 47*, 200–220.

Spink, K. S. (1990). Collective efficacy in the sport setting. *International Journal of Sport Psychology. 21*, 380–395.

Spitzberg, B. H., Canary, D. J., & Cupach, W. R. (1994). A competence-based approach to the study of interpersonal conflict. In D. D. Cahn (Ed.), *Conflict in personal relationships* (pp. 183–202). Hillsdale, NJ: Lawrence Erlbaum Associates, Inc.

Spreitzer, G. M., Cohen, S. G., & Ledford, G. E., Jr. (1999). Developing effective self-managing work teams in service organizations. *Group and Organization Management, 24*, 340–366.

Spreitzer, G. M., Noble, D. S., Mishra, A. K., & Cooke, W. N. (1999). Predicting process improvement team performance in an automotive firm: Explicating the roles of trust and empowerment. In R. Wageman (Ed.), *Research on managing groups and teams: Groups in context* (Vol. 2, pp. 71–92). Stamford, CT: Elsevier Science/JAI Press.

Srivastava, A. K., & Lalnunmawii [only]. (1989). Cooperative-competitive behaviour and conflict resolution style among Mizo children: A cultural perspective. *Psychology and Developing Societies, 1*, 191–205.

Srivastava, J. (2001). The role of inferences in sequential bargaining with one-sided incomplete information: Some experimental evidence. *Organizational Behavior and Human Decision Processes, 85*, 166–187.

Staber, U. (2004). Networking beyond organizational boundaries: The case of project organizations. *Creativity and Innovation Management, 13*, 30–40.

Stafford, M. C., & Gibbs, J. P. (1993). A theory about disputes and the efficacy of control. In R. B. Felson & J. T. Tedeschi (Eds.), *Aggression and violence: Social interactionist perspectives* (pp. 69–96). Washington, DC: American Psychological Association.

Stahl, D. O., & Wilson, P. W. (1995). On players' models of other players: Theory and experimental evidence. *Games and Economic Behavior, 10*, 218–254.

Stanford, W. (1995). A Note on the probability of k pure Nash Equilibria in matrix games. *Games and Economic Behavior, 9*, 238–246.

Stangor, C., & Duan, C. (1991). Effects of multiple task demands upon memory for information about social groups. *Journal of Experimental Social Psychology, 27*, 357–378.

Stangor, C., & Thompson, E. P. (2002). Needs for cognitive economy and self-enhancement as unique predictors of intergroup attitudes. *European Journal of Social Psychology, 32*, 563–575.

Stanton, N. A., Ashleigh, M. J., Roberts, A. D., & Xu, F. (2003). Virtuality in human supervisory control: Assessing the effects of psychological and social remoteness. *Ergonomics, 46*, 1215–1232.

Stapley, L. F. (2006). *Individuals, groups, and organizations beneath the surface: An introduction*. London: Karnac.

Stark, O. (2004). Cooperation and wealth. *Journal of Economic Behavior and Organization, 53*, 109–115.

Stark, O., & Wang, Y. Q. (2004). On the evolutionary edge of altruism: A game-theoretic proof of Hamilton's rule for a simple case of siblings. *Journal of Evolutionary Economics, 14*, 37–42.

Stasavage, D. (2004). Opendoor or closeddoor? Transparency in domestic and international bargaining. *International Organization, 58*, 667–703.

Stathi, S., & Crisp, R. J. (2008). Imagining intergroup contact promotes projection to outgroups. *Journal of Experimental Social Psychology, 44*, 943–957.

Staub, E. (2001). Individual and group identities in genocide and mass killing. In R. D. Ashmore, L. Jussim, & D. Wilder (Eds.), *Social identity, intergroup conflict, and conflict reduction* (pp. 159–184). New York: Oxford University Press.

Staub, E. (2008). The origins of genocide and mass killing, prevention, reconciliation, and their application to Rwanda. In V. M. Esses & R. A. Vernon (Eds.), *Explaining the breakdown of ethnic relations: Why neighbors kill* (pp. 245–268). Malden: Blackwell Publishing.

Stearns, L. B., & Almeida, P. D. (2004). The formation of state actor-social movement coalitions and favorable policy outcomes. *Social Problems, 51*, 478–504.

Stefan, S., Simon, B., Loewy, M., & Jörger, H. (2003). The Dual-Pathway Model of Social Movement Participation: The Case of the Fat Acceptance Movement. *Social Psychology Quarterly, 66*, 71–82.

Stein, N. L., Bernas, R. S., & Calicchia, D. J. (1997). Conflict talk: Understanding and resolving arguments. In T. Givon (Ed.), *Conversation: Cognitive, communicative and social perspectives. Typological studies in language* (Vol. 34, pp. 233–267). Amsterdam: John Benjamins Publishing Company.

Stein, N. L., Bernas, R. S., Calicchia, D. J., & Wright, A. (1996). Understanding and resolving arguments: The dynamics of negotiation. In B. K. Britton & A. C. Graesser (Eds.), *Models of understanding text* (pp. 257–287). Mahwah, NJ: Lawrence Erlbaum Associates.

Steiner, I. D. (1983). Whatever happened to the touted revival of the group? In H. H. Blumberg, A. P. Hare, V. Kent, & M. F. Davies (Eds.), *Small groups and social interaction* (Vol. 2, pp. 539–548). Chichester, UK and New York, NY: John Wiley & Sons.

Steinfeld, G. J. (1998). Personal responsibility in human relationships: A cognitive-constructivist approach. *Transactional Analysis Journal, 28*, 188–201.

Stellmacher, J., & Petzel, T. (2005). Authoritarianism as a Group Phenomenon. *Political Psychology, 26*, 245–274.

Stenstrom, D. M., Lickel, B., Denson, T. F., & Miller, N. (2008). The roles of ingroup identification and outgroup entitativity in intergroup retribution. *Personality and Social Psychology Bulletin, 34*, 1570–1582.

Stephan, W. G. (2008a). Psychological and communication processes associated with intergroup conflict resolution. *Small Group Research, 39*, 28–41.

Stephan, W. G. (2008b). The road to reconciliation. In A. Nadler, T. E. Malloy, & J. D. Fisher (Eds.), *The social psychology of intergroup reconciliation* (pp. 369–394). New York: Oxford University Press.

Stephan, W. G., Boniecki, K. A., Ybarra, O., Bettencourt, A., Ervin, K. S., Jackson, L. A., McNatt, P. S., & Renfro, C. L. (2002). The role of threats in the racial attitudes of Blacks and White. *Personality and Social Psychology Bulletin, 28*, 1242–1254.

Stephan, W. G., & Stephan, C. W. (1989). Antecedents of intergroup anxiety in Asian-Americans and Hispanic-Americans. *International Journal of Intercultural Relations, 13*, 203–219.

Stephan, W. G., & Stephan, C. W. (2000). An Integrated Threat Theory of Prejudice. In S. Oskamp (Ed.), *Reducing Prejudice and Discrimination* (pp. 23–46). Mahwah, NJ: Lawrence Erlbaum Associates.

Stephan, W. G., Ybarra, O., & Bachman, G. (1999). Prejudice toward immigrants. *Journal of Applied Social Psychology, 29*, 2221–2237.

Stephan, W. G., Ybarra, O., & Morrison, K. R. (2009). Intergroup threat theory. In T. D. Nelson (Ed.), *Handbook of prejudice, stereotyping, and discrimination* (pp. 43–59). New York: Psychology Press.

Stephen, A. T., & Pham, M. T. (2008). On feelings as a heuristic for making offers in ultimatum negotiations. *Psychological Science, 19*, 1051–1058.

Stephenson, G. M., & Tysoe, M. (1988). Social dimensions of industrial bargaining. In G. M. Breakwell, H. Foot, & R. Gilmour (Eds.), *Doing social psychology: Laboratory and field exercises* (pp. 202–221). New York: Cambridge University Press.

Sterman, J. D. (1988). Deterministic chaos in models of human behavior: Methodological issues and experimental results. *System Dynamics Review, 4*, 148–178.

Stettler, N., Signer, T. M., & Suter, P. M. (2004). Electronic games and environmental factors associated with childhood obesity in Switzerland. *Obesity Research, 12*, 896–903.

Stewart, G. L., & Barrick, M. R. (2000). Team structure and performance: Assessing the mediating role of intrateam process and the moderating role of task type. *Academy of Management Journal, 43*, 135–148.

Stewart, J. I. (2009). Cooperation when N is large: Evidence from the mining camps of the American West. *Journal of Economic Behavior and Organization, 69*, 213–225.

Stewart, N., Chater, N., Stott, H. P., & Reimers, S. (2003). Prospect relativity: How choice options influence decision under risk. *Journal of Experimental Psychology: General, 132*, 23–46.

Stewart, P. A., & Moore, J. C. (1992). Wage disparities and performance expectations. *Social Psychology Quarterly, 55*, 78–85.

Stinglhamber, F., & Vandenberghe, C. (2003). Organizations and supervisors as sources of support and targets of commitment: A longitudinal study. *Journal of Organizational Behavior, 24*, 251–270.

Stinglhamber, F., & Vandenberghe, C. (2004). Favorable job conditions and perceived support: The role of organizations and supervisors. *Journal of Applied Social Psychology, 34*, 1470–1493.

Stockard, J., van de Kragt, A. J., & Dodge, P. J. (1988). Gender roles and behavior in social dilemmas: Are there sex differences in cooperation and in its justification? *Social Psychology Quarterly, 51*, 154–163.

Stone, B., Jones, C., & Betz, B. (1996). Response of cooperators and competitors in a simulated arms race. *Psychological Reports, 79*, 1101–1102.

Stone, C. H., & Crisp, R. J. (2007). Superordinate and subgroup identification as predictors of intergroup evaluation in common ingroup contexts. *Group Processes and Intergroup Relations, 10*, 493–513.

Stott, C., & Drury, J. (2000). Crowds, context and identity: Dynamic categorization processes in the "poll tax riot." *Human Relations, 53*, 247–273.

Stott, C., Hutchison, P., & Drury, J. (2001). "Hooligans" abroad? Inter-group dynamics, social identity and participation in collective "disorder" at the 1998 World Cup Finals. *British Journal of Social Psychology, 40*, 359–384.

Stout, R. J., Salas, E., & Carson, R. (1994). Individual task proficiency and team process behavior: What's important for team functioning? *Military Psychology, 6*, 177192.

Stout, R. J., Salas, E., & Fowlkes, J. E. (1997). Enhancing teamwork in complex environments through team training. *Journal of Group Psychotherapy, Psychodrama and Sociometry, 49*, 163–186.

Straus, S. G., & McGrath, J. E. (1994). Does the medium matter? The interaction of task type and technology on group performance and member reactions. *Journal of Applied Psychology, 79*, 87–97.

Strauss, A. L. (1959, reprinted 1997). *Mirrors & masks: The search for identity*. New Brunswick, NJ: Transaction Publishers.

Stroebe, K., Spears, R., & Lodewijkx, H. (2007). Contrasting and integrating social identity and interdependence approaches to intergroup discrimination in the minimal group paradigm. In M. Hewstone, Schut, A. W. Henk, J. B. F. De Wit, K. Van Den Bos, & M. S. Stroebe (Eds.), *The scope of social psychology: Theory and applications* (pp. 173–190). New York: Psychology Press.

Stroebe, W., & Hewstone, M. (Eds.). (1998). *European Review of Social Psychology, Vol. 8*. Chichester, England UK: John Wiley and Sons, Inc.

Stroebe, W., Diehl, M., & Abakoumkin, G. (1996). Social compensation and the Koehler effect: Toward a theoretical explanation of motivation gains in group productivity. In E. H. Witte & J. H. Davis (Eds.), *Understanding group behavior, Vol. 2: Small group processes and interpersonal relations. Understanding group behavior* (pp. 37–65). Mahwah, NJ: Lawrence Erlbaum Associates, Inc.

Stroeker, N. E., & Antonides, G. (1997). The process of reaching an agreement in second-hand markets for consumer durables. *Journal of Economic Psychology, 18*, 341–367.

Stroessner, S. J., & Mackie, D. M. (1992). The impact of induced affect on the perception of variability in social groups. *Personality and Social Psychology Bulletin, 18*, 546–554.

Struch, N., & Schwartz, S. H. (1989). Intergroup aggression: Its predictors and distinctness from in-group bias. *Journal of Personality and Social Psychology, 56*, 364–373.

Struthers, C. Ward, Eaton, J., Ratajczak, A., & Perunovic, M. (2004). Social Conduct Toward Organizations. *Basic and Applied Social Psychology, 26*, 277–288.

Strutton, D., Pelton, L. E., & Lumpkin, J. R. (1993). The influence of psychological climate on conflict resolution strategies in franchise relationships. *Journal of the Academy of Marketing Science, 21*, 207–215.

Stuart, H. W., Jr. (1997). The supplier-firm-buyer game and its m-sided generalization. *Mathematical Social Sciences, 34*, 21–27.

Stuhlmacher, A. F., & Stevenson, M. K. (1997). Using policy modeling to describe the negotiation exchange. *Group Decision and Negotiation, 6*, 317–337.

Stuhlmacher, A. F., & Walters, A. E. (1999). Gender differences in negotiation outcome: A meta-analysis. *Personnel Psychology, 52*, 653–677.

Stürmer, S., & Simon, B. (2004). Collective action: Towards a dual-pathway model. In W. Stroebe & M. Hewstone (Eds.), *European review of social psychology* (Vol. 15, pp. 59–99). Hove, England: Psychology Press/Taylor & Francis (UK), 2004.

Subasic, E., & Reynolds, K. J. (2009). Beyond "practical" reconciliation: Intergroup inequality and the meaning of non-indigenous identity. *Political Psychology, 30*, 243–267.

Suchipriya [only], & Singh, D. (2001). Effect of spiritual tools in attitude building. *Abhigyan, 19*(3), 41–44.

Suen, W., Chan, W., & Zhang, J. (2003). Marital transfer and intra-household allocation: A Nash-bargaining analysis. *Journal of Economic Behavior and Organization, 52*, 133–146.

Sugiyama, L. S., Tooby, J., & Cosmides, L. (2004). Cross-cultural evidence of cognitive adaptations for social exchange among the Shiwiar of Ecuadorian Amazonia. In D. T. Kenrick & C. L. Luce (Eds.), *The functional mind: Readings in evolutionary psychology* (pp. 97–109). Auckland, New Zealand: Pearson Education New Zealand.

Suleiman, R. (1996). Expectations and fairness in a modified Ultimatum game. *Journal of Economic Psychology, 17*, 531–554.

Suleiman, R. (2004). Planned encounters between Jewish and Palestinian Israelis: A social-psychological perspective. *Journal of Social Issues, 60*, 323–337.

Suleiman, R., & Budescu, D. V. (1999). Common Pool Resource (CPR) dilemmas with incomplete information. In D. V. Budescu, I. Erev, & R. Zwick (Eds.), *Games and human behavior: Essays in honor of Amnon Rapoport* (pp. 387–410). Mahwah, NJ: Lawrence Erlbaum Associates Publishers.

Suleiman, R., & Rapoport, A. (1988). Environmental and social uncertainty in single-trial resource dilemmas. *Acta Psychologica, 68*, 99–112.

Suleiman, R., & Rapoport, A. (1992). Provision of step-level public goods with continuous contribution. *Journal of Behavioral Decision Making, 5*, 133–153.

Suleiman, R., Rapoport, A., & Budescu, D. V. (1996). Fixed position and property rights in sequential resource dilemmas under uncertainty. *Acta Psychologica, 93*, 229–246.

Sum, M., & Gil-White, F. J. (2004). Ultimatum game with an ethnicity manipulation: Results from Khovdiin Bulgan Sum, Mongolia. In J. Henrich, R. Boyd, S. Bowles, C. Camerer, E. Fehr, & H. Gintis (Eds.), *Foundations of human sociality* (pp. 260–304). New York: Oxford University Press.

Suman, H. C. (1989). The influence of non-verbal cues on impression formation. *Journal of the Indian Academy of Applied Psychology, 15*, 1–8.

Sundali, J. A., Rapoport, A., & Seale, D. A. (1995). Coordination in market entry games with symmetric players. *Organizational Behavior and Human Decision Processes, 64*, 203–218.

Sundstrom, E., & Altman, I. (1989). Physical environments and work-group effectiveness. *Research in Organizational Behavior, 11*, 175–209.

Sundstrom, E., De Meuse, K. P., & Futrell, D. (1990). Work teams: Applications and effectiveness. *American Psychologist, 45*, 120–133.

Sundstrom, E., Herbert, R. K., & Brown, D. W. (1982). Privacy and communication in an open-plan office: A case study. *Environment and Behavior, 14,* 379–392.

Susman, G. I. (1990). Work groups: Autonomy, technology, and choice. In P. S. Goodman & L. S. Sproull, *Technology and organizations* (pp. 87–108). San Francisco: Jossey-Bass Inc.

Susskind, J. E., & Hodges, C. (2007). Decoupling children's gender-based in-group positivity from out-group negativity. *Sex Roles, 56,* 707–716.

Sussman, G. (1997). *Communication, technology, and politics in the information age.* Thousand Oaks, Ca: Sage.

Sussman, S. W., & Siegal, W. S. (2003). Informational influence in organizations: An integrated approach to knowledge adoption. *Information Systems Research, 14,* 47–65.

Sutherland, M., Cowart, M. E., & Harris, G. J. (1997). Jackson County partnership: Developing an effective coalition. *International Quarterly of Community Health Education, 17,* 405–415.

Sutton, R. I., & Callahan, A. L. (1988). The stigma of bankruptcy: Spoiled organizational image and its management. In K. S. Cameron, R. I. Sutton, & D. A. Whetten (Eds.), *Readings in organizational decline: Frameworks, research, and prescriptions* (pp. 241–263). New York: Ballinger Publishing Co/Harper & Row Publishers.

Sveiby, K.-E., & Simons, R. (2002). Collaborative climate and effectiveness of knowledge work: An empirical study. *Journal of Knowledge Management, 6,* 420–433.

Sverke, M., Hellgren, J., & Näswall, K. (2002). No security: A meta-analysis and review of job insecurity and its consequences. *Journal of Occupational Health Psychology, 7,* 242–264.

Svyantek, D. J., Goodman, S. A., Benz, L. L., & Gard, J. A. (1999). The relationship between organizational characteristics and team building success. *Journal of Business and Psychology, 14,* 265–283.

Swaab, R. I., Postmes, T., & Spears, R. (2008). Identity formation in multiparty negotiations. *British Journal of Social Psychology, 47,* 167–187.

Swann, W. B., Jr., Kwan, Virginia S. Y., Polzer, J. T., & Milton, L. P. (2003). Fostering Group Identification and Creativity in Diverse Groups: The Role of Individuation and Self-Verification. *Personality and Social Psychology Bulletin, 29,* 1396–1406.

Swann, W. B., Jr., Polzer, J. T., Seyle, D. C., & Ko, S. J. (2004). Finding value in diversity: Verification of personal and social self-views in diverse groups. *Academy of Management Review, 29,* 9–27.

Swidler, A., & Arditi, J. (1994). The new sociology of knowledge. *Annual Review of Sociology, 20,* 305–329.

Swim, J. K., & Stangor, C. (Eds.). (1998). *Prejudice: The target's perspective.* San Diego, CA: Academic Press, Inc.

Swingle, P. G. (1989). The resolution of conflict. *Canadian Psychology/Psychologie canadienne, 30,* 650–661.

Sycara, K. P. (1990). Persuasive argumentation in negotiation. *Theory and Decision, 28,* 203–242.

Sze, W. C. (1990). Ego strength and coping capacity: Friend and social group affiliation. In J. D. Noshpitz & R. D. Coddington (Eds.), *Stressors and the adjustment disorders* (pp. 510–520). New York: John Wiley & Sons.

Tadepalli, R. (1992). Conflict management in organizational buying behavior: The role of coalitions. *International Journal of Conflict Management, 3,* 5–30.

Taggar, S. (2001). Group composition, creative synergy, and group performance. *Journal of Creative Behavior, 35,* 261–286.

Taggar, S. (2002). Individual creativity and group ability to utilize individual creative resources: A multilevel model. *Academy of Management Journal, 45,* 315–330.

Taggar, S., Hackett, R., & Saha, S. (1999). Leadership emergence in autonomous work teams: Antecedents and outcomes. *Personnel Psychology, 52,* 899–926.

Tajfel, H., Billig, M. G., Bundy, R. P., & Flament, C. (1971). Social categorization and intergroup behaviour. *European Journal of Social Psychology, 1,* 149–178.

Tajfel, H., & Turner, J. C. (1979). An Integrative Theory of Intergroup Conflict. In W. G. Austin & S. Worchel (Eds.), *The social psychology of intergroup relations.* Monterey, CA: Brooks-Cole.

Tajfel, H., & Turner, J. C. (1986). The social identity theory of inter-group behavior. In S. Worchel & L. W. Austin (Eds.), *Psychology of intergroup relations*. Chigago: Nelson-Hall.

Tajima, T. (1997). Expectation of others' reward allocation, and ingroup favoritism in reward allocation. *Japanese Journal of Psychology, 68*, 135–139.

Takao, A., & Okura, M. (2001). An experimental approach to the effectiveness of an incentive system against moral hazard in the insurance market. *Journal of Risk Research, 4*, 291–301.

*Talcott Parsons.* (2010, 27 November). Retrieved from http://en.wikipedia.org/wiki/Talcott[underline]Parsons#AGIL[underline]paradigm

Talmud, I., & Izraeli, D. N. (1999). The relationship between gender and performance issues of concern to directors: Correlates or institution? *Journal of Organizational Behavior, 20*, 459–474.

Tam, K.-P., Chiu, C.-Y., & Lau, I. Y.-M. (2007). Terror management among Chinese: Worldview defence and intergroup bias in resource allocation. *Asian Journal of Social Psychology, 10*(2), 93–102.

Tamir, Y., & Nadler, A. (2007). The role of personality in social identity: Effects of field-dependence and context on reactions to threat to group distinctiveness. *Journal of Personality, Vol 75*, 927–954.

Tanabe, Y. (2001). Effects of power cognition of the self in a group on perceived in-group variability. *Japanese Journal of Experimental Social Psychology, 41*, 37–44.

Tang, T. L.-P., Kim, J. K., & O'Donald, D. A. (2000). Perceptions of Japanese organizational culture: Employees in non-unionized Japanese-owned and unionized US-owned automobile plants. *Journal of Managerial Psychology, 15*, 535–555.

Tang, T. L.-P., Tollison, P. S., & Whiteside, H. D. (1993). Differences between active and inactive quality circles in attendance and performance. *Public Personnel Management, 22*, 579–590.

Tannenbaum, S. I., & Yukl, G. (1992). Training and development in work organizations. *Annual Review of Psychology, 43*, 399–441.

Tansky, J. W., & Cohen, D. J. (2001). The relationship between organizational support, employee development, and organizational commitment: An empirical study. *Human Resource Development Quarterly, 12*, 285–300.

Tarrant, M., & North, A. C. (2004). Explanations for Positive and Negative Behavior: The Intergroup Attribution Bias in Achieved Groups. *Current Psychology, 23*, 161–172.

Tasa, K., Taggar, S., & Seijts, G. H. (2007). The development of collective efficacy in teams: A multilevel and longitudinal perspective. *Journal of Applied Psychology, 92*, 17–27.

Tauer, J. M., & Harackiewicz, J. M. (2004). The effects of cooperation and competition on intrinsic motivation and performance. *Journal of Personality and Social Psychology, 86*, 849–861.

Tauman, Y. (2002). A note on k-price auctions with complete information. *Games and Economic Behavior, 41*, 161–164.

Tausch, N., Hewstone, M., Kenworthy, J., Cairns, E., & Christ, O. (2007). Cross-community contact, perceived status differences, and intergroup attitudes in Northern Ireland: The mediating roles of individual-level versus group-level threats and the moderating role of social identification. *Political Psychology, Vol 28*, 53–68.

Tausch, N., Hewstone, M., & Roy, R. (2009). The relationships between contact, status and prejudice: An integrated threat theory analysis of Hindu-Muslim relations in India. *Journal of Community and Applied Social Psychology, 19*, 83–94.

Tausch, N., Kenworthy, J., & Hewstone, M. (2006). Intergroup Contact and the Improvement of Intergroup Relations. In M. Fitzduff & C. Stout (Eds.), *The psychology of resolving global conflicts: From war to peace* (Vol. 2, pp. 67–107). Westport, CT: Praeger Security International, 2006.

Tausch, N., Tam, T., Hewstone, M., Kenworthy, J., & Cairns, E. (2007). Individual-level and group-level mediators of contact effects in Northern Ireland: The moderating role of social identification. *British Journal of Social Psychology, 46*, 541–556.

Tavuchis, N. (1991). *Mea culpa: A sociology of apology and reconciliation*. Stanford, CA: Stanford University Press.

Taylor, A., & Zwicker, W. (1997). Interval measures of power. *Mathematical Social Sciences, 33,* 23–74.

Taylor, I. A. (1959). The nature of the creative process. In P. Smith (Ed.), *Creativity: An examination of the creative process* (pp. 54–61). [A report on the 3rd communications conference of the Art Directors Club of New York]. New York: Hasting House.

Taylor, I. A. (1975). A retrospective view of creativity investigation. In I. A. Taylor & J. W. Getzels (Eds.), *Perspectives in creativity* (pp. 1–36). Chicago: Aldine.

Taylor, J., & MacDonald, J. (2002). The effects of asynchronous computer-mediated group interaction on group processes. *Social Science Computer Review, 20,* 260–274.

Taylor, P. D., & Day, T. (2004). Cooperate with thy neighbour? *Nature, 428,* 611–612.

Tedeschi, P. (1995). Bargained-correlated equilibria. *Games and Economic Behavior, 9,* 205–221.

Tedin, K. L., & Murray, R. W. (1994). Support for biracial political coalitions among Blacks and Hispanics. *Social Science Quarterly, 75,* 772–789.

Terry, D. J., & Callan, V. J. (1998). In-group bias in response to an organizational merger. *Group Dynamics, 2,* 67–81.

Terry, D. J., & Hogg, M. A. (2001). Attitudes, behavior, and social context: The role of norms and group membership in social influence processes. In J. P. Forgas & K. D. Williams (Eds.), *Social influence: Direct and indirect processes* (pp. 253–270). New York: Psychology Press.

Tesluk, P. E., Farr, J. L., & Klein, S. R. (1997). Influences of organizational culture and climate on individual creativity. *Journal of Creative Behavior, 31,* 27–41.

Tesluk, P. E, & Mathieu, J. E. (1999). Overcoming roadblocks to effectiveness: Incorporating management of performance barriers into models of work group effectiveness. *Journal of Applied Psychology, 84,* 200–217.

Tesser, A., Millar, M., & Moore, J. (1988). Some affective consequences of social comparison and reflection processes: The pain and pleasure of being close. *Journal of Personality and Social Psychology, 54,* 49–61.

Testé, B. (2001). Perspective socionormative sur la polarisation de groupe: Effets du consensus dans le cadre d'une activité de détection d'utilité sociale [A socionormative perspective on group polarization: Effects of consensus within the framework of a social utility detection activity]. *Revue Internationale de Psychologie Sociale, 14,* 91–129.

Tetlock, P. E. (1985). Integrative complexity of American and Soviet foreign policy rhetoric: A time-series analysis. *Journal of Personality and Social Psychology, 49,* 1565–1585.

Tetlock, P. E. (1997). Psychological perspectives on international conflict and cooperation. In D. F. Halpern & A. E. Voiskounsky (Eds.), *States of mind: American and post-Soviet perspectives on contemporary issues in psychology* (pp. 49–76). New York: Oxford University Press.

Tetlock, P. E., Kristel, O. V., Elson, S. Beth, Green, M. C., & Lerner, J. S. (2000). The psychology of the unthinkable: Taboo trade-offs, forbidden base rates, and heretical counterfactuals. *Journal of Personality and Social Psychology, 78,* 853–870.

Tetlock, P. E., McGraw, A. P., & Kristel, O. V. (2004). Proscribed Forms of Social Cognition: Taboo Trade-offs, Blocked Exchanges, Forbidden Base Rates, and Heretical Counterfactuals. In N. Haslam (Ed.), *Relational models theory: A contemporary overview* (pp. 247–262). Mahwah, NJ: Lawrence Erlbaum Associates Publishers.

Thakkar, B. M., & Kanekar, S. (1989). Dispositional empathy and causal attribution as determinants of estimated willingness to help. *Irish Journal of Psychology, 10,* 381–387.

Thavikulwat, P. (2004). The architecture of computerized business gaming simulations. *Simulation and Gaming, 35,* 242–269.

Thelen, H. A. (1954). *Dynamics of groups at work.* Chicago: University of Chicago Press.

Thiessen, E. M., Loucks, D. P., & Stedinger, J. R. (1998). Computer-assisted negotiations of water resources conflicts. *Group Decision and Negotiation, 7,* 109–129.

Thoits, P. A. (2003). Personal agency in the accumulation of multiple role-identities. In P. J. Burke, T. J. Owens, R. T. Serpe, & P. A. Thoits (Eds.), *Advances in identity theory and research* (pp. 179–194). New York: Kluwer Academic/Plenum Publishers.

Thomas, D. C. (1999). Cultural diversity and work group effectiveness: An experimental study. *Journal of Cross-Cultural Psychology, 30,* 242–263.

Thomas-Hunt, M. C., & Phillips, K. W. (2004). When what you know is not enough: Expertise and gender dynamics in task groups. *Personality and Social Psychology Bulletin, 30,* 1585–1598.

Thompson, L. (1990a). The influence of experience on negotiation performance. *Journal of Experimental Social Psychology, 26,* 528–544.

Thompson, L. (1990b). Negotiation behavior and outcomes: Empirical evidence and theoretical issues. *Psychological Bulletin, 108,* 515–532.

Thompson, L. L. (1991). Information exchange in negotiation. *Journal of Experimental Social Psychology, 27,* 161–179.

Thompson, L. L. (1992). A method for examining learning in negotiation. *Group Decision and Negotiation, 1,* 71–84.

Thompson, L. (1995a). The impact of minimum goals and aspirations on judgments of success in negotiations. *Group Decision and Negotiation, 4,* 513–524.

Thompson, L. (1995b). "They saw a negotiation": Partisanship and involvement. *Journal of Personality and Social Psychology, 68,* 839–853.

Thompson, L., & DeHarpport, T. (1994). Social judgment, feedback, and interpersonal learning in negotiation. *Organizational Behavior and Human Decision Processes, 58,* 327–345.

Thompson, L., & Fine, G. A. (1999). Socially shared cognition, affect, and behavior: A review and integration. *Personality and Social Psychology Review, 3,* 278–302.

Thompson, L. L., Mannix, E. A., & Bazerman, M. H. (1988). Group negotiation: Effects of decision rule, agenda, and aspiration. *Journal of Personality and Social Psychology, 54,* 86–95.

Thompson, L., Medvec, V. H., Seiden, V., & Kopelman, S. (2004). Poker face, smiley face, and rant 'n' rave: Myths and realities about emotion in negotiation. In M. B. Brewer & M. Hewstone (Eds.), *Emotion and motivation* (pp. 70–94). Malden: Blackwell Publishing.

Thompson, L. L., Nadler, J., & Kim, P. H. (1999). Some like it hot: The case for the emotional negotiator. In L. L. Thompson, J. M. Levine, & D. M. Messick (Eds.), *Shared cognition in organizations: The management of knowledge* (pp. 139–161). Mahwah, NJ: Lawrence Erlbaum Associates Publishers.

Thompson, L., Nadler, J., & Lount, R. B., Jr. (2006). Judgmental biases in conflict resolution and how to overcome them. In M. Deutsch, P. T. Coleman, & E. C. Marcus (Eds.), *The handbook of conflict resolution: Theory and practice* (2nd ed., pp. 243–267). Hoboken, NJ: Wiley Publishing.

Thompson, M. M., & Holmes, J. G. (1996). Ambivalence in close relationships: Conflicted cognitions as a catalyst for change. In R. M. Sorrentino & E. T. Higgins (Eds.), *Handbook of motivation and cognition, Vol. 3: The interpersonal context* (pp. 497–530). New York: Guilford Press.

Thompson, R. C., Bailey, L. L., & Farmer, W. L. (1998). Predictors of perceived empowerment: An initial assessment. *FAA Office of Aviation Medicine Reports,* FAA-AM–98–24, 1–5.

Thoron, S. (2004). Which acceptable agreements are equilibria? *Mathematical Social Sciences, 47,* 111–134.

Thye, S. R. (2000). A status value theory of power in exchange relations. *American Sociological Review, 65,* 407–432.

Thye, S. R., Yoon, J., & Lawler, E. J. (2002). The theory of relational cohesion: Review of a research program. In S. R. Thye & E. J. Lawler (Eds.), *Group cohesion, trust and solidarity* (pp. 139–166). San Diego, CA: Elsevier Science/JAI Press.

Tian, G. (2000). Incentive mechanism design for production economies with both private and public ownerships. *Games and Economic Behavior, 33,* 294–320.

Tian, G., & Li, Q. (1995). On Nash-Implementation in the presence of withholding. *Games and Economic Behavior, 9,* 222–233.

Tichy, N. M. (1981). Networks in organizations. In P. C. Nystrom & W. H. Starbuck (Eds.), *Handbook of organizational design* (Vol. 2, pp. 225–249). Oxford, England: Oxford University Press.

Tierney, P. (1997). The influence of cognitive climate on job satisfaction and creative efficacy. *Journal of Social Behavior and Personality, 12,* 831–847.

Timmerman, T. A. (2000). Racial diversity, age diversity, interdependence, and team performance. *Small Group Research, 31,* 592–606.

Tindale, R. S., Heath, L., Edwards, J., Posavac, E. J., Bryant, F. B., Suarez-Balcazar, Y., Henderson-King, E, & Myers, J. (Eds.). (1998). *Social psychological applications to social issues, Volume 4: Theory and research on small groups.* New York: Plenum Press.

Tindale, R. S., Kulik, C. T., & Scott, L. A. (1991). Individual and group feedback and performance: An attributional perspective. *Basic and Applied Social Psychology, 12,* 41–62.

Tindale, R. S., & Larson, J. R. (1992). Assembly bonus effect or typical group performance? A comment on Michaelsen, Watson, and Black (1989). *Journal of Applied Psychology, 77,* 102–105.

Tindale, R. S., & Sheffey, S. (2002). Shared information, cognitive load, and group memory. *Group Processes and Intergroup Relations, 5,* 5–18.

Ting-Toomey, S. (1993). Communicative resourcefulness: An identity negotiation perspective. In R. L. Wiseman & J. Koester (Eds.), *Intercultural communication competence. International and intercultural communication annual* (Vol. XVII, 1993, pp. 72–111). Newbury Park, CA: Sage Publications, Inc.

Ting-Toomey, S. (1994). Managing conflict in intimate intercultural relationships. In D. D. Cahn (Ed.), *Conflict in personal relationships* (pp. 47–77). Hillsdale, NJ: Lawrence Erlbaum Associates, Inc.

Ting-Toomey, S., Gao, G., Trubisky, P., Yang, Z., Kim, H. S., Lin, S.-L., & Nishida, T. (1991). Culture, face maintenance, and styles of handling interpersonal conflicts: A study in five cultures. *International Journal of Conflict Management, 2,* 275–296.

Tinoco, J. (1998). Effect of intergroup differentiation on participation with religious young people. *International Journal for the Psychology of Religion, 8,* 197–204.

Tinsley, C. H. (1997). Understanding conflict in a Chinese cultural context. In R. J. Lewicki, R. J. Bies, & B. H. Sheppard (Eds.), *Research on negotiation in organizations* (Vol. 6, pp. 209–225). San Diego, CA: Elsevier Science/JAI Press, 1997.

Tinsley, C. H. (2004). Culture and conflict: Enlarging our dispute resolution framework. In M. J. Gelfand & J. M. Brett (Eds.), *The handbook of negotiation and culture* (pp. 193–210). Stanford, CA: Stanford University Press.

Tipa, G., & Welch, R. (2006). Comanagement of natural resources: Issues of definition from an indigenous community perspective. *Journal of Applied Behavioral Science, 42,* 373–391.

Tjosvold, D. (1988). Effects of shared responsibility and goal interdependence on controversy and decisionmaking between departments. *Journal of Social Psychology, 128,* 7–18.

Tjosvold, D. (1997). Conflict within interdependence: Its value for productivity and individuality. In C. K. W. De Dreu & E. Van de Vliert (Eds.), *Using conflict in organizations* (pp. 23–37). London: Sage Publications, Inc.

Tjosvold, D. (1998). Cooperative and competitive goal approach to conflict: Accomplishments and challenges. *Applied Psychology: An International Review, 47,* 285–342.

Tjosvold, D., & Van de Vliert, E. (1994). Applying cooperative and competitive conflict theory to mediation. *Mediation Quarterly, 11,* 303–311.

Todorov, A., Lalljee, M., & Hirst, W. (2000). Communication context, explanation, and social judgment. *uropean Journal of Social Psychology, 30,* 199–209.

Tomala, T. (1999). Nash equilibria of repeated games with observable payoff vectors. *Games and Economic Behavior, 28,* 310–324.

Tomochi, M. (2004). Defectors' niches: Prisoner's dilemma game on disordered networks. *Social Networks, 26,* 309–321.

Tompkins, T. C. (1997). A developmental approach to organizational learning teams: A model and illustrative research. In M. M. Beyerlein, D. A. Johnson, & S. T. Beyerlein (Eds.), *Advances in interdisciplinary studies of work teams* (Vol. 4, pp. 281–302). Greenwich, CT: Jai Press, Inc.

Toranzo, F. M., Canto, J., & Gómez Jacinto, L. (2004). Internet y desindividuación. Nuevas perspectivas sobre la desindividuacion en la red: El modelo de identidad social de los fenómenos de desindividuación (SIDE) [Internet and deindividuation. New perspectives of deindividuation on the net: The social identity model of deindividuation effects (SIDE)]. *Revista de Psicología Social, 19,* 93–106.

Torenvlied, R., & Thomson, R. (2003). Is implementation distinct from political bargaining?: A micro-level test. *Rationality and Society, 15*, 64–84.

Torres, J. B. (2002). Creating a Latino/Hispanic alliance: Eliminating barriers to coalition building. *Journal of Human Behavior in the Social Environment, 5*, 189–213.

Totterdell, P., Wall, T., Holman, D., Diamond, H., & Epitropaki, O. (2004). Affect Networks: A structural analysis of the relationship between work ties and job-related affect. *Journal of Applied Psychology, 89*, 854–867.

Townsend, A. M., Demarie, S. M., & Hendrickson, A. R. (2001). Desktop video conferencing in virtual workgroups: Anticipation, system evaluation and performance. *Information Systems Journal, 11*, 213–226.

Townsend, J. M. (1993). Sexuality and partner selection: Sex differences among college students. *Ethology and Sociobiology, 14*, 305–329.

Tracer, D. P. (2004). Market integration, reciprocity, and fairness in rural Papua New Guinea: Results from a two-village Ultimatum game experiment. In J. Henrich, R. Boyd, S. Bowles, C. Camerer, E. Fehr, & H. Gintis (Eds.), *Foundations of human sociality* (pp. 232–259). New York: Oxford University Press.

Tracy, L. (1995). Negotiation: An emergent process of living systems. *Behavioral Science, 40*, 41–55.

Treviño, L. K., Brown, M., & Hartman, L. P. (2003). A qualitative investigation of perceived executive ethical leadership: Perceptions from inside and outside the executive suite. *Human Relations, 56*, 5–37.

Treviño, L. K., Butterfield, K. D., & McCabe, D. L. (2001). The ethical context in organizations: Influences of employee attitudes and behaviors. In J. Dienhart, D. Moberg, & R. Duska (Eds.), *The next phase of business ethics: Integrating psychology and ethics* (pp. 301–337). San Diego, CA: Elsevier Science/JAI Press.

Triandis, H. C., Bontempo, R., Villareal, M. J., Asai, M., & Lucca, N. (1988). Individualism and collectivism: Cross-cultural perspectives on selfngroup relationships. *Journal of Personality and Social Psychology, 54*, 323–338.

Tripp, T. M., & Sondak, H. (1992). An evaluation of dependent variables in experimental negotiation studies: Impasse rates and Pareto efficiency. *Organizational Behavior and Human Decision Processes, 51*, 273–295.

Troisi, A. (1993). Biological constraints on cooperation in large political groups. In M. T. McGuire (Ed.), *Human nature and the new Europe* (pp. 9–18). Boulder, CO: Westview Press.

Trope, Y., & Gaunt, R. (1999). A dual-process model of overconfident attributional inferences. In S. Chaiken & Y. Trope (Eds.), *Dual-process theories in social psychology* (pp. 161–178). New York: Guilford Press.

Tropp, L. R. (2003). The psychological impact of prejudice: Implications for intergroup contact. *Group Processes and Intergroup Relations, Vol 6*, 131–149.

Tropp, L. R. (2008). The role of trust in intergroup contact: Its significance and implications for improving relations between groups. In U. Wagner, L. R. Tropp, G. Finchilescu, & C. Tredoux (Eds.), *Improving intergroup relations: Building on the legacy of Thomas F. Pettigrew* (pp. 91–106). Malden: Blackwell Publishing.

Tropp, L. R., & Bianchi, R. A. (2007). Interpreting references to group membership in context: Feelings about intergroup contact depending on who says what to whom. *European Journal of Social Psychology, 37*, 153–170.

Tropp, L. R., & Brown, A. C. (2004). What benefits the group can also benefit the individual: Group-enhancing and individual-Enhancing motives for collective action. *Group Processes and Intergroup Relations, 7*, 267–282.

Tropp, L. R., & Wright, S. C. (1999). Ingroup identification and relative deprivation: An examination across multiple social comparisons. *European Journal of Social Psychology, 29*, 707–724.

Trost, M. R., Cialdini, R. B., & Maass, A. (1989). Effects of an international conflict simulation on perceptions of the Soviet Union: A FIREBREAKS backfire. *Journal of Social Issues, 45*(2), 139–158.

Troy, L. C., Szymanski, D. M., & Varadarajan, P. R. (2001). Generating new product ideas: An initial investigation of the role of market information and organizational characteristics. *Journal of the Academy of Marketing Science, 29*, 89–101.

Trubisky, P., Ting Toomey, S., & Lin, S. l. (1991). The influence of individualism/collectivism and self-monitoring on conflict styles. *International Journal of Intercultural Relations, 15*, 65–84.

Tsai, Y. (1993). Social conflict and social cooperation: Simulating "the Tragedy of the Commons." *Simulation and Gaming, 24*, 356–362.

Tschan, F. (2002). Ideal cycles of communication (or cognitions) in triads, dyads, and individuals. *Small Group Research, 33*, 615–643.

Tschan, F., Semmer, N. K., Nägele, C., & Gurtner, A. (2000). Task adaptive behavior and performance in groups. *Group Processes and Intergroup Relations, 3*, 367–386.

Tsuchiya, S., & Tsuchiya, T. (2000). A review of policy exercise interactive learning environments. *Simulation and Gaming, 31*, 509–527.

Tucker, A. L., Edmondson, A. C., & Spear, S. (2002). When problem solving prevents organizational learning. *Journal of Organizational Change Management, 15*, 122–137.

Tudge, C. (2003, 11 August). Why nasty guys rule and nice guys let them. *New Statesman*, 12–19.

Turdaliev, N. (2002). Calibration and Bayesian learning. *Games and Economic Behavior, 41*, 103–119.

Turner, D. A. (1988). A game theory model of student decisions to leave school at 16 plus. *Educational Research, 30*, 65–71.

Turner, D. B. (1992). Negotiator-constituent relationships. In L. L. Putnam & M. E. Roloff (Eds.), *Communication and negotiation* (pp. 233–249), Newbury Park, CA: Sage. [*Sage Annual Reviews of Communication Research*, Vol. 20.]

Turner, J. C. (2000). Social identity. In A. E. Kazdin (Ed.), *Encyclopedia of psychology* (Vol. 7, pp. 341–343). Washington, DC: American Psychological Association, 2000.

Turner, J. C., & Oakes, P. J. (1989). Self-categorization theory and social influence. In P. B. Paulus (Ed.), *Psychology of group influence* (2nd ed., pp. 233–275). Hillsdale, NJ: Lawrence Erlbaum Associates, Inc.

Turner, J. C., & Reynolds, K. J. (2004). The social identity perspective in intergroup relations: Theories, themes, and controversies. In M. B. Brewer & M. Hewstone (Eds.), *Self and social identity* (pp. 259–277). Malden: Blackwell Publishing.

Turner, M. E., & Pratkanis, A. R. (1997). Mitigating groupthink by stimulating constructive conflict. In C. K. W. De Dreu & E. Van de Vliert (Eds.), *Using conflict in organizations* (pp. 53–71). London: Sage Publications, Inc.

Turner, M. E., & Pratkanis, A. R. (1998). A social identity maintenance model of groupthink. *Organizational Behavior and Human Decision Processes, 73*, 210–235.

Turner, M. E., Pratkanis, A. R., Probasco, P., & Leve, C. (1992). Threat, cohesion, and group effectiveness: Testing a social identity maintenance perspective on groupthink. *Journal of Personality and Social Psychology, 63*, 781–796.

Turner, N., Barling, J., Epitropaki, O., Butcher, V., & Milner, C. (2002). Transformational leadership and moral reasoning. *Journal of Applied Psychology, 87*, 304–311.

Turner, N. E. (1998). Doubling vs. constant bets as strategies for gambling. *Journal of Gambling Studies, 14*, 413–429.

Turner, R. (2010). Imagining harmonious intergroup relations. *Psychologist, 23*, 298–301.

Turner, R., & Crisp, R. J. (2010). Imagining intergroup contact reduces implicit prejudice. *British Journal of Social Psychology, 49*, 129–142.

Turner, R. N., Crisp, R. J., & Lambert, E. (2007). Imagining intergroup contact can improve intergroup attitudes. *Group Processes and Intergroup Relations, 10*, 427–441.

Turner, R. N., Hewstone, M., & Voci, A. (2007). Reducing explicit and implicit outgroup prejudice via direct and extended contact: The mediating role of self-disclosure and intergroup anxiety. *Journal of Personality and Social Psychology, 93*, 369–388.

Turniansky, B., & Hare, A. P. 1998. *Individuals and groups in organizations*. London: Sage Publications.

Turnley, W. H., Bolino, M. C., Lester, S. W., & Bloodgood, J. M. (2003). The impact of psychological contract fulfillment on the performance of in-role and organizational citizenship behaviors. *Journal of Management, 29,* 187–206.

Tusing, K. J., & Dillard, J. P. (2000). The psychological reality of the door-in-the-face: It's helping, not bargaining. *Journal of Language and Social Psychology,* 19, 5–25.

Tutzauer, F. (1990). Integrative potential and information exchange as antecedents of joint benefit in negotiation dyads. *International Journal of Conflict Management, 1,* 153–173.

Tutzauer, F. (1992). The communication of offers in dyadic bargaining. In L. L. Putnam & M. E. Roloff (Eds.), *Communication and negotiation* (pp. 67–82). Thousand Oaks, CA: Sage Publications, Inc.

Tutzauer, F. (1993). Toughness in integrative bargaining. *Journal of Communication, 43*(1), 46–62.

Tutzauer, Frank, & Roloff, Michael E. (1988). Communication processes leading to integrative agreements: Three paths to joint benefits. *Communication Research, 15,* 360–380.

Twale, D. J. (1991). Southeast State University: A simulation for higher education administration courses. *Simulation and Gaming, 22,* 490–497.

Tyler, T. R. (1997). The psychology of legitimacy: A relational perspective on voluntary deference to authorities. *Personality and Social Psychology Review, 1,* 323–345.

Tyler, T. R., & Blader, S. L. (2001). Identity and cooperative behavior in groups. *Group Processes and Intergroup Relations, 4,* 207–226.

Tyler, T. R., & Blader, S. L. (2003). The Group Engagement Model: Procedural Justice, Social Identity, and Cooperative Behavior. *Personality and Social Psychology Review, 7,* 349–361.

Tyler, T. R., & Degoey, P. (1995). Collective restraint in social dilemmas: Procedural justice and social identification effects on support for authorities. *Journal of Personality and Social Psychology, 69,* 482–497.

Tyler, T., Degoey, P., & Smith, H. (1996). Understanding why the justice of group procedures matters: A test of the psychological dynamics of the group-value model. *Journal of Personality and Social Psychology, 70,* 913–930.

Tyler, T. R., & Smith, H. J. (1999). Justice, social identity, and group processes. In T. R. Tyler, R. M. Kramer, & O. P. John (Eds.), *The psychology of the social self* (pp. 223–264). Mahwah, NJ: Lawrence Erlbaum Associates Publishers.

Tyre, M. J., & von Hippel, E. (1997). The situated nature of adaptive learning in organizations. *Organization Science, 8,* 71–83.

Tyson, G. A., Schlachter, A., & Cooper, S. (1988). Game playing strategy as an indicator of racial prejudice among South African students. *Journal of Social Psychology, 128,* 473–485.

Uleman, J. S., Rhee, E., Bardoliwalla, N., Semin, G., & Toyama, M. (2000). The relational self: Closeness to ingroups depends on who they are, culture, and the type of closeness. *Asian Journal of Social Psychology, 3,* 1–17.

Urada, D. I., & Miller, N. (2000). The impact of positive mood and category importance on crossed categorization effects. *Journal of Personality and Social Psychology, 78,* 417–433.

Urada, D., Stenstrom, D. M., & Miller, N. (2007). Crossed categorization beyond the two-group model. *Journal of Personality and Social Psychology, 92,* 649–664.

Vaccaro, J. P., & Coward, D. W. F. (1993). Selling and sales management in action: Managerial and legal implications of price haggling: A sales manager's dilemma. *Journal of Personal Selling and Sales Management, 13*(3), 79–86.

Vaes, J., Paladino, M. P., Castelli, L., Leyens, J.-P., & Giovanazzi, A. (2003). On the Behavioral Consequences of Infrahumanization: The Implicit Role of Uniquely Human Emotions in Intergroup Relations. *Journal of Personality and Social Psychology, 85,* 1016–1034.

Vaes, J., & Wicklund, R. A. (2002). General threat leading to defensive reactions: A field experiment on linguistic features. *British Journal of Social Psychology, 41,* 271–280.

Valacich, J. S., Paranka, D., George, J. F., & Nunamaker, J. F. (1993). Communication concurrency and the new media: A new dimension for media richness. *Communication Research, 20,* 249–276.

Valenciano, F., & Zarzuelo, J. M. (1997). On Nash's hidden assumption. *Games and Economic Behavior, 21,* 266–281.

Valley, K., Thompson, L., Gibbons, R., & Bazerman, M. H. (2002). How communication improves efficiency in bargaining games. *Games and Economic Behavior, 38*, 127–155.

Van Aken, E. M., Monetta, D. J., & Sink, D. S. (1994). Affinity groups: The missing link in employee involvement. *Organizational Dynamics, 22*(4), 38–54.

Van Assen, M., & Snijders, C. (2004). Effects of risk preferences in social dilemmas: A game-theoretical analysis and evidence from two experiments. In R. Suleiman, D. V. Budescu, I. Fischer, & D. M. Messick (Eds.), *Contemporary psychological research on social dilemmas* (pp. 24–57). New York: Cambridge University Press.

Van Avermaet, E., Buelens, H., Vanbeselaere, N., & Van Vaerenbergh, G. (1999). Intragroup social influence processes in intergroup behavior. *European Journal of Social Psychology, 29*, 815–823.

Van Avermaet, E., & Van Nieuwkerke, S. (1989). Bijdragen of niet bijdragen tot een gemeenschappelijk goed: de rol van hebzucht en vrees nader onderzocht [To contribute or not contribute to a common good: The role of greed and fear of being cheated]. *Nederlands Tijdschrift voor de Psychologie en haar Grensgebieden, 44*, 217–224.

Van Bavel, J. J., & Cunningham, W. A. (2009). Self-categorization with a novel mixed-race group moderates automatic social and racial biases. *Personality and Social Psychology Bulletin, 35*, 321–335.

Van Beest, I., Van Dijk, E., & Wilke, H. (2004a). The interplay of self-interest and equity in coalition formation. *European Journal of Social Psychology, 34*, 547–565.

Van Beest, I., Van Dijk, E., & Wilke, H. (2004b). Resources and alternatives in coalition formation: The effects on payoff, self-serving behaviour, and bargaining length. *European Journal of Social Psychology, 34*, 713–728.

Van Beest, I., Wilke, H., & Van Dijk, E. (2003). The excluded player in coalition formation. *Personality and Social Psychology Bulletin, 29*, 237–247.

Van Boven, L., Gilovich, T., & Medvec, V. H. (2003). The illusion of transparency in negotiations. *Negotiation Journal, 19*, 117–131.

Van Buskirk, W., & McGrath, D. (1993). The culture focused T-group: Laboratory learning from the interpretive perspective. *Public Administration Quarterly, 17*, 316–338.

Van Cayseele, P., & Furth, D. (1996). Bertrand-Edgeworth duopoly with buyouts or first refusal contracts. *Games and Economic Behavior, 16*, 153–180.

Van Damme, E., & Hurkens, S. (1996). Commitment robust equilibria and endogenous timing. *Games and Economic Behavior, 15*, 290–311.

Van de Vliert, E. (1992). Questions about the strategic choice model of mediation. *Negotiation Journal, 8*, 379–386.

van de Vliert, E., & Euwema, M. C. (1994). Agreeableness and activeness as components of conflict behaviors. *Journal of Personality and Social Psychology, 66*, 674–687.

Van Der Krogt, F. J. (1998). Learning network theory: The tension between learning systems and work systems in organizations. *Human Resource Development Quarterly, 9*, 157–177.

Van Der Zee, K., & Paulus, P. (2008). Social psychology and modern organizations: Balancing between innovativeness and comfort. In L. Steg, A. P. Buunk, & T. Rothengatter (Eds.), *Applied social psychology: Understanding and managing social problems* (pp. 271–290). New York: Cambridge University Press.

Van Dijk, E., De Cremer, D., & Handgraaf, M. J. J. (2004). Social value orientations and the strategic use of fairness in ultimatum bargaining. *Journal of Experimental Social Psychology, 40*, 697–707.

Van Dijk, E., & Grodzka, M. (1992). The influence of endowments asymmetry and information level on the contribution to a public step good. *Journal of Economic Psychology, 13*, 329–342.

Van Dijk, E., & Van Knippenberg, D. (1996). Buying and selling exchange goods: Loss aversion and the endowment effect. *Journal of Economic Psychology, 17*, 517–524.

Van Dijk, E., & Van Knippenberg, D. (1998). Trading wine: On the endowment effect, loss aversion, and the comparability of consumer goods. *Journal of Economic Psychology, 19*, 485–495.

Van Dijk, E., & Wilke, H. A. (1993). Differential interests, equity, and public good provision. *Journal of Experimental Social Psychology, 29*, 1–16.

Van Dyne, L., & Saavedra, R. (1996). A naturalistic minority influence experiment: Effects of divergent thinking, conflict and originality in work-groups. *British Journal of Social Psychology, 35,* 151–167.

van Eck, R., & Dempsey, J. (2002). The Effect of Competition and Contextualized Advisement on the Transfer of Mathematics Skills in a Computer-Based Instructional Simulation Game. *Educational Technology Research and Development, 50*(3), 23–41.

Van Gastel, M. A., & Paelinck, J. H. (1992). Generalization of solution concepts in conflict and negotiation analysis. *Theory and Decision, 32,* 65–76.

Van Ginkel, W. P., & Van Knippenberg, D. (2009). Knowledge about the distribution of information and group decision making: When and why does it work? *Organizational Behavior and Human Decision Processes, 108,* 218–229.

Van Huyck, J. B., Battalio, R. C., & Walters, M. F. (1995). Commitment versus discretion in the peasant-dictator game. *Games and Economic Behavior, 10,* 143–170.

Van Knippenberg, A., & Ellemers, N. (1993). Strategies in intergroup relations. In M. A. Hogg & D. Abrams (Eds.), *Group motivation: Social psychological perspectives* (pp. 17–32). London: Harvester Wheatsheaf.

Van Knippenberg, D. (2000). Group norms, prototypicality, and persuasion. In D. J. Terry & M. A. Hogg (Eds.), *Attitudes, behavior, and social context: The role of norms and group membership* (pp. 157–170). Mahwah, NJ: Lawrence Erlbaum Associates Publishers.

Van Knippenberg, D., & Wilke, H. (1992). Prototypicality of arguments and conformity to ingroup norms. *European Journal of Social Psychology, 22,* 141–155.

Van Laar, C., Levin, S., & Sidanius, J. (2008). Ingroup and outgroup contact: A longitudinal study of the effects of cross-ethnic friendships, dates, roommate relationships and participation in segregated organizations. In U. Wagner, L. R. Tropp, G. Finchilescu, & C. Tredoux (Eds.), *Improving intergroup relations: Building on the legacy of Thomas F. Pettigrew* (pp. 127–142). Malden: Blackwell Publishing.

Van Lange, P. A. M. (2000). Cooperation and competition. In A. E. Kazdin (Ed.), *Encyclopedia of psychology* (Vol. 2, pp. 296–300). Washington, DC: American Psychological Association, 2000.

Van Lange, P. A. M., Bekkers, R., Schuyt, T. N. M., & Van Vugt, M. (2007). From games to giving: Social value orientation predicts donations to noble causes. *Basic and Applied Social Psychology, 29,* 375–384.

Van Lange, P. A. M., & Kuhlman, D. M. (1990). Expected cooperation in social dilemmas: The influence of own social value orientation and other's personality characteristics. In P. J. D. Drenth, J. A. Sergeant, & R. J. Takens (Eds.), *European perspectives in psychology, Vol. 3: Work and organizational, social and economic, cross-cultural* (pp. 239–250). Chichester, England: John Wiley & Sons.

Van Lange, P. A., & Liebrand, W. B. (1989). On perceiving morality and potency: Social values and the effects of person perception in a give-some dilemma. *European Journal of Personality, 3,* 2Causal attribution of choice behavior 09–225.

Van Lange, P. A., Liebrand, W. B., & Kuhlman, D. M. (1990). Causal attribution of choice behavior in three N-Person Prisoner's Dilemmas. *Journal of Experimental Social Psychology, 26,* 34–48.

Van Lange, P. A. M., & Semin-Goossens, A. (1998). The boundaries of reciprocal cooperation. *European Journal of Social Psychology, 28,* 847–854.

Van Leeuwen, E., Van Knippenberg, D. (2002). How a group goal may reduce social matching in group performance: Shifts in standards for determining a fair contribution of effort. *Journal of Social Psychology, 142,* 73–86.

Van Leeuwen, E., & Van Knippenberg, D., & Ellemers, N. (2003). Continuing and changing group identities: The effects of merging on social identification and ingroup bias. *Personality and Social Psychology Bulletin, 29,* 679–690.

Van Oudenhoven, J. P., Mechelse, L., & De Dreu, C. K. W. (1998). Managerial conflict management in five European countries: The importance of power distance, uncertainty avoidance, and masculinity. *Applied Psychology: An International Review, 47,* 439–455.

Van Prooijen, J.-W., & Lam, J. (2007). Retributive justice and social categorization: The perceived fairness of punishment depends on intergroup status. *European Journal of Social Psychology, 37*, 1244–1255.

Van Schaik, C. P., Pandit, S. A., & Vogel, E. R. (2004). A model for within-group coalitionary aggression among males. *Behavioral Ecology and Sociobiology, 57*, 101–109.

Van Schie, E. C. M., & Van der Pligt, J. (1995). Influencing risk preference in decision making: The effects of framing and salience. *Organizational Behavior and Human Decision Processes, 63*, 264–275.

Van Twuyver, M., & Van Knippenberg, A. (1998). Effects of group membership and identification on categorization and subtyping in memory. *European Journal of Social Psychology, 28*, 531–553.

Van Vianen, A. E. M., & Fischer, A. H. (2002). Illuminating the glass ceiling: The role of organizational culture preferences. *Journal of Occupational and Organizational Psychology, 75*, 315–337.

Van Vianen, A. E. M., & Kmieciak, Y. M. (1998). The match between recruiters' perceptions of organizational climate and personality of the ideal applicant for a management position. *International Journal of Selection and Assessment, 6*, 153–163.

Van Vugt, M., & De Cremer, D. (1999). Leadership in social dilemmas: The effects of group identification on collective actions to provide public goods. *Journal of Personality and Social Psychology, 76*, 587–599.

Van Vugt, M., & De C. (2002). Leader endorsement in social dilemmas: Comparing the instrumental and relational perspectives. In W. Stroebe & M. Hewstone (Eds.), *European review of social psychology* (Vol. 13, pp. 155–184). Hove, England: Psychology Press/Taylor & Francis (UK), 2002.

Van Vugt, M., De Cremer, D., & Janssen, D. P. (2007). Gender differences in cooperation and competition: The male-warrior hypothesis. *Psychological Science, 18*, 19–23.

Van Vugt, M., & Hart, C. M. (2004). Social identity as social glue: The origins of group loyalty. *Journal of Personality and Social Psychology, 86*, 585–598.

Van Zomeren, M., Fischer, A. H., & Spears, R. (2007). Testing the limits of tolerance: How intergroup anxiety amplifies negative and offensive responses to out-group-initiated contact. *Personality and Social Psychology Bulletin, 33*, 1686–1699.

Vanbeselaere, N. (1988). Reducing intergroup discrimination by manipulating ingroup/outgroup homogeneity and by individuating ingroup and outgroup members. *Communication and Cognition, 21*, 191–198.

Vanbeselaere, N. (1996). The impact of differentially valued overlapping categorizations upon the differentiation between positively, negatively, and neutrally evaluated social groups. *European Journal of Social Psychology, 26*, 75–96.

Vanbeselaere, N. (2000). The treatment of relevant and irrelevant outgroups in minimal group situations with crossed categorizations. *Journal of Social Psychology, 140*, 515–526.

Vanbeselaere, N., Boen, F., & Smeesters, D. (2003). Tokenism also works with groups as tokens, The impact of group openness and group qualification on reactions to membership in a low-status group. *Group Dynamics, 7*, 104–121.

Vandenberghe, C., Bentein, K., & Stinglhamber, F. (2004). Affective commitment to the organization, supervisor, and work group: Antecedents and outcomes. *Journal of Vocational Behavior, Vol 64*, 47–71.

Vanderschraaf, P., & Richards, D. (1997). Joint beliefs in conflictual coordination games. *Theory and Decision, 42*, 287–310.

Vanderslice, V. J. (1995). Cooperation within a competitive context: Lessons from worker cooperatives. In B. B. Bunker & J. Z. Rubin (Eds.), *Conflict, cooperation, and justice: Essays inspired by the work of Morton Deutsch* (pp. 175–204), San Francisco: Jossey-Bass.

Vannetelbosch, V. J. (1999). Alternating-offer bargaining and common knowledge of rationality. *Theory and Decision, 47*, 111–137.

Vassileva, J., Breban, S., & Horsch, M. (2002). Agent reasoning mechanism for long-term coalitions based on decision making and trust. *Computational Intelligence, 18*, 583–595.

Veenema, H. C., Das, M., & Aureli, F. (1994). Methodological improvements for the study of reconciliation. *Behavioural Processes, 31*, 29–37.

Veríssimo, M., Monteiro, L., Vaughn, B. E., & Santos, A. (2003). Qualidade da vinculaçao e desenvolvimento sócio-cognitivo [Quality of bonding and sociocognitive development]. *Análise Psicológica, 21*, 419–430.

Verkuyten, M. (1997). Intergroup evaluation and self-esteem motivations: Self-enhancement and self-protection. *European Journal of Social Psychology, 27*, 115–119.

Verkuyten, M. (2001). National identification and intergroup evaluations in Dutch children. *British Journal of Developmental Psychology, 19*, 559–571.

Verkuyten, M. (2007). Religious group identification and inter-religious relations: A study among Turkish-Dutch Muslims. *Group Processes and Intergroup Relations, 10*, 341–357.

Verkuyten, M., & Hagendoorn, L. (2002). In-group favoritism and self-esteem: The role of identity level and trait valence. *Group Processes and Intergroup Relations, 5*, 285–297.

Verkuyten, M., & Kwa, G. A. (1996). Ethnic self-identification, ethnic involvement, and group differentiation among Chinese youth in the Netherlands. *Journal of Social Psychology, 136*, 35–48.

Verkuyten, M., & Reijerse, A. (2008). Intergroup structure and identity management among ethnic minority and majority groups: The interactive effects of perceived stability, legitimacy, and permeability. *European Journal of Social Psychology, 38*, 106–127.

Verkuyten, M., & Yildiz, A. A. (2007). National (dis)identification and ethnic and religious identity: A study among Turkish-Dutch Muslims. *Personality and Social Psychology Bulletin, 33*, 1448–1462.

Verschuren, P., & Arts, B. (2004). Quantifying influence in complex decision making by means of paired comparisons. *Quality and Quantity: International Journal of Methodology, 38*, 495–516.

Vervaecke, H., De Vries, H., & Van Elsacker, L. (2000). Function and distribution of coalitions in captive bonobos (Pan paniscus). *Primates, 41*, 249–265.

Vescio, T. K., Hewstone, M., Crisp, R. J., & Rubin, J. M. (1999). Perceiving and responding to multiple categorizable individuals: Cognitive processes and affective intergroup bias. In M. A. Hogg & D. Abrams (Eds.), *Social identity and social cognition* (pp. 111–140). Malden, MA: Blackwell Publishers.

Vescio, T. K., Judd, C. M., & Kwan, V. S. Y. (2004). The crossed-categorization hypothesis: Evidence of reductions in the strength of categorization, but not intergroup bias. *Journal of Experimental Social Psychology, 40*, 478–496.

Vey, M. A., & Campbell, J. P. (2004). In-role or extra-role organizational citizenship behavior: Which are we measuring? *Human Performance, 17*, 119–135.

Vidal, J. M. (2004). The effects of co-operation on multiagent search in task-oriented domains. *Journal of Experimental and Theoretical Artificial Intelligence, 16*, 5–18.

Vieth, M. (2003). Die Evolution von Fairnessnormen im Ultimatumspiel: Eine spieltheoretische Modellierung [The Evolution of Norms of Fairness in the Ultimatum Game: A Game Theoretical Model]. *Zeitschrift für Soziologie, 32*, 346–367.

Vignoles, V. L., & Moncaster, N. J. (2007). Identity motives and in-group favouritism: A new approach to individual differences in intergroup discrimination. *British Journal of Social Psychology, 46*, 91–113.

Vinokur-Kaplan, D. (1995). Treatment teams that work (and those that don't): An application of Hackman's group effectiveness model to interdisciplinary teams in psychiatric hospitals. *Journal of Applied Behavioral Science, 31*, 303–327.

Visher, E. B., & Visher, J. S. (1989). Parenting coalitions after remarriage: Dynamics and therapeutic guidelines. *Family Relations, 38*, 65–70.

Viswesvaran, C., & Deshpande, S. P. (1995). Assessing the social determinants of negotiator preferences: The case of a collective bargaining simulation. *Journal of Psychology: Interdisciplinary and Applied, 129*, 249–259.

Vitell, S. J., & Paolillo, J. G. P. (2004). A cross-cultural study of the antecedents of the perceived role of ethics and social responsibility. *Business Ethics: A European Review, 13*, 185–199.

Vivian, J. E., & Berkowitz, N. H. (1992). Anticipated bias from an outgroup: An attributional analysis. *European Journal of Social Psychology, 22*, 415–424.

Voci, A., & Hewstone, M. (2002). Contatto intergruppi in ambito lavorativeo e riduzione del pregiudizio: Effetti di mediazione e moderazione [Intergroup contact at work and prejudice reduction: Mediational and moderational effects]. *Testing Psicometria Metodologia, 9*(1–2), 5–15.

Voci, A., & Hewstone, M. (2003). Intergroup contact and prejudice toward immigrants in Italy: The mediational role of anxiety and the moderational role of group salience. *Group Processes and Intergroup Relations, 6*, 37–52.

Vogelzang, L. N., Euwema, M. C., & Nauta, A. (1997). You, we, and I: Relationships between verbal expressions of communality and dyadic conflict behavior. *Journal of Language and Social Psychology, 16*, 456–463.

Volij, O., & Winter, E. (2002). On risk aversion and bargaining outcomes. *Games and Economic Behavior, 41*, 120–140.

Vollhardt, J. K., & Bilali, R. (2008). Social psychology's contribution to the psychological study of peace: A review. *Social Psychology, 39*, 12–25.

von Hippel, W., Sekaquaptewa, D., & Vargas, P. (1997). The linguistic intergroup bias as an implicit indicator of prejudice. *Journal of Experimental Social Psychology, 33*, 490–509.

Vonk, R. (1999). Effects of outcome dependency on correspondence bias. *Personality and Social Psychology Bulletin, 25*, 382–389.

Vonofakou, C., Hewstone, M., & Voci, A. (2007). Contact with out-group friends as a predictor of meta-attitudinal strength and accessibility of attitudes toward gay men. *Journal of Personality and Social Psychology, 92*, 804–820.

Vorauer, J. D., & Claude, S. D. (1998). Perceived versus actual transparency of goals in negotiation. *Personality and Social Psychology Bulletin, 24*, 371–385.

Vorauer, J. D., Gagnon, A., & Sasaki, S. J. (2009). Salient intergroup ideology and intergroup interaction. *Psychological Science, 20*, 838–845.

Vorauer, J. D., Martens, V., & Sasaki, S. J. (2009). When trying to understand detracts from trying to behave: Effects of perspective taking in intergroup interaction. *Journal of Personality and Social Psychology, 96*, 811–827.

Vorauer, J. D., & Sasaki, S. J. (2009). Helpful only in the abstract? Ironic effects of empathy in intergroup interaction. *Psychological Science, 20*, 191–197.

Vrugt, A., & Kraan, H. (1996). Vooroordeel op het voetbalveld: vertekende intergroepsattributies bij Surinaamse en blanke voetballers [Prejudice in the football field: Intergroup attributional bias in Surinamese and White football players]. *Nederlands Tijdschrift voor de Psychologie en haar Grensgebieden, 51*, 192–198.

Wade-Benzoni, K. A. (2002). A golden rule over time: Reciprocity in intergenerational allocation decisions. *Academy of Management Journal, 45*, 1011–1028.

Wageman, R. (1995a). Interdependence and group effectiveness. *Administrative Science Quarterly, 40*, 145–180.

Wageman, Ruth. (1995b). "Interdependence and group effectiveness": Erratum. *Administrative Science Quarterly, 40*, 367.

Wageman, R. (2001). How leaders foster self-managing team effectiveness: Design choices versus hands-on coaching. *Organization Science, 12*, 559–577.

Wagner, J. D., Flinn, M. V., & England, B. G. (2002). Hormonal response to competition among male coalitions. *Evolution and Human Behavior, 23*, 437–442.

Wagner, U., Christ, O., Pettigrew, T. F., Stellmacher, J., & Wolf, C. (2006). Prejudice And Minority Proportion: Contact Instead of Threat Effects. *Social Psychology Quarterly, 69*, 380–390.

Wagner, U., Tropp, L. R., Finchilescu, G., & Tredoux, C. (Eds.). (2008). *Improving intergroup relations: Building on the legacy of Thomas F. Pettigrew*. Malden, MA: Blackwell Publishing.

Wagner, U., van Dick, R., Pettigrew, T. F., & Christ, O. (2003). Ethnic prejudice in East and West Germany: The explanatory power of intergroup contact. *Group Processes and Intergroup Relations, 6*, 22–36.

Wagner, U., & Ward, P. L. (1993). Variation of out-group presence and evaluation of the in-group. *British Journal of Social Psychology, 32*, 241–251.

Wagner, U., & Zick, A. (1990). Psychologie der Intergruppenbeziehungen: Der "Social Identity Approach." [The psychology of intergroup relationships: The social identity approach]. *Gruppendynamik, 21*, 319–330.

Wagstaff, G. F., & Perfect, T. (1992). On the definition of perfect equity and the prediction of inequity. *British Journal of Social Psychology, 31*, 69–77.

Waldzus, S., Mummendey, A., Wenzel, M., & Weber, U. (2003). Towards tolerance: Representations of superordinate categories and perceived ingroup prototypicality. *Journal of Experimental Social Psychology, 39*, 31–47.

Walker, I., & Smith, H. J. (Eds.). (2002). *Relative deprivation: Specification, development, and integration*. New York: Cambridge University Press.

Wall, J. A., Jr. (1990). Mediation in the People's Republic of China. In M. A. Rahim (Ed.), *Theory and research in conflict management* (pp. 109–119). New York: Praeger Publishers.

Wall, J. A., Jr. (1991). Impression management in negotiations. In R. A. Giacalone & P. Rosenfeld (Eds.), *Applied impression management: How image-making affects managerial decisions* (pp. 133–156). Newbury Park, CA: Sage Publications, Inc.

Wall, J. A., & Blum, M. W. (1991). Negotiations. *Journal of Management, 17*, 273–303.

Wallach, T. (2006). conflict transformation: A group relations perspective. In M. Fitzduff & C. Stout (Eds.), *The psychology of resolving global conflicts: From war to peace (Vol. 1): Nature vs. nurture* (pp. 285–305). Westport, CT: Praeger Security International, 2006.

Waller, M. J., Giambatista, R. C., & Zellmer-Bruhn, M. E. (1999). The effects of individual time urgency on group polychronicity. *Journal of Managerial Psychology, 14*, 244–256.

Waller, M. J., Zellmer-Bruhn, M. E., & Giambatista, R. C. (2002). Watching the clock: Group pacing behavior under dynamic deadlines. *Academy of Management Journal, 45*, 1046–1055.

Walliban, J. (2003). Reverse bargaining: Some oddities that illustrate the "rules." *Negotiation Journal, 19*, 207–214.

Walther, J. B. (1997). Group and interpersonal effects in international computer-mediated collaboration. *Human Communication Research, 23*, 342–369.

Wang, S. H.-Y., & Chang, H.-C. (1999). Chinese professionals' perceptions of interpersonal communication in corporate America: A multidimensional scaling analysis. *Howard Journal of Communications, 10*, 297–315.

Washbush, J., & Gosen, J. (2001). An exploration of game-derived learning in total enterprise simulations. *Simulation and Gaming, 32*, 281–296.

Waskul, D. D. (2003). *Self-games and body-play: Personhood in online chat and cybersex*. New York: Peter Lang Publishing.

Watanabe, J. M., & Smuts, B. B. (2004). Cooperation, commitment, and communication in the evolution of human sociality. In R. W. Sussman & A. R. Chapman (Eds.), *The origins and nature of sociality* (pp. 288–309). Hawthorne, NY: Aldine de Gruyter.

Watkins, M., & Rosegrant, S. (1996). Sources of power in coalition building. *Negotiation Journal, 12*, 47–68.

Watson, C. (1994). Gender versus power as a predictor of negotiation behavior and outcomes. *Negotiation Journal, 10*, 117–127.

Watson, J. (1996). Reputation in repeated games with no discounting. *Games and Economic Behavior, 15*, 82–109.

Watson, W. E., & Michaelsen, L. K. (1988). Group interaction behaviors that affect group performance on an intellective task. *Group and Organization Studies, 13*, 495–516.

Watson, W. E., Johnson, L., Kumar, K., & Critelli, J. (1998). Process gain and process loss: Comparing interpersonal processes and performance of culturally diverse and non-diverse teams across time. *International Journal of Intercultural Relations, 22*, 409–430.

Watson, W. E., Johnson, L., & Merritt, D. (1998). Team orientation, self-orientation, and diversity in task groups: Their connection to team performance over time. *Group and Organization Management, 23*, 161–188.

Watson, W. E., Johnson, L., & Zgourides, G. D. (2002). The influence of ethnic diversity on leadership, group process, and performance: An examination of learning teams. *International Journal of Intercultural Relations, 26*, 1–16.

Waung, M., & Brice, T. S. (1998). The effects of conscientiousness and opportunity to caucus on group performance. *Small Group Research, 29*, 624–634.

Wayne, S. J., & Rubinstein, D. (1992). Extending game theoretic propositions about slack and scarcity in managerial decision making. *Human Relations, 45*, 525–536.

Weaver, G. R., & Conlon, D. E. (2003). Explaining façades of choice: Timing, justice effects, and behavioral outcomes. *Journal of Applied Social Psychology, 33*, 2217–2243.

Weaver, J. L., Bowers, C. A., Salas, E., & Cannon Bowers, Janis A. (1997). Motivation in teams. In M. M. Beyerlein, D. A. Johnson, & S. T. Beyerlein (Eds.), *Advances in interdisciplinary studies of work teams* (Vol. 4, pp. 167–191). Greenwich, CT: Jai Press, Inc.

Weber, U., Mummendey, A., & Waldzus, S. (2002). Perceived legitimacy of intergroup status differences: Its prediction by relative ingroup protypicality. *European Journal of Social Psychology, 32*, 449–470.

Weenig, M. W. H., Van Der Salm, C. A., & Wilke, H. A. M. (2004). The relationship between perceived in-group variability, number of contacts, and identification. *Journal of Applied Social Psychology, 34*, 872–886.

Weesie, J. (1994). Incomplete information and timing in the volunteer's dilemma: A comparison of four models. *Journal of Conflict Resolution, 38*, 557–585.

Weesie, J., & Franzen, A. (1998). Cost sharing in a volunteer's dilemma. *Journal of Conflict Resolution, 42*, 600–618.

Weg, E., & Smith, V. (1993). On the failure to induce meager offers in ultimatum games. *Journal of Economic Psychology, 14*, 17–32.

Weg, E., & Zwick, R. (1999). Infinite horizon bargaining games: Theory and experiments. In D. V. Budescu, I. Erev, & R. Zwick (Eds.), *Games and human behavior: Essays in honor of Amnon Rapoport* (pp. 259–296). Mahwah, NJ: Lawrence Erlbaum Associates Publishers.

Weg, E., Zwick, R., & Rapoport, A. (1996). Bargaining in uncertain environments: A systematic distortion of perfect equilibrium demands. *Games and Economic Behavior, 14*, 260–286.

Weigelt, K., Dukerich, J., & Schotter, A. (1989). Reactions to discrimination in an incentive pay compensation scheme: A game-theoretic approach. *Organizational Behavior and Human Decision Processes, 44*, 26–44.

Weiloch, N. (2002). Collective mobilization and identity from the underground: The deployment of "oppositional capital" in the harm reduction movement. *Sociological Quarterly, 43*, 45–72.

Weinberger, C. J. (2000). Selective acceptance and inefficiency in a two-issue complete information bargaining game. *Games and Economic Behavior, 31*, 262–293.

Weiner, B. (1996). Searching for order in social motivation. *Psychological Inquiry, 7*, 199–216.

Weingart, L. R. (1992). Impact of group goals, task component complexity, effort, and planning on group performance. *Journal of Applied Psychology, 77*, 682–693.

Weingart, L. R., Bennett, R. J., & Brett, J. M. (1993). The impact of consideration of issues and motivational orientation on group negotiation process and outcome. *Journal of Applied Psychology, 78*, 504–517.

Weingart, L. R., & Weldon, E. (1991). Processes that mediate the relationship between a group goal and group member performance. *Human Performance, 4*, 33–54.

Weisinger, J. Y., & Salipante, P. F. (1995). Toward a method of exposing hidden assumptions in multicultural conflict. *International Journal of Conflict Management, 6*, 147–170.

Weiss, B. P. (1996). A public health approach to violence prevention: The Los Angeles coalition. In R. L. Hampton, P. Jenkins, & T. P. Gullotta (Eds.), *Preventing violence in America* (pp. 197–208). Thousand Oaks, CA: Sage Publications, Inc.

Weitzman, E. A., & Weitzman, P. F. (2006). The PSDM model: Integrating problem solving and decision making in conflict resolution. In M. Deutsch, P. T. Coleman, & E. C. Marcus (Eds.), *The handbook of conflict resolution: Theory and practice* (2nd ed., pp. 197–222). Hoboken, NJ: Wiley Publishing.

Welbourne, T. M., & Cable, D. M. (1995). Group incentives and pay satisfaction: Understanding the relationship through an identity theory perspective. *Human Relations, 48*, 711–726.

Weldon, E. (2000). The development of product and process improvements in work groups. *Group and Organization Management, 25*, 244–268.

Weldon, E., & Weingart, L. R. (1993). Group goals and group performance. *British Journal of Social Psychology, 32*, 307–334.

Weldon, E., & Yun, S. (2000). The effects of proximal and distal goals on goal level, strategy development, and group performance. *Journal of Applied Behavioral Science, 36*, 336–344.

Wellen, J. M., Hogg, M. A., & Terry, D. J. (1998). Group norms and attitude-behavior consistency: The role of group salience and mood. *Group Dynamics, 2*, 48–56.

Wellington, W. J., & Faria, A. J. (1996). Team cohesion, player attitude, and performance expectations in simulation. *Simulation and Games, 27*, 23–40.

Wells, C. V., & Kipnis, D. (2001). Trust, dependency, and control in the contemporary organization. *Journal of Business and Psychology, 15*, 593–603.

Weltz, D. (2003). Call me antipsychiatry activist—not "consumer." *Ethical Human Sciences and Services, 5*, 71–72.

Wenzel, M., Mummendey, A., Weber, U., & Waldzus, S. (2003). The ingroup as pars pro toto : Projection from the ingroup onto the inclusive category as a precursor to social discrimination. *Personality and Social Psychology Bulletin, 29*, 461–473.

Werner, J. M., & Lester, S. W. (2001). Applying a team effectiveness framework to the performance of student case teams. *Human Resource Development Quarterly, 12*, 385–402.

Werner, S. (1999). Choosing demands strategically: The distribution of power, the distribution of benefits, and the risk of conflict. *Journal of Conflict Resolution, 43*, 705–726.

Werth, J. L., & Lord, C. G. (1992). Previous conceptions of the typical group member and the contact hypothesis. *Basic and Applied Social Psychology, 13*, 351–369.

Wesenberg, P. (1994). Bridging the individual-social divide: A new perspective for understanding and stimulating creativity in organizations. *Journal of Creative Behavior, 28*, 177–192.

West, M. A. (1990). The social psychology of innovation in groups. In M. A. West & J. L. Farr (Eds.), *Innovation and creativity at work: Psychological and organizational strategies* (pp. 309–333). Chichester, England: John Wiley & Sons.

West, M. A. (2008). Effective teams in organizations. In N. Chmiel (Ed.), *An introduction to work and organizational psychology: A European perspective* (2nd ed., pp. 305–328). Malden: Blackwell Publishing.

West, M. A., & Wallace, M. (1991). Innovation in health care teams. *European Journal of Social Psychology, 21*, 303–315.

West, R. L., Lebiere, C., & Sun, R. (2001). Simple games as dynamic, coupled systems: Randomness and other emergent properties. *Cognitive Systems Research, 1*, 221–239.

Westen, D. (1991). Social cognition and object relations. *Psychological Bulletin, 109*, 429–455.

Westerberg, K., & Armelius, K. (2000). Municipal middle managers: Psychosocial work environment in a gender-based division of labor. *Scandinavian Journal of Management, 16*, 189–208.

Westermark, A. (2003). Bargaining, binding contracts, and competitive wages. *Games and Economic Behavior, 43*, 296–311.

Westphal, J. D., & Khanna, P. (2003). Keeping directors in line: Social distancing as a control mechanism in the corporate elite. *Administrative Science Quarterly, 48*, 361–398.

Wetherell, M. (1996a). Group conflict and the social psychology of racism. In M. Wetherell (Ed.), *Identities, groups and social issues* (pp. 175–238). Milton Keynes, England: Open University Press; London: Sage Publications, Inc.

Wetherell, M. (Ed.). (1996b). *Identities, groups and social issues*. Milton Keynes, England: Open University Press; London: Sage Publications, Inc.

Wheatley, W. J., Hornaday, R. W., & Hunt, T. G. (1988). Developing strategic management goal-setting skills. *Simulation and Games, 19*, 173–185.

Wheeler, M. (2004). Anxious moments: Openings in negotiation. *Negotiation Journal, 20*, 153–169.

Whisman, M. A., & Allan, L. E. (1996). Attachment and social cognition theories of romantic relationships: Convergent or complementary perspectives? *Journal of Social and Personal Relationships, 13*, 263–278.

White, H. C. (1992). *Identity and control: A structural theory of social action*. Princeton, NJ: Princeton University Press.

White, K., & Watkins, S. C. (2000). Accuracy, stability and reciprocity in informal conversational networks in rural Kenya. *Social Networks, 22,* 337–355.

White, Ralph K., & Lippitt, R. O. (1960). *Autocracy and democracy: An experimental inquiry.* Oxford, England: Harper.

White, Robert W. (2001). Social and role identities and political violence: Identity as a window on violence in Northern Ireland. In R. D. Ashmore, L. Jussim, & D. Wilder (Eds.), *Social identity, intergroup conflict, and conflict reduction* (pp. 133–158). New York: Oxford University Press.

White, S. B. (1994). Testing an economic approach to resource dilemmas. *Organizational Behavior and Human Decision Processes, 58,* 428–456.

Whitehead, R., Butz, J. W., Vaughn, R. E., & Kozar, B. (1996). Implications of Gray's three factor arousal theory for the practice of basketball free-throw shooting. *Journal of Sport Behavior, 19,* 354–364.

Whiteley, T. R., & Faria, A. J. (1989). A study of the relationship between student final exam performance and simulation game participation. *Simulation and Games, 20,* 44–64.

Whitener, E. M. (2001). Do "high commitment" human resource practices affect employee commitment? A cross-level analysis using hierarchical linear modeling. *Journal of Management, 27,* 515–535.

Whitmeyer, J. M. (2004). The group control catastrophe. *Sociological Perspectives, 47,* 109–129.

Whitney, K. (1994). Improving group task performance: The role of group goals and group efficacy. *Human Performance, 7,* 55–78.

Widmeyer, W. N., Brawley, L. R., & Carron, A. V. (1985). *The measurement of cohesion in sport teams: The Group Environment Questionnaire.* London, Ontario, Canada: Sports Dynamics.

Widmeyer, W. Neil, & Ducharme, K. (1997). Team building through team goal setting. *Journal of Applied Sport Psychology. 9,* 97–113.

Wiersema, M. F, & Bantel, K. A. (1992). Top management team demography and corporate strategic change. *Academy of Management Journal, 35,* 91–121.

Wiesenfeld, E. (1997). From individual need to community consciousness: The dialectics between land appropriation and eviction threat. (A case study of a Venezuelan "barrio." *Environment and Behavior, 29,* 198–212.

Wigboldus, D., Spears, R., & Semin, G. (1999). Categorization, content and the context of communicative behaviour. In N. Ellemers, R. Spears, & B. Doosje (Eds.), *Social identity: Context, commitment, content* (pp. 147–163). Oxford, England: Blackwell Science.

Wiggins, J. S. (1991). Agency and communion as conceptual coordinates for the understanding and measurement of interpersonal behavior. In D. Cicchetti & W. M. Grove (Eds.), *Thinking clearly about psychology: Essays in honor of Paul E. Meehl, Vol. 1: Matters of public interest; Vol. 2: Personality and psychopathology* (pp. 89–113). Minneapolis, MN: University of Minnesota Press.

Wilberg, S. (1996). Favorisierung der "eigenen" Gruppe in einem deutsch-deutschen Vergleich [Preferential judgments of the "ingroup" in an East-West German comparison]. *Zeitschrift fuer Sozialpsychologie, 27,* 278–282.

Wilder, D. A. (1990). Some determinants of the persuasive power of in-groups and out-groups: Organization of information and attribution of independence. *Journal of Personality and Social Psychology, 59,* 1202–1213.

Wilder, D. A. (2001). Intergroup contact: The typical member and the exception to the rule. In M. A. Hogg & D. Abrams (Eds.), *Intergroup relations: Essential readings* (pp. 370–382). Philadelphia: Psychology Press.

Wilder, D. A., & Shapiro, P. (1989a). Effects of anxiety on impression formation in a group context: An anxiety-assimilation hypothesis. *Journal of Experimental Social Psychology, 25,* 481–499.

Wilder, D. A., & Shapiro, P. N. (1989b). Role of competition-induced anxiety in limiting the beneficial impact of positive behavior by an out-group member. *Journal of Personality and Social Psychology, 56,* 60–69.

Wilder, D. A., & Shapiro, P. (1991). Facilitation of outgroup stereotypes by enhanced ingroup identity. *Journal of Experimental Social Psychology, 27,* 431–452.

Wilder, D. A., & Simon, A. F. (1996). Incidental and integral affect as triggers of stereotyping. In R. M. Sorrentino & E. T. Higgins (Eds.), *Handbook of motivation and cognition, Vol. 3: The interpersonal context* (pp. 397–419). New York: Guilford Press.

Wildschut, T., Insko, C. A., & Gaertner, L. (2002). Intragroup social influence and intergroup competition. *Journal of Personality and Social Psychology, 82*, 975–992.

Wildschut, T., Pinter, B., Vevea, J. L., Insko, C. O., & Schopler, J. (2003). Beyond the group mind: A quantitative review of the interindividual-intergroup discontinuity effect. *Psychological Bulletin, 129*, 698–722.

Wilke, H. A., & Braspenning, J. (1989). Reciprocity: Choice shift in a social trap. *European Journal of Social Psychology, 19*, 317–326.

Wilke, H., Van Dijk, E., Morel, K., & Olde Monnikhof, M. (1996). Coalitieformatie in gesimuleerde organisaties [Coalition formation in simulated organizations]. *Gedrag en Organisatie, 9*, 82–99.

Wilkenfeld, J., Kraus, S., & Holley, K. M. (1998). The negotiation training model. *Simulation and Gaming, 29*, 31–43.

Wilkinson, S., & Kitzinger, C. (Eds.). (1996). *Representing the other: A feminism & psychology reader*. London: Sage Publications, Inc.

Williams, K. C. (1991). Advertising and political expenditures in a spatial election game: An experimental investigation. *Simulation and Gaming, 22*, 421–442.

Williams, W. M., & Sternberg, R. J. (1988). Group intelligence: Why some groups are better than others. *Intelligence, 12*, 351–377.

Williamson, D. A., Williamson, S. H., Watkins, P. C., & Hughes, H. E. (1992). Increasing cooperation among children using dependent group-oriented reinforcement contingencies. *Behavior Modification, 16*, 414–425.

Willson, S. J. (2000). Axioms for the outcomes of negotiation in matrix games. *Mathematical Social Sciences, 39*, 323–348.

Wilson, C., & Brewer, N. (1993). Individuals and groups dealing with conflict: Findings from police on patrol. *Basic and Applied Social Psychology, 14*, 55–67.

Wilson, S. R. (1992). Face and facework in negotiation. In L. L. Putnam & M. E. Roloff (Eds.), *Communication and negotiation* (pp. 176–205). Newbury Park, CA: Sage Publications, Inc.

Wilson, S. R., Aleman, C. G., & Leatham, G. B. (1998). Identity implications of influence goals: A revised analysis of face-threatening acts and application to seeking compliance with same-sex friends. *Human Communication Research, 25*, 64–96.

Wiltermuth, S. S., & Heath, C. (2009). Synchrony and cooperation. *Psychological Science, 20*, 1–5.

Winkler, J. D. (1999). Are smart communicators better? Soldier aptitude and team performance. *Military Psychology, 11*, 405–422.

Winquist, J. R., & Franz, T. M. (2008). Does the Stepladder Technique improve group decision making? A series of failed replications. *Group Dynamics: Theory, Research, and Practice, 12*, 255–267.

Winter, E. (1996). Mechanism robustness in multilateral bargaining. *Theory and Decision, 40*, 131–147.

Wischniewski, J., Windmann, S., Juckel, G., & Brüne, M. (2009). Rules of social exchange: Game theory, individual differences and psychopathology. *Neuroscience and Biobehavioral Reviews, 33*, 305–313.

Wiseman, T., & Yilankaya, O. (2001). Cooperation, secret handshakes, and imitation in the Prisoners' Dilemma. *Games and Economic Behavior, 37*, 216–242.

Wit, A. P., & Wilke, H. A. (1992). The effect of social categorization on cooperation in three types of social dilemmas. *Journal of Economic Psychology, 13*, 135–151.

Wit, A., & Wilke, H. A. (1990). The presentation of rewards and punishments in a simulated social dilemma. *Social Behaviour, 5*, 231–245.

Wit, A., & Wilke, H. A. (1992). The effect of social categorization on cooperation in three types of social dilemmas. *Journal of Economic Psychology, 13*, 135–151.

Wit, A., & Wilke, H. (1998). Public good provision under environmental social uncertainty. *European Journal of Social Psychology, 28*, 249–256.

Wit, A., Wilke, H. A. M., & Oppewal, H. (1992). Fairness in asymmetric social dilemmas. In W. B. G. Liebrand, D. M. Messick, & H. A. M. Wilke (Eds.), *Social dilemmas: Theoretical issues and research findings* (pp. 183–197). Oxford, England: Pergamon Press, Inc.

Witt, L. A., Hochwarter, W. A., Hilton, T. F., & Hillman, C. M. (1999). Team-member exchange and commitment to a matrix team. *Journal of Social Behavior and Personality, 14*, 63–74.

Witte, Erich H. (1989). Koehler rediscovered: The anti-Ringelmann effect. *European Journal of Social Psychology, 19*, 147–154.

Witte, E. H. (1994). Mediation (Regelungsberatung): Theoretische Grundlagen und empirische Ergebnisse [Mediation: Theoretical foundations and research results]. *Gruppendynamik, 25*, 241–251.

Witte, E. H., & Davis, J. H. (Eds.). (1996). *Understanding group behavior, Vol. 1: Consensual action by small groups*. Mahwah, NJ: Lawrence Erlbaum Associates, Inc.

Witteman, H. (1992). Analyzing interpersonal conflict: Nature of awareness, type of initiating event, situational perceptions, and management styles. *Western Journal of Communication, 56*, 248–280.

Wittenbaum, G. M., & Stasser, G. (1995). The role of prior expectancy and group discussion in the attribution of attitudes. *Journal of Experimental Social Psychology, 31*, 82–105.

Wittenbaum, G. M., & Stasser, G. (1996). Management of information in small groups. In J. L. Nye & A. M. Brower (Eds.), *What's social about social cognition? Research on socially shared cognition in small groups* (pp. 3–28). Thousand Oaks, CA: Sage Publications, Inc.

Wittenbaum, G. M., Stasser, G., & Merry, C. J. (1996). Tacit coordination in anticipation of small group task completion. *Journal of Experimental Social Psychology, 32*, 129–152.

Wolf, S. T., Cohen, T. R., Kirchner, J. L., Rea, A., Montoya, R. M., & Insko, C. A. (2009). Reducing intergroup conflict through the consideration of future consequences. *European Journal of Social Psychology, 39*, 831–841.

Wolf, S. T., Insko, C. A., Kirchner, J. L., & Wildschut, T. (2008). Interindividual-intergroup discontinuity in the domain of correspondent outcomes: The roles of relativistic concern, perceived categorization, and the doctrine of mutual assured destruction. *Journal of Personality and Social Psychology, 94*, 479–494.

Wolfe, J. (1993). On the propriety of forecasting accuracy as a measure of team management ability: A preliminary investigation. *Simulation and Gaming, 24*, 47–62.

Wolfe, J., & Box, T. M. (1988). Team cohesion effects on business game performance. *Simulation and Games, 19*, 82–98.

Wolfe, J., & Chanin, M. (1993). The integration of functional and strategic management skills in a business game learning environment. *Simulation and Gaming, 24*, 34–46.

Wolfe, J., & Roberts, C. R. (1993). A further study of the external validity of business games: Five-year peer group indicators. *Simulation and Gaming, 24*, 21–33.

Wolfensberger, W. (1995). An "if this, then that" formulation of decisions related to social role valorization as a better way of interpreting it to people. *Mental Retardation, 33*, 163–169.

Wolfenstein, E. V. (1998). Reflections on Malcolm X and Black feminism. *Journal for the Psychoanalysis of Culture and Society, 3*(2), 41–59.

Wolpert, L., & Richards, A. (1988). *A Passion for Science*. Oxford, England: Oxford University Press.

Wolsko, C., Park, B., Judd, C. M., & Bachelor, J. (2003). Intergroup contact: Effects on group evaluations and perceived variability. *Group Processes and Intergroup Relations, 6*, 93–110.

Womack, D. F. (1990). Communication and negotiation. In D. O'Hair & G. L. Kreps (Eds.), *Applied communication theory and research* (pp. 77–101). Hillsdale, NJ: Lawrence Erlbaum Associates, Inc.

Wong, Rosanna Y.-m., & Hong, Y.-y. (2005). Dynamic influences of culture on cooperation in the Prisoner's Dilemma. *Psychological Science, 16*, 429–434.

Wood, B. D., & Bohte, J. (2004). Political transaction costs and the politics of administrative design. *Journal of Politics, 66*, 176–202.

Wood, W. (2000). Attitude change: Persuasion and social influence. *Annual Review of Psychology, 51*, 539–570.

Wooders, J. (1998). Walrasian equilibrium in matching models. *Mathematical Social Sciences, 35*, 245–259.

Woody, R. H. (1998). Bartering for psychological services. *Professional Psychology: Research and Practice, 29*, 174–178.

Worchel, S. (1996). Emphasizing the social nature of groups in a developmental framework. In J. L. Nye & A. M. Brower (Eds.), *What's social about social cognition? Research on socially shared cognition in small groups* (pp. 261–282). Thousand Oaks, CA: Sage Publications.

Worchel, S. (1998). A developmental view of the search for group identity. In S. Worchel, J. F. Morales, D. Paez, & J.-C. Deschamps (Eds.), *Social identity: International perspectives* (pp. 53–74). London: Sage Publications, Inc.

Worchel, S., & Coutant, D. (2004). It Takes two to tango: Relating group identity to individual identity within the framework of group development. In M. B. Brewer & M. Hewstone (Eds.), *Self and social identity* (pp. 182–202). Malden: Blackwell Publishing.

Worchel, S., & Coutant, D. K. (2008). Between conflict and reconciliation: Toward a theory of peaceful coexistence. In A. Nadler, T. E. Malloy, & J. D. Fisher (Eds.), *The social psychology of intergroup reconciliation* (pp. 423–446). New York: Oxford University Press.

Worchel, S., Coutant-Sassic, D., & Wong, F. (1993). Toward a more balanced view of conflict: There is a positive side. In S. Worchel & J. A. Simpson (Eds.), *Conflict between people and groups: Causes, processes, and resolutions* (pp. 76–89). Chicago, IL: Nelson-Hall, Inc.

Worchel, S., Iuzzini, J., Coutant, D., & Ivaldi, M. (2000). A multidimensional model of identity: Relating individual and group identities to intergroup behaviour. In D. Capozza & R. Brown (Eds.), *Social identity processes: Trends in theory and research* (pp. 15–32). Thousand Oaks, CA: Sage Publications Ltd.

Worchel, S., Jenner, S. M., & Hebl, M. R. (1998). Changing the guard: How origin of new leader and disposition of ex-leader affect group performance and perceptions. *Small Group Research, 29*, 436–451.

Worchel, S., & Lundgren, S. (1991). The nature of conflict and conflict resolution. In K. G. Duffy, J. W. Grosch, & P. V. Olczak (Eds.), *Community mediation: A handbook for practitioners and researchers* (pp. 3–20). New York: Guilford Press.

Worchel, S., Rothgerber, H., Day, E. A., Hart, D., & Butemeyer, J. (1998). Social identity and individual productivity within groups. *British Journal of Social Psychology, 37*, 389–413.

Worchel, S., & Simpson, J. A. (Eds.). (1993). *Conflict between people and groups: Causes, processes, and resolutions.* Chicago, IL: Nelson-Hall, Inc.

Worchel, S. W., Wong, F. Y., & Scheltema, K. E. (1989). Improving intergroup relations: Comparative effects of anticipated cooperation and helping on attraction for an aid-giver. *Social Psychology Quarterly, 52*, 213–219.

Wright, S. C., Aron, A., & Brody, S. M. (2008). Extended contact and including others in the self: Building on the Allport/Pettigrew legacy. In U. Wagner, L. R. Tropp, G. Finchilescu, & C. Tredoux (Eds.), *Improving intergroup relations: Building on the legacy of Thomas F. Pettigrew* (pp. 143–159). Malden: Blackwell Publishing.

Wu, J.-J., Zhang, B.-Y., Zhou, Z.-X., He, Q.-Q., Zheng, X.-D., Cressman, R., & Tao, Y. (2009). Costly punishment does not always increase cooperation. *PNAS Proceedings of the National Academy of Sciences of the United States of America, 106*, 17448–17451.

Wyer, R. S., Jr., & Gruenfeld, D. H. (1995). Information processing in interpersonal communication. In D. E. Hewes (Ed.), *The cognitive bases of interpersonal communication* (pp. 7–47). Hillsdale, NJ: Lawrence Erlbaum Associates, Inc.

Xia, L., Yuan, Y. C., & Gay, G. (2009). Exploring negative group dynamics: Adversarial network, personality, and performance in project groups. *Management Communication Quarterly, 23*, 32–62.

Xue, L. (2002). Stable agreements in infinitely repeated games. *Mathematical Social Sciences, 43*, 165–176.

Yamagishi, T. (1988). Seriousness of social dilemmas and the provision of a sanctioning system. *Social Psychology Quarterly, 51*, 32–42.

Yamagishi, T. (1990). Factors mediating residual effects of group size in social dilemmas. *Japanese Journal of Psychology, 61*, 162–169.

Yamagishi, T. (1992). Group size and the provision of a sanctioning system in a social dilemma. In W. B. G. Liebrand, D. M. Messick, & H. A. M. Wilke (Eds.), *Social dilemmas: Theoretical issues and research findings* (pp. 267–287). Oxford, England: Pergamon Press, Inc.

Yamagishi, T., & Cook, K. S. (1993). Generalized exchange and social dilemmas. *Social Psychology Quarterly, 56*, 235–248.

Yamagishi, T., Gillmore, M. R., & Cook, K. S. (1988). Network connections and the distribution of power in exchange networks. *American Journal of Sociology, 93*, 833–851.

Yamagishi, T., Kanazawa, S., Mashima, R., & Terai, S. (2005). Separating trust from cooperation in a dynamic relationship: Prisoner's Dilemma with variable dependence. *Rationality and Society, 17*, 275–308.

Yamagishi, T., & Kiyonari, T. (2000). The group as the container of generalized reciprocity. *Social Psychology Quarterly, 63*, 116–132.

Yamaguchi, H. (1989). Coalition formation in the competition for power precedence. *Japanese Journal of Experimental Social Psychology, 29*, 83–91.

Yamaguchi, H. (1991a). Coalition formation in the competition for power precedence. *Japanese Journal of Experimental Social Psychology, 30*, 195–202.

Yamaguchi, H. (1991b). Coalition tactics of the weaks in the power struggle. *Japanese Journal of Psychology, 61*, 370–376.

Yamaguchi, H. (1992). Formation of grand coalition when consciousness of intragroup competition is activated. *Japanese Journal of Psychology, 62*, 357–363.

Ybema, J. F., & Buunk, B. P. (1993). Aiming at the top? Upward social comparison of abilities after failure. *European Journal of Social Psychology, 23*, 627–645.

Yeung, K.-T., & Stombler, M. (2000). Gay and Greek: The identity paradox of gay fraternities. *Social Problems, 47*, 135–152.

Yi, R., & Rachlin, H. (2004). Contingencies of reinforcement in a five-person prisoner's dilemma. *Journal of the Experimental Analysis of Behavior, 82*, 161–176.

Yi, S.-S. (1997). Stable coalition structures with externalities. *Games and Economic Behavior, 20*, 201–237.

Yi, S.-S. (1999). On the coalition-proofness of the Pareto frontier of the set of Nash equilibria. *Games and Economic Behavior, 26*, 353–364.

Yildiz, M. (2003). Walrasian bargaining. *Games and Economic Behavior, 45*, 465–487.

Yoo, Y., & Kanawattanachai, P. (2001). Developments of transactive memory systems and collective mind in virtual teams. *International Journal of Organizational Analysis, 9*, 187–208.

Yoshida, F., & Kubota, K. (1994). Minority versus majority: Intergroup discrimination in the minimal group paradigm. *Japanese Journal of Psychology, 65*, 346–354.

Young, C. K. (1989). Effectiveness of coalition building. In R. M. Friedman, A. J. Duchnowski, & E. L. Henderson (Eds.), *Advocacy on behalf of children with serious emotional problems* (pp. 79–88). Springfield, IL, England: Charles C Thomas, Publisher.

Young, I. M. (1994). Gender as seriality: Thinking about women as a social collective. *Signs, 19*, 713–738.

Young, S. A., & Parker, C. P. (1999). Predicting collective climates: Assessing the role of shared work values, needs, employee interaction and work group membership. *Journal of Organizational Behavior, 20*, 1199–1218.

Yuki, M. (2003). Intergroup comparison versus intragroup relationships: A cross-cultural examination of social identity theory in North American and East Asian cultural contexts. *Social Psychology Quarterly, 66*, 166–183.

Yzerbyt, V. Y., Judd, C. M., & Muller, D. (2009). How do they see us? The vicissitudes of metaperception in intergroup relations. In S. Demoulin, J.-P. Leyens, & J. F. Dovidio (Eds.), *Intergroup misunderstandings: Impact of divergent social realities* (pp. 63–83). New York: Psychology Press.

Yzerbyt, V., Dumont, M., Wigboldus, D., & Gordijn, E. (2003). I feel for us: The impact of categorization and identification on emotions and action tendencies. *British Journal of Social
Psychology, 42*, 533–549.

Yzerbyt, V. Y., Leyens, J. P., & Bellour, F. (1995). The ingroup overexclusion effect: Identity concerns in decisions about group membership. *European Journal of Social Psychology, 25*, 1–16.

Yzerbyt, V. Y., Rogier, A., & Fiske, S. T. (1998). Group entitativity and social attribution: On
translating situational constraints into stereotypes. *Personality and Social Psychology Bulletin,
24*, 1089–1103.

Zaccaro, S. J., Blair, V., Peterson, C., & Zazanis, M. (1995). Collective efficacy. In J. E. Maddux (Ed.), *Self-efficacy, adaptation, and adjustment: Theory, research, and application* (pp.
305–328). New York: Plenum Press.

Zacharias, G. L., Macmillan, J., Van Hemel, S. B., & Committee on Organization Modeling: From
Individuals to Societies (Eds.). (2008). *Behavioral modeling and simulation: From individuals
to societies*. Washington, DC: National Academies Press.

Zagefka, H., & Brown, R. (2006). Predicting comparison choices in intergroup settings: A new
look. In S. Guimond (Ed.), *Social comparison and social psychology: Understanding cognition, intergroup relations, and culture* (pp. 99–126). New York: Cambridge University Press.

Zajonc, R. B. (1965). Social facilitation. *Science, 149*, 269–274.

Zakaria, N., Amelinckx, A., & Wilemon, D. (2008). Navigating across culture and distance: Understanding the determinants of global virtual team performance. In V. I. Sessa & M. London
(Eds.), *Work group learning: Understanding, improving and assessing how groups learn in organizations* (pp. 175–191). New York: Taylor & Francis Group/Lawrence Erlbaum Associates.

Zander, A. F. (1977). *Groups at work: Unresolved issues in the study of organizations*. San Francisco: Jossey-Bass.

Zander, A. F. (1994). *Making groups effective (2nd ed.)*. San Francisco: Jossey-Bass Inc, Publishers.

Zander, A. F. (1997). *Groups at work*. San Francisco: Jossey-Bass.

Zani, B. (1992). Lo studio delle relazioni tra gruppi: "Dopo" e "Oltre" la teoria di Tajfel [The study
of intergroup relations: "After" and "beyond" Tajfel's theory]. *Giornale Italiano di Psicologia,
19*, 357–386.

Zapka, J. G., Marrocco, G. R., Lewis, B., McCusker, J., Sullivan, J., McCarthy, J., & Birch, F. X.
(1992). Inter-organizational responses to AIDS: A case study of the Worcester AIDS Consor-
tium. *Health Education Research, 7*, 31–46.

Zarate, M. A., Garcia, B., Garza, A. A., & Hitlan, R. T. (2004). Cultural threat and perceived realistic group conflict as dual predictors of prejudice. *Journal of Experimental Social Psychology,
40*, 99–105.

Zartman, I. W. (1991). The structure of negotiation. In V. A. Kremenyuk (Ed.), *International negotiation: Analysis, approaches, issues* (pp. 65–77). San Francisco: Jossey-Bass Inc, Publishers.

Zdaniuk, B., & Levine, J. M. (1996). Anticipated interaction and thought generation: The role of
faction size. *British Journal of Social Psychology, 35*, 201–218.

Zdaniuk, B., & Levine, J. M. (2001). Group loyalty: Impact of members' identification and contributions. *Journal of Experimental Social Psychology, 37*, 502–509.

Zeng, D.-Z. (2003). An amendment to final-offer arbitration. *Mathematical Social Sciences, 46*,
9–19.

Zenger, T. R., & Lawrence, B. S. (1989). Organizational demography: The differential effects of
age and tenure distributions on technical communication. *Academy of Management Journal,
32*, 353–376.

Zhang, J., & Norman, D. A. (1994). Representations in distributed cognitive tasks. *Cognitive Science: A Multidisciplinary Journal, 18*, 87–122.

Zhong, F., Wu, D. J., & Kimbrough, S. O. (2002). Cooperative agent systems: Artificial agents
play the ultimatum game. *Group Decision and Negotiation, 11*, 433–447.

Zick, C. D. (1992). Do families share-and-share-alike? The need to understand intrahousehold
resource allocations. *Journal of Family and Economic Issues, 13*, 407–419.

Zohar, D. (2000). A group-level model of safety climate: Testing the effect of group climate on
microaccidents in manufacturing jobs. *Journal of Applied Psychology, 85*, 587–596.

Zollman, K. J. S. (2008). Explaining fairness in complex environments. *Politics, Philosophy and Economics, 7*, 81–97.

Zott, C. (2002). When adaptation fails: An agent-based explanation of inefficient bargaining under private information. *Journal of Conflict Resolution, 46*, 727–753.

Zucchermaglio, C., & Talamo, A. (2000). Identità sociale e piccolo gruppo [Social identity and small groups]. *Giornale Italiano di Psicologia, 27*, 499–527.

Zumkley, H., & Zumkley-Muenkel, C. (1992). "Schlechte Laune", Aggressionskonfliktloesung und Altruismus ["Bad mood," aggression conflict resolutions, and altruism]. *Psychologische Beitraege, 34*, 113–126.

Zurcher, L. A., & Snow, D. A. (1990). Collective behavior: Social movements. In M. Rosenberg & R. H. Turner (Eds.), *Social psychology: Sociological perspectives* (pp. 447–482). New Brunswick, NJ: Transaction Publishers.

Zwick, R., Rapoport, A., & Howard, J. C. (1992). Two-person sequential bargaining behavior with exogenous breakdown. *Theory and Decision, 32*, 241–268.

Zwick, R., Rapoport, A., & Weg, E. (2000). Invariance failure under subgame perfectness in sequential bargaining. *Journal of Economic Psychology, 21*, 517–544.

# Index

H. Blumberg et al., *Small Group Research,* Peace Psychology Book Series,
DOI 10.1007/978-1-4614-0025-7, © Springer Science+Business Media, LLC 2012

CPSIA information can be obtained at www.ICGtesting.com
Printed in the USA
LVOW070236171211

259879LV00009B/4/P